Encyclopedia
of
Empiricism

ENCYCLOPEDIA
OF
EMPIRICISM

Edited by
Don Garrett
and
Edward Barbanell

Greenwood Press
Westport, Connecticut

Library of Congress Cataloging-in-Publication Data

Encyclopedia of empiricism / edited by Don Garrett and Edward
  Barbanell.
     p. cm.
  Includes bibliographical references and index.
  ISBN: 0–313–28932–8 (alk. paper)
    1. Empiricism—Encyclopedias. I. Garrett, Don. II. Barbanell,
  Edward.
  B816.E53   1997
  146'.44'03—dc21   96–50212

British Library Cataloguing in Publication Data is available.

Library of Congress Catalog Card Number: 96–50212
ISBN: 0–313–28932–8

First published in 1997

Greenwood Press, 88 Post Road West, Westport, CT 06881
An imprint of Greenwood Publishing Group, Inc.

Printed in the United States of America

The paper used in this book complies with the
Permanent Paper Standard issued by the National
Information Standards Organization (Z39.48–1984).

10 9 8 7 6 5 4 3 2 1

Copyright Acknowledgments

CONTENTS

PREFACE

In its most general sense, the term "empiricism" designates a philosophical emphasis on the relative importance of experience and processes grounded in experience, in contrast to reasoning and theorizing a priori. In its more specific use as a proper noun, "Empiricism" designates a particular philosophical movement or tendency of the seventeenth and eighteenth centuries, originating and centered in Great Britain, but with much broader influence. Its best-known and most important representatives are John Locke, George Berkeley, and David Hume. It should be emphasized that these philosophers did not use the term "empiricism" to describe their own views, for the term itself achieved currency only much later. Nevertheless, they and the thinkers most directly influenced by them clearly conceived of themselves as seeking a more experiential basis for philosophy. In that sense, although they lacked the term, they conceived of themselves as empiricists.

Empiricism as a particular philosophical movement of the seventeenth and eighteenth centuries is often contrasted with the seventeenth-century Rationalism of René Descartes, Benedict de Spinoza, and Gottfried Wilhelm Leibniz, each of whom placed less relative emphasis on sensory experience and more on reasoning and a priori theorizing. These two movements arise, in part, from different ways of drawing epistemological and methodological lessons from the ongoing progress of the scientific revolution inaugurated by Copernicus and consummated by Newton. Together, Rationalism and Empiricism constitute the two main tendencies of European philosophy in the period after Scholasticism and prior to Kant. Both movements were comprehensive, in the sense that its members discussed a wide range of philosophical issues, ranging from epistemology and metaphysics to ethics, aesthetics, and politics.

The simple classification of philosophers of the early modern period as either (Continental) Rationalists or (British) Empiricists is, of course, a crude one, necessarily ignoring many fundamental differences among philosophers classed together (e.g., consider the robust realism of Locke in comparison with the idealism of Berkeley) and, equally, many fundamental affinities among philosophers classified as members of opposite movements (e.g., consider the naturalism of Spinoza and Hume). It ignores as well the many lines of influence interconnecting Empiricist and Rationalist philosophers. Nevertheless, Empiricism does exhibit some distinctive and defining characteristics that set it apart from Rationalism: a methodological suspicion of philosophical theorizing not governed by experience; the project of tracing the content of all concepts to experience; a willingness to suppose that the laws of nature could be discovered only by observation; an acquiescence to the possibility of ''brute'' or unexplainable facts; and, above all, a rejection of the Rationalists' common distinction between intellect and imagination as two distinct representational faculties of the mind, according to which nonimagistic ideas of intellect can serve as a fertile source of nonexperiential cognitive content (see IMAGINATION).

The influence of Empiricism is by no means restricted to the seventeenth and eighteenth centuries. In addition to Empiricism's influence on Kant, its force persisted through the nineteenth century in such figures as John Stuart Mill and the associationist psychologists. Moreover, two dominant and closely intertwined movements of the first half of the twentieth century, Logical Positivism and Logical Empiricism, were deeply influenced by the Empiricism of Locke, Berkeley, and Hume. While many of the specific theses of these movements no longer exert the force that they once did, it is fair to say that the prevailing tendencies of twentieth-century philosophy remain broadly empiricist in character.

This encyclopedia is intended to serve four purposes. First, of course, it provides a convenient reference for scholars and students seeking information on particular figures, topics, or doctrines specifically in their relation to Empiricism as a historical movement or to empiricism as a broader tendency of thought. Because each entry contains a brief bibliography of primary and secondary sources, it can usefully serve as a point of first reference. Second, it illustrates the continuity and logical development of the Empiricist movement by examining, within topical articles, the contributions of a number of different philosophers related to the statement and solution of particular issues. Third, it explicates the relations, both logical and historical, between Empiricism as a movement of the seventeenth and eighteenth centuries and the various species of empiricism that preceded and succeeded it. Fourth, it explores some of the most important intellectual influences on empiricism as a tendency of thought.

Choices of entries for inclusion have been made with these aims in mind. In addition to entries on important Empiricist philosophers, detailing their views on a variety of subjects, and on concepts and doctrines that have important relations to Empiricism as a historical movement or empiricism as a broader tendency of thought, there are entries on broadly empiricist thinkers who either influenced Empiricism (such as Aristotle, Aquinas, and Ockham) or were influenced by Empiricism (such as Mill, Russell, and Mach). Also included are entries on a number of scientists (such as Galileo, Newton, and Darwin) who exerted an important influence on empiricism, as well as a number of philosophers (such as Adam Smith, Immanuel Kant, Ludwig Wittgenstein, and W.V.O. Quine) whose historical and/or critical relation to empiricism warrants discussion.

In each case, authors of individual entries have provided helpful bibliographies of primary and secondary sources for further research. References to other entries within the encyclopedia are indicated by the convention of using all capital letters on the first occurrence of the title term.

LIST OF CONTRIBUTORS

TODD L. ADAMS
Pennsylvania State University

JOSEPH AGASSI
York University

BRUCE AUNE
University of Massachusetts

DAVID BERMAN
Trinity College, Dublin

CHRISTOPHER J. BERRY
Glasgow University

JOHN I. BIRO
University of Florida

PANAYOT BUTCHVAROV
University of Iowa

NICHOLAS CAPALDI
University of Tulsa

HUGH CHANDLER
University of Illinois

C.A.J. COADY
University of Melbourne

WILLIAM C. DAVIS
Mt. Union College

WILLIAM DEMOPOULOS
University of Western Ontario

DOUGLAS J. DEN UYL
Bellarmine College

STEPHEN M. DOWNES
University of Utah

JOHN DUPRÉ
Stanford University

LORNE FALKENSTEIN
University of Western Ontario

JAMES FIESER
University of Tennessee at Martin

DANIEL E. FLAGE
James Madison University

ROGER GALLIE
University of Nottingham

DON GARRETT
University of Utah

ROGER F. GIBSON
Washington University

DOUGLAS R. GROOTHUIS
Denver Seminary

LEWIS E. HAHN
Southern Illinois University

GARY L. HARDCASTLE
Virginia Polytechnic Institute

BERNARD HARRISON
University of Utah/University of Sussex

GARY HATFIELD
University of Pennsylvania

ALAN HAUSMAN
Southern Methodist University

DAVID HAUSMAN
Southern Methodist University

CHRISTOPHER HOOKWAY
University of Sheffield

ROBERT G. HUDSON
University of Victoria

CHARLES HUENEMANN
Utah State University

DALE JACQUETTE
Pennsylvania State University

YUKIO KACHI
University of Utah

MIKAEL M. KARLSSON
University of Iceland

MANFRED KUEHN
Purdue University

CHARLES LANDESMAN
Hunter College

JAMES LENNOX
University of Pittsburgh

BERYL LOGAN
York University

E. J. LOWE
University of Durham

JEFF MALPAS
Murdoch University

PETER MENZIES
Australian National University

EMILY MICHAEL
City University of New York, Brooklyn College

FREDERICK S. MICHAEL
New York City

PETER MILLICAN
University of Leeds

WILLIAM E. MORRIS
University of Cincinnati

PAUL K. MOSER
Loyola University of Chicago

ROBERT MUEHLMANN
University of Western Ontario

DOUGLAS ODEGAARD
University of Guelph

L. J. O'NEILL
University of Melbourne

DAVID OWEN
University of Arizona

DAVID A. PAILIN
University of Victoria

DERK PEREBOOM
University of Vermont

ARNE FRIEMUTH PETERSEN
University of Copenhagen

ANTONY E. PITSON
University of Stirling

JOSEPH C. PITT
Virginia Polytechnic University

JEFFREY S. PURINTON
University of Oklahoma

QUENTIN QUESNELL
Smith College

ELIZABETH RADCLIFFE
Santa Clara University

SAMUEL RICHMOND
Cleveland State University

WADE L. ROBISON
Rochester Institute of Technology

PAUL RUSSELL
University of British Columbia

T. A. RYCKMAN
Northwestern University

JERRY SAMET
Brandeis University

ROBERT C. SCHARFF
University of New Hampshire

ROBERT SCHWARTZ
University of Wisconsin, Milwaukee

TOM SORELL
University of Essex

MARK STEINER
Hebrew University

M. A. STEWART
University of Lancaster

AVRUM STROLL
University of California, San Diego

DABNEY TOWNSEND
University of Texas, Arlington

SAUL TRAIGER
Occidental College

MARTIN TWEEDALE
University of Alberta

WAYNE WAXMAN
University of Colorado, Boulder

FRED WILSON
University of Toronto

K. BRAD WRAY
University of Western Ontario

Encyclopedia
of
Empiricism

A

A PRIORI/A POSTERIORI DISTINCTION. The distinction between a priori and a posteriori KNOWLEDGE marks the most fundamental division of epistemic categories. A priori knowledge in some sense is literally prior to, or independent of, experience; a posteriori knowledge by contrast comes after, or is literally posterior to, experience. There are different philosophical accounts of the way in which knowledge can depend, or not depend, on experience, and there is disagreement about whether knowledge or all knowledge is, or should be, a priori, a posteriori, or some combination of both.

The dichotomy between a priori and a posteriori knowledge is sometimes said to presuppose a distinction between contexts of knowledge acquisition and contexts of knowledge justification. Some defenders of a priori knowledge, primarily Socrates, Plato, and later Platonists, believe that all knowledge is acquired a priori. Socrates in Plato's dialogues the *Meno* and *Republic* argues that the immortal soul has perfect knowledge of the eternal Forms or Ideas by direct acquaintance in the realm of ideal entities prior to its embodiment in a particular human being in the world of appearance. Socrates' position presupposes both the immortality of the soul and a limitation of the concept of genuine knowledge to universals and raises difficulties about the way in which the soul is eternally possessed with such knowledge—apparently, merely by dwelling among the Forms or Ideas—that are not satisfactorily resolved in Plato's philosophy.

For those who do not share Socrates' views about the immortality of the soul and the limitation of genuine knowledge to knowledge of the eternal Forms or Ideas, it has seemed more reasonable to hold that while all knowledge is acquired by experience, a priori, unlike a posteriori, knowledge is not justified by experience but is warranted by pure reason and the understanding of meaning independent of the content of sensation and PERCEPTION. Typically, such a theory of knowledge provides for the possibility of both a priori and a posteriori knowledge, allowing that a priori and a posteriori knowledge alike require experience for the assimilation of CONCEPTS and true beliefs but distinguishing between the a priori and a posteriori justification of distinct types of knowledge, giving each its proper complementary place in cognition. A priori knowledge is also sometimes thought to be prior to experience in a non-Socratic sense as innate categories (see INNATENESS) presupposed by the possibility of experience, hardwired in the brain, so to speak, as part of the normal human genetic endowment.

A priori knowledge is usually thought to involve necessary truths (see MODALITY). These include, notably, analytic propositions ("All red objects are colored"), in which the predicate attributed to a subject is contained in, and constitutes part of, the meaning of the subject (see ANALYTIC/SYNTHETIC DISTINCTION), as well as logical truths or tautologies ("Either it is raining or it is not raining") and the propositions of mathematics ("2 + 2 = 4," "The interior angles of a right triangle add up to 180°"). Knowledge in this category, though experientially acquired, does not require justification that makes essential reference to specific information about the empirical world derived through sense experience ("Most swans are white"; "All non-Australian swans are white"). A posteriori knowledge is negatively characterized, by contrast, as all remaining knowledge that is not a priori, or more positively as knowledge justified by evidence about the contingent facts of the world gathered by empirical experience.

PRIMARY WORKS

Kant, Immanuel. *Critique of Pure Reason*. Translated by Norman Kemp Smith. New York: St. Martin's Press, 1965.
Leibniz, Gottfried Wilhelm. *New Essays concerning Human Understanding*. Edited and translated by Jonathan Bennett and Peter Remnant. Cambridge: Cambridge University Press, 1981.

BIBLIOGRAPHY

Dufrenne, Mikel. *The Notion of the* A Priori. Translated with an introduction by Edward S. Casey; preface by Paul Ricoeur. Evanston, IL: Northwestern University Press, 1966.
Hoche, Hans Ulrich. *Nichtempirische Erkenntnis, analytische und synthetische Urteile a priori bei Kant und bei Husserl*. Meiserheim am Glan: A. Hain, 1964.
Moser, Paul K., ed. *A Priori Knowledge*. Oxford: Oxford University Press, 1987.
Quine, W.V.O. "Two Dogmas of Empiricism." In *From a Logical Point of View: Logico-Philosophical Essays*, 2d ed., rev. Cambridge: Harvard University Press, 1961.

DALE JACQUETTE

ABSTRACTION. Abstraction is the ability of the mind to form a concept or attend to an aspect of a complex object or idea. In his *The Art of Thinking: Port-Royal Logic* (1662), Antoine Arnauld distinguishes between three meanings of the word "abstraction." (A1) One might attend to an integral part of an object, such as an arm or a leg, that can exist in separation from that of which it is a part. (A2) One might attend to a mode of a substance without attending to the substance of which it is a mode; for example, one might attend to the redness of an apple without attending to the apple. (A3) One might attend to one characteristic of a thing having several characteristics that are separable only in thought; for example, one might attend to the triangularity of a red triangle without attending to either the size or the color. Controversies regarding abstraction concern only (A2) and (A3).

Discussions of abstraction often occur within discussions of the problem of universals and discussions of the meaning of general terms. These metaphysical and semantic issues are not unrelated, but both must be distinguished from the epistemological issue of how general properties—properties common to many objects—come to be known. ARISTOTLE (384–322 B.C.), whose doctrine of forms is a type of metaphysical realism, held that a form of a particular kind is known by abstraction, even though a form cannot exist apart from some bit of matter (see *Metaphysics* K, 3, 1061^{a}29–1061^{b}4; *Posterior Analytics* A, 18, 81^{b}3; *De Anima* III, 7, 431^{b}12–19; *Nicomachean Ethics* VI, 8, 1142^{a}12–19). Aristotle describes the process of abstraction alternatively as stripping away the particularizing elements of an entity (matter) or as reaching a conclusion by INDUCTION.

Aristotle had an enormous impact on medieval philosophy. Boethius, Abelard, John of Salisbury, Avicenna, and AQUINAS follow Aristotle's basic lines, arguing that through abstraction one can conceive of an entity that, in reality, is inseparable from another, for example, form without matter. WILLIAM OF OCKHAM (c. 1285–1349), however, argued that whatever is separable in thought is separable in reality. He parted ways with many of his predecessors, contending (1) that all existents are particulars (there are no universals or forms) and (2) that the mind can selectively attend to one aspect of a complex object, even though the aspect in question cannot be conceived apart from that object.

While questions regarding abstraction were raised by other philosophers during the late medieval and early modern periods, John Locke's discussion of abstraction in the *Essay concerning Human Understanding* (1690) became a focal point of discussion in eighteenth-century British philosophy (see LOCKE). After claiming that all objects are particulars (III.iii.1), Locke wrote:

Words become general, by being made the signs of general *Ideas*: and *Ideas* become general, by separating from them the circumstances of Time, and Place, and any other *Ideas*, that may determine them to this or that particular Existence. By this way of abstraction they are made capable of representing more Individuals than one; each of which, having in it a conformity to that abstract *Idea*, is (as we call it) of that sort. (*Essay* III.iii.6)

This passage suggests that abstract ideas are constructed by mentally separating properties from objects and, in some cases, recombining such properties to form a complex, but general, idea. While recent scholars have argued that Lockean abstraction requires nothing more than selective attention (Mackie 1976: 107–18), his immediate followers assumed (1) that Locke was concerned with separability and (2) that whatever is separable is capable of independent existence. If one can separate a mode from a substance, or one of several aspects of an entity that cannot exist apart (the previous A2 and A3), then one is confronted with an inconsistency. This seems to be one of George Berkeley's points in the introduction to his *Principles of Human Knowledge* (1710; see BERKELEY), a point with which David HUME concurred in his *Treatise of Human Nature* (1739). Nonetheless, both held that abstraction as selective attention is possible (*Principles*, 2d ed. [1734], Intro., §16; *Treatise* I.i.7 on distinctions of reason).

The early eighteenth century was the high-water mark in discussions of abstraction. By the nineteenth century, many philosophers granted that humans engage in abstraction, while leaving open the question of how that is possible (see J. S. Mill, *A System of Logic*, Book IV, Chapter 2). The last bastion of critical discussion of abstraction was in the philosophy of mathematics, where Gottlob Frege (*Grundlagen der Arithmetik*, 1884) and Bertrand Russell (*Principia Mathematica*, 1914) argued that abstraction plays no role in number theory.

BIBLIOGRAPHY

Books

Doney, Willis, ed. *Berkeley on Abstraction and Abstract Ideas*. New York: Garland, 1989.
Mackie, J. L. *Problems from Locke*. Oxford: Clarendon Press, 1976.

Article

Weinberg, Julius. "Abstraction in the Formation of Concepts." In *Dictionary of the History of Ideas*, edited by Philip P. Wiener. 5 vols. New York: Charles Scribner's Sons, 1973: vol. 1: 1–9.

DANIEL E. FLAGE

ANALYTIC PHILOSOPHY. Analytic philosophy is historically and culturally rooted in the Enlightenment project. The Enlightenment project was the attempt to define, explain, and control the human predicament through SCIENCE and technology. This project originated among the French *philosophes* during the eighteenth century, among whom the most influential were Diderot, d'Alembert, La Mettrie, Condillac, Helvetius, d'Holbach, Turgot, and Condorcet. The *philosophes* were inspired by BACON's vision of the liberating power of science, HOBBES' materialism, NEWTON's physics, and LOCKE's empiricist epistemology. The project was epitomized in the nineteenth century by COMTE.

The Enlightenment project, as a philosophical movement, stood for philosophical materialism. That is, it took what science said about the physical world and made that knowledge primary, while knowledge of the subject was both secondary and derivative. In addition, it embraced the notion of the piecemeal growth of knowledge. All of these views were rejected by Hegel, who embraced KANT's Copernican turn, in which knowledge is a synthetic a priori structure imposed upon experience (see ANALYTIC/SYNTHETIC DISTINCTION), and advocated a holism, in which individual truths could not be understood apart from some knowledge of one all-encompassing truth.

Hegel's most prominent English follower was F. H. Bradley. Analytic philosophy's inaugural spokesman was Bertrand RUSSELL, and Russell's answer to Bradley, specifically Russell's defense of analysis, gave the movement its name. Russell defended the possibility of acquiring knowledge in a piecemeal fashion from experience and, further, that anything could be best understood by "analyzing" it or breaking it down into its constituent parts. Russell's programmatic conception of analytic philosophy was first articulated in *Our Knowledge of the External World* (1914). Russell's work as a logician was designed to develop a structure for atomistic truths.

The latter work inspired CARNAP, the leader of the Vienna Circle. Among the positivists of the circle, analysis was identified with the Enlightenment project, specifically in their "Manifesto" (1929) (see LOGICAL POSITIVISM/ LOGICAL EMPIRICISM). Positivism turned analytic philosophy into a movement that spread to Great Britain and the United States through direct influence on visiting scholars like AYER, QUINE, and Nagel and the emigration of its leaders (Carnap, Hempel, REICHENBACH, POPPER, and others).

As a program, analytic philosophy can be characterized as follows. It is naturalistic in maintaining that the world is self-explanatory and that we understand both ourselves and nature in the same way. It is scientistic in believing that all legitimate understanding is scientific understanding, and it is physicalistic in asserting that physical science is the basic science. Its ontology is mechanistic; that is, nature is alleged to consist of discrete entities that retain their character irrespective of context and whose interaction can be understood as a serial causal sequence. It adheres to the unity of science or the view that the social sciences are to be modeled after the physical sciences, within which subjects are to be treated as objects of a special kind.

In view of the unity of science, whatever account is given of the physical world supplies a basis for any account of the process by which human beings acquire knowledge. Knowing (cognition/methodology) is a reduction to discrete parts. Analysis is the epistemological analogue to ontological atomism. Experience is the internal processing of external stimuli. To be empiricist is to construe experience (not phenomenologically but) as the internal physical processing of an external physical structure. Through experience we can gain access to the truths that refer to objective structures. Our meaningful thoughts (or CONCEPTS), thus, either originate in, or cash out into, experience without remainder. The internal processing of external stimuli must be explainable without reference to an autonomous agent; that is, the world consists ultimately only of objects, and a putative subject must be a concatenation of subobjects.

As a consequence of scientism, theoretical knowledge is primary, and practical "knowledge" has a secondary status. Only factual judgments can be true;

value judgments are not truths, because they do not refer to structures independent of the observer or agents. However, given the primacy of theoretical knowledge and the derivative nature of the social sciences, there can be a physical-scientific and/or social-scientific factual account of the substructure of the context within which values function. This is how the realm of the practical will be explained, ultimately, in theoretical terms. There is a two-tier view of human psychology in which values are epiphenomena with a materialist substructure.

Analytic philosophy upholds the political agenda of the Enlightenment project. Despite differences, liberalism, socialism, and Marxism all subscribe to the two-tier view of human psychology in which values are epiphenomena with a materialist substructure that is transcultural and timeless and allows for a social technology that renders human beings compatible and cooperative.

The foregoing characterization should not be taken as a rigid body of doctrine to which all subscribe. It would be more accurate to say that there has been an analytic conversation initiated by the foregoing doctrines, but a conversation that consists of disparate and dissonant voices. To begin with, Russell's colleague G. E. MOORE also sought to circumvent the Copernican revolution in philosophy. What Moore did not share with Russell was a doctrinaire commitment to scientism. The lack of a shared commitment to doctrinaire scientism distinguished Moore from Russell, separated Moore from positivism and the Vienna Circle, led to Moore's championing of common sense, and finally established a separate philosophical movement known as ordinary language philosophy. While agreeing that philosophy is the clarification of common-sense presuppositions, the later WITTGENSTEIN insisted that a presupposition is not, and cannot be, an objective truth about the world independent of human projects in the world. From Wittgenstein's perspective, Moore erred not in believing in common sense but in believing that common sense could be subject to realist analysis.

Starting then with Moore, the ordinary language movement persistently obfuscated the differences between the clarification of presuppositions and advocacy of a particular theory about those presuppositions. As a consequence, positivist critics of ordinary language could always dismiss ordinary language philosophy as either a rationalization of prescientific prejudice or a failure in getting at the deep structure accessible only to "scientific" methods of analysis.

Analytic philosophy has in the later twentieth century undergone a period of self-criticism initiated by Thomas Kuhn's attack on its narrow conception of science and challenges to its realist doctrines by Richard Rorty, Hilary Putnam, and others.

PRIMARY WORKS

Feigl, H., and W. Sellars, eds. *Readings in Philosophical Analysis*. New York: Appleton-Century-Crofts, 1949.
Sarkar, Sahorta, ed. *Science and Philosophy in the Twentieth Century: Basic Works of Logical Empiricism*. 6 vols. New York: Garland, 1996.

BIBLIOGRAPHY

Books

Bell, D., and N. Cooper, eds. *The Analytic Tradition*. Oxford: Blackwell, 1990.
Rajchman, J., and C. West, eds. *Post-Analytic Philosophy*. New York: Columbia University Press, 1985.

Article

Capaldi, N. "Analytic Philosophy and Language." In *Linguistics and Philosophy: The Controversial Interface*, edited by R. Harre and R. Harris. Oxford: Pergamon Press, 1993: 45–107.

NICHOLAS CAPALDI

ANALYTIC/SYNTHETIC DISTINCTION. The analytic/synthetic distinction describes two different ways in which predicates are logically related to subjects. The terminology is self-consciously adopted by Kant in the "Introduction" to the *Critique of Pure Reason* from the vocabulary of eighteenth-century chemistry. Kant maintains that all subject-predicate judgments are either analytic or synthetic, depending on whether their predicates are contained within or external as something added to the meaning of their subjects.

An analytic judgment attributes to a subject an essential property that is a part of the subject's concept; it implies a contradiction when the judgment is negated or denied. Standard examples include such propositions as "All bachelors are unmarried" and "All triangles are three-sided." An analysis or breakdown of the component concepts that constitute the subjects "bachelors" or "triangles," as in the analysis of chemical substances, reveals that the predicates "being unmarried" and "being three-sided" are, respectively, already contained in the meanings of the subjects. When an analytic judgment is given, a property or concept that belongs to a subject as part of its essential meaning is attached (typically by the copula "is") to the subject term. Analytic judgments predicate properties of a subject that belong to, or are contained within, the subject as part of its meaning or ESSENCE and that are true of the subject analytically or by analysis of the subject's concept.

Synthetic judgments by contrast attribute properties to a subject that do not belong to, and are not already contained within, the subject as part of its meaning or essence but are added to the subject as something different from, and external to, its concept. A synthetic judgment, like a chemical synthesis, involves the putting together of different elements in order to make something new out of reassembled components. An example is the judgment that "Tom is a bachelor" or "This triangle is red." The assumption is that an analysis of the concept of Tom will not reveal the property of being a bachelor contained within it as part of Tom's essence or meaning, since Tom remains Tom whether or not he happens to be a bachelor. By contrast, no bachelor can be married and still be a bachelor. Similarly, it is not analytically true that this triangle is red, for it could presumably be red or blue or yellow without losing its essence as something triangular. The judgment that Tom is a bachelor synthesizes or puts together the concept of Tom with the property of being a bachelor, where the property of being a bachelor is not analytically contained within the concept of Tom. The same is true of the synthetic judgment that this triangle is red, in which the concept of this triangle is synthetically put together with the property of being red that is not analytically contained within it as part of its meaning or essence.

Analytic truths are necessary, and their negations are impossible. The negation of an analytic truth is an analytic falsehood, the necessarily false predication of a property analytically excluded from a subject's concept. This suggests that synthetic truths and synthetic falsehoods are logically contingent and never necessary or impossible (see MODALITY). Kant argues, on the contrary, that there are synthetic a priori judgments that are necessary but not analytic truths (see A PRIORI/A POSTERIORI DISTINCTION). Kant holds that the propositions of mathematics and metaphysics are synthetic a priori. The judgment that 7 + 5 = 12, in one of Kant's favorite examples, is a priori, because its necessary truth does not depend on sense experience. Kant interprets the proposition as synthetic rather than analytic, because the predicate ''being equal to 12'' is not contained in it as part of the meaning of the subjects 7, 5, or addition. Kant regards the discovery of the synthetic a priori as his chief contribution to the attempt to place philosophy on a scientific foundation, by identifying the proper sphere of metaphysics. The synthetic a priori offers a kind of compromise between the rival methodologies of rationalism and empiricism. Kant finds rationalism too impoverished in its limitation to strictly analytic judgments and empiricism too skeptical in its rejection of whatever cannot be directly experienced or reconstructed out of experience by reason and imagination. Synthetic a priori judgments go between the horns of this metaphilosophical dilemma by combining the necessity of analytic judgments as a priori with the greater interest of synthetic judgments. The necessity and nontriviality of synthetic a priori judgments restore the intuitive sense of what is valuable in mathematics and metaphysics. The propositions of mathematics and metaphysics are necessary, according to Kant, and are in some sense products of reason rather than empirical sense experience. But as synthetic a priori, the propositions of mathematics and metaphysics are more informative than analytic judgments, because they are not merely restatements of the properties that belong to judgment subjects.

The analytic/synthetic distinction has been disputed on philosophical grounds. For philosophers with a deeply rationalist orientation, like G. W. Leibniz, every judgment can be understood as analytic by virtue of a sufficiently probing analysis of the particular concept term in any predication or property attribution. Although it seems obvious that the property of being a bachelor (or not being one) is not contained in, or forthcoming from, an analysis of the concept of Tom as the subject of the judgment, in the sense that Tom could apparently either be a bachelor or not be a bachelor and still remain Tom, it is sometimes thought to be part of Tom's individual essence or *haecceity* that he either is or is not a bachelor at any particular time. If Tom is a bachelor, and we consider his not being a bachelor, it might be said, we are not really thinking about Tom, anymore than if we consider the concept of being a bachelor and try to imagine a bachelor as unmarried, we are not really thinking about bachelors or bachelorhood, but about some different, possibly confused, concept.

A related difficulty for the analytic/synthetic distinction is posed by W.V.O. QUINE in his important essay "Two Dogmas of Empiricism." Quine distinguishes between two subcategories of analytic statements. The first involves logical truths, such as "No unmarried man is married." These are necessarily true by virtue of their logical forms and hold true under any substitution of extralogical terms. The second subcategory concerns synonymous expressions, such as "No bachelor is married," which Quine maintains can be converted to a logical truth by intersubstituting synonyms for synonyms. In this case, appropriate substitution in the synonymy example of analyticity produces logical analyticity in the statement "No unmarried male adult is married." The analytic/synthetic distinction is doubtful for Quine because of problems connected with the concept of what he calls "cognitive synonymy." By this Quine means words or phrases having the same meaning for thought and not merely applying to the same things. The attempt to explain cognitive synonymy in terms of definition appears to involve a vicious circularity, because the concept of definition depends on cognitive synonymy, rather than the other way around. Quine considers alternative accounts but finds none acceptable and concludes that the distinction between analytic and synthetic judgments is an unfounded dogma of empiricism.

Quine's argument rests on assumptions that are not shared by all philosophers. The concept of cognitive synonymy and, with it, the analytic/synthetic distinction are rescued, among other ways, by referring to meanings as intensional entities in their own right or by interpreting cognitive synonymy as necessarily truth-preserving intersubstitutability of terms or phrases. Quine rejects both of these possibilities because of his general philosophical aversion to meanings and modalities (see MODALITY) as intensional entities, which many other logicians and philosophers find unproblematic.

PRIMARY WORKS

Kant, Immanuel. *Critique of Pure Reason*. Translated by Norman Kemp Smith. New York: St. Martin's Press, 1965.
———. *Prolegomena to Any Future Metaphysics That Will Be Able to Come Forward as Science*. Translated by Paul Carus; revised by James W. Ellington. Indianapolis, IN: Hackett, 1977.
Leibniz, Gottfried Wilhelm. *New Essays Concerning Human Understanding*. Edited and translated by Jonathan Bennett and Peter Remnant. Cambridge: Cambridge University Press, 1981.
Quine, W.V.O. "Two Dogmas of Empiricism." In *From a Logical Point of View: Logico-Philosophical Essays*, 2d ed.; rev. Cambridge: Harvard University Press, 1961.

BIBLIOGRAPHY

Books

Harris, James F., Jr., and Richard H. Severens, eds. *Analyticity*. Chicago: Quadrangle Books, 1970.

Martin, R. M. *The Notion of Analytic Truth*. Philadelphia: University of Pennsylvania Press, 1952.

Articles

Ebersole, F. B. "On Certain Confusions in the Analytic-Synthetic Distinction." *The Journal of Philosophy* 53 (1956): 485–94.

Gahringer, R. E. "Some Observations on the Distinction between Analytic and Synthetic Propositions." *The Journal of Philosophy* 51 (1954): 425–36.

Grice, H. P., and P. F. Strawson. "In Defense of a Dogma." *The Philosophical Review* 65 (1956): 141–58.

Hackett, S. C. "Contemporary Philosophy and the Analytic-Synthetic Dichotomy." *International Philosophical Quarterly* 7 (1967): 413–40.

Walsh, W. H. "Analytic-Synthetic." *The Proceedings of the Aristotelian Society* 54 (1958–1959): 77–96.

White, Morton G. "The Analytic and the Synthetic: An Untenable Dualism." In *John Dewey: Philosopher of Science and Freedom*. New York: Dial Press, 1950.

DALE JACQUETTE

AQUINAS, ST. THOMAS. St. Thomas Aquinas (1225–1274), born near Aquino, Sicily, was a scholastic philosopher and theologian of the first rank. He was a member of the Order of Preachers (Dominicans). Studies at the recently founded University of Naples and then at the international University of Paris exposed him to the scientific and philosophic materials then being translated from Greek and Arabic and plunged him into the then-raging controversies over the respective roles of faith and REASON and the relations of natural and supernatural. His mentor at Paris was Albertus Magnus, with whom he also did four years of private study in Cologne.

From 1256 to 1259 Thomas taught at the University of Paris, lecturing alternately on the works of ARISTOTLE and on individual books of the Bible, notably the Pauline letters. The following nine years, he served as theological adviser to the papal Curia in Italy. He taught again at Paris and then at Naples until the end of 1273. On his way to represent the pope at the second General Council of Lyons, he fell ill and died at Fossanova, Italy, on March 7, 1274. Many of his basic doctrines were condemned by church authority in Paris in 1277 and in Oxford shortly thereafter. The condemnations were revoked when Thomas was canonized in 1323.

The many varieties and schools of Thomism extend far beyond the narrow tradition of the classic Dominican fifteenth- and sixteenth-century commentators to include the "neo-Thomism" of the nineteenth-century Roman Jesuits and of Jacques Maritain; the twentieth-century critical renascence in textual studies of the Pontifical Medieval Institute at Toronto and especially of Étienne Gilson;

the ''transcendental Thomism'' of Joseph Maréchal, Karl Rahner, and Bernard LONERGAN; and, in the widest sense of Thomism, the lip-service allegiance paid to Thomas' principles and methods in all official Roman Catholic teaching since Leo XIII (1879).

This entry confines itself to the relation of Thomas' philosophy to empiricism. Confronting the questions of his time demanded of him a complete rethinking of the methodological issues concerning the origins and process of human knowledge. Thomas' unshakable position is that human intellectual knowledge takes its origin in the senses. It is not innate; it is not infused or reflected from elsewhere. It is always derived from sensible images in the imagination, which themselves result from the experience of material objects through the external senses.

However, Thomas rejects the position he identifies with Democritus, that the human mind is purely passive vis-à-vis the world of sense, a simple recorder on which experience makes its marks. He frequently quotes approvingly the Aristotelian dictum that the mind is at the beginning ''like a clean-wiped slate,'' but only in the sense that without sense experience, the mind is empty and has no informational content. In contrast to Democritus, Thomas—like Aristotle— is aware of the power and activity of the mind itself. This clean-wiped slate is alive and hungers to be filled. It also possesses an enormous transforming energy that plays a part in achieving its own fulfillment.

Material objects and sense experience, then, provide the material on which the mind works. But they alone cannot cause human understanding or explain human judgments of truth and falsehood. Full, true human knowledge comes from the active power of the mind, focusing on the images that result from sense experience, as part of its own perpetual drive to satisfy its natural desire to know, its ceaseless wonder about what, why, and whether. In this active search, the mind abstracts from place, time, and other particularities of this or that individual object to concentrate on the universal intelligibility it demands. The mind reflects on whatever understanding it comes to, in order to judge the accuracy of that understanding in the light of other experiences and of knowledge it has previously acquired.

These principles prevail in Thomas' best-known and most mature work, the *Summa Theologiae*. They are more fully explained in the *Disputed Questions on Truth*, roughly contemporaneous with the First Part of the *Summa*. In those two works, the basic method of investigation—the question—becomes the basic method of exposition. In the *Summa* hundreds of interrelated questions and thousands of subquestions are posed, with the answers to each appealing, one step at a time, to ever more fundamental, basic principles. Thomas refers to the foundational principles in traditional language as ''naturally known principles,'' principles ''known of themselves,'' and even says that understanding such principles is ''a natural habit.'' But in all these cases, he interprets the traditional language to mean only that the power of our intelligence implies the ability to recognize certain basic principles as true as soon as we hear them proposed and understand what the words mean. (His classic and Aristotelian example is "that a whole is greater than a part.") But his significant addition is that to know what is meant by "a whole" or "a part" is impossible unless one attends to the sensible images that come from sense experience (I–II, 51,1).

Finally, at the most crucial points of defending his system and method, Aquinas appeals to experience, not merely as an example but as the most irrefutable principle of all, especially when the experience called on is that of the reader. Thus:

Everyone experiences the fact that he himself is the one who is doing the understanding. (I, 76,1)

It is the very same man who perceives that he is understanding and perceives that he is sensing. (I, 76, 1)

This anyone can experience in himself, that when he is trying to understand something, he forms images for himself by way of examples in which he sees what he is striving to understand. (I, 84,7)

And we know this by experience, when we perceive that we abstract universal forms from particular conditions, which is to make them actually intelligible. (I, 79,4)

For we see that if the action of the imaginative power is hindered by an injury of the organ, . . . the man is hindered from actually understanding even things he already has learned. (I, 84,7)

The *Summa* is a theological work, which deals at length with objects as remote from experience as divine creation and providence, the Trinity, the Redemption, grace, and angels. It is at the same time a vigorous attempt to meet the challenges of its time by reconciling the possibility of faith and the supernatural with the claims of reason and a full vindication of the natural. Thomas' account of the basic process of human knowing, as rooted in sensation and regularly returning to experience as a norm, makes clear the criteria he expects his philosophical readers to use in judging the success of his efforts.

PRIMARY WORKS

The Disputed Questions on Truth. Translated from the definitive Leonine editions. Chicago: H. Regnery, 1952–1954.
Summa Theologiae. Latin text and English translation. Cambridge: Blackfriars, 1964–1981.

BIBLIOGRAPHY

Lonergan, Bernard. *Grace and Freedom: Operative Grace in the Thought of St. Thomas Aquinas*. New York: Herder and Herder, 1970.
———. *Verbum: Word and Idea in Aquinas*. Collected Works of Bernard Lonergan 2. Toronto: University of Toronto Press, 1996. Corrected edition of *Verbum: Word and Idea in Aquinas*. Notre Dame: University of Notre Dame Press, 1967.

QUENTIN QUESNELL

ARISTOTLE. Aristotle (384–322 B.C.) was born at Stagira. His father was the physician at the court of Macedon. Greek philosophy at the time of his birth was scarcely two centuries old, Socrates had died fifteen years before, and Plato was forty-four years old. In 367 B.C. the seventeen-year-old Aristotle entered Plato's school in Athens some two hundred miles to the south, and he remained there for nineteen years until Plato's death in 348. At that time, at age thirty-six, he left Athens. After several years in Asia Minor and several more years in Macedon, where he was tutor to Alexander, he returned to Athens in 335 B.C. to found his own school, the Lyceum. The year before his death marked the beginning of the Hellenistic Empire.

This entry consists of three parts. The first part explains Aristotle's perspective on philosophy and its divisions with a view to the modern conceptions of it and its divisions. The second part introduces his philosophy as a dialectic reaction to his predecessors, notably, Plato and Democritus, and attempts to locate his empiricism within his philosophical framework. The third part is a sketch of the influence of his philosophy.

Aristotle's outlook on philosophy is comprehensive. Philosophy is the systematic and self-reflective search for KNOWLEDGE. Knowledge so sought is of two kinds, substantive and methodological. Substantive knowledge in turn is of three kinds: ''theoretical'' (having the scientific knowledge of facts), ''practical'' (knowing how best to live as human beings), and ''productive'' (knowing how to make things). Methodological knowledge is knowing multifarious ways of language and LOGIC, both formal and informal, for the purpose of attaining, formulating, and communicating the three substantive kinds of knowledge.

It is a characteristic of Aristotle's conception and practice of philosophy that theory of knowledge does not enjoy the unity and theoretical priority it is given in modern Western philosophy in general and British Empiricism in particular. Thus, his observations on knowledge are found throughout his works in methodological, theoretical, practical, and productive sciences.

In general, it is important to keep in mind that Aristotle's conceptions of knowledge and SCIENCE are distinct from, and much broader than, those found in modern European philosophy. In particular, the following features of his perspectives upon knowledge seem especially noteworthy. First, Aristotle is epistemologically naive. The possibility of knowledge and the human capacity and desire for knowledge are among the starting points of his philosophizing. Without them, human beings might as well be beasts, he believes, and philosophy as he understands it would be futile. Those who deny them and would try to act accordingly would make poor fellow investigators, poor citizens, and poor cooks, who could prepare palatable and nutritious dishes only by accident. Radical SKEPTICISM would be self-defeating as a thesis and alien to philosophy as an attitude of mind. Second, Aristotle envisages a finished theoretical science as having the form of a system of syllogistic DEMONSTRATIONs. Accordingly, in the *Posterior Analytics*, his major work in philosophy of science, he devotes much attention to the application of syllogistic logic in scientific explanation and justification. Third, for Aristotle, what it is to know and what it is to be known are questions that call for certain human faculties and metaphysical structures. For actual knowledge is that matching of reality's knowability and human cognitive faculties in which these potentialities are actualized. Thus, he treats issues about knowledge not only with respect to the logic of scientific demonstration but also in the context of METAPHYSICS and philosophy of mind.

Aristotelianism stands in a similar relation to the unity and priority accorded philosophy of language in logical empiricism (see LOGICAL POSITIVISM). Like a linguistic philosopher, Aristotle does pay close and systematic attention to ways of language and logic, including what we say and how we say it. He does this partly to sharpen our tools for attaining, formulating, and communicating substantive knowledge and partly to use the ways of language and logic as preliminary evidence for principles in theoretical, practical, and productive sciences. Ultimately, logic and language have the instrumental and evidential values they do because of the *logos*-permeated way things are. Here again we have the primacy of metaphysics in Aristotle's outlook. His metaphysics, however, is not saddled with distinctions crucial to Empiricism, namely, those between "relations of ideas" and "matters of fact," language and reality, logic and experience, philosophy and science.

Aristotelianism is also innocent of the distinctions between *is* and *ought*, fact and value, science and ETHICS. What distinguishes theoretical and practical sciences for Aristotle is not HUME's guillotine but purpose and subject matter. Whereas the goal of theoretical science is fulfilled in giving correct and complete scientific explanation, that of practical science is fulfilled in the coordinated practices conducive to, or constitutive of, felicitous human life. As for the subject matter, whereas theoretical science treats only universals, leaving alone individuals qua individuals as unknowable, practical science treats us in our daily life, particular persons in particular situations. Moreover, practical science with its eudaemonistic foundation for ethics and politics has one of its tap roots in metaphysics. For the question whether or not a given individual thing is good would not be intelligible without reference to what kind of thing it is. But once we learn that it is, say, a pinch dog and what the pinch dog is for, what its proper function is, we can settle the question objectively. This inseparability of the kind of thing something is and its excellence or lack of it is at the heart of Aristotle's functionalist metaphysics and philosophy of nature.

To a considerable extent, Aristotle's philosophy is his dialectic response to his predecessors' thought systems. Democritus, two generations before him, postulated irreducible bits of matter called atoms and looked upon everything else as their configuration or mechanical interaction (see MATERIALISM). Plato postulated immaterial, unchangeable, and intelligible entities called Forms and looked upon sensible particulars as shifting reflections of independently existing Forms. Aristotle believed, on one hand, that these reductionisms, materialist and formalist, involved the two erroneous moves of treating matter or form in abstraction from that of which it is the matter or form, and then according independent EXISTENCE to it. The result was a fundamental distortion, oversimplification, and impoverishment of reality, a form-matter composite. He believed, on the other hand, that both Democritus and Plato had caught sight of an aspect of reality, inasmuch as it would be generally meaningful to ask about a given thing what its matter and form are. He insisted, however, that matter and form are ontological correlates. The question what matter or form is, without reference to the form of which it is the matter or the matter of which it is the form, would generally be unintelligible. Moreover, the matter of a matter-form composite, generally speaking, is itself another matter-form composite, something that has its own form. There is after all nothing so totally devoid of nature that it cannot do anything on its own but can have anything whatsoever done to it. But both reductionisms, Aristotle believed, would have to postulate such a thing.

Aristotle correlated matter to form as potential to actual: to be *informed* is actually to be such and such while matter is the potential to be such and such (see MODALITY). Change is matter-becoming-informed, and form-becoming-emmattered. In other words, change is the actualization of the potential to be such and such. This conceptual formula was Aristotle's answer to Parmenides, who, active one century before him, did away with potentiality and hence denied the possibility of change. Accordingly, whereas Parmenides bound reality with necessity, Aristotle enriched it with potentiality and potency.

As matter and form are correlated and nested, so are potentiality and actuality, or potency and act. This conceptual scheme finds a prime example in Aristotle's general theory of soul and body (see MIND–BODY PROBLEM). It holds that the body is the matter of the soul as form, and the soul is the matter of life-activity as form. In other words, the soul is the capacity a living organism has to perform the activities of living, whose presence requires the body to be in a certain physical configuration and physiological condition. In the conceptual dissolution of this matter-form correlation Aristotle locates the etiology of re-ductionist tendencies. Against those who hold the soul to be separable from the body, he reminds us that what engages in life-activity is not the soul but the living organism. Moreover, speaking and wrestling, though quite distinct in form, are alike in that to do either one needs a certain kind of functioning musculoskeletal system, which in turn requires functioning cardiovascular and digestive systems. Pythagoras' doctrine of transmigrating soul disregards this fact. The body of an earthworm, for instance, is ill equipped to do what an eagle can with its soul. Against those who reduce cognitive, linguistic, and psycho-logical processes to bodily ones, he points out that speaking is no more to be equated with emitting sounds than anger with the boiling of blood around the heart. Atomism, which would welcome such equations as steps toward reducing all phenomena to mechanical relations of atoms, despite its opposition to Pla-tonism, equally ignores the soul–body correlation.

In this dialectic context Aristotle's cosmology was formed. He envisioned the universe as a unified, spatially finite system of essence-instantiating substances. Because of the inner structure of an ESSENCE, its individual instances are objectively of a certain species and a certain genus, and the SUBSTANCEs taken as a whole form a system of grades ranging from the simple bodies of earth, water, air, and fire to the GOD. The simple bodies, which form the bottom layer of this cosmological hierarchy, serve as materials of some other sensible substances. The god is pure form, immaterial, and not subject to change.

Also because of the inner structure of an essence, there hold among natural kinds the relations of inclusion, exclusion, and subsumption. For a given individual substance there is a finite nest of natural kinds to which it belongs, ranging from the lowest species to the highest genus. The lowest species is the terminus of species individuation. Without it, every feature of the individual would be essential and taxonomically significant, every individual, sui generis. The highest genus of a given theoretical science determines its unity, scope, and subject matter. The god, being devoid of accidents and not subject to contingency, is in a sense not an individual but an essence, the essence that determines the unity, scope, and subject matter of theology.

Essences are manifested in the activities proper to the kinds of things their instances are. But in the sublunary realm they may fail to be manifested. They do fail and accidents do happen as teleological paths to essential activities interfere with one another, or the conditions necessary for successful travels along the paths otherwise fail to obtain. Such is the universe that we human beings inhabit and seek to comprehend. Thus, we see that Aristotle's picture of reality is not premised on the distinctions between mind and the external world, subjective and objective, private and public.

Aristotle's empiricism has two dimensions, one of which pertains to his conception of theoretical science. He conceives of a theoretical science as a finite, deductive, explanatory system. Its deep layer provides an explanation for the surface layer, "best knowable relative to us," and its deepest layer, "best knowable in the order of being," provides the ultimate explanation for the datum of observation insofar as that datum instantiates universals essential to that science. The greater the depth, the further from the senses (see PERCEPTION). The deepest layer has logico-epistemic as well as metaphysical priority; the surface layer, temporal and psychological priority.

Temporal and psychological beings that we humans are, we can start only with what is best knowable relative to us and closest to the senses. There is no such thing as an innate idea or knowledge (see INNATENESS). Having perceived several groups of singulars, we must draw out of them the essence embedded in them. This is the process Aristotle calls ἐπαγωγή, which is usually translated as "INDUCTION." The Aristotelian technical term used in this context, ἐμπειρία, to which the word "experience" is akin, refers to the faculty of concatenating singulars retained in memory. This concatenation precedes induction. Thus, on the part of the animal best cognitively equipped, there is the sequence of sense-perception, retention, concatenation, and induction. Of these terms, each of the last three presupposes all the others preceding it. The outcome of this sequence is the acquisition of the knowledge of the essence.

This acquisition is also pictured on the model of seeing: as sight is to a visible form, so is the intellect to an intelligible form. As seeing-being seen is the actualization of sight and visibility, so is knowing-being known the actualization of the intellect and intelligibility. But Aristotle does not articulate the connection between the sensible and the intelligible form and seems to leave the possibility open for a being without the faculty of sensory discrimination to possess theoretical knowledge.

We find the other dimension of Aristotle's empiricism in his emphasis on experience as the starting point of, and an evidential check upon, theory construction. The term "experience" here is used in a broad sense—bewilderingly and excessively broad from the perspective of British Empiricism—that includes not only directly observed natural phenomena but also reported observations, previous theories, conventional views, common sense, lexical data, and the logic of ordinary language. Accordingly, though he excelled in formal thinking and ventured to follow a line of thought in speculative theology well beyond the ken of experience, he generally distrusted a priori theorizing as a philosophical method, particularly when its outcome was paradoxical or bizarre. In investigating a problem he often made a point of collecting empirical data and subjected them to systematic analysis. Among prominent examples of this practice are his careful observation of the formation of chick embryos at different stages of incubation, his collection of the constitutions of 158 Greek city-states as the basis for his political science, his surveys of a wide variety of opinions and doctrines as the starting points of psychology, metaphysics, and ethics, and his observation of how the term "good" functions, from which he concluded that Plato was wrong to treat it as a universal. The following methodological remark of his accords well with this general practice: "The facts have not been sufficiently ascertained; and if at any time they are ascertained, then we must believe the senses more than the theories—and the theories if they show results in agreement with the observations" (*On the Generation of Animals*, III 10, 760 b 30–33).

We must face several closely related problems in trying to characterize Aristotle's empiricism precisely and systematically. First, although in the *Posterior Analytics* he conceives of scientific knowledge as having the form of nested demonstrations from the first principles, his works in theoretical sciences do not exemplify that conception. Why? Second, he does not work out a connection between that conception, in which the first principles are not explicitly pictured as empirically based, and his account of induction in *Posterior Analytics*, II 19. How would he amplify a sketch of this connection at I 18? Third, in his account of induction he assigns no role to the dialectic method so self-consciously employed elsewhere. Why? Fourth, how does he understand the connection and distinction between causation and justification with respect to knowledge? In his understanding of this matter, what role does his account of the two senses of "better known" play, and how does his doctrine of four causes apply to that role? Fifth, in his theory and practice concerning scientific knowledge and method, how are the faculties of REASON and sense-perception related? In the final analysis, is he an a priori foundationalist or an empirical one? If the latter, are we to think of him as more akin to the ordinary language analyst than to the sense-datum philosopher of science (see PHENOMENALISM)? How we are to understand Aristotelian empiricism in relation to British Empiricism depends on the answers to these questions.

Aristotle's influence is vast in scope and depth. An indication of this is the following array of tributes paid him. AQUINAS, in his attempt to systematize Christian theology in the thirteenth century, drew heavily on Aristotle, referring to him as "the Philosopher." Half a century later, Dante, the author of the monumental work of Christian literature, *The Divine Comedy*, called Aristotle "the master of those who know." In 1690 LOCKE, a champion of the emancipation from scholasticism and the classical tradition, wrote of Aristotle, "whose large views, acuteness, and penetration of thought and strength of judgment, few have equalled" (*An Essay concerning Human Understanding* IV.xvii.4). In 1882, upon reading *The Parts of Animals* by Aristotle, DARWIN, whose theory of evolution was pitted against the Aristotelian doctrine of eternal species, remarked: "Linnaeus and Cuvier have been my two gods . . . but they were mere schoolboys to old Aristotle" (in a letter to William Ogle). In 1956–1957, in expressing his hope to dispose of the problem of freedom by examining all the ways in which it will not do to say simply, "X did A," J. L. Austin acknowledged that he was following Aristotle's example ("A Plea for Excuses"). In general, Austin looked upon Aristotle as having anticipated his own brand of philosophizing, namely, ordinary language analysis. Writing in 1981, Alasdair MacIntyre called for virtue-centered communitarian ethics, declaring that "Aristotelianism is *philosophically* the most powerful of premodern modes of moral thought. If a premodern view of morals and politics is to be vindicated against modernity, it will be in *something like* Aristotelian terms or not at all" (*After Virtue*).

Most participants in the Western intellectual tradition have in fact come under the spells of the classical ideology of culture rationalism, the cultural force of the view that reason is the supreme human faculty. Aristotle was not the originator of this ideology. But much of his cultural influence can be attributed to the role he played, together with Plato, as a major proponent and exponent of this ideology. At its heart were the definition of man as the rational animal and the conception of the life of reason as the only one intrinsically worth living. The life of reason is the one in which reason, sufficiently developed, controls, coordinates, and utilizes other human faculties to achieve theoretical science.

The ramifications of this definition are numerous and far-reaching. Let us note just two of them here, one pertaining to the mode of theoretical discourse, the other to a hierarchy of power. First, since the operation of reason was supposed to be objective, impersonal, and disinterested, so was theoretical science. Thus, Aristotle envisaged a theoretical science as a logical system of universal, eternal, and necessary truths formulatable in a plain and precise language stripped of any elements of fancy or poetry, narratives or personal perspectives. Second, since reason is the supreme faculty definitive of humanity, those whose life is inadequately informed by rationality are only deficiently human. The highest good for man is simply out of reach for those who are constitutionally nonrational or irrational, like women and natural slaves. As subhumans they could only subserve humans.

Our division of learning and academic departments has its point of origin in Aristotle's notion and practice of a special science. For in the Western tradition he was the first to conceive of a branch of learning as having its own unity and identity with respect to the purpose, scope, subject matter, set of problems, and method of investigation proper to it. This is also true of branches of what we call philosophy today. Only from a post-Aristotelian perspective can we say, for instance, that in Plato's *Republic* metaphysics, ethics, political theory, and other fields of philosophy are fused into one.

Aristotle not only laid out a network of special sciences but also started investigations in a number of them. Among them perhaps the most monumental accomplishments are those in biology and logic. In biology, he operated with the logic of an essentialist taxonomy with respect to individual and kind, species and genus, extension and intension in laying out a classificatory scheme for animals, and he fleshed out this scheme with studies of animal morphology and behavior. Hence Darwin's observation quoted earlier. In formal logic, he had a clear understanding of logical form, used term-variables systematically, laid down the square of opposition, worked out an axiomatic system of syllogistic forms, and ventured upon modal logic. The Aristotelian assumption that subject-predicate is the fundamental sentential structure, and the view of the complete adequacy of the Aristotelian syllogistics persisted through the nineteenth century. The very notion of *informal* logic we have today and some of the subject matter treated under that heading are Aristotelian in origin.

No other philosopher contributed so much to the development of conceptual apparatus and terminology in the Western philosophical tradition as Aristotle did. Such terminology as "subject" and "predicate," "substance" and "attribute," "essence" and "accident," "genus" and "species," "universal" and "particular," "categories of being," "form" and "matter," "actuality" and "potentiality," "induction" and "demonstration," and "efficient and final causes" are of Aristotelian origin or the outcome of Aristotelian refinement. The view, which has persisted to this day despite criticisms from various quarters, that philosophy transcends history and culture, the personal and the political, is in part the legacy of Aristotle. His ability to raise significant issues, his manner of grappling with them while eschewing oversimplification, and the systematic correlation of his proposed solutions have been admired and emulated at different times and in different schools. The basic acceptability of Aristotelian essentialism, functionalism, and virtue-ethics is a live issue today.

The British Empiricists' outlook upon Aristotle's philosophy was negative. Their nominalistic (see NOMINALISM) tendency was antithetical to his realism and essentialism. Since they saw Aristotelianism as the straitjacket on Scholasticism, their project of emancipation from the latter involved the rejection of the former. Nevertheless, they inherited the Western tradition of philosophizing to the definition of which Aristotle had contributed in fundamental ways, and in their historical background Aristotle's empiricism stood as a rich stock of ideas. In particular, they accepted the medieval principle, traceable to Aristotle, that there is nothing in the intellect that was not previously in the senses. Other Empiricist tendencies and theses with Aristotelian antecedents include the tendency to isolate terms in considering the function of language, the understanding of cognition on the model of sight, and Locke's denial of innate ideas, his distinction between PRIMARY AND SECONDARY QUALITIES, and his theses that a quality requires a substratum and that the powers to bring about the experience of secondary qualities inhere in things.

PRIMARY WORK

The Complete Works of Aristotle. Edited by Jonathan Barnes. 2 vols. Princeton: Princeton University Press, 1984.

BIBLIOGRAPHY

Books

Ackrill, J. L. *Aristotle the Philosopher*. Oxford and New York: Oxford University Press, 1981.
Barnes, Jonathan, ed. *The Cambridge Companion to Aristotle*. Cambridge and New York: Cambridge University Press, 1995.
Barnes, Jonathan, Malcolm Schofield, and Richard Sorabji, eds. *Articles on Aristotle*. Vol. 1, *Science*. London: Duckforth, 1975.
Cohen, Sheldon M. *Aristotle on Nature and Incomplete Substance*. Cambridge: Cambridge University Press, 1996.
Edel, Abraham. *Aristotle and His Philosophy*. Chapel Hill: University of North Carolina Press, 1982.
Evans, J.D.G. *Aristotle's Concept of Dialectic*. Cambridge: Cambridge University Press, 1977.
Irwin, Terence. *Aristotle's First Principles*. Oxford: Clarendon Press; New York: Oxford University Press, 1988.
Lloyd, G.E.R. *Aristotelian Explorations*. Cambridge: Cambridge University Press, 1996.
Spelman, Elizabeth V. *Inessential Woman: Problems of Exclusion in Feminist Thought*. Boston: Beacon Press, 1988.

Articles

Burnyeat, M. F. "Aristotle on Understanding Knowledge." In *Aristotle on Science: The Posterior Analytics*, edited by Enrico Berti. Symposium Aristotelicum; Padova: Editrice Antenore, 1981: 97–139.
Owen, G.E.L. "ΤΙΘΕΝΑΙ ΤΑ ΦΑΙΝΟΜΕΝΑ." In *Aristote et les problèmes de la méthode*, edited by S. Mansion. Symposium Aristotelicum; Louvain: Editions Nauwelaerts, 1961: 83–103. Reprinted in *Aristotle: A Collection of Critical Essays*, edited by J.M.E. Moravcsik. Garden City, NY: Doubleday, 1967: 167–90; also in *Articles on Aristotle*, vol. 1, by Barnes et al.: 113–26.

Taylor, C.C.W. "Aristotle's Epistemology." In *Epistemology*, edited by Stephen Everson. Cambridge and New York: Cambridge University Press, 1990: 116–42.

YUKIO KACHI

ASSOCIATIONISM. Associationism is a theory of learning in psychology that was defended by many classical empiricists both as a theory and as providing accounts of certain facts alternative to those proposed by rationalists and Aristotelians. The theory was important in John LOCKE and was developed in detail as a psychological theory by David Hartley in his *Observations on Man* and by David HUME in his *Treatise of Human Nature*, which emphasized the philosophical implications. The theory was developed in the nineteenth century by James and John Stuart MILL. It subsequently became an important paradigm in psychological research. Important figures were H. Von Helmholtz and W. Wundt, as well as E. B. Titchener in the United States.

The theory was an empirical theory of learning and had its roots in Aristotle's account of memory (see ARISTOTLE) and in the well-known and useful facts concerning artificial associations established as memory aids for the classical orator. The theory states roughly this. If one has regularly observed As and Bs standing in relation R, then there comes to exist in one's mind a habitual connection between As and Bs such that if an A is presented to one, or if an idea of A is presented to one, then an idea of B will appear in consciousness. This habitual connection is an association. Thus, if the relation R is that of contiguity in space and time, then the habit that is formed is that of causal inference, the judgment that As cause Bs. Empiricists on the whole followed Hume in arguing that there are no objective necessary connections, that objectively all there is to causation is regularity. But why, then, do we think of causes as necessary? They responded by pointing to the habitual nature of causal judgments: subjectively, the mind is constrained in causal judgments by habits of association, and this is the source of the feeling of necessity.

Again, if the relation R is that of resemblance, then the As and Bs are associated by virtue of a common character. If, further, an artificial association is established between a certain sound or mark and the entities associated by virtue of R, then that mark or sound becomes a general term that applies to all the entities connected by the association. The classical empiricists thus proposed to account for how terms become general, that is, for general concepts, without invoking abstract universal ideas to which the Aristotelians and the rationalists appealed (see CONCEPTS).

BERKELEY used this theory of association to propose that our awareness of depth in space among physical objects arises not innately as the Cartesians had argued but through associational processes that bring together visual signs, tactile signs, and kinesthetic sensations of motion-toward. Our perceivings of depth are learned in much the same way that our causal judgments are learned. This became a standard theory in the emerging science of psychology, though it was to be challenged at times by forms of innatism deriving from KANT.

Other criticisms of associationism were based on phenomenology. Suppose that X is a form of thought—either, say, a causal judgment or a general concept—that is the product of an association between As and Bs. The first associationists tended to think of X as having the idea of A and the idea of B as literal parts, so that psychological analysis of an idea was akin to the logical analysis of a concept. Indeed, associationists such as John Locke and James Mill were often prone to confuse the two. Thomas REID defended a form of rationalist innatism against the associationists by arguing that since many judgments and mental states were phenomenologically simple rather than complex, they therefore could not have come about as a result of association. John Stuart Mill replied that the product of a process can well have properties that are not had by the genetic antecedents. The younger Mill argued that the genetic antecedents of mental states were not literal parts of the simple states but were present dispositionally and could be recovered through associational processes. This reconciled associationism with the phenomenology of mental states, on the one hand, and, on the other hand, made it clear that psychological analysis was an empirical method to be distinguished from logical analysis.

The associationists claimed in general that all mental states had sensory contents as their genetic antecedents and that these sensory contents could be recovered through psychological analysis. By the twentieth century it had become clear that many thoughts were irreducible to sensory contents (''imageless thoughts''). When it appeared that behaviorism was the appropriate methodological stance for psychology, if it was to be an objective science, associationism, insofar as it remained a viable research program, merged with varieties of classical conditioning and reinforcement theories of learning.

BIBLIOGRAPHY

Books

Boring, E. G. *A History of Experimental Psychology.* 2d ed. New York: Appleton-Century-Crofts, 1957.

Hartley, D. *Observations on Man* (1749). Gainsville, FL: Scholar's Facsimiles, 1966.

Mill, James. *Analysis of the Phenomena of the Human Mind.* 2d ed. Edited by John Stuart Mill, with additional notes by Mill et al. (1878). New York: A. M. Kelly, 1967.

Wilson, Fred. *Psychological Analysis and the Philosophy of John Stuart Mill.* Toronto: University of Toronto Press, 1990.

Article

Ward, James. ''Psychology.'' In *Encyclopedia Britannica,* 1886 ed., Peale (American) reprint. Chicago: R. S. Peale, 1892, vol. 20: 37–85.

FRED WILSON

AYER, SIR ALFRED JULES. Sir Alfred Jules Ayer (1910–1989), as he tells us in his ''Intellectual Autobiography,'' finished in July 1935 writing *Language, Truth and Logic*—arguably, the most influential single book written by a philosopher in the twentieth century. Although none of his other fifteen or twenty important volumes provoked the stir that this one did, they earned for him unusual distinction and numerous honors (see *Who's Who in the World*, 1989–1990). He wrote clearly, gracefully, and vigorously and showed exceptional capacity for self-criticism. He readily admitted inadequacies in earlier arguments and inability to formulate satisfactorily the VERIFICATION PRINCIPLE, although to the end he held fast to what he called the verificatory approach and remained an empiricist in the tradition of HUME and Bertrand RUSSELL. This entry sketches some of his major interests, ideas, and activities in roughly chronological order.

Ayer was educated at Eton College and Christ Church, University of Oxford, graduating from the latter in literary humanities in 1932. In this year he was appointed to a lectureship at Christ Church, the first of more than fifty years of appointments at Oxford and the University of London; but since he had no formal duties for two terms, he hesitated between going to Cambridge to study with WITTGENSTEIN or going to Vienna to learn what he could about the Vienna Circle. On Gilbert Ryle's recommendation, he chose the latter. Moritz Schlick arranged for him to attend lectures at the university and also invited him to participate in meetings of the Vienna Circle, a regular group of fewer than twenty philosophers and scientists concerned to strengthen links between philosophy and science, replace metaphysics with science, and develop a logic of science. The previous academic year Schlick was visiting professor at the University of California at Berkeley, where I took his year-seminar in logic devoted to Wittgenstein's *Tractatus* and sat in on his classes in theory of knowledge and philosophy of science. In philosophy the circle's leading members were Schlick, CARNAP, Neurath, Feigl, Waismann, Zilsel, and Victor Kraft, and for science and mathematics, Philipp Frank, Karl Menger, Kurt GÖDEL, and Hans Hahn.

After returning to Oxford for the 1933 summer term, Ayer gave a series of lectures on Wittgenstein and Carnap, drawing on what he had learned in Vienna, and Isaiah Berlin suggested that he put it all into a book before his enthusiasm waned. Accordingly, he plunged into writing a primer for LOGICAL POSITIV-ISM (see LOGICAL POSITIVISM/LOGICAL EMPIRICISM), *Language, Truth and Logic*, which turned out to be a mixture of Viennese positivism with a Wittgensteinian twist, the reductive empiricism of Hume and Russell, the analytical approach of G. E. MOORE, a little touch of the pragmatism of C. I. Lewis and F. P. Ramsey, and the conviction that all genuine philosophical problems can be solved by logical analysis. Significant propositions fell into two classes: formal propositions of MATHEMATICS and logic, which the positivists considered tautologies, and empirically verifiable factual propositions of SCIENCE and common sense. Other statements were neither true nor false but nonsensical or, at best, emotive. Ethical judgments, for example, were not statements of fact but rather expressions of approval or disapproval that its propounders hoped others would share. But the charge of nonsense was particularly directed against METAPHYSICS, with the verification principle being used to disqualify its statements. Unfortunately, this principle did not appear to be verifiable.

Ayer's favorite branch of philosophy was theory of knowledge, a topic central to most of his books. *Foundations of Empirical Knowledge* (1940) focused on problems of PERCEPTION and getting from sense-data to physical objects (see EXTERNAL WORLD), and *The Problem of Knowledge* (1956), his second most successful volume, treated theory of knowledge as a series of attempts to rebut the skeptic. Epistemological analysis is also focal in such other works as *The Concept of a Person and Other Essays* (1963); *Metaphysics and Common Sense* (1969); *The Central Questions of Philosophy* (1974), 1972–1973 Gifford Lectures; *Perception and Identity* (1979); and *Philosophy in the Twentieth Century* (1981).

During the war he served (1940–1945) as captain in the Welsh Guards with roving assignments to Military Intelligence in New York, Buenos Aires, Algiers, and France. He characterized it as more cloak than dagger.

In contrast to his critic J. L. Austin's form of language analysis, which elucidated ordinary linguistic usage, Ayer's emphasis was on achieving a different and clearer view of the facts language was used to describe. Also, he held that Austin's arguments do not refute the sense-datum theory.

Ayer credits PEIRCE the pragmatist with contributing to the development of his own position and finds much in James and C. I. Lewis consistent with his views. But he ignores John Dewey, even in *The Origins of Pragmatism*. Most of the interesting ideas he found in Dewey were ones he believed Dewey inherited from Peirce and James. Perhaps part of his lack of esteem for Dewey stems from their differing conceptions of philosophy. Whereas Ayer was convinced that the statements of philosophy are not empirically testable, the pragmatists think of them as ways of converting problematic situations into something better. Sharp differences between Ayer and the pragmatists on the possibility of moral knowledge further separate them. They thought that his contention that there is no moral knowledge, only "unproved moral assumptions," left him with no empirical warrant for his own humanitarianism. He was troubled also by what he saw as James' failure to distinguish adequately between the truth of a belief and there being some evidence for it. Further, contrary to Jamesian scholars, he was convinced that the only positive reason James offers for acceptance of religious hypotheses or judgments of value is his presumption that they satisfy emotional needs.

For fifty years Ayer participated in international philosophical meetings and spoke to highly diverse audiences in Russia, Bulgaria, China, South America, North America, and other parts of the world. He was for many years on panels for the British Broadcasting Company and was also invited to speak at high-level sessions in different parts of the world. For example, President John Kennedy invited him to speak on the nature of philosophy at one of a series of seminars that members of his family and his cabinet were expected to attend, and Ayer argued that his analytic conception of philosophy was squarely in the Socratic tradition.

PRIMARY WORKS

Language, Truth and Logic. London: Gollancz, 1936; rev. ed. 1946; London: Pelican Books, 1971.

The Foundations of Empirical Knowledge. London: Macmillan, 1940; London: St. Martin's Library ed., 1964.

The Problem of Knowledge. London: Macmillan; New York: St. Martin's Press, 1956; London: Penguin Paperback.

The Origins of Pragmatism. London: Macmillan and San Francisco: Freeman, Cooper, 1968.

Metaphysics and Common Sense. London: Macmillan and San Francisco: Freeman, Cooper, 1969.

Russell and Moore: The Analytical Heritage. Harvard 1970 William James Lectures. London: Macmillan and Cambridge: Harvard University Press, 1971.

Probability and Evidence. Columbia John Dewey Lectures for 1970. London: Macmillan and New York: Columbia University Press, 1972; paperback, 1979.

Russell. London: Fontana and New York: Viking Press, 1972. Under the title *Bertrand Russell*. Chicago: University of Chicago Press, 1988.

The Central Questions of Philosophy. Gifford Lectures at the University of St. Andrews, Scotland, 1972–1973. London: Weidenfeld and Nicolson and New York: Holt, Rinehart, and Winston, 1973; New York: Penguin Books, 1974.

Hume. Past Masters Series. Oxford: Oxford University Press and New York: Hill and Wang, 1980.

Philosophy in the Twentieth Century. London: Weidenfeld and Nicolson, 1981; New York: Random House, 1982; paperback, London: Allen and Unwin and New York: Vintage Books, 1984.

Freedom and Morality and Other Essays. Oxford: Clarendon Press and New York: Oxford University Press, 1984.

Wittgenstein. London: Weidenfeld and Nicolson and New York: Random House and Penguin Books, 1985.

Voltaire. London: Weidenfeld and Nicolson and New York: Random House, 1986.

The Meaning of Life and Other Essays [posthumously]. London: Weidenfeld and Nicolson. Under the title *The Meaning of Life*. New York: Scribner's, 1990.

Autobiographies

Part of My Life. London: Collins, 1977; paperback, Oxford: Oxford University Press, 1978.

More of My Life. London: Collins, 1984; paperback, Oxford: Oxford University Press, 1985.

"Intellectual Autobiography." In *The Philosophy of A. J. Ayer*, edited by Lewis Hahn. La Salle, IL: Open Court, 1992: 3–53.

Who's Who in the World, 9th ed., 1989–1990. Wilmette, IL: Marquis Who's Who, Macmillan Directory Division, 1989.

BIBLIOGRAPHY

Hahn, Lewis, ed. *The Philosophy of A. J. Ayer.* The Library of Living Philosophers, vol. 21. La Salle, IL: Open Court, 1992. Essays by twenty-five critics with his replies to twenty-two. Also provides a bibliography of his writings, pp. 661–80.

MacDonald, G. F., ed. *Perception and Identity: Essays Presented to A. J. Ayer with His Replies to Them.* London: Macmillan, 1979. Bibliography, pp. 334–46.

LEWIS E. HAHN

B

BACON, FRANCIS. Francis Bacon (1561–1626) was born to a well-to-do and influential family in London. He studied at Trinity College, Cambridge (1573–1575). There he encountered the new logic of Ramus, an alternative to the then-dominant Aristotelian logic. Being the second son of his father's second marriage, his father's death in 1579 left him dispossessed. He then enrolled at Grey's Inn and became a barrister in 1582, thus beginning an eventful and turbulent career in law and politics, which included his being a member of the House of Commons. Throughout his career he fell in and out of favor with the Crown, first with Queen Elizabeth I and then later with King James I. In addition, his life was marred by financial instability. He gained a reputation for ruthlessness when he represented the Crown against a once-close friend, the Earl of Essex, who had done much to advance Bacon's career. Essex was charged and subsequently executed for treason. Despite numerous setbacks, Bacon was knighted and ultimately became lord chancellor. But his political career ended in 1621, when he was convicted for bribery.

In addition to his political and legal career, Bacon began a literary career in 1597 with the publication of a series of essays. These and subsequent essays and books, most of which were written in Latin, addressed a range of topics including history, law, and SCIENCE. His most important scientific and philosophical works are *The Advancement of Learning* (1605), *Novum Organum* (1620) (The New Organon), *De Augmentis Scientiarum* (1623) (Of the Dignity and Advancement of Learning), and *New Atlantis* (1627). Bacon's contributions, strictly speaking, are contributions to the philosophy of science, rather than to science. In fact, Bacon neither had much contact with contemporary scientists nor engaged in much scientific experimentation himself, despite his insistence on the importance of experimentation. In 1626 Bacon died of bronchitis, which was brought on after he stuffed a chicken carcass with snow while attempting to test his hypothesis that snow could preserve flesh from putrefaction.

Bacon's own philosophical work is directed against two principal adversaries. First, he is critical of the Aristotelianism of the scholastics. He agreed with

neither their a priori approach to natural philosophy nor their reliance on AR-
ISTOTLE's syllogistic LOGIC. Deduction, Bacon felt, was not the appropriate
method for scientific inquiry. Second, Bacon was critical of the humanists. The
humanists, he maintained, were excessively occupied with style and were too
concerned with studying classical texts, rather than studying nature. Bacon's
work, though, is in the spirit of humanism. In particular, in Bacon's view science
had an as-yet untapped practical and liberating potential that promised to improve the condition of humanity.

Bacon believed that people were held back from exploiting the liberating
potential of science because of their own prejudices. People, he claimed, are
typically led into error by the following four types of prejudices, which in *Novum Organum* he refers to as the four idols: (1) *Idols of the Tribe* are prejudices
that are common to all people. For example, people have the tendency to notice
facts that support the beliefs they already hold and thus fail to perceive evidence
that would support a contrary view even when such evidence is available; (2)
Idols of the Market-Place are prejudices that result from taking language too
literally. That is, people often fail to realize that the words they use shape how
they perceive things, sometimes causing them to perceive things incorrectly; (3)
Idols of the Cave are prejudices that are unique to each person. People errone-
ously project various associations onto the world, personal associations that have
no ground in reality; and (4) *Idols of the Theatre* are prejudices that we acquire
from false systems of philosophy. For example, once educated in the philosophy
of Aristotle, one is apt to perceive the world in Aristotelian terms, despite the
fact that the world is otherwise. Because each of these idols gives rise to errors,
a correct understanding of the world requires that their effects be carefully monitored.

Bacon set himself a lifelong task that could be fully realized only by posterity.
He wanted to put humanity on the right track with respect to scientific inquiry,
and he referred to this project as ''the Great Instauration.'' He divided the
project into six distinct tasks: (1) to classify the existing sciences; (2) to devise
a method of inquiry; (3) to catalog all known facts and all experiments conducted; (4) to present applications of his new method; (5) to catalog the results
of his new method; and (6) to present a new science of nature.

In systematizing knowledge, Bacon provided a taxonomy of the various sciences. Most significantly, he drew a sharp distinction between natural matters
and supernatural matters, thus separating science from religion. Mistakenly,
some critics and commentators have assumed that Bacon was antireligious. In
fact, Bacon believed that a better understanding of nature would give us a better
understanding of God.

One of Bacon's most important contributions to the development of empiricism was due to his insistence on the importance of inductive reasoning for
scientific inquiry. INDUCTION was not something new. People had long been
familiar with the expounding approach to induction, generalizing from a number
of particular instances. But Bacon suggested a different approach to inductive

reasoning, an "eliminative" approach. Moreover, Bacon gave a structure to the eliminative approach to induction, thus making a method of it.

In *Novum Organum* Bacon demonstrates this new method. It works as follows. Imagine that we wish to determine the nature of some kind of phenomenon, heat, for instance. Bacon suggests that we draw up three comparative tables. First, on a "Table of Presence" we list as many instances of the phenomenon as we are aware of. Second, on a "Table of Absence" we list phenomena that are similar to those on the preceding table but that lack the nature we seek to understand. Finally, on a "Table of Degrees" we list instances in which the quality in question varies. The nature in question will be that which is present in all the instances listed on the first table and absent from all the instances on the second table. Further, the quality under investigation should vary as expected, which can be confirmed by the data on the third table. In this respect Bacon advocates an empirical method in scientific inquiry. We reason inductively to the nature of the thing that we wish to understand. Such a method invites active experimentation. Through carefully constructed experiments we could elicit an understanding of the nature of the things we wish to understand.

Bacon refers to these natures that we ultimately seek to identify as "forms." His use of this term has caused much confusion among his commentators and critics. Bacon does not have in mind transcendent forms like the forms of Plato's philosophy. Nor does he have in mind immanent forms as conceived by Aristotle. According to Bacon, forms are identified by explanations of a particular kind, specifically, to use the language of the British Empiricists, explanations of secondary qualities in terms of primary qualities (see PRIMARY AND SECONDARY QUALITIES). For example, as suggested earlier, using his method Bacon discovered that heat is matter in motion. Some of these natures, Bacon warns, can be discovered only with the assistance of instruments like telescopes.

An underlying assumption of Bacon's inductive method, an assumption that is now regarded as dubious, is that all the things in the world are composed of a finite number of simple natures. In *Abecadarium Naturae* (The Alphabet of Nature) Bacon compares these simple natures to the letters of the alphabet. Just as the finite number of letters of the alphabet are able to generate words and sentences of great complexity and variety, so too can the simple natures that constitute the world generate all the complexity and variety in the world. According to Bacon, unless this assumption were true, the world would be unknowable.

Bacon also anticipated the social nature of modern scientific inquiry. In *New Atlantis* Bacon describes a fictitious utopian society in which scientific inquiry is supported by the state. In his envisaged Utopia, teams of scientists work together, and there is a division of labor. Though Bacon was not a practicing scientist himself, he had tried to convince the king to support scientific inquiry as he envisaged it should be done, arguing that it would greatly benefit humanity. Although Bacon in his lifetime never saw scientific inquiry institutionalized in this way, he did inspire subsequent generations. In fact, the founding members of the Royal Society (the first of many important scientific academies in early modern Europe, established in England in 1662) acknowledged Bacon as a source of inspiration. Moreover, when the French Encyclopedists began their project of a catalog of all knowledge, they too attributed their inspiration to Bacon.

Bacon's contribution to modern science is thus threefold. First, he both inspired and anticipated the collective nature of modern scientific inquiry. The implications that the collective nature of inquiry has for empiricism, though, are just now being examined by philosophers like Helen Longino and Lynn Hankinson Nelson. Second, Bacon directed people's attention toward the significance of induction for scientific inquiry, though the particulars of his inductive method do not characterize the methods of modern science or even the science of his contemporaries. Third, as a consequence of a renewed interest in induction, scientific inquiry became more active, with scientists carefully constructing experiments to systematically elicit information about the phenomena under study.

Although Bacon represents a significant and progressive departure from the old Aristotelian scholastic approach to science, he is criticized on a number of accounts. First, it is generally agreed that Bacon neither understood MATHEMATICS sufficiently nor appreciated the significance that mathematics has for science. Second, it is generally believed that Bacon failed to appreciate the significant role of hypotheses in inquiry. His approach to science, though rightly empirical, is naively empirical. Finally, more recently, numerous feminist philosophers of science, including Carolyn Merchant and Evelyn Fox Keller, have criticized Bacon for the aggressive, sometimes brutal, objectifying metaphors he uses in describing how we are to go about understanding nature. They argue that these metaphors have shaped not only our understanding of nature but also our conception of, and practices in, scientific inquiry.

PRIMARY WORKS

The Works of Francis Bacon. Edited by James Spedding, R. L. Ellis, and D. D. Heath. 14 vols. London: Longmans, 1857–1874.
A Selection of His Works. Translated and edited by Peter Urbach and John Gibson. Chicago: Open Court, 1994.

BIBLIOGRAPHY

Books

Broad, C. D. *The Philosophy of Francis Bacon.* New York: Octagon Books, 1976.
Merchant, Carolyn. *The Death of Nature.* San Francisco: Harper and Row, 1980.
Peltonan, Markku, ed. *The Cambridge Companion to Bacon.* Cambridge: Cambridge University Press, 1996.
Perez-Ramos, Antonio. *Francis Bacon's Idea of Science.* Oxford: Clarendon Press, 1988.
Quinton, Anthony. *Francis Bacon.* Oxford: Oxford University Press, 1980.
Rossi, Paolo. *Francis Bacon: From Magic to Science.* Translated by Sacha Rabinovitch. London: Routledge and Kegan Paul, 1968.

Articles

Hesse, Mary. "Francis Bacon's Philosophy of Science." In *Essential Articles for the Study of Francis Bacon*, edited by B. Vickers. London, 1968.

Keller, Evelyn Fox. "Baconian Science: A Hermaphroditic Birth." *Philosophical Forum* 11 (1980): 299–307.

K. BRAD WRAY

BEATTIE, JAMES. James Beattie (1735–1803), Scottish commonsense philosopher, was born in the village of Laurencekirk, Kincardineshire, Scotland, and educated at Marischal College, Aberdeen. After teaching at a school in Fourdon and Aberdeen, Beattie became a professor of moral philosophy and logic at Marischal College in 1760 (after having been first appointed to the chair of natural philosophy). Thomas REID was his colleague at Marischal College until 1764. Beattie was a member of a philosophical club (the Wise Club), which also included Thomas Reid, George Campbell, and John Gregory. In the meetings of this club many of the doctrines that made these men famous were first put forward and discussed. Beattie first became known as a poet. In 1770 he published *An Essay on the Nature and Immutability of Truth in Opposition to Sophistry and Scepticism*, a highly popular attack on George BERKELEY and David HUME, and in 1771 the first part of *The Minstrel* appeared, which solidified his fame as a poetic genius. Though Hume called him a "silly and bigoted fellow," and Adam SMITH found only "a few good lines" in his poetry, Beattie was a great success not only in England but also in America and Germany. As a result, he was elected to the American Philosophical Society, and George III gave him a pension of two hundred pounds. His later works were not quite as successful, but they contributed to his reputation as a writer on literary and aesthetic subjects. His life was not without tragedy: his oldest son, in whom he had great hopes, died at the age of twenty-two, and his other son died soon after. His wife suffered from mental illness for most of her life, and he took care of her until she had to be institutionalized for her violent behavior.

Beattie is usually considered to be simply a follower of Reid, and his philosophical works are regarded as shallow and rightly forgotten. He is often lumped together with James Oswald as well, and KANT made the phrase "Reid, Oswald, and Beattie" famous. In Kant's view, Beattie misunderstood both Berkeley and Hume, and Beattie's critique of their positions can be safely disregarded. Perhaps Kant is correct. But since Beattie's works were highly successful, not only in Scotland but throughout Europe, he is important for understanding the spread of Humean ideas. Kant, for instance, may have learned of some of Hume's doctrines through Beattie (see Wolff 1960 and Kuehn 1987). Furthermore, many of his criticisms, while perhaps not well put, have turned out to be influential, such as his attack on the criterion of "liveliness" for the distinction of impressions and IDEAS, his criticism of the copy thesis, and the claim that ideas represent the meanings of concepts (see Sprague 1967). Beattie does follow Reid in assuming that we have a faculty, called common sense, that provides us with a number of fundamental truths without which we cannot know anything. These truths are truly first principles, which, as such, cannot be defended or justified in any way. "All reasoning terminates in first principles. All evidence ultimately intuitive. Common Sense the standard of Truth to Man" (title of Chapter 2 of Beattie, *Essay on the Nature of Immutability of Truth*). Unless "we believe many things without proof, we never can believe anything at all" (Beattie, *Essay*: 51). Trying to justify these basic principles or beliefs will lead inevitably to skepticism. This is shown by the philosophical theories of Descartes, Malebranche, Berkeley, and Hume. Beattie appears to place greater emphasis on the instinctual nature of common sense than Reid, who, especially in his later works, assimilates common sense more to the rational faculty.

Whereas Beattie claims that "common sense is the ultimate judge of truth, to which reason must continually act in subordination" (Beattie, *Essay*: 51), Reid wants to show that it is a function of reason itself, saying that we "ascribe to reason two offices, or two degrees. The first is to judge of things self-evident; the second to draw conclusions from those that are. The first of these is the province, and the sole province, of common sense" (Reid, *Works* I: 425).

Reid's earlier *Inquiry into the Human Mind on the Principles of Common Sense* (Edinburgh, 1764) seems to be closer to Beattie's position, however; and the change in emphasis may well have been occasioned by Joseph Priestley's vigorous attack on Reid, Oswald, and Beattie in 1774, calling special attention to Reid's "general system of instinctive principles of truth, which they all accept, and which is not only prejudicial to the cause of that very truth . . . he means to support, and favouring that very scepticism . . . he imagined he was overthrowing" (Priestley, *An Examination of Dr. Reid's Inquiry. Dr. Beattie's Essay. and Dr. Oswald's Appeal*: 115f.).

PRIMARY WORKS

An Essay on the Nature and Immutability of Truth in Opposition to Sophistry and Scepticism. Edinburgh: William Creech, 1770.

An Essay on the Nature and Immutability of Truth in Opposition to Sophistry and Scepticism; Poetry and Music, as They Affect the Mind; on Laughter, on Ludicrous Composition; on the Utility of Classical Learning. 2 vols. Edinburgh: William Creech, 1776.

Dissertations Moral and Critical. London: W. Strahan, T. Cadell, and W. Creech, 1783.

The Theory of Language. London: A. Strahan, 1788.

Elements of Moral Science. Vol. 1. Edinburgh William Creech, 1790.

OTHER PRIMARY WORKS

Oswald, James. *An Appeal to Common Sense in Behalf of Religion.* 2 vols. Edinburgh: A. Kincaid and W. Creech, 1766, 1772.

Priestley, Joseph. *An Examination of Dr. Reid's Inquiry. Dr. Beattie's Essay. and Dr. Oswald's Appeal.* London: J. Johnson, 1774.

Reid, Thomas. *Philosophical Works.* 2 vols. Edited by William Hamilton, with an introduction by Harry Bracken. Hildesheim: Olms, 1967.

BIBLIOGRAPHY

Books

Graham, Henry Gray. *Scottish Men of Letters in the Eighteenth Century*. London: Adam and Charles Black, 1908.
Kuehn, Manfred. *Scottish Common Sense in Germany, 1768–1800: A Contribution to the History of Critical Philosophy*. Preface by Lewis White Beck. Kingston and Montreal: McGill-Queen's University Press, 1987.

Articles

Kloth, Karen, and Bernhard Fabian. "James Beattie; Contributions toward a Bibliography." *Bibliotheck* 5 (1970): 234–45.
Sinclair, William. "The Bibliography of James Beattie." *Records of the Glasgow Bibliographical Society* 7 (1923): 27–35.
Sprague, Elmer. s. v. "Beattie, James." In *Encyclopedia of Philosophy*, edited by Paul Edwards. New York: Macmillan, 1967.
Wolff, Robert Paul. "Kant's Debt to Hume via Beattie." *Journal of the History of Ideas* 21 (1960): 117–23.

MANFRED KUEHN

BEAUTY. "Beauty" played a central role in classical philosophy, but, as Paul Oskar Kristeller pointed out, as a concept it was not distinguished from the good and thus functioned differently from the modern concept associated with art and the aesthetic. According to Plotinus, for example, perceptible beauty is the soul's recognition of its own nature in the forms, and intelligible beauty is just the nature of the forms themselves. The good is distinguished from beauty only as a source is distinguished from the forms (*Ennead* I.6). The Neoplatonic conception of beauty informs most subsequent discussions of beauty through the Middle Ages and Renaissance, and it reappears in a somewhat different form in the Cambridge Platonists of the seventeenth century and in romanticism. It is a key part of a METAPHYSICS that locates reality as fundamentally different from perceptual appearances. A hierarchy of beauty leads from sense to intelligible and moral beauty and ultimately to a mystical contemplation of the good.

The empiricist revolution in SCIENCE and philosophy in the course of the seventeenth and eighteenth centuries transformed the concept of beauty. "Beauty" is so deeply rooted in the thought of the period that initially efforts are directed at incorporating it into the new way of conceiving of the importance of experience. The third earl of Shaftesbury, for example, continues to link beauty and virtue and to regard both as higher forms superior to sense. However, he relies much more on "sentiment" understood as a feeling immediately available to an inner sense than any earlier Neoplatonist could, and sensual beauty is thus given a more important role. Subsequently, Francis Hutcheson completes the transformation by postulating an inner sense of beauty that makes beauty a direct object of experience. Beauty is simply the response of this sense to the properties of uniformity amid variety that our experience of objects and ideas provides. Beauty is thus transformed from a metaphysical reality that is accessible only by leaving sense behind to a feeling or emotion directly perceptible by a special sense.

Once beauty becomes a perceptual property of objects, the question immediately arises as to what property or properties it corresponds to. Classically, certain properties had always been regarded as beautiful—particularly the proportion represented by A:B as B:A + B, and Renaissance painters entertained the idea that some colors and proportions were particularly beautiful. These claims rested on the importance of harmony and proportion as ways of transcending mere sense, however. In the eighteenth century, beauty was sought in those properties that would be immediately pleasing to the senses. William Hogarth proposed that a sensual line, essentially a gentle curve, was the visual form that stimulated pleasure. In a somewhat different vein, Edmund Burke contributed to the speculation about the nature of beauty by distinguishing the beautiful from the sublime. Beauty was a pleasure produced by the small, refined, and delicate. The sublime, in contrast, was vast, grand, and frightening. In every case, beauty is thought of as a pleasant emotion stimulated in individuals by external objects. As such, it need have no moral or metaphysical significance beyond the significance of the human desire for pleasure and happiness.

In the empiricist scheme, beauty is subordinate to taste. Taste is an immediate judgment, either of a sense analogous to the gustatory sense of taste or of the reflective powers of the mind. Taste combines experience with a valuing of an object or action and is itself a subject of judgment as good or bad taste. Thus, taste reflects both moral character and aesthetic ability to feel and discriminate. The concept of beauty is linked to taste as its intentional object, but increasingly beauty is eliminable. Aesthetic feeling and experience are conceived as pleasurable expressions of the mind's own powers actively engaged by some object or activity. These powers involve the ability both to organize sensory input into coherent perception and to respond sensitively to stimuli that are pleasurable. The problem is that taste is individual and subjective in a way that beauty is not. A quest for a standard of taste largely bypasses the concept of beauty and goes directly to the mental operations themselves. David HUME, for example, characterizes the sound judge as one who combines strong sense with delicacy of sentiment, extensive practice, judicious comparison, and freedom from prejudice. These are properties of the judge, not of the object, and beauty plays no role in their description. Immanuel KANT brings together the elements of this new empiricist aesthetic in his *Critique of Judgment*, in which the analytic of the beautiful is essentially an analysis of aesthetic intuition rather than a metaphysical description. Although ''beauty'' continues to be the object of the analysis, it could be replaced by ''aesthetic experience'' with little loss, and that is essentially what happens in the subsequent tradition. Hegel and romanticism revert to a metaphysical form of beauty, but both are rejecting the empiricist forms of philosophy in the process.

Taste itself comes to be questioned in twentieth-century forms of empiricism.

Aesthetic concepts are linked to subjective experience of a perceiver, and increasingly it appears that no set of properties is either necessary or sufficient to justify aesthetic concepts. Not only are they not empirical in the way that color or shape is empirical, but they are not "rule-governed" at all in the way that they fit into our language. Either they are noncognitive expressions, or they are an irreducibly subjective expression of a perceptual gestalt that one must just "see" for oneself. In that context, beauty ceases to have any role at all to play in aesthetics. If taste is not a perception of some property that can be described as beautiful, then "beauty" is no longer anything more than an honorific term. That was the conclusion reached by Clive Bell, who proposed to drop it from the aesthetic vocabulary altogether. Others, including R. G. Collingwood and Benedetto Croce, tried to save beauty by identifying it with expression and denying that there was any such thing as natural beauty. In their usage, beauty was simply expression itself, so it presupposed an active mind. The breadth of that usage and the anomaly that nature could not be beautiful demonstrate how completely the empiricist conception of beauty had been divorced from its classical and metaphysical roots.

Recently, there have been attempts to resurrect the concept of beauty by arguing that it is essential to our critical language. The critique of taste and beauty made all aesthetic properties essentially noncognitive. That is inconsistent with the way that critical language works, so some concept of beauty is required if we are to make sense of that language. Mary Mothersill argues, for example, that beauty is what she calls a "standing concept" that is taken for granted in critical discussions and that it is conceptually indispensable (*Beauty Restored*: 247). Guy Sircello has proposed a new analysis of properties of beauty in terms of what he calls properties of qualitative degree, so that beauty is a function of a high degree of positive qualitative properties (*A New Theory of Beauty*: 43). At the very least, these attempts demonstrate that an empiricist analysis of beauty continues to be an issue in spite of the change of its place in aesthetics after the rise of empiricism.

PRIMARY WORKS

Bell, Clive. *Art*. New York: Capricorn Books, 1958.

Burke, Edmund. *A Philosophical Enquiry into the Origin of Our Ideas of the Sublime and Beautiful*. Notre Dame, IN: University of Notre Dame Press, 1968.

Collingwood, R. G. *Principles of Art*. Oxford: Oxford University Press, 1938.

Cooper, Anthony Ashley, third earl of Shaftesbury. *Characteristics of Men, Manners, Opinions, Times*. Edited by John M. Robertson. Indianapolis: Library of Liberal Arts, 1964.

Croce, Benedetto. *Aesthetic*. Translated by Douglas Ainslie. New York: Noonday Books, 1968.

Hogarth, William. *The Analysis of Beauty*. Oxford: Clarendon Press, 1955.

Hume, David. "Of the Standard of Taste." In *Essays Moral, Political and Literary*, edited by Eugene Miller. Indianapolis: Liberty Classics, 1987.

Hutcheson, Francis. *An Inquiry into the Original of Our Ideas of Beauty and Virtue* (1725). New York: Garland, 1971.
Kant, Immanuel. *Critique of Judgment.* Translated by Werner S. Pluhar. Indianapolis: Hackett, 1987.
Plotinus. "Beauty, *Ennead* I.6." Translated by Timothy Mahoney and Sherry Blum in *Aesthetics: Classic Readings from the Western Tradition,* edited by Dabney Townsend. Boston: Jones and Bartlett, 1996.

BIBLIOGRAPHY

Books

Mothersill, Mary. *Beauty Restored.* Oxford: Clarendon Press, 1984.
Sircello, Guy. *A New Theory of Beauty.* Princeton: Princeton University Press, 1975.

Articles

Kristeller, Paul Oskar. "The Modern System of the Arts, I and II." *Journal of the History of Ideas* 12 (1951) and 13 (1952). Reprinted in *Essays on the History of Aesthetics,* edited by Peter Kivy. Rochester, NY: University of Rochester Press, 1992.
Townsend, Dabney. "From Shaftesbury to Kant." *Journal of the History of Ideas* 48 (1987). Reprinted in *Essays on the History of Aesthetics,* edited by Peter Kivy. Rochester, NY: University of Rochester Press, 1992.

DABNEY TOWNSEND

BEHAVIORISM. "Behaviorism is not the science of human behavior; it is the philosophy of that science" (Skinner, *About Behaviorism*: 3). Moreover, according to that philosophy, psychology is the science of behavior. So, behaviorism is a philosophy of psychology, an investigation into the metaphysical, epistemological, and semantic aspects of the science of behavior. The science of behavior (variously referred to as "praxiology," "behavioristics," and "anthroponomy") "consists of the findings, principles, laws, and theories formulated through the study of behavior [of animals and humans]" (Zufiff, *Behaviorism: A Conceptual Reconstruction*: 2).

PSYCHOLOGICAL BEHAVIORISM

Consider the following (partial) explanation of why John just ate: John had not eaten for some time, which caused him to feel hungry, which, in turn, caused him to eat. One way of understanding this kind of explanation of behavior—where a physical event (deprivation of food) causes a mental event (a feeling of hunger), and the latter event causes another physical event (eating)—is in terms of Cartesian causal interactionism. According to this seventeenth-century view, bodies are extended unthinking substances, while minds are thinking unextended substances, and yet these two radically different substances somehow (notoriously!) causally interact. Furthermore, it is part of this view that one has introspective access to the contents of one's own mind. Cartesian causal interactionism is a paradigm case of mentalism, but today there are many other approaches toward understanding explanations of behavior.

A number of questions have been raised about these mentalistic approaches, however. Even if we shelve numerous puzzling, metaphysical questions regarding the old mind–body causal interactionism (see MIND–BODY PROBLEM) and the existence, nature, and causal powers of mental events (e.g., a feeling of hunger), troublesome epistemological questions associated with mental events remain. For example, how reliable is introspection as a method for acquiring knowledge about one's own mental life, and if introspected mental events are probative, of what are they probative? Furthermore, since we cannot introspect other people's mental events, how are we to justify *our* explanations of *their* behavior? Mentalists' inability to satisfactorily answer these and related questions regarding the metaphysical, epistemological, and semantical presuppositions of mentalistic explanations of behavior led many twentieth-century psychologists and philosophers to embrace one or another version of behaviorism—including classical, methodological, radical, teleological, and theoretical behaviorism.

Classical behaviorism is associated with Clark A. Hull (1884–1952) and Edward Chase Tolman (1886–1959), but especially with John Broadus Watson (1878–1958). In his seminal article "Psychology as the Behaviorist Views It" (1913), in which he coined the term "behaviorism," Watson wrote:

Psychology as the behaviorist views it is a purely objective experimental branch of natural science. Its theoretical goal is the prediction and control of behavior. Introspection forms no essential part of its methods, nor is the scientific value of its data dependent upon the readiness with which they lend themselves to interpretation in terms of consciousness. The behaviorist, in his efforts to get a unitary scheme of animal response, recognizes no dividing line between man and brute. (158)

In this passage, Watson is reacting to the introspectionist psychology of his day by insisting that psychology be both objective and empirically based (i.e., intersubjectively observable). Watson believed that if psychology is to become a natural science, then, like all such sciences, its data must be intersubjectively observable. Thus, there is no place in the science of behavior for mental events that allegedly cause behavior but that are accessible only to introspection. Rather, the behavior of organisms and their environments are intersubjectively observable. Watson allowed that a subject's covert muscular movements were to count as behavior—so that thought might be mostly covert speech, that is, movement of the vocal cords.

Influenced by the work on conditioned reflexes by Ivan P. Pavlov (1849–1936) and by the preference for simple mechanistic explanations of his former teacher at the University of Chicago, Jacques Loeb (1859–1924), Watson maintained that all complex human behavior (i.e., molar behavior) is itself the result of simple conditioned reflexes (i.e., molecular behavior). Indeed, he thought that psychology is, in principle, reducible to physics. The key to such reduction lay with the physiological investigation of an organism's mechanisms intervening between its environmental stimulus and its behavioral response.

Subsequent to his seminal 1913 essay, Watson articulated and defended this environmentally oriented stimulus–response version of behaviorism in a number of influential publications, including *Behavior: An Introduction to Comparative Psychology* (1914), *Psychology from the Standpoint of a Behaviorist* (1919), *Behaviorism* (1924), and *The Psychological Care of Infant and Child* (1928). Watson prematurely left academe when, as the result of a personal scandal, he was forced to resign from Johns Hopkins University in 1920. Nevertheless, his version of behaviorism continued to exert a powerful influence on the American psychological scene for another thirty years.

Methodological behaviorism, like classical behaviorism, responds to mentalism by focusing on the prior physical causes of a subject's behavior, thereby circumventing (but not repudiating) a subject's subjective mental events altogether. "Thus, if we know that a child has not eaten for a long time, and if we know that he therefore feels hungry and that because he feels hungry he then eats, then we know that if he has not eaten for a long time, he will eat" (*About Behaviorism*: 13). Like classical behaviorism, this approach has the effect of turning attention away from the pseudoexplanations of mentalism and toward a systematic analysis of lawlike connections between subjects' genetic and environmental history and their behavior. However, because it does not share Watson's tendency to identify thought and consciousness with individual muscular movements, it seems to endorse epiphenomenalism—the controversial view that there are mental events that are caused by physical events but that there are no physical events caused by mental events.

Radical behaviorism, identified with Burrhus Frederick Skinner (1904–1990), mediates the diametrically opposed orientations of mentalism and methodological behaviorism:

Mentalism kept attention away from the external antecedent events which might have explained behavior, by seeming to supply an alternative explanation. Methodological behaviorism did just the reverse: by dealing exclusively with external antecedent events it turned attention away from self-observation and self-knowledge. Radical behaviorism restores some kind of balance. It does not insist upon truth by agreement [i.e., intersubjectivity] and can therefore consider events taking place in the private world within the skin. It does not call these events unobservable, and it does not dismiss them as subjective. It simply questions the nature of the object observed and the reliability of the observations. (*About Behaviorism*: 16–17)

According to Skinner, the "objects" that introspection reveals are states of the observer's own body. Thus, Skinner avoids both mentalism and the epiphenomenalism of methodological behaviorism. Unfortunately for the science of behavior, however, these introspected "objects" are, according to Skinner, typically not the causes of one's behavior. Furthermore, Skinner maintains that introspection is an unreliable method since it utilizes the links between private events and verbal responses, which are themselves unreliable. Thus, though Skinner's radical behaviorism broadens the scope of the science of behavior in principle, in practice his attitude toward introspection is hardly different from that of the methodological behaviorists.

Skinner's ideas, as articulated in his many publications and lectures over his long academic career, had a profound impact on the science of behavior and on psychology in general. For example, his innovations of operant conditioning (namely, reinforcing or inhibiting behavior selectively) and the so-called Skinner box elevated radical behaviorism to a dominant position not only within behaviorism but within American psychology during the 1950s. "Since the 1950s, Skinner's influence on American psychology has been monumental. Laboratories and journals devoted to operant conditioning have thrived, and Skinnerian research has been applied to a wide variety of programs of 'behavioral modification' " (Smith, *Behaviorism and Logical Positivism*: 259–60).

Nevertheless, behaviorism was destined to be undermined by the cognitive revolution of the 1970s. Why did this happen?

Two things seem to have favored the cognitive movement: First, the digital computer, which for the first time allowed mentalistic ideas to be simulated and overcame behavioristic criticisms that cognitive theories were inexact and anecdotal. Secondly, the takeover of behaviorism by Skinnerian radical behaviorism with its strong bias against formal theory and its belief that psychology is nothing but the collection of orderly experimental data. (Staddon, *Behaviorism: Mind, Mechanism and Society*: 109)

Today cognitive psychology—the new mentalism that likens one's brain to the hardware of a digital computer and one's mental life to its software—appears to dominate the American psychological scene. Even so, some psychologists and philosophers profess to sense the waning of cognitive psychology and the waxing of a new behaviorism.

New behaviorism comes in (at least) two varieties: teleological and theoretical. The former is associated with Howard Rachlin; the latter with John Staddon.

According to Rachlin, there are two modern psychological sciences: cognitive or physiological psychology and behaviorism. The former "aims at the discovery of internal mechanisms, including complex mental mechanisms and representational systems"; the latter "aims at scientific explanation, prediction, and control of overt behavior, including complex patterns of overt behavior that . . . form our mental lives" (*Behavior and Mind*: v). Rachlin characterizes *teleological* behaviorism as

[t]he belief that mental terms refer to overt behavior of intact animals. Mental events are not supposed to occur inside the animal at all. Overt behavior does not just *reveal* the mind; it *is* the mind. Each mental term stands for a pattern of overt behavior. This includes such mental terms as "sensation," "pain," "love," "hunger," and "fear" (terms considered by the mentalist to be "raw feels"), as well as terms such as "belief" and "intelligence" that are sometimes said to refer to "complex mental states," sometimes to "propositional attitudes" and sometimes to "intentional acts." (*Behavior and Mind*: 15–16)

Thus, for example, to say that John is hungry *is* to say that John is manifesting a particular pattern of behavior. The "is" here is the "is" of identity, so John's hunger is identical to a particular pattern of behavior. Moreover, Rachlin claims that "[t]eleological behaviorism does not deny the validity of the physiological and the cognitive viewpoints. The teleological view may be complementary to the others" (*Behavior and Mind*: 18). So, while the physiological and the cognitive viewpoints try to explain *how* John manages to behave as he does, the teleological viewpoint tries to explain *why* he behaves as he does. The former viewpoint focuses on the efficient cause of John's behavior; the latter focuses on the final cause of his behavior.

According to Staddon, "The clearest division within contemporary behaviorism is between those who continue to believe in a fundamentally purposive (teleological) approach to reinforcement learning, and those with a renewed commitment to behavioral mechanisms" (*Behaviorism: Mind, Mechanism and Society*: 92). He refers to the latter approach as *theoretical* behaviorism. Thus, unlike Rachlin, Staddon does not relegate to the cognitive camp all psychologists who concern themselves with behavioral mechanisms. He refrains from doing so because he distinguishes classical computationalism—with its talk of computations over sentencelike mental representations—from connectionism (or parallel distributed processing). While classical computationalism is the cornerstone of the antibehaviorist cognitive approach, connectionist modeling of internal states and processes of an organism is fully consistent with a behaviorism that "promises to provide theoretical links between behavior and the brain that rest on real understanding, rather than on mentalistic presumptions about how brain–behavior relations 'must' be arranged" (*Behaviorism: Mind, Mechanism and Society*: 92).

PHILOSOPHICAL BEHAVIORISM

A number of philosophers who shared the psychological behaviorists' repudiation of Cartesian causal interactionism felt a need to furnish a behavioristic semantics for mentalistic terms. Some of these philosophers were associated with LOGICAL POSITIVISM, some with ordinary language philosophy.

Logical behaviorists, identified with some of the logical positivists—Rudolf CARNAP (1891–1970), for example—put forth semantic theories for mentalistic terms based on the verificationist criterion of meaningfulness (see VERIFICATION PRINCIPLE), in hopes of incorporating mentalistic terms into scientific discourse.

One such theory held that a sentence containing mentalistic terms is empirically meaningful if, and only if, it is synonymous with some intersubjectively verifiable set of sentences devoid of mentalistic terms. So, for example, the sentence "John is hungry" is empirically meaningful if, and only if, it is synonymous with such a set of sentences that includes, say, the sentence "John is eating." If this account were found acceptable, then, in principle, sentences containing mentalistic terms could be eliminated in favor of their respective synonym sets.

However, an apparent difficulty with this analysis is that no such set of sentences is sufficient for conferring empirical MEANING on "John is hungry." Suppose, for example, that John is not hungry, but he is eating anyway (e.g., to gain his parents' permission to go outside to play). Then the verification of "John is eating" (together with the verification of the other sentences in the relevant set) is *insufficient* for verifying "John is hungry." In short, John may not be hungry but may eat anyway (and, alternatively, he may not eat and be hungry). Once logical behaviorists realized the shortcomings of this account of the meaning of mentalistic terms, they developed a dispositional account, but that account, too, fails to eliminate mentalistic terms altogether.

Analytic behaviorists, identified with ordinary language philosophy—Gilbert Ryle (1900–1976), for example—focused their attention on mentalistic terms as they occur in ordinary (i.e., nonphilosophical) language. Ryle argues that the belief that the ordinary use of mentalistic terms commits one to mind–body dualism "is one big mistake and a mistake of a special kind. It is, namely, a category-mistake. It represents the facts of mental life as if they belonged to one logical type or category (or range of types or categories), when they actually belong to another" (*The Concept of Mind*: 16). Treating mental terms as though they belonged to the same category (or range of categories) as physical terms leads to absurdities, for example, that one person cannot know that another person has a mental life, the problem of other minds.

According to Ryle, the correct way to construe mentalistic terms is as referring to behavior and behavioral dispositions, not to private mental events. Therefore, the proper analysis of "John is hungry" involves construing the mentalistic term "hungry" as referring to John's eating or to his disposition to eat, not to some private mental event.

There is an important difference between the dispositional account proffered by logical behaviorists and that proffered by analytic behaviorists: for the former, a mentalistic term *means* the associated behavior and disposition; for the latter, the associated behavior and disposition are merely "criterial" for the application of the term (see Zuriff *Behaviorism: A Conceptual Reconstruction*: 209). Dispositional accounts of mentalistic terms have, in general, been roundly criticized as inadequate (see Chisholm, *Perceiving: A Philosophical Study*).

PRIMARY WORKS

Books

Chisholm, Roderick M. *Perceiving: A Philosophical Study*. Ithaca, NY: Cornell University Press, 1957.

Rachlin, Howard. *Behavior and Mind*. New York: Oxford University Press, 1994.

Ryle, Gilbert. *The Concept of Mind*. New York: Barnes and Noble, 1949.

Skinner, Burrhus Frederick. *About Behaviorism*. New York: Alfred A. Knopf, 1974.

———. *Beyond Freedom and Dignity*. New York: Bantam/Vintage, 1971.

———. *Verbal Behavior*. New York: Appleton-Century-Crofts, 1957.

Staddon, John. *Behaviorism: Mind, Mechanism and Society*. London: Gerald Duckworth, 1993.

Articles

Carnap, Rudolf. "Psychology in Physical Language." *Erkenntnis* 3 (1932–1933): 107–42.

Chomsky, Noam. "Review of B. F. Skinner's *Verbal Behavior*." *Language* 35 (1950): 26–58.

Watson, John Broadus. "Psychology as the Behaviorist Views It." *Psychological Review* 20 (1913): 158–77.

BIBLIOGRAPHY

Smith, Laurence D. *Behaviorism and Logical Positivism*. Stanford, CA: Stanford University Press, 1986.

Zufiff, Gerald E. *Behaviorism: A Conceptual Reconstruction*. New York: Columbia University Press, 1985.

ROGER F. GIBSON

BERGMANN, GUSTAV. Gustav Bergmann (1906–1985), a member of the Vienna Circle, was a strong defender of the central claims of logical positivism (see LOGICAL POSITIVISM/LOGICAL EMPIRICISM). He fled Europe in 1938 for the United States, where he found a collaborator in the psychologist K. W. Spence. The other positivists championed the idea of an objective science of human beings, but Bergmann alone of the positivists actively participated in development of psychological research in the 1940s and 1950s. Bergmann used his analytical tools to show how one could accept the experimental genius of the gestalt psychologists while rejecting their antipositivistic philosophy of science. He and Spence were able to give a clear analysis of the theories of C. L. Hull, making their methodological structure more evident and placing them in a context where they could be fruitfully developed by experimental psychologists, Spence included.

Bergmann defended the positivist idea that the language of science is empirically meaningful to the extent that it can be translated into an empiricist's language, that is, a language whose logical framework is that of the logic of Russell and Whitehead's *Principia Mathematica* and whose primitive descriptive constants are interpreted to refer to things and sorts of things that are presented in ordinary experience. A commonsense realism was defended by insisting that reference could be made to unpresented things and sorts by means of definite descriptions of the Russellian sort (see RUSSELL). All other concepts were to be introduced by means of explicit definitions. For example, a concept such as "x is soluble" is introduced as short for "If x is in water, then x dissolves." R. CARNAP argued that this condition ought to be relaxed, to allow "soluble" to be introduced by "If x is in water, then if x dissolves, then x is soluble." Bergmann argued that, since this way of introducing concepts did not allow for their eliminability, it in effect is a return to the unanalyzable DISPOSITIONS of the Aristotelians against which LOCKE and HUME argued so vigorously (see ARISTOTLE). As for Carnap's reason for abandoning the requirement of explicit definition—it permitted the inference that untested matches are soluble—Bergmann argued that this failed to take into account the context of use of such concepts, that they would not be introduced unless they appeared in such statements of law as "Sugar is soluble" and "Wood is insoluble." The apparently odd predications arise only as a sign that the objects in question are untested.

Bergmann also rejected Carnap's claim that there was a logical sense of "probability" in terms of which one could evaluate the cognitive worth of assertions. Bergmann argued that science proceeded not by simple enumeration but by a process of eliminative induction—falsification guided by a theory confirmed by past successes in discovering laws. Further, since the sense of "probability" proposed by Carnap depended on the logical form of the language used, it was a priori and could therefore provide no guide for matters of fact. Finally, he also argued that the languages that Carnap allowed as candidates for the language of science—languages that contained only first-order logic without relations—were far too impoverished in logical power to be of any use—one needed both relations and higher-order logic, as the earlier positivists had insisted.

Bergmann also defended the traditional empiricist distinction between the analytic and the empirical ("relations of ideas" and "relations of matters of fact") against the criticisms of W.V.O. QUINE. Bergmann argued, on one hand, that a nonfoundationalist account of verification that appealed to coherence did not require, pace Quine, a coherence theory of MEANING, in which the meaning of a CONCEPT was given by the statements of laws in which it appears rather than the presented entities to which it refers. Nor does the absence of a behavioral criterion for distinguishing those statements of ordinary language that are true by definition require one to give up the idea that there is in fact a clear distinction; all that follows is the fact that people at different times use words in different ways and that there is no "once for all" translation of the concept into the empiricist's ideal language.

The traditional doctrine of psychophysiological parallelism enabled Bergmann to defend both the notion of an objective behavioristic science of human beings (see BEHAVIORISM) and also the notion that mental states are irreducible to nonmental states. Contrary to the suggestions of many positivists, then, he argued that the empiricist's ideal language must contain terms and predicates that refer to mental states, including mental acts. By introducing terms that referred to irreducible moral sentiments, he was able to accommodate both something like the emotivism of other positivists and also the notion deriving from F. Brentano, G. E. MOORE, and others that moral judgments are irreducible to something nonmoral, such as pleasure.

Bergmann proposed to recognize the cognitive legitimacy of many traditional metaphysical problems, such as that of universals, in terms of discourse about the undefined descriptive constants of the ideal language. He aimed to reconcile the common sense that there are tables and chairs—expressed as statements in the ideal language—and the odd philosophical statements that, for example, only

SENSE-DATA exist—claims about what ought to be the referents of the undefined terms of the empiricist's ideal language.

The concern with mental states led Bergmann to focus increasingly on the "relation" of intentionality connecting mental states to their objects. This led him to argue that even in the cases of false belief the object must have some sort of ontological status. He came, too, to hold that something like K. Gödel's doctrine of the objective reality of sets and of arithmetic truths (see GÖDEL) is necessary if we are to defend the ANALYTIC/SYNTHETIC distinction. It is often felt that this introduction of a shadowy realm of being beyond what is given in ordinary experience is contrary to Bergmann's earlier strong defense of empiricism.

PRIMARY WORKS

The Metaphysics of Logical Positivism. New York: Longmans Green, 1954.
Philosophy of Science. Madison: University of Wisconsin Press, 1957.
Meaning and Existence. Madison: University of Wisconsin Press, 1960.
Logic and Reality. Madison: University of Wisconsin Press, 1964.

BIBLIOGRAPHY

Book

Gram, M., and E. D. Klemke, eds. *The Ontological Turn.* Iowa City: University of Iowa Press, 1974.

Article

Sellars, W. "Naming and Saying." In *Science, Perception and Reality.* London: Routledge and Kegan Paul, 1963.

FRED WILSON

BERKELEY, GEORGE

LIFE AND WORKS

George Berkeley (1685–1753) was born in or near Kilkenny, Ireland, on March 12, 1685. He attended Kilkenny College at the age of eleven and entered Trinity College, Dublin, in March 1700. He received his bachelor of arts in 1704. Upon receiving his master's degree, he was made a junior fellow of Trinity College in 1707, and upon receiving his doctorate, he became a senior fellow in 1717. Consistent with academic practices of the time, Berkeley was ordained an Anglican deacon in 1709 and a priest in 1710. His ordination was not uncontroversial. Berkeley was ordained by St. George Ashe, bishop of Clogher and vice-chancellor of Trinity College, rather than by William King, archbishop of Dublin. King took this as a personal affront: Berkeley and King differed significantly on both philosophical and theological issues.

The years between 1706 and 1713 were extremely productive, and the development of his philosophy is illustrated in the notebooks he made between 1706 and 1709, the *Philosophical Commentaries* (PC). In 1709 he published *An*

Essay toward a New Theory of Vision (NTV). In 1710, he published Part I of *A Treatise Concerning the Principles of Human Knowledge* (PHK). The projected second and third parts were never completed, and "Part I" was dropped from the title of subsequent editions of the *Principles*. In 1712 he published *Passive Obedience*, three discourses delivered in the Trinity College Chapel on moral and political issues (see Olscamp 1970). In 1713 he published the *Three Dialogues between Hylas and Philonous* (DHP), a popular restatement of his immaterialism and IDEALISM.

Berkeley left Dublin in January 1713 and went to London, where he befriended Jonathan Swift, Joseph Addison, Richard Steele, Alexander Pope, and other persons of note. He contributed several short pieces against "freethinking"—nontheistic accounts of the world—to Steele's *Guardian* that year, although which pieces were Berkeley's remains a matter of scholarly debate (Berman 1994: 72–79). In October 1713, Berkeley left London for a tour of the Continent as chaplain to Lord Peterborough, who had been appointed ambassador-extraordinary to Sicily on the occasion of the coronation of King Victor Amodeus. Berkeley returned to London in August 1714 and remained there for two years. In the autumn of 1716, he returned to the continent as companion to, and tutor of, the son of Dr. Ashe. During this sojourn, Berkeley told his American correspondent Samuel Johnson in 1729, he lost the manuscript for the second part of the *Principles*, "and I never had leisure since to do so disagreeable a thing as writing twice on the same subject" (*Works* II: 282). In 1720, he and young Ashe began their trip back to England, stopping in Lyon, France, where Berkeley finished *De Motu*, his argument that SCIENCE makes no ontological commitments and that scientific hypotheses are nothing more than instruments for prediction and control of the physical world. *De Motu* was published in 1721.

Berkeley became the dean of Derry on May 4, 1724, and resigned his fellowship at Trinity College. Berkeley was not a dean in residence. He devoted the mid-1720s and early 1730s to the Bermuda Project, a plan to found a college or seminary in Bermuda for children of the colonial planters and a certain number of Native Americans. As he describes it in his *Proposal for the Better Supplying of Churches in Our Foreign Plantations* (London, 1724), the sons of the planters were to serve in the understaffed churches in the colonies, and the Native Americans were to become missionaries to their own people. His project received considerable support in Ireland, and he was co-heir with Swift of Esther Vanhomrigh's estate. Between 1724 and 1728, he received a charter for his college, private contributions, and the promise of a grant of twenty thousand pounds from the British Parliament. On August 1, 1728, he married Anne Forster, and in September they sailed for America. Berkeley bought a farm in Rhode Island and built a house called Whitehall—which is still standing—a few miles outside Newport. His plan was to wait in Rhode Island until the promised grant was procured. In 1731 he received a letter from Edmund Gibson, bishop of

London, informing him that the promised grant never would be paid. Berkeley and his family returned to London in October 1731.

While the Bermuda Project itself was a failure, it was not without fruit. His presence in America generated interest in his philosophy. Samuel Johnson's *Elementa Philosophica* reflects the intellectual debt Berkeley's American correspondent owed him. Berkeley gave large collections of books to Harvard University and Yale University, and he gave his Rhode Island farm to Yale. Further, the Bermuda Project was personally beneficial to Berkeley: together with the defenses of theism he published in 1732–1735, it significantly enhanced his moral image. The philosopher whose early works were primarily objects of ridicule was eulogized by both philosophers and poets (Berman 1994: 120–22).

The period between 1731 and 1735 was also very productive. In addition to second editions of the *Principles* (1734) and the *Three Dialogues* (1734), Berkeley published *A Sermon before the Society for the Propagation of the Gospel in Foreign Parts* (1732), *Alciphron: or the Minute Philosopher* (1732), *The Theory of Vision or Visual Language Showing the Immediate Presence and Providence of a Deity, Vindicated and Explained* (TVV, 1733), *The Analyst; or, a Discourse Addressed to an Infidel Mathematician* (1735), *A Defense of Free-Thinking in Mathematics* (1735), and *Reasons for Not Replying to Mr. Walton's Full Answer* (1735). These publications reflect the broad range of Berkeley's intellectual interests: from religious apologetic (*Alciphron*), to philosophy, to mathematics.

Berkeley remained in London until early 1734. In addition to his writing, it was a period of waiting for a mark of royal favor to overshadow the failure of the Bermuda Project. In January 1734, he was appointed bishop of Cloyne. In February he resigned his position as dean of Derry and was consecrated bishop of Cloyne on May 19, 1734. Berkeley was a good bishop. He was concerned with the material as well as the spiritual well-being of the people in the diocese of Cloyne, Roman Catholic as well as Anglican. He set up a spinning school and tried to establish the manufacture of linen. His *Querist* (1735–1737) is concerned primarily with social and economic issues. There he argued for the need of an Irish national bank and proposed an early version of the credit theory of money. He continued his campaign against freethinking in the *Discourse Addressed to the Magistrates . . . Occasioned by the Enormous License, and Irreligion of the Times* (Dublin, 1738). In 1744 he published *Siris: A Chain of Philosophical Inquiries concerning the Virtues of Tar-water and Divers Subjects Connected Together and Arising One from Another*. During his lifetime, *Siris* was Berkeley's most popular work, due to its arguments for the medicinal virtues of tar-water. Berkeley considered tar-water a panacea or, at least, a useful substitute for intoxicating beverages. His philosophical reflections in the last third of the work are among the most obscure of his writings, and there is little scholarly agreement regarding either the focus of his late philosophy or the relationship it bears to his earlier philosophy.

Berkeley remained at Cloyne until his retirement in 1752. During that time he left the area only twice. In 1737 he visited Dublin to take a seat in the Irish House of Lords and speak against the Blasters (a group of freethinkers). In 1750 he made a brief excursion to Killarney for a holiday with family and friends.

In August 1752, Berkeley and his family left Cloyne for Oxford, ostensibly to oversee the education of his son George. He arranged for the republication of the *Alciphron* and the publication of his *Miscellany*, a collection of essays on various topics. Berkeley died on January 14, 1753, while his wife read him a sermon. He was buried in the Christ Church cemetery on January 20. In accordance with his will, his body was "kept five days above ground, . . . even till it grow offensive by the cadaverous smell" (*Works* VIII: 381), a provision that was intended to prevent premature burial.

In 1709, Berkeley published *An Essay toward a New Theory of Vision* (NTV). It is an empirical theory of vision. It was written, in part, in response to the geometrical theory of vision presented in Descartes' *Optics* (VI: §13) and Malebranche's *Search after Truth* (I.ix.3). It also raises issues on which Berkeley expands in the *Principles* and the *Three Dialogues*, so it is an appropriate place at which to begin an examination of Berkeley's philosophy.

Descartes and Malebranche argued that humans perceive depth in accordance with a natural geometry: one, in effect, calculates the distance from the perceiver to an object at a distance by means of a triangle in which the pupils of the eyes define the base, and the object seen is at the apex. Such a view holds that there are necessary connections between the visual world and the tactile world, that there is literally one thing that is both seen and touched. Berkeley challenges that position. He argues that "depth perception" is a function of judgment based on experience. If I see

a great number of intermediate objects, such as houses, fields, rivers, and the like, which I have experience to take up a considerable space, I thence form a judgment or conclusion that the object I see beyond them is at a great distance. Again, when an object appears faint and small which at a near distance I have experienced to make a vigorous and large appearance, I instantly conclude it to be far off. And this, it is evident, is the result of experience without which, from the faintness and littleness, I should not have inferred anything concerning the distance of objects. (NTV §3).

The "experience" to which Berkeley refers is the correlation of visual and tactile sensations. Consistent with the epistemic assumptions of the time, the Berkeley of NTV assumes for the sake of the argument that one has primary access to the physical world by means of the sense of touch. (This is an assumption he explicitly rejects in subsequent writings.) Depth is not literally in a visual sensation; one learns that there are certain visual signs of tactile distance. By repeatedly observing small and faint images that grew larger and stronger as one has those tactile sensations known as "walking toward the object," one develops a psychological association between aspects of the visual images and the tactile sensations by which distance is measured. Visual objects and tactile objects are numerically distinct (heterogeneous). A visual object represents a tactile object in a way analogous to that in which a word represents an object. Just as it is a historical accident that the word "cat" represents a furry creature rather than a table or an aardvark, it is a contingent fact that the visual cat represents the tangible cat. In both cases the representation is arbitrary; it is representation without resemblance. Vision functions as a divine language whereby the Author of Nature informs us how to regulate our lives "to attain those things that are necessary to the preservation and well-being of our bodies, and also to avoid whatever may be hurtful and destructive of them" (NTV §149; cf. TVV §§38–40).

Berkeley's argument for his linguistic theory of vision proceeds by showing, first, that it is not unreasonable to suggest that one idea can represent—that one can mediately perceive—another without presuming a resemblance between them: the redness of a person's face can show shame or fear (NTV §§9–10). Second, if distance is perceived by sight, it cannot be perceived on the basis of lines and angles (natural geometry), since the lines and angles are not so perceived (NTV §§12–15). Third, there is a constant correlation between tactile distance, kinesthetic sensations in the eyes (NTV §18), and the degree of confusion in the visual image (NTV §§21–26). Fourth, he argues that his theory of vision can solve a problem for mathematical optics posed by Isaac Barrow; namely, he can explain why an object seen through a lens can appear to become nearer when it is actually farther from the eye (NTV §§29–51; TVV §§62–68). Fifth, he argues that his theory of vision can explain the illusion that the moon on the horizon appears larger than the moon at the median, a phenomenon that cannot be explained on the basis of the geometrical theory (NTV §§52–87; TVV §§53–61). Finally, he argues for the heterogeneity thesis, that the objects of sight are numerically distinct from (not necessarily connected with) the objects of touch. This argument proceeded along two tracks. (1) He argues that it is impossible to abstract a common idea of extension from visual and tangible objects. This anticipates the more complete argument against abstraction in the Introduction to the *Principles*. (2) He considers the Molyneux problem (NTV §§132–43): if there were a person born blind who had learned the meanings of the words "sphere" and "cube" on the basis of the sense of touch, would he or she be able to distinguish a visual sphere from a visual cube if his or her sight were suddenly restored? Like Molyneux and Locke (*Essay* II.ii.8), Berkeley contends that the blind person made to see could not distinguish the visual sphere from the visual cube prior to touching both. Berkeley explains this on the basis of the numerical distinction between the objects of sight and touch and the need to learn that certain objects of sight represent objects of touch that are called by the same general term. In the *Theory of Vision, . . . Vindicated* (1734), he cites a reported case of a blind person who was made to see as evidence that his account of the Molyneux problem and the theory of visual signs were correct (TVV §71).

Berkeley's theory of vision can stand by itself. Recent studies tend to show that depth perception is learned in much the way Berkeley suggests. But the

NTV is also a propaedeutic to the philosophical position developed in the *Principles* and the *Three Dialogues*. If the objects of the several sensory modalities are numerically distinct, then ordinary perceptual objects—apples, tables, chairs—are inherently complex: they are composed of distinct objects of sense, and there is no empirical ground for claiming that ordinary objects are substantially simple.

AGAINST ABSTRACTION

In the Introduction to the *Principles of Human Knowledge*, Berkeley develops an extended criticism of the doctrine of ABSTRACTION, the doctrine of concept formation that contends that one forms general ideas by stripping away the particularizing aspects of particular ideas. As John LOCKE described it, abstract ideas provide the meanings of general terms, they are necessary for knowledge, and the ability to abstract distinguishes humans from nonhuman animals.

Berkeley claims that virtually all philosophical error proceeds from the doctrine of abstraction (Intro. §6). While Berkeley's criticisms are most clearly directed at Locke's account of abstract ideas in the *Essay concerning Human Understanding*, Book III, it is reasonable to suggest that they are intended to attack the entire tradition, since he claimed that Locke was the best of the abstractionists (PC §§564–67), and he does not limit his criticisms to Locke's account (see Flage 1987: 13–53).

The attack on abstractionism begins in Section 7 of the Introduction, where Berkeley indicates the point on which he and the abstractionists agree. He writes:

It is agreed, on all hands, that the qualities or modes of things do never really exist each of them apart by itself, and separated from all others, but are mixed, as it were, and blended together, several in the same object. But we are told, the mind being able to consider each quality singly, or abstracted from those other qualities with which it is united, does by that means frame to itself abstract ideas. . . . Not that it is possible for colour or motion to exist without extension: but only that the mind can frame to itself by abstraction the idea of colour exclusive of extension, and of motion exclusive of both colour and extension. (PHK, Intro. §7)

Berkeley alludes to the doctrine of modes and SUBSTANCE, a doctrine accepted in one form or another by virtually all the abstractionists. According to this doctrine, it is impossible for a mode or a quality of a substance to exist apart from a substance. Nonetheless, the abstractionists hold it is possible to conceptually separate modes from a substance and attend to that separated mode. As we shall see, Berkeley draws out the consequences of holding this pair of claims.

In the next two sections, Berkeley summarizes the abstractionists' position. In forming an abstract idea of color in general, one "considers apart or singles out by itself that which is common" to all colors (Intro. §8). One proceeds in the same way in forming the idea of a human being, which includes "colour, . . . but then it can be neither white, nor black, nor any particular colour" and "stature, but then it is neither tall stature nor low stature, nor yet middle stature, but something abstracted from all these" (Intro. §9). In Sections 10–13, Berkeley engages in a three-pronged attack on the doctrine of abstraction.

In Section 10 he claims that while he can imagine a proper part of an object apart from that object, he can form an idea neither of a human being that has no determinate color or size nor of motion apart from a thing moved. Since abstraction is said to be difficult, Berkeley takes the fact that *he* cannot abstract as good evidence that very few people can. At minimum, the passage shows that there is some empirical evidence that no one can form abstract ideas. Some commentators read more into the passage. Winkler, for example, contends that Berkeley accepted the principle that a state of affairs is conceivable if, and only if, it is possible (conceivability$_s$), and takes the difficulties Berkeley describes as indicative that abstract ideas are inconceivable and therefore impossible (Winkler 1989: 30–31). Conceivability$_s$ is too strong: the fact that a given person cannot actually conceive of a state of affairs x does not show that it is impossible to conceive of x. For example, you might be able to conceive (form ideas) of things that I cannot conceive. However, Berkeley, like most philosophers of the time, accepts the weaker principle that if x is conceivable, then x is possible (conceivability$_w$)—and, therefore, if x is impossible, then x is inconceivable. Given conceivability$_w$, there is a conceptual tension between the theory of abstraction and the contention that it is impossible for modes to exist apart from a substance (Intro. §7): given the doctrine of abstraction and conceivability$_w$, it follows that if one can conceive of a mode apart from a substance, it is possible for a mode to exist apart from a substance. Berkeley seems to have recognized this, for he wrote, "But I deny that I can abstract one from another, or conceive separately, those qualities which it is impossible should exist so separated" (Intro. §10).

Locke's theory of abstract ideas was developed, in part, to account for the meaning of general terms. A Lockean abstract idea contains all and only those general ideas that correspond to the properties mentioned in an intensional definition of a term. In Sections 11–12, Berkeley sketches an extensional theory of MEANING, a theory of meaning that does not require abstract ideas. Since the ontology assumed by Berkeley's theory is simpler than Locke's, Berkeley's account shows that abstract ideas are not needed to account for linguistic meaning.

In Section 13, Berkeley examines Locke's account of the abstract idea of a triangle, which "must be neither oblique nor rectangle, neither equilateral, equicrural, nor scalenon, but *all and none* of these at once. In effect, it is something imperfect that cannot exist, an idea wherein some parts of several different and *inconsistent* ideas are put together" (*Essay* IV.vii.9). Berkeley then asks his reader whether he or she can form such an idea. Given the emphasis on the inconsistencies in Locke's description of the idea, Berkeley clearly held that it is logically impossible to form the idea. In the NTV, Berkeley notes that Locke's views entail that Locke himself could not form the idea (NTV §125).

While Berkeley's discussion continues—he argues that abstraction is not necessary for knowledge (Intro. §15), that selective attention does not require separation (Intro. §16, 2d ed.), and that there are functions of language other than communication (Intro. §20)—Berkeley deemed the argument in Section 13 the "killing blow" to the doctrine of abstraction (PC §687). As we shall see later, this three-stage argument pattern found in the Introduction—I cannot form the idea, the doctrine is not necessary to explain the phenomenon, and the doctrine is inconsistent—appears again in the critique of material substance.

IDEALISM AND IMMATERIALISM

In the body of the *Principles* and the *Three Dialogues*, Berkeley develops his case for immaterialism and idealism. Immaterialism is the doctrine that material substances do not exist. Idealism is the doctrine that all existents either are, or depend for their existence on, minds. The primary case for idealism and immaterialism is developed in the first thirty-three sections of the *Principles*, and this entry focuses on those sections.

Beginning with a survey of the objects of human knowledge (ideas of sense, reflection, and imagination), Berkeley acknowledges that different kinds of ideas arise from the different senses, and "as several of these are observed to accompany each other, they come to be marked by one name, and so to be reputed as one thing" (PHK §1). Berkeley distinguished these objects of knowledge (ideas) from the mind or soul in which they exist—that is, which perceives them (PHK §2). He then argues for his famous principle *esse* is *percipi*: to be is to be perceived. Everyone will grant that thought, passions, and ideas of the imagination exist only in a mind. "And it seems no less evident that the various sensations or ideas imprinted on the sense, however blended or combined together (that is, whatever objects they compose), cannot exist otherwise than in a mind perceiving them" (PHK §3). Berkeley supports this by noting that one ascribes existence to the objects of each of the senses only if the object is actually perceived by that sense. "Their *esse* is *percipi*" (PHK §3).

Several points should be noticed about Berkeley's argument in the first three sections. First, without argument, Berkeley construes both objects of knowledge and sensible objects in terms of IDEAS (but see DHP I). Second, in identifying sensible objects with ideas, one all but grants *esse* is *percipi*, since the mind-dependence of ideas was widely granted (see Locke, *Essay* I.i.8). Third, Berkeley assumes that ordinary sensible objects are composites of ideas of different kinds (see PHK §44). This develops a theme from the NTV, and it paves the way for the attack on material substance. Finally, Berkeley's notion of perception is very broad. It might more readily be understood as awareness or consciousness of an idea: conceiving is a species of perceiving (see PHK §§5 and 22). Perceiving is a necessary connection between a mind and an idea.

There are several immediate consequences of the assumptions presented in the first three sections of the *Principles*. "[T]he absolute existence of unthinking things without any relation to their being perceived . . . seems perfectly unintelligible'' (PHK §3). Since one's knowledge is limited to ideas, one has no intellectual access to nonthinking things distinct from ideas. It is a ''manifest contradiction'' to claim that ''houses, mountains, rivers, and in a word sensible objects have an existence natural or real, distinct from their being perceived by the understanding'' (PHK §4), for Berkeley identified complex sensible objects with collections of (simple) sensible objects—ideas—which exist only in a mind. Given the attack on abstraction, Berkeley cannot allow that ''two'' entities that are necessarily connected to one another can be conceived separately (PHK §5). So sensible objects (ideas) that do not exist in the mind of a finite spirit ''must either have no existence at all, or else subsist in the mind of some eternal spirit'' (PHK §6).

In Section 8 of the *Principles*, Berkeley argues that an idea can be like, or resemble nothing other than, another idea, although his argument shows only that there can be no grounds for claiming a likeness between an idea and a nonideational entity (but see Cummins 1968). Given his likeness principle, however, Berkeley has grounds for attacking the primary/secondary qualities distinction (see PRIMARY AND SECONDARY QUALITIES).

At least since Locke and BOYLE, some philosophers had argued that material objects are composed fundamentally of shape, extension, figure, motion, and number—the primary qualities—and the secondary qualities (colors, sounds, tastes, etc.) arise solely from the interaction of material objects and functioning sense organs. Secondary qualities, as known, are merely ideas in the mind. In Sections 10–15, Berkeley argues that one cannot conceive of the primary qualities apart from the secondary qualities. He writes:

But I desire any one to reflect and try, whether he can, by any abstraction of thought, conceive the extension and motion of a body, without all other sensible qualities. For my own part, I see evidently that it is not in my power to frame an idea of a body extended and moved, but I must withal give it some colour or other sensible quality which is acknowledged to exist only in the mind. In short, extension, figure, and motion, abstracted from all other qualities, are inconceivable. Where therefore the other sensible qualities are, there must these be also, to wit, in the mind and nowhere else. (PHK §10)

Insofar as one can conceive of (visible) extension only by means of the limits of colored patches, there is no ground for claiming that color and extension can exist in separation from one another. Hence, there is no ground for claiming extension (extended things) can exist apart from color, and therefore apart from the mind. Given the likeness principle, there is no ground for claiming that there are material objects that are like, but distinct from, ideas. This is Berkeley's most general attack. In Sections 11–15 he argues that qualities such as motion, number, and unity cannot be understood apart from relative concepts such as swiftness and slowness or a standard of measure, which are mental constructs. Since the primary qualities cannot be conceived apart from secondary qualities, the primary/secondary qualities distinction collapses.

In Sections 16–23 Berkeley attacks the substratum theory of material SUB-

STANCE. It is a three-pronged attack, following the same pattern as the attack on abstraction in the Introduction, Sections 10–13. First, Berkeley asks, can one have a positive idea (image) or relative idea of a material substratum? Can one, at least, single out a material substance that supports sensible qualities without knowing its inherent properties? To do so, the notion of *support* must be made clear, which Berkeley argues cannot be done (PHK §16). So one has no idea of a material substratum. Second, does the doctrine of material substance increase one's understanding of the world? Berkeley answers no and argues that construing physical objects as collections of ideas is both ontologically simpler and intellectually more illuminating than the doctrine of material substance (PHK §§18–20). Finally, he promises that if one could so much as conceive of a material substance existing unperceived, he would grant its existence (PHK §22). But "to make out this, it is necessary that you conceive them existing unconceived or unthought-of, which is a manifest repugnancy" (PHK §23). If conceivability$_w$ is the mark of possibility, whatever you would claim to exist unperceived is perceived: it is related to the conceiver's mind. So, Berkeley concludes that there are no material substances, since material substances fulfill no theoretical purpose, and it is impossible to show that they are even possible entities. These are the central arguments for immaterialism, the criticism of the various doctrines of material substance.

Berkeley continues by completing the sketch of his idealism. He argues that ideas are "visibly inactive" (PHK §25). So ideas cannot be causes. Nonetheless, because "we perceive a continual succession of ideas" (PHK §26), this succession of ideas must have a cause. Since ideas cannot be causes, and since there are no material substances, "the cause of ideas is an incorporeal active substance or spirit" (PHK §26; see also §29). But how are these spirits known? Because an incorporeal substance is active, and because ideas are passive and can be like nothing but ideas, one cannot have an idea of a spirit. "Such is the nature of *spirit*, or that which acts, that it cannot be of itself perceived but only by the effects which it produceth" (PHK §27). In the second edition of the *Principles*, Berkeley adds that although we do not have an idea of spirit, "we have some *notion* of soul, spirit, and the operations of the mind, such as willing, loving, hating, inasmuch as we know or understand the meaning of those words" (PHK §27, emphasis added; see also §§89, 140, 142). What is the nature of notional knowledge? Berkeley gives little more than clues in the 1734 editions of the *Principles* and *Three Dialogues*, and the nature of Berkeleian notions remains a matter of considerable controversy (see Park 1972; Flage 1987; Muehlmann 1992; 224, 235–40).

Although Berkeley claimed that ordinary objects are nothing but collections of ideas in the first section of the *Principles*, in Sections 30–33 he distinguishes those collections we call "real things" from imaginary things. He distinguishes ideas of sensation from ideas of the imagination on the basis of the strength, liveliness, distinctness, steadiness, order, and coherence of the former *vis-à-vis* the latter (PHK §30; see also §62). Real things are composed of ideas of sensation and subject to the laws of nature (PHK §§32–33). As I read Berkeley, real things are human constructs. As one discovers that more and more distinct kinds of ideas are correlated in experience, one constructs an increasingly complex object of thought in much the same way that Locke claimed one constructs a nominal essence (see Locke, *Essay* III.vi.6; but cf. Luce 1945). Your idea of the table "in front of both of us" is numerically distinct from mine. Given the differences between your experience of tables and mine, your table might be "richer" than mine; that is, your expectations regarding what you would perceive regarding the table under various circumstances might differ from mine. Nonetheless, given that God causes ideas uniformly, given that humans tend toward a significant degree of uniformity in joining ideas together into objects, and given that the word "identity" is ambiguous (DHP 3, *Works* 2: 247), whether you and I see the same table is primarily a verbal issue.

While the primary cases for immaterialism and idealism are set forth in the first thirty-three sections of the *Principles*, Berkeley strengthens his case in the remaining sections by raising and replying to objections and by elaborating various points. He develops much the same case in his *Three Dialogues between Hylas and Philonous*, although there are differences in emphasis.

CONCLUDING REMARKS

George Berkeley was an intellectually complex figure. The champion of immaterialism and idealism was also the critic of Newtonian theories of fluxions and infinitesimals (the *Analyst*; see NEWTON). The religious apologeticist of the *Alciphron* was also an early proponent of the credit theory of money and an instrumentalist philosophy of science. Though Berkeley died in 1753, his intellectual legacy continues to impact on areas as diverse as philosophy and economics.

PRIMARY WORKS

The Works of George Berkeley, Bishop of Cloyne. Edited by A. A. Luce and T. E. Jessop. 9 vols. London: Thomas Nelson and Sons, 1948–1957.
Three Dialogues between Hylas and Philonous. Edited by Robert Merrihew Adams. Indianapolis: Hackett, 1979.
A Treatise concerning the Principles of Human Knowledge. Edited by Kenneth Winkler. Indianapolis: Hackett, 1982.
Notebooks of George Berkeley, Bishop of Cloyne, with Postscript by Désirée Park. Tercentenary facsimile ed. Oxford: Alden Press, 1984.
George Berkeley's Manuscript Introduction: An Editio Diplomatica. Edited with introduction and commentary by Bertil Belfrage. Oxford: Doxa, 1987.
De Motu and the Analyst: A Modern Edition with Introduction and Commentary. Edited and translated by Douglas M. Jesseph. Dordrecht and Boston: Kluwer Academic, 1992.

BIBLIOGRAPHY

Books

Atherton, Margaret. *Berkeley's Revolution in Vision*. Ithaca, NY: Cornell University Press, 1990.

Bennett, Jonathan. *Locke, Berkeley, Hume: Central Themes*. Oxford: Clarendon Press, 1971.

Berman, David. *George Berkeley: Idealism and the Man*. Oxford: Clarendon Press, 1994.

Bracken, Harry. *Berkeley*. Philosophers in Perspective. New York: St. Martin's Press, 1974.

———. *The Early Reception of Berkeley's Philosophy, 1710–33*. The Hague: Martinus Nijhoff, 1965.

Dancy, Jonathan. *Berkeley: An Introduction*. Oxford: Basil Blackwell, 1987.

Flage, Daniel E. *Berkeley's Doctrine of Notions: A Reconstruction Based on His Theory of Meaning*. London: Croom Helm, 1987.

Grayling, A. C. *Berkeley: The Central Arguments*. LaSalle, IL: Open Court, 1986.

Johnston, Joseph. *Bishop Berkeley's* Querist *in Historical Perspective*. Dundalk: Dundalgan Press (W. Tempest), 1970.

Luce, A. A. *Berkeley and Malebranche: A Study in the Origins of Berkeley's Thought*. Oxford: Clarendon Press, 1934.

———. *Berkeley's Immaterialism*. London: Thomas Nelson and Sons, 1945.

———. *The Life of George Berkeley, Bishop of Cloyne*. London: Thomas Nelson and Sons, 1949.

Muehlmann, Robert G. *Berkeley's Ontology*. Indianapolis, IN: Hackett, 1992.

———, ed. *Berkeley's Metaphysics: Structural, Interpretive, and Critical Essays*. University Park: Pennsylvania State University Press, 1995.

Olscamp, Paul J. *The Moral Philosophy of George Berkeley*. The Hague: Martinus Nijhoff, 1970.

Park, Désirée. *Complementary Notions: A Critical Study of Berkeley's Theory of Concepts*. The Hague: Martinus Nijhoff, 1972.

Pitcher, George. *Berkeley*. The Arguments of the Philosophers. London: Routledge and Kegan Paul, 1977.

Tipton, I. C. *Berkeley: The Philosophy of Immaterialism*. London: Methuen, 1974.

Turbayne, Colin Murry, ed. *Berkeley: Critical and Interpretive Essays*. Minneapolis: University of Minnesota Press, 1982.

Urmson, J. O. *Berkeley*. Past Masters. Oxford: Oxford University Press, 1982; reprinted in *The British Empiricists: Locke, Berkeley, Hume* by John Dunn, J. O. Urmson, and A. J. Ayer. Oxford: Oxford University Press, 1992.

Warnock, G. J. *Berkeley*. London: Penguin Books, 1953.

Winkler, Kenneth P. *Berkeley: An Interpretation*. Oxford: Clarendon Press, 1989.

Articles

Cummins, Phillip D. "Berkeley's Likeness Principle." In *Locke and Berkeley: Collection of Critical Essays*, edited by C. B. Martin and D. M. Armstrong. Garden City, NY: Doubleday Anchor Books, 1968: 353–63.

———. "Berkeley's Manifest Qualities Thesis." *Journal of the History of Philosophy* 28 (1990): 385–401.

DANIEL E. FLAGE

BOYLE, ROBERT. Robert Boyle (1627–1691), English natural philosopher, was a pioneer in the theory and practice of experimental method. He was one of the earliest fellows of the Royal Society (1662) and after removing to London in 1668 was always close to the center of its activities. His writing was an important influence on early modern epistemology as it sought to understand the implications of the corpuscularian theory of matter. The motives behind his work were partly practical and humanitarian, partly theological.

Boyle was born into an Anglo-Irish landed family and for much of his life was supported by the income of family estates in Dorset and Connaught. He was mostly privately educated, traveling and residing on the Continent with a French Calvinist tutor during the early years of the English civil war. An early competence in mathematics was not maintained. He studied Aristotelian and Stoic philosophy (see ARISTOTLE and STOICISM) at that time and followed the contemporary controversy over the work of GALILEO. Returning to England in 1744, he joined a group of educational reformers trained in the traditions of Christian humanism who believed in moral improvement without sectarian divisions. This resulted in a series of early ethical papers concerned with virtue and godliness, articulating attitudes that informed his subsequent life and work.

Self-taught studies in husbandry led Boyle to natural philosophy, at first particularly chemistry, which he was instrumental in reforming as an experimental study founded in the philosophical principles of the new science. His experiments were recorded in meticulous detail. He pursued these studies particularly while living in Oxford during the Cromwellian period. His theory of matter was partly a priori, partly experimental (see A PRIORI/A POSTERIORI DISTINCTION). It starts from the notion of a "universal matter" whose essence is or includes extension, but in his best-known exposition in *The Origin of Forms and Qualities* (1666) he added impenetrability, a conception later redefined as "solidity" by LOCKE.

It is observable that some of the parts of matter are in motion and that motion is of variable speeds and direction. Boyle therefore postulated that motion in all its variety is the immediate cause of the division and diversity apparent in the bodies that constitute these parts. Matter and motion are the "most catholic principles" among bodies; but motion, not being inherent (since matter could have been uniformly at rest), has to be attributable to an external cause. Since motion is a fact, matter must be actually fragmented, and its fragments must necessarily be bounded and therefore characterized by shape and size. The four characteristics of motion, rest, shape, and size are variously called the "primary moods" or "primary affections" of matter. Of these, motion is the "first and chief mood"; shape and size are the "inseparable accidents" of every part. The smaller parts that make up larger parts or individual bodies are then related to one another in respect of posture and order, and the sum of the smaller parts so related and characterized as previously is called the "texture" of the whole; where the parts are not homogeneous, the composition is called a "mixture." The primary affections along with these further features are collectively called the "mechanical affections" of matter. It is thus not Boyle's account of the primary moods, but the complete scheme of the mechanical affections combined with the initial essential characteristic(s) of matter, that corresponds to Locke's later account of primary qualities (see PRIMARY AND SECONDARY QUALITIES); but Boyle himself excluded these from the category of qualities.

From an early point in his exposition, Boyle introduced the assumption that helped give the corpuscularian theory its name—that the smallest parts of matter, variously called "corpuscles" and "particles," are individually imperceptible. A corpuscle is for practical purposes undivided, and a particle is indivisible, but it appears to be a contingent fact rather than a theoretical necessity that these are imperceptibly small. Although they are, Boyle considered that the evidence for them still lies in experience—sometimes from microscopes but more often from chemical experiments, where observable changes are presumed traceable to unobserved causes analogous to others that are observable. The line between theory and evidence is particularly blurred in Boyle's constant assumption that changes brought about by, for instance, fire, hammering, or chemical admixture are transparently changes of texture, but he sought to support it with evidence from those cases where further treatment restored the original state.

This led him into his theory of qualities ("properties" in modern scientific parlance). The chemical, medicinal, and other qualities of different kinds of substances are all relational properties that we colloquially call powers—powers of bodies to affect other bodies in specified ways in virtue of the mechanical affections of their respective parts and other concurrent circumstances. Where the second member of the relation is not present, what remains is nothing but the mechanical affections of the parts of the first, so that Boyle admitted nothing but matter modified in various ways, characterized counterfactually in terms of what would be its effects in other circumstances. This ultimate elimination of powers in favor of texture was the reverse of Locke's view, according to which qualities were themselves analyzed as irreducible powers, and was most fully spelled out by Boyle in relation to what he called "sensible" qualities (color, taste, sound, etc.). In terms of all such qualities we identify things by species, and therefore the corpuscularian theory of matter can dispense with the Aristotelian concept of form, just as it can explain the phenomena of substantial and accidental change (see SUBSTANCE).

Locke's portrayal of the mind compounding like and unlike ideas, decompounding (i.e., compounding from compounds) and associating its ideas, appears to have been based on analogies from Boyle's chemistry. Boyle and Locke shared a common view of science as probabilistic and of scientific theory as largely hypothetical and recommended lessons from this for much of the political and religious factionalism of the day. Boyle wrote indefatigably but repetitiously on what he considered the broad religious lessons to be learned from science, seeing God's existence proved both from the existence of motion and from the evidence of design, alike in the parts of nature and in the whole, while the design in turn was a motive to further research. He had a lifelong interest in the topic of miracles and in a late work, *The Christian Virtuoso* (1690), which Locke had reviewed in manuscript, Boyle defended the empirical foundations of revealed RELIGION. Miracles are meant not to convert the atheist to theism but to convince the theist to accept a particular dispensation worthy of acceptance. We learn both by personal experience and from history to recognize on the evidence of often humble persons that events contrary to our habitual expectations can occur; what is acceptable in ordinary life is essential in religion, and the greater our natural knowledge, the better able we are to identify what is supernatural.

PRIMARY WORKS

The Works of the Honourable Robert Boyle. 6 vols. London: 1772. Reprinted Hildesheim: Olms, 1965–1966. A new collected edition by Michael Hunter and Edward Davis is in preparation for the firm of Pickering and Chatto.

Robert Boyle on Natural Philosophy. Edited by Marie Boas Hall. Bloomington: Indiana University Press, 1965.

Selected Philosophical Papers of Robert Boyle. Edited by M. A. Stewart. Manchester: Manchester University Press, 1979. Reprinted with new Preface, Indianapolis: Hackett, 1991.

The Early Essays and Ethics of Robert Boyle. Edited by John T. Harwood. Carbondale: Southern Illinois University Press, 1991.

Robert Boyle by Himself and His Friends. Edited by Michael Hunter. London: Pickering and Chatto, 1994.

BIBLIOGRAPHY

Books

Alexander, Peter. *Ideas, Qualities and Corpuscles: Locke and Boyle on the External World*. Cambridge: Cambridge University Press, 1985.

Hunter, Michael, ed. *Robert Boyle Reconsidered*. Cambridge: Cambridge University Press, 1994. Includes a comprehensive bibliography from 1940.

Sargent, Rose-Mary. *The Diffident Naturalist: Robert Boyle and the Philosophy of Experiment*. Chicago: University of Chicago Press, 1995.

Articles

McCann, Edwin. "Lockean Mechanism." With Appendix, "Was Boyle an Occasionalist?" In *Philosophy, Its History and Historiography*, edited by A. J. Holland. Dordrecht: Kluwer, 1985: 209–31.

McGuire, J. E. "Boyle's Conception of Nature." *Journal of the History of Ideas* 33 (1972): 523–42.

MacIntosh, J. J. "Perception and Imagination in Descartes, Boyle and Hooke." *Canadian Journal of Philosophy* 13 (1983): 327–52.

———. "Robert Boyle's Epistemology: The Interaction between Scientific and Religious Knowledge." *International Studies in the Philosophy of Science* 6 (1992): 91–121.

O'Toole, F. J. "Qualities and Powers in the Corpuscular Philosophy of Robert Boyle." *Journal of the History of Philosophy* 12 (1974): 295–315.

Shanahan, Timothy. "God and Nature in Robert Boyle." *Journal of the History of Philosophy* 26 (1988): 547–69.

———. "Teleological Reasoning in Boyle's *Disquisition about Final Causes*." In *Rob-

ert Boyle Reconsidered, edited by Michael Hunter. Cambridge: Cambridge University Press, 1994: 177–92.

Stewart, M. A. ''Locke's 'Observations' on Boyle.'' *Locke Newsletter* 24 (1993): 21–34.

Wojcik, Jan W. ''The Theological Context of Boyle's *Things above Reason*.'' In *Robert Boyle Reconsidered*, edited by Michael Hunter. Cambridge: Cambridge University Press, 1994: 139–55.

M. A. STEWART

C

CARNAP, RUDOLF. Rudolf Carnap (1891–1970), a leading proponent of logical positivism, published extensively on empiricism, semantics, probability theory, inductive logic, and the nature of philosophical problems. By 1913 Carnap had studied logic with Frege at Jena and, after doing experimental work in physics, had come to hold that the scientific method was the only method of acquiring well-founded knowledge. Beginning his philosophical work in 1919, Carnap soon came under the influence of Bertrand Russell's work (see RUSSELL), especially *Our Knowledge of the External World* (1914). He was guided by the logical-analytic method, whereby one applies the logic of Frege and Russell to analyzing scientific concepts and clarifying philosophical problems. Carnap regarded the latter as the essential aim of his philosophical activity.

In 1926 Carnap joined the Vienna Circle, a group known for an antimetaphysical attitude that gave primacy to logic, mathematics, and the empirical sciences. Moritz Schlick started the circle at the University of Vienna and enlisted Carnap, Otto NEURATH, Herbert Feigl, Friedrich Waismann, Kurt GÖDEL, and Hans Hahn. The circle's members favored an approach to their problems that was analytical, scientific, and antimetaphysical.

In 1929, Carnap, Neurath, and Hahn published a manifesto for the circle entitled "The Scientific Conception of the World: The Vienna Circle." They identified the eighteenth-century empiricist David HUME as one of their main forerunners. With the exception of Gödel, the circle's members shared Hume's antipathy to metaphysics. They used modern logic and various analytical techniques to restrict philosophical pursuits to the advancement of "scientific" knowledge, thereby excluding metaphysical concerns from philosophy. Following Hume's concept of empiricism, the circle denied the cognitive meaningfulness of experience-transcendent, metaphysical notions and claims.

Ludwig WITTGENSTEIN decisively influenced Carnap and the circle. In his *Tractatus Logico-Philosophicus* (1921), Wittgenstein enunciated various doctrines attractive to the circle, including: "4.11 The totality of true propositions is the whole of natural sciences (or the whole *corpus* of the natural sciences)."

Carnap especially welcomed Wittgenstein's view that knowledge of logical propositions is not a special kind of metaphysical knowledge about the world. Wittgenstein proposed: "The propositions of logic are tautologies. . . . Therefore the propositions of logic say nothing. (They are the analytic propositions.)" (6.1–6.11). Later, in the 1950s and 1960s, Carnap would vigorously defend the philosophical significance of analyticity against objections from W.V.O. QUINE and others (see ANALYTIC/SYNTHETIC DISTINCTION).

The basis of the circle's positivism was a principle of verification regarding MEANING, recommended by Wittgenstein. In 1929, Wittgenstein claimed:

[I]f I can never verify the sense of a proposition completely, then I cannot have meant anything by the proposition either. Then the proposition signifies nothing whatever. In order to determine the sense of a proposition, I should have to know a very specific procedure for when to count the proposition as verified. (McGuinness: 47)

Since metaphysical claims about gods, souls, essences, values, and the like lack a method of verification, the Verification Principle dispenses with them as meaningless. The circle did indeed dispense with them as meaningless, holding that every meaningful claim can be expressed via observational claims, claims susceptible to confirmation or disconfirmation on the basis of observation. Carnap suggested that the principle of verification is a "convention" resting on a choice about how to use certain language. He recommended a kind of scientism implying that the empirical sciences can, in principle, say all that can be said.

The members of the circle divided over the nature of the fundamental observational claims—so-called protocol statements—that set the standard for confirmation and meaningfulness. One key issue was whether these observational claims are solely about what is given in subjective, private experience or can include intersubjectively testable claims about physical states of affairs.

In his *The Logical Structure of the World* (1928), Carnap aimed to show in detail how all meaningful concepts could be reduced to "the given," that is, "experiences themselves in their totality and undivided unity." In particular, Carnap sought to define a range of observationally relevant concepts (e.g., color concepts, visual spatial concepts) on the basis of the single fundamental concept of "recollection of similarity" between elementary experiences. More generally, he sought to analyze concepts of ordinary language that relate to things in our environment and to define these concepts in observational terms with the help of modern symbolic logic. Influenced by Ernst MACH and phenomenalist philosophers (see PHENOMENALISM), his analyses proceeded from complexes to smaller components, for example, from physical bodies to visual fields, then to color patches, and lastly to single positions in a visual field.

During the 1930s, under the influence of Gestalt psychology, Carnap came to reject attempts to analyze material things into separate SENSE-DATA. He then held that a visual field is given as a unit and that sense-data result from a process of ABSTRACTION. Still, his aim in *Logical Structure* was to give not a description of actual concept formation but a rational reconstruction. He aimed to be ontologically neutral: neither materialist (see MATERIALISM) nor phe-nomenalist. This attitude of ontological neutrality became the "principle of tol-erance" toward alternative languages in *The Logical Syntax of Language* (1934). Carnap thus aimed not to take sides on ontological issues, as he regarded on-tological claims as exceeding the bounds of science. Carnap abandoned the project of *Logical Structure* upon coming to hold that scientific concepts should have a physicalist, rather than a phenomenalist, base. By the early 1930s, Carnap proposed that protocol statements be formulated in intersubjectively shared lan-guage about physical situations.

From 1936 to 1952 Carnap held a position at the University of Chicago, where Russell taught in 1939. In 1940–1941, Carnap became a U.S. citizen and visited at Harvard, where Russell and Tarski were also visiting. By this time, the role of convention in Carnap's epistemology supported a kind of PRAGMATISM—an emphasis on purpose-relative, practical considerations. Questions about which linguistic conventions to adopt are naturally understood as questions about which conventions best serve one's linguistic and theoretical purposes. By 1936, Carnap held that the acceptance and the rejection of a synthetic sen-tence always contain a conventional component, inasmuch as one must decide what degree of confirmation is adequate for acceptability.

By 1950 Carnap's pragmatism was explicit. Realists about the external world affirm that there really are observable spatiotemporal things and events. Subjec-tive idealists question the reality of the thing-world itself. Carnap gave the re-alist-idealist controversy a pragmatic spin in "Empiricism, Semantics, and Ontology" (1950):

Those who raise the question of the reality of the thing world itself have perhaps in mind not a theoretical question . . . , but rather a practical question, a matter of practical de-cision concerning the structure of our language. We have to make the choice whether or not to accept and use the forms of expression in the [linguistic] framework in question. (207)

Carnap acknowledged that "the thing language" efficiently serves many pur-poses of everyday life and that it is advisable to accept the thing language on this pragmatic basis. He rejected, however, any suggestion that such a pragmatic basis can provide confirming evidence for "the reality" of the thing world. A statement of the reality of the total system of certain entities (e.g., spatiotemporal things), according to Carnap, is a "pseudo-statement without cognitive content." Questions about the total system of certain entities—what Carnap called "ex-ternal questions"—make sense, on this view, only as practical questions about whether to adopt certain ways of using language. By the 1950s, then, Carnap's LOGICAL POSITIVISM had moved toward pragmatism in epistemology, thus reviving themes from an American movement that antedated the Vienna Circle. Carnap's work on the pragmatic components in theory-formation has had en-during value.

PRIMARY WORKS

The Logical Structure of the World (1928). Translated by R. A. George. Berkeley: University of California Press, 1967.

The Logical Syntax of Language (1934). Translated by A. Smeaton. London: Kegan Paul.

"Empiricism, Semantics, and Ontology" (1950). In *Carnap, Meaning and Necessity*, 2d ed. Chicago: University of Chicago Press, 1956: 205–21.

(and W.V.O. Quine.) *Dear Carnap, Dear Van.* Berkeley: University of California Press, 1990.

BIBLIOGRAPHY

Books

Coffa, J. Alberto. *The Semantic Tradition from Kant to Carnap: To the Vienna Station.* Cambridge: Cambridge University Press, 1991.

McGuinness, B. F., ed. *Wittgenstein and the Vienna Circle.* Conversations recorded by Friedrich Weismann, translated by B. F. McGuinness and J. Schulte. Oxford: Basil Blackwell, 1979.

Schilpp, P. A., ed. *The Philosophy of Rudolf Carnap.* LaSalle, IL: Open Court, 1963.

PAUL K. MOSER

CAUSATION/POWER. Each time we hear a sound or turn our heads to glance about, each time the wind moves through the leaves, one thing seems causally to affect another. We seem to experience the power to affect our body and other things in the world and the power of things in the world to affect us and other things in it.

John LOCKE distinguishes active from passive power "as able to make, or able to receive any change" (*An Essay concerning Human Understanding* II.xxi.2), but he says that when faced with the question how mind can affect matter or be affected by it, "our understanding sticks and bogles and knows not what way to turne" (*An Early Draft of Locke's Essay Together with Excerpts from His Journals*: 90). When we ask how matter can affect other matter, however, we discover it is "by motion," so that it "would be then, perhaps, no more difficult to know, than it is to a Smith to understand, why the turning of one Key will open a Lock, and not the turning of another" (*Essay* IV.iii.25).

Yet we do not know much of how one object affects another or even how the parts of any one thing are related. We know that gold has the properties of "great Ductility, Fusibility, Fixedness, and Solubility, in *Aqua Regia*," but we do not know how these are connected together and so how something so easily shaped and readily fused is also soluble and resistant to change.

[I]f the formal Constitution of this shining, heavy, ductil Thing (from whence all these its Properties flow) lay open to our Senses, as the formal Constitution, or Essence of a Triangle does, the signification of the word *Gold*, might as easily be ascertained, as that of *Triangle*. (*Essay* III.xi.22)

When we understand "why the turning of one Key will open a Lock, and not the turning of another," we perceive the geometrical relations between the parts.

That the one and not the other will open the lock is "evident from the shape of the rigid parts, together with the idea of a body's defining property to push others out of its way" (Ayers, *Locke: Epistemology and Ontology*: 147). Had we the capacity to discern the minute particles of gold as clearly as we perceive the key and the parts of its lock, we would know how all the properties are related, one to another. The mechanical lock is a paradigm for knowledge of the world and fails, Locke seems to be saying, only because we are ignorant of the minute parts that make up such substances as gold.

But, Locke says:

Motion, according to the utmost reach of our *Ideas*, being able to produce nothing but Motion, so that when we allow it to produce pleasure or pain, or the *Idea* of a Colour, or Sound, we are fain to quit our Reason, go beyond our *Ideas*, and attribute it wholly to the good Pleasure of our Maker. (*Essay* IV.iii.6)

What is Locke about here? He may be saying that though we could understand the relations within objects, such as the key and the lock, the relations between objects and us are unintelligible because we cannot conceive how motion can produce something completely different from motion, such as IDEAS. But if such relations "are out of reach of reason," as Leibniz puts it, "that would be a backdoor through which to re-admit 'over-occult qualities' " (Leibniz, *New Essays on Human Understanding*: 379–83). Mechanism would have its limits because our understanding here "sticks and bogles." But Locke might be suggesting only that we are as ignorant of such connections as we are of those between particles of gold.

Between these two possibilities lies all the difference regarding the pretensions of the new SCIENCE of GALILEO, BOYLE, and NEWTON. If God provides the connections between us and the world, and we cannot understand them, no new science is possible regarding whatever involves us as causal agents or objects. The world would be split in two, one subject to mechanistic explanation, and the other not. But if only our ignorance is at issue, the new science can take the entire observable world as its field of play, the relations between the world and us as well as the relations within the world. Scientists could work to mitigate or remove our ignorance by new scientific instruments, such as "Microscopical Eyes," that would give us access to what our own limited observational capacities prevent us from observing (*Essay* II.xxiii.12).

But is mechanism even possible? The power of Locke's lock metaphor is that the relation between turning the key and opening the lock seems intelligible, because necessary. How could the proper key not open the lock? But what actually happens when a cause produces an effect? When one billiard ball hits another, Locke says,

it only communicates the motion it had received from another, and loses in it self so much, as the other received; which gives us but a very obscure *Idea* of an *active Power* of moving in Body, whilst we observe it only to transfer, but not produce any motion.

For it is but a very obscure *Idea* of *Power*, which reaches not to the Production of the Action, but the Continuation of the Passion. (*Essay* II.xxi.4)

To get "the Idea of the beginning of motion, we have . . . [to reflect] on what passes in our selves, where we find by Experience, that barely by willing it, . . . we can move the parts of our bodies, which were before at rest" (*Essay* II.xxi.4). Causation requires production, it seems. But objects that impact on each other do not produce anything new. They only transfer motion. We create something new when we move "the parts of our Bodies" and have something new created in us when "moved" by something external.

We thus have a problem. To get the production Locke thinks a causal relation requires, we must look to the WILL, but then the mind "bogles," unable to see how we can create motion by an act of will or how pleasure or pain or any ideas can be produced by motion. But where we have intelligibility, as when a billiard ball transfers motion to another, we lack production. We cannot have both production and intelligibility—if by "intelligibility" is meant that we can see connections such as those we see regarding triangles. The motion between the billiard balls is not part of their ESSENCE. In seeing one ball transfer motion to the other, we see nothing about the balls that could make intelligible what it is about the one that causes it or the other to move. The motion is added to them. As Locke says, we can have but "experimental Knowledge" of these relations (*Essay* IV.iii.30). How then is the new science possible?

In BERKELEY and HUME we see two different ways of coming to grips with the apparently incoherent set of propositions about causation with which Locke struggled. There are various ways one could cut that set, and Berkeley cuts it by maintaining that a cause produces an effect, a new entity, not previously existent (*Philosophical Commentaries*, §499 and §699).

So when one billiard ball hits another, Berkeley argues, it does not cause that second ball to move. Using Locke's terminology, the second ball is passive, "able to receive . . . change," but the first ball is not active. There is nothing in our ideas, Berkeley argues, but what we perceive, and we perceive nothing of an agent in the first billiard ball. Were we to do that, we should have to perceive the first ball deciding to move and then moving itself into the second ball of its own volition. But, in fact, we can trace back motion to motion to motion among such objects, never reaching a point in them where motion begins through an act of will. For the production of motion we must look at least to the person with the cue stick. Billiard balls are not agents, and so we perceive no active power in them. Since we perceive none, and there is nothing there but what we perceive, there is none, Berkeley concludes (*Principles of Human Knowledge*, §25).

The paradigmatic instance of a causal agent is GOD. Whatever God wills must occur (*Principles* §152). It is not necessary that God will anything since if it were, that would limit his power. So what is produced is not of his essence, and the relationship between God and what is produced is not like that between the properties of a triangle. So, though it is necessary that what God wills occur, it is contingent that God wills anything. We thus could not predict, even if we knew God's essence, what God would will.

Though Berkeley is reluctant to admit it, we are, predictably, worse off than God. We seem to be causal agents. When I turn my head to glance about, willing that my head turn seems to suffice to produce that effect. It may even seem that what I will must happen because what we will has content: I will that my head turn, and my head turns. But it is no more part of my essence that I will that effect than it is part of God's essence that he will anything, and it is equally a contingent matter that when I will, something happens. We do not even need imagine a Cartesian evil genius who disconnects me from my will and my will from the world. We all too often find our will impotent—enough to deny the necessity of a relation between it and its object. For all we can know, God produces what we seem to will, our will being the occasion of God's acts.

Only contingent relations exist between our essence, what we will, and what happens. In insisting that a cause produces an effect, a new entity, and in taking as his paradigm of a causal relation the necessity of the connection between God's will and what God wills, Berkeley seems to have committed himself to a SKEPTICISM he would be loath to embrace. First, he has ensured that we cannot know we are causal agents. For we cannot know we produce anything. Second, though God is a causal agent, the world is as potentially arbitrary as it would be were God an evil genius, because only a contingent relation exists between his essence and what he wills. Even if we knew God's essence, we could infer nothing about what he has willed about the world—why he willed one thing rather than another. Even when we discover regularities in the world and in us, we have no guarantee that these speak to any intelligible connection between God and the world, for the relation between his essence and the features of the world is not like that between the properties of a triangle. The new science promises intelligibility by uncovering the causal connections in the world, but, on Berkeley's view, the only causal connections we could uncover lack the intelligibility we need to give us understanding of the world.

Hume argues that whenever we judge that one thing, a, causes another, b, we perceive that a and b are contiguous in time. That is all we perceive that is common to any one instance of what we call a causal relation, whatever the relata are—whether they are things in the world (one billiard ball hitting another) or things in us (one thought causing another) or things between us and the world (my willing that my head move or something making a noise). "Passions," as he puts it, "are connected with their objects and with one another; no less than external objects are connected together. The same relation, then, of cause and effect, which belongs to one, must be common to all of them" (*A Treatise of Human Nature* I.iii.2).

When the causal relata are capable of spatial relations—as PASSIONS are not, but billiard balls are—we also perceive that a and b are contiguous in space (see SPACE). Were this conjunction not constant—were it not true, that is, that whenever we perceive anything relevantly similar to a, we perceive something relevantly similar to b—we would not judge the one the cause of the other.

Hume argues as Berkeley does, from our lack of perception of any connection between a cause and its effect, but he also argues that whatever the relata of a causal relation, the one can exist without the other. We can readily conceive of the world changing or ceasing at any particular instant so that a would occur, and nothing would follow, or we can conceive of b's beginning without a's occurring. In short, there can be no necessary connection between any cause and any effect.

Why do we think there is? The perception of a constant conjunction of what we call a cause and an effect causes us to have a ''propensity, . . . to pass from an object to the idea of its usual attendant'' (Hume, *Treatise* I.iii.14). This propensity determines us to believe that the second billiard ball will move upon our perceiving the first moving toward it. So the necessity we attribute to the causal relation is in us.

One consequence is that the presumption that causal relations are like the relations between the properties of a triangle is false. Another consequence is what we now call the problem of INDUCTION. Since an a could occur without its ''usual attendant,'' we have no way of inferring from what we perceive to what we do not perceive, whether that is in the future, the past, or the present, unless we assume that what we have experienced as happening still holds. But this assumption we cannot justify. It is not a necessary truth, and the only evidence we have for it is that past experiences have continued to be as they were, and we cannot infer from that anything about what we have not experienced without assuming what we are to prove.

A third consequence is that a universal science is possible. We have no reason to exclude ourselves and our causal relations from the world, and part of Hume's enterprise was to show that a scientific understanding is possible in every corner of human activity—history, economics, political science, and art, among others. Our understanding need not ''stick and bogle'' no matter what it investigates.

All of these implications remain as contentious as any interpretation of Locke, Berkeley, and Hume. The problem of induction, for instance, is a classic example of a vexing philosophical issue, and cognitive scientists and philosophers continue to debate whether the passions, as Hume would put it, are as subject to causal understanding as objects in the world.

PRIMARY WORKS

Berkeley, George. *The Works of George Berkeley, Bishop of Cloyne*. Edited by A. A. Luce and T. E. Jessop. 9 vols. London: Thomas Nelson and Sons, 1948–1957.

Hume, David. *An Enquiry concerning Human Understanding*. In *Enquiries concerning Human Understanding and concerning the Principles of Morals*, edited with an analytical index by L. A. Selby-Bigge; rev. with notes by P. H. Nidditch. Oxford: Clarendon Press, 1975.

———. *A Treatise of Human Nature*, 2d ed., edited with an analytical index by L. A. Selby-Bigge; rev. with notes by P. H. Nidditch. Oxford: Clarendon Press, 1978.

Leibniz, *New Essays on Human Understanding*. Edited by Peter Remnant and Jonathan Bennett. Cambridge: Cambridge University Press, 1981.

Locke, John. *An Early Draft of Locke's Essay Together with Excerpts from His Journals*. Edited by R. I. Aaron and Jocelyn Gibb. Oxford: Clarendon Press, 1936.

———. *An Essay concerning Human Understanding*. Edited with an introduction by P. H. Nidditch. Oxford: Clarendon Press, 1975.

BIBLIOGRAPHY

Ayers, Michael. *Locke: Epistemology and Ontology*. London: Routledge, 1991.

Chappell, V. C., ed. *Hume: A Collection of Critical Essays*. Garden City, NY: Doubleday, 1966.

Foster, John, and Howard Robinson. *Essays on Berkeley: A Tercentennial Celebration*. Oxford: Clarendon Press, 1985.

Mackie, J. L. *The Cement of the Universe: A Study of Causation*. Oxford: Clarendon Press, 1974.

Winkler, Kenneth P. *Berkeley: An Interpretation*. Oxford: Clarendon Press, 1989.

WADE L. ROBISON

COLLINS, ANTHONY. Anthony Collins (1676–1729), a leading British freethinker and critic of religion, is important philosophically for his defense of determinism and freethinking and for his materialist account of the mind. Perhaps his main interest for empiricism was his close connection with John LOCKE.

Born in Middlesex on June 21, 1676, Collins was educated at Eton. He then went to King's College, Cambridge, which he left without taking a degree, and to the Middle Temple, where he continued the family tradition of studying law. In 1703 his wife died, leaving him with three children. Also in this year Collins met Locke, probably the main influence on his thought. In his cordial letters to Collins—published in 1720—Locke expresses a high regard for Collins' amiable character, love of truth, and grasp of Locke's philosophy. Indeed, Locke seems to have looked on Collins as his intellectual heir or chief interpreter. Thus, in a letter of April 3, 1704, Locke says that he knows no one who understands his *Essay concerning Human Understanding* (London, 1690) "so well, nor can give me better light concerning it" than Collins; see also Locke's letter of October 29, 1703.

Collins' authorship falls into two periods of about a decade each. His philosophical works are from the first period, from 1707 to 1717. From 1720 to his death in 1729 his writings are chiefly historical, mainly concerned with questioning the authority of Christianity.

The first period is relevant here, especially Collins' first published work, *An Essay concerning the Use of Reason* (London, 1707), where he draws on Locke's accounts of MEANING and TRUTH, that is, that all meaningful words stand for IDEAS and that truth and falsity consist in seeing the agreement or disagreement of our ideas. For Collins, all our judgments are based on our ideas, on how things appear to us. Hence, perception is the only criterion of truth: I cannot know something "to be true but by my own Perception" (*An Essay concerning the Use of Reason*: 10). He is, however, aware that this subjective theory could lead to extreme SKEPTICISM. But he seems to assume that no sane person would go that way, since, as he puts it in a later pamphlet, it would "destroy all Knowledge or Science relating to things existing" (*Answer to Clark's Third Defence*, London, 2d ed., 1711: 8). Perhaps the main advantage of this theory for Collins is that it excludes any external authority or religious mysteries above our understanding. Collins, I suggest, is drawing out the rationalistic implications of Locke's theories of meaning and knowledge, not so much for the "quieting of disputes"—as Locke expressed it (*Essay* IV.iii.22)— but for firmly settling them.

At least partly by means of this epistemological rationalism, as it may be called, Collins is able to argue (1) for the materiality of the mind in his 1707–1708 duel with Samuel Clarke, (2) against Archbishop William King's negative theology in his *A Vindication of the Divine Attributes* (London, 1710), and (3) for determinism in his influential *Philosophical Inquiry concerning Human Liberty* (London, 1717), which draws on Locke and also on HOBBES and Spinoza. The work for which Collins is probably best known is *A Discourse of Free-Thinking* (London, 1713), which also continues his defense of reason by opposing restrictions on intellectual inquiry.

There is some dispute about Collins' theological position. Although he is usually described as a deist (see DEISM), George BERKELEY claimed that he was a speculative atheist, indeed, that he heard Collins say that he (Collins) had a proof for the nonexistence of God—a judgment that is supported by the present author in *A History of Atheism from Hobbes to Russell* (London, 1990), Chapter 3. It is likely that some of Berkeley's criticisms of materialism and determinism are aimed at Collins and that Collins alerted Berkeley to the irreligious implications of Locke's philosophy.

PRIMARY WORK

An Essay concerning the Use of Reason. London: s.n., 1707.

BIBLIOGRAPHY

Berman, David. "Anthony Collins: Aspects of His Thought and Writings." *Hermathena* 119 (1975): 49–70.
O'Higgins, James. *Anthony Collins: The Man and His Works*. The Hague: Nijhoff, 1970.

DAVID BERMAN

COMTE, AUGUSTE. Auguste Comte (1798–1857), child of postrevolutionary France, student at the École Polytechnique (expelled), youthful associate of St.-Simon, first positivist, pioneer for "sociology" (his term), epistemologist-historian of science, political theorist, social visionary, advocate of a "religion of humanity," and among the most influential nineteenth-century philosophers, is now typically felt to deserve little more than a scholarly footnote. Classical positivism's core teachings—for example, its scientism, its social-engineering optimism, its antimetaphysical dogmatism—are out of favor. Even the connection between Comte and later positivisms seems tenuous. During his lifetime, positivists already split into two camps. Some, like Littré and John Stuart Mill, embraced the scientific epistemology more prominent in Comte's early *Cours* and rejected the later moral-political works like his *Système* as sentimental, authoritarian embarrassments. Others, with Comte's blessing, dubbed such followers "abortive positivists," insisting the *Cours* is only an "indispensable preamble" to Comte's grand system of "social reorganization." Ultimately, the scientific-epistemic construal of positivism prevailed, and Comte is now vaguely remembered, if at all, for anticipating logical positivism. Yet logical positivists themselves refused to honor him, called their philosophy logical empiricism, and traced their roots to HUME.

Recent work, however, has challenged this portrait of an inconsequential Comte. New editions of his writings, several book-length studies, an intellectual biography, an English translation of the Comte–Mill correspondence, and even a few respectful essays on his political and religious views have appeared. Under this scrutiny, he reemerges as a substantial thinker with contemporary relevance.

To begin with, despite his famous slogan, "All real knowledge rests on observed facts," Comte is no empiricist of the Humean or Logical Empiricist sort. Though antispeculative—he calls theologico-metaphysical efforts to "transcend" sense, "mysticism"—he rejects all attempts to view cognition as transformed sensation. Such "empiricism" reduces knowledge to "a barren accumulation of unrelated facts." Reason must be put in service of experience, not enslaved by it. Mysticism and empiricism distort the nature of this service because they both dichotomize "speculative" and sense-based propositions—truths of reason and truths of fact—thereby perpetuating prescientific misestimations of both sense and reason. In Comtean positivism, "observation" has as "objects" everything from stars and molecules to language and social customs; scientists "only employ observations connected with some law or hypothesis"; and true science "dispenses with observation as soon as phenomena permit," since its "dogmatical aim" is to "deduce the greatest number of results from the smallest amount of immediately given data."

What mysticism and empiricism obscure is that science is not a rejection of theology and metaphysics but a transformation, and its applications are simply a more successful regulation of nature and the social order. In giving a historical-reflective dimension to positivism, Comte avoids the later positivists' hostility toward traditional philosophy. This difference traces to his famous three-stage law, according to which human intelligence successively utilizes three methods of philosophizing in three developmental stages—the theological (fictive), metaphysical (abstract), and scientific (positive). This "fundamental law" describes human development in several ways. Psychologically, it identifies stages of individual intellectual growth. Historically, it depicts these stages in the whole race. Epistemologically, it explains how each science realizes its ultimate aim by passing through the stages. Sociopolitically, it depicts the rise of human societies in their religious, military, industrial, and legal activities as following, with a time lag, intellectual progress.

In the theological era, three substages are roughly chronological. During a fetishistic (animistic) substage, experientially disturbing ruptures in a presumably predictable relation between ourselves and our surroundings evoke spontaneous expressions of feelings and instinct. Next, imagination reworks these animistic notions, wondering why the mysterious things we encounter act as they do and creating polytheistic conceptions about their causes. Finally, the intelligence grows dissatisfied with polytheistic theory—for its chronic unclarity and inconsistency and its implication that everything operates by arbitrary powers—and develops monotheism. Reason now constrains imagination by conceiving the cosmos as created by one God who acts not capriciously, but through invariable universal laws.

For Comte, theology forms the necessary "childhood" of humanity. At first, lacking either reliable theory based on previous observation or fruitful observation guided by established theory, we would have remained forever caught in a "vicious circle" without the spontaneous conceptualizations of primitive peoples. Here, all human faculties achieve their original expression, and it becomes clear for the first time that we have them. "Overstimulation" of the mind by feelings and imagination conquers initial mental lethargy by appearing to promise answers to life's great mysteries. Ultimate answers are never found, but imaginative speculation teaches us how to theorize. Moreover, by guiding rituals and social rules, theologies ground a first form of universal praxis.

Two major limitations of the theological stage condition the beginnings of the metaphysical. Ultimately, every theology is intellectually unsatisfying; and if there is universal cosmic necessity, then its laws, not God's use of them, constitute the real topic. Metaphysics has no substages; but it does have earlier and later forms. Initially, it construes natural powers as moved by God's agency; later, "nature itself" is conceived as the power behind everything. The metaphysical era is a transitional, essentially unstable period. It occasions reason's liberation from religious authority and superstition and valorizes argument and abstraction. Yet the metaphysical mind remains concerned with "inner essences" and hidden causes. It produces competing dogmatic systems—each logically consistent, none practically satisfying, and all so inattentive to what is actually observable that nothing seems at stake in choosing among them. Ultimately, this free use of reason offers neither true science nor better social life. Metaphysics, like "adolescence," is fundamentally abstract and individualistic. If it fosters any form of universal praxis, it is merely contemplation and love of argument.

Eventually, the metaphysical stage passes over into the scientific. Reason must not be slave to feelings, but it cannot be its own authority. Comte cites Francis BACON as pioneering the turn toward observation, away from old prejudices ("idols"). Yet for reason to properly serve observation, its basic concern must be methodological. Descartes is cited for turning philosophy toward epistemology. Finally, a fusion of theory and practice requires the growth (and application) of positive sciences. Metaphysical naturalism (which only thinks teleologically why things work) yields to scientific naturalism (which explains mechanistically how things work). GALILEO is cited on this task of "discovering" nature's laws (and again, Bacon, for "knowledge is power"). As the mind turns from life's ultimate mysteries toward observed phenomena, a hierarchy of sciences develops, from simplest and most abstract (mathematics) to most complex (sociology). Comte stresses sociology's special importance, for knowledge of social behavior will finally enable us to establish truly peaceful, prosperous societies. The third and last form of universal praxis will thus be a truly global technology, achieving what humanity has desired since its earliest experiences of cosmic disruption—control of material nature and the means for "social engineering."

Comte has been attacked, probably rightly, for claiming empirical warrant for his law, but wrongly as promoting speculative philosophy of history. The latter criticism has long obscured the role he gives his law in arguing philosophy's need for self-understanding. This reflective dimension of Comte's thinking is what keeps his positivism historically sensitive and nonformalist concerning philosophy's relation to science. Many of his substantive ideas—for example, the natural inferiority of women, the dream of becoming high priest of a humanistic religion—are hopelessly dated; but his demand that philosophers be historico-critically reflective about their practice still makes him interesting. He reminds us that no philosophy escapes its origins; and he joins, before the fact, the many contemporary inheritors of the empiricist-positivist tradition who now struggle to put hostility to tradition, rational reconstruction, and a monological conception of epistemology behind them.

PRIMARY WORKS

Cours de philosophie positive. 6 vols. Paris: Bachelier, 1830–1842. Reprinted in 2 vols. as *Philosophie prémier: Cours de philosophie positive, leçons 1 à 45,* edited by Michel Serres, François Dagonet, and Allal Sinaceur; and *Physique sociale: Cours de philosophie positive, leçons 46–60,* edited by Jean-Paul Enthoven. Paris: Hermann, 1975. There is no complete English translation.

Discours sur l'esprit positif. Paris: Carilian-Goeury and Victor Dalmont, 1844. Translated by Edward Spencer Beesly as *A Discourse on the Positive Spirit.* London: William Reeves, 1903.

Système de politique positive, ou traité de sociologie, instituant la religion de l'humanité. 4 vols. Paris: L. Mathias, 1851–1854. Translated by J. H. Bridges et al., as *System of Positive Polity,* 4 vols. London: Longmans, Green, 1875–1877.

The Correspondence of John Stuart Mill and Auguste Comte [1841–47]. Edited and translated by Oscar Haac. New Brunswick, NJ: Transaction, 1995.

BIBLIOGRAPHY

Ficquelmont, Gérard Marie de, et al. *Auguste Comte: Qui êtes-vous?* Lyon: La manufacture, 1988. Extensive bibliography.

Gouhier, Henri. *La jeunesse d'Auguste Comte et la formation du positivisme*. 3 vols. (Vol. 3, 2d ed.) Paris: J. Vrin, 1933, 1936, 1941 (1970). Extensive bibliography.

Kremer-Marietti, Angèle. *Le concept de science positive. Ses tenants et ses aboutissants dans les structures anthropologiques du positivisme*. Paris: Klincksieck, 1983.

La vie d'Auguste Comte. 2d ed. Paris: J. Vrin, 1965.

Mill, John Stuart. *Auguste Comte and Positivism* (1865). Edited by J. M. Robson. Vol. 10 of *The Collected Works of John Stuart Mill*. Toronto: University of Toronto Press; and London: Routledge and Kegan Paul, 1969: 261–368.

Pickering, Mary. *Auguste Comte: An Intellectual Biography*. Vol. 1. Cambridge: Cambridge University Press, 1993. Extensive bibliography.

Scharff, Robert C. *Comte after Positivism*. Cambridge: Cambridge University Press, 1995. Extensive bibliography.

ROBERT C. SCHARFF

CONCEPTS. To have a concept is, in one respect, simply to have the capacity to use a word, the word that, as one says, expresses that concept. Having a concept is having the ability to use a word to reidentify things and sorts when they are re-presented and to refer to things and sorts of things that are not present.

But we often think without speaking; in that case the capacity to use the word that expresses the thought is present but unexercised. Nonetheless, we *are* thinking of the object: that state is not dispositional (see DISPOSITIONS). The concept is what is present to consciousness when we think about things; it is what is present to consciousness when we are disposed to use a word.

The traditional doctrine of concepts deriving from ARISTOTLE is that a concept is the form or essence of the thing known. The form or essence is not given in ordinary sense experience or inner awareness; it transcends ordinary experience, though at the same time accounting for its structure. According to this doctrine, when the mind knows or thinks of the thing, the form or essence of the latter is literally in the mind; it is this form or essence *qua* characterizing the mind that constitutes the concept by virtue of which we can refer to the thing in its absence and can reidentify it when it is re-presented. Formally, as Descartes would put it, the concept as the concept characterizes a state of consciousness, whereas, objectively or materially, the concept is literally the thing known or thought about. This form or essence is either innate, as Descartes, following Plato, argued; or it is derived from sense by means of a process of ABSTRACTION, as Aristotle argued.

The classical empiricists, from LOCKE to HUME, criticized this doctrine. The main objection was the claim that we somehow have access to entities that lie outside the realm of ordinary experience. Forms or essences were thus subjected to a skeptical attack, along with the doctrines of abstraction and innatism (see INNATENESS). The empiricists had therefore to develop an alternative account of what is involved in the capacity to use words. Specifically, they argued that what is before the mind is a sensory *image* of the thing thought about. By virtue of relations of resemblance among things and among sorts of things, we come to be able to use words to refer to things that are not present and to reidentify things or sorts of things when they are re-presented. The connections between the relations of resemblance and the words are established through acquired or learned conventions. The theory of learning that the empiricists defended was ASSOCIATIONISM. If we regularly observe As and Bs standing in a relation of resemblance, then we acquire a habit by which an observed A or an idea (image) of A will call up the image of a B. If, further, an artificial association is established between a certain sound or mark and the entities associated by virtue of the relation of resemblance, then that mark or sound becomes a general term that applies to all the entities connected by the association. The classical empiricists proposed thus to account for general concepts without invoking the abstract forms or essences to which the Aristotelians and the rationalists appealed. The classical empiricists thus argued, in effect, that the aboutness of thought, its intentionality, is to be understood in terms similar to the aboutness of language, in terms of internalized conventions of syntax and semantics.

Gottlob Frege argued, however, that this could not be correct. If a concept is an image, then, since images are private, it follows that two persons cannot have the same concept: no two persons can think the same thoughts, and, indeed, no one person can have the same thought on separate occasions. But, of course, thoughts *are* public: we *can* think the same thing. Frege concluded that the empiricist account of concepts in terms of images had to be wrong and that concepts or senses or meanings had to be neither in the mind nor physical but were objective entities inhabiting a third realm.

The notion of entities outside ordinary experience has always troubled empiricists, who insist that philosophical problems cannot be solved by postulating entities inhabiting some shadowy world beyond sense. Frege's solution to the problem posed by the fact that concepts, thoughts, and meanings are public is therefore not acceptable to the empiricist.

G. E. MOORE offered an alternative. It is necessary, he argued, to treat the characteristics of things as universal rather than particular. If the characteristics of things are universals, then one and the same character can be shared by several things. This would apply equally to concepts. The concept as present to consciousness is a characteristic of consciousness, but since this characteristic is, like all others, universal, it follows that the same concept considered as a universal can be in several minds—that is, public—as Frege insisted.

This solves Frege's problem in a way that is compatible with empiricism. There remains the problem, however, of how the concept is about, refers to, or intends, its object. This was handled by the classical empiricists by means of associative ties established through the learning of certain linguistic (social) conventions. Some empiricists continue to defend this view, even if they at the same time tend to reject many of the details of associationist learning theory. Others have argued that the aboutness of concepts or thoughts is a unique relation that cannot be analyzed in terms of linguistic regularities and dispositions, not even if we allow that those patterns are often rule-governed. If, however, it is some unique relation, then there is a temptation to say that there is an entity to which the concept is related, even when what the concept is of or about—for example, mermaids or Belerophon—does not exist. This reintroduces Frege's shadowy third realm.

The "aboutness" of concepts is an issue of continuing debate among empiricists.

BIBLIOGRAPHY

Books

Dummett, M. *Origin of Analytical Philosophy*. Cambridge: Harvard University Press, 1994.
Grossman, R. "Conceptualism." In *Essays in Ontology*, by E. B. Allaire et al. The Hague: Nijhoff, 1963.
―――. *The Structure of Mind*. Madison: University of Wisconsin Press, 1965.
Hume, David. *A Treatise of Human Nature*. 2d ed., edited with an analytical index by L. A. Selby-Bigge; revised with notes by P. H. Nidditch. Oxford: Clarendon Press, 1978: Book. I, Part I, especially section vii.
Russell, B. *The Analysis of Mind*. London: Allen and Unwin, 1921.

Article

Frege, G. "Sense and Reference" and "Concept and Object." In *Translations from the Philosophical Writings of Gottlob Frege*, 2d ed., edited and translated by P. T. Geach and M. Black. Oxford: Blackwell, 1960.

FRED WILSON

COPERNICUS, NICOLAUS. Nicolaus Copernicus (1473–1543) was born in Poland. He studied the liberal arts, including astronomy, at the university in Cracow (1491–1494). He continued his studies at the universities in Bologna (1496–1500) and Padua (1501–1503) and received a doctorate in canon law from the University of Ferrara in 1503. While in Italy, Copernicus became significantly influenced by the renewed interest in Platonism and Neoplatonism. After finishing his studies in Italy, he returned to Poland, earning a living as a clergyman and physician but continuing research in astronomy. His reputation as an astronomer led Pope Leo X to seek his assistance in reforming the calendar, which Copernicus declined on the grounds that there were insufficient data available. His most important work, *De Revolutionibus Orbium Coelestium* (On the Revolutions of the Heavenly Spheres), was published just before he died, in 1543, though his principal ideas circulated among European astronomers decades before in his *Commentariolus* (The Little Commentary).

Astronomy in medieval Europe was constrained by a number of factors: Christian Scripture, the teachings of ARISTOTLE, and Ptolemy's *Almagest*. This combination supported a picture of the heavens that was geocentric—that is, earth-centered—and in which the earth was static. A significant part of astronomy was concerned with explaining the observed motions of the planets. In fact, this had been Ptolemy's principal objective. In particular, Ptolemy was concerned to address "the problem of the planets," that is, to explain the apparent retrograde, or backward, motion that was occasionally observed. Through the centuries, astronomers had tried to improve the predictive success of Ptolemy's system. In doing so, they had to invoke various irregularities, such as epicycles. Thus, the planets were thought to rotate around a point that, in turn, simultaneously rotated around the earth. Because these epicycles seemed to be added in an ad hoc fashion and greatly complicated the Ptolemaic theory, some medieval astronomers, notably Buridan, Oresme, and Cusa, began to question the theory.

Copernicus' research is a response to the problem of the planets. He was determined to provide a better explanation for the available data. Reviving an alternative theory from ancient Greek astronomers, Copernicus developed a heliocentric theory, that is, a sun-centered model. Strictly speaking, according to Copernicus, the sun was not in the center of the solar system but was slightly off-centered. His theory enabled him to explain the apparent retrograde motion of the other planets. When, from the perspective of the earth, a planet appears to change directions, it is because the earth, the place from which our observations of the other planet are made, is moving. The key to Copernicus' solution to the problem of the planets was his rejection of the Ptolemaic assumption that the earth was the center of the universe.

Anticipating the empirical methods characteristic of early modern SCIENCE, Copernicus was committed to practical astronomy, collecting new data by observing the phenomena. This approach to inquiry subsequently became the norm in astronomy and natural science in general. Though Copernicus' concern was to account for the observables, it would be a mistake to treat his solution as merely arising out of the data. Copernicus did not question many of the assumptions of his predecessors. For example, he believed that the motions of the planets were regular and circular, two assumptions that Kepler would later prove to be false. Further, the source of his theory was not observation but a careful study of classical texts.

For a number of reasons, the Copernican system did not initially create a revolution in astronomy. First, because Copernicus' work was quite technical, it was not very accessible and thus remained known only to scholars. Second, after centuries of refinements made to the Ptolemaic theory, astronomers had produced a very effective system. In fact, neither theory proved to be predictively superior until the late 1500s. In addition, even some who felt that Copernicus' theory was predictively superior argued that it did not describe the real motion of the planets. Andreas Osiander, for example, took such an instrumentalist view (see INSTRUMENTALISM), treating the theory as a system for making effective predictions but denying that it described the actual nature of the solar system. Further, in order to produce a system that was predictively comparable to the most effective contemporary versions of the Ptolemaic theory, Copernicus had to invoke epicycles and other irregularities, thus undermining the elegance of his theory. Most significantly, people were reluctant to accept Copernicus' system because of the implausible implications it had for terrestrial physics. People, including many scholars, were unprepared to believe that the earth was moving, given that there were no phenomenal indications of this motion.

The astronomical significance of Copernicus' work is twofold. He both provided a solution to the problem of the planets and revived and developed the heliocentric model that we accept today. Copernicus' influence, though, extends beyond astronomy. Methodologically, he demonstrated a commitment to the mathematical rigor that characterizes the quantitative nature of modern science. Moreover, Copernicus' research enabled people to think about themselves and the world quite differently. In a heliocentric solar system people could no longer view themselves as occupying the center of the universe. Further, the authority of the medieval world was challenged, as the Ptolemaic theory had been grounded on, and supported by, Scripture and the teachings of Aristotle and Ptolemy. Copernicus' theory, thus, contributed to the process by which Europeans began to see themselves from a very different perspective.

PRIMARY WORKS

Three Copernican Treatises. 2d ed.; revised, edited, and translated by Edward Rosen. New York: Dover, 1959.
Complete Works. Edited by Pawel Czartoryski; translated by Z. Nierada, E. Hilfstein, and E. Rosen. 3 vols. London: Macmillan Press, 1972.

BIBLIOGRAPHY

Armitage, Angus. *Copernicus: The Founder of Modern Astronomy.* London: George Allen and Unwin, 1938.
Beer, Arthur, and K. A. Strand, eds. *Copernicus: Yesterday and Today.* Oxford: Pergamon Press, 1975.
Kuhn, Thomas S. *The Copernican Revolution.* Cambridge: Harvard University Press, 1957.
Westman, Robert S., ed. *The Copernican Achievement.* Berkeley: University of California Press, 1975.

K. BRAD WRAY

D

DARWIN, CHARLES. Charles Darwin (1809–1882) was born in Shrewsbury, England, son of Dr. Robert Darwin and grandson of Dr. Erasmus Darwin, Enlightenment advocate of progressive evolution. Charles attended Shrewsbury School before spending two years in medical school at Edinburgh. He graduated from Christ's College, Cambridge, in 1831. During his college years Charles avidly pursued natural history, studying marine invertebrates with Robert Grant in Edinburgh and, in Cambridge, botany with Rev. John Henslow and geology with Rev. Adam Sedgwick. Henslow secured for Darwin an unexpected invitation to be naturalist on HMS *Beagle*, a surveying vessel that circumnavigated the globe between December 1831 and October 1836. Shortly after his return, he began a series of notebooks that eventuated in the first formulations of the theory of evolution by natural selection. Married in 1838 to a cousin, Emma Wedgwood, the Darwins moved to the village of Downe, southeast of London, where Darwin carried out continuous experimental research until his death. A premier geologist, zoologist, and botanist, he is best known for the evolutionary theory presented in *On the Origin of Species* (1859) and *The Descent of Man and Evolution in Relation to Sex* (1871).

The question of Darwin's empiricism is complicated. In the Introduction to *On the Origin of Species*, Darwin recalls that "it occurred to me, in 1837, that something might perhaps be made out on this question [the origin of species] by patiently accumulating and reflecting on all sorts of facts which could possibly have any bearing on it" (1). In his autobiography he proclaims he worked "on true Baconian principles, and without any theory collected facts on a wholesale scale." Yet those notebooks are theory driven from the start, and the following comment, from a review of the *Origin* by Sedgwick, voices a common complaint: "Darwin's theory is not inductive,—not based on a series of acknowledged facts pointing to a general conclusion" (Hull 1973: 160). Upon reading this review, Darwin wrote to Henslow, asking

whether it was not allowable (and a great step) to invent the undulatory theory of light, i.e., hypothetical undulations, in a hypothetical substance, the ether. And if this be so, why may I not invent the hypothesis of Natural Selection (which from analogy of domestic productions, and from what we know of the struggle for existence and of the variability of organic beings, is, in some very slight degree, in itself probable) and try whether this hypothesis of Natural Selection does not explain (as I think it does) a large number of facts in geographical distribution—geological succession, classification, morphology, embryology, etc. (Hull 1973: 156)

Here, then, are three distinct pictures of Darwin's empiricism: Darwin the Baconian inductivist; the Darwin who fails the inductive test; Darwin the Newtonian empiricist. They can be reconciled, however.

Darwin sees empirical research as part of the search for a theory to account for previously established "facts." Darwin correctly notes that he began his notebooks without a specific theory "to be tested." Nevertheless, he did begin with established laws from geology, biogeography, and comparative anatomy, which suggested that past and present species were all related by patterns of descent, laws that called out for explanation. Darwin's theory of natural selection is the product of "wholesale fact gathering" driven by the search for some theory to explain a vast set of established "facts."

Origin is organized as we would expect from Darwin's letter to Henslow. The first four chapters develop a theory of natural selection based on a study of the *vera causa* (true cause) of domestic selection. But in the summary of Chapter 4, Darwin admits that his theory "must be judged by the general tenour and balance of evidence given in the following chapters." The convincing empirical support derives from three chapters that counter evidence that might suggest the impossibility of new species arising naturally; and five chapters that show that the laws of geological succession, geographic distribution, classification, morphology, and embryology follow naturally from his theory. Here Darwin presents the empirical support for his theory.

From whence comes this form of empiricism? Pretty surely from Sir John Herschel's *A Preliminary Discourse on the Study of Natural Philosophy*, which "stirred up in me [Darwin] a burning zeal to add even the most humble contribution to the noble structure of Natural Science." Herschel's ideas on scientific method come to life in Charles Lyell's *Principles of Geology*, which Darwin read on the *Beagle*. It is not going too far to say that the method of *Origin* derives from these two sources. Both men viewed themselves as Newtonians (see NEWTON), arguing for basing new theories on *verae causae* through analogical reasoning and supporting new theories by displaying their ability to unite under one theory many diverse and apparently unconnected facts. Here we find the origins of Darwin's empiricism.

PRIMARY WORKS

On the Origin of Species: A Facsimile of the First Edition. Cambridge: Harvard University Press, 1964.

Charles Darwin's Notebooks: 1836–1844. Edited by Paul H. Barrett et al. Ithaca, NY: Cornell University Press, 1989.

Herschel, J.F.W. *A Preliminary Discourse on the Study of Natural Philosophy*. London: Longman et al., 1831.

BIBLIOGRAPHY

Books

Desmond, Adrian, and James Moore. *Darwin: The Life of a Tormented Evolutionist.*
    New York: W. W. Norton, 1992. The best biography of Darwin available.
Hull, David. *Darwin and His Critics: The Reception of Darwin's Theory of Evolution
    by the Scientific Community.* Chicago: University of Chicago Press, 1973. Con-
    tains many crucial reviews of Darwin's *On the Origin of Species* written by his
    contemporaries.
Kohn, David, ed. *The Darwinian Heritage.* Princeton: Princeton University Press, 1985.
    Thirty-one essays on Darwin and Darwinism; those in Part One by Gruber,
    Schweber, Hodge and Kohn, and Beatty and in Part Two by Rudwick are the
    most important for the themes of this *Encyclopedia.*

JAMES LENNOX

DAVIDSON, DONALD HERBERT. Donald Davidson (1917–), one of the
most important philosophers writing in English during the latter half of the
twentieth century, is a philosopher whose work may at first sight give the appearance of an aggregation of different papers on diverse and sometimes rather
narrowly constrained topics. Such an appearance belies the real unity, integrity,
and breadth of Davidson's work as a whole. In fact, one can see Davidson's
many articles on the philosophy of language and of mind, on ethics (see MO-
RALITY) and the philosophy of action and on epistemology and METAPHYS-
ICS as part of a single body of work that is bound together by a small set of
closely intertwined ideas concerning the relation between action, CAUSATION,
mind, MEANING, and TRUTH.

Born in Springfield, Massachusetts, Davidson completed his undergraduate
study at Harvard, graduating in 1939. He served with the U.S. Navy in the
Mediterranean from 1942 to 1945. He completed his doctoral studies at Harvard
with a dissertation on Plato's *Philebus*, graduating in 1949. He has held teaching
positions at Stanford, Princeton, and Rockefeller Universities, as well as at the
University of Chicago and, since 1981, at the University of California at Berkeley. Davidson has visited and held fellowships at many institutions around the
world and in 1991 was awarded the Hegel Prize by the city of Stuttgart—an
indication of the depth of interest in his work not only in the English-speaking
philosophical world but also in Europe.

Davidson's work is strongly influenced by that of W.V.O. QUINE, as well
as by American pragmatist thinking, particularly as exemplified in the work of
C. I. Lewis and John Dewey (see PRAGMATISM). Wittgensteinian and Kantian
themes are also echoed at many points in Davidson's writing. Although his work
is clearly connected with the empiricist tradition, through Quine in particular, it
can also be regarded as constituting a critique of that tradition—a critique that
is sometimes quite explicit.

Quine famously identified two "dogmas" that he took to be characteristic of
empiricism: the idea of reductionism (the idea that the meaning of a statement

can be reduced to some sensory content) and the ANALYTIC/SYNTHETIC DISTINCTION. Following Quine, Davidson rejects both these dogmas, but in addition he identifies a third and final dogma of empiricism for the rejection of which he also argues—the distinction between conceptual scheme and empirical content. In rejecting this distinction, Davidson asserts a form of holism affecting truth, meaning, and BELIEF that goes far beyond the epistemic holism that underlies Quine's rejection of the first two dogmas, one that has important consequences in both epistemology and philosophy of language: Davidson claims that neither the evidential grounding for particular beliefs nor the meaning of particular utterances is to be found in the proximal sensory stimulations to which beliefs or utterances may be causally related; instead Davidson holds that beliefs are identified and utterances interpreted through their being related to the distal causes of belief and of utterance, that is, through being related to the objects and events that are the publicly accessible features of the world. In fact, Davidson marries epistemology to the philosophy of language in such a way that it becomes impossible to develop a theory of meaning for a speaker's language (a theory that Davidson proposes should take the form of a Tarski-style truth theory in which the underlying structure of the language would be revealed) independently of providing an account of the beliefs and other attitudes possessed by the speaker. Thus, both epistemology and semantic theory become part of the project of what Davidson calls, echoing Quine, "radical interpretation." Moreover, identifying a speaker's beliefs cannot proceed independently of what the interpreter believes—independently, that is, of what the interpreter holds true. Consequently, a requirement of successful interpretation is that most of the beliefs and utterances attributed to the speaker must be true and consistent by the interpreter's lights—a requirement known as the principle of charity. The holistic interdependence of meaning, belief, and truth is not merely a matter of interpretation—these notions are defined only in relation to one another in such a way that a creature to whom these notions and the interpretive constraints with which they are associated could not be applied would not be a creature capable of believing, meaning, or knowing. A number of important conclusions follow further from this position: (1) any strong form of SKEPTICISM or relativism is rendered incoherent since overall truth and widespread agreement in beliefs is a prerequisite for belief itself; (2) meaning and belief are both dependent on the possibility of "triangulation," that is, on there being appropriate connections between speakers, interpreters, and objects and events in the world; (3) since meanings, beliefs, and other attitudes form a holistic system governed by the principle of charity, it is impossible to reduce such psychological notions to the concepts of physical theory, but as psychological states are nevertheless causally enmeshed with other states and with objects and events in the world, they must also be part of a single causal order—Davidson thus espouses a position in regard to the MIND–BODY PROBLEM that he calls "anomalous monism," according to which mental events are identical with physical events (and reasons are identical with causes), even though talk of mental events is neither reducible to, nor replaceable by, talk of physical events.

Davidson's ideas have often provoked strong criticism, although this criticism has sometimes tended to focus on particular ideas in isolation rather than taking account of Davidson's thought as a whole. While it is generally acknowledged that Davidson has made significant and lasting contributions in many central areas of contemporary philosophy, as it becomes easier with the passing of time to view Davidson's work in its entirety, so it is likely that his work will be appreciated as even more significant in years to come.

PRIMARY WORKS

Essays on Actions and Events. Oxford: Clarendon Press, 1980.
Inquiries into Truth and Interpretation. Oxford: Clarendon Press, 1984.
"Three Varieties of Knowledge." In *A. J. Ayer: Memorial Essays*, edited by A. Phillips Griffiths. *Royal Institute of Philosophy Supplement* 30 (1991): 153–66.

BIBLIOGRAPHY

Evnine, Simon. *Donald Davidson*. Cambridge: Polity Press, 1991.
LePore, Ernest, ed. *Truth and Interpretation: Perspectives on the Philosophy of Donald Davidson*. Oxford: Basil Blackwell, 1986.
LePore, Ernest, and Brian McLaughlin, eds. *Actions and Events: Perspectives on the Philosophy of Donald Davidson*. Oxford: Basil Blackwell, 1985.
Malpas, J. E. *Donald Davidson and the Mirror of Meaning*. Cambridge: Cambridge University Press, 1992.
Ramberg, Bjørn. *Donald Davidson's Philosophy of Language: An Introduction*. Oxford: Basil Blackwell, 1989.

JEFF MALPAS

DEISM. The earliest reference to "deists" appears to be in Peter Viret's *Instruction Chrétienne* of 1564, where he states that while "they believe, that there is a God, whom they own to be the creator," and while they outwardly conform to religious practices, at heart they "laugh at all religion" and, in particular, scorn Christianity. As for the term "deist," it should be noted that in the seventeenth century the terms "deist" and "theist" were sometimes used interchangeably, the former having its etymological root in the Latin word for "God" (*deus*) and the latter in the Greek word (*theos*). In 1683, for instance, Henry Hallywell, having described the "deists" as holding the Bible and Christianity in "mean and low esteem," asserts that this "theism" is opposed to authentic Christian faith. Similarly, William Nicholls' preface to the first volume of his *Conference with a Theist* of 1696 characterizes "theists" as those who "disown a Revelation, make our whole Religion an Imposture, and all that have to do with it either Cheats or Fools." With the passage of time, however, the terms acquired different senses. While "theism" is now used in a basically neutral way to refer straightforwardly to belief in the reality of God, "deism" has kept the pejorative connotation of its earliest usage.

In spite of the widespread use of the term ''deist,'' the great variety of (sometimes incompatible) opinions held by those who have commonly been called ''deists'' means that attempts to define the notion of deism by reference either to what doctrines and attitudes all deists are supposed to hold in common or to what they are supposed to deny are unsatisfactory. Hence, while any use of the term should be expected to be pejorative, it should not be treated as affixing a label identifying a set of specific doctrines (or a set of denials). Although current usage today generally implies by the description ''deist'' the belief that there is a deity who was responsible for the creation of the world but who does not influence the course of nature, history, or the lives of individuals in particular ways (including through miraculous interventions and revelatory communications), the term is best understood, not least in relation to its use in earlier times, as being similar to the way in which the terms ''radical'' and ''unbeliever'' are employed. The material content of these apparent descriptions varies with the persons using them. What, for example, is a dangerous ''radical'' for one is a harmless ''liberal'' for another; an ''unbeliever'' for the adherent of one faith may be a fellow traveler for the adherent of another. Similarly, the specific deficiency in belief expressed by the description ''deist'' seems to be largely determined by contrast with what those using it regard as the requirements of authentic faith in God: ''deists,'' that is, are those whose beliefs about the will and activity of God and about human destiny are deemed deficient by those so describing them. In what way they are deemed deficient depends, however, on the critics' own position.

While Viret's remark shows that the term ''deist'' was used to identify some deriders of faith in the middle of the sixteenth century, ''deism'' is generally considered to have flourished mostly in England in the period from John LOCKE to David HUME (i.e., during the last three decades of the seventeenth and the first half of the eighteenth centuries). The canon of major deists seems, furthermore, to a large extent to have been determined by surveys made by two of their critics at the end of this period, Philip Skelton in *Ophiomaches: or Deism Revealed* (1749) and John Leland in *A View of the Principal Deistical Writers* (1754). Although their lists start with HERBERT OF CHERBURY (1583?–1648), it is questionable whether his reputation for being the father of English deism is warrantable in view of the fact that he apparently believed in revelation (claiming in his *Autobiography* only to have published his *De Veritate* after a sign from heaven), immortality, specific providences, and the power of prayer. Leland discusses the opinions of Charles Blount (1654–1693), John Toland (1670–1722), Anthony, earl of Shaftesbury (1671–1713), Anthony COLLINS (1676–1729), Thomas Woolston (1670–1731), Matthew Tindal (1657?–1733), Thomas Morgan (?–1743), Henry Dodwell (?–1784), Thomas Chubb (1679–1746), and Henry St John, Viscount Bolingbroke (1678–1751).

Skelton includes Bernard Mandeville (1670–1733) in his more thematic treatment. Others who are often classed among the deists include William Wollaston (1660–1724) and Peter Annet (1693–1769). While both Leland and Skelton consider the views of Thomas HOBBES (1588–1679), and Leland also deals at length with David Hume (1711–1776), later opinion has tended to distinguish the positions of these philosophers from that of the ''deists,'' whatever it is supposed to be. Whereas, for instance, Hume's views on miracles, immortality, and the origin of belief in God parallel ideas typically found in the writings of the deists, his analyses of the arguments purporting to justify theistic belief suggest that he is rather to be classed as a skeptical critic of all attempts to establish a reasonable theistic belief.

The problem with such lists is that they tend to imply that those not on them are not to be so categorized. In practice the concept of ''deism'' has such fuzzy edges because those so classed put forward positions so divergent that it is difficult to show why, if some on the preceding list are to be classed as deists, others (e.g., John LOCKE [1632–1704], John Tillotson [1630–1694], and some of the Cambridge Platonists) should not also be included with them. The variety of what is supposed to be deism becomes more apparent still when American and Continental writers who are usually held to be ''deists'' are taken into account. They include, in America, Benjamin Franklin (1706–1790), George Washington (1732–1809), Thomas Jefferson (1743–1826), and Thomas Paine (1737–1809); and on the Continent, Voltaire (1694–1778), Hermann Samuel Reimarus (1694–1768), Jean-Jacques Rousseau (1712–1778), Gotthold Ephraim Lessing (1729–1781), and, in some respects, Immanuel KANT (1724–1809).

The views characteristic of these authors range from Toland's point that people cannot believe what does not make sense to them and Wollaston's attempt to delineate ''the religion of nature'' that all rational persons can recognize, through Tindal's thesis that the ''infinitely Wise and Good'' God must have given all people from the beginning the means to ascertain the true religion, to Collins' use of ''freethinking'' to attack priestcraft and orthodox doctrines and Woolston's increasingly vigorous attacks on stories about miracles. Some of the works by those listed as deists are primarily negative, being rational (in some cases one should say rationalist) challenges to traditional beliefs and religious practices and the arguments supposed to justify them; others attempt to identify what empirical observation and rational reflection show to be the truth about God and humankind. The latter have considerable overlap with others generally regarded as more orthodox who recognize the significance of ''natural religion'' (another term that is used to label over a dozen distinct positions) and of the ''natural theology'' that emerges from pondering on the character of the natural world. One lesson that arises from recognizing the variety of what is labeled ''deist'' is that the term is most unsatisfactory as an intellectual description and that studies of the history of thought might do well to avoid it; another, however, is that those described as ''deists,'' their fellow travelers, and their opponents created a lively debate about the relationship of faith and rational reflection that remains stimulating, provocative, and amusing.

PRIMARY WORKS

[Collins, Anthony]. *A Discourse of Free-Thinking, Occasion'd by the Rise and Growth of a Sect Call'd Free-Thinkers*. London: J. Morphew, 1713.

[Tindal, Matthew]. *Christianity as Old as the Creation: Or, The Gospel a Republication of the Religion of Nature*. London: n.s., 1730.

Toland, John. *Christianity Not Mysterious: Or, a Treatise Shewing That There Is Nothing in the Gospel Contrary to Reason, Nor Above It: And That No Christian Doctrine Can Be Properly Call'd a Mystery*. London: n.s., 1696.

Wollaston, William. *The Religion of Nature Delineated*. London: S. Palmer, 1722.

BIBLIOGRAPHY

Byrne, Peter. *Natural Religion and the Nature of Deism: The Legacy of Deism*. London and New York: Routledge, 1989.

Creed, John M., and John S. Boys Smith, eds. *Religious Thought in the Eighteenth Century*. Cambridge: Cambridge University Press, 1934.

Leland, John. *A View of the Principal Deistical Writers That Have Appeared in England in the Last and Present Century; with Observations upon Them*. London: B. Dod, 1754.

Redwood, John. *Reason, Ridicule and Religion: The Age of Enlightenment in England 1660–1750*. London: Thames and Hudson, 1976.

Stephen, Leslie. *A History of English Thought in the Eighteenth Century*. London, 1902. While old, this is still the best comprehensive study.

Stromberg, Roland N. *Religious Liberalism in Eighteenth-Century England*. London: Oxford, 1954.

DAVID A. PAILIN

DEMONSTRATION. Roughly speaking, from ARISTOTLE right through the scholastic tradition, a demonstration was a valid syllogism with necessarily true, self-evident, or certain premises. The conclusion thus retained the certainty, though not the self-evidentness, of the premises. Descartes, following the Renaissance humanists, rejected syllogism as an account of the way we REASON. LOCKE took on board this rejection, saying, ''God has not been so sparing to Men to make them barely two-legged Creatures, and left it to Aristotle to make them Rational'' (*An Essay concerning Human Understanding* IV.xvii.4). Locke gave his own account of demonstrative reasoning, based on the perceived agreement between ideas. When we can immediately perceive the agreement between two ideas, we have intuitive knowledge; when our perception of the agreement of two ideas is mediated by the intervention of other ideas or ''proofs,'' we have demonstrative knowledge (*Essay* IV.ii.17). Thus, a demonstration for Locke is a chain of ideas, each idea being intuitively linked to its neighbor.

As the scholastic conception of demonstration required two ingredients—formal validity of the argument according to syllogistic and necessary or certain premises—it is tempting to think of Locke's account as similarly having two features: deductive validity of the argument and certain or necessary premises. But nothing in Locke's account resembles deductive validity; he uses ''deduction'' just as a synonym for ''argument,'' either demonstrative or probable. The inferential links hold between ideas, with each idea being intuitively linked to its neighbor. A proposition (e.g., ''The three internal angles of a triangle equal two right angles'') is demonstrated not by showing how it follows from some other propositions but by showing how the idea that makes up the subject (''three internal angles'') agrees in size with the idea that makes up the predicate (''two right angles''). If this agreement could be perceived immediately, the proposition would be known intuitively. But human reason can discover the agreement only via the intervention of some one or more ideas, and thus we know the proposition demonstratively. In this case, the relevant intermediate idea would be of some other angles, equal to both the internal angles of a triangle, and to two right angles (*Essay* IV.ii.2).

HUME by and large took over Locke's account of demonstration. They diverge not just in Hume's limitation of demonstration to relations of quantity and number but also in Hume's tendency to collapse demonstration into INTUITION. This is due to the fact that ideas for Locke were the equivalent of traditional terms; they were ingredients of propositions. But Hume thought that ideas themselves could be propositional in nature. So one propositional idea might be seen to stand in the right relation to another propositional idea; it makes little difference, for Hume, whether one calls this intuition or demonstration. This provides Hume's account with the capacity to deal with a class of cases that creates a difficulty for Locke's account. Consider any argument that we would call deductively valid but with a clearly contingent or noncertain premise. The agreement between the ideas that make up that premise is thus not intuitive. So the argument could not be classified by Locke as demonstrative. The only alternative is probable, which seems odd, at least to modern ears. But Hume could lump the premises together as one idea and treat the conclusion as another idea and at least raise the question whether the relation between them is demonstrative. So Hume's theory of demonstration allows him to raise the question of whether the existence of one object could be demonstratively inferred from the existence of another, even though he is there concerned with contingent, nonnecessary items. Of course, he frequently does raise such questions when speaking of CAUSATION.

PRIMARY WORKS

Hume, David. *A Treatise of Human Nature*. 2d ed., edited with an analytical index by L. A. Selby-Bigge; revised with notes by P. H. Nidditch. Oxford: Clarendon Press, 1978.

Locke, John. *An Essay concerning Human Understanding*. Edited with an introduction by P. H. Nidditch. Oxford: Clarendon Press, 1975.

BIBLIOGRAPHY

Book

Ayers, Michael. *Locke: Epistemology and Ontology*. Vol. 1, *Epistemology*. London and New York: Routledge, 1993.

Articles

Jardine, Lisa. ''Humanistic Logic.'' In *The Cambridge History of Renaissance Philosophy*, edited by C. B. Schmitt and Q. Skinner. Cambridge: Cambridge University Press, 1992.

Owen, David. ''Hume on Demonstration.'' In *Logic and the Workings of the Mind*, edited by P. Easton. North American Kant Society Studies in Philosophy. Atascadero, CA: Ridgeview, forthcoming.

DAVID OWEN

DISPOSITIONS. A disposition is the power of an object to affect or be affected by another thing in some specific way. For example, the fragility of a glass is the power of the glass to break if struck by something; in other words, it is a property of the glass in virtue of which it would break if it were struck. The breaking of the glass is the *manifestation* of the disposition of fragility; the striking of the glass is the *activation-condition* of the disposition, and the property of the glass in virtue of which the striking would cause the breaking—its crystalline structure or whatever—is the *ground* or *basis* of the disposition.

Dispositions play a central role in both common-sense and scientific views of the world. However, the concept of a disposition has posed a number of difficulties for traditional versions of empiricism. These difficulties all stem from the empiricist stricture that a concept is meaningful only if it is a sensory concept or can be exhaustively analyzed in terms of sensory (and logical) concepts.

One such difficulty concerns the fact that the concept of a disposition seems to be the concept of a theoretical or unobservable entity. LOCKE was one of the first empiricists to grapple with this difficulty. In *An Essay concerning Human Understanding* he argued that the idea of disposition or power results from the need to explain regularities in the observable behavior of objects and that the explanation of such regularities may involve reference to properties that are unobservable. ''Since whatever change is observed, the mind must collect a power somewhere, able to make that change, as well as a possibility in the thing itself'' (*Essay* II.xxi.4). Locke treated the idea of a power as a dummy or placeholder concept, which is useful because we are ignorant of the intrinsic properties of objects. Indeed, in his discussion of PRIMARY AND SECONDARY QUALITIES he states that secondary qualities are powers in objects to produce sensory experience in perceivers and identifies these powers (or at least their grounds) with the primary qualities of the unobservable corpuscles that make up matter (*Essay* II.viii.15).

These views are in tension with the empiricist stricture about the meaningfulness of concepts that Locke accepted. Locke's resolution of the tension was to argue that while the idea of disposition implicitly refers to what lies behind observable changes, the only positive content of the idea of a particular disposition is supplied by its observable manifestation. Thus, the idea of the power of a piece of wax to melt when heated implies that some property of the wax causes its melting; but the only positive content of the idea of this power is given by the observable effect of melting. For Locke the idea of this observable effect comes to represent and stand for whatever it is in the wax that causes it (*Essay* II.xxii.11).

In this way Locke tried to reconcile his conception of dispositions with the empiricist stricture about meaningfulness by adopting a form of PHENOME-NALISM about them: the idea of a disposition is to be analyzed in terms of the idea of its observable manifestation. In contrast, BERKELEY adopted a form of INSTRUMENTALISM about dispositions: he thought that the terms referring to theoretical entities such as dispositions misleadingly appear to refer to objects when, in fact, they do not refer to anything at all. When we talk about force, gravity, and attraction, we are not talking about objects at all: "Force, gravity, attraction, and terms of this sort are useful for reasonings and reckonings about motion and bodies in motion, but not for understanding the simple nature of motion itself or for indicating so many distinct qualities" (*De Motu*, §17). On this view, the dispositional notions of force and gravity are mere conceptual devices that help us organize known phenomena and predict new phenomena, but they do not correspond to anything in reality. Both Locke's and Berkeley's antirealist treatments of dispositions are heir to all the deficiencies of phenomenalist and instrumentalist treatments of theoretical entities.

Another difficulty raised by the concept of a disposition for traditional empiricists is that this concept essentially involves the notion of CAUSATION: a disposition is a power possessed by an object to *cause* an appropriate manifestation when appropriately activated. However, the conception of causation as a relation holding in singular instances and consisting in the activation of a causal power has raised empiricist suspicions. Hume famously criticized this conception of causation on the grounds that we do not experience any sensory impressions of such singular causal relations (*A Treatise of Human Nature* I.iii.14 and *An Enquiry concerning Human Understanding* VII). He argued that the only positive empirical content in the idea of causation is given by the ideas of spatial contiguity, temporal priority, and regularity. He sought to explain our idea of causal necessity—the kind of causal connection that consists in the operation of a causal power—as arising from "a felt determination of the mind" to pass from cause to effect, a determination that results from observing regularities between similar things. One implication of Hume's views is that the notion of a causal power, as a discrete property existing in an object, is called into question:

Tho' the several resembling instances, which give rise to the idea of power, have no influence on each other, and can never produce any new quality *in the object*, which can be the model of that idea, yet the *observation* of this resemblance produces a new impression *in the mind*, which is its real model. (*Treatise* I.iii.14: 165)

Hume's repudiation of objective, mind-independent singular causal connections and of causal powers has been questioned by subsequent philosophers.

A third difficulty the concept of disposition poses for empiricists is that it essentially involves the concept of MODALITY, in particular the concept of unactualized possibility: a fragile glass is one that *would* break if it *were* struck, even if as a matter of fact it never is struck. Traditionally, empiricists have sought to banish unactualized possibilities from meaningful scientific discourse because of their unobservability. The logical empiricists (see LOGICAL POSITIVISM AND LOGICAL EMPIRICISM) of the twentieth century were especially vexed by the modal character of dispositional discourse. In his paper "Testability and Meaning," CARNAP sought to translate such discourse into the purely extensional language of first-order classical logic that avoids reference to unactualized possibilities. He considered whether a sentence such as "a is fragile" could be analyzed as: (For all times t) (if a is struck at t, then it breaks at t). But he concluded that this is not a suitable translation, as it implies that anything that is never struck is fragile. In its place Carnap proposed an analysis in terms of the following "reduction sentence": (For all times t) (if a is struck at t, then [a is fragile if and only if a breaks at t]). This analysis is defective too, however. Its defect is its incompleteness: it says what fragility is only for those things that are struck but does not say what it is for those things that are never struck. Notwithstanding the efforts of Carnap, GOODMAN, and QUINE, the logical empiricists and their successors did not succeed in offering completely satisfactory analyses of dispositional discourse that avoid unactualized possibilities.

The difficulties that the concept of disposition has posed for empiricists are indicative of the more general difficulties empiricists have had in reconciling the apparent meaningfulness of the concepts of theoretical entities, singular causal connexions, and modality with their strict criterion of meaningfulness in terms of sensory concepts (see VERIFICATION PRINCIPLE). The intractable nature of these difficulties casts suspicion on this empiricist criterion of meaningfulness.

PRIMARY WORKS

Books

Berkeley, George. *The Works of George Berkeley, Bishop of Cloyne*. Edited by A. A. Luce and T. E. Jessop. 9 vols. London: Thomas Nelson and Sons, 1948–1957.

Goodman, Nelson. *Fact, Fiction, and Forecast*. London: University of London Press, 1955.

Hume, David. *An Enquiry concerning Human Understanding*. In *Enquiries concerning Human Understanding and concerning the Principles of Morals*, edited with an analytical index by L. A. Selby-Bigge; revised with notes by P. H. Nidditch. Oxford: Clarendon Press, 1975.

———. *A Treatise of Human Nature*. 2d ed., edited with an analytical index by L. A. Selby-Bigge; revised with notes by P. H. Nidditch. Oxford: Clarendon Press, 1978.

Locke, John. *An Essay concerning Human Understanding*. Edited with an introduction by P. H. Nidditch. Oxford: Clarendon Press, 1975.

Articles

Carnap, Rudolf. "Testability and Meaning." *Philosophy of Science* 3 (1936): 439–53.
Quine, Willard Van Orman. "Natural Kinds." In *Essays in Honor of Carl G. Hempel*, edited by N. Rescher. Dordrecht: Reidel, 1969.

BIBLIOGRAPHY

Alexander, Peter. *Ideas, Qualities, and Corpuscles: Locke and Boyle on the External World*. Cambridge: Cambridge University Press, 1985.
Ayers, Michael. *Locke: Epistemology and Ontology*. London: Routledge, 1991.
Cartwright, Nancy. *Nature's Capacities and Their Measurement*. Oxford: Clarendon Press, 1989
Harre, Rom, and Edward Madden. *Causal Powers*. Oxford: Basil Blackwell, 1975.
Prior, Elizabeth. *Dispositions*. Aberdeen: Aberdeen University Press, 1985.
Tuomela, Raimo, ed. *Dispositions*. Dordrecht: Reidel, 1978.

PETER MENZIES

E

EPICURUS. Epicurus (341–271 B.C.), the founder of one of the four major schools of Hellenistic philosophy, was an atomist in his physics, a hedonist in his ethics, and an empiricist in his "canonics." His "canonics," as he called his foundationalist epistemology, was set out in *The Canon*, where, according to Diogenes Laertius (DL) (10.31), he claimed that "the criteria of truth are sensations, notions, and affections." I explain later what this claim amounts to and how Epicurus' canonics provides the foundations for his atomism and hedonism.

LIFE

Born on Samos of Athenian parents, Epicurus "turned to philosophy after stumbling onto the works of Democritus" (DL 10.2). He studied for a time under Nausiphanes, a Democritean who had studied under Pyrrho the skeptic. But he fell out with Nausiphanes, and eventually set up his own school, first in Asia Minor, then, in 307 B.C., in an enclosed garden in Athens. There the members of the school, which included women and slaves, lived together as a sort of extended family, following Epicurus' admonitions to live simply (eschewing "vain desires" for luxuries) and to "live unnoticed" (eschewing fame and political involvement). In this peaceful setting, Epicurus proved most prolific, filling about three hundred papyrus rolls with his writings.

SOURCES

Of Epicurus' writings, surviving intact are three philosophical letters, a compendium of forty "Key Doctrines," and a second collection of apothegms. Fortunately, there are many quotations from his lost works and many reports of his views, in later Epicureans (like Lucretius and Philodemus), critics of Epicureanism (like Cicero, Plutarch, and SEXTUS EMPIRICUS), and doxographers (like Diogenes Laertius). Most of these are collected in Usener. The most important are presented and translated in Long and Sedley.

SENSATIONS

Epicurus famously claimed that all sensations are true. He made this claim, says Cicero (*De Natura Deorum* 1.70), because "he feared that, if one sensation were false, none would be true"; that is, none would be immune to skeptical doubt. The claim amounts to this: every "sense-object" (*aistheton*) really is just as it appears in the "sensation" (*aisthesis*) it causes. Its justification is this: "[S]ensation is non-rational and involves no memory" (DL 10.31); hence, it does not interpret the sense-object but merely registers its features passively. Interpretation enters only as "added opinion," the result of a "motion in us" that, though "conjoined" to the "impression-producing focusing of the sense-organs," which results in sensation, "is distinct" from it (*Letter to Herodotus* 51).

What is the "sense-object" that really is as it appears? It seems it cannot be the "solid-body" (*steremnion*), for example, the square tower that appears round from a distance. Hence, Everson et al. have argued that it must rather be the "idols," the material films that flow from the solid-body into our eyes and that change shape, from square to round, in transit. The problem with this view is that, as Lucretius notes (*De Rerum Naura* 4.257–58), we do not see idols; we see solid-bodies or, at any rate, the colors of these bodies. The round-shaped color of the tower seen from a distance, then, must be the "sense-object" that really is as it appears. This is confirmed by Sextus Empiricus' report of Epicurus' position (*Adversus Mathematicos* 7.207–9):

[I]t is not the whole solid-body which is seen, . . . but the color of the solid-body. And, of color, some is on the solid-body, as in things seen from nearby . . . and some exists outside the solid-body, as in things viewed from a great distance. This color, having been altered in the intervening space and taking on its own shape, produces an impression such as it in truth is.

So vision "tells the truth" when "from a great distance it sees the tower as small and round." Those who suppose that this sensation is false mistakenly suppose that it has the same "sense-object" as the sensation from nearby. It doesn't: the latter's object is the square-shaped color "on" the solid-body; the former's is the round-shaped color "outside" it. But both *are* colors *of* the solid-body, and it is not the idols, but "the tower"—though not "the whole" tower—that is seen "as small and round" from a distance. With Sextus' report compare Plutarch's: "One should resist no sensation, for they all make contact with something, each taking from the 'multiple-mixture' . . . what fits and agrees with itself. And, making contact with parts, we should make no assertions about the whole." That is, depending on what fits the pores of their sense-organs, different perceivers receive different impressions from "the multiple-mixtures of seeds dispersed in all flavors, odors, and colors" (*Against Colotes* 1109c–e). Thus, when a drink tastes sweet to one man, bitter to another, neither man is mistaken; they have simply made contact with different sense-objects, that is, different parts of the multiple-mixture. As with tastes of flavors, so with smells of odors, visions of shaped colors, and so on: every sensation is caused by some part (quality or feature) of the body sensed and accurately reports the truth about that part.

NOTIONS

"By a 'notion' (*prolepsis*)," we are told (DL 10.33), the Epicureans mean "a concept or stored universal idea, i.e., a memory of something often having appeared from without, e.g., that man is such-and-such a thing. For, as soon as 'man' is said, the image of man comes to mind in accordance with the notion." This notion is empirically acquired from repeated sensations of men. It is a criterion of truth, because it is that to which one makes reference in judging whether what one sees is a man or not. It is "the primary idea" underlying the term "man" and, to serve as a criterion, must be "recognized and need no demonstration" (*Letter to Herodotus* 38). It must not, that is, await clarification by some definition of the word "man," for example, "rational animal." For these words would themselves require definition. Hence, Epicurus "abolishes definition" as useless (if only some words are defined) or impossible (if all must be) and satisfies himself with having a clear "notion" (literally, "pre-grasping") of what underlies the word "man."

On the Epicurean view, "all ideas come from the senses, by encounter, analogy, similarity, and combination, with reasoning contributing something too" (DL 10.32). Our idea of "man," for example, arises by "encounter" with men, of "centaur" by "combination" of man and horse, and of "atom" by "analogy" with macroscopic body. (Atomic bodies are analogous to the bodies we sense but, as reasoning tells us, are smaller and indivisible.) This suggests that all notions are empirically acquired, but the Epicureans speak of some as "innate." On this, see later.

AFFECTIONS

Any passive experience, for example, a sensation, is an "affection" (*pathos*), broadly speaking, but the "primary" affections are ("kinetic") pleasure and pain. A kinetic pleasure is a "smooth motion (*kinesis*) of the flesh," and a pain is a rough one. Nonrational animals and infants sense that kinetic pleasure feels good and is "choiceworthy." Hence, reports Cicero (*De Finibus* 1.30), Epicurus "denies the need for argument or proof that pleasure is choiceworthy," insisting that this is immediately "sensed, as that fire is hot." But some Epicureans, Cicero adds, "deny that it is enough that what is good or bad be judged by sensation"; they say that we have an innate "notion" that pleasure is choiceworthy. This notion must be innate, however, only in a weak, dispositional sense: we are born so disposed as to recognize, on first sensing kinetic pleasure, that it is good.

Infants enjoy only kinetic pleasures. Rational adults, however, recognize that "the greatest and most secure joy" is found in "painlessness" and "undisturbedness'' and hence make obtaining these ''states'' (*katastemata*)—''the katas-tematic pleasures'' of the body and soul—their ''end'' (*telos*), though with the understanding that they will still enjoy kinetic pleasures (e.g., in the tongue as they eat) in the course of ridding themselves of pains. This is still hedonism, but of a quietist sort, emphasizing the need for the ''undisturbedness'' (*ataraxia*) that comes from freeing the mind of fears of death, vengeful gods, pain, and unsatisfied desire.

MENTAL IMPRESSIONS

After reporting that Epicurus posited three criteria of truth in *The Canon*, Diogenes Laertius notes that ''the Epicureans'' added a fourth: ''impression-producing focusings (*phantastikai epibolai*) of the mind.'' This term, which is act/result ambiguous, must here refer to the results of mental ''focusings'': non-sensory ''impressions'' (*phantasiai*), for example, dreams, hallucinations, and ''visions'' of gods. The addition of these as a fourth criterion should not be judged unorthodox, for Epicurus did hold that nonsensory impressions are al-ways true: just as ''sensations'' are caused by ''sense-objects,'' so mental im-pressions are caused by ''impression-objects'' (*phantasta*) and accurately report their features. Error, for example, the false opinion that the god one ''sees'' is a ''solid-body,'' is again explained as ''added opinion.'' The gods, then, really do exist, for we get mental impressions of them when idols of huge, anthro-pomorphic beings enter our minds. But in what sense does a god (say, Zeus) exist for Epicurus? Not as a body, reports Cicero, but as a ''quasi body'' (*Nat. Deorum* 1.49), that is, not as a ''solid-body'' with ''numerical identity'' but as that ''nature'' that our focusing minds grasp through the influx of an ''infinite series of similar images.'' Cicero's testimony squares with that of Philodemus, that Epicurus posited ''natures from similar elements'' as well as ''natures from the same elements.'' Solid-bodies, it seems, are the latter, made up of (roughly) the same material parts from instant to instant; gods are the former, made up of matter, to be sure (for everything is), but not of the same material parts from instant to instant, but only of similar ones. An atheist would conclude from this that Zeus does not really exist; all there really is, is an endless stream of Zeus-shaped idols, which flow from no body and yet produce the impression of one. But Epicurus concludes that Zeus *does* exist, albeit only as a quasi body.

Lucretius explains as follows mankind's acquisition of its notion of gods as immortal and blessed (*Nat.* 5.1169–82): early men, asleep and awake, had ''vi-sions'' of great anthropomorphic beings and ''endowed them with eternal life'' and blessedness, ''because their appearance was perpetually supplied,'' and they appeared invulnerable and fearless. Given this empirical account, we must un-derstand in the weak, dispositional sense the Epicurean claim that men's ''no-tion'' of god is ''innate.'' This notion serves as the criterion by which to judge false the superstitious belief that the gods meddle in human affairs: their bless-edness rules out their having the troublesome job of governing our world.

ATOMISM

Divine providence, then, must be rejected. Its explanatory role is filled by infinity: in the infinite void, the infinitely many atoms must combine in all possible ways, producing infinitely many "worlds" (*cosmoi*), some like ours, some different, but all merely transitory. There must be void, for otherwise there would not be motion. This empty space must be infinite, for a space can be bounded only by more space or by a body in space. This void is the only "incorporeal" admitted into Epicurus' ontology; everything else is a body (or quasi body) or property thereof. Macroscopic bodies exist and truly have both the primary and secondary qualities they appear to have, though composed of atoms, which have only primary qualities (see PRIMARY AND SECONDARY QUALITIES). Living things exist, though their souls are perishable compounds of lifeless atoms. Since living things move with three kinds of motion (rebounding from collisions, falling due to their weight, and moving voluntarily), atoms too must move with three kinds of motion (rebounding from collisions, falling due to their weight, and swerving indeterministically) so as to cause these macroscopic motions from the bottom up.

METHOD

Truths about such "nonevident things" are obtained by entertaining all possible explanations of a given phenomenon and then endorsing only those that are verified by "noncontestation," that is, that are not inconsistent with any phenomena. In some cases, there is only one such explanation; for example, only void can explain motion. In others, there are many; for example, thunderbolts could be caused by ignition of vortices in clouds or by collisions of wind with clouds or in other ways. In these cases, all possible explanations should be endorsed, since all possibilities are actualized somewhere in the universe. We cannot know which such explanation applies to the lightning in *our* cosmos, but it is enough that we can rule out explanations in terms of angry gods.

INFLUENCE

Epicureanism flourished in Greece and Rome for many centuries, its adherents insisting that its main critics, Stoic fatalists (see STOICISM) and academic skeptics (see SKEPTICISM), were "self-refuting." It could not compete, however, with the otherworldly promises of Neoplatonists and Christians, who derided Epicurus as an atheistic sensualist. It was revived, however, by GASSENDI and influenced the corpuscularism of "the new science" and the epistemology of the British empiricists.

BIBLIOGRAPHY

Books

Long, A. A., and D. N. Sedley. *The Hellenistic Philosophers*. Cambridge: Cambridge University Press, 1987. Contains a good bibliography.

Usener, H. *Epicurea*. Leipzig, 1887. A sourcebook with extensive exegetical commentary and a good bibliography.

Articles

Everson, S. "Epicurus on the Truth of the Senses." In *Epistemology*, edited by S. Everson. Cambridge: Cambridge University Press, 1990.
Purinton, J. S. "Epicurus on the *Telos*." *Phronesis* 38 (1993): 281–320.

JEFFREY S. PURINTON

ESSENCE. The concept of essence originates in Aristotelian and Scholastic philosophy, where it forms part of the theory of SUBSTANCE. The essence is the property of an individual or a quantity of stuff that determines what kind of substance it is. The essence of a thing was distinguished from its properties, which flow directly from its essence, and its accidents, which are not necessarily connected to the essence. Thus, for ARISTOTLE the essence of the species (or substance) man was to be a rational animal; properties such as possession of language followed necessarily from this; and accidents, such as being tall or bald, were possessed by some men but not others.

The Aristotelian concept of essence has generally been perceived by empiricists as a major obstacle to empirical science and was later ridiculed in Voltaire's famous jibe about the *virtus dormitiva* of opium. The *locus classicus* is LOCKE's *Essay concerning Human Understanding*. Locke's discussion is based on the distinction between real and nominal essence, which he defines, respectively, as "the very being of any thing, whereby it is, what it is" and "the abstract idea which the general, or sortal . . . name stands for," that is, a set of properties associated with the term (*Essay* III.iii.15). Whereas the former comes close to the Aristotelian notion of an essence, Locke argued that only in the sense of a nominal essence was there any essence associated with a general term. Thus, attributions of essential properties to kinds involved only claims about language, not about the real nature of the objects. Locke was in fact highly skeptical about real essences. He held that the property of an object from which its properties derived was the arrangement of its microstructural constituents. Since we lack microscopical eyes (*Essay* II.xxiii.12), even if there were real essences, we would be unable to discover what they were. Moreover, he saw no reason to assume that the kinds we distinguished by means of nominal essences would share a common microstructure. Thus, he claimed, "The boundaries of the Species, whereby Men sort them, are made by Men" (*Essay*, III.vi.37).

Some more recent philosophers, as they have become more optimistic about the possibility of exploring the microstructural constitution of things, have been inclined to revive the concept of essence. Most notable in this regard is work by Hilary Putnam. Putnam (1975) argued that natural kind terms (roughly, substance terms) should be understood as referring to a kind the extension of which was determined by a real essence, even prior to the scientific specification of that essence. This idea has been welcomed by contemporary philosophers of science as a solution to the apparent incommensurability of kind terms across changes in scientific theory. However, the assumption, contra Locke, that such an essence is there to be discovered might violate reasonable empiricist scruples. In a range of central cases, most notably in biology, scientific inquiry strongly suggests that there is indeed no such essential property to be found.

PRIMARY WORK

Locke, John. *An Essay concerning Human Understanding*. Edited with an introduction by P. H. Nidditch. Oxford: Clarendon Press, 1975.

BIBLIOGRAPHY

Ayers, Michael. "Locke vs. Aristotle on Natural Kinds," *Journal of Philosophy* 78 (1981): 247–72.
Putnam, Hilary. "The Meaning of 'Meaning.' " In *Mind, Language, and Reality. Philosophical Papers*. Vol. 2. Cambridge: Cambridge University Press, 1975.

JOHN DUPRÉ

EXISTENCE. The concept of existence comprises all there is. Empiricists argue that the domain of what there is, the realm of existence, is delimited by the range of our experience. All our concepts derive from experience, and so we cannot think about things that are somehow outside the limits of our experience: for us, such discourse is literally nonsense.

This does not mean that nothing exists besides what we actually experience. There are, of course, things that are too small to see, too far away to hear, things that are in the past or in the future, that we quite reasonably believe to exist and that we have not, or even, given the limits of our senses, cannot, experience. The point is that we infer the existence of these entities from the existence of things that we do experience on the basis of principles whose truth is justified by the things that we experience. As a consequence, those things that exist but that we do not actually experience are like, or similar—if not specifically then at least generically—to things that we do actually experience. By forming generic concepts of these entities we can think about them in general terms at least, even if they are specifically things "I know not what," as John LOCKE put it. The notion that there are entities that cause the entities that we do experience or cause us to have certain sense-data is captured by referring to them by means of what David HUME and others referred to as "relative ideas"; they are, for example, "the small material objects that *cause* the entities that we experience," where the concept of "cause" is a relational concept whose meaning derives from the world presented to us in ordinary experience. Earlier empiricists had difficulty explaining the logic of references based on generic and relative concepts, but Bertrand RUSSELL solved those logical problems with his well-known theory of definite descriptions. As he would put it, our knowledge of the nonexperienced entities is knowledge by description rather than knowledge by acquaintance.

Some philosophers have argued that besides the things that exist, there is another realm of things that merely subsist or merely *have being* rather than existence. For example, Plato and others have argued that in order to account for the sameness of things we need to introduce Forms or Ideas that transcend the world of ordinary or sense experience and that these Forms have a different kind of being from ordinary things. Or again, others such as Meinong have argued that when we think of things that do not exist—mermaids, for example— these thoughts have objects or are about entities that even if they do not exist, must have some sort of being; otherwise the thoughts would be about nothing.

Empiricists have generally argued that philosophical problems of this sort have to be resolved without appeal to entities that inhabit a shadowy world of being that lies outside the realm of existence as delimited by our ordinary human experience. Thus, they have argued that the problem of sameness can be solved by recognizing the existence of a relation of resemblance among the properties of things or else by recognizing that the characteristics of things as given in experience are already universal. Or again, they have argued that the aboutness of thought can be dealt with in much the same way as the aboutness of language; since a scientific explanation of the semantics and therefore of the aboutness of language does not require the introduction of another world of entities beyond those of ordinary experience, so we can hold that the aboutness of thought does not presuppose such a world.

Among empiricists, some have argued that only certain very special entities exist. They have suggested, for example, that only atoms exist or that only sense- data exist. These sorts of claims have an air of paradox, since, as G. E. MOORE argued vigorously, these same philosophers recognize—when they sit down, for example—that there are chairs and tables. There seems to be an ordinary sense of ''exist'' in which tables and chairs exist and a philosophical sense of ''exist'' in which only atoms or only sense-data exist. In order to understand what these philosophers were trying to say in a way that avoided the air of paradox that it generated, a number of empiricists made what has been termed the ''linguistic turn.'' Upon this view, the philosophical claims are claims *about* the (structure and interpretation of an) ideal language, while the ordinary claims are claims made *within* the ideal language. W.V.O. QUINE argued that we can best ex- plicate the philosophical use of ''exist'' in terms of the formula that ''to be is to be the value of a variable.'' Gustav BERGMANN, in contrast, argued that we should understand what exists in the philosophical sense as what is referred to by the primitive descriptive terms of the ideal language. Thus, for example, the philosophical claim that only sense-data exist is to be understood, on Quine's view, as claiming that we quantify over nothing other than sense data or, on Bergmann's view, is to be understood as claiming that sense-data alone are referred to by the primitive terms of one's ideal language. As for the common- sense claim that here is a chair, this is reconstructed in the philosopher's ideal language as a very complicated claim about extended patterns of sense-data, while such commonsense claims as that there are atoms or objects in the past or other minds are reconstructed as references made by means of Russellian definite descriptions. The linguistic turn thus shows how the realism of common sense can be reconciled with the philosopher's phenomenalist claim that only sense-data exist (see PHENOMENALISM). Other philosophical claims, such as there being only atoms, can similarly be reconstructed.

The linguistic turn has been a very helpful tool in the attempts by empiricists to establish a dialectically adequate understanding of existence.

BIBLIOGRAPHY

Books

Grossman, R. *The Existence of the World*. London: Routledge, 1992.
Orenstein, A. *Existence and the Particular Quantifier*. Philadelphia: Temple University Press, 1978.
Williams, C.J.F. *What Is Existence?* Oxford: Oxford University Press, 1981.

Articles

Bergman, G. "Particularity and the New Nominalism." In *Meaning and Existence*. Madison: University of Wisconsin Press, 1960.
Hochberg, H. "A Note on the Empty Universe." *Mind*, n.s. 66 (1957).
Quine, W.V.O. "On What There Is" (a symposium with P. T. Geach). *Proceedings of the Aristotelian Society* 25, supplement (1951).
Sellars, W. "Grammar and Existence: A Preface to Ontology." In *Science, Perception and Reality*. London: Routledge and Kegan Paul, 1963.

FRED WILSON

EXTERNAL WORLD. The concept of the external world has played a central role in empiricist epistemology and metaphysics. The world in question is "external" in the sense of being external to human consciousness; it has been the object of empiricist concern because, when distinctively empiricist epistemic principles and conceptions of cognitive MEANING are assumed, it is difficult to see how it can possibly be known or even conceived of. Different conceptions of "the" external world and different claims about whether or how it can be known to exist have characterized the history of empiricism.

The pertinent epistemological and metaphysical problems received their classic statement in HUME's philosophy. According to him, there are two rival systems of ideas regarding the external world, a popular system and one involved in what he called "the modern philosophy," but there are insuperable epistemological problems with the claim that either represents the world as it actually is. In his *An Enquiry concerning Human Understanding* he claimed that owing to a powerful natural instinct, we always suppose that the colored expanses we see are objects genuinely external to our consciousness, not images or impressions that merely represent such objects. But this universal and primary opinion "of all men" is destroyed, he said, "by the slightest philosophy, which teaches us that nothing can ever be present to a mind but an image or perception and that the senses are only inlets through which these images are conveyed"

(*Enquiry* XII.i: 152). The trouble with the new system is that the external objects causing our impressions are unknowable and incomprehensible. We cannot know them because we can neither perceive them directly nor infer their existence by an acceptable form of "experimental" inference. They are incomprehensible to us because we can form no idea of something that we cannot possibly perceive: the ideas we do have can always be traced back to "original impressions."

The conception of experimental inference to which Hume appealed is causal inference (see CAUSATION/POWER), a form of reasoning based on causal principles such as "Scratching dry matches causes them to light." Principles of this kind cannot be known to be true a priori (see A PRIORI/A POSTERIORI DISTINCTION), Hume argued; they require empirical support. Although a given causal principle might gain such support from another, more general causal principle, empirical support is ultimately derived from the experience of a "constant conjunction" between events. Since the experience of such a conjunction is not possible when one of the events occurs outside human consciousness, there is no way of adding support to a causal principle that bridges the gap between mental impressions and mind-independent causes. An experimental inference could not, therefore, support the belief that an external world— a world of objects external to human consciousness—actually exists.

In the early twentieth century, philosophers such as Bertrand RUSSELL and Rudolf CARNAP made sophisticated attempts to avoid the skeptical consequences of Hume's empiricism. Relying on techniques involving the new mathematical logic developed in *Principia Mathematica*, Russell in *Our Knowledge of the External World* (1929) and Carnap in *Der Logische Aufbau der Welt* (1928) argued that the external world could be regarded as a "logical construction" whose existence could be supported empirically. So understood, the external world is not really external to human consciousness; it is a construct built up (as it were) out of human consciousness. As such, it is importantly similar to the world of BERKELEY's "subjective IDEALISM." Although Carnap was an earnest opponent of metaphysical theories such as Berkeley's, he was committed to verificationism (see VERIFICATION PRINCIPLE), a theory of meaning that was essentially a linguistic version of Hume's thesis that (genuine) IDEAs can always be traced back to original impressions (see Carnap 1932). Since an external world genuinely independent of human consciousness could not possibly be verified experientially, Carnap could make no sense of such a world. He had to follow Russell and regard the "external" world as a construct out of experience.

In "Testability and Meaning" (1936) Carnap explicitly abandoned both verificationism and the thesis that our knowledge of the world (SCIENCE, as he called it) must be founded on the data of subjective experience. Meaningful discourse had to be "confirmable" by experience, he now said, not conclusively verifiable by it, and confirming experience may be understood as the experience (the perception) of physical things, not merely the experience of a perceiver's

sensory states. Russell, in *An Inquiry into Meaning and Truth* (1940), held to
the view that basic confirming experience is the experience of a perceiver's
sensory states, but he rejected the idea that meaningful discourse must be verifiable or confirmable. As he saw it, a sentence has meaning if every "constant"
it contains has a meaning derived from experience, and unverifiable propositions
of physics satisfy this condition (see *An Inquiry Into Meaning and Truth*: 304f).
In conceding that there are true propositions about the world that are not verifiable, he admitted that he was abandoning "pure empiricism." Such empiricism
is "believed by no one," he said, "and if we are to retain beliefs that we all
regard as valid, we must allow principles of inference which are neither demonstrative nor derivable from experience" (*Inquiry*: 305). In *Human Knowledge: Its Scope and Limits* (1946) he identified five "postulates" that, in his
view, govern scientific inference. These postulates cannot be shown to be true,
he said, and they are not "based upon experience"; but they are presupposed
by inferences that are regarded as acceptable in science as well as in everyday
life, and they allow us to distinguish absurd inductions from those deemed useful
and legitimate.

Although Hume did not use the word "INDUCTION," his famous claim,
that the sort of arguments from experience to which this word is now applied
cannot be shown to be truth-preserving, has long been standard empiricist doctrine. Russell accepted this assessment of arguments from experience, but he
may have been the first to see that patterns of inference conforming to textbook
paradigms yield false conclusions from true premises more often than not. He
proved this point in *Human Knowledge* (Part V, Chapter 7), but he illustrated
it nicely in a later essay on John Stuart MILL when he said that although all
the sheep Kant ever saw were within ten miles of Königsberg, it would have
been absurd for Kant to conclude that all sheep were within ten miles of Königsberg (*Portraits from Memory*: 126). In Russell's view, the "inductive" inferences people actually make are commonly not of the objectionable sort; but
since the familiar inductive principle permits bad inferences as well as good
ones, the good inferences people commonly make must be warranted by something other than that principle. Russell argued that the source of this warrant is
the mathematical theory of PROBABILITY together with the postulates of scientific inference that he identified. He did not, of course, mean to imply that
people who make acceptable "inductive" inferences are generally aware of this
warrant; his claim was merely that they generalize by means of inferential habits
that accord with it. These inferential habits are formed, he thought, in the process
of adaptation to the environment that enable the human species to survive (*Human Knowledge*: 526).

The abandonment by Carnap and other "logical empiricists" (see LOGICAL
POSITIVISM/LOGICAL EMPIRICISM) of Hume's subjective basis for empirical knowledge was reinforced by Ludwig WITTGENSTEIN's influential contention that empirical thought is carried out in language and that a private
language is impossible. As Wittgenstein argued in his *Philosophical Investiga-*

tions, we can think about the world only by means of concepts that are rooted in the classificatory practice of a community, and such concepts are applied primarily to community-accessible things, not to subjective images or impressions. The traditional empiricist idea, which Russell never abandoned, that our knowledge and justifiable opinions about the world ultimately rest on subjective sensory data (the late Russell merely added structural postulates to this foundation) became extremely unpopular as Wittgenstein's ideas began to dominate Anglo-American philosophy in the 1960s, and many philosophers who considered themselves empiricists began to agree that Hume's problems about the external world did not actually make sense.

Widespread conviction that Hume's problems are actually nonsensical or incoherent has persisted into the 1990s, but one of the sources of Hume's problems is not the difficulty of founding the popular system (the view of the world that Wittgenstein defended) on the subjective data of a single consciousness but the implications of physics and physiology (the new scientific system of ideas). Hume argued that the popular system is not theoretically satisfactory: we begin with the assumption that it is true, but critical reflection leads us to reject it in favor of a sophisticated alternative, which is indefensible and incomprehensible. Russell described the breakdown of the popular system as follows:

We all start from "naive realism," the doctrine that things are what they seem. We think that grass is green, that stones are hard, and that snow is cold. But physics assures us that the greenness of grass, the hardness of stones, and the coldness of snow are not the greenness, hardness, and cold that we know in our experience, but something very different. The observer, when he seems to himself to be observing a stone, is really, if physics is to be believed, observing the effects of the stone upon himself [since the qualities he perceives "in" the stone do not actually belong to it]. Thus science seems to be at war with itself: when it most means to be objective, it finds itself plunged into subjectivity against its will. Naive realism leads to physics, and physics, if true, shows that naive realism is false. Therefore naive realism, if true, is false; therefore it is false. (*Inquiry into Meaning and Truth*: 15)

If naive realism is false, the question arises, How can we know that the swarms of imperceptible entities postulated by physics actually exist? To answer this question, we have to identify the sort of evidence that entitles us to believe in such things. Only by doing so can we dismiss the possibility that in spite of our firm natural beliefs about ourselves and the community to which we belong, we might be (in Hilary Putnam's words) mere "brains in vats" reacting to experiences produced by the diabolical devices of scientific maniacs. What is the evidence, then, that I am not, in fact, a brain in a vat and that I do have the attributes that current physics attributes to me? This is a question about the external world, and it is not rendered otiose or nonsensical by Wittgenstein's arguments.

Philosophers who have attempted to dispose of the Hume–Russell problem by arguing that it cannot coherently arise generally have little to say about the kind of inference that can add rational support to the claims of physics, and, in proceeding as they do, they tacitly overlook a basic empiricist doctrine. The doctrine they overlook is that matters of empirical fact can be ascertained only a posteriori—by some kind of observational input or argument from experience. That we and our world are even approximately as we are described by physics and cognitive science is a matter of empirical fact not ascertainable a priori or by direct observation. An ''argument from experience'' is therefore required. But what can it be?

It is obvious that the required argument must be different from the kind Hume considered, for that sort of argument merely permits one to generalize about the domain of observation. Recent work in the spirit of Russell has shown that a logic of experimental inference is adequately supplied by probability theory (see Salmon), but serious problems remain about how the required premises for inference can ultimately be justified (see Aune: Chapter 7) and whether the theories adequately supported by experimental inference should be interpreted ''realistically'' (as telling us what the world is really like), or whether they should be understood as merely a source of reliable predictions about what is observable (see van Fraassen). In view of the problems that still exist about the relevant ''arguments from experience,'' it is fair to say that empiricist problems about the external world have not yet been fully resolved.

PRIMARY WORKS

Books

Carnap, Rudolf. *Der Logische Aufbau der Welt*. Berlin: Weltkreis-Verlag, 1928.
Hume, David. *An Enquiry concerning Human Understanding*. In *Enquiries concerning Human Understanding and concerning the Principles of Morals*, edited with an analytical index by L. A. Selby-Bigge; revised with notes by P. H. Nidditch. Oxford: Clarendon Press, 1975.
———. *A Treatise of Human Nature*. 2d ed., edited with an analytical index by L. A. Selby-Bigge; revised with notes by P. H. Nidditch. Oxford: Clarendon Press, 1978.

Articles

Carnap, Rudolf. ''Testability and Meaning, I–IV.'' *Philosophy of Science* 3 (1936): 419–71; 4 (1937): 1–40. Reprinted, in part, in *Readings in the Philosophy of Science*, edited by H. Feigl and M. Broadbeck. New York: Appleton-Century-Crofts, 1953: 47–92.
———. ''Überwindung der Metaphysik durch Logische Analyse der Sprache.'' *Erkenntnis* 2 (1931–1932): 219–41. Translated by Arthur Pap in *Logical Positivism*, edited by A. J. Ayer. New York: Free Press, 1959: 60–81.
Russell, Bertrand. *Human Knowledge: Its Scope and Limits*. London: Allen and Unwin, 1946.
———. *An Inquiry into Meaning and Truth*. London: Allen and Unwin, 1940.
———. *Our Knowledge of the External World*. London: Allen and Unwin, 1929.
———. *Portraits from Memory*. New York: Simon and Schuster, 1956.

BIBLIOGRAPHY

Aune, Bruce. *Knowledge of the External World*. London: Routledge, 1991.

Putnam, Hilary. *Reason, Truth, and History*. Cambridge: Cambridge University Press, 1981.

Salmon, Wesley. *The Foundations of Scientific Inference*. Pittsburgh: University of Pittsburgh Press, 1979.

van Fraassen, Bas C. *The Scientific Image*. Oxford: Clarendon Press, 1980.

BRUCE AUNE

F

FERGUSON, ADAM. Adam Ferguson (1723–1816), the only member of the Scottish Enlightenment to come from the Highlands and the only Gaelic speaker, attended St. Andrews University, intending to follow in his father's footsteps in the ministry. He served with the newly formed Black Watch regiment as a chaplain. He did not in fact succeed his father, and he left the ministry. After a break he briefly succeeded David HUME at the Advocates' Library before becoming, in 1759, a professor (initially of natural philosophy and then five years later of pneumatics and moral philosophy) at Edinburgh. His most important book is the *Essay on the History of Civil Society* (1767), but he also published in 1768 a brief edition of his lectures (*Institutes of Moral Philosophy*) and a compendious two-volume edition in 1792 (*Principles of Moral and Political Science*). Apart from various pamphlets, his other major intellectual enterprise was a five-volume *History of the Progress and Termination of the Roman Republic*, published in 1783.

The opening chapter of the *Essay* establishes Ferguson's empiricist credentials. His aim there is to criticize the assumptions and methods of those theorists who talk of a State of Nature. The theorists he has in mind, although they are not named, are Rousseau and HOBBES. Though different, these two share the same fatal weakness, in his view. They have each erected a "system" based upon selecting "one or few particulars on which to establish a theory." In adopting this approach, Ferguson says, they have deviated from the practice of the "natural historian," who thinks the "facts" should be collected, and general rules should be derived from "observations and experiments." In contrast to this proper BACONIAN procedure (see the opening sections of the *Institutes*) Hobbes and Rousseau resort to "hypothesis" or "conjecture" or "imagination" or "poetry." To these Ferguson juxtaposes, respectively, "reality," "facts," "reason," and "science," and the latter list "must be admitted as the foundation of all our reasoning relative to man." Just as Hume saw in the "science of man" the center of the moral sciences, so Ferguson saw "man's nature" as "the foundation of every science relating to him." To execute that science we must turn to evidence. The evidence uniformly returns the same verdict: "[B]oth the earliest and latest accounts collected from every quarter of the earth represent mankind as assembled in troops and companies" (*Essay* I.1).

By "earliest" accounts, Ferguson means those of the ancient historians, with Thucydides among the Greeks and Tacitus among the Romans being especially favored. By the "latest," he means the reports and journals of various travelers and missionaries, preeminent among which were the accounts of the various tribes of North America supplied by many authors, especially by Lafitau and Charlevoix. To rely (not uncritically) on such sources is to accept that experience provides the evidence. On this basis we have "no record" of a time when humans were not social. With respect to a "wild man" caught in the woods or a feral child, a number of whom were causes célèbres in the eighteenth century, Ferguson denied they constituted authentic counterevidence. In line with the principle of INDUCTION—the practice of the "natural historian"—it is clear, he affirms, that every "experiment" should be made with "entire societies not with single men" (*Essay* I.1).

For Ferguson, humans are not social as a consequence of some rational calculation (as social contract theory was held to suppose). Rather, human sociality is the combined product of instinct, of the permanency of familial relationships, and, most characteristically, of the "resolute ardour" with which individuals attach themselves to each other. This ardor is expressed in friendship and patriotism, and since these are found when relationships are under threat, it demonstrates that society is not valued simply because of the conveniences it supplies (*Essay* I.3).

Ferguson's moral theory is relatively underdeveloped. He subscribes to a version of the "moral sentiment" theory; as "actors or spectators" we "feel" the differences in human conduct. Such feeling is empirically indisputable. The selfish system of Mandeville or Hobbes is thus contrary to the evident presence of a "principle of affection" or "amicable disposition" in human nature (*Essay* I.6). More generally, Ferguson's work as a whole exhibits a pervasive moralism. He is strongly imbued with "civic republican" sensitivities. While not denying the merits of commerce and the rule of law, he is far less sanguine than Adam SMITH or Hume about their effects on human character. He fears public duty will be neglected, and political tranquillity will ensue, an outcome that runs counter to the fact that "man is not made for repose" but for action on the public stage (*Essay* V.2). In broad terms, Ferguson thus subscribes more to a "positive" view of liberty than to the "negative" view more typically associated with empiricists.

In his own time, Ferguson, along with Thomas REID, had some influence on Dugald Stewart's version of "common sense philosophy" (see STEWART), but his later renown rests on his being seen as a pioneer in sociology. Auguste COMTE knew his work, but those who champion Ferguson's case do so often because they see him representing a more fertile line of speculation than that actually provided by Comte.

PRIMARY WORK

Essay on the History of Civil Society. Edited by F. Oz-Salzburger. Cambridge: Cambridge
  University Press, 1996. An older edition of this work, edited by D. Forbes (Edinburgh: Edinburgh University Press, 1966), contains a valuable introduction;
  there is also a modern German translation edited by H. Medick (Frankfurt: Suhr-
  kamp, 1988).

BIBLIOGRAPHY

Berry, Christopher J. *Social Theory of the Scottish Enlightenment*. Edinburgh: Edinburgh
  University Press, 1997.
Bryson, Gladys. *Man and Society: The Scottish Enquiry of the Eighteenth Century*.
  Princeton: Princeton University Press, 1945.
Kettler, David. *The Social and Political Thought of Adam Ferguson*. Columbus: Ohio
  State University Press, 1965.
Sher, Richard. *Church and University in the Scottish Enlightenment*. Edinburgh: Edin-
  burgh University Press, 1985.

CHRISTOPHER J. BERRY

FREE WILL. The problem of ''free will'' (see WILL) has generally been interpreted in modern times in terms of the question of whether or not moral
freedom and responsibility are compatible with causality and determinism. Philosophers in the empiricist tradition have defended, with remarkable consistency,
a compatibilist position on this issue. Moreover, most of the major figures of
the empiricist tradition are understood to have endorsed and contributed to a
single, unified strategy on this subject. The philosophers concerned include, most
prominently, HOBBES, LOCKE, HUME, MILL, RUSSELL, Schlick, and
AYER. (BERKELEY is a notable exception to the generalization that empiricists
have supported the compatibilist position.) The position that these philosophers
developed reflects, in large measure, the ''antimetaphysical'' (see METAPHYS-
ICS) and naturalistic (see NATURALISM) orientation of empiricist philosophy.

   The two most basic elements in the classical empiricist-compatibilist strategy
concern their interpretation of ''freedom'' and their account of ''causal necessity'' (see CAUSATION). The fundamental claim is that incompatibilism is a
product of (related) confusions concerning both these aspects of the ''free will''
problem. It is argued, moreover, that erroneous incompatibilist conclusions have
encouraged the (obscure) metaphysical system building that characterizes the
''libertarian'' or ''free will'' position. In this way, there are a positive, constructive aspect and a negative, destructive aspect to classical empiricist-
compatibilism. On one hand, it aims to articulate and defend a plausible account
of freedom and responsibility, and, on the other hand, it seeks to discredit ''free
will'' metaphysics and expose the confusions that lead to it.

   Historically, the most influential figures in the empiricist-compatibilist tradition are Hobbes and Hume. These two thinkers are generally taken to have laid
the foundations of the classical strategy. Hobbes argued that ''a free agent is he
that can do if he will, and forbear if he will; and that liberty is the absence of

external impediments'' (*Works* IV: 275–76). On this understanding of freedom—what Hume refers to as ''liberty of spontaneity'' (*Treatise*: 407)—an agent is free so long as she is able to act according to the *determination* of her own will. Freedom of this kind is opposed to force or compulsion, such as when a prisoner cannot escape because of the external constraints on her actions (e.g., chains, bars, etc.). This kind of freedom (''spontaneity'') is to be contrasted with a freedom that presupposes the absence of causes and necessity—what Hume terms ''liberty of indifference'' (*Treatise*: 407—compare Hobbes's *Works* IV: 261). Hume maintains that ''liberty of indifference'' has no existence and that it is not what we ordinarily *mean* by liberty. ''Liberty of spontaneity''—freedom to act without external constraint—captures our everyday understanding of freedom.

Clearly, then, properly understood, the conditions of freedom involve the absence of any (external) obstacles to *action*. Free action is *caused* by the will of the agent. Failing this, the behavior in question is a product of external causes (i.e., causes other than the agent's desires and willings) and is thus unfree. The distinction between free and unfree action, therefore, depends not on the presence or absence of causation but rather on the *type* of cause that gives rise to it. It follows that it is a mistake to suppose that freedom requires the absence of causation. On the contrary, free action must be caused by the agent, and, hence, freedom *requires* causation.

The question arises, in light of this, why so many philosophers have supposed that (moral) freedom requires the absence of causation and necessity (i.e., ''liberty of indifference''). Hume's famous and influential explanation for this is that confusion about the nature of freedom has its roots in misunderstanding about the nature of causation and necessity (*Treatise*: 407, 409–10; *Enquiry*: 93–94, 97; compare Ayer: 21–22). Freedom properly understood—liberty of spontaneity—does require the absence of any force or compulsion. Traditional metaphysical views of causation, however, seem to imply that causes (somehow) compel or force their effects to occur. It would seem to follow from this, that if our actions are caused, then they cannot be free—because they would then be forced or compelled to occur. Causation and necessity, Hume maintains, are simply a matter of constant conjunction or the regular union of like objects. On the basis of such regularities we are able to make inferences from causes to effects. In the case of human conduct, our experience of certain characters serves as a basis for making inferences as to how these individuals will act in given circumstances or conditions. None of this, however, implies that the actions of these agents were in any way forced or compelled to occur. In short, confusion about the nature of causal necessity has led to confusion about the conditions of moral freedom. With this confusion eliminated, we can conclude that there is no conflict between freedom and necessity.

The preceding account of the conditions of free action serves to explain why the alternative conception of freedom—''liberty of indifference''—must be rejected. Defenders of ''free will'' (i.e., ''libertarians'') maintain that moral

freedom requires that our actions are not caused or necessitated. Empiricist-compatibilists argue that this is obviously an inadequate basis for moral responsibility. If our actions are uncaused, then they are merely chance occurrences—lacking *any* explanation. Occurrences of this kind would "just happen," rather than being brought about or produced by some cause. However, actions that just happen cannot be attributed to an agent or to anyone or anything else. Moreover, the effectiveness of rewards and punishments—which are essential to moral life and society—depends on the fact that these motives *cause* agents to act in some ways and not others. Accordingly, it is evident that freedom understood in terms of "indifference" would make both morality and society impossible (Hume, *Treatise*: 411; *Enquiry*: 98; Ayer: 18).

Empiricist-compatibilist concern with the efficaciousness of rewards and punishments indicates that there are important (historical) links between this strategy and utilitarian moral theory. This linkage is apparent in the work of both Hobbes and Hume, but it is especially clear in the work of Schlick (who was a leading member of the Vienna Circle). According to Schlick, all concern with "backward-looking" considerations such as *desert* and *retribution* is based on a combination of metaphysical confusion and a primitive desire for vengeance (compare Hobbes, *Works* IV: 255–56). Responsibility, however, should be understood in terms of the efficaciousness of praise and blame, rewards and punishments, with a view to altering an agent's conduct in socially desirable ways. These sorts of (forward-looking) considerations, it is argued, explain the general rationale of excusing considerations. The reason we do not condemn or punish individuals who act in ignorance or accidentally or who are mentally disabled or disturbed is that in these circumstances these practices are ineffective and thus unjustified.

Although Hume is generally regarded as the leading representative of classical compatibilism, his own strategy differs from it in important respects. On the classical interpretation, Hume's effort to "reconcile" liberty and necessity is essentially *conceptual* in nature. That is, Hume is understood to be primarily concerned to remove certain "verbal" obstacles regarding the meaning of (the terms) "liberty" and "necessity"—obstacles that stand in the path of his (independent) project of a "science of man." Although this understanding of Hume's intentions has been widely accepted and hugely influential, it nevertheless overlooks the most interesting and important aspect of his general strategy—and in doing so misrepresents the nature of his arguments. More specifically, Hume was concerned to *describe* the circumstances under which people are *felt* to be responsible (this was a particularly important aspect of his "science of man"). The key element in this account is the workings of moral sentiment. The moral sentiments, Hume holds, operate according to the more general principles of the mechanism of the indirect passions (e.g., love and hate). Hume's account of the way in which "liberty" and "necessity" are essential to ascriptions of responsibility must be understood within the framework of his naturalistic account of how the moral sentiments are generated. For this reason his "reconciliation" strategy needs to be interpreted in terms of his naturalistic commitments, rather than in terms of conceptual analysis.

The naturalistic interpretation of Hume's compatibilism brings his position much closer to the recent influential work of P. F. Strawson on this subject ("Freedom and Resentment") and distinguishes it sharply from the more orthodox line of Hobbes and Schlick. Hume's naturalistic approach suggests that a proper understanding of the "free will" problem must be grounded in a more adequate (empirical) account of the role of human emotion in this sphere. This contrasts with the classical strategy's emphasis on the conceptual analysis of "freedom" as the basis of any adequate account of the conditions of moral responsibility. However, although Hume's naturalism suggests an approach that is quite distinct from the classical strategy, it nevertheless remains faithful to empiricism's more general antilibertarian and compatibilist orientation.

The critical issue that separates compatibilists and incompatibilists was well captured by Hobbes in the following terse statement: "Again the whole question of free-will is included in this, 'Whether the will determine itself?' " (*Works* V: 4). Hobbes maintained that the notion of free *will* (i.e., a person having the power to determine his own will, as opposed to freedom to act according to its dictates) was *absurd* (compare *Works* V: 450–51). Moral freedom is nothing more than freedom of *action*; it does not require any further (incoherent) notion of free *will*. Two of the great attractions of this position are its simplicity and the (apparent) clarity of its metaphysical commitments. The position, however, suffers from a number of well-known difficulties. Contemporary compatibilists, for example, generally acknowledge that the classical "solution" fails to account for the sort of "freedom" that distinguishes rational, responsible adults from children and animals. Similarly, it is widely recognized that it is necessary to account for "internal barriers" to moral freedom and responsibility (e.g., compulsive desires). In light of these deficiencies in the classical "solution," contemporary compatibilists generally agree that the most pressing task at present is to explain how agents can be said to be in control of their character and will in a way that is consistent with a naturalistic and necessitarian framework (compare Dennett, *Elbow Room*). These developments in contemporary compatibilism—along with efforts to naturalize our understanding of moral responsibility (i.e., in the manner suggested by Hume and Strawson)—certainly constitute a sophisticated advance in the general position. However, they in no way abandon traditional empiricist doubts about the metaphysics of libertarianism, nor do they in any way compromise the more fundamental commitment to compatibilism itself.

PRIMARY WORKS

Books

The Questions concerning Liberty, Necessity, and Chance (1656). In *The English Works of Thomas Hobbes*, 11 vols., edited by W. Molesworth. London: Bohn, 1839–1845; vol. 5.

Hume, David. *An Enquiry concerning Human Understanding*. In *Enquiries concerning Human Understanding and concerning the Principles of Morals*, edited with an analytical index by L. A. Selby-Bigge; revised with notes by P. H. Nidditch. Oxford: Clarendon Press, 1975.

———. *A Treatise of Human Nature*. 2d ed., edited with an analytical index by L. A. Selby-Bigge; revised with notes by P. H. Nidditch. Oxford: Clarendon Press, 1978.

Locke, John. *An Essay concerning Human Understanding*. Edited with an introduction by P. H. Nidditch. Oxford: Clarendon Press, 1975.

Mill, John Stuart. *A System of Logic*. 8th ed. London: Longmans, Green, 1898.

Russell, Bertrand. "On the Notion of Cause." In *Mysticism and Logic and Other Essays*, 2d ed. London: Allen and Unwin, 1917.

Schlick, Moritz. *The Problems of Ethics* (1930). Translated by David Rynin. New York: Dover, 1962.

Articles

Ayer, A. J. "Freedom and Necessity" (1954). In *Free Will*, edited by Gary Watson. Oxford: Oxford University Press, 1982.

Hobbes, Thomas. "Of Liberty and Necessity" (1646). In *The English Works of Thomas Hobbes*, 11 vols., edited by W. Molesworth. London: Bohn, 1839–1845, vol. 4: 229–78.

BIBLIOGRAPHY

Books

Dennett, Daniel. *Elbow Room: The Varieties of Free Will Worth Wanting*. Oxford: Clarendon Press, 1984.

Honderich, Ted. *How Free Are You?: The Determinism Problem*. New York and Oxford: Oxford University Press, 1993.

Russell, Paul. *Freedom and Moral Sentiment: Hume's Way of Naturalizing Responsibility*. New York and Oxford: Oxford University Press, 1995.

Article

Strawson, P. F. "Freedom and Resentment." In *Free Will*, edited by Gary Watson. Oxford: Oxford University Press, 1982.

PAUL RUSSELL

G

GALILEI, GALILEO. If we are to characterize Galileo Galilei (1564–1642) as an empiricist, it must be done without his blessing. It is important to recognize that "empiricism" and "empiricist" are terms he did not recognize and would not know how to parse. As a philosophical stance, empiricism was not a fully developed and recognized position in late sixteenth- and early seventeenth-century Italy. So, in attempting to view him in these clothes we must acknowledge a full-blown case of Whig historiography.

Galileo's empiricism was fairly basic. Out of his methodological pronouncements we can construct two principles, articulated most prominently in three works: *The Assayer*, *Dialogue on Two Chief World Systems*, and *Two New Sciences*, with the *Dialogue* being the primary methodological text. One principle proclaims the superiority of observation to dogmatic assertion. Galileo also has two corollaries to this reliance on observation. The first is a criterion of evidential uniformity. All observations are to be understood in terms of terrestrial phenomena. This is essential in order for him to reject the classic two-sphere Aristotelian universe with its various kinds of objects in different domains. The second corollary is his rejection of appeals to occult causes. Galileo was so opposed to explanatory accounts that invoked unobservable causes that it is sometimes possible to read him as rejecting causal explanations of any type. In the end, this is too strong a position to impose on him, for he did allow causal explanations, but not Aristotelian ones with their appeals to many different kinds of causes. For Galileo, "ultimately one single true and primary cause must hold good for effects which are similar in kind" (*Opere* VII: 444). Further, his rejection of occult causes for purposes of explanation is highlighted by his own characteristic explanatory maneuver, which was to construct a diagram and then interpret it in terms of a readily observable everyday set of phenomena.

A second principle, however, can be considered equally basic for purposes of exploring Galileo's empiricism. For Galileo the fundamental feature of that form of knowledge that we will eventually come to call science is mathematics.

In fact, the main thrust of his argument in the *Dialogue* is to reject discursive first principles in favor of mathematical demonstrations. This case is most forcefully presented in *Two New Sciences*, where the quantificational move is cashed out in terms of measurement. The emphasis on measurement is consistent with his rejection of occult causes and his reliance on commonsense observation.

It might appear possible to reject the view that Galileo is a protoempiricist, especially in light of his notorious comments on the Book of Nature:

Philosophy is written in this grand book—I mean the universe—which stands continually open to our gaze, but it cannot be understood unless one first learns to comprehend the language and interpret the characters in which it is written. It is written in the language of mathematics, and its characters are triangles, circles, and other geometrical figures. (Drake and O'Malley 1960: 183–84; *Opere* VI: 232)

Here, however, Galileo is merely emphasizing the importance of mathematics for the doing of science. Our focus should be on his insistence on the need to interpret the characters in which the language of the universe is written. He is not claiming that there are no stars, only mathematical characters. Rather, he argues here and elsewhere that to understand the universe one must use mathematics. This in itself does not sound much like empiricism. But when coupled with his insistence that what gets quantified is what is observable, we have the nub of a stark but classic empiricism and the prelude to modern science.

PRIMARY WORK

Le Opere. Edited by Antonio Favaro. 20 vols. Florence: Barbera, 1890–1909.

BIBLIOGRAPHY

Clavelin, M. *The Natural Philosophy of Galileo; Essay on the Origin and Formation of Classical Mechanics*. Translated by A. J. Pomerans. Cambridge and London: MIT Press, 1974. First published in French by Librairie Armand Colin, 1968.

Drake, S. *Galileo at Work*. Chicago: University of Chicago Press, 1978.

Drake, S., and C. D. O'Malley, eds. and trans. *The Controversy of the Comets of 1618*. Philadelphia: University of Pennsylvania Press, 1960.

Pitt, J. C. *Galileo and the Book of Nature; Method Replaces Metaphysics*. Dordrecht: Kluwer, 1992.

Wallace, W. A. *Galileo and His Sources; The Heritage of the Collegio Romano in Galileo's Science*. Princeton: Princeton University Press, 1984.

JOSEPH C. PITT

GASSENDI, PIERRE. Pierre Gassendi (1592–1655), French philosopher and scientist, advocate of Epicurean atomism, and the principal adversary of Descartes in his time, was the first modern empiricist. Gassendi was born on January 22, 1592, in Champtercier, a village in Provence. He entered the College of Digne (1519), then the University of Aix (1609), and was appointed professor of rhetoric at Digne by the age of twenty-one. In 1614, he received his doctorate of theology from Avignon and was appointed canon of the church of Notre Dame du Bourg in Digne; he was ordained a priest two years later.

In 1615, Gassendi took his first trip to Paris, and, for the remainder of his life, his time was divided about equally between Paris and Provence. He held the chair of philosophy at Aix from 1617 until 1623, when the Jesuits acquired control of the university. His lectures at Aix provided the foundation for his first publication, *Exercitationes Paradoxicae Adversus Aristoteleos* (Grenoble, 1624). This was planned as a work in seven books, but only two were ever written, and only the first book, which is largely a polemic against Aristotelian philosophy (especially seventeenth-century scholasticism), was published in Gassendi's lifetime. While teaching at Aix, Gassendi lodged with astronomer Joseph Gaultier, and he met Nicolaus-Claude Fabri de Peiresc, who became, until his death in 1637, Gassendi's patron, friend, and associate. Gassendi published a groundbreaking intellectual biography of Peiresc in 1641. Peiresc and Gaultier inspired Gassendi's lifelong interest in astronomy and, with this, his commitment to the fundamental role of observation and experiment in science.

During a visit to Paris in 1625, Gassendi began a lifelong friendship with Marin Mersenne, who, like Gassendi, was an enthusiastic supporter of the scientific work of GALILEO. Mersenne was the center of the most important circle of progressive thinkers and scientists of the time, including Galileo, HOBBES, Henry More, Fermat, PASCAL, Descartes, and Gassendi. At the urging of Mersenne, Gassendi wrote a study attacking Robert Fludd's "Mosaic" philosophy; and it is probably also at the request of Mersenne that Gassendi wrote a much admired refutation of the claims of astrology. Finally, Mersenne solicited the objections published with the second edition of Descartes' *Meditations,* together with Descartes' responses. The author of the fifth and arguably the most important set of objections was Gassendi. Descartes' contemptuous response to Gassendi's objections led Gassendi to publish in 1644 a greatly expanded version of his original objections, the *Disquisitio Metaphysica,* which at once became the basic source of arguments for opponents of Cartesian metaphysics.

Gassendi, after a variety of publications in astronomy and physics, was, in 1645, appointed to the chair of mathematics (actually, astronomy) at the College Royal in Paris, but a recurring pulmonary illness, dating from 1639, forced his return to the milder climate of Provence in 1648. In the last years of his life Gassendi published the Epicurean philosophy that he had been developing since 1627. In 1647, he published an influential work on the life and morality of EPICURUS, defending Epicurus from attacks on his character, and in 1649 appeared the massive *Animadversiones in Decimum Librum Diogenis Laertii,* which contains the text, translation, and an extended commentary on Diogenes Laertius' *Life of Epicurus* and, in addition, gathers together the results of the more than twenty years that Gassendi had devoted to the development of his Epicurean philosophy. Particularly noteworthy in this work is the atomistic physics that Gassendi developed using Epicurean principles. Published as an appendix to this work was the *Syntagma Philosophiae Epicuri,* a rational reconstruction of Epicurus' philosophy, perhaps the first work in this genre. The *Animadversiones* was to be the basis for the posthumously published *Syntagma*

Philosophicum, a work encyclopedic in scope and systematic in structure, covering the whole of philosophy as it was at that time understood. Gassendi, dividing philosophy into logic, physics, and ethics, as Epicurus had, gives a wide range of opinions on each subject, drawing principally on classical sources, and from this foundation he develops his own position.

During Gassendi's last visit to Paris (beginning in April 1653), he resided with Henri-Louis Habert de Montmor, a member of the French Academy, and, with the aid of a disciple, Samuel Sorbiere, he worked on his *Syntagma Philosophicum*. After a serious illness and treatment by frequent blcedings, Gassendi died on October 24, 1655.

AGAINST THE DOGMATISTS

In his early work attacking ARISTOTLE, Gassendi's empiricist tendencies are already evident. In this work, Gassendi attacks Aristotelian disputation or argumentation as useless for the discovery of truth, claiming instead that experience alone can lead us to truth. But, Gassendi here claims, we can acquire truth only about appearances, for with respect to ESSENCES or the real nature of things, as the skeptics maintain, we have no knowledge at all.

Gassendi's empiricism is further developed in his writings against Descartes. Gassendi argues against the Cartesian criterion of truth, according to which we can have knowledge of the real nature of things by clear and distinct IDEAS. He denies that any ideas are innate (see INNATENESS), holding instead that ideas are either derived directly from sense or formed from other ideas that themselves are derived directly from sense. He rejects Descartes' ontological argument for the existence of GOD, arguing that existence is neither a perfection nor a property, so that a being with all perfections does not, on that account, have to exist. KANT is usually thought to have been the first to have offered this criticism of the ontological argument. What Gassendi takes to be evidence for the existence of God is the presence in the world of purpose or design. Against Descartes, who argues that animals are mere automata, Gassendi argues that there is evidence that animals have cognitive powers similar to those of human beings, and he even claims for animals some rudimentary powers of reasoning. Finally, he denies the Cartesian view that mind is a SUBSTANCE whose nature it is to think, holding that we have no knowledge of the real nature of mind. He contends that Descartes does not show that mind cannot be some sort of subtle matter (like a vapor animating the whole body) or perhaps the brain, which controls the body.

SCIENTIFIC OBSERVATION AND EXPERIMENT

Gassendi recorded observations, between 1618 and 1655, of, for example, satellites of Jupiter, the moon's surface, sunspots, and eclipses. His most significant contribution was his 1631 observation of the transit of Mercury across the sun, which confirmed a prediction made by Kepler in 1629 and which showed that Mercury was about one-fifteenth of the magnitude that it was expected to be, a finding that inspired the seventeenth-century recalculation of the sizes of the planets.

In addition to being a keen observer of astronomical phenomena, Gassendi was an avid experimentalist. He was the first to publish a correct version of the law of inertia, and he supported this by an experiment of dropping a lead ball from the top of the mast of a ship to its base, demonstrating that in addition to its downward motion, the ball in free fall also has a forward motion, corresponding to the motion of the ship when the ball was released. Apart from conducting this dramatic experiment, Gassendi took part in anatomical demonstrations, conducted dissections, and studied the movement of the blood and the structure and functions of the eye; he examined the formation and dissolution of crystals and the nature of color, fossils, salt water, and springs. Finally, Gassendi was the originator of the term "molecule," which concept enabled him to provide an atomistic foundation for chemical phenomena and to thereby make an important contribution to the development of modern chemical theory.

GASSENDI'S MIDDLE WAY

Gassendi's early SKEPTICISM with regard to our knowledge of the nature of things gives way in his mature writings to a search for a middle ground between skepticism and dogmatism. If truth is the goal of logic, but Aristotelian disputation does not lead to truth, and there are no Cartesian clear and distinct ideas to reveal it to us, how may any truth about the nature of things be known? Gassendi's mature view is that truth of this sort can be known by a sign. A sign is something perceptible by sense, through which what is hidden from sense may be known. Of course, we have no guarantee that things grasped in this way are as we suppose them to be. Knowledge by signs is not infallible, but, Gassendi believes, this is the only kind of knowledge we have. There are two kinds of signs. An empirical sign points to the presence of something temporarily hidden, as smoke indicates the presence of fire; an indicative sign reveals the presence of something naturally hidden, something that cannot be directly perceived by our senses, as we know by perspiration that there are pores in the skin. Also by indicative signs we know of atoms, the void or space, and other things not directly perceptible by sense. This is not skepticism, since by indicative signs, we do acquire some knowledge about the nature of things; nor is it dogmatism, since it is always possible that a belief supported by an indicative sign may be mistaken. This middle way between skepticism and dogmatism is fallibilism, a position Gassendi seems to have been the first to articulate. Ideas, insofar as they are capable of leading us to truth, are indicative signs. Truth, insofar as it can be attained, can be reached only by way of ideas.

THE EPICUREAN CANONS

Gassendi's empiricism has its source in his reconstruction of the Epicurean canonic. The canonic, derived from Epicurus and other ancient sources, is a series of rules concerned with KNOWLEDGE, MEANING, and truth. The canonic was intended by Epicurus as a substitute for the logic of Aristotle and the Stoics (see STOICISM), but Gassendi makes it the basis for a logic of his own. Aristotle and most Aristotelians take an empiricist position in maintaining that there is nothing in the intellect that was not first in sense, but at the same time they hold that an opinion can be shown to be true only by deriving it from first principles or first truths. The Epicurean canonic recognizes no first truths, tracing our knowledge of truth to experience alone.

The first set of canons or rules, as represented by Gassendi, are the canons of sense. These explain the empiricist criterion of truth. According to the first of these canons, sense is never mistaken, since it neither affirms nor denies anything; truth and falsity, properly speaking, pertain only to opinions, in which something is either affirmed or denied. An opinion or judgment is something that is added to sensation and that is capable of truth and falsity (Canon II). Canon III states that an opinion is true if supported by sense, either directly or indirectly; and Canon IV states that an opinion is false if directly or indirectly opposed by sense. What is not directly known by sense can be known by reasoning, as we infer the existence of atoms. So there are two criteria of truth, sense and REASON. But still all our knowledge of truth derives ultimately from the senses.

What has been perceived by sense produces an image in the mind. These images provide a conceptual framework for the apprehension of future perceptions, for which reason they may be called anticipations of PERCEPTION or prenotions. They are what Gassendi calls ideas. There is a group of four canons concerned with ideas. The first asserts that ideas are images that are derived directly from sense impressions or else are formed from these by increase or diminution (as we acquire the idea of a giant or pygmy), by composition (as we obtain the idea of a golden mountain), or by analogy (as we form the idea of a town we have never seen from one we have). The second canon holds that the idea is the very notion of a thing, fundamental to its definition, and that without an idea, we cannot inquire about, think about, or even name anything. The last two canons concerning ideas spell out the connection of ideas with logic. The third asserts that the idea is what is fundamental in all reasoning, and so in logic. It is what we consider when we infer that one thing is the same as another or different, joined to another or separated from it. Finally, the fourth canon affirms that what is not directly evident to sense must be demonstrated from the idea of something that is evident to sense, as the observation of perspiration on the skin enables us to infer the existence of pores. The canonic may be seen as a kind of blueprint for an empiricist logic, and that is just the kind of logic that Gassendi was to develop.

THE LOGIC OF IDEAS

Gassendi, in his *Institutio Logica*, a late work, first published in the posthumous *Opera Omnia* of 1658, defines logic as *ars bene cogitandi*, the art of thinking well. Thinking well involves the following four skills: imagining well, that is, forming correct images or ideas of things; posing propositions well, that is, advancing propositions that are correct; inferring well; and ordering well. Accordingly, logic is divided into four parts: the first concerns simple apprehension by means of images or ideas; the second, propositions; the third, syllogism; and the fourth, method. This was a new form of logic, the logic of ideas, based on a theory of the nature, origin, and formation of ideas. It was to be the model for the *Port-Royal Logic*, through which the logic of ideas would become the dominant form of logic for more than a century.

Gassendi's theory of ideas is in Part I of the *Institutio Logica*, entitled "Of the Simple Imagination of Things." Simple IMAGINATION, Gassendi explains, is a form of simple apprehension, by corporeal images, of a thing without anything affirmed or denied of it. As there can be falsehood only when something is affirmed or denied, the simple imagination of things cannot be false. It is the simple imagination of a thing that Gassendi calls its idea.

The idea of a thing, Gassendi tells us, is genuine, legitimate, and true when it conforms to the thing itself. This is not the thing as it really is in itself; for, Gassendi holds, its real nature is not known to us. What we want are ideas that will correctly represent things as our senses apprehend them. Also to represent things correctly, we want them to be as clear and distinct as possible, and the more frequent, recent, and striking are the experiences we have of a thing, the more clear and distinct is the idea we form of it likely to be. A Cartesian clear and distinct idea guarantees that the idea we have of a thing represents that thing as it really is in itself; a Gassendist clear and distinct idea represents only the thing as we sense it.

Gassendi, following Epicurus, maintains that sense perception is the original source of all our ideas. Sense perception is caused by an external object that affects a sense organ, nerves, and brain and thereby produces a double effect: a *species impressa*, an impression described as a trace or fold in the brain; and a *species expressa*, the awareness associated with that trace or fold. Further, Gassendi distinguishes native or primary qualities—for example, of magnitude, figure, weight, and motion—which are real qualities of things, from affective or secondary qualities, such as color, sound, odor, and savor, which are nothing other than ways that combinations of atoms are able to affect sense organs.

The mind is a tabula rasa on which nothing has been engraved or depicted, Gassendi says, and those who hold that there are ideas that are naturally imprinted or innate, not acquired by sense, do not at all prove what they say. In support of the view that all our ideas originate in sensation, Gassendi offers the following inductive argument: blind men have no idea of color, and deaf men no idea of sound; so if there could be a person with no senses at all, that person would have no ideas either. Similar arguments are given by LOCKE, HUME, and other empiricists. Gassendi goes further than most empiricists, however, in holding that even necessary truths must be discovered to be true by experience.

Principles such as "the whole is greater than the part" come to be believed not because they are necessary but because, one by one, we have observed that a whole man is greater than his head, a whole house is greater than a room, a whole forest is greater than a tree, the whole sky is greater than a star, and so forth.

In addition to ideas acquired directly by sensation, ideas can be formed from ideas we already have by increase or diminution, composition, analogy, or similitude, as Epicurus had maintained and as Locke later also claims. Ideas of incorporeals, such as God, according to Gassendi, are always analogical. Thus, we form the idea of God from the image of some such thing as a grand old man or a blinding light. We do not, of course, believe that he is any of these things, only that in some respects he is like them.

Gassendi, as a nominalist (see NOMINALISM), holds that whatever exists is singular, and consequently any idea derived directly from sense will be singular as well. Yet he maintains that we can form general ideas and, in fact, that we can do so in two ways, by collection and by ABSTRACTION. Collection is putting together the ideas of many similar things and so forming the idea of the collection to which they belong; abstraction is comparing a group of similar ideas, determining what features they have in common, and, disregarding differences between them, constructing a separate idea of the common features. The idea is general, since it represents the features that a group of singular ideas shares. Once general ideas have been formed, others still more general can be formed from these in the same two ways; and by proceeding in this manner, we ultimately reach the most general idea of all, that of being. Irrational animals, Gassendi believes, can form ideas of collections of things; they cannot, however, form general ideas by abstraction.

GASSENDI'S INFLUENCE

Gassendi was influential through his disciples and through his works, as a humanist, scientist, and philosopher. François Bernier, a follower of Gassendi, translated substantial portions of Gassendi's *Syntagma Philosophicum* into French in his seven-volume *Abregé de la Philosophie de Gassendi*. There were early English translations of Gassendi's Epicurean *Syntagma*, his ethics, his life of Peiresc, and his writings against astrology. His views on physics, physiology, and psychology were propagated in many works by Walter Charleton, an English physician, who was the principal proponent of Gassendism in England. His physiology and his views on the soul were promoted also by the English physician Thomas Willis, while the antidogmatic strain in Gassendi's work is represented by the English divine Joseph Glanvill. The first book of the Logic of the *Syntagma Philosophicum*, on the "Origin and Varieties of Logic," was recognized as a pioneering work by historians of logic with humanist inclinations, and Thomas Stanley credits the very extensive historical material incorporated in Gassendi's *Animadversiones* as his chief inspiration in his highly influential work, *The History of Philosophy*. Robert BOYLE developed Gassendi's molecular theory and was a champion of the approach to natural religion for which Gassendi had argued. Gassendi's atomism provided the ontological foundation for Newtonian physics.

John Locke, who had been an associate of Robert Boyle, had carefully read works by Charleton and Willis and had studied medicine under Willis at Oxford. He had also read Gassendi directly—there are passages from Gassendi's *Physics* in early notebooks of Locke. Leibniz says of Locke that he accepts the system of Gassendi, and it was indeed taken for granted until the end of the eighteenth century that Locke was heavily indebted to Gassendi. Recently, with the revival of interest in Gassendi after more than a century of neglect, some have questioned whether Locke had any familiarity with Gassendi's logic. This much is clear, however: virtually every canon in Part I of the *Institutio Logica*, which constitutes Gassendi's theory of ideas, is found in Locke's *Essay concerning Human Understanding* in some form or other.

The logic of ideas, which Gassendi originated, had a long and fruitful career, taking many different forms, including, for instance, the Cartesian *Port-Royal Logic*, the Lockean logic of Jean LeClerc, and the Leibnizian logic of Christian Wolff. In the influential anti-Aristotelian eighteenth-century philosophy of Antonio Genovese, obviously under the influence of Gassendi, Epicurus is portrayed as a more trustworthy guide in logic than Aristotle.

The late seventeenth-century *Novantiqua* movement sought to incorporate Gassendist or Cartesian elements into a basically Aristotelian framework. Eclectics, before Kant, sought a reconciliation between the Cartesian, Gassendist, and Aristotelian approaches. The roots of British empiricism, modern atomism, and fallibilism are in Gassendi. But Gassendi was to be eclipsed by those who developed what he had begun. Still, his writings constitute a treasure trove of material of inestimable value for his age and subsequent philosophy, a source of fruitful leads for later ages to explore.

PRIMARY WORKS

Disquisitio Metaphysica. Amsterdam: apud J. Blaeu, 1644; edited and translated by Bernard Rochot as Recherches métaphysiques. Paris: J. Vrin, 1962.

Opera Omnia. 6 vols. Lyons, 1658. Photoreproduction, Stuttgart, 1964.

Syntagma Philosophiae Epicuri (1649). Translated into English in Thomas Stanley's *The History of Philosophy*, vol. 3, London: n.s., 1660.

Abregé de la philosophie de Gassendi. 7 vols. Edited by François Bernier. Paris: Jacques Langlois, 1674; new edition, edited by S. Murr and G. Stefani. Paris: Fayard, 1992.

The Selected Works of Pierre Gassendi. Edited and translated by C. B. Brush. New York and London: Johnson Reprint, 1972.

Pierre Gassendi's "Institutio Logica." Translated by Howard Jones. Assen, the Netherlands: Van Gorcum, 1981.

BIBLIOGRAPHY

Books

Bloch, Olivier-René. *La Philosophie de Gassendi: nominalisme, matérialisme et méta-physique*. The Hague: Martinus Nijhoff, 1971. Extensive bibliography.

Brundell, Barry. *Pierre Gassendi: From Aristotelianism to a New Natural Philosophy*. Dordrecht: D. Reidel, 1987.

Jones, Howard. *Pierre Gassendi, 1592–1655: An Intellectual Biography*. Nieuwkoop: B. DeGraaf, 1981.

Joy, Lynn Sumida. *Gassendi the Atomist, Advocate of History in an Age of Science*. Cambridge: Cambridge University Press, 1987.

Lennon, Thomas M. *The Battle of the Gods and Giants: The Legacies of Descartes and Gassendi, 1655–1715*. Princeton: Princeton University Press, 1993.

Osler, Margaret J. *Divine Will and the Mechanical Philosophy: Gassendi and Descartes on Contingency and Necessity*. Cambridge: Cambridge University Press, 1994.

Pintard, René. *Le Libertinage érudit dans la premiere moitié du XVIIe siecle*. Paris: Boivin, 1943.

Puster, Rolf W. *Britische Gassendi-Rezeption am Beispiel John Lockes*. Stuttgart: Frommann-Holzboog, 1991.

Collections of Articles

Corpus, no. 20/21, *Bernier et les gassendistes*, mis en oeuvre par Sylvia Murr, 1992.

Pierre Gassendi, 1592–1655, sa vie et son oeuvre. Centre international de synthèse. Paris: A. Michel, 1955.

Pierre Gassendi 1592–1655, 2 vols. Société Scientifique et Litteraire des Alpes de Haute-Provence. Digne-Les-Bains, 1994.

Articles

Glidden, David K. "Hellenistic Background for Gassendi's Theory of Ideas." *Journal of the History of Ideas* 49 (1988): 405–24.

Kroll, Richard W. F. "The Question of Locke's Relation to Gassendi." *Journal of the History of Ideas* 45 (1984): 341–59.

Michael, Fred S., and Emily Michael. "Hierarchy and Early Empiricism." *Anti-Foundationalism Old and New*. Philadelphia: Temple University Press, 1991: 85–104.

———. "The Theory of Ideas in Gassendi and Locke." *Journal of the History of Ideas* 51 (1990): 379–99.

EMILY MICHAEL and FREDERICK S. MICHAEL

GOD. A belief in a supernatural Deity, often with the characteristics of omniscience, omnipotence, omnibenevolence, infinitude, and so on, is central to a RELIGION. Three of the predominant proofs for the existence of such a Deity, or God, are the ontological, the cosmological, and the teleological.

The ontological argument purports to prove God's existence from the idea of God a priori (See A PRIORI/A POSTERIORI DISTINCTION). Anselm, an eleventh-century monk, argued that what we mean by "the Deity" is the Greatest Conceivable Being. Such a being that exists in reality is greater than one that exists only in the understanding, so in order to be the Greatest Conceivable Being, such a being must necessarily exist in reality. For René Descartes, the seventeenth-century rationalist, God's existence cannot be separated from God's nature, just as three-sidedness cannot be separated from a triangle or a mountain from a valley.

The cosmological and teleological arguments, on the other hand, proceed a posteriori, grounded in facts in and about the world. The cosmological argument begins with the fact that the universe exists at all, and the teleological argument draws inferences from the universe as an effect that exhibits certain features to its cause and the nature of that cause.

These arguments are found in St. Thomas AQUINAS' (1225–1274) Five Ways, or proofs of God's existence (although elements of these proofs may be found in Plato and ARISTOTLE). They begin with the empirical fact that the universe exists and, from given certain known facts about that existence, prove the existence of God. The cosmological argument is the basis of four of the Five Ways: that there is motion in the world shows there must be an Unmoved Mover; causal chains prove an Uncaused Cause; the contingency of the world leads to a necessary Being; and varying goodness in the world leads to an all-good being.

Aquinas' fifth way is the teleological argument, or Argument from Design, that the orderly character of worldly events entails the existence of an intelligent Orderer. Found also in Cicero's *De Natura Deorum* (The Nature of the Gods) and William Paley's *Natural Theology*, this argument is given its fullest expression and criticism in David HUME's *Dialogues concerning Natural Religion*. In this text, the Argument from Design is presented by Cleanthes, who urges us to look to the world for evidence of God's existence and nature. As the world resembles machines of human design, in that they exhibit similar features of means-to-ends relations and coherence of parts, and as we know that such machines have intelligent designers, we can infer by "all the rules of analogy" that the world has a similarly intelligent designer. A second formulation shows that as order in humanly designed objects has only, from our experience, come about from the work of a mind (e.g., bits of steel will never come together without the intervention of a mind to form a watch), so too the order in the divinely designed object—the world—has come about from the work of a mind.

In either formulation, this argument has several consequences; for example, because it concludes similarity of causes from similarity of effects, it should conclude that the divine mind is just like a human mind, "only much greater in proportion to the grandeur of the work." This anthropomorphic (as resembling humans) Deity must be limited as humans are in power, knowledge, and so on, in proportion to the known effects. Much of our experience of humanly designed objects is that they are the work of teams of designers, so the data do not justify an inference to a unitary designer of the world. Also, as the inference is being made from effects to causes, no more can be inferred in the cause than can be found in the effect. The inference cannot be made from finite order to an infinite orderer or from a world that contains evil to a Deity who is free of evil.

This conclusion is drawn so eloquently by Hume:

[I]t must evidently appear contrary to all rules of analogy to reason, from the intentions and projects of men, to those of a Being so different, and so much superior. In human nature, there is a certain experienced coherence of designs and inclinations; so that when, from any fact, we have discovered one intention of any man, it may often be reasonable, from experience, to infer another, and draw a long chain of conclusions concerning his past or future conduct. But this method of reasoning can never have place with regard to a Being, so remote and incomprehensible, who bears much less analogy to any other being in the universe than the sun to a waxen taper, and who discovers himself only by some faint traces or outlines, beyond which we have no authority to ascribe to him any attribute or perfection. (*An Enquiry concerning Human Understanding*: 146)

While George BERKELEY claims that the harmony and contrivance in the works of nature convince us of the Deity's attributes (*Principles of Human Knowledge* §§62–63, §151), he argues to God's existence by considering the existence of the sensible world. As a response to the materialism of LOCKE that leaves no room for God in the world, Berkeley wished to turn our minds back to God by making the Deity, not matter, the cause of our perceptual experience. There are two main aspects to Berkeley's argument. First, perceptions can be caused only by a mind, but our sensory ideas are not produced by, nor are they dependent on, the wills of human perceivers. As an idea cannot be caused by another idea (since only minds have agency) but can be caused only by a mind, there is some other mind that causes them, the infinite mind of God. Second, as existence is to be found only in a mind, the only assurance we have that objects continue to exist when they are not being perceived by a finite (human) mind lies in their continuing to be perceived (and thus to exist) in the infinite (divine) mind. God is thus central to our lives: "That in God we live and move and have our being" (*Three Dialogues between Hylas and Philonous*).

PRIMARY WORKS

Aquinas, St. Thomas. *Summa Theologica*. New York: Benziger Brothers, 1947–1948.

Berkeley, George. *The Works of George Berkeley, Bishop of Cloyne*. Edited by A. A. Luce and T. E. Jessop. 9 vols. London: Thomas Nelson and Sons, 1948–1957.

Cicero. *De Natura Deorum* (*The Nature of the Gods*). New York: Hammondsworth Penguin, 1972.

Hume, David. *Dialogues concerning Natural Religion*. Edited by S. Tweyman. London: Routledge, 1992.

———. *An Enquiry concerning Human Understanding*. In *Enquiries concerning Human Understanding and concerning the Principles of Morals*, edited with an analytical index by L. A. Selby-Bigge; revised with notes by P. H. Nidditch. Oxford: Clarendon Press, 1975.

Locke, John. *An Essay concerning Human Understanding*. Edited with an introduction by P. H. Nidditch. Oxford: Clarendon Press, 1975.

Paley, William. *Natural Theology, Evidence for the Existence and Attributes of the Deity.* Farnborough: Gregg International, 1970.

BERYL LOGAN

GÖDEL, KURT. Kurt Gödel (1906–1978) was a mathematical logician of the first rank and a member of the Vienna Circle of logical positivists (see LOGICAL POSITIVISM). He established a number of important theorems, including the completeness of first-order logic, the incompleteness of higher-order logic (including arithmetic), and the consistency of the axiom of choice and of the continuum hypothesis. What is important in each case is not only the theorem that was proved but Gödel's invention of new techniques of proof that turned out to be powerful tools in the subsequent development of logic and mathematics. The proof that had the most important impact on empiricism was the proof of the incompleteness of arithmetic.

Gottlob Frege and Bertrand RUSSELL hoped to establish that arithmetic was free from any of the sort of contradictions that had previously been discovered by philosophers such as BERKELEY in the foundations of analysis but eliminated in the nineteenth century. To this end, Frege and Russell proposed to deduce arithmetic from the fundamental truths of LOGIC. They translated Peano's axioms for arithmetic into set theory and succeeded in deducing these from logic or, at least, as they discovered, from elementary logic supplemented by some nonelementary set-theoretical axioms, for example, the axiom of choice. This was the logicist program in the philosophy of mathematics. This program was adopted by many empiricists, particularly the logical positivists of the Vienna Circle. Among these was one of the founders of the circle, the mathematician Hans Hahn; Gödel was his student. These philosophers argued that all truths of logic, now including those of arithmetic, were analytic (see ANALYTIC/SYNTHETIC DISTINCTION), vacuously true by virtue of the meanings of the terms they contain. They held that empiricism now had available what had eluded David HUME and John Stuart MILL, namely, an account of the necessity of arithmetic that was compatible with the central tenets of empiricism.

Unfortunately, although the logicist program was designed to ensure the absence of contradictions in arithmetic, Russell discovered new contradictions and paradoxes in the foundations of set theory. These paradoxes were eliminated, but only in ways that were not always intuitive and that sometimes seemed ad hoc.

D. Hilbert proposed a revised program. Mathematicians had developed proofs in geometry that established that various axiomatizations of geometrical systems were consistent. Hilbert extended this idea to arithmetic. He proposed that freedom from contradiction could be ensured if one could prove the axiomatized system of arithmetic consistent using only the weak logical principles of elementary (first-order) logic. Gödel's proof of the incompleteness of arithmetic demonstrated that this revised program for establishing the foundations of arithmetic could not be completed.

Gödel's proof established, with regard to a certain sentence **G**, that neither it nor its negation can be derived from the axioms of arithmetic. On one hand, **G** is an ordinary arithmetical sentence the truth of which is clear, as clear as, say, the statement that "two is an even number." On the other hand, by virtue of an ingenious coding system for the sentences of arithmetic that Gödel devised, **G** says about itself that it has no proof. In this way Gödel proved that there is a true sentence of arithmetic for which a proof from the axioms does not exist. He proved, moreover, that if one adds **G** to the list of axioms, making it trivially provable, then there is *another* arithmetical truth that cannot be proved from the axioms. Arithmetic is thus incomplete, in the sense that no axiomatization can capture all of its known truths.

It follows that Hilbert's aim of capturing all arithmetical statements in an axiomatic system and proving that the latter is consistent using only elementary logic cannot be fulfilled. To be sure, it can be shown that if one uses more powerful systems of logic, then consistency can be proven. But that does not achieve the aim of Hilbert's original program.

It follows from Gödel's incompleteness theorem, on the assumption that the truths of arithmetic are analytic, that the set of analytic sentences cannot be captured in an axiomatic system or, what amounts to the same, that the set of analytic truths is not exhausted by the set of *provably* analytic truths. Since the interest of mathematicians is in proofs, they immediately lost interest in the analytic.

Many philosophers, perhaps too impressed by MATHEMATICS, followed this lead. This was not true of Gödel himself. He came to reject the positivist account of analyticity and proposed a sort of Platonic view of mathematical entities—as well as the properties of, and relations among, those entities—as existing in a realm of their own outside the world of ordinary experience. This realm of entities that mathematics considers is one that is presented to us in thought as opposed to the realm that is presented to us in ordinary experience. The truths of arithmetic are necessary because they are about timeless entities.

Gödel's solution to the problem of the necessity of arithmetical truth is, however, not one that is generally acceptable to empiricists, who argue that there are no entities outside the realm of ordinary experience. They have tended to hold that such truths are somehow linguistic, as the positivists argued, or somehow truths about pure structures. But there is no consensus. In this respect, Gödel has bequeathed to empiricism a continuing problem about the nature of arithmetical truths and of the nature of their necessity.

Moreover, if Gödel is correct, then there is a sharp distinction between the analytic and the empirical (or synthetic). This was the position of earlier empiricists such as Hume and Mill, as well as the positivists of the Vienna Circle. W.V.O. QUINE has argued that if necessary truths are linguistic, as these philosophers all tended to argue, then there is no sharp distinction between the analytic and the empirical. The challenge to empiricists who wish to defend with

Gödel the analytic/empirical distinction, is to find a way of meeting Quine's challenge while not having recourse to the nonempirical metaphysics of Gödel.

PRIMARY WORKS

Book

Collected Works, 2 vols., English and German. Oxford: Oxford University Press, 1986.

Article

"Russell's Mathematical Logic." In *The Philosophy of Bertrand Russell*, edited by P. A. Schilpp. Evanston, IL: Northwestern University Press, 1944.

BIBLIOGRAPHY

Benacerraf, P., and Hilary Putnam, eds. *Philosophy of Mathematics: Selected Writings.* Englewood Cliffs, NJ: Prentice-Hall, 1964.
Russell, B. *Introductioin to Mathematical Philosophy.* London: Allen and Unwin, 1930.
Van Heijenhoort, J. *From Frege to Gödel: A Source Book in Mathematical Logic 1879–1931.* Cambridge: Harvard University Press, 1967.

FRED WILSON

GOODMAN, NELSON. Nelson Goodman (1906–   ) was born in Massachusetts. He received his undergraduate and graduate degrees from Harvard University, where C. I. Lewis was perhaps the most important influence on his studies. His doctoral thesis, "A Study of Qualities," served as the basis for his first book. Before assuming an academic position, Goodman managed an art gallery. A serious concern for art has been an abiding interest.

Goodman's philosophical writings are far-ranging, including work in epistemology, philosophy of science, philosophy of language, and aesthetics. Although most of his papers and books can stand on their own, common threads of argument, as well as commitments to NOMINALISM, constructivism, and a form of relativism, run throughout. A brief chronological summary of this follows some consideration of where and how Goodman's philosophy fits into the empiricist tradition.

Goodman's views have numerous points of contact with central empiricist doctrines. For example, Goodman rejects claims for an a priori truth (see A PRIORI/A POSTERIORI DISTINCTION), denies that KNOWLEDGE is ever certain, and insists that our hypotheses be constrained by the experiences they help organize. On more particular issues, he joins LOCKE in repudiating innate ideas, champions BERKELEY'S *New Theory of Vision*, and claims a close kinship with Hume's approach to the problem of INDUCTION (see HUME).

At the same time, it is somewhat inappropriate to label Goodman an "Empiricist." Along with QUINE, Goodman questions two of the "dogmas of empiricism": the appeal to an ANALYTIC/SYNTHETIC DISTINCTION and the presupposition of a reductionist/foundationalist relationship of theory to observation. Applying the "empiricist" label is even more misleading if it is taken to suggest that knowledge is simply a matter of experience and that the contribution of the knowing subject can be ignored. Here Goodman is closer to KANT in emphasizing the essential role played by the concepts and categories we bring to ordering our world. Unlike Kant, however, we need not, and must not, postulate a thing-in-itself. Most significantly, the schemes of interpretation that embody our contribution are neither fixed nor final. They are constantly evolving to meet new problems and expand our intellectual horizons.

Goodman's empiricism, if it is to be called that, is perhaps best seen as allied with that of the pragmatists (see PRAGMATISM). In fact, in later writings Goodman's ideas are stated in terms quite close to those of James and Dewey. Knowledge is always a matter of reconstruction—we must build on what earlier theories and schemes of organization provide. In doing so, there is no pure experiential element or given that we can rely on to constrain our hypotheses. TRUTH cannot be insightfully explained as correspondence between ideas and reality, for there is no coherent notion of "the world" independent of the constructions we impose on it. In this sense, we may be said to "make" our worlds. The plural is emphasized here to call attention to the fact that there is no single best or complete account of reality. We develop different theories for different domains and can even construct alternative acceptable theories for the same domain. Relativism holds sway; however, it is a relativism with constraints. Our theories must work. But the working of a theory, like the working of a car, is not a subjective feature determined by whim or fiat.

Goodman's first book, *The Structure of Appearance*, is both a criticism and development of CARNAP'S *Aufbau* project. In it, Goodman shows how to overcome numerous problems that had undermined earlier phenomenalist programs (see PHENOMENALISM). The book also provides a framework for doing philosophy from a constructivist perspective. Structural isomorphism is proposed as the proper criterion for definitions. The core features of this account foreshadow ideas found in later philosophical discussions of scientific reduction, the indeterminacy of translation, and the ontological status of numbers. Other parts of the book include a calculus of individuals, providing the formal mechanism for Goodman's nominalism; a calculus of simplicity for measuring the simplicity of formal systems; and an original system of psychophysical scaling.

Goodman's paper "The Problem of Counterfactual Conditionals" (reprinted with other major early papers in *Problems and Projects*) is a classic statement of the issues and has been a basis for much of the subsequent literature on the topic. The problems dealt with also served as a springboard for Goodman's own consideration of questions of lawlikeness and projectibility, topics taken up in his book *Fact, Fiction, and Forecast*. This revolutionary work brought to a head Goodman's earlier thoughts on the problem of induction, culminating in his elaboration of a "new riddle of induction." Goodman showed how for every seemingly acceptable inductive inference there were equally well supported conflicting hypotheses. Further, he argued that there was no syntactic or semantic way to distinguish the competitors. Choice among hypotheses depends on the prior use or "entrenchment" of the predicates employed. At root, inductive validity rests on habit and related pragmatic considerations like simplicity. The book provoked a firestorm of controversy, but even most of its critics now recognize that the problems and solution Goodman presented are not easily challenged.

With *Languages of Art*, Goodman began to focus more on issues of art, embedding this work in his own general theory of symbols. This book is arguably the most important attempt to develop a theory of symbols since that of PEIRCE. Moreover, the topics considered and proposals made have relevance to a host of problems in epistemology, cognitive psychology, aesthetics, and education. They have served as the guiding light for Harvard's Project Zero, a research project organized by Goodman.

A constant theme in Goodman's aesthetic writings is the cognitive nature of art. In turn, Goodman's later writings, collected in *Of Mind and Other Matters* and *Ways of Worldmaking*, have enriched and elaborated earlier doctrines. Pictures, sculpture, dance, music, and so on inform and shape our conceptions and experiences. A linguistic or propositional mode of representation is thus but one among many ways to describe our world. So the pluralism of acceptable schemes and theories is given even wider scope. Correspondence accounts of truth are further subverted, metaphor and exemplification assume a prominent role in science, and Irrealism is offered as a way to turn a deaf ear to the bankrupt blandishments of both Idealism and Realism. Our notion of ''understanding'' must be broadly reconceived to encompass nonlinguistic symbols and nonpropositional modes of thought. Finally, as elaborated in *Reconceptions in Philosophy*, constructive analyses of these varied and various forms of understanding replace traditional epistemological concerns.

Future work on the numerous issues Goodman has explored cannot help but build on his pioneering contributions.

PRIMARY WORKS

A Study of Qualities. Cambridge: Harvard University, 1941. Reprint, New York: Garland Press, 1990.
The Structure of Appearance. Cambridge: Harvard University Press, 1951.
Fact, Fiction, and Forecast. Cambridge: Harvard University Press, 1955.
Languages of Art. Indianapolis: Bobbs-Merrill, 1968.
Problems and Projects. Indianapolis: Bobbs-Merrill, 1972.
Ways of Worldmaking. Indianapolis: Hackett, 1978.
Of Mind and Other Matters. Cambridge: Harvard University Press, 1984.
(with Catherine Elgin). *Reconceptions in Philosophy and Other Arts and Sciences*. Indianapolis: Hackett, 1988.

ROBERT SCHWARTZ

H

HELMHOLTZ, HERMANN VON. Hermann von Helmholtz (1821–1894) made major contributions to physics, physiology, and sensory psychology. An early formulator of the law of the conservation of energy, he did important work in auditory physiology, and he established a theoretical framework for the physiology and psychology of color and spatial vision (see SPACE, COGNITION OF). He published lectures on the epistemology of PERCEPTION in light of his theories of the senses.

Helmholtz adopted broadly "empiricist" positions with respect to the justification of general laws in natural science, the human ability for spatial perception, the determination of the geometrical curvature (in Riemann's sense) of physical space, and the interpretation of SENSATIONS as "signs" for an EXTERNAL WORLD, the meaning of which must be learned from experience. Specifically, he held that laws in physics or psychology attain no better than inductive warrant (see INDUCTION); that all visual spatial ability is acquired through learning during the lifetime of each individual perceiver, including both the ability to localize in a direction (two-dimensionally) and to perceive objects in depth and distance; that, on the assumption that "rigid" bodies can be identified, various sets of empirical observations can be conceived that would lead respectively to the conclusion that physical space has positive, negative, or zero curvature; and that all our knowledge is mediated by aspatial sensations (originally varying only in quality and intensity) that acquire meaning and spatial organization through association with other sensations. In his view, the same unconscious processes of learning and inference operate in spatial perception and in the formulation of scientific hypotheses: inductive inferences by analogy from previous experience to new and similar instances.

Nonetheless, it is incorrect to assimilate Helmholtz to a classical empiricist position (such as that of, say, HUME), for two important reasons. First, Helmholtz explicitly distinguished his own epistemological stance from that of LOCKE and Hume, which he described as "sensualist" and criticized for leading to SKEPTICISM (*Physiological Optics*, §§26, 28). Second, he considered his epistemological position to be inspired by KANT, with respect to the "subjectivity" of our perceptual representations (cutting us off from the "thing in itself") and to the crucial role of the law of cause in mediating cognition of the physical world. Helmholtz's conception of his relation to Kant changed, and his descriptions of Kant's position and his relation to it reveal misconceptions. Still, any understanding of Helmholtz's relation to empiricism must evaluate his self-ascribed, limited Kantianism.

Helmholtz contended that with the failure of the metaphysical systems of German Idealism, theoretical philosophy should be restricted to the problem of knowledge. His most articulated discussion of *Erkenntnistheorie*, or epistemology, is the 1878 lecture "The Facts in Perception," in which he asserts both that natural SCIENCE cannot eschew epistemological questions and that it can help to answer them. He stated the fundamental question of epistemology as follows: "What is true in our intuition and thought?" or "In what sense do our representations correspond to actuality?" (*Epistemological Writings*: 117). Both forms of the question concern intuition, thought, or mental representations in general, not specific judgments about particular objects. Examples are whether color sensation, as a kind of sensation, directly reveals a fundamental physical property or is instead to be seen as a mere "sign" (the phenomenal character of which is wholly subjective) of an external cause whose characteristics must be inferred from other knowledge; and whether spatial representations directly reveal the real spatial character of the world or merely represent sets of external relations that cannot be known to be genuinely spatial. Thus, Helmholtz was raising a question about the representational accuracy of kinds of sensory representation, as philosophers previously had sought to assess the informativeness of perceptual representations of PRIMARY AND SECONDARY QUALITIES.

Helmholtz remained always committed to the principle that "sensations are only signs for the state of the external world, whose interpretation must be learned through experience" ("Autobiographical Sketch" 1892, in *Science and Culture*). He changed his view of how fully we can read these signs. He uniformly held that color sensations are merely arbitrary signs for their causes. His position on spatial perception varied from a robust realism to an epistemically modest PHENOMENALISM. In his 1855 lecture, "On Human Vision" ("Über das Sehen des Menschen," in *Vorträge und Reden*), he held that we use the law of cause as "a law of thought given prior to all experience" to infer the spatial properties of the external world. In 1867, he denied that spatial representations provide an "image" of real spatial relations: they inform us of real external relations but do not tell us whether these relations are in fact spatial (he asserted that TIME relations do correspond to an objective temporal sequence) (*Physiological Optics*, §26). In his 1878 lecture, he treated realism about the external world as a merely useful hypothesis that could not be firmly established over its idealist competitor, advising the epistemologically sophisticated natural scientist merely to chart the lawful relations among sensory representations, without affirming realism. The law of cause, reduced merely to a belief in the continued lawfulness of nature, now becomes a working presupposition of all perception and of empirical investigation in natural science, not a principle warranting an inference to the existence of the external world.

Although Helmholtz often set perceptual and scientific inferences on a par, his own writings on the geometry of physical space (in *Epistemological Writings*) provide the basis for separating the psychological theory of "empirism"— which teaches that human visual spatial abilities are acquired through experience—from the epistemological question of whether the structure of physical space can be determined empirically. In these writings he showed that an observer whose visual system is tuned to a Euclidean space could, if introduced into a space of significant curvature, make observations to reveal that curvature. This implies that even if human visual spatial abilities are innate (a "nativist" as opposed to "empirist" position), one can remain empiricist about the structure of physical space, although Helmholtz did not himself state this implication.

Helmholtz's final position treats physical space as a set of regular relations (such as repeatable, reversible sequences) among phenomenally given sensations. It is far removed from his early adherence to the law of cause as an a priori principle that could warrant a realist inference to an external world of objects in space. His 1878 position that the law of cause is a presupposition of empirical research and amounts to "faith" in the lawfulness of nature moves him in the direction of classical empiricism, though in the same lecture he described this presupposition in the Kantian language of "transcendental law." In evaluating Helmholtz's position and his descriptions of it, readers must balance the latent empiricism in Helmholtz's treatment of the law of cause as a working presupposition against his use of Kantian terminology and the understanding (or lack thereof) of Kant's position revealed thereby.

PRIMARY WORKS

Treatise on Physiological Optics. Translated by James P. C. Southall. 3 vols. Milwaukee: Optical Society of America, 1924–1925; 1st German ed., 1867.

Wissenschaftliche Abhandlungen. 3 vols. Leipzig: Barth, 1892–1895.

Vorträge und Reden. 4th ed., 2 vols. Braunschweig: Vieweg, 1896.

Epistemological Writings. Edited by Robert Cohen and Yehuda Elkana. Boston: Reidel, 1977.

Science and Culture: Popular and Philosophical Essays. Edited by David Cahan. Chicago: University of Chicago Press, 1995.

BIBLIOGRAPHY

Cahan, David, ed. *Hermann von Helmholtz and the Foundations of Nineteenth-century Science.* Berkeley: University of California Press, 1993.

Hatfield, Gary. *The Natural and the Normative: Theories of Spatial Perception from Kant to Helmholtz.* Cambridge: MIT Press, 1990.

Turner, R. Steven. *In the Mind's Eye: Vision and the Helmholtz-Hering Controversy.* Princeton: Princeton University Press, 1994.

GARY HATFIELD

HERBERT, EDWARD (BARON HERBERT OF CHERBURY). Edward Herbert (1583?–1648) was a courtier, soldier, diplomat, poet, historian, philosopher, and theologian. Probably born in 1583, as a young man he paid several visits to the Continent, where he became aware of the threats of philosophical SKEPTICISM and the problems of religious conflicts over the determination of true belief. While ambassador to the French court he completed his major philosophical work, *De Veritate, Prout Distinguitur a Revelatione, a Verisimili, a Possibili, et a Falso* (On Truth in Distinction from Revelation, Possibility, and Error). The first edition was published in 1624 in Paris; an enlarged third edition was published in 1645 in London. Dismissed from his post without explanation and fobbed off with peerages, he declined to take an active part in the civil war. In 1645 his *De Religione Laici* (On the Religion of the Laity) appeared. His important history of Henry VIII (1649); a pioneering study of other faiths, *De Religione Gentilium* (On the Religion of the Nations) (1663), and an amusing but partial autobiography (1764) were published after his death in 1648. It is also generally agreed that he was the author of another study of religion, *A Dialogue between a Tutor and His Pupil*, which was published in 1768.

In *De Veritate* Herbert considers himself an independent thinker for whom the only authority is "right reason" (*recta ratio*). Taking up ideas from a variety of sources in classical, scholastic, and Renaissance literature, he combines epistemological, psychological, and methodological factors in an attempt to show how people may avoid the traps of dogmatism, fideism, and skepticism in using "right reason" to determine true understanding. Holding that the mind contains as many preestablished latent modes of thought (which he calls "faculties" [*facultates*]) as there are discriminable objects to be known, he defines truth in terms of the exact "conformity" (*conformitas*) between an object and a faculty. He also holds that people are created in such a way that they feel satisfied only when their faculties correctly correspond (*recte conformitae*) to what they seek to grasp. By this means he puts forward a theory of KNOWLEDGE that acknowledges the activity of the mind in knowledge while upholding the "commonsense" view that true knowledge is a matter of apprehending things as they are.

A basic doctrine for Herbert's understanding of how people are to determine to what they should assent is that of the "common notions" (*notitiae communes*). The common notions are marked by priority, independence, universality, certainty, necessity in the sense of being needed for human survival, and immediacy in the sense that they do not require to be justified by discursive reasoning (*prioritas, independentia, universalitas, certitudo, necessitas, et modus conformationis*). Herbert maintains that the common notions are latent in every whole mind, having been implanted by divine providence, and that when they come to a person's attention, they are immediately perceived to be true. By the common notions of religion people are able (and in principle have been able always and everywhere) to judge which religious claims are to be believed. Contrary to widespread allegations, Herbert is probably not to be classed as an early "deist" (see DEISM) but as a rational theologian who was suspicious of the pretensions of priestcraft and who perceived that proper acknowledgment of the Deity sees God as benevolently concerned with all humankind.

PRIMARY WORKS

The Antient Religion of the Gentiles. Translated by William Lewis. London: n.s., 1705.
A Dialogue between a Tutor and His Pupil: London: W. Bathoe, 1768.
De Veritate. Translated with an introduction by M. H. Carré. London: Routledge/Thoemmes Press and Tokyo: Kinokuniya, 1992.

BIBLIOGRAPHY

Books

Bedford, R. D. *The Defence of Truth: Herbert of Cherbury and the Seventeenth Century.* Manchester: Manchester University Press, 1979.
Harrison, Peter. *"Religion" and the Religions in the English Enlightenment.* Cambridge: Cambridge University Press, 1990: 61–98.

Articles

Pailin, David A. "Herbert of Cherbury and the Deists." *The Expository Times* 94 (1983): 196–200.
————. "Herbert von Cherbury." In *Grundriss der Geschichte der Philosophie, Band 3: Die Philosophie des 17. Jahrhunderts*, edited by J.-P. Schobinger. Basel: Schwabe, 1988: 224–39, 284–85.

DAVID A. PAILIN

HOBBES, THOMAS. Thomas Hobbes (1588–1679) contributed to the movement of ideas in seventeenth-century Europe sometimes known as "the scientific revolution." From the 1630s he started to propose hypotheses about the nature of light and vision; and he claimed that his theories of the PASSIONS, natural right, and natural law combined to form the first genuinely scientific politics. He is primarily remembered today as a political philosopher. His *Leviathan* (1651) is widely considered one of the great works in the history of political thought, though Hobbes himself always cited *De Cive* (1642) as the best statement of his political science. He also worked on unifying and systematizing science as a whole. In a trilogy that dominated two decades of his working life (from the late 1630s to the late 1650s) he claimed to present the elements of SCIENCE in something like the sense that Euclid had presented the elements of geometry.

Both his scientific practice and his views about the nature and organization of science were heavily influenced by scientific innovators in Continental Europe. He was a great admirer of GALILEO, and during the 1640s he was an active member of the Parisian intellectual circle around Marin Mersenne. This circle included Pierre GASSENDI, Gilles Roberval, and also, through correspondence, René Descartes. When Hobbes returned to England and tried to attach himself to the fledgling Royal Society in London, expecting it to function rather as Mersenne's circle had in Paris, he found himself ostracized. The members of the Royal Society suspected him of atheism, distrusted his politics, questioned his competence in mathematics, and were at odds with him over method.

His differences with the Royal Society over method raise the question of whether Hobbes can be regarded as an empiricist. This entry begins with those differences, tracing them to a philosophy of science that distinguished reason sharply from experience and that favored reason over experience in the conduct of science. Hobbes did not minimize the influence of experience on thought and on such faculties as memory, IMAGINATION, and passion, but he tended to think that experience had to be corrected and revised by reason in order to benefit people. He distrusted experience as a basis for natural science, and he distrusted experience even more as a basis for civil and moral philosophy.

HOBBES AND NATURAL SCIENTIFIC METHOD

Experiment was not essential to science, according to Hobbes, and he thought members of the Royal Society such as BOYLE were overimpressed with scientific equipment and the effects that could be produced with it. Again, writing some years before the controversy with Boyle, he said it was no objection to the principle of the instantaneous propagation of very small motions through infinite distance that the very small motions would get weaker and weaker "till at last [they] can no longer be perceived by sense; for motion may be insensible; and I do not here examine things by sense and experience, but by reason" (*De Corpore*, Chapter 15: vii). Hobbes believed that it was perfectly legitimate to postulate types of motion that were beyond the reach of the senses if doing so helped to explain a natural phenomenon. Members of the Royal Society associated these unseen entities with the hidden properties sometimes invoked by exponents of premodern science to explain phenomena that eluded their theories. For the Royal Society, observable matters of fact and experiment were required to combat the dogmatic new science of the Continent just as much as the bankrupt old science of the Aristotelians.

In the 1660s Hobbes became involved in a controversy about the proper interpretation of experiments conducted by Robert Boyle to establish the properties of air, in particular its "spring" (roughly, its pressure). These experiments were conducted with a specially designed air pump apparatus and were reported in Boyle's *New Experiments Physico-Mechanical* (1660), to which Hobbes responded in *Dialogus physicus* (1661). To give a sketch of the background for Boyle's experiments, it had been observed by Evangelista Torricelli that a tube sealed at one end and filled with mercury could be placed, sealed end up, on a dish containing mercury. Once the tube stood upright on the dish of mercury, the column of mercury within the tube would appear to fall somewhat, creating a space between the seal and the top of the column of mercury. One question raised by the experiment was whether the space above the mercury in the column was empty; another was whether the space above the mercury counted as a "vacuum" in some sense, for example, the sense in which certain versions of the new philosophy—Descartes', for example—denied that there was a vacuum. Boyle was able to show that when the Torricellian experiment was performed within a glass globe from which air could be sucked out, the column of mercury could be made to fall even farther, to a level close to the surface of the dish. What is more, the column could be made to rise when a valve designed to keep air out of the glass globe was opened. In some sense the experiments told in favor of the answer yes to the question of whether the space above the mercury was empty. Hobbes took Boyle to interpret his experiments as showing that a vacuum could exist in nature, a conclusion that Hobbes ruled out by definition and a priori argument.

Hobbes had a long-standing intellectual investment in denying the existence of a vacuum. Far from believing that nature contained perfectly empty spaces, he was, like Descartes and others, a plenist, that is, a believer in a physical world filled entirely by matter. Successive optical treatises by Hobbes composed before the 1660s had worked on the assumption that light was action that displaced a medium with no spaces but microscopic ones. This conception made no room for a macroscopic void, which is what Hobbes took Boyle to be saying was created by the action of sucking air out of the glass globe. Hobbes could concede that the experiment created a space that *seemed* empty, but this did not rule out a filling for the space that was too subtle to be seen. So long as something filled the space and had an existence without the mind, it would be a body—a fluid body—albeit an invisible one.

The postulate of the plenum was not only impossible to *rule out* by experiment, Hobbes thought; adopting it simplified the foundations of physics. All physical CAUSATION could be regarded as some variation of displacement. In other words, and as Hobbes insists in Part Two of *De Corpore*, one could say that there was a single universal cause of all difference and change, namely, "motion" in the sense of change of place of bodies or their parts. Or as it is put in the preface to the reader of *Dialogus physicus*, "Nature does all things by the conflict of bodies pressing each other mutually with their motions." Hobbes' simplifying postulate seemed from Boyle's point of view to be simple dogma; and Boyle wished his experiments with the air pump to be approached open-mindedly—not as if they were interventions, let alone partisan interventions, in the controversy between plenists and vacuists. Boyle believed that unless one's mind were already made up in this controversy, the nature of the space above the mercury in the tube had to be squared with the observed "matters of fact" that the air was sucked out of the globe, the globe was visibly empty; and the level of mercury descended. This attitude toward "matters of fact"—that is, toward observations of competent witnesses—together with a refusal to give credence to postulates just for their power of simplifying explanation, seems to make Boyle more of an empiricist than Hobbes in the controversy over the air pump, and the character of Hobbes' reaction may even make Hobbes appear an outright antiempiricist.

HOBBES THE RATIONALIST?

The impression that Hobbes was antiempiricist is reinforced when one considers the importance he attached to "DEMONSTRATION" in science, his very elaborate theory of acceptable ingredients of demonstration, and his divorce of demonstration in the strict sense from observation. According to *The Elements of Law*, Chapter 13, demonstration in the strict sense is a matter of studied name imposition, studied combination of names into propositions, and studied combination of propositions into syllogisms according to rules of inference. Demonstration along these lines is what one finds in geometry, according to Hobbes, which explains why geometry is so free from controversy and therefore so splendid an example of science. While physics cannot aspire to the same freedom from controversy as geometry, it still involves—as any science according to Hobbes must involve—demonstration. Physical demonstration differs from geometrical in involving hypotheses as premises. Hobbes connects the need for hypotheses with the fact that effects in physics are sense-experiences with causes outside us and causes subject to an omnipotent GOD. While we cannot say that an omnipotent God could have produced the effect in only one way—that would be to limit a will we have agreed is without limit—we *can* say that any way of producing the effect would have involved a kind of motion: this follows from the fact that it is an effect we are explaining and from the definition of "cause" and "effect." Not only can the Hobbesian physicist be sure that some type of motion is responsible for an effect, but he can be sure that the motion relevant to a selected effect is one of a small range of types of motion: either the simple motion studied by geometry, the intermediate kind studied by pure mechanics, or motions inside and between bodies interacting with the senses.

It is indeed a precept of Hobbes' method of physics as stated in the very late *Decameron Physiologicum* (1678) that an inquirer *start* any investigation of the causes of a particular phenomenon with the definitions of "cause," "efficient cause," "place," and "time" and a knowledge of the nature of motion and the different types of motion. The physicist is then to draw from "these definitions, and from whatsoever truth else [he knows] by the light of nature, such general consequences as may serve for axioms, or principles of [his] ratiocination." Only after the general principles and properties of motion are added to these axioms is the inquirer to collect relevant additional observations with which his would-be explanations must be consistent, observations that are best drawn directly from nature rather than from experimental apparatus. At this stage, the physicist is in a position to arrive at a hypothesis concerning the cause of the phenomenon he started with.

The method described in *Decameron Physiologicum* does not give observation an important role in physics; and when Hobbes turns to similar matters in the much more authoritative work, *De corpore*, it is clear that the real work in science is done by reason:

[T]o those that search after science indefinitely, which consists in the knowledge of the causes of all things, as far forth as it may be attained (and the causes of singular things are compounded of the causes of universal or simple things) it is necessary that they know the causes of universal things, or of such accidents as are common to all bodies, that is, to all matter, before they can know their causes. Moreover, seeing universal things are contained in the nature of singular things, the knowledge of them is to be acquired by reason, that is, by resolution. (*English Works of Thomas Hobbes* I: 68–69)

Superficially at least, Hobbes comes rather close in this passage to Descartes in the *Discourse on the Method*. In the *Discourse*, the second and third rules of the preferred Cartesian logic are ''to divide each of the difficulties into as many parts as possible and as may be required to resolve them better'' and ''to direct my thoughts in an orderly manner, by beginning with the simplest and most easily known objects in order to ascend little by little, step by step, to the knowledge of the most complex'' (*Philosophical Writings* I: 120).

Is the resemblance more than superficial, so that Hobbes' method commits him to a kind of rationalism, perhaps even a Cartesian rationalism? Yes and no. Hobbes *can* be regarded as a kind of rationalist; but he has a radically un-Cartesian theory of the medium of REASON and reasoning, and the senses he attaches to the terms ''simple,'' ''complex,'' ''resolution,'' and so on are importantly different from those in Descartes.

In Hobbesian resolution, one looks for what a particular phenomenon has in common with others. This is a matter of looking for the most general terms that apply to an observed thing and for the cause of the aspect that makes that general term applicable to the observed thing as well as everything else named by the term. Hobbes gives the example of an idea of a particular square. When reason gets to work in the required way,

this square is to be resolved into a *plane, terminated with a certain number of equal and straight sides and right angles*. For by this resolution we have these things universal or agreeable to all matter, namely *line, plane* (which contains *superfices*) *terminal, angle, straightness, rectitude*, and *equality*; and if we can find out the causes of these, we can compound them together into the causes of a square. (*English Works* I: 69)

He is describing something like the analysis of the concept of a square. What would come next is the identification of the motions that produce all of the universals analyzed out, that is, the motions required to construct any square. Hobbes goes on to give a second example illustrating resolution in physics:

Again, if any man propound to himself the conception of *gold*, he may, by resolving, come to the ideas of *solid, visible, heavy*, (that is, tending to the centre of the earth, or downwards) and many other more universal than gold itself; and these he may resolve again, till he comes to such things as are most universal. (*English Works* I: 69)

Knowing the nature of gold would consist of knowing why gold presents (i.e., what motions produce) that combination of solidity, visibility, heaviness, and so on.

Descartes' conception of resolution, on the other hand, is usually applied to formulations of *problems* rather than particular appearances, and it often consists of the mathematization of the problem formulation, that is, its redescription as an equation between numerical knowns and unknowns or, more characteristically, as a relation between geometrical figures. In Hobbes, resolution is mostly understood on the much cruder model of definition, that is, where a combination of terms breaks down the sense of a single term by being a combination of terms more general than the definiendum. Associated with these two different models of resolution are very different conceptions of where we get our knowledge of universals and of what has to exist metaphysically for such knowledge to be possible. In Descartes the knowledge of universals appears to be regarded as innate (see INNATENESS), and some or all of the universals—in the form of "simple" natures—are supposed to be full-fledged abstract existents, rather as the nature of the triangle is supposed at the beginning of Meditation Five to be real independently of Descartes' thought. For Hobbes, on the other hand, no knowledge is innate: it all originates in the senses (*Leviathan*, Chapter 1); and everything that exists is concrete and particular. There can be universal names— names that apply to many or all particulars; and there can be general conceptions, that is, images of particular things made general by the conceiver's disregarding some of the distinguishing features of those particulars (see ABSTRACTION). But no ideas are originally ideas of universals; the closest one comes in nature to an idea of body in general is the idea of some particular body as seen from such a distance that nothing besides the aspect for which it is given the name "body"—that is, appearing to be something out there and independent of one in space—registers.

REASONING AND NAMES

What conception of scientific reasoning is open to Hobbes if the thoughts that enter into pieces of reasoning have to have a content derived from sense experience of particulars? Hobbes thinks that the scientific conclusion par excellence, the conclusion of a geometrical proof, is perfectly general and, if true, true at all times and places; but if the terms in the premises of the proof only ever signify ideas of particular things, seen at particular times and places, how can the thoughts ever have a content required by a universal truth? Hobbes' answer is, "[B]y being expressed by terms that apply wherever and whenever the aspects that make *us* apply them present themselves." Thus, "All triangles have angles adding up to two right angles" can be true because wherever "triangle" applies, "thing with angles adding to two right angles" also applies. The term/thing relation "applies" or "is a name of"—as opposed to the user/term/audience relation "signifies"—can hold even when the last sentient being with a memory of triangles dies, and his conceptions of triangles die with him.

More important, perhaps, a geometrical conclusion reached by an individual on the basis of the construction of a particular triangle and a consideration of its properties can be true in all other cases that are relevantly similar, even if it is impossible for one person to carry out all of the relevant constructions and observe all of the relevant properties.

What goes for geometrical conclusions goes for scientific conclusions in general. An item of science is a true proposition reached as a conclusion of a piece of syllogistic reasoning, and Hobbes says that only universal affirmative propositions can serve as the premises or conclusions of scientific syllogisms (*De Corpore*, Chapter 4: vii). A universal proposition is one "whose subject is affected with the sign of a universal name," that is, a proposition of the form "All Fs are G" where F and G are universal names, names of each of a plurality of things, like "horse," "man," or "tree." Since only universal names are allowed to figure in the grammatical subject position of a proposition of science, since any such proposition is true, and since predicates of all propositions have to have extensions at least as wide as those of subject terms (*De Corpore*, Chapter 3: vii), the predicates must also be universal names. Universal names, then, are *the* items of scientific vocabulary. The proper name and the singular proposition have no place in a scientific syllogism at all (*De Corpore*, Chapter 4: iv, vii).

Universal names are imposed on many things "for their similitude to one another in some quality or accident" (*Leviathan*, Chapter 4). Although outside science the same name can be imposed by different speakers in view of different accidents, producing equivocal universal names, within science all universal names are defined in terms of a fixed set of accidents and therefore enjoy univocity. Different universal names that belong to the same logical category or "predicament," such as "body," "man," and "living creature," have "extents" that contain one another or that overlap. The extent of a universal name is the plurality of things to which a name applies severally. Because certain affirmations built out of names with overlapping extents can be reexpressed as assertions about how the extents are related, it is possible, by means of universal propositions, to bring relations between the extents into a train of reasoning. Extralinguistically, or in experience, we never have access to an extent at a single time, let alone relations between extents. All our prelinguistic conceptions are particular and of one thing at a time. Consequently, while experience can disclose facts concerning as many of a plurality of things as have been observed or remembered, it cannot convert that long conjunction of known facts about Fs into facts about all Fs, even if the observed and remembered Fs are all the Fs there are. As Hobbes puts it in *The Elements of Law*, "[E]xperience concludeth nothing universally."

Without names and name-combinations, without universal names and their possibilities of combination in particular, human beings would only ever have experience and never science. They would be able to perceive, remember, and imagine, and, on the strength of these capacities, they would be able to form some expectations and achieve some ends. But their expectations would often prove mistaken, and when correct, they would be so accidentally. By perception, memory, and imagination we are at most able to hit upon useful generalizations; infallible rules depend on science (*Leviathan*, Chapter 6). By experience, memory, and imagination we are at most able to hit upon the characteristic antecedents of a type of event, not its causes or the conditions that, if satisfied, necessitate the event. Only science discloses causes. Science is based on reason, the capacity for putting together propositions composed of aptly imposed names. As Hobbes says in *Leviathan*:

Reason is not as Sense and Memory, borne with us; nor gotten by experience onely, as Prudence is; but attayned by Industry; first in apt imposing of Names; and secondly by getting a good and orderly Method in proceeding from the Elements, which are Names, to Assertions made by Connexion of one of them to another; and so to Syllogismes, which are the Connexions of one Assertion to another, till we come to a knowledge of all the Consequences of names appertaining to the subject in hand; and that is it, men call SCIENCE. (*Leviathan* I.v.17)

EXPERIENCE AND CIVIL PHILOSOPHY

There is some reason to think that Hobbes was prepared to give experience a greater role in civil philosophy than in natural philosophy. He says in more than one place that the assumptions he uses in civil philosophy can be confirmed by experience (*Leviathan*, Intro., Chapter 13); and he also insists on the relevance of records of experience—civil histories—to the conclusions of civil philosophy. But while this is so, it is also true that he insists on the limitations of experience as a guide to the good things in life.

Experience alerts us to sources of pleasure, but something pleasant is good only in relation to an occasion and the constitution of the one who experiences the pleasure (*Leviathan*, Chapter 6). A person may find a thing pleasant on one occasion and call it "good" then, only to change his mind later (*De cive*, Chapter 14: xvii; *Leviathan*, Chapter 15). The very thing a person calls "good" on one occasion, another person may call "bad" on the same occasion. Experience cannot be expected to generate consistent valuations over time or between people. It tends to suggest not only fluctuating, but defeasible, valuations. That is, people can pursue what is pleasant and avoid what is painful and yet pursue and avoid the wrong things. Something that seems to be worth avoiding because it is unpleasant may turn out to be worth suffering, all things considered; and something that seems to be worth pursuing because it is gratifying may not really be worth pursuing when all relevant considerations, including all calculable considerations, are allowed to weigh. To give some illustrations important to Hobbes' civil philosophy, the felt unpleasantness of losing one's liberty under government does not by itself show that the loss of liberty is an evil and to be avoided (*Elements of Law*, Part 2, Chapter 5: ii). Symmetrically, the fact that it is pleasant to people to compete with one another and highly gratifying to win does not mean that competing and winning are good things. On the contrary, the all-out competition of the state of nature is the worst of the avoidable bad things, according to Hobbes' civil philosophy.

Experience is not a trustworthy indicator of ends because pleasure and pain are not sure guides to what is worth pursuing and avoiding. But pain and pleasure are the only guides people naturally have. When their fallible guidance is followed, there is no guarantee that agents who pursue and avoid the relevant goods and evils will succeed in getting the one or in steering clear of the other. This is because, by nature, people have only experience to inform them about means–ends relations and the only means–ends relation revealed by experience is a loose relation of succession. It takes reason to show what means *must* bring about a certain effect, as opposed to what things regularly follow the implementation of the means. Systematic knowledge of these "musts" is available only through science.

Just how much of a difference reason and its product, science, make, when added to the accumulation of experience, is supposed to be revealed in the differences between the way of life of the native peoples of North America and the commodious existence of Western Europeans in the seventeenth century. At one time, according to Hobbes, all of humanity lived as in his day the Indians of America lived. They had a command of speech and a limited ability to reason. But they could arrive at only a small number of "true, general and profitable" speculations:

[M]en lived on gross experience; there was no method; that is to say, no sowing or planting of knowledge by itself, apart from the weeds, and common plants of error and conjecture. And the want of it being the want of leisure from procuring the necessities of life, and defending themselves against their neighbours, it was impossible, till the erecting of great commonwealths it should be otherwise. *Leisure* is the mother of *philosophy;* and Commonwealth is the mother of *peace* and *leisure*. (*Leviathan*, Chapter 46)

To live "on gross experience" is to live in Hobbes' famous state of nature. When one is not at the mercy of an uncooperative natural environment, one is at the mercy of other people, among whom one can at best live insecurely.

Hobbes thinks that experience provides no solution to the insecurity of life within groups, just as it offers no solution to the problem of getting what one wants and avoiding what one dislikes. Experience may help us to *recognize* a problem of insecurity, for experience can disabuse us of the complacent Aristotelian doctrine that people are naturally suited to society. As Hobbes points out in the opening chapter of *De cive*, it takes only a little observation of human beings to reveal that some people are given to backbiting, that they tend to have a better opinion of themselves than of their fellows, that they quickly come to blows over very little, and so on. But it takes reason and science to see that there are the makings of war even in the dispositions of the meek, in fact in human beings of any temperament. Reason reveals the so-called *right of nature*, the right of all persons to be the judge of the means to their survival and well-being (cf. *Leviathan*, Chapter 14). This right justifies the greedy and the over-bearing in appropriating as much as they can and disabling as many competitors as they can. The same right justifies everyone else, the mild-mannered included, in taking preemptive action against anyone who, for all one knows, *might* be greedy and overbearing—that is, anyone at all. The right of nature, then, leads from the whole variety of temperaments and "manners" to war. War, in Hobbes' sense, is the known disposition to fight for one's survival and well-being. To overcome the danger of war is to overcome the problem of insecurity of life within groups. Once more, reason is required. Reason identifies a good—namely, peace—that all people can acknowledge as good no matter what the rest of their conception of well-being is. Reason can also show that the key to obtaining this good is a certain kind of collective transfer of the right of nature. As soon as the many delegate the right of judging what is for the best, the prospects of everyone's enjoying a reasonable share of the good things in life increase. Delegating the right of nature is the effect of submission to government. Each of the many allows a ruler or governing body to decide what is the best means to the security and collective well-being of all, and the ruler or governing body is well placed to do this, as he or it is detached from the passions that magnify the personal good of each of the many and make each person's interests seem more important to that person than anyone else's. Of course, the ruler or governing body must also keep his or its own interests from outweighing those of the subjects, but reason indicates that this is in the interest of the ruler or governing body, as not to do so could provoke the insecurity that led the many to agree to give their submission. If the insecurity returns, and the many are disappointed, then the right of nature reverts to the many, and the ruler or governing body's status dissolves, making the holders of this office extremely vulnerable. It is in the interest of the ruler or rulers to govern impartially, and it is in the interest of those under government to stay submissive. If they do not, they must reckon on war and the high risk of dispossession of the good things in life, including life itself.

Reason alerts one to both the general form of the problem to which Hobbes' political philosophy is a solution and also the general form of the solution itself. The problem—the war of all against all—arises from the right of nature; the solution arises from a conditional laying down of this right: people will abide by the sovereign's judgment of what is for the best—as embodied in civil laws—if it is not too dangerous to do so, if doing so actually promotes security and well-being. There is a role for experience in confirming that the ingredients of the war of all against all are manifest in some human behavior, and there is also a role for experience in identifying in oneself the passions that matter to understanding war (cf. *Leviathan*, Intro.); but beyond this it is for reason to show us the path to peace.

PRIMARY WORKS

The Elements of Law Natural and Politic (1640). Edited by F. Tones. London: 1889.

Elementorum philosophiae sectio tertia de cive. Paris: n.s., 1642. English translation: *Philosophical Rudiments concerning Government and Society* (1651) in *English Works*, vol. 2.

Leviathan, or the Matter, Form and Power of a Commonwealth, Ecclesiastical and Civil (1651). Edited by Richard Tuck. Cambridge: Cambridge University Press, 1991.

Philosophiae sectio prima de corpore (1655). English translation: *Elements of Philosophy, the First Section concerning Body* (1656) in *English Works*, vol. 1.

Decameron Physiologicum (1678). In *English Works*, vol. 7.

The English Works of Thomas Hobbes. Edited by William Molesworth, 11 vols. London: Bohn 1839.

OTHER PRIMARY WORKS

Descartes, René. *Discourse on Method.* In *The Philosophical Writings of René Descartes*, edited by J. Cottingham, R. Stoothoff, and D. Murdoch, vol. 1. Cambridge: Cambridge University Press, 1985.

BIBLIOGRAPHY

Books

Shapin, S., and S. Shaffer. *Leviathan and the Air-Pump: Hobbes, Boyle and the Experimental Life.* Princeton: Princeton University Press, 1985. Contains, as an appendix, the first English translation of Hobbes' *Dialogus Physicus*.

Sorell, T. *Hobbes.* London: Routledge, 1986.

———, ed. *The Cambridge Companion to Hobbes.* Cambridge: Cambridge University Press, 1996.

Watkins, J.W.N. *Hobbes's System of Ideas.* London: Hutchinson, 1965.

Woolhouse, R. *The Empiricists.* Oxford: Oxford University Press, 1988.

Article

Jesseph, Douglas. "Hobbes and the Method of Natural Science." In *The Cambridge Companion to Hobbes*, by T. Sorell. Cambridge: Cambridge University Press, 1996: Chapter 4.

TOM SORELL

HUME, DAVID. David Hume (1711–1776) was a Scottish philosopher, historian, and essayist. Generally regarded as the most important philosopher ever to write in English, Hume was a master stylist in any genre and one of the greatest philosophers "in all nations and ages." His contemporaries—when they read his philosophical works—found them shocking; "the zealots" denounced him as a Pyrrhonist (see SKEPTICISM) and an atheist, even as they enjoyed his *Essays* and made his *History of England* a best-seller.

Though he awakened KANT from his "dogmatic slumbers" and "caused the scales to fall" from Bentham's eyes, a long tradition—beginning with Thomas REID—has insisted on reading Hume as a philosopher whose purpose was entirely negative. On this reading, Hume's achievement was to expose the latent skepticism in the "way of ideas" he inherited from LOCKE and BERKELEY, in order to push their empiricism to its logical, absurd conclusions. Thomas Hill

Green ensured that this picture became orthodoxy by making it the focal point of the lengthy introduction to his and Thomas Grose's edition of Hume's *Works*. Green called Hume "the last great English philosopher," with the emphasis on "*last*": Green intended to display the poverty of the British philosophical tradition and ready England for the invasion of German Absolute Idealism.

Despite this traditional treatment and relative neglect, Hume's philosophical views were widely and deeply influential. He helped shape the moral philosophy and economic writings of his close friend Adam SMITH, as well as the work of the utilitarians. His *Essays* resound significantly in the writings of James Madison and Thomas Jefferson: Hume's voice can be heard, however faintly, in the *Federalist Papers*, the Declaration of Independence, and the Constitution of the United States. Charles DARWIN counted Hume as a central influence, as did "Darwin's bulldog," Thomas Henry Huxley. The diverse directions in which these writers took what they gleaned from reading Hume reflect not only the richness of their sources but also the wide range of topics that Hume's empiricism addresses.

Though Hume's star was in eclipse during the heyday of Absolute Idealism, it rose with the advent of logical atomism, logical empiricism, and the logical positivist movement (see LOGICAL POSITIVISM/LOGICAL EMPIRICISM). The positive aspect of his philosophy was finally recognized by Norman Kemp Smith, who championed him as a "naturalist." In a rather different sense of "naturalist," Hume's views have been appreciated by many contemporary philosophical naturalists, including W.V.O. QUINE. The old image of Hume as arch skeptic still persists to some degree, however, and debate continues as to the proper characterization and relative importance of the strains of skepticism and naturalism in his work.

LIFE AND WORKS

Born in Edinburgh, Hume spent his childhood at Ninewells, the family's modest estate on the Whitadder River in the border Lowlands near Berwick. His father died just after David's second birthday, "leaving me, with an elder brother and a sister under the care of our Mother, a woman of singular Merit, who, though young and handsome, devoted herself to the rearing and educating of her Children."

Katherine Falconer Hume realized that David was "uncommonly wake-minded"—precocious, in her Lowland dialect—so when his brother went up to Edinburgh University, David, not yet twelve, joined him. He studied mathematics and contemporary science and read widely in history, literature, and ancient and modern philosophy.

Hume's family thought him suited for a career in the law, but he preferred reading classical authors, especially Cicero, whose *Offices* became a secular substitute for *The Whole Duty of Man* and his family's strict Calvinism. Pursuing the goal of becoming "a Scholar and Philosopher," Hume followed a rigorous program of reading and reflection for three years until "there seem'd to be open'd up to me a New Scene of Thought."

The intensity of developing this philosophical vision precipitated a psychological crisis in the isolated scholar. Believing that "a more active scene of life" might improve his condition, Hume made "a very feeble trial" in the world of commerce, as a clerk for a Bristol sugar importer. But his psychological crisis passed, and he remained intent on articulating his "new scene of thought." He moved to France, where he could live frugally, and settled in La Flèche, a sleepy village in Anjou best known for its Jesuit college. Here, where Descartes and Mersenne had studied a century before, Hume read French and other Continental authors, especially MALEBRANCHE, Dubos, and Bayle; he occasionally baited the Jesuits with iconoclastic arguments; and, between 1734 and 1737, he drafted *A Treatise of Human Nature*.

Hume returned to England in 1737 to ready his *Treatise* for the press. Probably to curry favor with Bishop Butler, he "castrated" his manuscript, deleting his controversial discussion of miracles (see RELIGION), along with other "nobler parts." Book I (*Of the Understanding*) and Book II (*Of the Passions*) were published anonymously in 1739. Book III (*Of Morals*) appeared in 1740, when an anonymous *Abstract* of the first two books of the *Treatise* also appeared. Though other candidates, especially Adam Smith, have been proposed as the *Abstract*'s author, scholars now agree that it is Hume's work. The *Abstract* features a clear, succinct account of "one simple argument" concerning CAUSATION and the formation of belief, an elegant summary that presages Hume's "recasting" of this argument in the first *Enquiry*.

The *Treatise* was no literary sensation, but it did not "fall dead-born from the press," as Hume disappointedly described its reception. Despite his surgical deletions, the *Treatise* attracted enough of a "murmour among the zealots" to fuel his lifelong reputation as an atheist and skeptic.

Back at Ninewells, Hume published two modestly successful volumes of *Essays, Moral and Political* in 1741 and 1742. When the chair of ethics and pneumatical ("mental") philosophy at Edinburgh became vacant in 1745, Hume hoped to fill it, but his reputation provoked a vocal and ultimately successful opposition to his candidacy. Six years later, he stood for the chair of logic at Glasgow, only to be turned down again. Hume never held an academic post.

In the wake of the Edinburgh debacle, Hume made an unfortunate decision to tutor the marquess of Annandale, only to find that the young marquess was insane, and the estate manager dishonest. Extricating himself from this situation, Hume accepted an invitation from a cousin, Lieutenant General James St. Clair, to be his secretary on what promised to be a military expedition against the French in Quebec. Contrary winds delayed St. Clair's fleet until the Ministry canceled the plan, only to "spawn a new expedition" that ended as an abortive raid on the coastal town of L'Orient in Brittany.

Hume also accompanied St. Clair on an extended diplomatic mission to Vienna and Turin in 1748. While he was in Italy, the *Philosophical Essays concerning Human Understanding* appeared. A recasting of the central ideas of Book I of the *Treatise*, the *Philosophical Essays* were read and reprinted, eventually becoming part of Hume's *Essays and Treatises* under the title by which they are known today, *An Enquiry concerning Human Understanding*. In 1751, this *Enquiry* was joined by a second, *An Enquiry concerning the Principles of Morals*. Hume described the second *Enquiry*, a substantially rewritten version of Book III of the *Treatise*, as "incomparably the best" of all his works. More essays, the *Political Discourses*, appeared in 1752, and Hume's correspondence reveals that a draft of the *Dialogues concerning Natural Religion* was under way at this time.

An offer to serve as librarian to the Edinburgh Faculty of Advocates gave Hume the opportunity to work steadily on another project, a *History of England*, which was published in six volumes in 1754, 1756, 1759, and 1762. The *History* became a best-seller, giving him long-sought financial independence.

Even as a librarian, Hume continued to arouse the ire of the "zealots." In 1754, his order for several "indecent Books unworthy of a place in a learned Library" prompted a move for his dismissal, adding fuel to an unsuccessful attempt to excommunicate him in 1756. The library's trustees canceled his order for the offending volumes, which Hume regarded as a personal insult. Since he needed the library's resources for his *History*, Hume did not resign his post; he did turn over his salary to Thomas Blacklock, a blind poet he befriended and sponsored. When research for the *History* was done in 1757, Hume quickly resigned to make the position available for Adam FERGUSON.

Hume's publication of *Four Dissertations* (1757) was also surrounded by controversy. In 1755, he was ready to publish a volume that included "Of Suicide" and "Of the Immortality of the Soul." He suppressed the controversial essays when his publisher, Andrew Millar, was threatened with legal action, due largely to the machinations of the minor theologian William Warburton. Hume added "Of Tragedy" and "Of the Standard of Taste" to round out the volume, which also included *The Natural History of Religion* and *A Dissertation on the Passions*.

In 1763, Hume accepted an invitation from Lord Hertford, the ambassador to France, to serve as his private secretary. During his three years in Paris, Hume became secretary to the embassy and eventually its chargé d'affaires. He also become the rage of the Parisian salons, enjoying the conversation and company of Diderot, D'Alembert, and d'Holbach, as well as the attentions and affections of the *salonnières*, especially the Comtesse de Boufflers.

Hume returned to England in 1766, accompanied by Jean-Jacques Rousseau, then fleeing persecution in Switzerland. Their friendship ended quickly and miserably when the paranoid Rousseau became convinced that Hume was masterminding an international conspiracy against him.

After a year (1767–1768) as an undersecretary of state, Hume returned to

Edinburgh to stay. His autumnal years were spent quietly and comfortably, dining and conversing with friends and revising his works for new editions of his *Essays and Treatises*, which contained his collected essays, the two *Enquiries*, *A Dissertation on the Passions*, and *The Natural History of Religion*. In 1775, he added an ''Advertisement'' to these volumes, in which he disavowed the *Treatise*. Though he regarded this note as ''a compleat Answer'' to his critics, especially ''Dr. Reid and that biggotted, silly fellow, Beattie'' (see BEATTIE), subsequent readers have wisely chosen to ignore Hume's admonition to ignore his greatest philosophical work.

Upon finding that he had intestinal cancer in 1775, Hume prepared for his death with the same peaceful cheer that characterized his life. He arranged for the posthumous publication of his most controversial work, the *Dialogues concerning Natural Religion*; it was seen through the press by his nephew and namesake in 1779, three years after his uncle's death.

THE TREATISE AND THE ENQUIRIES

Hume's apparent disavowal of the *Treatise* raises a question as to how we should read his works. Should we take his ''Advertisement'' *literally* and let the *Enquiries* represent his considered view? Or should we take him *seriously* and conclude—whatever *he* may have said or thought—that the *Treatise* is the best statement of his position?

Both responses presuppose that there are substantial enough differences between the works to warrant our reading them as disjoint. This is highly dubious. Even in the ''Advertisement,'' Hume says that ''most of the principles, and reasonings, contained in this volume, were published'' in the *Treatise* and that he has ''cast the whole anew in the following pieces, where some negligences in his former reasoning and more in the expression, are . . . corrected.'' Despite his protests, this hardly sounds like the claims of one who has genuinely repudiated his earlier work.

Hume reinforces this perspective when he writes Gilbert Elliot of Minto that ''the philosophical principles are the same in both . . . by shortening and simplifying the questions, I really render them much more complete.'' In ''My Own Life,'' he opined that the *Treatise*'s lack of success ''proceeded more from the manner than the matter.'' Hume's ''recasting'' of the *Treatise* was probably designed primarily to address this point. This brief overview of Hume's central views on method, epistemology, and ETHICS therefore follows the structure— ''the manner''—of the *Enquiries* and emphasizes ''the matter'' they have in common with the *Treatise*.

METHOD

In his Introduction to the *Treatise*, Hume bemoans the sorry state of philosophy, evident even to ''the rabble without doors,'' which has given rise to ''that common prejudice against metaphysical reasonings of all kinds.'' He hopes to correct this miserable situation by introducing "the experimental method of reasoning into moral subjects," establishing "a science of human nature" that will put philosophy on a "solid foundation" of "experience and observation."

Hume's positive, naturalistic project has much in common with contemporary cognitive science. Recent readers have paid more attention to these aspects of his philosophy than his earlier critics apparently did. As a result, no contemporary Hume scholar entirely accepts the traditional view that Hume was solely a negative philosopher whose goal was to make manifest the skeptical consequences of the views of his empiricist predecessors. But there remain considerable disagreement about the role and extent of skepticism in his philosophy and disagreement about its relation to the naturalistic elements of his system. What Hume says about his aims and method helps clarify these issues.

In *An Enquiry concerning the Principles of Morals*, Hume says that he will "follow a very simple method" that will nonetheless bring about "a reformation in moral disquisitions" like that already accomplished in natural philosophy, where we have been cured of "a common source of illusion and mistake"— our "passion for hypotheses and systems." To make parallel progress in the moral sciences, we should "reject every system . . . however subtle or ingenious, which is not founded on fact and observation," and "hearken to no arguments but those which are derived from experience."

The "hypotheses and systems" Hume rejects cover a wide range of philosophical and theological views. These theories, Hume realized, were too entrenched, too influential, and too different from his proposed science of human nature to permit him just to present his "new scene of thought" as their replacement. He needed to show why we should reject these theories, so that he might have space to develop his own.

Hume outlines this strategy in the first section of *An Enquiry concerning Human Understanding*. He considers two prominent types of "false metaphysics." Though each type has as its basis an appealing human characteristic, both views extend their accounts of these characteristics beyond their basis in experience and so beyond the bounds of cognitive content.

The first view looks at humans as active creatures, driven by desires and feelings. It paints a flattering picture of human nature, easy to understand and even easier to accept. These philosophers make us *feel* what they *say* about our feelings, and what they say is so useful and agreeable that ordinary people who encounter these views are readily inclined to accept them. This view might be called *sentimentalism*. It is a generic characterization of the position defended in Hume's time by Shaftesbury and Francis Hutcheson.

The other view downgrades sentiment to concentrate on *rationality*, which it treats as the distinctive human characteristic. This view glorifies the reasonable aspects of our natures and appeals to them in its emphasis on rarefied speculation and abstract argument. The systems of Descartes and other rationalist philosophers fit this general description. Given its emphasis on the role of the intellect, this view might be called *intellectualism*.

Intellectualism and sentimentalism seem to be exhaustive alternatives, ways of characterizing the ancient debate as to whether REASON or passion (see PASSIONS) is, or should be, the dominant force in human life. Hume saw that *both* approaches capture important aspects of human nature but that *neither* tells the whole story. We are active *and* reasonable creatures. A view that mixes both styles of philosophy will be best, so long as it gets the mixture right.

But getting the mixture right, Hume realized, is no easy task. Intellectualism is too abstract, too remote from ordinary life to have any practical application. It can indulge the worst excesses of human vanity, especially when it treats matters that are beyond the limits of human understanding. It can be co-opted by popular superstitions, peddling religious fears and prejudices cloaked in profound-sounding but meaningless metaphysical jargon.

It is tempting to react to these features of intellectualism by arguing that we should abandon metaphysics altogether. But ordinary life does not equip us to do good metaphysics, and without some measure of accurate metaphysical description, sentimentalism cannot be as precise as it should be. Delicate sentiment requires just reasoning, and an adequate account of just reasoning requires an accurate and precise metaphysics. The only way to correct sentiment and to avoid the sources of error and uncertainty rooted in intellectualism is to do more metaphysics—but of the right kind. We must pursue *true* metaphysics if we want to jettison these false and deceptive views.

Hume's insight was to see that getting the correct mixture requires a twofold task, with negative and positive aspects. To develop a science of human nature, it is first necessary to undermine the foundations of all forms of false and misleading metaphysics. When we are rid of these sources of superstition, prejudice, and error, the stage will be clear for the kind of mental geography that constitutes true metaphysics. Accurate, just reasoning about human nature—the descriptive project of true metaphysics—requires us to examine the scope and limits of our cognitive capacities, so that we may at last obtain an exact picture of the powers and limitations of human understanding.

The negative phase of Hume's project scrutinizes the central arguments of the dominant philosophical and theological views of his day and exposes the lack of cognitive content in their key notions. Hume's skeptical arguments are an important part of this negative phase. Since these arguments are among the most prominent and powerful Hume has to offer, it is not surprising that they are often mistaken for his final view. But these arguments function as *reductios* of theories he rejects, not as parts of the positive position he offers in their place. They point up the poverty of false metaphysics to rid us of the temptation of doing metaphysics this way. Only then will we be ready for the positive phase—true metaphysics, which will replace the old, incoherent metaphysics with the careful, accurate description that is the proper goal of philosophy.

EMPIRICISM

This combination of negative and positive aims is a distinguishing feature of Hume's particular brand of empiricism: the strategy he devised to achieve these aims is revelatory of his philosophical genius.

For Hume, all the materials of thinking—"perceptions"—are derived from "sensation" ("outward sentiment") or from "reflection" ("inward sentiment"). He divides perceptions into two categories, distinguished by their different degrees of force and vivacity (see PERCEPTION). Our "more feeble" perceptions, IDEAS, are ultimately derived from our livelier *impressions.*

Though we permute and combine ideas to form complex ideas of things we have not experienced, our creative powers extend no further than "the materials afforded us by the senses and experience." Complex ideas are composed of simple ideas, fainter copies of the simple impressions from which they are derived, to which they correspond and exactly resemble. Hume offers this "general proposition," his "first principle . . . in the science of human nature," as an empirical thesis. He even offers a counterexample—the infamous missing shade of blue.

Hume's empiricism is usually identified with this principle. Generally called "the Copy Principle," it is indeed the cornerstone of his empiricism, though his use of its *reverse*—in his account of definition—is the most distinctive element of his empiricism.

Believing that "the chief obstacle . . . to our improvement in the moral or metaphysical sciences is the obscurity of the ideas, and ambiguity of the terms," Hume argued that conventional definitions—defining terms in terms of other terms—replicate philosophical confusions by substituting synonyms for the original and thus never break out of a narrow definitional circle. Determining the cognitive content of an idea or term requires something else.

Hume supplied what was required with his account of definition, which offers a simple series of tests to determine cognitive content. First, find the idea to which a term is annexed. If none can be found, then the term has no content, however prominently it may figure in philosophy or theology. If the idea is complex, break it up into the simple ideas of which it is composed. Then trace the simple ideas back to their original impressions: "These impressions are all strong and sensible. They admit not of ambiguity. They are not only placed in a full light themselves, but may throw light on their correspondent ideas, which lie in obscurity" (*An Enquiry concerning Human Understanding*: 62).

If the process fails at any point, the idea in question lacks cognitive content. When carried out successfully, it yields a full account—a "just definition"— of the troublesome idea or term; a Humean definition gives us its exact cognitive content. So, whenever we are suspicious that a

philosophical term is employed without any meaning or idea (as is too frequent), we need but enquire, *from what impression is that supposed idea derived?* And if it be impossible to assign any, this will serve to confirm our suspicion. By bringing ideas into offso clear a light we may reasonably hope to remove all dispute, which may arise, concerning their nature and reality. (*An Enquiry concerning Human Understanding*: 22)

Hume's account of definition is not only the distinctive feature of his empiricism; it is also a brilliant strategic device. He regards it as "a new microscope or species of optics, by which, in the moral sciences, the most minute, and most simple ideas may be so enlarged as to fall readily under our apprehension, and be equally known with the grossest and most sensible ideas, that can be the object of our enquiry" (*An Enquiry concerning Human Understanding*: 62).

ASSOCIATION

The Copy Principle accounts for the origins of our ideas. But our ideas are also regularly connected: "[T]here is a secret tie or union among particular ideas, which causes the mind to conjoin them more frequently together, and makes the one, upon its appearance, introduce the other" (*Abstract of a Treatise of Human Nature*: 662).

A science of human nature should account for these connections. Otherwise, we are stuck with an eidetic atomism that fails to explain how ideas are "bound together." The inadequacy of eidetic atomism encourages us, as Hume thought it encouraged Locke, to postulate theoretical notions—power, SUBSTANCE— to account for the connections we find among our ideas. Eidetic atomism is thus a prime source of the philosophical "hypotheses" Hume aims to eliminate.

Hume saw that the required principles were not theoretical and rational; they were natural operations of the mind, *associations* we experience in "internal sensation," or reflection (see ASSOCIATIONISM). Hume's introduction of these "principles of association" is the other distinctive feature of his empiricism, so distinctive that in the "Abstract" he advertises it as his most original contribution: "If any thing can intitle the author to so glorious a name as that of an inventor, 'tis the use he makes of the principle of the association of ideas."

Hume locates "three principles of connexion" or association: resemblance, contiguity, and cause and effect. Of the three, causation is the only principle that takes us "beyond the evidence of our memory and senses." It establishes a link or connection between past and present experiences with events that we predict or explain, so that "all reasonings concerning matter of fact seem to be founded on the relation of cause and effect." But causation and the ideas closely related to it also raise serious metaphysical problems: "[T]here are no ideas, which occur in metaphysics, more obscure and uncertain, than those of power, force, energy or necessary connexion" (*An Enquiry concerning Human Understanding*: 61–62).

Hume wants to "fix, if possible, the precise meaning of these terms, and thereby remove some part of that obscurity, which is so much complained of in this species of philosophy" (*An Enquiry concerning Human Understanding*: 62). This project provides a crucial experiment for Hume's metaphysical microscope. If successful, it will prove the worth of his method, will provide a paradigm for investigating problematic philosophical and theological notions, and will supply valuable material for these inquiries.

CAUSATION: THE NEGATIVE PHASE

Hume's strategy dictates that he first show that alternative accounts of our "causal reasonings" are inadequate. This negative project directs his metaphysical microscope toward the intellectualist view that causal connections are made on the basis of the operations of the understanding. Hume proceeds by examining all of the possible ways in which our "causal reasonings" might be based on reason.

Reasoning concerns either *relations of ideas* or *matters of fact*. Hume quickly establishes that, whatever assures us that a causal relation obtains, it is not reasoning concerning relations between ideas. Effects are distinct events from their causes: we can always conceive of one such event occurring and the other not. So causal reasoning cannot be a priori reasoning (see A PRIORI/A POSTERIORI DISTINCTION).

Causes and effects are discovered not by reason but through experience, when we find that particular objects are constantly conjoined with one another. We tend to overlook this because most ordinary causal judgments are so familiar; we have made them so many times that our judgment seems immediate. But when we consider the matter, we realize that "an (absolutely) unexperienced reasoner could be no reasoner at all" (*An Enquiry concerning Human Understanding*: 45n). Even in applied mathematics, where we use abstract reasoning and geometrical methods to apply principles we regard as laws to particular cases in order to derive further principles as consequences of these laws, the discovery of the original law itself was due to experience and observation, not to a priori reasoning.

Even after we have experience of causal connections, our conclusions from those experiences are not based on any reasoning or on any other process of the understanding. They are based on our past experiences of similar cases, without which we could draw no conclusions at all.

But this leaves us without any link between the past and the future. How can we justify extending our conclusions from past observation and experience to the future? The connection between a proposition that summarizes past experience and one that predicts what will occur at some future time is surely not an intuitive connection; it needs to be established by reasoning or argument. The reasoning involved must either be *demonstrative* (see DEMONSTRATION), concerning relations of ideas, or *probable* (see PROBABILITY), concerning matters of fact and existence.

There is no room for demonstrative reasoning here. We can always conceive of a change in the course of nature. However unlikely it may seem, such a supposition is intelligible and can be distinctly conceived. It therefore implies no contradiction, so it cannot be proven false by a priori demonstrative reasoning.

Probable reasoning cannot establish the connection, either, since it is based on the relation of cause and effect. What we understand of that relation is based on experience, and any inference from experience is based on the supposition that nature is uniform—that the future will be like the past.

The connection could be established by adding a premise stating that nature is uniform. But how could we justify such a claim? Appeal to experience will either be circular or question-begging. For any such appeal must be founded on some version of the uniformity principle itself—the very principle we need to justify.

This argument exhausts the ways reason might establish a connection between cause and effect and so completes the negative phase of Hume's project. The explanatory model of human nature that makes reason prominent and dominant in thought and action is indefensible. Skepticism about it is well founded: the model must go.

Hume insists that he offers his "sceptical doubts about the operations of the understanding," not as "discouragement, but rather an incitement . . . to attempt something more full and satisfactory" (*An Enquiry concerning Human Understanding*: 26). Having cleared a space for his own account, Hume is ready to do just that.

CAUSATION: THE POSITIVE PHASE

Hume's negative argument showed that our causal expectations are not formed on the basis of reason. But we do form them, and "if the mind be not engaged by argument . . . it must be induced by some other principle of equal weight and authority."

This principle cannot be some "intricate or profound" metaphysical argument Hume overlooked. For all of us—ordinary people, infants, even animals—"improve by experience," forming causal expectations and refining them in the light of experience. Hume's "sceptical solution" limits our inquiries to common life, where no sophisticated metaphysical arguments are available, and none are required.

When we examine experience to see how expectations are actually produced, we discover that they arise after we have experienced "the constant conjunction of two objects"; only then do we "expect the one from the appearance of the other." But when "repetition of any particular act or operation produces a propensity to renew the same act or operation . . . we always say, that this propensity is the effect of *Custom*."

So the process that produces our causal expectations is itself causal. Custom or habit "determines the mind . . . to suppose the future conformable to the past." But if this background of experienced constant conjunctions was all that was involved, then our "reasonings" would be merely hypothetical. Expecting that fire will warm, however, is not just *conceiving* of its warming; it is *believing* that it will warm.

Belief requires that there also be some fact present to the senses or memory that gives "strength and solidity to the related idea." In these circumstances, belief is as unavoidable as is the feeling of a passion; it is "a species of natural instinct," "the necessary result of placing the mind" in this situation.

Belief is "a peculiar sentiment, or lively conception produced by habit" that results from the *manner* in which ideas are conceived and "in their feeling to the mind." It is "nothing but a more vivid, lively, forcible, firm, steady conception of an object, than what the imagination alone is ever able to attain." Belief is thus "more an act of the sensitive, than of the cogitative part of our natures," so that "all probable reasoning is nothing but a species of sensation." This should not be surprising, given that belief is "so essential to the subsistence of all human creatures." "It is more conformable to the ordinary wisdom of nature to secure so necessary an act of the mind, by some instinct or mechanical tendency" than to trust it "to the fallacious deductions of our reason." Hume's "sceptical solution" thus gives a descriptive alternative, appropriately "independent of all the laboured deductions of the understanding," to philosophers' attempts to account for our causal "reasonings" by appeal to reason and argument. For the other notions in the definitional circle, "either we have no idea of force or energy, and these words are altogether insignificant, or they can mean nothing but that determination of the thought, acquir'd by habit, to pass from the cause to its usual effect."

NECESSARY CONNECTION AND THE DEFINITION OF CAUSE

It remains only for Hume to "confirm and illustrate" his positive account by providing a precise definition of our idea of causation. In doing so, he accounts in his own terms for the "necessary connection" so many philosophers have taken to be an essential component of the idea of causation.

As we should expect from the preceding discussion, when we examine a single case of two events we regard as causally related, our impressions are only of their *conjunction*; the single case, taken by itself, yields no notion of their *connection*. When we go beyond the single case to examine the background of experienced constant conjunctions of similar pairs of events, we find little to add, for "there is nothing in a number of instances, different from every single instance, which is supposed to be exactly similar." How can the mere repetition of *conjunctions* produce a *connection*?

While there is indeed nothing added to our *external* senses by this exercise, something does happen: "[A]fter a repetition of similar instances, the mind is carried by habit, upon the appearance of one event, to expect its usual attendant, and to believe that it will exist." We *feel* this transition as an impression of *reflection*, or *internal* sensation, and it is this feeling of determination that is "the sentiment or impression from which we form the idea of power or necessary connexion. Nothing farther is in the case."

Though the impression of reflection—the internal sensation—is the source of our idea of the connection, that experience would not have occurred if we had not had the requisite impressions of sensation—the external impressions of the current situation, together with the background of memories of our past impressions of relevant similar instances.

All the impressions involved are relevant to a complete account of the origin of the idea, even though they seem to be "drawn from objects foreign to the cause." Hume sums up all of the relevant impressions in not one but two definitions of *cause*.

The relation—or the lack of it—between these definitions has been a matter of considerable controversy. If we follow his account of definition, however, the first definition, which defines a cause as *"an object, followed by another, and where all objects similar to the first are followed by objects similar to the second,"* accounts for all the external impressions involved in the case. His second definition, which defines a cause as *"an object followed by another, and whose appearance always conveys the thought to that other,"* captures the internal sensation—the feeling of determination—involved. Both are definitions, by Hume's account, but the "just definition" of *cause* he claims to provide is expressed only by the conjunction of the two: only together do the definitions capture all the relevant impressions involved.

Hume's account of causation provides a paradigm of how philosophy, as he conceives it, should be done. He goes on to apply his method to other thorny traditional problems of philosophy and theology: liberty and necessity (see FREE WILL), miracles, and design (see GOD and RELIGION). In each case, the moral is that a priori reasoning and argument get us nowhere: "[I]t is only experience which teaches us the nature and bounds of cause and effect, and enables us to infer the existence of one object from that of another. Such is the foundation of moral reasoning, which forms the greater part of human knowledge, and is the source of all human action and behaviour." Since we all have limited experience, our conclusions should always be tentative, modest, reserved, and cautious. This conservative, fallibilist position, which Hume calls "mitigated scepticism," is the proper epistemic attitude for anyone "sensible of the strange infirmities of human understanding."

MORAL PHILOSOPHY

The cautious attitude Hume recommends is noticeably absent in moral philosophy, where "systems and hypotheses" have also "perverted our natural understanding," the most prominent being the views of the moral rationalists (Samuel Clarke, Locke, and William Wollaston), the theories of "the selfish schools" (HOBBES and Mandeville), and the pernicious theological ethics of "the schools," whose promotion of the dismal "monkish virtues" frame a catalog of virtues that is diametrically opposed to Hume's.

Though he offers arguments against the "systems" he opposes, Hume thinks the strongest case against them is to be made descriptively: all these theories offer accounts of human nature that "experience and observation" prove false.

Against the moral rationalists—the intellectualists of moral philosophy—who hold that moral judgments are based on reason, Hume maintains that it is difficult even to make their "hypothesis" intelligible. Reason, Hume argues, judges either of *matters of fact* or of *relations* (see RELATIONS). Morality never consists in any single matter of fact that could be immediately perceived, intuited, or grasped by reason alone; morality for rationalists must therefore involve the perception of relations. But inanimate objects and animals can bear the same relations to one another that humans can, though we do not draw the same moral conclusions from determining that objects or animals are in a given relation as we do when humans are in that same relation. Distinguishing these cases requires more than reason alone can provide. Even if we could determine an appropriate subject matter for the moral rationalist, it would still be the case that, after determining that a matter of fact or a relation obtains, the understanding has no more room to operate, so the praise or blame that follows cannot be the work of reason.

Reason, Hume maintains, can at most inform us of the tendencies of actions. It can recommend means for attaining a given end, but it cannot recommend ultimate ends. Reason can provide no motive to action, for reason alone is insufficient to produce moral blame or approbation. We need sentiment to give a preference to the useful tendencies of actions.

Finally, the moral rationalists' account of justice fares no better. Justice cannot be determined by examining a single case, since the advantage to society of a rule of justice depends on how it works in general under the circumstances in which it is introduced.

Thus, the views of the moral rationalists on the role of reason in ethics, even if they can be made coherent, are clearly false.

Hume then turns to the claims of the "selfish schools," that morality either is altogether illusory (Mandeville) or can be reduced to considerations of self-interest (Hobbes). He argues that an accurate description of the social virtues, benevolence and justice, will show that these views are false.

There has been much discussion over the differences between Hume's presentation of these arguments in the *Treatise* and the second *Enquiry*. "Sympathy" is the key term in the *Treatise*, while "benevolence" does the work in the *Enquiry*. But this need not reflect any substantial shift in doctrine. If we look closely, we see that benevolence plays much the same functional role in the *Enquiry* that sympathy plays in the *Treatise*. Hume sometimes describes benevolence as a manifestation of our "natural" or "social sympathy." In both texts, Hume's central point is that we experience this "feeling for humanity" in ourselves and observe it in others, so "the selfish hypothesis" is "contrary both to common feeling and to our most unprejudiced notions."

Borrowing from Butler and Hutcheson, Hume argues that, however prominent considerations of self-interest may be, we do find cases where, when self-interest is *not* at stake, we respond with benevolence, not indifference. We approve of benevolence in others, even when their benevolence is not, and never will be, directed toward us. We even observe benevolence in animals. Haggling over *how much* benevolence is found in human nature is pointless; that there is *any benevolence at all* refutes the selfish hypothesis.

Against Hobbes, Hume argues that our benevolent sentiments cannot be reduced to self-interest. It is true that, when we desire the happiness of others and try to make them happy, we may enjoy doing so. But benevolence is necessary for our self-enjoyment, and though we may act from the combined motives of benevolence and enjoyment, our benevolent sentiments are not identical with our self-enjoyment.

We approve of benevolence in large part because it is *useful*. Benevolent acts tend to promote social welfare, and those who are benevolent are motivated to cultivate the other social virtue, justice. But while benevolence is an original principle in human nature, justice is not. Our need for rules of justice is not universal; it arises only under conditions of relative scarcity, where property must be regulated to preserve order in society.

The need for rules of justice is also a function of a society's size. In very small societies, where the members are more of an extended family, there may be no need for rules of justice, because there is no need for regulating property— no need, indeed, for our notion of *property* at all. Only when society becomes extensive enough that it is impossible for everyone in it to be part of one's "narrow circle" does the need for rules of justice arise.

The rules of justice in a given society are "the product of artifice and contrivance." They are constructed by the society to solve the problem of how to regulate property; other rules might do just as well. The real need is for some set of "general inflexible rules . . . adopted as best to serve public utility."

Hobbesians try to reduce justice to self-interest, because all people recognize that it is in their interest that there be rules regulating property. But even here, the benefits for each individual result from the whole scheme or system being in place, not from the fact that each just act benefits each individual directly. As with benevolence, Hume argues that we approve of the system itself even where our self-interest is not at stake. We can see this not only from cases in our own society but also when we consider societies distant in space and time.

Hume's social virtues are related. Sentiments of benevolence draw us to society, allow us to perceive its advantages, provide a source of approval for just acts, and motivate us to do just acts ourselves. We approve of both virtues because we recognize their role in promoting the happiness and prosperity of society. Their functional roles are, nonetheless, distinct. Hume compares the benefits of benevolence to "a wall, built by many hands, which still rises by every stone that is heaped upon it, and receives increase proportional to the diligence and care of each workman," while the happiness justice produces is like the results of building "a vault, where each individual stone would, of itself, fall to the ground."

"Daily observation" confirms that we recognize and approve of the utility of acts of benevolence and justice. While much of the agreeableness of the utility we find in these acts may be due to the fact that they promote our self-interest, it is also true that, in approving of useful acts, we do not restrict ourselves to those that serve our particular interests. Similarly, our private interests often differ from the public interest, but, despite our sentiments in favor of our self-interest, we often retain our sentiment in favor of the public interest. Where these interests concur, we observe "a sensible increase of the sentiment," so "the interests of society are not . . . entirely indifferent to us."

With that final nail in Hobbes' coffin, Hume turns to develop his account of the sources of morality. Though we often approve or disapprove of the actions of those remote from us in space and time, it is nonetheless true that, in considering the acts of, say, an Athenian statesman, the good he produced "affects us with a less lively sympathy," even though we judge their "merit to be equally great" as the similar acts of our contemporaries. In such cases our judgment "corrects the inequalities of our internal emotions and perceptions; in like manner, as it preserves us from error, in the several variations of images, presented to our external senses." Adjustment and correction are necessary in both cases if we are to think and talk consistently and coherently.

"The intercourse of sentiments" that conversation produces is the vehicle for these adjustments, for it takes us out of our own peculiar positions. We begin to employ general language that, since it is formed for general use, "must be moulded on some general views." In so doing, we take up a "general" or "common point of view," detached from our self-interested perspectives, to form "some general unalterable standard, by which we may approve or disapprove of characters and manners." We begin to "speak another language"—the language of morals, which

implies some sentiment common to all mankind, which recommends the same object to general approbation, and makes every man, or most men, agree in the same opinion or decision concerning it. It also implies some sentiment, so universal and comprehensive as to extend to all mankind, and render the actions and conduct, even of the persons the most remote, an object of applause or censure, according as they agree or disagree with that rule of right which is established. These two requisite circumstances belong alone to the sentiment of humanity here insisted on. (*An Enquiry concerning the Principles of Morals*: 272)

It is the "extended" or "extensive" sentiment of humanity—"benevolence" or "sympathy"—that for Hume is ultimately "the foundation of morals."

But even if the *social* virtues move us from a perspective of self-interest to one more universal and extensive, it might appear that the *individual* virtues do not. But since these virtues also receive our approbation because of their usefulness, and since "these advantages are enjoyed by the person possessed of the character, it can never be self-love which renders the prospect of them agreeable to us, the spectators, and prompts our esteem and approbation."

Just as we make judgments about others, we are aware, from infancy, that others make judgments about us. We desire their approval and modify our behavior in response to their judgments. This "love of fame" gives rise to the habit of reflectively evaluating our own actions and character traits. We first see ourselves as others see us, but eventually we develop our own standards of evaluation, keeping "alive all the sentiments of right and wrong," which "begets, in noble natures, a certain reverence" for ourselves as well as others, "which is the surest guardian of every virtue."

The general character of moral language, produced and promoted by our social sympathies, permits us to judge ourselves and others from the general point of view, the proper perspective of morality. For Hume, that is "the most perfect morality with which we are acquainted."

Hume summarizes his account in this definition of virtue, or "Personal Merit": "[E]very quality of the mind, which is *useful* or *agreeable* to the *person himself* or to *others*, communicates a pleasure to the spectator, engages his esteem, and is admitted under the honourable denomination of virtue or merit" (*An Enquiry concerning the Principles of Morals*: 277). That is, as observers—of ourselves as well as others—to the extent that we regard certain acts as manifestations of certain character traits we consider the usual tendencies of acts done from those traits and find them useful or agreeable, to the agent or to others, and approve or disapprove of them accordingly. A striking feature of this definition is that it is precisely parallel to the two definitions of cause that Hume gave as the conclusion of his central argument in the first *Enquiry*. Both definitions pick out features of events, and both record a spectator's reaction or response to those events.

POLITICS, CRITICISM, HISTORY, AND RELIGION

The "advertisement" for the first two books of the *Treatise* promised subsequent books on morals, politics, and criticism, but Hume abandoned this ambitious project after Book III "fell dead-born from the press"; his *Political Discourses*, "On Tragedy," and "Of the Standard of Taste" are our only hints as to his views on those topics.

Hume's political essays range widely, not only covering the constitutional issues one might expect but also venturing into what we would now call economics, dealing with issues of commerce, luxury, and their implications for society. His treatments of these scattered topics exhibit a unity of purpose and method that makes the essays much more than the sum of their parts and links them not only with his more narrowly philosophical concerns but also with his earlier moral and literary essays.

Hume adopts a causal, descriptive approach to each of the problems he discusses, stressing that current events and concerns can be best understood by tracing them historically to their origins. This approach contrasts sharply with the discussions of his contemporaries, who treated these events as the products of chance or—worse—of providence. Hume substitutes a concern for the "moral causes"—human choices and actions—of the events, conditions, or institutions he discusses. This thoroughly secular approach is accentuated by his willingness to point out the bad effects of superstition and enthusiasm on society, government, and political and social life.

"Of the Standard of Taste" is a rich contribution to the then-emerging discipline of what we now call aesthetics. This complex essay contains a lucid statement of Hume's views on what constitutes "just criticism," but it is not just about criticism, as readers are now beginning to realize. Though Hume's account of aesthetic judgment precisely parallels his account of causal and moral judgment, the essay also contains a discussion of how a naturalistic theory might deal with questions of normativity and so is important not just as a significant contribution to Hume's overall view but also for its immediate relevance for pressing problems in contemporary empirical naturalism.

Hume's *History of England*, published in six volumes over as many years in the 1750s, recalls Hume's characterization, in the first *Enquiry*, of history as "so many collections of experiments." Hume not surprisingly rejects the theoretical commitments of both Tory and Whig accounts of British history and offers what he believes is an impartial account that looks at political institutions as historical developments responsive to Britons' experience of changing conditions, evaluating political decisions in the contexts in which they were made, instead of second-guessing them in the light of subsequent developments.

The *Natural History of Religion* is also a history in a sense, though it has been described as "philosophical" or "conjectural" history. It is an account of the origins and development of religious beliefs, with the thinly disguised agenda not only of making clear the nonrational origins of religion but also of exposing and describing the pathology of its current forms. Religion began in the postulation, by primitive peoples, of "invisible intelligences" to account for frightening, uncontrollable natural phenomena, such as disease and earthquakes. In its original forms, it was polytheistic, which Hume regards as relatively harmless because of their tolerance of diversity. But polytheism eventually gives way to monotheism, when the followers of one deity hold sway over the others. Monotheism is dogmatic and intolerant; worse, it gives rise to theological systems which spread absurdity and intolerance but that use reason to corrupt philosophical thought. But since religion is not universal in the way that our nonrational beliefs in causation or physical objects are, perhaps it can eventually be dislodged from human thinking altogether.

Hume's *Natural History* cemented his reputation as a religious skeptic and atheist, even before its publication. Prompted by his own prudence, as well as the pleas of his friends, he resisted publishing the *Dialogues concerning Natural Religion*, which he had worked on since the early 1750s, though he continued revising the manuscript until his death. An expansion and dramatic revision of the argument he previewed in Section XI of the first *Enquiry*, the *Dialogues* is riddled with irony to the extent that controversy still rages as to what character, if any, speaks for Hume. But his devastating critique of the argument from design leaves no doubt that—scholarly details about its enigmatic final section aside—the conclusions philosophers and theologians have drawn from that argument go far beyond any evidence the argument itself provides.

A fitting conclusion to a philosophical life, the posthumously published *Dialogues* alone ensures the philosophical and literary immortality of its author: Hume not only shows himself to be a master of the dialogue form, but his last book also is *the* preeminent work in the philosophy of religion.

PRIMARY WORKS

There is at present no standard critical edition of Hume's philosophical writings. The closest thing to a complete edition remains the edition of Green and Grose.

The Philosophical Works of David Hume. 4 vols., edited by T. H. Green and T. H. Grose. London: Longman, Green, 1874–1875.

The Letters of David Hume. 2 vols., edited by J.Y.T. Greig. Oxford: Clarendon Press, 1932.

Dialogues concerning Natural Religion. Edited by Norman Kemp Smith. Oxford: Oxford University Press, 1935.

New Letters of David Hume. Edited by Raymond Klibansky and Ernest C. Mossner. Oxford: Clarendon Press, 1954.

The Natural History of Religion. Edited by H. E. Root. Stanford, CA: Stanford University Press, 1967.

Enquiries concerning Human Understanding and concerning the Principles of Morals. Edited with an analytical index by L. A. Selby-Bigge; revised with notes by P. H. Nidditch. Oxford: Clarendon Press, 1975.

A Treatise of Human Nature. 2d ed., edited with an analytical index by L. A. Selby-Bigge, revised with notes by P. H. Nidditch. Oxford: Clarendon Press, 1978. Also contains Hume's "Abstract" of the *Treatise.*

The History of England, from the Invasion of Julius Caesar to the Revolution of 1688. Edited by William B. Todd. Indianapolis: Liberty Classics, 1983.

Essays, Moral, Political, Literary. Edited by Eugene F. Miller. Indianapolis: Liberty Classics, 1985.

BIBLIOGRAPHY

Hall also prepared annual bibliographies of the Hume literature for *Hume Studies*, a journal specializing in work on Hume, for the years 1977–1986; these bibliographies appeared in the November issues of that journal from 1978 to 1988. *Hume Studies* revived the practice of including bibliographies with its November 1994 issue, which contained a comprehensive bibliography of the Hume literature from 1986 to 1993. Subsequent volumes contain annual supplements to this bibliography.

Árdal, Páll S. *Passion and Value in Hume's* Treatise. Edinburgh: Edinburgh University Press, 1966; 2d ed., 1989.

Baier, Annette C. *A Progress of Sentiments: Reflections on Hume's* Treatise. Cambridge: Harvard University Press, 1991.

Beauchamp, Tom L., and Alexander Rosenberg. *Hume and the Problem of Causation.* New York: Oxford University Press, 1981.

Bennett, Jonathan. *Locke, Berkeley, Hume: Central Themes.* Oxford: Oxford University Press, 1973.

Box, Mark A. *The Suasive Art of David Hume.* Princeton: Princeton University Press, 1990.

Bricke, John. *Hume's Philosophy of Mind*. Princeton: Princeton University Press, 1980.

Capaldi, Nicholas. *Hume's Place in Moral Philosophy*. New York: Peter Lang, 1989.

Fogelin, Robert. *Hume's Scepticism in the* Treatise of Human Nature. London: Routledge and Kegan Paul, 1985.

Garrett, Don. *Cognition and Commitment in Hume's Philosophy*. New York: Oxford University Press, 1997.

Hall, Roland. *Fifty Years of Hume Scholarship: A Bibliographical Guide*. Edinburgh: Edinburgh University Press, 1978. A useful bibliography of work on Hume.

Jones, Peter. *Hume's Sentiments*. Edinburgh: Edinburgh University Press, 1982.

Livingston, Donald W. *Hume's Philosophy of Common Life*. Chicago: University of Chicago Press, 1984.

Mossner, Ernest Campbell. *The Life of David Hume*. London: Nelson, 1954.

Norton, David Fate. *David Hume, Common Sense Moralist, Sceptical Metaphysician*. Princeton: Princeton University Press, 1982.

———, ed. *The Cambridge Companion to Hume*. Cambridge: Cambridge University Press, 1993.

Noxon, James. *Hume's Philosophical Development*. Oxford: Oxford University Press, 1973.

Passmore, John. *Hume's Intentions*. Cambridge: Cambridge University Press, 1952.

Pears, David. *Hume's System: An Examination of the First Book of His* Treatise. Oxford: Oxford University Press, 1990.

Penelhum, Terence. *Hume*. London: Macmillan, 1975.

Phillipson, Nicholas. *Hume*. London: Weidenfeld and Nicolson, 1989.

Russell, Paul. *Freedom and Moral Sentiment*. New York: Oxford University Press, 1995.

Smith, Norman Kemp. *The Philosophy of David Hume*. London: Macmillan, 1941.

Stewart, John B. *Opinion and Reform in Hume's Political Philosophy*. Princeton: Princeton University Press, 1992.

Stewart, M. A., and John P. Wright. *Hume and Hume's Connexions*. Edinburgh: Edinburgh University Press, 1994.

Strawson, Galen. *The Secret Connexion: Causation, Realism and David Hume*. Oxford: Oxford University Press, 1989.

Stroud, Barry. *Hume*. London: Routledge and Kegan Paul, 1977.

Wright, John P. *The Sceptical Realism of David Hume*. Minneapolis: University of Minnesota Press, 1983.

WILLIAM E. MORRIS

I

IDEALISM. Idealism is, fundamentally, the metaphysical (ontological) thesis that reality is ideational, sensational, or otherwise made of "mental stuff." In this sense, idealism is opposed to at least three other views about the nature of reality: materialism (only material things exist), dualism (both material and mental things exist), and neutral monism (the stuff of the world is "neutral," neither material nor mental). Of course, philosophers rarely confine themselves to ontology, and, in fact, the earliest form of idealism, PLATO's, is a blend of ontology and epistemology, a theory of what exists combined with a theory of knowledge.

Plato held that the objects of knowledge (real objects) are eternal, unchanging, and transcendental Ideas (or Forms). In the *Timaeus* Ideas are held to be coexistent with, but independent of, both humanity (human souls) and the δημιονργοζ (the "craftsman/artisan" or maker of the world). Ideas are sui generis, that is, literally without generation, for they are *absolute existents*, items having no existential dependence on anything else. Ideas are, moreover, both *universals* and *exemplars*: they are what is common to many individuals as well as that toward which those individuals are teleologically directed (all things strive for "that which is best"). In the dialogues *Meno* and *Phaedo*, the account presupposes that our original knowledge of Ideas, the knowledge our souls acquire "before we were born," is a kind of direct or immediate cognitive acquaintance. As Plato's "Socrates" then explains, in this life (incarnation) we come to know of Ideas through a process of recollection: the sensory perception of (imperfect) copies of Ideas, namely, the various perceptible qualities of sensible things, serves to remind us of their originals, the Ideas (see INNATE-NESS). Since the former are in constant flux, sense perception is not a state of knowledge but only one of opinion.

In the early years of the eighteenth century, George BERKELEY advanced a version of idealism that, in three fundamental ways, turned the Platonic theory upside down. Berkeley argued, first, that Platonic knowledge, the pure contemplation of Ideas, is impossible (see ABSTRACTION). He argued, second, that (most of) the real objects of knowledge are fleeting, momentary sensible things (precisely Plato's objects of mere opinion). He argued, third, that ideas (identified, neutrally, with sensible qualities and sensible things) are mind-dependent. Although Berkeley never used the term "idealism" to describe his theory, it is with this third thesis—specifically, with the thesis that sensible things cannot exist apart from being perceived (their *esse* is *percipi*)—that we now most closely associate the term. The expression Berkeley preferred, "immaterialism," serves better to emphasize his PHENOMENALISM, that is, his immaterialist analysis of bodies. According to this analysis, bodies are not material substances with causal powers and sensible qualities inhering in them—a view that, Berkeley argues, is incoherent. Rather, bodies are constituted entirely of sensed qualities from the various different modes of sense perception. On this account, bodies are nothing but coherently and lawfully related collections of sensible qualities.

Berkeley's idealism, properly speaking, resides in an additional set of claims, the most important of which are these: (1) sensible qualities are sensational—it is impossible for them to exist beyond the duration of one's perceptual consciousness; (2) there is no act–object distinction in sense perception; (3) it is incoherent to speak of an absolutely existing sensible thing (the argument for this is nowadays referred to as the "master argument"; see *Principles*: 22–23 and *Three Dialogues*: 200); and (4) all real causes are mental activities. In Berkeley's philosophy, the phenomenalistic analysis of bodies interacts with several of these theses. For example, it interacts in two ways with (4). The first way is this: Berkeley insists that though the qualities of sensible things are inseparable from our minds, we are not causally responsible for their existence; their causes, he argues, are the volitional activities of a Deity. (However, he assumes, rather than proves, that the volitional activities causing sensible qualities are all activities of a *single* Deity.) The second way phenomenalism interacts with (4)—a way that is of special significance for the later development of idealism—resides in Berkeley's account of the source of the *coherence* of sensible qualities, that is, in the cause of the *unity* of sensible things. He vacillates between an "objective" idealist position that this coherence is not something for which the perceiver is causally responsible and a "subjective" idealist position that it is. For example, Berkeley has "Philonous" say, of the sensible qualities constituting a cherry, that they "are united into one thing (or have one name given them) by the mind" (*Three Dialogues between Hylas and Philonous*: 249). This passage seems unproblematically to support a subjectivist reading of Berkeley: not only are the individual sensible qualities of a thing ideas, but the very coherence of those qualities is brought about by the perceiver, via the causal activities of his or her cognitive or imaginative faculty. However, since Berkeley officially acknowledges only volitional causation, the subjectivist alternative cannot be a serious possibility: we can no more be said to will the order in which sensible qualities appear to us than we can be said to will their existence. In fact, Berkeley is more attracted here to the objectivist alternative, since he holds that God, not the finite perceiver, via orderly (lawful) creation, does the collecting of sensible qualities into sensible things.

A more thoroughly idealist position regarding the coherence of sensible things (and more generally, the unity of the world) nevertheless finds its opening in Berkeley's suggestion; and KANT took the first firm steps in this direction. His *transcendental idealism* includes the view that CAUSATION, SPACE, and TIME are among the categories that make perceptual experience possible: they are "the a priori conditions of the possibility of experience." While Kant did not (and could not consistently) speak of this in terms of process or describe it as a case of "mental contribution" to the objects of perception—indeed, his official view is that the mind (and its operations) is as much an unknown, a *noumenon*, as the body (the *Ding an sich*)—that did not prevent his successors from drawing this conclusion.

The nineteenth century saw the development of various forms of *absolute idealism*, the view that mind (usually God's) is the ultimate principle of reality. In Germany the principal successors of Kant combined this ontological position with epistemological, ethical, political, and sometimes even aesthetic components as well as "libertarian" responses to the doctrine of determinism. J. G. Fichte (1762–1814) argued that mind (especially cognitive thought and intelligence) cannot be causally explained but must be taken as sui generis in any attempt to give a fundamental account of the world. F.W.J. von Schelling (1775–1854) maintained that our capacity for aesthetic appreciation reveals the mind as the only unconditioned, undetermined, and therefore absolute being. In some of the most impenetrable prose of the period, G.W.F. Hegel (1770–1831) insisted, in his *Science of Logic* (I.i.2) that "the finite is not genuinely real" and, in the same work, tried to show how a deduction of Kant's categories could be achieved. Britain's principal absolute idealists were T. H. Green (1836–1882) and F. H. Bradley (1846–1924). Green blended Berkeleian, Kantian, and Hegelian theses, respectively, in arguing that mind is the source of all order (relational and otherwise) in the world; denying that there is a "given" in experience; and affirming that the world of finite (natural) objects is not ultimate. In *Appearance and Reality* (1893) Bradley seconded many of these themes while arguing overall that commonsense realism is self-contradictory. He concluded that the only way to avoid antinomies is by adopting a thoroughgoing holism involving both a doctrine of internal relations and a coherence theory of truth (and knowledge).

Idealism had already in the eighteenth century come under attack from both skeptical and realist quarters: David HUME undermined Berkeley's arguments for (1) and (4) and cast doubt on (3) as well, while Thomas REID (1710–1796) attacked the entire tradition of "the way of ideas," a tradition he traced back to Plato. But idealism had to run its course through the nineteenth century before a significant realist backlash was to be initiated by G. E. MOORE (1873–1958) in his seminal 1903 paper "The Refutation of Idealism" (*Philosophical Studies*: 1–30). Moore took "*esse* is *percipi*" to be the core idealistic doctrine, and his main counterargument consisted in a rejection of (2). Even in the simple sensation of a color, he insists, a distinction can be drawn between sensation, or act of mind, and object. Thus, Moore writes, "Merely to have a sensation is already to *be* outside of . . . the circle of our own ideas and sensations" (*Philosophical Studies*: 27). (Perhaps because he focused on such positive arguments for realism, Moore did not call attention to the principal fallacy in Berkeley's argument against the act–object distinction, namely, the illicit replacement of "act" with "action"; see *Three Dialogues*: 195.) Within the past several decades commentators have identified a modal fallacy at the heart of Berkeley's argument for thesis (3)—at the heart of his move from the sentence "[I]t is impossible to conceive of O without conceiving of O" to the sentence "[I]t is impossible to conceive of O as unconceived." While the soundness of Moore's argument may be questioned, and the modal-fallacy objection challenged, it seems clear that Berkeley requires a real distinction between act and object, if only to secure a consistent account of the knowledge we are supposed to have of God. Moore and the critics of Berkeley's argument for (3) are certainly right to this extent: insofar as *"esse* is *percipi"* is held to be some sort of conceptual, a priori, or necessary truth—a stance on its modal status commonly taken by idealists and one that is implicit in the argument for (3)—idealism founders on the bare possibility that a state of awareness (of any kind) is distinct from its object.

PRIMARY WORKS

Berkeley, George. *The Works of George Berkeley, Bishop of Cloyne*. Edited by A. A. Luce and T. E. Jessop. 9 vols. London: Thomas Nelson and Sons, 1948–1957.
Hume, David. *A Treatise of Human Nature*. 2d ed., edited with an analytical index by L. A. Selby-Bigge; revised with notes by P. H. Nidditch. Oxford: Clarendon Press, 1978.
Moore, G. E. *Philosophical Studies*. London: George Allen and Unwin, 1959.

BIBLIOGRAPHY

Ewing, A. C., ed. *The Idealist Tradition: Berkeley to Blanshard*. Glencoe, IL: Free Press, 1969.

ROBERT MUEHLMANN

IDEAS. LOCKE used the term "idea" "to stand for whatsoever is the Object of the Understanding when a Man thinks" (*Essay concerning Human Understanding* I.i.8). Although theorizing about ideas figures prominently in philosophy before him, Locke introduced what became known as the "New Way of Ideas," by considering all metaphysical and epistemological questions through an examination of the nature and origin of the mind's content. Although sometimes disagreeing with him on important details, other empiricists of the modern era follow Locke by first theorizing about the origin of ideas and second by classifying ideas into types, based on origin and characteristics discovered by mental inspection. The shared features of the empiricist notion of ideas is that ideas are not innate and that they are the result of sensation and reflection (see INNATENESS).

In contrast to Plato, for whom ideas were archetypes abstracted from experience and obscured by it, for the empiricist, ideas are first and foremost particular mental contents founded on experience; abstract ideas (see ABSTRACTION) are not given in experience but derive from mental operations involving particular ideas that are so given. The origins of this conception of ideas can be traced to SEXTUS EMPIRICUS and the ancient skeptics. Sextus distinguished between the apprehensive nature of sense perception, which furnishes us with appearances, and the intellect, by means of which we attempt to judge truth and falsity. When we try to judge, for example, whether external objects have the properties we sense them as having, we find that the senses can contradict themselves. For Sextus, we ought doubt not the appearances but rather "the account given of the appearances" (*Outlines of Pyrrhonism*: 15). Here we find an early skeptical answer to the question of the relation between ideas and external objects. Sextus also allowed that we can apprehend the intellect itself, thus anticipating the modern notion of ideas of reflection.

René Descartes (1596–1650), although not an empiricist, did much to introduce theorizing about ideas. Descartes initially defines ideas as belonging to a subclass of the class of thoughts, those that are "images of things." The examples of ideas he gives are the thought of "a man, or a chimera, or the sky, or an angel, or God" (*Philosophical Writings* II: 25). Emotions, volitions, and judgments are not mere ideas. They include ideas as their content but also contain an additional attitude or stance.

Like Sextus Empiricus, Descartes holds that ideas by themselves cannot introduce falsehood or error. Ideas are modifications of the mind, properties of the mental SUBSTANCE that are revealed through clear and distinct perception. Unlike Sextus, however, Descartes does not hold that all ideas originate in sense perception. His tripartite classification of ideas in the *Meditations on First Philosophy* is based on their origin: ideas are innate, adventitious, or made up. Only adventitious ideas are acquired through sense perception. Descartes grants that our ideas appear to come from sense perception, but he argues that such a view is the result not of "reliable judgment" but rather of a "blind impulse." Our most important ideas, including the idea of God and the idea of oneself as a thinking thing, are innate.

Descartes' philosophy forms the backdrop for the theories of ideas of his followers, the Cartesians, and their critics. GASSENDI, an early modern empiricist, took issue with Descartes' tripartite classification. In the *Objections and Replies* to Descartes' *Meditations*, Gassendi argued that all ideas are adventitious; ideas of the imagination, "made up" ideas, are simply concatenations of sensory ideas. Descartes responded that only ideas that are images are derived from the senses. The idea of a chiliagon, Descartes had argued in Meditation VI, is perfectly intelligible, though not imaginable as a construct of sensory perceptions. It is an idea of the intellect.

Controversy arose over the extent to which the mind could author its ideas. Descartes himself had argued that some ideas are the result of external objects' impinging on our senses, for if that were not the case, God would be a deceiver. Following Descartes, Arnauld held that some ideas are authored by the mind, for example, the ideas of existence and thought. Other ideas come from the senses and are signs of the objects they represent. One difficulty with the Cartesian view is that sensory ideas, though mental, are caused by physical things, external objects. Although our knowledge that our ideas are so caused depends on our knowledge that God is no deceiver, it is still the case that a mental phenomenon, an idea, is brought about by entirely different substance, matter.

Malebranche, another Cartesian, sought to resolve the ontological mismatch between ideas and their causes with the doctrine that we see all things in God. We do not perceive external objects, such as the sun and the stars. To do so, Malebranche argued, our souls would have to leave our bodies and "stroll about the heavens" (*The Search after Truth* III.ii.1). What we perceive are our ideas, which are the mind's immediate objects, the "object closest to the mind, when it perceives something." Further, we do not author any of our ideas, even in response to the "impressions that objects make on the body" (*Search* III.ii.3). The claim of human authorship gives us powers that God does not have, since it means that we can create ideas that were not already created by God. Malebranche concludes that all our ideas are those works of God that are revealed to us.

The philosophical treatment of ideas did not, then, begin with Locke. On the contrary, Locke, as well as BERKELEY and HUME, attempts to explain human understanding in terms of ideas, fully aware of the controversies raging about their origin and ontological status. Malebranche had argued that ideas are spiritual items, not material items, and our having ideas is a matter of the uniting of our souls with God's soul. Locke takes this account of the having of ideas to be more problematic than his own, in which sensory ideas are the effects of external objects. For Locke, Malebranche's "intimate union" of our minds with God's "signifies literally nothing" (*Opinion*: 223). Locke has another difficulty with Malebranche's account. Malebranche distinguishes sensations from the ideas of the intellect but vacillates on whether sensations are ideas or physical states accounted for in terms of human physiology. Yet this leads to the same problem Malebranche's doctrine of seeing everything in God was supposed to avoid: if sensations are physical, then how can we see all things in God when we perceive the scent of a rose? If sensations are not physical, how can he distinguish the ideas of the intellect from the sentiments?

Locke's own theory of ideas attempts to avoid these difficulties by using the term "idea" in a broad sense to cover anything about which one thinks and by taking "thinks" to include both sensation and reflection. Accordingly, for Locke, there are two types of ideas, ideas of sensation and ideas of reflection. Examples of the former are "*Yellow, White, Heat, Cold, Soft, Hard, Bitter, Sweet*, and all those which we call sensible qualities" (*Essay* II.i.3). The source of ideas of sensation is external objects. Reflection, "the other Fountain" of ideas, supplies us with ideas such as "*Perception, Thinking, Doubting, Believing, Reasoning, Knowing, Willing*," that is, ideas of the mind's own operations. The source of ideas of reflection is the mind itself, not external objects. Yet Locke insists that this source is also a matter of experience. Our first ideas must be ideas of sensation, since the mind cannot reflect on its operations until there are some operations on which to reflect. Introspection reveals that sensation and reflection are the only sources of ideas; therefore all ideas are either simple ideas of sensation or reflection or complex ideas concatenated from simple ideas (see SIMPLE/COMPLEX).

External objects have the power to bring about ideas in us, but the ideas themselves are not in the external objects; only the power to produce ideas, which Locke calls "qualities," are in the objects. The qualities in external objects produce ideas in us by the motion of matter in those objects, which motion brings about further motions in our bodies. Qualities that produce ideas that resemble qualities that the objects really have Locke calls "primary qualities." Other ideas, of "secondary qualities" such as heat and light, do not resemble actual properties of the objects. The same object can feel hot to one hand and cold to another. Locke explains that this happens because the ideas of secondary qualities arise from the combination of the motions in the object and the motions of the affected part of the body (see PRIMARY/SECONDARY QUALITIES). Fully aware of Malebranche's worry about how matter can cause ideas, Locke sees no difficulty in explaining ideas of sensation in terms of such interaction: "It being no more impossible, to conceive, that God should annex such *Ideas* to such Motions, with which they have no similitude; than that he should annex the *Idea* of Pain to the motion of a piece of Steel dividing our Flesh, with which that *Idea* hath no resemblance" (*Essay* II.viii.13).

Locke's insistence that an account of the nature and origin of ideas provides the starting point for any theory of human understanding was novel enough that Locke offers a preemptive defense of his widespread use of the term "idea" in the Introduction to the *Essay* (*Essay* I.i.8). Some readers found Locke's wide use of the term radical and puzzling. Lee and Sergeant interpreted Locke's emphasis on ideas as a commitment to idealism. Others, such as Stillingfleet and Toland, argued that Locke's use of the term "ideas" deviated from common usage. Others, however, found that Locke provided a framework for understanding how experience brings about the entire range of mental phenomena, and the appeal to ideas gained widespread acceptance in modern British philosophy.

Berkeley, like Locke, takes the objects of human understanding to be ideas. He also follows Locke in recognizing ideas of sense, reflection, and ideas formed from these two sources. Ideas are either "imprinted on the senses, or else such as are perceived by attending to the passions and operations of the mind, or lastly, ideas formed by help of memory and imagination, either compounding, dividing, or barely representing those originally perceived in the aforesaid ways" (*Principles*, Part I, section 1). Ideas are had by the mind and depend on the mind for their existence. This view of the dependence of ideas on the mind is close to Descartes' view that ideas are accidents of the soul as substance. It is a consequence of this dependence that, as Berkeley famously puts it, "the existence of an idea consists in its being perceived" (*Principles*, Part I, §2).

Whereas Locke understood ideas of sense to represent external objects, the final objects of sense for Berkeley are the ideas themselves. Berkeley's insistence that the only things we perceive are our ideas leads him to the conclusion that we do not perceive external objects at all, even through the mediation of ideas. To perceive such external objects would mean either that we perceive nonideas or that things we perceive, external objects, as nonideas, exist unperceived. Either way we have a contradiction. Berkeley's conception of ideas as the sole objects of perception is clearly at work in his rejection of the existence of an external world. Berkeley took his system to avoid the SKEPTICISM engendered by a theory such as Locke's, where ideas represent external objects but where one cannot show that the objects represented exist as represented.

If ideas are not caused by external objects, how can Berkeley account for the fact that ideas come to us against our will and that the interconnections we perceive appear not to be our own cognitive inventions? Here Berkeley resurrects a version of Malebranche's theory that we see all things in God. The order we perceive in the having of ideas, as well as their independence of our will, is proof of God's existence. God, as omniscient perceiver, has created all the ideas there are through divine perception. Human perception is access to God's mind. God provides ideas directly. There is no need for external objects to mediate our insight into God's ideas.

David Hume thought that the generality of Locke's theory of ideas threatened one of its central claims, the claim that there are no innate ideas. Some of the items Locke takes to be ideas, namely, the passions, are, on Hume's view, perceptions that arise "immediately from nature" (*Abstract of a Treatise of Human Nature*: 10). If they are ideas, they are innate. At the same time, Hume criticizes Malebranche's narrow conception of ideas for failing to account for the role of sensation in the origin of ideas. Hume reconciles the narrow and the wide theories of ideas by dividing perceptions into two classes, impressions and ideas. Impressions include "all our sensations, passions, and emotions, as they make their first appearance in the soul" (*Treatise of Human Nature* I.i.1). Ideas are the "faint images" of impressions. We have ideas when we think or remember. Impressions are original; ideas are copies of impressions and are distinguished from them phenomenologically by having less force and vivacity.

The distinction between sensation and reflection is maintained by Hume, although, unlike Locke, Hume does not distinguish *ideas* of sensation and reflection but only *impressions* of sensation and reflection. All simple ideas derive from simple impressions. It is a basic principle of Hume's philosophy "[t]hat all our simple ideas in their first appearance, are derived from simple impressions, which are correspondent to them, and which they exactly represent" (*Treatise* I.i.1). Ideas can, in turn, bring about impressions. An impression of desire may result from the idea of pleasure. The idea of pleasure, however, must itself derive from an antecedent impression of pleasure. About the origin of our impressions themselves Hume has little to say. He appears to think that determining the origins of impressions is outside the bounds of philosophical inquiry. Some commentators take Hume to hold that impressions of sensation are caused by external objects, as Locke held ideas of sense are caused. However, in the *Treatise* Hume criticizes this view, which he calls the doctrine of double existence, as an obscure philosophical invention that derives simultaneously from our vulgar or ordinary conception and the philosopher's rejection of that very conception.

The principle that all simple ideas derive from simple impressions is put to use in Hume's examination of rival philosophical systems. It plays an important role in Hume's rejection of rationalist accounts of causation (see CAUSATION/POWER) and SUBSTANCE, in addition to the more obvious employment in arguments against innate ideas. Hume rejects the claim that we have simple ideas of causation and substance by showing that there are no corresponding antecedent simple impressions. Hume's treatment of ideas, like Berkeley's and Locke's, emphasizes both the limitations of the mind—the only ideas we can have are those that arise from sensation and reflection—and the mind's great imaginative power to go beyond what is given in sensation and reflection by the ASSOCIATION and concatenation of ideas.

Both logical positivism and logical empiricism acknowledge their debt to the empiricist account of ideas (see LOGICAL POSITIVISM/LOGICAL EMPIRICISM). A. J. Ayer interprets Berkeley's use of the term "idea" to mean sense content or sense data and takes sense content to be metaphysically neutral, neither mental nor physical, but rather the basis on which the mental and physical must be defined. Ayer, CARNAP, and REICHENBACH, among others, saw in the theory of ideas the germ of their VERIFICATION PRINCIPLE of meaning, which holds that the only terms that are meaningful are those that can be empirically verified, that is, defined in terms of sense contents. While acknowledging that the twentieth-century positivists and empiricists took themselves to be advancing the views of Locke, Berkeley, and Hume with the tools of modern physics and logic, many commentators hold that Ayer and others oversimplified and misunderstood the range of views understood as the theory of ideas.

Postpositivist critiques of foundationalism and PHENOMENALISM find fault with any theory of ideas that attempts to treat ideas both as sensations and as thoughts. Wilfrid Sellars argues that Locke, Berkeley, and Hume each took our ability to have and recognize determinate ideas or impressions—such as an idea of a particular instance of the color red—to be given and unproblematic and explained our ability to form abstract ideas in terms of it. But what are the criteria for the correct identification of a particular idea as the idea of this particular shade of red? Sellars argues that our ability to master the logic of sensations—for sensations to play a role in our thought—presupposes the mastery of higher-level concepts, including the concept of external objects.

PRIMARY WORKS

Arnauld, Antoine. *The Art of Thinking; Port-Royal Logic*. Indianapolis: Bobbs-Merrill, 1964.

Ayer, A. J. *Language, Truth, and Logic*. New York: Dover, 1952.

Berkeley, George. *The Works of George Berkeley, Bishop of Cloyne*. Edited by A. A. Luce and T. E. Jessop. 9 vols. London: Thomas Nelson and Sons, 1948–1957.

Descartes, René. *The Philosophical Writings of Descartes*. Edited and translated by John Cottingham, Robert Stoofhoff, and Dugald Murdoch. 3 vols. Cambridge: Cambridge University Press, 1984–1985.

Empiricus, Sextus. *Outlines of Pyrrhonism*. Translated by Robert Gregg Bury. Cambridge: Harvard University Press, 1933–1949.

Hume, David. *An Abstract of a Treatise of Human Nature, 1740, A Pamphlet Hitherto Unknown*. Edited by John Maynard Keynes and Sraffa Piero. Cambridge: Cambridge University Press, 1938.

———. *A Treatise of Human Nature*. 2d ed., edited with an analytical index by L. A. Selby-Bigge; revised with notes by P. H. Nidditch. Oxford: Clarendon Press, 1978.

Locke, John. *An Essay concerning Human Understanding*. Edited with an introduction by P. H. Nidditch. Oxford: Clarendon Press, 1975.

———. *An Examination of P. Malebranche's Opinion of Seeing All Things in God*. In *The Works of John Locke*, vol. 8. London: C. and J. Rivington, 1824.

Malebranche, Nicolas. *The Search after Truth*. Translated by Thomas M. Lennon and Paul J. Olscamp. Columbus: Ohio State University Press, 1980.

Reichenbach, Hans. *The Rise of Scientific Philosophy*. Berkeley: University of California Press, 1951.

BIBLIOGRAPHY

Books

Winkler, Kenneth P. *Berkeley: An Interpretation*. Oxford: Oxford University Press, 1989.

Yolton, John W. *John Locke and the Way of Ideas*. Oxford: Clarendon Press, 1968.

Article

Sellars, Wilfrid. "Empiricism and the Philosophy of Mind." In *Minnesota Studies in the Philosophy of Science*. Vol. 1, *The Foundations of Science and the Concepts of Psychology and Psychoanalysis*, edited by Herbert Feigl and Michael Scriven. Minneapolis: University of Minnesota Press, 1956.

SAUL TRAIGER

IDENTITY. It is difficult, arguably even impossible, to give a noncircular definition of the concept of identity, which is one reason it has proved problematical for empiricist thinkers. One can say, for instance, quite truly, that identity is the relation that everything necessarily bears to itself and to no other thing: but "otherness" is simply nonidentity and so not an independent concept. Again, one could appeal to Leibniz's principle of the identity of indiscernibles—contentious though that principle is—to define identity as the relation that holds between things that do not differ in respect of any of their properties. But this presupposes the notion of one property's differing from—that is, being non-identical with—another. Arguably, then, the concept of identity is primitive and unanalyzable. That might well suit a rationalist such as Descartes, who could urge the INNATENESS of the concept. But it poses a problem for any empiricist who thinks that the concept must be acquired from experience. For it is not plausible to suppose that one could simply acquire the concept through observation, as one might acquire other concepts that are arguably primitive and unanalyzable, such as the color concept of *redness* or the relational concept of *being to the left of*. This is because, as was remarked before, identity is a relation that *everything* necessarily bears to itself, and accordingly nothing is empirically distinguishable from anything else in virtue of its possession of identity.

This consideration might lead a tough-minded empiricist to conclude that identity is not a ''real'' relation at all and that our talking as if it were is a mere artifact of language. In support of this, it may be pointed out that we customarily talk of identity *as if* it were a relation between *different* things, when strictly this cannot be so. We ask, for instance, how we can tell that one material object is the same as ''another,'' answering, perhaps, that ''they'' are the same just in case ''they'' exist in the same place at the same time; and the very use of the plural pronoun ''they'' here seems to imply, of course, plurality and hence diversity. Some philosophers would urge, on this account, that wherever questions seemingly about ''identity'' have real import, they are really questions about something else, such as *unity*—for instance, questions about the unity of a thing's spatial parts at a moment of time or about the unity of a thing's temporal parts over time. These questions, they hold, are at least genuine and substantive ones, whose answers can be based on empirically determinable facts. Thus, the unity of a thing's spatial parts at one moment may be held to consist in certain spatiotemporal and causal relations between them, such as relationships of contiguity and adhesion.

The first major empiricist philosopher to discuss the concept—or, as he describes it, the IDEA—of identity in a systematic way was John LOCKE, in his *An Essay concerning Human Understanding* (II.xxvii). One of his most important insights was that ''such as is the *Idea* belonging to [a] Name, such must be the *Identity*'' (*Essay* II.xxvii.7). What he means by this is that the criteria we should apply to judge whether or not x is the same F as y—where F is a general term (''name'') signifying our idea of a certain *sort* or *kind* of things, such as ''tree'' or ''mountain'' or ''table''—will depend on just what that idea is and hence will be different for different such ideas. Thus, the considerations—all of them empirical, of course—that should lead us to judge that one *tree* is the same as ''another'' may be expected to differ from those that should lead us to judge that one *table* is the same as ''another.'' A particularly graphic illustration of this thesis is provided by Locke's own account of PERSONAL IDENTITY, which he urges must be distinguished from the identity of a human being or ''man,'' conceived purely as a kind of living organism. This raises the question of whether Locke can be seen as an early proponent of the thesis of the *relativity* of identity, defended in recent times by Peter Geach. According to this thesis, x may be the same F as y and yet not the same G: for instance, the river I stepped into yesterday is the same *river* as the river I stepped into today, but not the same *water*. Advocates of the *absoluteness* of identity, such as David Wiggins, urge that this example is misleadingly expressed, holding that to say that rivers x and y are "not the same water" is merely to imply that they are *constituted* by different water. However, an implication of the absolutist position is that two different things—such as a river and the body of water currently "constituting" it—can exist in exactly the same place at the same time and hence that two empirically indistinguishable objects can "coincide." Empiricist-minded philosophers will inevitably be unhappy about such a claim, and so it may be reasonable to surmise that Locke would have been unhappy about it too.

Locke has interesting things to say about the identity of material objects and of living organisms. Concerning the notion of a piece or "mass" of matter, he remarks: "[W]hilst [a number of atoms] exist united together, the Mass, consisting of the same Atoms, must be the same Mass, let the parts be never so differently jumbled: But if one of these Atoms be taken away, or one new one added, it is no longer the same Mass" (*Essay* II.xxvii.3). Clearly, what Locke is providing here is what we spoke of earlier as an account of the *unity* of a piece of matter, in terms of certain relations between its parts—relations that are in principle, even if not in practice, empirically discernible. He contrasts this account with his corresponding account of the unity of a *living organism*, saying: "In the state of living Creatures, their Identity depends not on a Mass of the same Particles; but on something else. For in them the variation of great parcels of Matter alters not the Identity" (*Essay* II.xxvii.3). Locke's point, of course, is that processes of growth and metabolism do not normally disrupt the unity of a living organism, provided that its constantly changing material constituents continue to sustain the life of the whole. In these passages of the *Essay*, Locke provides the starting point for all modern discussion of the metaphysics of material objects and organisms, at least for those philosophers who seek to combine empiricism with scientific realism.

David HUME, of course, either rejected such realism altogether or, at most, espoused "skeptical" realism, and this difference between him and Locke is reflected not least in their contrasting views about identity, especially identity over time. For Hume, strict identity is incompatible with change, and what we *call* identity is often nothing more than *similarity* between different things (see his *A Treatise of Human Nature* I.iv.6). In modern times, this view—shorn of its idealist clothing—finds voice in the doctrine of temporal parts, as defended by such philosophers as David Lewis. In support of the doctrine, Lewis has raised the "problem of intrinsic change": how can one and the same object literally have different and incompatible intrinsic properties, such as different shapes, at two different times? On the face of it, this conflicts with Leibniz's principle of the indiscernibility of identicals, but one might think to avoid such conflict by indexing properties to times—saying, for instance, that x is bent-at-t_1 but straight-at-t_2 and thus that x does not, after all, have two *incompatible* properties. To this Lewis objects that such time-indexed properties are no longer *intrinsic* properties, but rather *relational* ones. His solution is to retain the intrinsicness of shape properties and put the time indices, instead, into the terms denoting the *subjects* of these properties—saying, thus, that x-at-t_1 is bent while x-at-t_2 is straight, where "x-at-t_1" and "x-at-t_2" denote two different *temporal parts*, or *time-slices*, of the persisting object x. Many empiricist-minded philosophers now believe that an ontology of temporal parts is more consistent with the theories of contemporary physics, such as Einstein's theory of relativity, than is the traditional ontology of enduring substances (see SUBSTANCE) that was inherited from ARISTOTLE and incorporated into the metaphysical framework of Newton's kinematic and dynamic theories (see NEWTON). Partly at issue here, of course, are differing views about the nature of, and relationships between, SPACE and TIME.

The concept of identity has perhaps given rise to more philosophical puzzles than any other metaphysical notion, and in the minds of empiricists these puzzles often serve to reinforce their doubts about the empirical validity of the concept. Perhaps the best-known such puzzle is that of the ship of Theseus, given prominence by HOBBES in his *De Corpore*:

[I]f, for example, that ship of Theseus, concerning the difference whereof made by continued reparation in taking out the old planks and putting in new, the sophisters of Athens were wont to dispute, were, after all the planks were changed, the same numerical ship it was at the beginning; and if some man had kept the old planks as they were taken out, and by putting them afterwards together in the same order, had again made a ship of them, this, without doubt, had also been the same numerical ship with that which was at the beginning; and so there would have been two ships numerically the same, which is absurd. (*De Corpore* II.11)

What is at issue here is whether continuity of form or sameness of material parts carries greater weight in determining the identity of a composite object, such as a ship, over time. It seems that the satisfaction of each criterion is sufficient for identity in the absence of the satisfaction of the other, so that when both criteria seem to be satisfied but deliver different answers, we are perplexed. If a ship were merely dismantled, without replacement of parts, and its parts later put together again, we would be happy to describe the reassembled ship as being identical with the original ship. On the other hand, if the parts of a ship were gradually replaced, and the old ones destroyed, then, equally, we would be happy to describe the renovated ship as being identical with the original ship. In Hobbes' puzzle case, however, we have both a "reassembled" ship and a "renovated" ship, which are clearly not identical with each other, whence either one or both of them cannot be identical with the original ship. But how can we justify selecting the renovated ship, say, as being identical with the original ship when, it seems, the reassembled ship is still related to the original ship in exactly the way that would have sufficed for *its* identity with the original ship if the latter had merely been gradually dismantled, and its parts had later been reassembled without being replaced? How can the identity or nonidentity of one thing with "another" depend in this way upon *what else* is the case? If we judge the renovated ship to be identical with the original, then it might seem that we must say, of the ship put together from the old parts, that although it *actually* came into existence for the first time when those parts were reassembled, it *would* have come into existence earlier if the process of renovation had not occurred, for then *it* would have been the original ship. To this it may be replied that the "reassembled" ship that would have existed if renovation had not occurred is not to be identified with the "reassembled" ship that *actually* exists alongside the renovated ship, precisely because that other reassembled ship would have *been* the very ship that, in actuality, now exists in renovated form. This seems a sensible reply, but from an empiricist point of view it has the perhaps unpalatable implication that two possible objects can differ in their identity, even though the histories of the parts composing them are empirically indistinguishable.

The puzzle of the ship of Theseus is just one example of the problems posed for our everyday concept of identity by cases of *fission* and *fusion*, in which one object divides into two, or two objects merge into one. In the light of such puzzles, an empiricist may be inclined to judge that there often are no "facts of the matter" about the identities of objects over time and that our judgments of identity are often backed by little more than arbitrarily chosen convention. That seems to have been Hume's opinion, though by his own confession the attempt to extend it to judgments of personal identity threatens to be paradoxical.

PRIMARY WORKS

Hobbes, Thomas. *The English Works of Thomas Hobbes*. Edited by W. Molesworth. London: John Bohn, 1839–1845.

Hume, David. *A Treatise of Human Nature*. 2d ed., edited with an analytical index by L. A. Selby-Bigge; revised with notes by P. H. Nidditch. Oxford: Clarendon Press, 1978.

Locke, John. *An Essay concerning Human Understanding*. Edited with an introduction by P. H. Nidditch. Oxford: Clarendon Press, 1975.

BIBLIOGRAPHY

Books

Geach, P. T. *Reference and Generality*. 3d ed. Ithaca, NY: Cornell University Press, 1980.

Lewis, David. *On the Plurality of Worlds*. Oxford: Blackwell, 1986.

Lowe, E. J. *Kinds of Being: A Study of Individuation, Identity and the Logic of Sortal Terms*. Oxford: Blackwell, 1989.

Wiggins, David. *Sameness and Substance*. Oxford: Blackwell, 1980.

Articles

Chappell, V. C. "Locke and Relative Identity." *History of Philosophy Quarterly* 6 (1989): 69–83.
Lowe, E. J. "On the Identity of Artifacts." *Journal of Philosophy* 80 (1983): 220–32.

E. J. LOWE

IMAGINATION. The imagination is a faculty for having imagistic representations or IDEAS; in a broad sense that includes not only visual representations but also auditory, gustatory, olfactory, and tactile ones, as well as "images" of internal sensations and feelings such as hunger and pain. Some philosophers—Spinoza, for example—use the term "imagination" to cover all imagistic representation, including even sensation and memory. Others—like Descartes—use it to designate all imagistic representation except sensation. HUME distinguishes imagination from both memory and sensation. When the imagination is understood as a representational faculty distinct from sensation, its ability to produce imagistic representations is generally explained through its ability to retain and rearrange traces of imagistic mental content first acquired in sensation (see PERCEPTION) or (in some cases) introspective reflection on the mind's own operations.

Imagination is often contrasted with the intellect, where the latter is understood as a faculty for having radically nonimagistic representations or ideas. Both imagination and intellect are to be contrasted with other cognitive faculties that, while sometimes or always operating on representations, are not themselves primarily faculties for having particular kinds of representations. Examples of such faculties are REASON (the inferential faculty) and WILL (the conative or volitional faculty). Many of the differences between early modern Empiricists and early modern Rationalists result from the fact that the former deny, while the latter affirm, the existence of an intellect as a representational faculty distinct from the imagination.

The distinction between intellect and imagination dates at least to ARISTOTLE. Descartes introduces his version of the distinction near the end of his Second Meditation, in the course of his famous discussion of a piece of wax. There he argues that he can *conceive* by intellect the substance that underlies the wax's changing properties even though he cannot *imagine* it; and he concludes that it is also by intellect, rather than imagination, that he conceives of himself as a thinking thing. While Aristotle had held that nothing is in the intellect that is not first in the senses, Descartes makes the distinction more radical by arguing that the contents of the most distinctive ideas of intellect—including those of God, infinity, substance, relations, mind, and even extension in general (as opposed to particular shapes or extended things)—are innate and not derived from sensation or perception. Spinoza and Leibniz also emphasize the distinction between intellect and imagination and the superiority of the former over the latter. The most distinctive Rationalist metaphysical doctrines—

Descartes' affirmation that the mind always thinks and his denial of the vacuum, Spinoza's monism and necessitarianism, and Leibniz's affirmation of the phenomenal character of extension and his denial of substantial interaction, as well as their common affirmation of the necessary existence of God—are all intended to be consequences of the rich cognitive content of ideas of intellect.

LOCKE employs the term ''intellect'' only once in his published writings, and then not in the technical Cartesian sense but simply as a synonym for human cognitive faculties in general (*An Essay concerning Human Understanding* II.i.24). He regularly uses the term ''imagination'' to designate a representational faculty, however; and the only representational faculties he mentions are sensation, reflection, memory, and imagination. In general, it is clear that Lockean ideas are far more similar to Cartesian ideas of imagination than they are to Cartesian ideas of intellect. Book II of the *Essay* can be read as an attempt to explain, using a variety of strategies, how the content of each of Descartes' alleged innate ideas of intellect can be produced instead through a representational faculty like the imagination, operating on the contents of sensation and reflection. One of these Lockean operations is ABSTRACTION. Although this operation renders representations less determinate, Locke still seems to think of the results as less determinate (and cognitively poorer) images, rather than as the cognitively richer and nonimagistic representations of Cartesian intellect.

BERKELEY explicitly distinguishes all ideas into those of sensation and those of intellect (*Principles of Human Knowledge* §30, §33), and he argues against Locke that indeterminate abstract ideas cannot exist because all ideas are determinate images. (In Berkeley's theory, the generality of thought is accomplished with selective attention to, and use of, determinate images.) In his early notebooks, he writes: ''Pure intellect I understand not'' (*Philosophical Commentaries* §810). In his *Three Dialogues between Hylas and Philonous*, however, Philonous (representing Berkeley) declares:

Since I cannot frame abstract ideas at all, it is plain, I cannot frame them by the help of *pure intellect* whatsoever faculty you understand by those words. Besides—not to inquire into the nature of pure intellect and its spiritual objects, as *virtue, reason, God*, or the like—thus much seems manifest, that sensible things are only to be perceived by sense, or represented by the imagination. (*Dialogues* II: 193–94)

As this passage indicates, Berkeley's published writings avoid denying the existence of intellect by leaving open (rather unenthusiastically) the possibility that the term ''intellect'' could be used to designate our capacity to understand spiritual substances and qualities of which we cannot form ideas in the imagination. Berkeley's reluctance to use the word ''intellect'' for this purpose is understandable, inasmuch as his underlying view is that we understand such things directly, by participation, without representations at all.

According to Hume, the imagination is the ''faculty by which we repeat our impressions'' in the form of ideas having less force and liveliness than those of memory (*A Treatise of Human Nature* I.i.3). In a passage at *Treatise* I.iii.1, he indicates his reasons for rejecting the intellect as a representational faculty separate from the imagination or ''fancy'' (an equivalent term in eighteenth-century usage) and for affirming that all ideas are derived from sensory or reflective experience (i.e., from ''impressions''):

> 'Tis usual with mathematicians, to pretend, that those ideas, which are their objects, are of so refin'd and spiritual a nature, that they fall not under the conception of the fancy, but must be comprehended by a pure and intellectual view, of which the superior faculties of the soul are alone capable. The same notion runs thro' most parts of philosophy, and is principally made use of to explain our abstract ideas, and to shew how we can form an idea of a triangle, for instance, which shall neither be an isosceles nor scalenum, nor be confin'd to any particular length and proportion of sides. 'Tis easy to see, why philosophers are so fond of this notion of some spiritual and refined perceptions; since by that means they cover many of their absurdities, and may refuse to submit to the decision of clear ideas, by appealing to such as are obscure and uncertain. But to destroy this artifice, we need but reflect on that principle so oft insisted on, *that all our ideas are copy'd from our impressions.* For from thence we may immediately conclude, that since all impressions are clear and precise, the ideas, which are copy'd from them, must be of the same nature, and can never, but from our fault, contain any thing so dark and intricate. An idea is by its very nature weaker and fainter than an impression; but being in every other respect the same, cannot imply any very great mystery. (*Treatise*: 72)

Hume rejects the traditional doctrine that distinguishes sharply between conception, judgment, and reasoning (*Treatise*: 96n) in terms of the number of ideas involved and the operations performed on them. In his view, judgment and reasoning are particular ways of conceiving or coming to conceive—that is, to have ideas of imagination. Even causal reasoning—according to Hume, a process in which custom operates to enliven ideas to the level of belief—is therefore, in a broad sense, ''founded on the imagination'' (*Treatise*: 265). Hume also recognizes a narrower sense of ''imagination,'' however (*Treatise*: 117n), in which demonstrative and causal reasoning can be *opposed* to the many (other) distinctive belief-enhancing or -weakening aspects and operations of the imagination, such as the influence of surprise and wonder.

Willingness to reject the existence of intellect and to construe all operations on mental representations as operations on imagelike representations has a number of important consequences for eighteenth-century Empiricism. First, because the intellect generally serves Rationalists as a source of higher concepts capable of determining theory and placing constraints on the interpretation of observations, the rejection of intellect played a significant role for Empiricists in elevating observation over theory. Second, the rejection of ideas of intellect makes it easier for Empiricists to argue that the semantic content of thought is derived entirely from objects of sensory or reflective experience. Third, by doing away with a source of richer, higher-level representations, the rejection of intellect leads Empiricists (particularly Berkeley and Hume) to the view that the laws of nature cannot be known, even in principle, a priori (see A PRIORI/A POSTERIORI DISTINCTION), and can be discovered only by experience. Fourth, by reducing "conceivability" to "imaginability," the rejection of intellect leads those Empiricists who treat conceivability as the criterion of possibility to expand the realm of the possible and thus to admit that more of what is actually the case could have been otherwise (see MODALITY).

Most contemporary cognitive scientists grant that there are distinctively imagistic representations derived from those of sensation and in that sense that there is an "imagination." The exact nature, operation, and extent of that faculty in human understanding remain a subject of serious debate and investigation.

PRIMARY WORKS

Berkeley, George. *The Works of George Berkeley, Bishop of Cloyne*. Edited by A. A. Luce and T. E. Jessop. 9 vols. London: Thomas Nelson and Sons, 1948–1957.
Descartes, René. *The Philosophical Writings of Descartes*. Translated by John Cottingham, Robert Stoothoff, and Dugald Murdoch. 3 volumes. Cambridge: Cambridge University Press, 1985.
Hume, David. *A Treatise of Human Nature*. 2d ed., edited with an analytical index by L. A. Selby-Bigge; revised with notes by P. H. Nidditch. Oxford: Clarendon Press, 1978.
Locke, John. *An Essay concerning Human Understanding*. Edited with an introduction by P. H. Nidditch. Oxford: Clarendon Press, 1975.
Spinoza, Benedict. *Spinoza's Collected Works*. Vol. 1. Edited and translated by Edwin Curley. Princeton: Princeton University Press, 1985.

BIBLIOGRAPHY

Flage, Daniel. *Berkeley's Theory of Notions: A Reconstruction Based on Theory of Meaning*. London: Croom Helm, 1987.
Fogelin, Robert. *Hume's Skepticism in the Treatise of Human Nature*. London: Routledge and Kegan Paul, 1985: Chapter 5.
Garrett, Don. *Cognition and Commitment in Hume's Philosophy*. New York: Oxford University Press, 1997: Chapter 1.
Wilbanks, Dennis. *Hume's Theory of Imagination*. The Hague: M. Nijhoff, 1968.

DON GARRETT

INDUCTION. The word "induction" is derived from Cicero's *inductio*, itself a translation of Aristotle's *epagôgê*. In its traditional sense this denotes the inference of general laws from particular instances, but within modern philosophy it has usually been understood in a related but broader sense, covering any nondemonstrative reasoning that is founded on experience. As such it encompasses reasoning from observed to unobserved, both inference of general laws and of further particular instances, but it excludes those cases of reasoning in which the conclusion is logically implied by the premises, such as induction by complete enumeration.

The question of the foundation of inductive inference so defined came to center stage with HUME, though earlier philosophers such as GASSENDI, Arnauld, Nicole, and LOCKE had also been aware that "inductions" other than by complete enumeration were inherently fallible. But Hume was the first to raise "sceptical doubts" about inductive reasoning, leaving a puzzle as to why the concerns he highlighted had earlier been so completely overlooked. (By contrast, the main skeptical arguments of Descartes and Bayle, e.g., had various ancient antecedents.) Hacking (1975) attributes this to the unavailability before the late seventeenth century of the concept of "internal evidence" (i.e., evidence other than testimony), combined with the lingering influence until then of a traditional assumption that fundamental causal connections must be demonstrable (see CAUSATION). Milton (1987) instead attributes Hume's novelty to his philosophical courage, his freedom from theological constraint, and his willingness to follow through the logical implications of the conceptual NOMINALISM characteristic of the empiricist tradition—if "everything which exists, is particular," as BERKELEY had insisted (*Three Dialogues between Hylas and Philonous*: 192), then unobserved entities cannot straightforwardly be known about in virtue of knowing the universals that they instantiate, and Hume's new problem of how we can learn about such unobserved entities comes into focus.

THE CONTEXT AND TOPIC OF HUME'S ARGUMENT

Hume's argument concerning induction is perhaps the single best-known and most influential argument in the entire corpus of empiricist writings and occupies a central place within his philosophical system. He presents it three times, in the *Treatise of Human Nature* (1739: 86–92), the anonymously published *Abstract* of the *Treatise* (1740: 649–52), and finally in the *Enquiry concerning Human Understanding* (1748: 25–39). Each of these presentations differs in important respects from the others, as the argument is progressively clarified and refined. In the *Treatise* it appears as a detour in Hume's search for the impression of necessary connection—as a result, its emphasis is psychologistic, and it is closely entangled with the working out of his analysis of causation (though its force turns out, at pp. 90–91, to be quite independent of Hume's new understanding of necessary connection). The *Abstract* version of the argument loosens this entanglement, with the argument's primary impetus now coming from questions not about the origin of our ideas but instead about the foundation of our inferences concerning hitherto unobserved "matter of fact" (*Abstract*: 649). In the *Enquiry* this development is completed—the argument is detached entirely from the analysis of causation, substantially expanded and clarified, and centered exclusively around the one central epistemological issue: "what is the nature of that evidence, which assures us of any real existence and matter of fact, beyond the present testimony of our senses, or the records of our memory" (*Enquiry*: 26).

Hume does not use the word "induction" to characterize the topic of his famous argument; indeed his few uses of that word (*Treatise*: 27; *Treatise*: 628; *Enquiry*: 170) indicate that he sees it as merely a synonym for "inference" in general. For the specific form of inference from observed to unobserved he employs three different terms, all interpreted equivalently: "probable reasoning," "moral reasoning," and "reasoning concerning matter of fact and existence." Regrettably, all three are to some extent infelicitous to modern ears, especially the last—*deductive* reasoning that concerns matters of fact, such as "That is a large book; therefore that is a book," is certainly not what Hume had in mind here (and such reasoning would presumably fall on the "demonstrative," rather than the "probable," side of his official dichotomy, despite differing from most of his own examples of "demonstration" in having a posteriori premises). Such infelicities give ample justification for preferring the modern term "induction" except when discussing Hume's writings themselves, for which purpose it seems more appropriate to adopt his own most consistent choice, namely, "probable" inference. However, again it should be noted that this does not mean "probable" in the technical sense (involving the mathematical calculation of odds and so forth): Hume's "probable reasoning" is simply everyday factual inference, taking us from premises about observed things to conclusions about unobserved things and universally founded, according to him, upon the supposition that the two will resemble each other.

THE STRUCTURE OF HUME'S ARGUMENT

Although the interpretation of Hume's argument concerning induction is a controversial matter, with major implications for the understanding of his philosophy, nevertheless the argument's general structure can be established with reasonable confidence. The *Enquiry* version can be spelled out as follows. (For details and a diagrammatic representation, together with extensive interpretative discussion, see Millican 1995 or 1996.)

1. Only the relation of cause and effect can take us beyond the evidence of our memory and senses—*Enquiry*: 26.

2. All probable arguments are founded on the relation of cause and effect—*Enquiry*: 26, 35. (from 1)

3. The sensible qualities of objects do not reveal their causes or effects, and there is no known connection between an object's sensible qualities and its "secret powers"—*Enquiry*: 27, 33.

4. Any effect is quite distinct from its cause, and for any given cause, many alternative effects are from an a priori point of view just as conceivable and natural as the actual effect—*Enquiry*: 30.

5. Causal relations cannot be known a priori, but can be discovered only by experience (of constant conjunctions)—*Enquiry*: 27, 28, 30. (from 3 and 4)

6. All probable arguments are founded on experience—*Enquiry*: 27, 30. (from 2 and 5)

7. All arguments from experience proceed upon the supposition that the future will be conformable to the past—*Enquiry*: 33, 35, 37.

8. All probable arguments proceed upon the supposition that nature is uniform and, in particular, that similar causes will in the future have similar effects to those that they have had in the past (henceforth: the "Uniformity Principle")—*Enquiry*: 35. (from 6 and 7)

9. The Uniformity Principle cannot be rationally founded on anything that we learn through the senses about objects' "secret powers"—*Enquiry*: 33. (from 3)

10. The Uniformity Principle is not intuitively certain—*Enquiry*: 34.

11. The Uniformity Principle can be rationally founded only on the basis of a good argument (hence, if it is to be founded on reason, there must be a *medium* for proving it)—*Enquiry*: 34. (from 9 and 10)

12. All (good) reasonings are either demonstrative or probable—*Enquiry*: 35.

13. The contrary of the Uniformity Principle can be distinctly conceived and is therefore possible—*Enquiry*: 35.

14. There can be no demonstrative argument for the Uniformity Principle—*Enquiry*: 35. (from 13)

15. If there is a good argument for the Uniformity Principle, it must be a probable argument—*Enquiry*: 35. (from 12 and 14)

16. Any probable argument for the Uniformity Principle would be circular—*Enquiry*: 35–36. (from 8)

17. There is no good argument of any kind for the Uniformity Principle—*Enquiry*: 35. (from 15 and 16)

18. The Uniformity Principle cannot be founded on reason—*Enquiry*: 39. (from 11 and 17)

19. No probable argument is rationally founded, and hence it is not reason (but custom or habit, an instinct) that engages us to make probable inferences—*Enquiry*: 32. 43. (from 8 and 18)

The argument falls into five main stages. First (1 to 6), Hume proves that inferences about the unobserved cannot legitimately be a priori (see A PRIORI/A POSTERIORI DISTINCTION). Second (7 to 8), he uses this result to conclude that probable reasoning must presuppose, in some sense, a "Uniformity Principle." Third (9 to 11), he eliminates what he sees as the possible noninferential sources of this principle, namely, sensation and intuition. Fourth (12 to 17), he shows that inference too is powerless to provide a rational ground for it. Finally (18 to 19), he puts together the results of the previous stages to conclude that the Uniformity Principle and hence also the probable reasoning of which it is a presupposition cannot be founded on REASON.

THE INTERPRETATION OF HUME'S ARGUMENT

The interpretation of Hume's argument has been particularly contentious because its logic has been widely seen as revealing fundamental presuppositions of his thought in general. Stove, for example, presents his well-known analysis of the argument as a basis for claiming that Hume is a "deductivist"—if true, this would suggest that Hume's celebrated skeptical doubts are just a fairly direct consequence of an underlying crude assumption that only deductive evidence has any weight and thus would make those doubts easy to dismiss for philosophers (such as Stove himself) who see no reason to start from such an extreme and manifestly skeptical premise. It is philosophically significant, therefore, that Stove's analysis can be decisively rejected.

The most significant interpretive issue in the first stage of Hume's argument concerns his grounds for denying the possibility of a priori causal knowledge (5). Stove (1965: 194; 1973: 31) sees that denial as based on the mere *logical conceivability* of causes and effects being differently combined and accordingly adduces this as powerful evidence that Hume is a deductivist. But in fact the premises here (3 and 4) are far stronger than Stove realizes: Hume says that a priori there is *nothing at all* to link cause with effect—not only can the one not be deductively inferred from the other, but a priori their combination seems "entirely arbitrary" (*Enquiry*: 30). Premises as strong as this, if granted, are clearly sufficient to license Hume's denial of a priori causal knowledge without the slightest hint of deductivism.

The second stage of Hume's argument raises another important issue: what does he mean when he states that probable arguments "proceed upon the supposition" that nature is uniform? Flew (1961: 70–89) has been followed by many, including Stove, in viewing the Uniformity Principle here as a middle premise in a would-be deductive syllogism, but this deductivist interpretation is not warranted, as Flew appears to believe, by Hume's talk of a "medium," for on the Lockean logic that Hume inherited, probable arguments as well as demonstrative standardly contain such "middle terms" or "proofs" (*An Essay concerning Human Understanding* IV.xv.1, IV.xvii.15–16). Nevertheless a deductivist understanding of Humean presupposition can seem tempting, because it renders Hume's (8) as stating a manifest truth: that any argument that passes from observed to unobserved will be deductively invalid unless it is supplemented by a "principle of uniformity" that asserts a similarity between them. However, a second manifest truth, likewise evident to Hume, should give us pause, namely, that no "principle of uniformity" can possibly be sufficiently specific to transform inductions into valid deductions, without at the same time being far too strong to be at all plausible. Or conversely, even if nature is indeed uniform, this in no way implies that any particular induction, even one that is well corroborated, will turn out to have a true conclusion, because there will always remain the possibility of unknown causal factors that have not been taken into account (cf. *Treatise*: 175; *Enquiry*: 86–87).

If Hume does not see his Uniformity Principle as a means of transforming inductions into valid deductions, then how does he see it? The answer suggested by its role as a presupposition of probable inference turns out to be quite straightforward. For what is evidently being presupposed by anyone who relies on a probable inference is that the premise (concerning observed entities) is *evidentially relevant* to the conclusion (concerning unobserved entities) and is, moreover, evidentially relevant in a *positive* manner—the unobserved are expected to be *similar* to the observed rather than, say, contrasting with them. Hume's Uniformity Principle, therefore, can most simply be understood as a statement of *positive evidential relevance*, asserting that unobserved instances can indeed properly be expected to resemble observed instances. Such an interpretation does not give the principle deductive force but is quite sufficient to account for its role within Hume's argument.

Thus, the first two stages of Hume's argument do not, after all, provide support for the once-dominant deductivist skeptical interpretations by Stove and others. These have indeed lost favor in recent years, but the reasons for this have had less to do with the logic of Hume's reasoning than with the overall tenor of his philosophy. His famous argument may purport to prove that induction "is not founded on reason," but if this conclusion is interpreted in an extreme skeptical manner, it seems very hard to reconcile with Hume's positive attitude to inductive reasoning elsewhere in his writings. How could a radical inductive skeptic subtitle his *Treatise* "An attempt to introduce the experimental method of reasoning into moral subjects" (*Treatise*: xi), or present "Rules by which to judge of causes and effects" (*Treatise*: 173), or criticize natural theologians and believers in miracles for failing to "proportion their belief" to the *empirical* evidence (*Enquiry*: 110)? How could a deductivist, who rejects all but deductive evidence, overtly propose arguments (most notably on "scepticism with regard to reason" and on miracles) that seem to depend quite crucially on the idea (stated very explicitly at *Treatise*: 31 and *Enquiry*: 113) that such evidence can have intermediate degrees?

Two main responses have emerged. The first and more popular interprets Hume as employing two (or more) quite different conceptions of "reason," one of which features within his famous argument while another provides his own norm of empirical reasonableness. The second response is more radical and involves denying that Hume's conception of reason is essentially normative at all.

A number of writers, from Beauchamp and Mappes (1975) to Baier (1991), have claimed that Hume's argument is in effect a reductio ad absurdum, intended to demonstrate only the empirical impotence of the non-Humean "rationalist" conception of reason that it employs and thus devoid of serious skeptical consequences for Hume himself. Most of these accounts have followed Stove in identifying a deductivist notion of "reason" within the argument but differ from him in seeing this as a rationalist straw man rather than Hume's own notion. However, the structure of the argument is hard to reconcile with *any* kind of deductivist interpretation, because it seems highly unlikely that Hume would employ such a complicated argument to prove the evident truth that no inductive inference has deductive force, when he could prove this immediately with precisely the sort of "argument from distinct conceivability" that he himself uses in the fourth stage, to infer (14) from (13).

A more promising interpretation of the notion of "reason" within the argument takes inspiration from Locke, who considers our faculty of reason to be capable of "perceiving" both demonstrative and probable relations (*Essay* IV.xvii.2, IV.xx.16). Interpreting reason in this way, as a faculty of intellectual *perception*, appears to be entirely compatible with the structure of Hume's argument and, moreover, explains why he would consider its skeptical conclusion to be radical and "extraordinary" (*Treatise*: 139) even in a context in which Lockean inductive fallibilism was perfectly familiar (*Essay* IV.xv.2). The claim that no form of intellectual perception can give us any understanding whatever about the unobserved, either a priori or a posteriori, is far more potentially unsettling than the trivial observation that inductive inference is less than deductively certain. Of course, this still leaves the task of giving a plausible account of Hume's own main sense of "reason" outside the context of his famous argument, inevitably on this interpretation a different sense because it treats induction as entirely respectable (e.g., *Treatise*: 96n, 225, 459; *Enquiry*: 110). Although there is some evidence to support the claim that Hume's notion of "reason" is ambiguous in just this way (e.g., *Treatise*: 117n), nevertheless it is obviously the case that an interpretation that had no need to postulate such an ambiguity would be, to that extent, preferable.

Garrett (1997: Chapter 4) has recently proposed such an interpretation, in which he reconciles Hume's argument with his advocacy of induction by taking the conclusion of that argument to be descriptive rather than normative: "[I]t is not a direct denial of the evidential value of inductive inferences on *any* conception of them, but is instead a straightforward negative conclusion, within cognitive psychology, about the causes of the mechanism of inductive inference." From this perspective there is no conflict between Hume's argument and his endorsement of the inductive method: in proving that induction is not grounded in reason, Hume is just showing that it cannot be accounted for by reference to "our inferential/argumentative faculty"—that there is, literally, "no *argument*, which determines me to suppose" (*Abstract*: 652) that the future will be conformable to the past. This is perfectly compatible with the claim that induction is warranted, albeit based on custom or habit rather than on inference.

Garrett's interpretation is elegant, but not without difficulties. First, it is in tension both with the structure of Hume's argument (notably its third stage, which seems to be denying more than just that induction is founded on *inference*) and also with some of Hume's apparently skeptical paraphrases of its conclusion (e.g., *Treatise*: 139; *Enquiry*: 162). More fundamentally, it is not clear how Garrett can explain away Hume's often apparently normative view of reason, manifested both in explicit claims about its reliability (e.g., *Treatise*: 193, 209), but especially in implicit assumptions about its scope—if "reason" is just our actual inferential faculty, interpreted nonnormatively, then what right has Hume to be confident that only certain specific kinds of reasoning can have that faculty as their source? (One notable example is his assertion of (12), which takes for granted that a priori probabilistic reasoning is impossible. Millican (1996: Part II) provides a survey and critique of modern attempts to circumvent Hume's argument by means of such reasoning (see PROBABILITY for some relevant background).

This is not the place to attempt to adjudicate these debates, for only careful analysis of Hume's texts and arguments can ultimately show whether Garrett's radical hypothesis is tenable or whether instead it is necessary, in order to render Hume consistent, to attribute to him an ambiguity in his notion of "reason." What is clear, however, is that the interpretation of Hume's argument concerning induction is far from resolved but is crucial for the interpretation of his entire philosophical project.

PRIMARY WORKS

Berkeley, George. *Three Dialogues between Hylas and Philonous* (1713). In *The Philosophical Works of George Berkeley*, edited by A. A. Luce and T. E. Jessop, vol. 2. Nelson, 1949.

Hume, David. *Abstract of a Book Lately Published, Entitled, A Treatise of Human Nature, etc.* (1740). Reprinted as pp. 641–62 of Hume (1739).

———. *Enquiries concerning Human Understanding and concerning the Principles of Morals*. Edited with an analytical index by L. A. Selby-Bigge; revised with notes by P. H. Nidditch. Oxford: Clarendon Press, 1975. First publication by Hume 1748 and 1751, respectively—1777 was the last edition to incorporate new authorial corrections, and all quotations in the text have been corrected to it.

———. *A Treatise of Human Nature*. 2d ed., edited with an analytical index by L. A. Selby-Bigge; revised with notes by P. H. Nidditch. Oxford: Clarendon Press, 1978.

Locke, John. *An Essay concerning Human Understanding*. Edited with an introduction by P. H. Nidditch. Oxford: Clarendon Press, 1975.

BIBLIOGRAPHY

Books

Baier, Annette C. *A Progress of Sentiments: Reflections on Hume's Treatise*. Cambridge: Harvard University Press, 1991.

Flew, Antony. *Hume's Philosophy of Belief*. London: Routledge and Kegan Paul, 1961.

Garrett, Don. *Cognition and Commitment in Hume's Philosophy*. New York: Oxford University Press, 1997.

Hacking, Ian. *The Emergence of Probability*. Cambridge: Cambridge University Press, 1975.

Millican, J. R. "Hume, Induction, and Probability." Diss., University of Leeds, and in preparation as a monograph under the same title, 1996.

Stove, D. C. *Probability and Hume's Inductive Scepticism*. Oxford: Oxford University Press, 1973.

Articles

Beauchamp, Tom, and Thomas Mappes. "Is Hume Really a Sceptic about Induction?" *American Philosophical Quarterly* 12 (1975): 119–29.

Millican, J. R. "Hume's Argument concerning Induction: Structure and Interpretation." In *David Hume: Critical Assessments*, ed. Stanley Tweyman. London: Routledge, 1995, vol. 2: 91–144.

Milton, J. R. "Induction before Hume." *British Journal for the Philosophy of Science* 38 (1987): 49–74.

Stove, D. C. "Hume, Probability, and Induction." *Philosophical Review* 74 (1965): 160–

77. Reprinted in *Hume*; edited by V. C. Chappell. New York: Macmillan, 1968: 187–212.

PETER MILLICAN

INNATENESS

NATIVISM, EMPIRICISM, AND RATIONALISM

The innateness doctrine (henceforth: ''nativism'') holds that our understanding of the world is significantly based on our innate mental endowment. To turn this vague formulation into a specific theory, one must answer (at least) the following questions. (1) What exactly does this innate mental endowment comprise? (2) Which aspects of our understanding are innately based? (3) How does our innate endowment contribute to our mature knowledge? Individual nativists have answered these questions in very different ways, and nativism is therefore best seen as a family of related doctrines. Indeed, empiricists themselves implicitly include nativist elements in their thinking: they agree that innate structures make it possible for us to perceive the world and to build our knowledge on the foundation of experience. What then ultimately distinguishes the two camps? Many philosophers have expressed skepticism about whether any clear-cut distinction is possible. They are right to this extent: empiricists are really *minimal* nativists, as opposed to *anti*nativists. But it is an important matter where one draws the line. Empiricists have traditionally held that only the general architecture and processes of thought are innate. Experience alone provides the IDEAS out of which knowledge is constructed, and, more important, experience alone can provide evidence for our knowledge claims.

It is really this last claim that best defines empiricism's position against its great rival rationalism. Traditional rationalism holds that REASON can discover a priori necessary truths about the intelligible structure of the mind-independent world (see A PRIORI/A POSTERIORI DISTINCTION). Reason has this ability to go beyond what PERCEPTION alone could teach us, because it can draw on another information source: our innate endowment. Nativism is in this way a crucial working part in the larger rationalist machine.

THE HISTORICAL DEFENSE OF NATIVISM

Although nativist theories differ in detail, they have a common weapon: the poverty-of-the-stimulus argument. The nativist points out that our knowledge encompasses x and argues that our experience of the world processed through empiricist learning mechanisms cannot account for how we come to know x. So our knowledge must to some extent also rest on a nonexperiential, innate basis.

Plato first applied this argument scheme in the *Meno*. He shows us an untutored slave discovering a nonobvious geometrical truth and argues that this can be explained only on the hypothesis that geometrical knowledge is innate. For Plato, experience and instruction simply ''jog'' our innate memories; learning is really recollection (*anamnesis*). This argument is extended in the *Phaedo* to show that concepts like "equality" are innate and ultimately generalized to all our concepts.

Two millennia later we find Descartes arguing that such concepts as infinity and, ultimately, our idea of GOD cannot be derived from experience and must therefore be innate. Leibniz extends the poverty-of-the-stimulus argument to the whole class of necessary truths. If our knowledge were solely based on particular experiences, as the empiricist claims, how is it that we have certain knowledge of necessary truths of MATHEMATICS, logic, METAPHYSICS, and so on? In his positive account Leibniz suggests that even our ordinary empirical concepts contain an innate element. Our concept of a table, for instance, draws upon our innate general concept of SUBSTANCE as well as on the specific features of tables that we discover in experience. General metaphysical truths about substance can in this way be a priori, because they are independent of the idiosyncratic features of specific substances.

RESPONSES TO NATIVISM

LOCKE's *Essay concerning Human Understanding* represents the most important sustained empiricist response to nativism. Locke argues first that the theory has debilitating internal problems. It takes as critical evidence the fact that some principles command universal assent, but in actual fact there are no such principles. Furthermore, the notion of innateness itself inevitably leads to a dilemma: nativists must accept either the patently absurd view that we are literally born knowing things—a clear violation of the Cartesian identification of thought with consciousness—or else see their claim reduced to the innocuous point that we are born with the ability to discover truths. Locke's preemptive arguments are in turn challenged by Leibniz in his *New Essays on Human Understanding*. But the more important empiricist response, which is the main thrust of Locke's *Essay*, is that nativism is unnecessary because empiricism offers a more parsimonious explanation of how knowledge is acquired. As we come to understand more about the origins of individual ideas and the learning mechanisms that convert experience into knowledge (and about the true nature and extent of our knowledge), the need for the innateness hypothesis vanishes. The subsequent empiricist tradition can be viewed as a detailed working out of Locke's "adequacy-of-the-stimulus" response.

A very different sort of response does not challenge nativism head-on but instead questions its proposed role in the overall rationalist scheme. The argument, originally proposed by Samuel Parker in the seventeenth century, is that even if there are innate beliefs or principles, their innateness cannot establish their truth, and certainly not their necessity. Nativism, therefore, cannot of itself underwrite a priori knowledge. This rather obvious point is generally ignored in rationalist defenses of nativism—it is surprisingly not even raised by Locke— perhaps because it is taken for granted that if God has placed something in our minds innately, its falsehood is unthinkable. But this is certainly not an obvious principle; Parker makes the nice point that fields sometimes require clearing of naturally growing weeds before useful crops can be planted.

Historically, this introduction of a deus ex machina to help nativism play its assigned epistemological role is symptomatic of a larger problem. Nativism was already associated, rightly or wrongly, with Plato's claims about the immortal soul's having learned all things in a previous existence. Various moralists and religious authorities were not above citing the authority of the innate to impose their pet beliefs and principles. Last but not least, rationalism had to deal with the growing success of Newtonian science, constructed on a supposedly empiricist foundation. Taken together, nativism came to seem philosophically and culturally out of step with the modern temperament.

It is therefore important to point out that these problems do not in any way undermine the core nativist claim. Whether the innate can ground the a priori or not, the core question—and it is ironically a purely "empirical" question—remains open: are all our ideas, beliefs, and so on derived solely from experience, or are some traceable to the mind's initial endowment? From this perspective, rationalism (and whatever religious or moral agenda it may have inspired) is a millstone unfairly hung around the neck of a wholly innocent nativist hypothesis.

CONTEMPORARY NATIVISM

If we take this perspective, then the real issue that divides nativists and empiricists must be settled by empirical research and not by armchair philosophy. This, in fact, reflects the current status of the debate. In the last decades, the nativist cause has been championed by Noam Chomsky's groundbreaking work in linguistics. Chomsky has argued persuasively that the linguistic evidence available to the child learning a language underdetermines the grammar. Despite this evidence-theory gap, normal children arrive at the right set of rules with relatively little effort and instruction, during a period in which they cannot master much else. Chomsky's conjecture is that as part of our specieswide biological endowment we each have innate language-specific information that mediates acquisition. In this respect, there is nothing obscure or unscientific about nativism. It is, on the contrary, very much in line with our understanding of the way brains evolve to equip organisms to function in their evolutionary niche.

Because of such work in language acquisition, traditional questions about the development of knowledge in areas like mathematics and physical causality (see CAUSATION) are now being reopened, and many argue that there are domain-specific innate factors that mediate the growth of our knowledge in these areas as well. This sort of nativism is often presented as a revived rationalism because it resuscitates claims made by seventeenth-century forebears, but it is rationalism without aprioricity. To this extent, nativism has now been stripped of what is really extraneous theoretical baggage and is being evaluated on its own merits.

PRIMARY WORKS

Descartes, René. *Meditations on First Philosophy* (1641). In *The Philosophical Works of Descartes*, edited by Haldane and Ross. Cambridge: Cambridge University Press, 1911.

Leibniz, Gottfried Wilhelm. *New Essays on Human Understanding* (1704). Translated and edited by Peter Remnant and Jonathan Bennett. Cambridge: Cambridge University Press, 1981.

Locke, John. *An Essay concerning Human Understanding*. Edited with an introduction by P. H. Nidditch. Oxford: Clarendon Press, 1975.

BIBLIOGRAPHY

Books

Chomsky, N. *Aspects of a Theory of Syntax*. Cambridge: MIT Press, 1965.
Samet, J. *Nativism*. Cambridge: MIT Press, forthcoming.
Stich, S., ed. *Innate Ideas*. Berkeley: University of California Press, 1975.

Articles

Edgley, R. "Innate Ideas." In *Knowledge and Necessity*, Royal Institute of Philosophy Lectures, vol. 3. London: Macmillan, 1970.
Fodor. J. "The Present Status of the Innateness Controversy." In *Representations*. Cambridge: MIT Press, 1981.

JERRY SAMET

INSTRUMENTALISM. In its most recent incarnation, instrumentalism is a way of understanding a scientific theory in which the theory's distinctively theoretical terms or phrases—those that denote things in principle unobservable to us—are to be understood as mere linguistic or logical instruments that exist solely to facilitate the derivation of one set of observation sentences from another. According to instrumentalism, a theoretical term does not refer to an extralinguistic object, no more than a hammer or any other tool so refers. It is thus nonsensical to ask if sentences that contain theoretical terms are true or false (see Boyd, CARNAP, Gardner, Nagel, and van Fraassen for discussions of instrumentalism).

Instrumentalism so defined is distinguished from various empiricist "reductionisms" (represented in this century by verificationism, OPERATIONISM, and Carnap's bilateral reduction sentences), which affirm that theoretical terms refer to complexes of experience, sense-data, primitive observations, or observation sentences, as well as from versions of empiricism that urge that a theory's theoretical terms be taken "literally" but that the correct attitude toward claims containing those terms is something short of belief. All these versions of empiricism address only the question of how a *scientific theory* is to be understood; they are therefore distinct from metaphysical views like idealism or realism, which concern the nature of the world. In fact, instrumentalists have typically been metaphysical *realists*.

INSTRUMENTALISM'S HERITAGE

This definition of instrumentalism presents it in the language and concepts of twentieth-century philosophy of SCIENCE, but the idea that theories are tools, not truths, is at least four centuries old. Osiander's infamous, anonymous, un-solicited, and unauthorized Preface to COPERNICUS' *De revolutionibus orbium coelestium* (On the Revolutions of the Celestial Spheres) is a prominent state-ment of the position: "[T]he astronomer's job," wrote Osiander, "is [to] think up or construct whatever hypothesis he pleases such that . . . the [clestial] move-ments can be calculated." Planetary motions were to be regarded as "fictive causes," conceived "solely to set up correct computation" (*To Save the Phe-nomena*: 67). Osiander's instrumentalist perspective was not Copernicus', but it was shared by the astronomers of Protestant reformer Philipp Melanchthon's "Wittenberg School" of the mid-sixteenth century (see Duhem, Westman). In-strumentalism thus can not only interpret scientific practice but inform it as well.

Some pre–sixteenth-century thinkers can be understood as instrumentalists, and indeed Pierre Duhem's 1908 *To Save the Phenomena*, perhaps this century's most significant examination and defense of instrumentalism, traces the instru-mentalist attitude from "Geminus, Ptolemy, and Proclus," through Maimonides, to "the tradition of Paris that was born in the teaching of Thomas Aquinas and Bonaventura and handed on by John of Jandun and Lefevre d'Etaples" (*To Save the Phenomena*: 67), and finally to the admonitions Urban VIII offered GALI-LEO.

Since the sixteenth century, instrumentalism has surfaced especially in debates surrounding physical theory. In the nineteenth century, for example, Dalton's atomic hypothesis was understood by many (although not by all and not by Dalton) as a mere summarization of the laws governing the ways elements com-bined into compounds; much debate concerned whether this understanding was warranted (see Nye for a historical treatment and Gardner for its philosophical import; see MACH and Whewell for nineteenth-century discussions of instru-mentalism).

INSTRUMENTALISM IN THE TWENTIETH CENTURY

Much of the impetus for, and historical understanding of, instrumentalism in this century is owed to Duhem, but Duhem's influence may in turn owe some-thing to philosophical positions that were sympathetic to, but developed inde-pendently of, instrumentalism and also to the emergence of special problems in the physical sciences. Chief among the former is the PRAGMATISM associated with Charles PEIRCE, William James, and John Dewey, which emphasized the tool-like nature of language, scientific language included; and logical positivism (see LOGICAL POSITIVISM/LOGICAL EMPIRICSM), within which the re-casting of scientific theories as uninterpreted formal calculi provided for per-spicuous definition of instrumentalism. An identification of instrumentalism with either position would be mistaken, however, for logical positivists often claimed that the question of how the theoretical terms of a theory should be understood was a pseudoquestion (see Nagel, discussed later), while pragmatists found in the successful employment of a scientific theory grounds for asserting the truth of the theory's claims. In the scientific realm, various conceptual difficulties that arose in the course of interpreting the formalism of quantum mechanics (e.g., the understanding of matter as collapsing wave packets) motivated instrumentalism for scientific theories generally.

OBJECTIONS TO INSTRUMENTALISM

It might have been expected that the move in recent decades away from the formulation of philosophical problems as problems of language would have promoted instrumentalism, for a theory's theoretical parts may be more naturally regarded as tools when they are not linguistic. In fact, though, the turn away from language was a turn toward detailed studies of scientific practice, and scientists often resisted an understanding of their theories as mere tools. The combination of a drive toward the literal interpretation of scientific practice and a rejection of the linguistic turn has been philosophically fruitful, but it has not promoted instrumentalism.

Against this background, a range of criticisms of instrumentalism has accumulated. Instrumentalism neither supports nor explains the motivation for theories that unify disparate phenomena; indeed, instrumentalists ought to prefer disparate theories for disparate phenomena (provided they make for effective predictions) on the assumption that tools are better designed when they are designed for a specific task. Further, instrumentalism cannot account for cases in which theoretical claims have been established to such an extent or in such distinctive manner that they lose their status as theoretical claims and take on the epistemological status of observation sentences. It is appropriate (and common) to say that in such cases the *truth* of the claim was established beyond scientific doubt, but instrumentalists can say no such thing.

Finally, a view militating against instrumentalism holds that the debate between realists and antirealists and hence between realism and instrumentalism is a false debate, since the acceptance of either position makes no difference in practice; a realist and an antirealist would be indistinguishable in the lab (see Nagel and, for a contemporary view close to this, Fine). While the two may be indistinguishable in practice, that in itself would not show the debate to be empty, since realism denies that two different accounts of science could be equivalent with respect to their observational consequences. If being a realist or an instrumentalist made no difference in practice, then that would tell against realism.

PRIMARY WORKS

Copernicus, N. *On the Revolutions of Celestial Spheres*. Edited by J. Dobrzyzki; translation and commentary by E. Rosen. London: Macmillan, 1978.

Dalton, J. *New System of Chemical Philosophy*. Manchester: Rickerstaff, 1808/1810.

Duhem, P. *To Save the Phenomena: An Essay of the Idea of Physical Theory from Plato to Galileo*. Edited with an introduction by Stanley Jaki; translated by E. Doland and C. Maschler. Chicago.: University of Chicago Press, 1908/1969.

Mach, E. *Die Analyse der Empfindungen*. Jena: G. Fischer, 1886.

van Fraassen, B. *The Scientific Image*. Oxford: Oxford University Press, 1980.

Whewell, W. *The Philosophy of Inductive Sciences, Founded upon Their History.* London, 1840.

BIBLIOGRAPHY

Books

Carnap, R. *An Introduction to the Philosophy of Science.* Edited by M. Gardner. New York: Basic Books, 1966.

Fine, A. *The Shaky Game: Einstein, Realism, and the Quantum Theory.* 2d ed. Chicago: University of Chicago Press, 1997.

Leplin, J., ed. *Scientific Realism.* Berkeley: University of California Press, 1984.

Nagel, E. *The Structure of Science: Problems in the Logic of Scientific Explanation.* Indianapolis, IN: Hackett, 1979/1961.

Suppe, F. *The Semantic Conception of Theories and Scientific Realism.* Urbana: University of Illinois Press, 1989.

Articles

Boyd, R. "On the Current Status of Scientific Realism." *Erkenntnis* 19 (1983): 45–90.

Gardner, M. R. "Realism and Instrumentalism in 19th-Century Atomism." *Philosophy of Science* 46 (1979): 1–34.

Hesse, M. "Is There an Independent Observation Language?" In *The Nature of Scientific Theories*, edited by R. Colodny. Pittsburgh: University of Pittsburgh Press, 1970: 35–77.

Maxwell, G. "The Ontological Status of Theoretical Entities." In *Minnesota Studies in the Philosophy of Science*, vol. 3, edited by H. Feigl and G. Maxwell. Minneapolis: University of Minnesota Press, 1962.

Nye, M. J. "The Nineteenth-Century Atomic Debates and the Dilemma of an 'Indifferent Hypothesis.' " *Studies in History and Philosophy of Science* 7 (1976): 245–68.

Westman, R. "The Melanchthon Circle, Rheticus, and the Wittenberg Interpretation of the Copernican Theory." *Isis* 66 (1975): 165–93.

GARY L. HARDCASTLE

INTUITION. In LOCKE (*An Essay concerning Human Understanding*), intuition and DEMONSTRATION are two faculties of the understanding or REASON that result in the most certain KNOWLEDGE. Locke defines knowledge as "the perception of the connexion and agreement, or disagreement and repugnancy of any of our Ideas" (*Essay* IV.i.2). Intuition is the direct or immediate perception of such an agreement or disagreement, whereas demonstration is indirect, the perception of the agreement being mediated by intervening ideas (see IDEAS). But as any two adjacent ideas in a demonstrative chain must be directly seen to agree by intuition, intuitive knowledge is the more fundamental of the two.

It is also more certain. Locke seems to follow Descartes in thinking that intuitive knowledge is the most certain because of its lack of complexity. This simplicity and directness leave no room for error or doubt: "This part of Knowledge is irresistible, and like the bright Sun-shine, forces it self immediately to be perceived, as soon as ever the Mind turns its view that way; and leaves no room for Hesitation, Doubt, or Examination, but the Mind is presently filled with the clear light of it'' (*Essay* IV.ii.1). The visual metaphor is also found in Descartes, and there it is perhaps more illuminating. What is known by Cartesian intuition are ideas of the intellect or reason; the faculty and its objects are made for each other. But Lockean intuition perceives agreement or disagreement between ideas that come from experience, that is, ideas of sensation or reflection. Just what intuition is for Locke and how it produces knowledge of the highest degree of certainty are unclear.

One strategy is to look at Locke's examples of intuitive knowledge and try to see just what sort of agreement is immediately perceivable. By and large, his examples involve identity, either pure or partial. Examples of pure identity (or its denial) include ''[W]hite is not black,'' ''[T]hree is equal to one or two'' (*Essay* IV.ii.1), and ''A Law is a Law'' (*Essay* IV.viii.3). Examples of partial identity are ''Lead is a metal'' and ''All gold is fusible'' (*Essay* IV.viii.4–5). The former cases involve the same idea twice, whereas the latter cases involve predicating one idea on another that contains the first idea as a part. In both cases we might characterize the way the ideas agree as analytic, considered as idea containment (see ANALYTIC/SYNTHETIC DISTINCTION). Thus, we might explain Locke's account of intuition as the immediate awareness of self-evident analytic agreement between ideas.

An advantage of this account, apart from giving an explanation of Locke's account of intuition, is that it allows us to classify Locke's ''trifling propositions'' (which by and large are intuitive) as analytically self-evident, without classifying his ''instructive'' propositions as synthetic. Of instructive propositions, Locke says that ''he that would enlarge his own, or another's Mind, to Truths he does not yet know, must find out intermediate Ideas, and then lay them in such order one by another, that the Understanding may see the agreement, or disagreement of those in question'' (Essay IV.viii.3). So the distinction between instructive and trifling seems to come down to the distinction between demonstration and intuition, where demonstration is accounted for by a string of intuitions, and intuition is accounted for by the immediate awareness of self-evident, analytic agreement between ideas.

PRIMARY WORK

Locke, John. *An Essay concerning Human Understanding*. Edited with an introduction by P. H. Nidditch. Oxford: Clarendon Press, 1975.

BIBLIOGRAPHY

Book:

Ayers, Michael. *Locke: Epistemology and Ontology*. Vol. 1, *Epistemology*. London and New York: Routledge, 1993.

Article

Wolfram, Sybil. "On the Mistake of Identifying Locke's Trifling-Instructive Distinction with the Analytic-Synthetic Distinction." *The Locke Newsletter* 9 (1978): 27–53.

DAVID OWEN

K

KANT, IMMANUEL. Immanuel Kant (1724–1804) was the most important philosopher of the German Enlightenment. With an encyclopedic grasp of classical and contemporary intellectual developments, Kant advanced one of the most complete and comprehensive philosophical systems since Aristotle. After his work in the monumental *Critique of Pure Reason, Critique of Practical Reason, Critique of Judgment,* and related scientific, philosophical, and theological writings, all later European philosophy divides into two mainstreams. These were fully integrated in Kant's own thought but subsequently split apart as German idealism (and its successors in phenomenology, existentialism, hermeneutics, deconstructionism, and postmodernism, as so-called Continental philosophy), and Austrian and Anglo-American scientific empiricism, logical positivism, and linguistic analysis (so-called analytic philosophy).

Kant was born on April 22, 1724, in Königsberg, then East Prussia, where he died on February 12, 1804. He attended the Collegium Fridericianum and the Universität Königsberg, studying philosophy, theology, and mathematics. He left the university in 1746 to work as a private tutor to several families, returning to earn his master's degree in 1755. Kant began his university teaching as *Privatdozent* (fee-paid lecturer) at this time and was later appointed professor of logic and metaphysics in 1770. Kant's learning was so extensive that at the height of his career he was certified by the university to teach every course in its curriculum, and he lectured frequently on logic, metaphysics, history of philosophy, ethics, natural theology, philosophy of religion, mathematics, physics, physical geography, and mineralogy. He was president of the university from 1786 to 1788. When he retired, he was carried about the town in triumph on the shoulders of enthusiastic students as a token of their respect for a local scholar who had become a distinguished philosopher of international reputation.

The *Critique of Pure Reason* (1781, 1787) inaugurated Kant's so-called critical philosophy or philosophy of "critical idealism." The *Critique* advances a bold synthesis of rationalism and empiricism. In the *Prolegomena to Any Future Metaphysics That Will Be Able to Come Forward as Science*, written in 1783 as a preparatory study to the first edition of the *Critique*, Kant criticizes the unscientific character of pure rationalism and the poverty and SKEPTICISM entailed by radical empiricism. The rationalists, wary of the potential delusions and uncertainty of sense experience, professed to use pure REASON to arrive at metaphysical conclusions about such questions as the nature of SUBSTANCE, the necessity of CAUSATION, the SELF as a unitary subject of thought, and the existence and essence of GOD (see METAPHYSICS). Kant pronounces rationalism unscientific and hence dogmatic on the grounds that its results, unlike the findings of public scientific observation and repeatable experiment, when practiced by such distinct philosophical personalities as Descartes, Spinoza, and Leibniz, are so different as to be mutually logically contradictory. The empiricists, by contrast, in response to these limitations, caused the methodological pendulum to swing too far in the opposite direction away from pure reason, by restricting KNOWLEDGE to what is directly perceived or constructible by other faculties of mind out of the data of the senses. Empiricism anchors SCIENCE and philosophy to experience, where rationalism's reliance on pure reason offers only noncontradiction with no guarantee of truth. In its extreme formulations in BERKELEY and HUME, Kant complains that radical empiricism leads to excessive skepticism about entities for which there is no sensory experiential evidence, including the existence of a world outside, and independent of, the mind's IDEAS, the necessity (in some sense) of efficient causal connection (see CAUSATION), the concept of a unitary self, and the existence of God. Kant accepts a version of Leibniz's rationalist system, as transmitted by the teachings of Christian Wolff, in which most of these commonsense beliefs are affirmed. But Kant regards rationalist methodology as inadequate to uphold its conclusions. It is Hume the empiricist whom Kant credits as having opened his eyes to the limitations of rationalism, as Kant acknowledges in the *Prolegomena* when he states: "I openly confess that my remembering David Hume was the very thing which many years ago first interrupted my dogmatic slumber and gave my investigations in the field of speculative philosophy a quite new direction" (5).

To make philosophy scientific as against pure rationalism and nonskeptical as against radical empiricism, Kant proposes to identify the proper subject matter of metaphysics as the realm of nonmathematical synthetic a priori judgments (see ANALYTIC/SYNTHETIC DISTINCTION and A PRIORI/A POSTERIORI DISTINCTION). Kant claims to discover these propositions by a new method of transcendental argument in a critique of pure reason. The critique sets limits to what can and cannot be known by logic and reflection on the MEANING of CONCEPTS, thereby highlighting the importance of sense experience and faith in human belief. The method of transcendental argument fuses sense experience ("intuition") with reason in a special type of inquiry. Kant's transcendental method begins with something indisputably given in empirical experience and asks reason to determine what must be true in order for the experience or some particular aspect of experience to be possible. Kant's slogan in achieving his grand synthesis of pure rationalism and radical empiricism in the *Critique* is, "Thoughts without content are empty, intuitions without concepts are blind" (A51/B75). In the "Transcendental Aesthetic," *Critique*, Book I, First Part, Kant illustrates the method of transcendental argument. He begins with the experience of objects perceived as distinctly individuated things, contrasted with the background against which they are discriminated in the flux of impressions that Kant calls the "sensory manifold." Kant asks the transcendental question, What must be true in order for such objectifying experience to be possible? He deduces as the central synthetic a priori conclusion of his transcendental aesthetic that space and time are pure forms of intuition innate to the mind, which the mind brings to, and superimposes on, experience and without which sensation would be totally unformed and chaotic. Space and time by Kant's critique are therefore not real things or real properties of things, as they are in themselves independent of thought. Space and time are rather presupposed by the mind's ability to make sense of the world by imposing its own order on the data of sensation as the world appears to thought and, in that broad sense, are mental or ideal.

Kant is nevertheless at pains to distinguish his limited version of idealism from Berkeley's more radically empiricist and mentalistic (albeit theological) idealism (see BERKELEY). Kant distances himself from Berkeley's idealism by offering a proof of the thing-in-itself (*Ding an sich*) in a section of the first *Critique* appropriately titled, "The Refutation of Idealism." Kant argues transcendentally by beginning with the given experience of consciousness as determined in time. Asking what must be true in order for this fact of experience to be possible, Kant concludes that there must be something external to the mind, a reality that transcends the flow of consciousness, by reference to which the events occurring within thought are determined. The reference point by which occurrences in consciousness are fixed in time must be something outside, and other than, consciousness, a thing unto itself, external to, and independent of, thought. If whatever it is that determines the time at which consciousness occurs were just a part of consciousness, then it would equally stand in need of being temporally determined, whereas Kant assumes that the entire stream of consciousness with all its contents is experienced as determined in time. The occurrence of consciousness could no more be determined in time by something within thought as a part of consciousness than we could fix our location along a highway if we were to carry the distance-marking road signs along with us in the car.

The proof of the thing-in-itself establishes Kant's most fundamental metaphysical distinction between the noumenal and phenomenal world. As a bare existence claim, Kant's refutation of idealism proves only that the thing-in-itself exists. But because the thing-in-itself exists outside thought, it is by definition noumenal or representationally unknowable. The world of empirical experience filtered through, informed by, and made intelligible by the mind's forms of intuition and by the concepts and categories of the understanding, Kant denotes as the phenomenal world. The phenomenal world is that aspect of reality available to empirical study as the proper subject of natural science. It is the knowable aspect of the world within the bounds of sense to which the mind is limited in its empirical investigations, as established by a critique of pure reason. The noumenal world is the representationally unknowable thing-in-itself, by the transcendental proof of which Kant's critical idealism is preserved from a Berkeleian, radically empiricist, purely mentalistic idealism. The non-Berkeleian idealism of Kant's critical idealism amounts to the claim Kant himself declares a kind of Copernican revolution in philosophy, that the mind brings to, and imposes its ideas of space and time on, the world as it appears to thought, along with the concepts and categories of the understanding, as the transcendental ground of empirical experience.

Kant's critical idealism thus combines the idealism implied by radical empiricism with rationalist belief (inadequately justified by rationalist methods) of pure reason in the existence of substance, matter, or a real world outside, and independent of, thought. In similar ways, Kant seeks to prove the transcendental ground of the other elements of experience. He thereby establishes the necessity of causation as a concept of pure understanding and the existence of the self, invisible to empirical experience, as what he calls "the transcendental unity of apperception." The conclusions of Kant's critical idealism are alike transcendental in establishing the existence of something not empirically discoverable in the content of sensation but that transcends and is presupposed by the occurrence and nature of empirical experience. The limits of pure reason are reinforced by Kant's critique of the paralogisms and antinomies of reason, in which rationally unsupportable or contradictory conclusions appear equally justified by the resources of reason alone. Having proved the existence of a transcendent unknowable world outside thought, the necessity of causation as a requirement of reasoning about phenomena, and the self as transcendental unity of apperception, Kant remarkably does not apply the method of transcendental argument to demonstrate the existence of God. In the section of the *Critique* on "The Ideal of Pure Reason," Kant instead systematically considers and refutes four styles of rationalist and empiricist proofs for the existence of God, which he considers to exhaust the possibilities, concluding, as he states in the Preface to the second edition of the *Critique*, "I have therefore found it necessary to deny *knowledge*, in order to make room for *faith*" (Bxxx).

The synthesis of reason and experience that Kant advances in his critical idealism is undoubtedly one of the most ambitious projects ever to have been undertaken in the history of philosophy. Kant brings together empiricism and rationalism in the transcendental method, by which he uncovers the pure forms of intuition and the concepts and categories of the understanding presupposed as the transcendental ground of experience. By itself, Kant finds neither pure reason nor pure intuition satisfactory as a basis for science or philosophy. One complements the other, and one needs and implies the other. Only by recognizing the symbiotic interaction and involvement of reason and intuition does Kant believe we can arrive at a correct understanding of mind and world. Kant performs much the same investigation of the transcendental ground of empirical experience in metaphysics or speculative philosophy as for the metaphysics of moral or practical philosophy and the aesthetic appreciation of beauty and the sublime in the theory of judgment.

In considering the implications of Kant's philosophy for empiricism, it is finally noteworthy that in the metaphysics of MORALS, Kant does not conclude, as in his critical, idealist, speculative philosophy, that moral philosophy must combine reason with intuition or sense experience, but instead he proposes a doctrine self-consciously based solely on reason. Kant is unequivocal in denouncing any trace of empirical consideration as a theoretical impurity to be purged from moral philosophy so as to make ethics a thoroughly formalist enterprise. The *Foundations of the Metaphysics of Morals* leaves no room for doubt about Kant's demand that reason alone in the form of what he thereafter refers to as the categorical imperative must autonomously dictate its own morality. Kant holds:

Is it not of the utmost necessity to construct a pure moral philosophy which is completely freed from everything which may be only empirical and thus belong to anthropology? That there must be such a philosophy is self-evident from the common idea of duty and moral laws. . . . [Everyone] must concede that the ground of obligation here must not be sought in the nature of man or in the circumstances in which he is placed, but sought a priori solely in the concepts of pure reason, and that every other precept which rests on principles of mere experience, so far as it leans in the least on empirical grounds (perhaps only in regard to the motive involved), may be called a practical rule but never a moral law. Thus not only are moral laws together with their principles essentially different from all practical knowledge in which there is anything empirical, but all moral philosophy rests solely on its pure part. (5)

It must be concluded that Kant's attitude toward empiricism is complex. Kant distinguishes between the integration of empirical elements in the transcendental foundations of metaphysics in speculative philosophy and its sharp exclusion from the transcendental foundations of the metaphysics of morals in practical philosophy. The distinction reflects Kant's requirement of perfect freedom or autonomy of reason in ethical decision making. In choosing to act, practical reason must be uninfluenced by empirical, psychological considerations of pleasure and pain that threaten to make moral judgment heteronomous, giving reason an external motivation to act, beyond the demands reason makes of itself. The impure empiricism appropriate to Kant's synthesis of empiricism and rationalism in speculative philosophy is thereby necessarily excluded from the transcendental foundations of practical philosophy in what Kant believes must be the pure nonempiricism of the metaphysics of morals.

PRIMARY WORK

Kants gesammelte Schriften. Edited by the königlich preussischen Akademie der Wissenschaften. Berlin: G. Reimer, 1901–1910.

Foundations of the Metaphysics of Morals. Translated with an introduction by Lewis White Beck. New York: Macmillan, 1959.

Critique of Pure Reason. Translated by Norman Kemp Smith. New York: St. Martin's Press, 1965.

Prolegomena to Any Future Metaphysics That Will Be Able to Come Forward as Science. Translated by Paul Carus; revised by James W. Ellington. Indianapolis, IN: Hackett, 1977.

BIBLIOGRAPHY

Books

Allison, Henry E. *Kant's Transcendental Idealism: An Interpretation and Defense.* New Haven, CT: Yale University Press, 1983.

Beck, Lewis White. *A Commentary on Kant's Critique of Practical Reason.* Chicago: University of Chicago Press, 1960.

————. *Essays on Kant and Hume.* New Haven, CT: Yale University Press, 1978.

Buchdahl, Gerd. *Kant and the Dynamics of Reason: Essays on the Structure of Kant's Philosophy.* Oxford: Basil Blackwell, 1992.

Cassirer, Ernst. *Kant's Life and Thought.* Translated by James Haden. New Haven, CT: Yale University Press, 1981.

Guyer, Paul, ed. *The Cambridge Companion to Kant.* Cambridge: Cambridge University Press, 1992.

Henrich, Dieter. *The Unity of Reason: Essays on Kant's Philosophy.* Edited by Richard L. Velkley; translated by Jeffrey Edwards. Cambridge: Harvard University Press, 1994.

Paton, H. J. *The Categorical Imperative: A Study in Kant's Moral Philosophy.* New York: Harper and Row, 1967.

Strawson, P. F. *The Bounds of Sense: An Essay on Kant's Critique of Pure Reason.* London: Methuen, 1975.

Article

Schopenhauer, Arthur. "Criticism of the Kantian Philosophy." In *The World as Will and Representation*, 2 vols., translated by E.F.J. Payne. New York: Dover, 1966: 413–534: vol. 1 (Appendix).

DALE JACQUETTE

KNOWLEDGE. LOCKE famously defines knowledge as "*the perception of the connexion and agreement, or disagreement and repugnancy of any of our Ideas*" (*An Essay concerning Human Understanding* IV.i.2), but his subsequent discussion significantly extends this somewhat vague and unclear definition. He starts by suggesting that knowledge always concerns one of four types of agreement or disagreement, namely, "Identity, or Diversity," "Relation," "Co-existence, or necessary connexion," and "real Existence"—his examples of the first two of these (perceiving the self-identity and distinctness of ideas, and the relations between ideas) fit relatively comfortably with his definition, but knowledge of "co-existence" (Locke instances the fixedness of gold and the magnetizability of iron) and knowledge of "real existence" (e.g., of physical objects, or of GOD) both seem to involve the "agreement" of ideas with external things rather than merely among themselves.

Locke then points out (*Essay* IV.i.8) that knowledge can involve not only current "perception of agreement or disagreement," which he calls *actual knowledge*, but also remembered perception, which he calls *habitual knowledge*. Some habitual knowledge, so-called *intuitive knowledge* (see INTUITION), is such that its truth is immediately apparent whenever it is brought to mind; but other habitual knowledge, for example, of geometrical theorems, relies on memory (which "is but the reviving of some past knowledge") to provide the assurance that it has indeed been perceived to be true in the past, as well as on an awareness of "the immutability of the same relations between the same immutable things" (see RELATIONS) to extend that assurance to the present and future. Locke admits to having had doubts about the status of remembered truths, which "seem'd formerly to me like something between Opinion and Knowledge, as sort of Assurance which exceeds bare Belief, for that relies on the Testimony of another; Yet upon a due examination I find it comes not short of perfect certainty, and is in effect true Knowledge" (*Essay* IV.i.9).

Locke's fundamental assumption, made explicit here, that "true knowledge" requires "perfect certainty" generates an obvious tension when he comes to discuss "the Degrees of our Knowledge" (*Essay* IV.ii). For then he distinguishes three such degrees, namely, *intuitive knowledge, demonstrative knowledge* (or "*knowledge by intervening proofs*"; see DEMONSTRATION), and *sensitive knowledge*. A truth known intuitively is (as mentioned earlier) immediately and irresistibly apparent—"like the bright Sun-shine," it "forces it self immediately to be perceived, as soon as ever the Mind turns its view that way; and leaves no room for Hesitation, Doubt, or Examination." Demonstrative knowledge, by contrast, becomes evident only through the mediation of intervening "proofs," and although such a "demonstration" must consist of intuitively certain steps to merit the name, nevertheless the fact that "pains and attention" are required to keep the reasoning in view (and hence that "Men embrace often Falshoods for Demonstrations"—*Essay* I.ii.7) implies that this is in some sense a lesser degree of knowledge. Unable to attribute its inferiority to any descent from "perfect certainty," however, Locke instead explains that, as compared with INTUITION, DEMONSTRATION is only less *clear and distinct* or less *evidently* certain. Likewise, his account of sensitive knowledge, "of the existence of particular external Objects, by that perception and Consciousness we have of the actual entrance of *Ideas* from them" (*Essay* IV.ii.14), displays a similar awkwardness. He seems torn between, on one hand, his desire to confer on it the honorific title of "knowledge," and, on the other, his awareness that, in the face of skepticism about the external world, sensation appears, in some respects at least, to be significantly less secure than intuition.

HUME largely takes over Locke's understanding of knowledge but because of his skeptical outlook, shows far less interest in it. Thus, although the longest part of his *A Treatise of Human Nature* is entitled "Of Knowledge and Probability,'' only the first few pages of this are devoted to knowledge proper, and all the remainder to PROBABILITY.

Like Locke, Hume begins his discussion of knowledge by specifying the kinds of relation that are susceptible of it, namely, on his account *"resemblance, contrariety, degrees in quality, and proportions in quantity or number"* (*Treatise*: 70). The first three of these, he says, "fall more properly under the province of intuition than demonstration''—only the fourth, which underlies the "sciences'' of algebra and arithmetic, yields ideas sufficiently precise and distinct to enable us to "carry on a chain of reasoning to any degree of intricacy, and yet preserve a perfect exactness and certainty.'' (However, in his first *Enquiry* [1748]: 25, 163, Hume admits geometry as a third science depending only on quantity or number and therefore capable of demonstration—he no longer sees geometrical ideas as being contaminated with the vagueness and imprecision of our sensory impressions.)

For Hume, therefore, knowledge has only a very restricted scope—the vast bulk of our beliefs falls within the realm of probability, being dependent not on one of the four knowledge-yielding relations but instead on CAUSATION and on causal reasoning by INDUCTION. Hume sees such beliefs as capable of being certain in a *psychological* sense—indeed he uses language highly reminiscent of Locke's account of *intuition* in describing some of them as "entirely free from doubt and uncertainty'' (*Treatise*: 124) and as irresistible, like "seeing the surrounding bodies, when we turn our eyes toward them in bright sunshine'' (*Treatise*: 183). But this kind of certainty carries no rational guarantee and hence cannot merit the title of "knowledge.''

Modern epistemologists have retreated from the early empiricists' assumption that beliefs can count as knowledge only if rationally certain and have tried to give a coherent account of our commonsense notion of "knowledge'' that sets no such extreme constraint. However, the seminal paper of Gettier (1963) showed that the then-popular analysis of knowledge as "justified true belief'' is dubious, essentially because a true belief that is "justified'' on the basis of a prior (justified but) false belief cannot intuitively be described as knowledge. The massive literature generated on the topic since then gives little ground for confidence that the quest for a precise analysis of the commonsense notion of knowledge will ever be successful.

PRIMARY WORKS

Hume, David. *A Treatise of Human Nature.* 2d ed., edited with an analytical index by L. A. Selby-Bigge; revised with notes by P. H. Nidditch. Oxford: Clarendon Press, 1978.

———. *An Enquiry concerning Human Understanding.* In *Enquiries concerning Human Understanding and concerning the Principles of Morals*, edited with an analytical index by L. A. Selby-Bigge; revised with notes by P. H. Nidditch. Oxford: Clarendon Press, 1975. First publication by Hume 1748 and 1751, respectively—1777 was the last edition to incorporate new authorial corrections.

Locke, John. *An Essay concerning Human Understanding*. Edited with an introduction by P. H. Nidditch. Oxford: Clarendon Press, 1975.

BIBLIOGRAPHY

Books

Ayers, Michael. *Locke*. Vol. 1, *Epistemology*. London: Routledge, 1991.
Kemp Smith, Norman. *The Philosophy of David Hume*. New York: Macmillan, 1941: Chapter 15.

Article

Gettier, Edmund, Jr. "Is Justified True Belief Knowledge?" *Analysis* 23 (1963): 121–23.

PETER MILLICAN

L

LOCKE, JOHN. John Locke (1632–1704), arguably the greatest of all English philosophers, was the first of the triumvirate of British philosophers known as "the British Empiricists," the remaining two being BERKELEY and HUME. In his magnum opus, *An Essay concerning Human Understanding* (1689), he was the first major philosopher to combine a thoroughgoing critique of the rationalist doctrine of the INNATENESS of IDEAS with a systematic empiricist account of the derivation of all human KNOWLEDGE and understanding from their source in our ideas of sensation and reflection. Following a brief account of Locke's life and work, this entry focuses successively on Locke's attack on innate ideas, his theory of PERCEPTION, his contributions to METAPHYSICS, his views about language, and his theory of knowledge.

LIFE AND WORK

Locke's social origins were quite humble, as he was the son of a minor landowner and attorney from Somerset, but patronage enabled him to receive an excellent education, first at Westminster School and then at Christ Church, Oxford, where he graduated with a B.A. in 1656. An excellent scholar, he retained his Studentship at Christ Church after graduating and entered upon an academic career, combining teaching with further study in theology, philosophy, and medicine. Locke's extensive knowledge of medicine (he was awarded the Oxford degree of M.B. in 1675) led to his friendship with Lord Ashley (later the earl of Shaftesbury), a prominent and wealthy Whig politician of the period. This association began in 1666 and lasted until a constitutional crisis over the succession to the throne compelled Shaftesbury to flee the country in 1682. These were dangerous times for Shaftesbury's associates, several of whom were arrested for treason for their part in the Rye House plot against Charles II in 1683. Locke himself was not directly involved in this conspiracy but wisely departed for the Netherlands in that year, returning only in 1689, after the last Stuart king, James II, had been replaced by William of Orange and his wife, Mary. In the remaining years of his life Locke accepted public office under a government more in line with his political convictions but spent most of his time quietly pursuing intellectual interests.

Besides the *Essay*, Locke wrote many other works, the most notable being his *Two Treatises of Government* (1689), the *Second Treatise* expounding his view that legitimate civil government is founded on a social contract and defending the right of subjects to overthrow a ruler who abuses their trust. Locke's concern for political liberty and religious toleration—the latter made famous by his *Letter on Toleration* (1689)—was partly the product of his association with Shaftesbury but had its deeper roots in his Protestant upbringing. Though unmarried and without children of his own, Locke's interest in the humane education of children and in their intellectual development manifests itself in his enormously influential *Some Thoughts concerning Education* (1693), as well as, indirectly, in the *Essay* itself. His best-known religious work is *The Reasonableness of Christianity* (1695).

The *Essay* provoked widespread reaction from its first publication and was issued in three further revised editions in Locke's own lifetime, the fourth edition of 1700 being the version most closely studied today. Many of the more conservative readers of the *Essay* attacked it as a threat to established religious authority, not least on account of Locke's hostility to the doctrine of innate ideas. In the eyes of these critics, Locke's views about human knowledge appeared dangerously skeptical. But in fact Locke was by no means an enemy of religious faith and merely sought to reconcile such faith with the evidence of experience and the dictates of REASON. Of his more philosophical contemporary critics, the most prominent were Berkeley and Leibniz, the former famous for his attack on Locke's belief in matter and abstract ideas, the latter famous for his defense of innatism against Locke's criticisms of it. (Leibniz presents this defense in his *New Essays on Human Understanding*, an extended commentary on Locke's *Essay* in dialogue form, unpublished in his own lifetime.)

INNATE IDEAS

Turning now to look in more detail at Locke's attack on the doctrine of innate ideas, we need to consider the arguments he presents in Book I of the *Essay*. Even in Locke's time the doctrine already had a long pedigree, stretching back to Plato's defense of it in one of his dialogues, the *Meno*. The medieval Scholastics, taking their inspiration more from ARISTOTLE than Plato, had on the whole been sympathetic to empiricism; but by the seventeenth century the influence of Aristotle was on the wane, and Neoplatonism was undergoing a revival. The Platonic esteem for MATHEMATICS and distrust of sensory experience are echoed in the rationalist thought of this period, above all in the works of Descartes, who was then the leading proponent of the doctrine of innate ideas. Descartes, thus, must have been one of Locke's prime targets, even if Locke did not discuss Descartes' writings on these matters directly.

Locke's basic objection to the doctrine of innate ideas is twofold: that there is no evidence to support it (and there is much against it) and that it serves no explanatory purpose. On the first point, he urges that the only evidence that *would* support the doctrine would be evidence of universal assent, by all human beings, to certain principles of a logical, metaphysical, or moral nature (see *Essay* I.ii). However, even the best candidates for principles thus universally assented to, such as the logical laws of IDENTITY and of noncontradiction, are *not* in fact assented to by children, the uneducated, and the mentally defective. To say that such people do nevertheless know the truth of these principles but are unaware of their knowledge is, for Locke, tantamount to a contradiction. Nor will it help to urge that children (at least those of sound mind) come to assent to these principles upon attaining the age of reason, for even if true, this is perfectly explicable in terms of their *discovering* the truth of the principles for themselves. On the second point, Locke suggests that to posit the existence of innate ideas in an attempt to explain certain features of our knowledge and understanding is not really to *explain* those features at all but just to take them for granted. Moreover, he believes that a genuine explanation of all these features is available anyway, in terms of his empiricist theory of concept-formation and knowledge-acquisition, the exposition and defense of which occupy the remaining three Books of the *Essay*.

How compelling are Locke's criticisms of the doctrine of innate ideas? In modern times, some psychologists and linguists, such as Noam Chomsky, have attempted to revive the doctrine in order to account, among other things, for the capacity of all human children to learn a language. They point out that children learn languages rapidly and on the basis of degraded, fragmentary, and limited data in the form of the sentences that they hear their elders uttering. Moreover, all human languages share certain universal grammatical principles, despite their widespread diversity of vocabulary. The modern innatists or nativists urge that a child's capacity to learn a language so easily can be explained only by supposing that these universal principles are innately (albeit only tacitly) known by all humans, being part of their genetic inheritance much in the way that bipedal locomotion is. This is supposed to explain, too, why it is that human languages are unteachable to creatures of other species. It is likely that Locke would have remained skeptical in the light of these claims, urging the absurdity of supposing that children learn their native tongue analogously to the way in which a theoretical linguist might attempt to decode the utterances of a newly discovered tribe: that is, by (tacitly) testing the members of a family of grammatical hypotheses against the linguistic data. Alternative explanations of an empiricist stamp have more recently begun to find some favor, since it has been discovered that artificial neural networks can be trained, for instance, to learn the rules for forming the past tense of English verbs and acquire mastery of these rules in a fashion that interestingly mimics that of human children (see Bechtel and Abrahamsen, Chapter 6).

THEORY OF PERCEPTION

We should next look at Locke's account of sense perception, this being for him one of the two sources of all our ideas, the other being reflection or (as we now call it) introspection. Here we need to note a certain fluidity in Locke's use of the term "idea," whereby it sometimes denotes an ingredient in the content of sensory (or else introspective) experience and sometimes an ingredient in the content of IMAGINATION or thought. Of course, such fluidity is to be expected in the light of Locke's basic empiricist thesis that our capacities for thought and understanding are all dependent on prior experience. Locke defines an idea as "Whatsoever the Mind perceives in itself, or is the immediate object of Perception, Thought or Understanding" (*Essay* II.viii.8). In thus calling ideas *objects* of perception and thought, does he literally mean to say that they are "things" of a certain sort to which the mind is somehow related in an act of perceiving or thinking? Many passages in the *Essay* suggest this interpretation of Lockean ideas as mental *images*, closely akin to the SENSE-DATA of some more recent theories of perception. Modern theorists of perception who agree that perceptual experiences possess sensory content differ over whether to interpret that fact in terms of an "act-object" analysis of sensation or in terms of an "adverbial" analysis. On the act-object analysis, a sensing of pain or of color involves an act of awareness of some inner mental *object*, whereas on the adverbial analysis such a sensing is a *mode* or *manner* of sensory awareness without any such object. Thus, on the former view a sensing of pain involves an awareness of a *painful sensation*, whereas on the latter view it involves sensing *painfully*. It may be possible to interpret Locke's theory of sense perception in line with the adverbial analysis and thus in a way that does not commit him to an imagistic or "inner object" account of perceiving and thinking. If so, Locke need not be credited with an "indirect" realist theory of perception, with all the skeptical implications that such a theory is commonly believed to harbor. In fact, however, it is debatable whether "indirect" realism is really any more vulnerable to skeptical challenge than is "direct" realism: for however strongly one urges that "external" objects are the "direct" objects of perception, the skeptic may raise doubts as to whether we ever *do* perceive such objects—doubts that are entirely parallel to those he or she may raise for the "indirect" realist as to whether sense-data or mental images ever faithfully represent the nature of their supposed "external" causes.

An important feature of Locke's theory of sense perception is his treatment of the distinction between PRIMARY AND SECONDARY QUALITIES. According to Locke, a secondary quality, such as the red color of a rose, is a power (or, as we would now say, DISPOSITION) that an external object has, in virtue of the primary qualities of its microstructural parts, to produce a certain sensation in us in suitable circumstances (see *Essay* II.viii.10). He holds that whereas our idea of that quality, deriving from that sensation, in no way resembles the quality itself as it is in the object, our ideas of *primary* qualities such as shape do indeed resemble the qualities in question. Berkeley objected to this doctrine as incoherent, on the grounds that "an idea can be like nothing but an idea" (*Philosophical Works*: 79). However, Locke's contention is not as indefensible as his critics suppose, provided we interpret his use of the term "resemblance" charitably in this context. What he can be taken to be claiming is not, absurdly, that our visual ideas of shape *look like* external objects possessing those shapes but rather that some sort of structural isomorphism obtains between a primary quality such as squareness and the sense-content that characteristically represents that quality in our experience (see Lowe: Chapter 3).

METAPHYSICS

I now consider the implications of Locke's theory of perception for his metaphysical views. Some of the most important notions in metaphysics, such as those of identity, SUBSTANCE, and CAUSATION, were held by the rationalists, such as Descartes, to be innate ideas. An important test of Locke's empiricism was, therefore, whether it was able to account for such ideas as arising wholly from experience (see also PERSONAL IDENTITY). A difficulty that Locke faced over the idea of *substance* was that he believed, just as Descartes did, that sense perception at best reveals to us only certain *properties or qualities* of external objects, not the "substratum" in which such qualities supposedly "inhere." Locke is therefore forced to say that we do not possess any "positive" idea of substance, but only a "relative" idea of it as "something we know not what," which is necessary for the support and union of a thing's qualities (see *Essay* II.xxiii.2). Critics, from Berkeley onward, have poked fun at Locke for his supposed embarrassment over this difficulty, but in fact his account can be seen to be stronger than has been alleged, provided one recognizes that Locke is not contending that a thing's "substratum" is a featureless "something" that exists independently of all that thing's qualities. Rather, in accordance with Locke's theory of ABSTRACTION (of which more later), we do better to think of the idea of "substratum" as that aspect of our idea of a thing that remains when we abstract from the latter all of our ideas of its particular qualities.

As for our idea of *causation* or *power*, Locke's view is that this arises from *reflection* upon our own voluntary agency. As he puts it, "The *Idea* of the beginning of motion, we have only from reflection on what passes in our selves, where we find by Experience, that barely by willing it, . . . we can move the parts of our Bodies" (*Essay* II.xxi.4). It might be thought that this would commit Locke to an unacceptably animistic conception of the causal powers of material objects, but I do not see that such a charge can be sustained. What we experience in ourselves, according to Locke, is the exercise of a particular causal power, that of the WILL: this is enough to give us the idea of what it is for some motion in an object to be *initiated or brought about*, but we can perfectly well separate that idea from the idea of volition as a distinctive kind of mental cause.

LANGUAGE

Book III of the *Essay*, "Of Words," has many interesting things to say about language and thought. For Locke, language is a two-edged sword: a necessity and convenience for society but at the same time subject to pernicious abuses. Given that all human knowledge and understanding arise from the many and varied experiences of individuals, it is imperative that there be a means of communicating this knowledge and understanding from one person to another, so that society at large may collectively benefit from the individual experience of its members through processes of education and testimony. On the age-old question of whether thought precedes language or language thought, Locke comes down firmly in favor of the priority of thought. By his account, thinking just is the having of ideas, that is, a process of imagination. The function of words is to operate as "signs" of ideas and thereby to provide publicly accessible evidence of the thoughts we engage in privately. "The use . . . of Words, is to be sensible Marks of *Ideas*; and the Ideas they stand for, are their proper and immediate Signification" (*Essay* III.ii.1). Locke has been unjustly mocked in recent times for proposing, in effect, a solipsistic theory of MEANING, whereby the meaning of a word in any speaker's mouth is constituted by a private idea in that speaker's mind, inaccessible to any other person. In fact, however, Locke is quite properly aware that the privacy of ideas is no barrier to the successful use of language in communication, as is demonstrated by his handling of the notorious "inverted spectrum" problem: "[I]f the *Idea*, that a *Violet* produced in one Man's Mind by his Eyes, were the same as that a *Marigold* produced in another Man's, and *vice versa*, . . . since this could never be known . . . neither the *Ideas* . . . nor the Names, would be at all confounded" (*Essay* II.xxxii.15). Locke's point, we may take it, is that it is possible for a third party to judge, on the basis of publicly accessible evidence, that two people both consistently use the same word—say, "yellow"—when confronted by objects with the same color (such as marigolds) and thereby reasonably infer that each of them experiences a distinctive visual idea upon seeing this color and that each of them uses the word "yellow" to indicate that such an idea is present in his or her mind. We need not know what these ideas are "like" for the persons concerned in order to be able to judge that their ideas are both ideas of *yellow*.

Locke maintains that *general* terms in a language are signs of "abstract general ideas" and that these are generated by the mental process of abstraction, whereby the distinguishing features of a number of different but similar ideas are stripped away to leave an idea that contains only the features that they have in common. Thus, the abstract general idea of a triangle will leave out any idea of the relative lengths of a triangle's sides and retain only the idea of its being a plane figure with three rectilinear sides (see *Essay* III.iii). The notorious passage in the *Essay* (IV.vii.9) where Locke describes the general idea of a triangle as one "wherein some parts of several different and inconsistent *Ideas* are put together"—unjustly pounced upon by Berkeley—should be regarded as unrepresentative of Locke's considered opinion, which is that abstraction merely *leaves out* those respects in which a number of similar ideas differ. In many ways, Lockean abstract general ideas function very much like the "prototypes" postulated by some modern psychologists to explain our capacities for categorization and classification (see Lakoff: Chapter 2). They are by no means as vulnerable to criticism as philosophers from Berkeley onward have supposed.

One important use to which Locke puts his theory of abstract general ideas is in his account of the notion of ESSENCE. According to Locke, we need to distinguish, in the case of substances, between *real* and *nominal* essence—the former being the (in Locke's day) unknown microstructural constitution of a substance that is the cause of its observable properties and the latter being the abstract general idea by reference to which we classify that substance as being of a certain sort or kind (see *Essay* III.iii). Thus, Locke holds, we classify a lump of metal as being *gold* just in case it has observable properties corresponding to the ideas that we have included in the abstract general idea signified by our word "gold"—properties such as yellow color, shininess, and ductility. He believes that it would be impossible, or at best impractical, for us to classify substances by reference to their *real* essences—first because we do not know what those essences are (and certainly this was true in Locke's day) but also because, even if we did manage to discover them, this could not be expected to alter our linguistic practices, "since Languages, in all Countries, have been established long before Sciences" (*Essay* III.vi.25). On this point Locke has been challenged in recent times by philosophers, such as Hilary Putnam, who contends that, owing to what he calls the "division of linguistic labor" among members of a speech community, ordinary members of that community may be expected to defer to experts on the question of the extension of a general term like "gold." Indeed, it does seem to be the case that any ordinary speaker of English would be prepared to be corrected by a metallurgist or chemist on the question of whether a certain lump of metal was "really" gold. However, Putnam himself sees a role for "stereotypes" in the psychological explanation of our recognitional capacities very much akin to the role that Locke accords to abstract general ideas, so that the differences between the two philosophers may not be quite as great as might first appear. Indeed, some of the differences may arise from the fact that Locke is, in any case, much more interested in how *individuals* use language to communicate the contents of their own thoughts than in the wider social dimensions of linguistic meaning and "correct" usage.

THEORY OF KNOWLEDGE

We may turn, finally, to Book IV of the *Essay*, "Of Knowledge and Opinion," which is probably the least discussed part of the work. This relative neglect is unfortunate, both because it has led to some important misunderstandings about Locke and also because, after all, one of the main motivations for Locke in writing the *Essay* was to explore the relations between—and as far as possible to reconcile—reason, experience, and religious faith. Knowledge, according to Locke—and in this he was articulating the standard view of his day—has three distinct sources, in INTUITION, DEMONSTRATION, and experience. By *intuition* we know, for instance, that black is not white or that a circle is not a triangle (*Essay* IV.ii.1). By *demonstration* we can know such geometrical truths as Pythagoras' theorem, which we can arrive at by a chain of intuitively certain steps of reasoning from premises that are themselves intuitively certain. (Locke holds that moral knowledge, as well as mathematical knowledge, may be had through demonstration.) By *experience* we can know, for instance, that external things possess certain observable properties and indeed that such things really do exist: "For I think no body can, in earnest, be so sceptical, as to be uncertain of the Existence of those Things which he sees and feels" (*Essay* IV.xi.13). Here we need to appreciate that, for Locke, knowledge—properly so called—requires *certainty*: and where certainty is absent, we can have at best only probable belief or opinion. (Thus, for example, whatever we learn by way of *testimony* can at most qualify as probable belief, according to Locke.) In addition to knowledge and probable belief, however, there is also *faith*, though this never (Locke thinks) has the intuitive certainty that is characteristic of knowledge (see *Essay* IV.xv.3). But because knowledge requires certainty, the scope of our knowledge is "very narrow" (*Essay* IV.xv.2), and this, at bottom, is why we must leave room for faith. For the claims of faith may only be conclusively overridden by those of knowledge, not those of mere probable belief.

Modern philosophers may criticize Locke's assumption that knowledge requires certainty—either because they are fallibilists who think that a less rigorous standard of justification is required to warrant a knowledge claim or because they reject altogether a "justified true belief" account of knowledge in favor of some form of "externalist" or "reliabilist" account. But to some extent this sort of dispute may just be a terminological one: what a fallibilist means by saying that we *know* that the earth is not flat is perhaps not so very different from what Locke would mean by saying that we "believe" this, with a high degree of PROBABILITY. A more interesting point to make about Locke's account of knowledge is that it is wholeheartedly "empiricist" only in the sense that, by that account, all the "materials" of our understanding—all our *ideas*—arise from experience, either from sensation or from reflection. He does not, as we have just seen, maintain that all *knowledge* is acquired through the senses, since it may also be acquired by intuition or demonstration working upon our ideas. Thus, although it is true enough that, by Locke's account, no one can know that red is not green who has not experienced these colors, the knowledge itself is "intuitive"—that is, it is the sort of knowledge that arises when, as Locke puts it, "the Mind perceives the Agreement or Disagreement of two *Ideas* immediately" (*Essay* IV.ii.1)—and thus differs entirely from the kind of knowledge we have of external objects by means of our senses. There is, then, a perfectly good sense in which Locke acknowledges the possibility of a priori knowledge (see A PRIORI/A POSTERIORI DISTINCTION) even while denying the doctrine of innate ideas and principles. Thus, Locke cannot be construed as believing, with J. S. MILL, that mathematical knowledge is a posteriori and founded on INDUCTION from experience.

Locke was not, of course, at all original in defending the cause of empiricism in the seventeenth century: in this respect, he was following in the footsteps of BACON, HOBBES, GASSENDI, and many others. On the other hand, it would not be fair to say that he was merely a synthesizer of other philosophers' views. The greatness of the *Essay* does partly lie in its systematicity and comprehensiveness as a presentation of the empiricist program. But in certain other respects it is more clearly groundbreaking. For instance, in one way it represents the beginnings of the modern science of psychology, being an attempt to understand the workings of the human mind from first principles and as an intellectual end in itself. The modernity of Locke's enterprise in this regard consists in his implicit commitment to a wholly *naturalistic* account of the mind, not least in consequence of his repudiation of those supposedly God-given features of its makeup, innate ideas. Even more important, perhaps, the *Essay* represents the beginnings of a fundamental change in the relationship between science and philosophy or rather a separation between them into two distinct disciplines. Locke, in the Epistle to the Reader that prefaces the *Essay*, famously describes himself as a humble "underlabourer," clearing the ground of rubbish in order that the work begun by the great scientists of his day—such as NEWTON, BOYLE, and Huygens—might proceed more smoothly and effectively. The role of the philosopher, in Locke's eyes, is not to contribute directly to the production of scientific knowledge—as Descartes had assumed—but is, rather, to adopt a critical, self-reflective perspective on the nature of human knowledge and to determine its scope and limits by examining its sources in the mind's own capacities of sense and reason. In a way, then, Locke's approach may be seen as prefiguring the "critical" philosophy of KANT, as well as the naturalism that informs much of twentieth-century philosophy. This, no doubt, is why Locke still speaks to us so powerfully today, despite the quaintness of his seventeenth-century language to the modern ear. On all sorts of issues, whether it be personal identity, perception, thought and language, or real essence, Locke's *Essay* provides the starting point of modern debate. As a systematic presentation and defense of an empiricist program it still holds up remarkably well.

PRIMARY WORK

An Essay concerning Human Understanding. Edited with an introduction by P. H. Nidditch. Oxford: Clarendon Press, 1975.

Two Treatises of Government. Edited by P. Laslett. Cambridge: Cambridge University Press, 1967.

OTHER PRIMARY TEXTS

Berkeley, George. *Philosophical Works.* Edited by M. R. Ayers. London: Dent, 1975.

Descartes, René. *The Philosophical Writings of Descartes.* Translated by J. Cottingham, R. Stoothoof, and D. Murdoch. 3 vols. Cambridge: Cambridge University Press, 1984.

Leibniz, Gottfried Wilhelm. *New Essays on Human Understanding.* Edited and translated by P. Remnant and J. Bennett. Cambridge: Cambridge University Press, 1981.

BIBLIOGRAPHY

Books

Aaron, R. I. *John Locke.* 3d ed. Oxford: Oxford University Press, 1971.

Alexander, Peter. *Ideas, Qualities and Corpuscles.* Cambridge: Cambridge University Press, 1985.

Ayers, M. R. *Locke*. 2 vols. London: Routledge, 1991.

Bechtel, W., and A. Abrahamsen. *Connectionism and the Mind*. Oxford: Blackwell, 1991.

Chappell, V. C., ed. *The Cambridge Companion to Locke*. Cambridge: Cambridge University Press, 1994.

Chomsky, Noam. *Language and Mind*. New York: Harcourt Brace Jovanovich, 1972.

Cranston, Maurice. *John Locke: A Biography*. London: Longman, 1957.

Hall, R., and R. S. Woolhouse. *Eighty Years of Locke Scholarship*. Edinburgh: Edinburgh University Press, 1983.

Lakoff, George. *Women, Fire and Dangerous Things*. Chicago: University of Chicago Press, 1987.

Lowe, E. J. *Locke on Human Understanding*. London: Routledge, 1995.

Mackie, J. L. *Problems from Locke*. Oxford: Clarendon Press, 1976.

Rogers, G.A.J., ed. *Locke's Philosophy: Content and Context*. Oxford: Clarendon Press, 1994.

Tipton, I. C., ed. *Locke on Human Understanding*. Oxford: Oxford University Press, 1977.

Woolhouse, R. S. *Locke*. Brighton: Harvester Press, 1983.

Yolton, J. W. *Locke and the Compass of Human Understanding*. Cambridge: Cambridge University Press, 1970.

Articles

Ashworth, E. J. "Locke on Language." *Canadian Journal of Philosophy* 14 (1984): 45–73.

Bennett, J. "Substratum." *History of Philosophy Quarterly* 4 (1987): 197–215.

Martin, C. B. "Substance Substantiated." *Australasian Journal of Philosophy* 58 (1980): 3–10.

Putnam, Hilary. "The Meaning of 'Meaning.' " In *Mind, Language and Reality*. Cambridge: Cambridge University Press, 1975.

E. J. LOWE

LOGIC. The word "logic" as used today is commonly taken to refer to a *formal* discipline, as indeed it was almost universally from the time of ARISTOTLE until at least the sixteenth century. But the writings of Descartes and his followers (notably, Malebranche and the authors of the *Port-Royal Logic*, Arnauld and Nicole) undermined this understanding of the word, preparing the ground for LOCKE to reinterpret it most influentially in his *Essay concerning Human Understanding*. Locke adopted from the Cartesians a contempt for the alleged barrenness of Aristotelian syllogistic theory and aspired to replace it with a discipline focused not on the formal relations of words but instead on the powers of the human mind and the improvement of our cognitive faculties. This kind of informal discipline, therefore, is most commonly referred to as "logic" by the empiricist authors from Locke to MILL, and indeed their understanding of the logical enterprise persisted until the turn of the twentieth century, when FREGE and RUSSELL firmly reestablished the discipline of formal logic in a new, more powerful, and non-Aristotelian guise.

Locke's own understanding of Aristotelian logic seems to have been drawn not primarily from Aristotle himself or from the medieval schoolmen but instead from modern scholastic authors such as Robert Sanderson and Philippe du Trieu (see Milton 1984). This helps to explain both his low regard for its admittedly second-rate supporters and also the manner of his criticism. For later scholastic thought had stressed the supposed role of formal logic not only in the presentation of argument but also in "invention" or "discovery," and this is the aspect of syllogistic theory of which Locke is most critical:

The Rules of *Syllogism* serve not to furnish the Mind with those intermediate *Ideas*, that may shew the connexion of remote ones. This way of reasoning discovers no new Proofs, but is the Art of marshalling, and ranging the old ones we have already. . . . A Man knows first, and then he is able to prove syllogistically. So that *Syllogism* comes after Knowledge, and then a Man has little or no need of it. (*Essay concerning Human Understanding* IV.xvii.6)

By contrast Locke does allow some value to syllogism as a means of presenting and showing the validity of arguments, and he is careful to express his considerable respect for Aristotle himself,

whom I look on as one of the greatest Men amongst the Antients. . . . And who in this very invention of Forms of Argumentation . . . did great service against those, who were not ashamed to deny any thing. And I readily own, that all right reasoning may be reduced to his Forms of Syllogism. (*Essay* IV.xvii.4)

But Locke sees syllogisms as far from ideal even for the purpose of presenting arguments and suggests instead (*Essay* IV.xvii.4) that reasoning can better be presented as a chain of connected ideas with the "middle term" appearing explicitly as such (e.g., "man-animal-living") rather than in syllogistic form (e.g., "animals are living; man is an animal; therefore man is living"), in which the premises force the ideas involved into an unnatural sequence ("animal-living-man-living").

In place of a syllogistic understanding of reasoning, Locke sees it as founded on "a native Faculty to perceive the Coherence, or Incoherence of its *Ideas*" (*Essay* IV.xvii.4; see DEMONSTRATION), a Faculty whose objects, IDEAS, are one and all particular, so that the universality that is a fundamental characteristic of formal reasoning becomes merely "accidental" on Locke's informal conception (*Essay* IV.xvii.8). Hence, "logic" ceases to be a study of formal patterns of inference and becomes instead the study of the cognitive faculties of the mind, a "facultative logic" (Buickerood 1985) whose aim is to yield principles for the correct employment of those faculties. Since ideas are the material with which they work, the study of ideas is at the heart of this discipline, and Locke's *Essay* (together with his posthumous *On the Conduct of the Understanding*) thus itself appears to be a work of "logic" so conceived, which he also calls the "*Doctrine of Signs*" or semiotics—this name being appropriate on the grounds that an idea is "a Sign or Representation of the thing [the Understanding] considers" (*Essay* IV.xxi.4).

HUME very explicitly followed the Lockean interpretation of "logic" and evidently saw the first book of his *Treatise of Human Nature* as a contribution to it:

The sole end of logic *is to explain the principles and operations of our reasoning faculty, and the nature of our ideas.* . . . This treatise therefore of human nature seems intended for a system of the sciences. The author has finished what regards logic. (*Abstract of a Treatise of Human Nature: 646*, quoting *A Treatise of Human Nature*: xv)

Hume likewise follows Descartes and Locke in viewing the traditional logic as barren, on the grounds that any "pretended syllogistical reasoning" that purports to extend our knowledge is in reality "nothing but a more imperfect definition" (*An Enquiry concerning Human Understanding*: 163).

Given the scholastic authors with whom they were acquainted, it is perhaps not surprising that the classical empiricists were so contemptuous of formal logic. But after a century that has seen a rigorous and fertile discipline rise from the ashes, while the alternative informal search for natural principles of reasoning has little of substance to show, one can only conclude that their dismissal of formal logic as a worthwhile subject of study was certainly, if understandably, premature.

PRIMARY WORKS

Hume, David. *Abstract of a book lately published, entitled A Treatise of Human Nature, etc.* (1740). Reprinted as pp. 641–62 of Hume [1739].
————. *An Enquiry concerning Human Understanding.* In *Enquiries concerning Human Understanding and concerning the Principles of Morals* [1777]. Edited with an analytical index by L. A. Selby-Bigge; revised with notes by P. H. Nidditch. Oxford: Clarendon Press, 1975; first publication by Hume 1748 and 1751, respectively—1777 was the last edition to incorporate new authorial corrections.
————. *A Treatise of Human Nature* [1739]. 2d ed., edited with an analytical index by L. A. Selby-Bigge; revised with notes by P. H. Nidditch. Oxford: Clarendon Press, 1978.
Locke, John. *An Essay concerning Human Understanding* [1690]. Edited with an introduction by P. H. Nidditch. Oxford: Clarendon Press, 1975.

BIBLIOGRAPHY

Book

Howell, Wilbur Samuel. *Eighteenth-Century British Logic and Rhetoric.* Princeton: Princeton University Press, 1971.

Articles

Buickerood, James G. "Locke and the Rise of Facultative Logic." *History and Philosophy of Logic* 6 (1985): 157–90.
Milton, J. R. "The Scholastic Background to Locke's Thought." *Locke Newsletter* 15 (1984): 25–34.
0Passmore, J. A. "Descartes, the British Empiricists, and Formal Logic." *Philosophical Review* 62 (1953): 545–53.

PETER MILLICAN

LOGICAL POSITIVISM/LOGICAL EMPIRICISM. Logical positivism and logical empiricism are two closely related philosophical doctrines that originated in Vienna early in the twentieth century. For ease of exposition, we associate the term "logical positivism" with the verifiability criterion of meaning (see VERIFICATION PRINCIPLE) and the attempt to produce a scientific philosophy rid of METAPHYSICS and the term "logical empiricism" with the attempt to provide a sound empiricist foundation for scientific knowledge. Definitions for these further concepts will be provided later, but first some historical background is necessary.

Logical positivism and logical empiricism have their philosophical roots in two distinct strands of thought. The first is the empiricism of HUME, via the PHENOMENALISM of MACH; the second is the LOGIC of Frege, RUSSELL, and WITTGENSTEIN as presented in his *Tractatus Logico-Philosophicus*. A third important influence was the positivism of COMTE. The group of philosophers, scientists, and social scientists who first discussed the fruitful combination of these strands of thought was the Vienna Circle, formed by Moritz Schlick in 1922. Schlick took Mach's chair in the philosophy of the inductive sciences at Vienna in 1922 and started the meetings that came to be known as the Vienna Circle. Some notable members of the Vienna Circle were A. J. AYER, Rudolf CARNAP, Herbert Feigl, Kurt GÖDEL, Otto NEURATH, and Friedrich Waismann. The group shared beliefs in logical empiricism or positivism, physicalism, and the possibility of a unified SCIENCE. The group was broken up in the early 1930s largely due to the fact that many of its members were Jewish and the Nazi Party was beginning to assert its influence in Austria. The doctrines were kept alive by members of the circle and their students moving to universities in the United States and Britain and through the publication of logical empiricist ideas in the influential journal *Erkenntnis* and the series of monographs entitled the *International Encyclopedia of Unified Science*.

One of the central doctrines of the Vienna Circle was the verifiability criterion of meaning. The doctrine was first pronounced by Waismann and popularized by A. J. Ayer in his *Language, Truth and Logic*. The verifiability criterion of meaning states that all meaningful propositions must be empirically verifiable. According to the logical positivist there are two other kinds of propositions: those that are analytically true (see ANALYTIC/SYNTHETIC DISTINCTION) and hence are meaningful (see MEANING) and those that are meaningless, for example, the statements of metaphysics and ETHICS. The two kinds of meaningful propositions echo Hume's two kinds of ideas: matters of fact and relations of ideas. The advance over Hume was the introduction of powerful new techniques in logic to present analytic truths. The influence of Wittgenstein's *Tractatus Logico-Philosophicus* is clear in this regard, although Wittgenstein never explicitly stated a verifiability criterion. Wittgenstein's use of truth tables to establish the truth of complex propositions was a highly influential and simple method for addressing analyticity.

Some examples may make these points clearer. The proposition "The Chicago Bulls won the 1996 NBA championship" is meaningful on the grounds that it is empirically verifiable. Simply put, we can check if it is true or not. Ayer and others claimed that propositions such as "God is infinitely powerful and omniscient" were not empirically verifiable. Logical positivists were not proponents of ontological arguments for God's existence. There are more implications than this latter one for the view. No statements of abstract metaphysics and, perhaps more worrying, no statements about the character of the "good" are meaningful: the propositions of metaphysics and many of the propositions of ethics are meaningless. This view is consistent with the logical positivist goal of placing philosophy on a scientific foundation. Philosophy should consist of the analysis of meaningful propositions in terms of experientially verifiable truths or by the use of logic.

What of ethics and metaphysics? Wittgenstein's enigmatic statement at the end of the *Tractatus* is relevant here: "What we cannot speak about we must pass over in silence." The scientific philosophy could address metaphysical or ethical issues only insofar as they could be addressed by using meaningful propositions. The foundations of MATHEMATICS, for example, need not now focus on the existence of numbers in a Platonic realm; rather, the focus would be on establishing formally that all mathematical truths were logical truths. Several logical positivist proposals were made about ethical propositions, Ayer's being a form of emotivism.

The most damaging criticisms of logical positivism come from problems with the verifiability criterion of meaning. Perhaps for some, the loss of ethics and metaphysics is not such a great one, and so that alone is not a sufficient criticism of the view. There are, however, two important problems with the criterion that seriously undermined logical positivism. The first is to ask the question, How is the criterion itself established as meaningful? Clearly, the criterion is not analytic, and it is hard to see how it could be empirically verified. This criticism was addressed by logical positivists by appealing to the techniques of logic. They argued that the criterion was part of the metalanguage and not the object language. In logic, Tarski introduced this distinction to avoid some of the more problematic paradoxes. The idea was that when we say, " 'The sky is blue' is true," the term "is true" is not part of the language under study, which includes sentences such as "The sky is blue" and other empirically verifiable sentences. This distinction is very useful in logic and especially metamathematics, where we want to talk about characteristics of the propositions of mathematics, such as their provability. The logical positivists argued that the verifiability criterion of meaningfulness was part of the metalanguage we use to analyze sentences in our ordinary object language. Philosophical literature is full of uses of this influential distinction. Certainly, appealing to this distinction goes some way to vindicating the logical positivists, but suspicions with the view were now aroused. The following criticism is more damning.

Science rests on laws or empirical generalizations, on most accounts, and yet these statements are neither analytic nor empirically verifiable. The statement "All H_2O has a boiling point of 100°C" cannot be conclusively verified, because of the problem of INDUCTION. Biology and archaeology are sciences that rest on evidence from past events, and sentences characterizing those events are very difficult to verify empirically. For example, how do we verify the statement "The first protozoa existed three billion years ago"? There are also difficulties envisaging verifiability criteria for scientific statements such as "The wave function exists." Despite many efforts to address these problems, the verifiability criterion was forever suspect after the realization that the sciences, the very disciplines logical positivists championed, contained unverifiable statements, according to the criterion.

Versions of the verifiability criterion of meaning have some contemporary adherents—for example, Michael Dummett's theory of meaning bears a close resemblance—but most philosophers have abandoned the positivists' attempt to reformulate philosophy according to this criterion. The more pervasive and successful doctrines stemming from the Vienna Circle are those in the philosophy of science. Here we collect these under the term "logical empiricism."

Rudolf CARNAP was the most influential member of the Vienna Circle. We will discuss his views along with those of Hans REICHENBACH and Carl Hempel. Together these three philosophers and their students shaped much of twentieth-century philosophy of science. Reichenbach used the term "logical empiricism" to refer to his own views, but we use the term for all three philosophers' views. Although very few philosophers are still logical empiricists, the view has set the agenda for most twentieth-century philosophy of science. Logical empiricists concentrated on confirmation, explanation, prediction, and the nature of scientific theories, as well as the unification thesis, or the reduction of all sciences to physics. The combined view is often referred to as the "received view" in philosophy of science. Here we discuss some of the main philosophical tenets of logical empiricism; other entries provide more detail about individual logical empiricists (see Carnap and Reichenbach).

Logical empiricists conceived of theories as sets of sentences expressing laws, hypotheses, and principles connecting these hypotheses to empirical phenomena. The view was modeled on the axiomatization of mathematics, with laws taking the place of axioms. Carnap wanted to show that science could be rationally reconstructed using only logic and observation sentences. The relations between laws and hypotheses were characterized deductively. This part of the account seemed to be borne out by examples from science: Kepler's third law can be deduced from NEWTON's laws. Problems in rationally reconstructing scientific knowledge come in providing an account of confirmation: how do observations confirm hypotheses or indeed laws? A simple inductive model would fall foul of the problem of induction and the relation between theory and observation could not be straightforwardly deductive and yet still informative. A further problem here is that theoretical terms often refer to unobservable or unobserved entities. The theory may hold together deductively, but some relation has to be established between observables and the hypotheses of the theory for the theory to make sense empirically. The first set of concerns was addressed by various logics of confirmation, and the second was addressed by an appeal to correspondence rules or, as Hempel later called them, bridging principles.

First, let us consider confirmation. The universal generalization "(x) $(Px \rightarrow Qx)$" is confirmed by the observation sentence "Pa & Qa" and disconfirmed by "Pa & $-$Qa." On this account the confirmation relation is a simple, logical one. This notion of confirmation falls prey to logical criticisms, and several were presented. One relies on logical equivalence: "(x) $(Px \rightarrow Qx)$ $\leftrightarrow$ $(x)(-Qx \rightarrow -Px)$"; "$-$Qa & $-$Pa" is a confirming instance of the latter and so should be a confirming instance of the former. Let us consider an example: "All ravens are black" should be confirmed by the observation of any object that is both not black and not a raven; my blue and white striped coffee mug would suffice. This and other paradoxes of confirmation relied on the disparities that could be shown between satisfying the dictates of deductive logic and providing a coherent account of confirmation by empirical observations. One way around the paradoxes is to develop reformulations of the confirmation criteria; another is to suggest completely different criteria. Logical empiricists took both approaches. The latter was more productive. An approach initiated by Carnap was to treat the confirmation relation probabilistically. This approach is still pervasive in philosophy of science. Exactly how it is spelled out depends on one's conception of probability. The approach Hempel favored was to propose several mutually applicable criteria of confirmation: for example, the number and variety of confirming instances, new test implications, the level of theoretical support for the hypothesis under test, and the simplicity of the hypothesis. Although this approach looks workable and consistent with scientific practice, it departs from the strict dictates of logical empiricism, as it invokes concepts other than observation sentences and deductive logic.

Before turning to bridge principles, let us look at one final perspective on confirmation. Karl POPPER rejected the logical empiricists' approach altogether, arguing that falsification, rather than confirmation, should be the central feature in the rational reconstruction of scientific testing. Popper proposed that any account of confirmation would fall foul of the problem of induction but that falsification could be expressed deductively without paradox. Falsification can be expressed using *modus tollens*: if this hypothesis is true, then the following will be observed; there was no such observation; and so the hypothesis is false. Popper's idea was that if scientific hypotheses and their test situations could be reconstructed in this way, then the hypotheses were appropriately testable. His favorite example was Einstein's general theory of relativity, which was testable by empirical observation of the curvature of light around the sun. Most philosophers of science acknowledge the role of both confirmation and falsification in testing scientific hypotheses, although the logical empiricist agenda of rationally reconstructing scientific testing entirely in terms of one of these concepts has been abandoned.

For the logical empiricist, theoretical terms, just like any other terms, must derive their meaning from experience. The broad dictates of the verifiability criterion constrained the investigation of science. Scientific theories are formulated from theoretical terms, which are related logically within the theory. The logical empiricists proposed that theoretical terms are connected to observations by means of correspondence rules or bridging principles. According to Hempel, bridge principles connect theoretical entities with observable entities. There is a problem with this proposal: to concur with the broad dictates of verifiability, the bridging principles themselves must be analytic or conventional (a suggestion of Hempel's). An examination of the history of science reveals that bridging principles change with changing empirical findings and hence are not analytic or entirely conventional. The logical empiricists were again thwarted by their own stringent dictates.

Most philosophers assume that scientific theories have an explanatory role. For logical empiricists, explanation, like confirmation, would have to be reconstructed as a logical relation. So logical empiricists proposed the deductive-nomological model of explanation. The deductive-nomological model, or "D-N model," says that an empirical phenomenon E is explained by various laws and statements about particular facts. The explanatory relation is a deductive one: the phenomenon E can be deduced from the laws and statements of facts. For example, "This copper bar expanded on heating" is explained by the law that all metals expand on heating and the particular fact that copper is a metal. The logical empiricists also proposed that the logic of explanation was the same as the logic of prediction, both being deductive. We can predict from the law that all metals expand on heating, that copper is a metal, and that this metal bar will expand on heating.

The proposals that explanation is deductive and that explanation and prediction are logically equivalent drew a great deal of criticism. First, critics inquired how we can distinguish between simple deductions and explanations. They also asked whether prediction or explanation was the predominant relation. Several attempts were made by Hempel, among others, to shore up the purely logical account of explanation, but criticisms of the proposed symmetry between explanation and prediction still remained problematic. For example, we can deductively predict the height of a flagpole from the length of its shadow and the sun's angle of elevation, but this information does not explain the height of the flagpole. Facts about flagpole manufacturing and government regulations do this latter job. The logical empiricist account of explanation faced further criticism from philosophers of science who emphasized the pragmatic aspects, rather than the purely logical aspects of explanation. These philosophers argued that an explanation constituted a satisfactory answer to a "why?" question. Such criticisms were consistent with ordinary language philosophy and PRAGMATISM. By the 1960s these latter were both gathering strength as alternative philosophical views to logical empiricism.

The underlying theoretical principle of logical empiricism was the verifiability criterion of meaning, and the aspiration of logical empiricists was that, guided by this principle and their account of science, the unification of science would be realizable. If all science could be reduced to physics, and physics could be reduced to the logical reconstruction of theories and their relations to observation, then all physics and all science would be placed on sound empirical foundations. What logical empiricists aimed at was the demonstration that such a reduction was in principle possible. The unity of science and its close relative reductionism are familiar themes in all discussions of science. Many physicists think that ultimately all scientific explanations will be explanations in physics. Logical empiricists were interested not in whether it is in fact the case that quantum mechanics explains chemistry but rather whether chemical theory, construed as a set of axioms, is logically reducible to quantum physics, similarly construed. One reason for the failure of this project in the short term was the immense difficulty in appropriately axiomatizing any branch of science in preparation for the relevant reduction. These difficulties are exemplified by the complexity of Carnap's axiomatic presentation of thermal expansion, a relatively simple component of physics. Despite these difficulties logical empiricists produced several axiomatizations of branches of the sciences, including axiomatizations of evolutionary biology.

Logical empiricism provided a strong set of directives for how philosophy of science should proceed. In the terms of one of logical empiricism's most vocal critics, Thomas Kuhn, logical empiricism provided a paradigm for normal philosophy of science. The numerous logical difficulties with the approach, coupled with the increasing number of alternative approaches to philosophy of science, such as Kuhn's, led to a situation where no one view dominates. Philosophers of science still work on confirmation, explanation, and reduction, but they no longer share any one set of guiding principles. Anglo-American philosophy in general has inherited much of the logical positivist and empiricist legacy despite repeated attempts to reject it wholesale.

PRIMARY WORKS

Ayer, A. J. *Language, Truth and Logic*. New York: Penguin Books, 1946/1971.

Carnap, Rudolf. *The Logical Structure of the World*. Berkeley and Los Angeles: University of California Press, 1928/1967.

————. *Philosophical Foundations of Physics: An Introduction to the Philosophy of Science*. New York: Basic Books, 1966.

Hempel, Carl G. *Aspects of Scientific Explanation and Other Essays in the Philosophy of Science*. New York: Free Press, 1965.

Reichenbach, Hans. *Experience and Prediction: An Analysis of the Foundations of Science*. Chicago: University of Chicago Press, 1938/1961.

BIBLIOGRAPHY

Books

Ayer, A. J. *Logical Positivism*. Glencoe, IL: Free Press, 1959.
Giere, R. N., and A. Richardson, eds. *Origins of Logical Positivism*. Minnesota Studies in Philosophy of Science, vol. 16. Minneapolis: University of Minnesota Press, 1996.
Hanfling, O., ed. *Essential Readings in Logical Positivism*. Oxford: Blackwell, 1981.
————. *Logical Positivism*. New York: Columbia University Press, 1981.
Joergensen, J. *The Development of Logical Empiricism*. Chicago: University of Chicago Press, 1951.
Salmon, W. C. *Hans Reichenbach: Logical Empiricist*. Dordrecht: Reidel, 1979.
Stadler, F. ed. *Scientific Philosophy*. Dordrecht: Kluwer, 1993.

Article

Galison, P. "Aufbau/Bauhaus: Logical Positivism and Architectural Modernism." *Critical Inquiry* 16 (1990): 709–52.

STEPHEN M. DOWNES

LONERGAN, BERNARD J. F. Bernard Lonergan (1905–1984) was a Canadian philosopher and theologian and a member of the Society of Jesus (Jesuits). He received his S.T.D. from Gregorian University, Rome (1940), and was a companion of the Order of Canada, fellow of the British Academy, and the recipient of seventeen honorary doctorates. He served as professor at Regis College, Toronto, and at the Gregorian University, Rome, was Stillman Professor at Harvard University, and Distinguished Professor at Boston College. His best-known works are *Insight: A Study of Human Understanding* and *Method in Theology*.

Lonergan is a major representative of what has become known as "transcendental Thomism," a school that concentrates on the conscious psychological realities implied and presupposed by the objective language of AQUINAS's metaphysical analyses of knowledge. In Lonergan's analysis, these psychological realities are all experiential, and experience indeed has absolute primacy in knowing. But Lonergan insists on the important fact, often passed over lightly, that human experience includes far more than the experience of the senses.

What I experience is what I am aware of, and vice versa. Being conscious and having experience are but two names for the same reality. Data of consciousness, then, are just as empirical as data of sense and must be accounted for by the philosopher. I, who am consciously trying to understand, am as much a part of my own experience as I who am consciously tasting or feeling or seeing. Understanding and the effort to understand are as obvious an experience, as powerful an experience, and as philosophically significant an experience as any experience of sensation.

Concretely, it is clear that under such an analysis no philosopher can plausibly describe himself or herself as totally absorbed in sense experience and sense-consciousness. More typically, in philosophers as in other human beings, sense experience provokes questions about the meaning, reality, and importance of what is experienced—questions that are not answered by the sensation itself. One is concerned for what one's own experience means; and that concern is itself a part of experience. The concern leads one, through questioning, to trying to understand, to passing judgment on the validity of one's sense experiences and on the reality of what one has experienced. This questioning and these efforts to understand and to judge correctly are functionally interrelated elements of human consciousness, quite as universal as sense experience and at least equally basic, hence, not plausibly reducible to sense experience. If "empirical method" is the term used to characterize the empirical sciences, which concern themselves with sensibly verifiable laws and expectations, then the same method, applied to the data of consciousness, could be called "generalized empirical method." This is the method Lonergan describes and recommends in *Insight*.

He reprobates the tendency of philosophers to model their analysis of knowledge less on their own mature and actual experience than on the supposed experiences of infants. The only psychological world that could perhaps be adequately described in terms of sense experience alone is the world of the nursery and, indeed, the crib. The actual starting place of philosophy is the questioning provoked by the mature experience of wonder.

In his foundational work, *Insight*, Lonergan classifies empiricism among the "directive" methods, that is, as basically constituted by the universal advice it gives: "Observe the significant facts." But a principal theme of *Insight* is that observation yields not facts but only data. To find facts in the data or conclude facts from the data is not a matter of observing but of understanding and of exercising critical judgment. Moreover, to determine which data are significant requires further understanding and additional judgments. To reduce knowing to observation, to looking, is to ignore the more important but more subtle realities of insight (the act of understanding) and of judgment ("This is a fact"). In the context of *Insight*, then, Lonergan's dry conclusion on empiricism is: "Empiricism amounts to the assumption that what is obvious in knowing is what knowing obviously is. That assumption is false."

Most of Lonergan's other works also include discussions of empiricism, because he considered empiricism a basic "counter-position," that is, one of a handful of basic erroneous options possible in philosophy. A counterposition is a principle or theory that is incompatible with the functionally interrelated elements of human consciousness. As such, a counterposition can be disproved only by deliberately and consciously putting it into practice. Because the functionally interrelated elements of human consciousness always prevail in the end, the counterposition will in practice ultimately reverse itself.

For instance, to practice empiricism one must follow through on the principle that what cannot be derived or validated from sense experience is to be rejected. But that principle itself cannot be derived or validated from sense experience. No single sense experience and no addition or multiplication of sense experiences ever yields that universally binding principle. Therefore the thoroughgoing observance of the principle of empiricism involves rejecting the principle of empiricism, and empiricism is recognizable as a counterposition.

PRIMARY WORKS

Insight: A Study of Human Understanding. Toronto: University of Toronto Press, 1992. In *Collected Works of Bernard Lonergan 3.* 5th ed., revised and augmented. Original edition London: Longmans, Green, and Co., 1957.
Method in Theology. New York: Herder and Herder, 1972.

BIBLIOGRAPHY

Novak, Michael. "Lonergan's Starting Place: The Performance of Asking Questions." In *Spirit as Inquiry: Studies in Honor of Bernard Lonergan,* edited by Frederick E. Crowe. Chicago: Continuum, 1964.
Quesnell, Quentin. "On Not Neglecting the Self in the Structure of Theological Revolutions." In *Religion and Culture: Essays in Honor of Bernard Lonergan, S.J.,* edited by Timothy P. Fallon and Philip Boo Riley. Albany: State University of New York Press, 1987.

QUENTIN QUESNELL

M

MACH, ERNST. Ernst Mach (1838–1916), German experimental physicist and philosopher, was born in Moravia (today's Czech Republic) in 1838. He taught as a *privatdozent* in Vienna during 1861–1864 and then as professor of mathematics and physics at the University of Graz. In 1867 he joined the University of Prague as professor of experimental physics and also served twice as rector of the university. In 1895 he became professor of philosophy at the University of Vienna. A severe stroke paralyzed half of his body in 1898. He retired in 1901 and continued writing, corresponding, and experimenting until his death from heart disease in 1916. In addition to his importance to empiricist philosophy, he is known for significant contributions to a variety of scientific disciplines: cosmology (Mach's principle), gas dynamics (the Mach number), physiology (the Mach–Breuer–Brown theory regarding the function of the inner ear's semicircular canals), psychology of perception (Mach bands), and, of course, physics and its history (Mach's principle and his criticism of Newtonian mechanics).

Mach became interested in philosophy upon reading KANT's *Prolegomena to Any Future Metaphysics* as a teenager. Although he came to disagree fundamentally with Kant, he allowed that no other philosophical work made so deep an impression upon him. His adult life was devoted almost exclusively to SCIENCE and philosophy. Mach resisted political involvement, despite growing frictions between Germans and Czechs in pre–World War I Europe. (However, he was embroiled in some controversy as rector, splitting the University of Prague into German and Czech halves; to avoid further controversy, he resigned his second rectorate.) He showed consistent concern for the suffering of animals; when certain hypotheses regarding the inner ear's role in bodily equilibrium called for vivisection, he declined and remained content with textbook accounts of the ear's physiology. (He was especially fond of half-tamed sparrows.) When William James met Mach, he wrote to his wife that Mach "has an absolute simplicity of manner and winningness of smile when his face lights up, that are charming." And: "I don't think anyone ever gave me so strong an impression of pure intellectual genius."

For the sake of convenience, Mach's philosophical thought can be divided into three parts: PHENOMENALISM, philosophy of science, and social and religious views and influence (see RELIGION).

PHENOMENALISM

Antimetaphysical Stance

Mach showed both his affinity for Kant and his temperament as an experimental scientist as he tried repeatedly to distance himself from any metaphysical doctrine. Only experience, according to Mach, provides the facts upon which all observers can agree; the slightest departure from experience into metaphysics risks dogmatism, division, and delusion. For Mach, the ideal philosophy—for both intellectual and social concerns—discloses nothing more than regularities among phenomena. His antimetaphysical stance is vivid in the way he distinguished himself from BERKELEY and Kant: "Berkeley regards the 'elements' [of experience] as conditioned by an unknown cause external to them (God); accordingly Kant, in order to appear a sober realist, invents the 'thing-in-itself'; whereas, on the view which I advocate, a dependence of the 'elements' on one another is theoretically and practically all that is required" (*Analysis of Sensations*: 361–62n).

Mach also made great use of a particular notion of *economy*. For Mach, scientists should concern themselves only with phenomena that might make some difference in human experience; anything too small, too remote, or too subtle for measurement does not fall properly within science's domain. Similarly, scientific theories should be constructed as simply and clearly as possible for the sake of utility and for ease of learning. Mach's underlying sentiment seems to have been that science—or, indeed, any human endeavor—is valuable only to the extent that it benefits humanity in some measurable way (see the later discussion of his social views). Mach thought that METAPHYSICS, in a traditional sense, is therefore of no value.

Ontology

Mach was a phenomenalist: he believed in sensations and the relations among them and denied the existence of material objects. Mach wrote often of the "elements" of sensation, but it is not clear what these elements are supposed to be. At one extreme, they could be, for example, the tiniest perceivable pixels in the visual field, the smallest increments in pitch, and so on. At another extreme, the elements could be more inclusive sensory packages, perhaps as described by Gestalt psychology. There are, of course, intermediate candidates as well: patches of color, discrete sounds, and so forth. Mach seems to have been content to leave empirical psychology to determine which portions of experience should count as elements and to distinguish simple sensory objects from complex ones (see SIMPLE/COMPLEX DISTINCTION). At any rate, Mach is quite clear that the sensations, not any material objects, are at the foundation of his ontology: "Properly speaking, the world is not composed of 'things' as its elements, but of colors, tones, pressures, spaces, times, in short what we ordinarily call individual sensations" (*Science of Mechanics*: 579).

Mach believed that, in addition to the elements, there also exist mathematical functions among those elements; but the ontological status of these functions is also unclear (see RELATIONS). They serve to allow elements to be grouped into objects. For example, "A body," Mach wrote, "is a relatively constant sum of touch and sight sensations associated with the same space and time sensations" (*Science of Mechanics*: 611). A function thus connects the sensations so as to yield a fixed conglomerate that becomes identified with a table, a face, and so on. But the functions are not themselves elements of sensations, since they do not appear in experience: one sees the table's shape and feels its texture, but one does not directly sense the function connecting the two. How and why certain elements become combined through functions are questions Mach did not pursue; his empiricism urged him to accept the connections in the world as brute facts.

Phenomenalists must find some way to account for the truth of claims regarding objects that are not now being observed. For example, suppose it is true that water is boiling next door, unobserved. How can this be true if only elements of sensation and functions connecting them exist? One possible answer to this question is through a counterfactual: it is true that the water is boiling, because *were* an observer to go next door, the observer *would* see the water boiling. But what makes this counterfactual true? J. S. MILL appealed to possible observations; but Mach resisted this move and instead relied on his mathematical functions to provide an account. According to Mach, if it is true that unobserved water boils next door, then it is true because the functions connecting elements that are actually sensed imply that if one were to travel next door, one would observe water boiling there. For instance, perhaps one remembers putting the kettle on the stove; perhaps the whistling of the kettle is heard from that direction; and perhaps the local temperature is very slightly increased because of the boiling next door. Combine these observed facts with observed facts regarding the observer's body and its location, and the overall circumstance will fall within the scope of a function that determines that if the observer were to travel next door, the observer would see water boiling. The point is that this function, not the existence of possible (but nonactual) observations, determines the truth of the claim in question. Generally, Mach believed that all truths regarding unobserved phenomena can be treated in this way. If one were to posit some unobserved event too remote to have any connection to anything being observed now, Mach would simply deny that it is within science's scope to deal with such phenomena. This is a manifestation of his notion of "economy," mentioned earlier.

As will be seen later, consciousness itself is a function among elements; and so, according to Mach, the division between the mental and physical realms is a division within the domain of elements. Elements themselves, said Mach, are mental or physical with respect to the kinds of functions that incorporate them. With this in mind, Mach provided a clear summary of his ontology:

[E]verything we can know about the world is necessarily expressed in the sensations, which can be set free from the individual influence of the observer in a precisely definable manner. Everything that we can want to know is given by the solution of a problem in mathematical form, by the ascertainment of the functional dependence of the sensational elements on one another. This knowledge exhausts the knowledge of "reality." The bridge between physics, in the widest sense, and scientific psychology, is formed of these very elements, which are physical and psychical objects according to the kind of combination that is being investigated. (*Analysis of Sensations*: 369)

Neutral Monism

In this way, Mach was neither idealist nor materialist (see IDEALISM and MATERIALISM); for the division of experience into either mental or physical events is logically subsequent to the ontology of elements. The elements themselves are within a single category—that of "experience"—and by themselves are neither mental nor physical; hence, Mach's view can be called "neutral monism." Mach's view was influenced by Gustav Fechner's "psychophysics," which sidestepped the MIND–BODY PROBLEM by aiming only to describe the functional relations that obtain among bodily states and mental events. (He was also quite sympathetic to Wilhelm Wundt's experimental approach to introspection; and no reader of *The Analysis of Sensations* can fail to appreciate Mach's unflagging precision in relating his own subjective experiences, no matter how unusual.)

Elements, according to Mach, are either mental or physical, depending on the functional relation that incorporates them: "A color is a physical object as soon as we consider its dependence, for instance, upon its luminous source, upon other colors, upon temperatures, upon spaces, and so forth. When we consider its dependence on the retina, it is a psychological object, a sensation" (*Analysis of Sensations*: 17). This is not to say, as some commentators suggest, that whether an element is mental or physical is arbitrary or conventional; rather, each element is truly mental, in virtue of its belonging to one set of functional relations; and it is also truly physical, in virtue of its belonging to another set of functional relations. The distinction is no more subjective than is the distinction between being tall and being an uncle; one can be truly both, in any context, in virtue of different sets of relations.

It should be noted that Mach favored neutral monism because it seemed that only such an approach could allow for a science that unifies physics and psychology and because it easily dissolves the mind–body problem.

The Self and Other Minds

As mentioned before, Mach understood consciousness to consist in a function over elements. But Mach did not describe how a function is capable of playing the role of consciousness; presumably, again, he left this for empirical psychology to determine. Mach wrote that "out of this fabric [of sensations], that which is relatively fixed and permanent *stands prominently forth, engraves itself* on the memory, and *expresses itself* in language" (*Analysis of Sensations*: 2; emphasis added). There is something of a miracle here, to be sure, but clearly the idea is supposed to be that consciousness consists in the complexity of relations among elements. Why some complexes of relations are conscious and others are not is again an issue Mach did not resolve. Mach welcomed the consequence that the self is not sharply marked off from its environment, since the elements that compose it also compose other objects (through other sets of functions); indeed, he thought that this understanding of the self bypassed some other philosophical problems:

If we regard the ego as a real unity, we become involved in the following dilemma: either we must set over against the ego a world of unknowable entities (which would then be quite idle and purposeless), or we must regard the whole world, the egos of other people included, as comprised in our own ego (a proposition to which it is difficult to yield serious assent). (*Analysis of Sensations*: 28)

Mach avoided this dilemma by taking the ego to be merely a practical unity, employed only for convenience.

Because Mach took the elements to be ontologically fundamental and understood selves to be constructed out of functions ranging over those elements, he saw no urgent need to disprove SOLIPSISM. When the question of other minds arose, he usually offered a generic argument by analogy; but clearly, he did not ever doubt that there were elements of sensation other than those involved in whatever function characterized his own mind. He also took some nonhuman animals to have minds, that is, to experience, and he thought it is empirical psychology's task to describe the sensations animals may have (again through a kind of argument by analogy). Mach's views of the self and other minds had interesting ramifications for his social and religious views (discussed later).

PHILOSOPHY OF SCIENCE

Criticisms of Newton

Mach believed that the evident grace and strength of NEWTON's physics could be augmented with firmer connections to the elements of sensation. For example, while Newton had defined mass to be a certain quantity of matter, Mach (as a phenomenalist) found that definition utterly vacuous so far as experience is concerned. Mach therefore defined mass as follows: "All those bodies are bodies of equal mass, which, mutually acting on each other, produce in each other equal and opposite reactions" (*Science of Mechanics*: 266). Similarly for force: "Force is any circumstance of which the consequence is motion" (*Science of Mechanics*: 95), with the allowance that several of these circumstances can be conjoined so that the result is no motion (equilibrium). These definitions ground the basic terms of Newtonian mechanics in sensory experience—as any good definitions should:

As soon therefore as we, our attention being drawn to the fact by experience, have *perceived* in bodies the existence of a special property determinative of accelerations, our task with regard to it ends with the recognition and unequivocal designation of this *fact*. Beyond the recognition of this fact we will not get, and every venture beyond it will only be productive of obscurity. (*Science of Mechanics*: 271)

Mach further believed that Newton's arguments for absolute SPACE were inconclusive. Newton had argued that since the surface of water in a rotating bucket changes as the bucket rotates more rapidly (namely, a meniscus forms), there must be some absolute frame of reference. Mach responded that Newton's experiment showed only that the meniscus forms when the bucket rotates with respect to the fixed stars (the largest frame of reference available); perhaps the same meniscus would form if the bucket were held still (relative to an even larger frame of reference) and the stars were rotated about the bucket; or perhaps the meniscus would not form if the walls of the bucket were astronomically thick. In short, there are a variety of hypotheses, in addition to that of absolute space, to explain the formation of the meniscus. At most, experience can tell us only that a change occurs upon rotation relative to a larger frame of reference and not, of course, that there is a largest frame of reference.

Mach labored to explain in some detail how observers progress from understanding space, as it is subjectively experienced, to understanding the space described by physics and eventually the space described by geometry (see SPACE COGNITION). One begins with *primary space*, or what one experiences while inertial: objects in the visual field grow, shrink, and distort, and tactile experiences register only when objects collide with (what comes to be understood as) the observer's own body. When the observer experiences kinesthetic changes (through the observer's acceleration), the observer experiences *secondary space*. Only experience in secondary space can bring the observer to an understanding of the third dimension and the notion of an unbounded space. Once the observer is able to manipulate solids in space and therefore measure, then the observer begins to develop the concept of the space described by physics, or *metric space*. A variety of ABSTRACTIONs and INDUCTIONs leads the observer finally to a conception of *geometrical space*, where the physical properties of bodies (other than size and shape) become irrelevant. Thus, geometrical knowledge is predicated upon physical experience: "Geometry, therefore, is concerned with *ideal objects* produced by the schematization of *experiential objects*" (*Space and Geometry*: 68). Geometry, like physics, "can become an exact, deductive science only on the condition of its representing the objects of experience by means of schematizing and idealizing concepts" (*Space and Geometry*: 124).

Mach also disagreed with Newton about absolute TIME. Mach understood time as an abstraction reached through the study of memory and change: "the connection of that which is contained in the province of our memory with that which is contained in the province of our sense-perception'' (*Science of Mechanics*: 274–75). He also noted that the increase in entropy (as described by the second law of thermodynamics) is what gives us the idea of the direction of time. But since the notion of time is drawn from experience alone, there can be no evidence for Newton's *absolute* time, which would transcend possible experience.

Functional Laws, Mathematics, and Intuition

The importance of functions for Mach's views has been seen. But Mach was not able to explain in any detail how observers arrive at knowledge of those functions. Mach believed that mathematical knowledge is drawn from experience; and when this knowledge is combined with the proper amount of experimental evidence, the mind is led to a sudden apprehension of, in Mach's words, "the main thing," that is, the lawful relationship displayed in the evidence. How, why, and when such sudden apprehension occurs are, again, a matter for empirical psychological research.

The path from evidence to enlightenment is lined with provisional theories: observers might initially invent relatively complex, mechanical theories that connect the phenomena; for example, observers might (and do) employ a cumbersome atomic theory in explaining the phenomenon of boiling water. Eventually, Mach believed, such "developing" sciences would throw off these theoretical distractions, and there would emerge an "end" science consisting purely of functions. Theories are thus, at best, provisionally useful and, at worst, positively misleading; Mach recognized the science of mechanics, for example, to be an extraordinarily useful provisional theory and also extremely well developed (because of its employment of MATHEMATICS). But he also maintained that mechanics reaches no deeper than explanations involving thermal, chemical, magnetic, or electrical principles. All theories obscure the essential, functional relationships: "The object of natural science is the connexion of phenomena; but the theories are like dry leaves which fall away when they have long ceased to be the lungs of the tree of science" (*History and Root of the Principle of the Conservation of Energy*, Preface). Science, according to Mach, is "the completest possible presentation of the facts with the *least possible expenditure of thought*" (*Science of Mechanics*: 586); and while this is in part an expression of Mach's sense of economy (mentioned before), it also expresses his reluctance to employ unobservable phenomena, hidden mechanisms, occult phenomena, or any metaphysics in scientific theories.

Mach has been criticized (by no less a thinker than Einstein) for producing a catalog instead of a system—and description instead of explanation. But this criticism is misguided. Mach did not recommend merely recording and cataloging correlations among events but instead recommended finding the deepest and most general functional laws that *integrate* the phenomena. Mach's ideal science can be viewed as science purged of the last remnants of an influx theory of

CAUSATION, promoted by some philosophers in the medieval and early modern periods. In Mach's words, "There is no cause nor effect in nature; nature has but individual existence; nature simply is" (*Science of Mechanics*: 580). It is science's job, then, to describe the simplest mathematical structure that can encompass the broad diversity of experience.

Empirical Stance

As has been seen, it is characteristic of Mach to leave many details of his theories for further research to discover. This is a defect, in a way, since a theory just is its details. But it is also a virtue, since Mach tried to develop a theory that would be consistent with new insights. His understanding of even the best available theories as provisional is best seen in his observations that

the apparently simplest mechanical principles are of a very complicated character, that these principles are founded on uncompleted experience, nay on experience that never can be fully completed, that practically, indeed, they are sufficiently secured, in view of the tolerable stability of our environment, to serve as the foundation of mathematical deduction, but that they can by no means themselves be regarded as mathematically established truths but only as principles that not only admit of constant control by experience but actually require it. (*Science of Mechanics*: 290)

Mach was thus anything but dogmatic in the sciences he favored.

Objections to Atoms and the Theory of Relativity

Mach never believed in atoms except as theoretical constructs. Because he saw atoms as purely theoretical, he resisted Boltzmann's efforts to reduce the second law of thermodynamics to atomic activity and also any attempt to account for shock waves in terms of atoms. He simply did not think the theoretical benefits of atoms worth the ontological investment, and he did not like the probabilistic underpinnings of the atomic theory of gases—and presumably he saw a more straightforward, phenomenalistic account of shock waves. Also, there was the plain fact that, in his day, there was only indirect evidence for the existence of atoms; a story is told that when people tried to persuade Mach of the existence of atoms, he would ask, "Have you seen one?" and the discussion would be over.

Mach's objections to Einstein's theory of relativity are more complex. In the Preface to *The Principles of Physical Optics*, Mach wrote: "The reason why, and the extent to which, I reject the present-day relativity theory, which I find to be growing more and more dogmatical, together with the particular reasons which have led me to such a view—considerations based on the physiology of the senses, epistemological doubts, and above all the insight resulting from my experiments—must remain to be treated in the sequel." The sequel was never published, and Mach's son was requested by his father to destroy the papers documenting those experiments. But a plausible conjecture is that (1) Mach thought (very probably mistakenly) that he had demonstrated in experiments that the speed of light is relative; that (2) the theory of relativity came to employ a conception of space-time developed by Minkowski, which Mach believed was misguided because it was non-Euclidean and four-dimensional and hence far removed from the physiological account of our perception of physical space and time; and that, more generally, (3) Mach thought the general outlook of the theory of relativity, as it was coming to be understood in the physics community, was not based firmly on empirical principles.

INFLUENCE AND SOCIAL AND RELIGIOUS VIEWS

Mach was influenced by DARWIN and maintained that scientists' efforts should be directed toward only what humans need to promote their ability to survive. This in turn led him to accept a pragmatic notion of truth: the value of a scientific claim lies in its contribution to human survival (see PRAGMATISM). (Mach's notion of economy, mentioned earlier, is central to these concerns.) Perhaps the strongest motivation for Mach's phenomenalism was that he believed that only such an approach would lead to a unified science to which all rational minds would assent, thereby obviating controversy and strife.

Mach saw organized religions as counterproductive to this utopian goal: they encouraged superstition and dogmatism. But his philosophy was not devoid of religious themes. First, he believed that truly important ideas discovered by one person will, after that person's death, continue to exist in the minds of others— and so there is a weak substitute for immortality. Second, in his later years Mach became aware (through Paul Carus) of the affinities of his philosophy to Buddhism. Mach and Buddhists would agree that the ego is in some sense less real than the experience that conditions it, and both would agree that the totality of reality is itself an inclusive being. In fact, many of Mach's works were translated into Asian languages (without his knowledge) by Buddhists who saw the similarities. But Mach, of course, rejected Buddhism's rejection of science's utility in solving human problems.

Mach had a tremendous influence on early analytic philosophy (see ANALYTIC PHILOSOPHY, LOGICAL POSITIVISM/LOGICAL EMPIRICISM); indeed, CARNAP's *The Logical Construction of the World* can be viewed as a technically precise development of Mach's philosophy (though Mach favored a "heteropsychological construction" to Carnap's "autopsychological construction"). Nietzsche admired Mach's stance against materialism and the notion of a unitary ego; but Mach disdained Nietzsche's conception of the *Übermensch*. William James' neutral monism and pragmatic notion of truth were, at least in part, influenced by Mach. Of course, many of Mach's contributions to the exact sciences continue to be employed today. Finally, because of the broad extent of his learning and utter originality of his thought, no serious consideration of the empirical basis of science can afford to ignore Mach.

PRIMARY WORKS

Space and Geometry. Translated by T. J. McCormack. Chicago: Open Court, 1906.

Popular Scientific Lectures. 3d ed., translated by T. J. McCormack. Chicago: Open Court, 1910.
History and Root of the Principle of the Conservation of Energy. Translated by Ph.E.B. Jourdain. Chicago: Open Court, 1911.
The Principles of Physical Optics. Translated by J. S. Anderson and A.F.A. Young. New York: Dover, 1953.
The Science of Mechanics. 6th ed., incorporating changes in the 9th German ed., translated by Ph.E.B. Jourdain. LaSalle: Open Court, 1960.
The Analysis of Sensation. Translated by C. M. Williams; revised and supplemented from the 5th German ed. by S. Waterlow. London: Routledge/Thoemmes Press, 1996 (reprint of the 1914 edition).

BIBLIOGRAPHY

Books

Blackmore, J. *Ernst Mach: His Work, Life, and Influence*. Berkeley: University of California Press, 1972.
———. *Ernst Mach—A Deeper Look: Documents and New Perspectives*. Boston Studies in the Philosophy of Science, vol. 143. Dordrecht: Kluwer, 1992.
Bradley, J. *Mach's Philosophy of Science*. London: Athlone, 1971.
Cohen, R., and Seeger, R., eds. *Ernst Mach: Physicist and Philosopher*. Boston Studies in the Philosophy of Science, vol. 6. Dordrecht: D. Reidel, 1970.

Articles

Blackmore, J. "Ernst Mach Leaves 'The Church of Physics.' " *The British Journal for the Philosophy of Science* 40 (1989): 519–40.
———. "An Historical Note on Ernst Mach." *The British Journal for the Philosophy of Science* 36 (1985): 299–305.
Feyerabend, P. "Mach's Theory of Research and Its Relation to Einstein." *Studies in History and Philosophy of Science* 15 (1984): 1–22.
Holton, G. "Ernst Mach and the Fortunes of Positivism in America." *Isis* 83 (1992): 27–60.
Loparic, Z. "Problem-Solving and Theory Structure in Mach." *Studies in History and Philosophy of Science* 15 (1984): 23–49.
Mitchell, S. "Mach's Mechanics and Absolute Space and Time." *Studies in History and Philosophy of Science* 24 (1993): 565–83.

CHARLES HUENEMANN

MATERIALISM. Materialism about some realm is the thesis that everything in that realm is ultimately and completely materially constituted. Materialism about human beings, for example, is the claim that human beings are wholly materially constituted. Materialism about human beings would thus exclude dualism about human beings, the view that they are constituted partly materially and partly immaterially, as well as immaterialism about human beings, the claim that they are wholly immaterially constituted. Materialism without qualification is the thesis that everything that exists is wholly materially constituted.

The proposal that something is ultimately and completely materially constituted begs for a characterization of the material. The early modern philosophers provide various attempts at an account. For example, Descartes conceives of the material as that which is extended in three dimensions, while BERKELEY took the material to be inert, senseless stuff that is outside any mind. Such characterizations, however, have been eclipsed by more recent physical theorizing. According to the understanding of contemporary physics, the material realm includes energy, and energy may very well be the sole fundamental constituent of the material world. But energy is not clearly extended in three dimensions. If one were to claim that energy is so extended by virtue of having causal efficacy in three dimensions, then God's power would also have to be so extended and thereby material. But God's power is paradigmatically immaterial. Against Berkeley's view, energy is material and yet not inert. One might amend Berkeley's characterization by defining the material as senseless stuff that is outside any mind, but the élan vital of the vitalists was supposed to be immaterial and yet senseless and outside any mind.

Difficulties such as these have led philosophers to despair of such accounts in favor of less specific characterizations of the material, such as "that over which a completed physics quantifies." But this too is inadequate. If a completed physics were to require that God exist in order to provide an explanation for the existence of the most basic physical laws, God would not thereby be rendered material. If Berkeley were right, and all entities over which physics quantifies are in some sense identical to, or reducible to, sensations, then perhaps nothing over which physics quantifies would be material.

Perhaps we should admit that if there is an essence of the material, we do not now know what it is. However, physics might be brought in as a prima facie reference-fixing device. It may be, then, that all we can say at this point is that the material is prima facie that which is constituted of whatever kind of entity physics typically quantifies over, whatever that may be. This leaves open what the essence of the material is, but it also allows for Berkeley's claim that there is nothing material at all.

The attractiveness of materialism lies in the promise of a materialist research program. Over the past three hundred years physics has seen spectacular progress, which might encourage the view that materialist suppositions will yield the best prospect for advance in our understanding of reality. But traditionally, four problems have cast doubt on the prospects of materialism. (1) The most prominent challenge for materialism is to provide an account of thought and consciousness. For centuries, materialists remained content with highly speculative claims on this topic (such as that thoughts are made up of very fine atoms) that provide no significant explanation of the target phenomena. Not until the twentieth century did an advancing materialist research program in psychology become a reality. (2) A second problem for materialism is to provide an account of living processes. Up until the twentieth century, many held the vitalist view that life could never be explained materialistically. But advances in biochemistry have undermined the vitalist program in favor of a materialist one. (3) A third challenge to materialism is to explain order and apparent design, for example, the apparent teleological organization in biological organisms. It was long thought that such phenomena would require the existence of a divine author of nature. (4) Finally, it has often been argued that theories of mathematics and predication require abstract entities such as universals, numbers, and sets. This claim has sometimes been viewed as inconsistent with materialism, and some materialists have attempted to develop theories in these areas that do not make reference to abstract entities.

Materialism has had a long history. Among the pre-Socratic philosophers, Thales, Anaximander, and Anaximines were materialists by virtue of holding that everything is made up of some fundamental material element or elements, such as water or air. Later, Empedocles claimed that everything is made up of four basic material elements—earth, air, fire, and water. Another materialist tradition, atomism, was developed by Leucippus and Democritus. In the Democritean conception, everything that exists is made up of atoms, literally "uncuttables," fundamental particles that are indestructible and in themselves lifeless, senseless, and inert. Atoms have various sizes, shapes, and motions, and every event that occurs and the nature of everything that exists can be explained as a function of the sizes, shapes, and motions of atoms. Materialism of the atomistic variety was accepted by EPICURUS and his followers, most notably, Lucretius, who provides an extensive atomistic account of the universe in his poem *De Rerum Natura*. In the materialist conception of the Stoics, matter is not inert but rather has dynamic characteristics, which they claimed to allow for a plausible materialist account of life and mind (see STOICISM). But even here, explanations of life and mind, for example, were mere gestures, and only the very rudiments of a materialist research program had been proposed.

Due to the influence of Platonism and dualist versions of Aristotelianism, together with religious concerns, materialism about the universe or about human beings had few prominent advocates during the medieval period. During the seventeenth century, HOBBES advocated materialist views but made no significant progress over the Greeks in accounting for life, mind, and teleology. Nevertheless, although philosophers such as GALILEO, Descartes, LOCKE, and BOYLE did not endorse a materialist account of the mind and were thus not materialists, they did develop the conception of matter that characterized the scientific revolution and that in turn inspired a revival of materialism. In particular, they developed a conception of matter that could conceivably allow its existence and nature to be independent of any human cognitive or sensory perspective on it. Berkeley's challenge to this conception was deeply influential—empiricists such as HUME, MILL, MACH, and Schlick all accepted some version of it—and a defense against his arguments is required for materialism's plausibility.

The modern conception of matter challenged two fundamental components of the view advanced by the medieval Aristotelians. First, according to the Aristotelians, matter is largely as we sense it to be—it is characterized by qualities that resemble our sensations of primary qualities, such as extension, size, shape, motion, location, and duration, as well as of secondary qualities, such as color, taste, odor, and temperature (see PRIMARY AND SECONDARY QUALI-TIES). Second, the kind of CAUSATION that is most important for understanding the physical world—formal causation—is modeled on the psychological. Just as the sculptor's idea of the statue, together with the intentions associated with it, is efficacious in the statue's production, so the characteristics of material things are idea- and intention-like forms that make changes in things by being impressed on them. Descartes set the tone for the modern period by rejecting these two features of the Aristotelian account. What motivates the Cartesian conception is a vision of physics that consists solely of mathematics together with a limited number of laws of motion. Matter, for Descartes, is exactly like the space of geometry. Primary qualities can be characterized geometrically, whereas the Aristotelian secondary qualities—properties that resemble our secondary quality sensations—cannot, and hence we have reason to believe that the primary qualities, not the Aristotelian secondary qualities, are features of the physical world. Empiricist intuitions might lead one to suspect that Descartes' claims are simply artifacts of mystic Pythagoreanism. But as we shall see, this is not so, and mathematical expressibility has impressive empiricist credentials.

Descartes, as well as Galileo, Locke, and Boyle, agree that the formal causal model for explanation in physics should be replaced by the mechanistic one. Boyle, in particular, is very explicit about rejecting the Aristotelian view because of its psychological inspiration. According to early conceptions of mechanistic science, all features of the physical world can be explained by the motion and mechanical interaction of various parts of matter, where typical mechanical interactions are impact, pushing, and pulling. In addition, there is a link between mechanistic causal explanation and the modern conception of matter. Mechanistic science, its proponents argued, allows us to explain all of the features of the physical world, including the physical aspect of the causal history of sensory ideas in us, in terms of the primary qualities alone. Secondary qualities are consequently not explanatorily primary, if they exist in the physical world at all.

Siding with Descartes, Locke also argues that the real characteristics of the material are the primary qualities, such as extension and motion, and that by contrast with the Aristotelian view, matter has no qualities that resemble secondary quality ideas, such as the ideas of color, shape, sound, taste, odor, and temperature. Locke presents a much-discussed perceptual relativity argument for claims of this sort: if one hand is initially warm, and the other cold, and both are placed in the same bowl of water, it will feel cooler to one hand than the other. Since the water could not have a quality that resembles the temperature sensations of each of the hands, one should conclude that the water really has no such quality at all. The reality of primary qualities, by contrast, cannot be undermined by analogous arguments.

The modern conception of mind-independent matter was challenged by Berkeley, who argued that there does not, and could not, exist any matter at all in the universe. Perhaps Berkeley's most important consideration against the existence of matter involves his attack on the supposed mind-independence of primary qualities. In reference to Locke's argument from perceptual relativity, Berkeley argues that perception of primary qualities also varies with the state or nature of the perceptual organs and that consequently primary qualities are as mind-dependent as the secondary qualities are. For instance, in the case of size, a mite sees its foot as big, whereas a human being sees it as small. No quality in the foot could resemble the idea of big and the idea of small at the same time, so big and small are no different from the secondary qualities after all.

On behalf of Locke, however, one can reply that Berkeley is correct in claiming that big and small cannot count as primary qualities. Indeed, their relativity to the perceptual mechanism counts as strong evidence that they lack mind-independent existence. Yet, Berkeley has not recognized two very significant points. First, there is a related quality that escapes the argument from perceptual relativity, and it is mathematically expressible. Big is not a primary quality, but having a volume of five million cubic feet is. Second, the mathematically expressible qualities of volume in cubic feet and length in millimeters are immune to perceptual relativity arguments because all perceivers can come to agree about these qualities. We and the mite can agree that the mite's foot is .01 millimeters long, even though our judgment about whether it is big or small is relative to the state or nature of the perceptual mechanism. Hence, according to this Lockean (and Cartesian) reply to Berkeley, not all aspects of size, duration, and motion, as we perceive them, are primary qualities. Rather, in order to distinguish what is merely perspectival from what is real in our ideas of primary qualities, we can focus on the mathematically expressible (or scalar) features of the contents of these ideas. Finding the mathematically expressible feature is a way of isolating a quality on which we can all agree, one that is therefore immune to the perceptual relativity arguments. This agreement can typically be secured by an empirical argument to the best explanation. Consequently, it appears that the modern conception of mind-independent matter can be rescued from the Berkeleian attack.

The materialist revival began in earnest during the eighteenth century, when the *philosophes* La Mettrie and Holbach defended it, but again without any significant progress on the crucial issues of life and mind. Perhaps the most significant nineteenth-century event for the progress of materialism was the publication of DARWIN's *Origin of Species*. Prior to Darwin, it was often argued that the best explanation of biological teleology involves the existence of an intelligent designer. Darwin's theory, that biological order is due to natural selection together with variation of traits, undermined the prevailing orthodoxy.

During the twentieth century, three important advances made materialism the dominant view. The first was the development of biochemistry, which provided a successful material research project for the various processes characteristic of living organisms. For example, the discovery of DNA allowed for a biochemical explanation of the inheritance of physical characteristics. The second advance was the invention of the modern digital computer, which provided a material model for certain aspects of mental functioning, such as information processing. The third was rapid progress in neurophysiology, which many claimed to yield a yet more powerful research program for mental phenomena. Twentieth-century physics, with the development of relativity theory and quantum mechanics, resulted in profound changes in the conception of matter, but these changes did not have any significant impact on the main problems for materialist theory. Some theorists claim that quantum theory will help to explain consciousness, but such views remain speculative and have not gained wide acceptance.

Twentieth-century materialism has several important varieties. One important division separates reductive from nonreductive materialism. According to reductive materialism, all natural kinds—including those, for example, in biology and psychology—bear some strong relation such as identity or causal equivalence to natural kinds in physics. By contrast, nonreductive materialists argue that while everything that exists is wholly constituted by entities over which physics quantifies, it is not the case that all natural kinds bear a relation such as identity to natural kinds in physics.

One influential reductive conception was developed by the logical positivists (see LOGICAL POSITIVISM/LOGICAL EMPIRICISM). The logical positivists themselves were not materialists in the true sense, for, in their conception, the materialist thesis, that everything is constituted solely of matter, has no meaning because it is not empirically verifiable. Immaterialism, they claimed, is as unverifiable as materialism is. Nevertheless, the logical positivists advanced a view that was to influence subsequent materialist theories: that every meaningful sentence can be translated without loss of content into a sentence of physics. This thesis was dubbed "the unity of science." The psychological part of this program became known as logical BEHAVIORISM. In Hempel's classic formulation of this position, every sentence about mental states can be translated without loss of content into a sentence about behavioral and neural states. Realist reductionists, such as J.J.C. Smart, eschewed the linguistic aspect of the positivist program. Mental kinds of entities, they argued, are identical to physical kinds, while at the same time mental state terms are not identical in meaning to physical state terms. The most prominent model for this realist sort of reductionism requires that kinds in special sciences, such as psychology, be appropriately connected with kinds in physics by virtue of bridge principles. Bridge principles specify a metaphysical relation, such as "being identical to" or "being a necessary and sufficient condition for" between the kinds of the special science and those of physics. Materialists of this reductionist type claim that there are bridge principles that will secure the reducibility of every kind of entity to a kind in physics.

Beginning in the 1960s, philosophers such as Hilary Putnam, Jerry Fodor, and Richard Boyd defended a nonreductive model for materialism. Their argument against reductionism arises from the phenomenon of multiple realizability.

An automobile part, such as a carburetor, provides a simple example of this phenomenon. A carburetor might be constructed of steel, aluminum, or copper, and hence the kind "carburetor" is multiply realizable at the level of physics. Similarly, the psychological kind "pain" might be realized in brains of different sorts—octopus, cat, and human. Because such brains have different neurophysiologies, the kind "pain" is multiply realizable at the neurophysiological level. Consequently, the bridge principles linking psychology to neurophysiology would identify neurophysiological kinds with disjunctions, and possibly indefinitely long disjunctions, of neurophysiological kinds. But then, the neurophysiological laws to which the psychological laws "reduce" would involve indefinitely long disjunctions, as would the physical laws to which, in the end, the psychological laws "reduce." But statements involving such indefinitely long disjunctions are not laws, because the indefinitely long disjunctive "laws" are not explanatory.

What the phenomenon of multiple realizability suggests is that the essence of the kinds of special sciences is not to be identified with the stuff of which instances of the kinds are composed. Instead, the essence of such kinds is to be found at a higher level of abstraction, a level that abstracts from the details of the physical realization of its instances. The core nonreductivist claim is that there are causal powers at the level of the special sciences that emerge from, but do not appear at, the physical level. A project that would reduce all laws to physical laws would miss out on certain causal powers and on laws and explanations that involve them. This nonreductive picture gives rise to a form of materialism that currently enjoys widespread popularity. Its central claim is that although not all laws and kinds reduce to laws and kinds in physics, nevertheless everything that exists is wholly materially constituted.

Among the challenges to materialism, the problem of accounting for consciousness is widely regarded as the most serious. Some philosophers have argued that there can be no materialist account of the mental. According to the "knowledge argument," if materialism is true, someone who possesses complete physical knowledge will know every fact about mental states there is to know. But because there are facts about mental states that will not be known by someone who possesses complete physical knowledge but has never enjoyed certain experiences, it follows that materialist accounts of the mental are inadequate. Early resistance to the knowledge argument aimed to show that what distinguishes a subject who has had certain sensory experiences from someone who is physically omniscient but has never had them is not factual knowledge but merely an ability, such as an ability to imagine, recognize, or remember or an ability to apply a concept, and that hence, there is no fact about mental states that eludes a materialist account. A second strategy concedes that the special knowledge that certain sensory experiences provide might well be factual knowledge, but it insists that all of the facts known by means of these experiences will also be known by someone who has complete physical knowledge but has never had the experiences at issue. Complete physical knowledge, all by itself, fails to supply only certain ways that facts can be represented, not knowledge of these facts themselves. Accordingly, many philosophers believe that the knowledge argument can be answered. Nevertheless, most will also agree that a materialist account of consciousness does not now exist. Yet materialists argue that because of the successes of the materialist program in psychology, together with the absence of a rival dualist research program, we have very good reason to believe that materialism is true.

There is currently no consensus on whether there are accounts of mathematics and predication that avoid reference to abstract entities. Philosophers have doubted, however, whether the truth of materialism requires accounts of this sort. Progress has yet to be made in defining the issues in this area and in carefully laying out the various options for resolving them.

BIBLIOGRAPHY

Boyd, Richard. "Materialism without Reductionism: What Physicalism Does Not Entail." In *Readings in Philosophy of Psychology*, vol. 1. edited by Ned Block. Cambridge: Harvard University Press, 1980: 67–106.

Fodor, Jerry. "Special Sciences." *Synthese* 28 (1974): 97–115.

Hempel, Carl. "The Logical Analysis of Psychology." In *Readings in Philosophy of Psychology*, vol. 1, edited by Ned Block. Cambridge: Harvard University Press, 1980: 14–23.

Kim, Jaegwon. "The Myth of Nonreductive Materialism." *Proceedings and Addresses of the American Philosophical Association* 63, no. 3 (1989): 31–47.

Nagel, Thomas. "What Is It Like to Be a Bat?" *The Philosophical Review* 83 (1974): 435–50.

Putnam, Hilary. "The Nature of Mental States." In *Philosophical Papers*, vol. 2. Cambridge: Cambridge University Press, 1975.

Smart, J.J.C. "Sensations and Brain Processes." *The Philosophical Review* 67 (1959): 141–56.

DERK PEREBOOM

MATHEMATICS. It sounds paradoxical, but empiricists have generally avoided empiricist theories of arithmetic. Only John Stuart MILL straightforwardly asserted that arithmetical propositions are empirical (albeit very general) laws. But Mill's view has not found many adherents: arithmetical propositions seem far more certain than any available empirical evidence for them (what observation could verify that one million plus one million equals two million?). Indeed, arithmetical truths are generally believed to be necessary. Also, arithmetical propositions are universal, valid for anything that can be counted, whether empirical or not. For the most part, therefore, empiricists, from LOCKE to CARNAP, have conceded the rationalist claim that arithmetic is a necessary and an a priori subject (see A PRIORI/A POSTERIORI DISTINCTION) but have argued that no metaphysical consequences follow from this. For example, HUME maintained that arithmetical propositions assert "relations of ideas," rather than "matters of fact." Contemporary empiricists who are also analytic philosophers (Carnap, Hempel; see ANALYTIC PHILOSOPHY) have held that they are analytic truths, tautologies (see ANALYTIC/SYNTHETIC DISTINC- TION). (According to KANT, of course, Hume also held that arithmetical truths are analytic, but in his *Treatise of Human Nature*, Hume explicitly denies that "The shortest distance between two points is a straight line" is a definition.) Ironically, the tenability of the contemporary empiricist view is based on the "logicist" work of the celebrated philosopher-mathematician Gottlob Frege, who was not an empiricist at all. Once arithmetic had been reduced to logic, as in Frege, the empiricists then argued (in opposition to Frege) that the validity of logic itself was a linguistic matter, grounded in semantic rules rather than in metaphysics. Problems, however, remain with logicism itself: technical and phil- osophical problems have persuaded most philosophers that Frege's program to reduce arithmetic to logic cannot be carried out.

For geometry, the empiricist case is far stronger. Geometry has not the uni- versality of arithmetic but (as its name means) is the science of measuring regions of a planar surface or of three-dimensional SPACE. The empiricist need not concede to the rationalist that geometry is either a priori or necessary. The discovery of consistent non-Euclidean geometries in the nineteenth century by Gauss, Riemann, and Lobachevsky was a blow to these two claims. Worse, from the perspective of the rationalist, the Einsteinian approach to space-time presupposed that Euclidean geometry was actually false, though not observably false in a very small region in which the gravitational field (which curves space) is, further, weak. The view, then, that the propositions of geometry are empirical facts has much to recommend it. Nevertheless, some empiricists have adopted some form or other of conventionalism, according to which the choice between Euclidean and non-Euclidean geometry is not a matter of fact at all but a choice between two ways of describing the same facts: for example, instead of saying that Euclidean geometry is false, since Einstein's theory predicts that the sum of the angles of a triangle of three light rays near a heavy body is not 180 degrees, we can say instead that Euclidean geometry is true—what happens is that the light rays are "bent" as a result of the strong gravitational field.

BIBLIOGRAPHY
Bennaceraf, Paul, and Hilary Putnam. *The Philosophy of Mathematics: Selected Read- ings*. 2d rev. ed. Cambridge: Cambridge University Press, 1983.

MARK STEINER

MEANING. Theories of meaning, construed with respect to human languages, stipulate the conditions under which concepts and propositions become in- telligible to human knowers. Meaning may be distinguished from truth. A proposition such as "Green ideas sleep furiously" does not refer to any com- prehensible state of affairs; it is conceptually unintelligible because it categori- cally misapplies predicates. (Ideas do not have color.) A good case can be made that such meaningless statements are neither true nor false. On the other hand, the proposition "Unicorns exist" does mark out a comprehensible state of affairs and is therefore meaningful (but false). In any event, questions of meaning logically precede questions of truth. To determine whether p is true or false, I must know the meaning of p. If an intelligible state of affairs is stipulated by p, one can begin to assess the truth-value of p.

The meaning of concepts and propositions is necessarily related to the communicative intentions and propositional attitudes of those articulating them. Authorial intention theories of meaning have been criticized by poststructuralists, deconstructionists, and postmodernists. Nevertheless, the successful translation of texts or speeches from one language to another and the achievement of everyday spoken and written communication depend on the premise that the primary meaning of a statement consists in the author's propositional intentions and what can be logically derived from them. The job application means what the employer says it means. So also for the newspaper column and the cookbook. To untether meaning from authorial intent is to court linguistic nihilism, for this removes all controls on interpretation. Furthermore, the deconstructionists become hypocritical when they protest being misinterpreted by those employing their own deconstructionist techniques against them.

Besides disputing the importance of authorial intent with respect to meaning, philosophers also disagree on the necessity of other features to make language meaningful. Empiricist theories of meaning maintain that empirical data of some kind—as opposed to a priori and/or innate ideas—are fundamental to meaning.

Empiricist theories can be roughly divided into those that allow concepts and propositions to possess supraempirical meaning and those that do not. The latter view is typified by HUME's approach in *A Treatise on Human Nature*, whereby he denies meaning in the absence of ideas derived directly or indirectly from sensory impressions. All ideas must originate in impressions. Putative ideas lacking this genetic pedigree—such as "substance" and "the soul"—are fictions, even if philosophically hallowed. Therefore, as Hume avers in *An Enquiry concerning Human Understanding*, any volume of metaphysics or divinity that lacks "abstract reasoning concerning quantity or number" (the relation of ideas) or "experimental reasoning concerning matters of fact and existence" should be committed to the flames, "for it can contain nothing but sophistry and illusion." It is meaningless. Recently, Kai Nielsen has argued in a like manner against the meaningfulness of theism. Hume's basic approach was adopted by the logical positivists (see LOGICAL POSITIVISM/LOGICAL EMPIRICISM), whose verificationist theory (see VERIFICATION PRINCIPLE) denied meaning to statements that are neither necessarily true nor empirically verifiable.

Such theories suffer from at least two primary defects. First, they often deny meaning to matters that are intuitively taken to be meaningful but are neither necessarily true nor verifiable by empirical confirmation—such as objective moral principles and objective aesthetic properties. The field of meaning is narrowed illegitimately. Second, these theories typically suffer from self-referential incoherence. The logical positivist's verificationist theory cannot be taken as necessarily true or true by virtue of observation. It renders itself meaningless, as has been widely recognized.

Other empirical theories avoid these problems by grounding meaning in empirical conditions without limiting meaning to concepts and propositions about empirical states of affairs. For instance, AQUINAS claimed that there is "nothing in the intellect which was not previously in the senses"; yet for him "God" was not a meaningless term but an intelligible, supraempirical concept that is at least partially derivable through the evidence of the senses.

PRIMARY WORKS

Hume, David. *An Enquiry concerning Human Understanding.* In *Enquiries concerning Human Understanding and concerning the Principles of Morals*, edited with an analytical index by L. A. Selby-Bigge; revised with notes by P. H. Nidditch. Oxford: Clarendon Press, 1975.

————. *A Treatise of Human Nature.* 2d ed., edited with an analytical index by L. A. Selby-Bigge; revised with notes by P. H. Nidditch. Oxford: Clarendon Press, 1978.

Locke, John. *An Essay concerning Human Understanding.* Edited with an introduction by P. H. Nidditch. Oxford: Clarendon Press, 1975.

BIBLIOGRAPHY

Groothuis, Douglas. "Questioning Hume's Theory of Meaning." *Kinesis* 18 (1992): 27–38.

Nielsen, Kai. "No! A Defense of Atheism." In *Does God Exist? The Great Debate*, edited by J. P. Moreland and Kai Nielsen. Nashville: Thomas Nelson, 1990: 48–56.

DOUGLAS R. GROOTHUIS

METAPHYSICS. Metaphysics traditionally has been ontology in Aristotle's sense, the study of being as being, a science that attempted to set down the common characters of all that existed. For many philosophers this involved the inference to the existence and characterization of entities that lie outside the world of experience. Thus, for KANT metaphysics was the study of self (rational psychology), the world (cosmology), and God (theology). It was often argued that the world of ordinary experience is merely the appearances of some underlying or transcendent reality and that in order to discover the truth of the world of experience, one must turn away from it to the deeper and more real world that lies beyond it. Metaphysicians of this sort generally dislike and distrust the world of ordinary experience. Empiricists, in contrast, embrace that world. Empiricists, such as EPICURUS and SEXTUS EMPIRICUS in the ancient world and those from LOCKE onward in the early modern period, employed skeptical arguments to attack the very notion that a science of beings outside the realm of ordinary experience was possible or even, as David HUME argued, intelligible. The question of psychology is to be decided not by appeal to pure reason but through empirical means, those of natural SCIENCE. So, too, the structure of the world is to be found in what natural science tells us about it; pure reason cannot, for example, reveal an underlying teleological structure or meaning. Nor can pure reason take us to an ultimate cause, God, that lies outside the world of ordinary experience. For the empiricist, truth and reality are to be found within the world of experience, and if metaphysics is possible at all, it is restricted to the world we know by ordinary experience, including the mental events presented in inner consciousness and the nonmental events given in sense awareness.

This is not to say that there are no parts of the world of ordinary experience that are not given in such experience—there are parts that are too small to see or too far away or in the past or the future. The point is that these parts, while they might be specifically different from things that we experience, are at least of the same generic kinds as the things of ordinary experience. In contrast, the entities of the traditional metaphysician are totally different in kind from ordinary things: they are things that are accessible not by means of ordinary experience but only by means of a REASON that goes beyond the world of ordinary experience.

In an empiricist metaphysics, then, some of the traditional problems disappear. Others remain. But the range of solutions is restricted. Thus, for example, there is the problem of the sameness of things: why do we apply the same general term, for example, "white," to two different things? Empiricists such as Hume and Herbert Spencer argued that it is because the properties of things, though intrinsically different, stand in relations of resemblance to each other. Others, such as John Stuart MILL, argued to the contrary that the characteristics of things are not themselves intrinsically different; they are to the contrary universals, given in experience. The dialectic is difficult, but for the empiricist one answer is not possible, that of Plato, who argued that the sameness of things is to be accounted for in terms of Forms that transcend the world of ordinary experience.

Empiricists have argued a number of other metaphysical issues. For example, they have disagreed on whether the ultimate constituents of the world are material things (MATERIALISM) or SENSE-DATA (PHENOMENALISM). Again, empiricists have generally argued, following Hume, that CAUSATION is objectively nothing more than regularity; but others have followed John LOCKE and argued that there is given in experience some sort of causal tie over and above regularity.

One group of empiricists, the logical positivists, including Rudolf CARNAP, argued that even these questions were nonsense and that metaphysics is therefore not a legitimate pursuit (see LOGICAL POSITIVISM/LOGICAL EMPIRICISM). The so-called metaphysical questions were to be answered not by any appeal to experience but by fiat, by deciding to adopt one framework rather than another as a tool to describe the world. It could be phenomenalistic or materialistic; it could assume a resemblance account of sameness or one that took characteristics to be universals; it could use a logic with causal modalities (see MODALITY) or one without such necessities. Cognitively, it makes no difference; one simply chooses the framework that is most convenient. Since the problems are solved by decision, those problems are, cognitively speaking, nonsense. Other empiricists, however, such as W.V.O. QUINE and Gustav BERGMANN, have argued that some frameworks do solve such traditional problems as that of sameness while others do not. Insofar as we can thus offer reasons for adopting one framework rather than another, the decision is not merely a fiat: it has cognitive content. Metaphysics therefore remains a legitimate pursuit, even for an empiricist.

BIBLIOGRAPHY

Books

Ayer, A. J. *Language, Truth and Logic*. 2d ed. New York: Dover, 1952.
Bergmann, G. *Meaning and Existence*. Madison: University of Wisconsin Press, 1960.
Quine, W.V.O. *From a Logical Point of View*. Cambridge: Harvard University Press, 1953.
Russell, B. *The Problems of Philosophy*. London: Oxford University Press, 1962.
Sellars, W. *Science, Perception and Reality*. London: Routledge and Kegan Paul, 1963.

Article

Russell, B. "Lectures on Logical Atomism." In *Logic and Knowledge*, edited by R. C. Marsh. London: Allen and Unwin, 1956.

FRED WILSON

MILL, JOHN STUART. The philosophy of John Stuart Mill (1806–1873) was in the tradition of the British empiricism of LOCKE, BERKELEY, and HUME. However, he made strenuous efforts to incorporate what he called the reaction of the nineteenth century upon the eighteenth into his thought. In his mind, the eighteenth century was represented by the ethical and social thought of Jeremy Bentham (1748–1832) and the nineteenth by the thought of Samuel Taylor Coleridge (1772–1834). (See Mill's essays "Bentham" and "Coleridge" in *The Collected Works of John Stuart Mill*, vol. 10.) As an empiricist, he adopted a position close to the PHENOMENALISM of Berkeley. He was influenced by Hume's views on CAUSATION, but he was close to Locke in his lack of interest in skeptical moves in epistemology and in his rejection of innate principles. Like Locke and Hume, he had an extraordinary breadth of interest, making major contributions to ETHICS, political and social philosophy, and economics as well as to topics in logic and epistemology. He was the outstanding spokesman of his time for liberal policies and practices in politics, economics, and the moral life.

He was educated by his father, James Mill (1773–1836), who was close to Bentham and an advocate of political reform in the direction of greater democratic representation. John Stuart Mill describes his remarkable education in the first chapter of his autobiography (*Collected Works* I). He began to learn Greek by the age of three and Latin by the age of eight. Soon after, he was reading the Greek poets and learning geometry and algebra. By the age of thirteen he was familiar with the intricacies of the then-new science of political economy. Mill's father, however, did not aim at cramming information into his young mind. "Anything which could be found out by thinking, I never was told, until I had exhausted my efforts to find it out for myself" (*Collected Works* I: 35). He was brought up from the first without any religious belief, and his major philosophical views are quite independent of the influence of any religious position. "I am thus one of the very few examples, in this country, of one who has not thrown off religious belief, but never had it" (*Collected Works* I: 45).

Mill describes his early education as "a course of Benthamism" (*Collected Works* I: 67). The most important thing he learned from Bentham is to reject a priori reasoning in matters of morals and legislation (see A PRIORI/A POSTERIORI DISTINCTION). Terms like "law of nature" and "the moral sense" he came to believe were "dogmatism in disguise" (*Collected Works* I: 67). Bentham's standard of the greatest happiness superseded that of all previous moralists. Mill felt that he had acquired a mission in life to contribute to the reform of British institutions according to the political liberalism and utilitarian morality that Bentham and his father advocated.

In 1823 Mill received an appointment from the East India Company to work in the office of the examiner of East India Correspondence, a position he held until his retirement thirty-five years later.

In 1826, Mill experienced what he described as a crisis in his mental history. He asked himself whether he would be happy if his mission in life was actually realized, and he answered "No!"

At this my heart sank within me: the whole foundation on which my life was constructed fell down. All my happiness was to have been found in the continual pursuit of this end. The end had ceased to charm, and how could there ever again be any interest in the means? I seemed to have nothing left to live for. (*Collected Works* I: 139)

He thought that the deep depression he was then experiencing was caused by an education that had failed to inculcate the ability to experience emotional identification with the good of others. "My education, I thought, had failed to create these feelings in sufficient strength to resist the dissolving influence of analysis, while the whole course of my intellectual cultivation had made precocious and premature analysis the inveterate habit of my mind" (*Collected Works* I: 143).

Gradually, his depression lifted, and, as a result of his crisis, he modified his views of life in two ways. First, even though he retained Bentham's view that happiness is the end of life, he realized that in order to attain happiness, one must not aim at it directly; it is most reliably experienced as a by-product of the realization of other ends. Second, he recognized the importance of the cultivation of the feelings and a balance between intellect and emotion in the development of the personality, and he emphasized "the importance of poetry and art as instruments of human culture" (*Collected Works* I: 147). In particular,

Mill credited his reading of the poetry of Wordsworth as one of the major factors in the lifting of his depression.

At about this time, Mill modified his strict adherence to Benthamism. "The influences of European, that is to say, Continental, thought, and especially those of the reaction of the nineteenth century against the eighteenth, were now streaming in upon me" (*Collected Works* I: 169). From his reading of Coleridge, Goethe, and Carlyle, he came to the conclusion that "all questions of political institutions are relative, not absolute, and that different stages of human progress not only will have, but ought to have, different institutions" (*Collected Works* I: 169). He became more sympathetic to socialism through his study of the St. Simonian school in France, particularly the writings of Auguste COMTE, although late in his life (1879) he composed a series of papers on socialism (*Collected Works* V) that were severe in their criticisms of it.

In 1830, Mill was introduced to Mrs. Harriet Taylor, "the most admirable person I had ever known" (*Collected Works* I: 193), with whom he established a close emotional and intellectual relationship that persisted through the twenty-one subsequent years that she continued to be married to Mr. Taylor. After her husband's death, they were married in April 1851; the marriage lasted until her death seven years later. Mill credited his wife with being the source of some of his most important ideas. "All my published writings," he says, "were as much her work as mine" (*Collected Works* I: 251). Mill was elected to a seat in Parliament in 1865 as a member of the Liberal Party but failed to be reelected in 1868. While in Parliament, he became a strong advocate for female suffrage and in general defended positions characteristic of advanced Liberalism. He died in 1873.

The major text for Mill's epistemology is his *A System of Logic* (*Collected Works* VII and VIII), first published in 1843 and frequently revised in subsequent editions. It contains original ideas about MEANING, the foundations of MATHEMATICS, and scientific reasoning, with special emphasis on INDUCTION. The central thesis of *A System of Logic* is that all knowledge is founded either on the observation of particulars or on inductive inference whose premises are furnished by observation of particulars. In this respect he differs from both Locke and Hume. Locke allowed that we can have a priori knowledge of the relations of the contents of our ideas and that while some of this knowledge is trifling (what KANT later classified as analytic; see ANALYTIC/SYNTHETIC DISTINCTION), some of it, especially mathematical knowledge, is instructive and real (what Kant labeled as synthetic) (Locke, *An Essay concerning Human Understanding* IV.viii.8). Following Locke, Hume claimed that the truths of mathematics are intuitively and/or demonstratively certain, that they are discoverable "by the mere operation of thought" (Hume, *An Enquiry concerning Human Understanding*: 25). Mill, on the contrary, doubted that there is a faculty of intuition and insisted that mathematical knowledge consists of generalizations derived from experience by inductive reasoning.

Mill distinguished between real and verbal propositions. A verbal truth is a proposition of universal affirmative subject-predicate form "in which the predicate connotes the whole or part of what the subject connotes, but nothing besides" (*Collected Works* VII: 113). A real proposition states a matter of fact. He recognizes that the distinction between real and verbal corresponds to Kant's distinction between synthetic and analytic (*Collected Works* VII: 116n). The existence of verbal propositions does not, Mill thinks, represent a challenge to empiricism because they do not convey any knowledge. They

do not relate to any matter of fact, in the proper sense of the term, at all, but to the meaning of names. Since names and their signification are entirely arbitrary, such propositions are not, strictly speaking, susceptible of truth or falsity, but only of conformity or disconformity to usage or convention. (*Collected Works* VII: 108)

Thus, the very propositions that Locke took as paradigm cases of knowledge Mill takes as mere expressions of verbal conventions.

Mill rejected the then-dominant view of mathematics put forward by Kant that mathematical truths are necessary, synthetic a priori, and absolutely certain and also the view of Hume that they are analytic and thus a priori. For Mill, "there is in every step of an arithmetical or algebraic calculation a real induction, a real inference of facts from facts" (*Collected Works* VII: 254). He interpreted a statement of numerical equality such as "2 + 1 = 3" as a statement of identity but argued that this character did not mean that it is trifling or analytic.

The expression "two pebbles and one pebble," and the expression "three pebbles," stand indeed for the same aggregation of objects, but they by no means stand for the same physical fact. They are names of the same objects, but of those objects in two different states: though they denote the same things, their connotation is different. (*Collected Works* VII: 256)

Mill here anticipates Frege's explanation (in his "Sense and Reference") of how identity statements can be informative.

Similarly, a geometrical truth such as "Two straight lines do not enclose a space" is an inductively confirmed approximate truth: "it receives confirmation in almost every instant of our lives, since we cannot look at any two straight lines which intersect one another, without seeing that from that point they continue to diverge more and more. Experimental proof crowds in upon us in such endless profusion" (*Collected Works* VII: 231–32). Because mathematical truths have such a high level of confirmation, they possess a greater degree of certainty than do truths of the other sciences. There is, therefore, no need to postulate a faculty of intellectual intuition to account for their certainty.

The friends of a priori knowledge claim, in opposition to Mill, that we are in possession of a criterion for determining a priori that a proposition is true: if we are unable to conceive or imagine its falsehood, if we cannot represent to ourselves a possible world in which its negation is true, then it follows that it is necessarily true and that we know it to be true, not by induction from observed instances but by intellectual intuition. Mill argues against this criterion by asserting that the fact that something is inconceivable depends not on any objective necessity it is alleged to possess but on associations established by experience. The profusion of observed confirmations of mathematical truths causes us to be unable to conceive what it would be like for them to be false.

Although Mill's theory of mathematical truths as empirical generalizations ultimately verified by experience was later rejected by LOGICAL POSITIVISM, which argued that they are analytic, it was subsequently revived by QUINE, who, like Mill, denied that any knowledge of the world is necessary. But whereas Mill claimed that these truths are direct inductions from observed instances, Quine adopted a holistic and pragmatic point of view according to which mathematical truths occupy a central role in our system of beliefs whose epistemic worth is determined by its overall success in prediction and explanation.

Mill utilized the distinction between connotation and denotation in order to explain how arithmetical equalities can be both true and informative. A connotative general term such as "white" connotes the attribute whiteness and denotes all white things. Our knowledge of the connotation enables us to apply general terms to a variety of different particulars. Mill also claimed that proper names are not connotative; "they do not indicate or imply any attributes as belonging to those individuals" (*Collected Works* VII: 33). Mill accepted the existence of attributes but denied the Platonistic view that regarded them "as a peculiar kind of substances, having an objective existence distinct from the individual objects classed under them" (*Collected Works* VII: 174). However, Mill was a realist in thinking of an attribute as a universal, that is, as a "One in the Many" (*Collected Works*, Vol. VII: 179n), and explicitly rejected the idea that an attribute is a particular, though an abstract one. Mill rejected both the conceptualism or IDEA theory of Locke according to which a proposition represents a relation among ideas and the NOMINALISM of HOBBES that attempts to account for our ability to apply general terms without bringing universals into the picture. Mill's moderate realism concerning the existence of universals distinguishes his ontology from the nominalism of Locke, Berkeley, and Hume, according to which everything that exists is particular.

His realism, however, is not consistent with his conventionalist theory of verbal or analytic truths. Given his account of the meanings of concrete general terms, the proposition that a square has four sides is true in virtue of the fact that the attribute of having four sides is included within the attribute of being a square. Since attributes are actual entities, this fact of inclusion is a fact about a relation among realities and is not to be confused with the statement that the word "square" in English means, among other things, being four-sided. The latter is a formulation of a verbal convention and is an empirical truth whereas the former is known in virtue of our knowledge of the content of an attribute and is true a priori.

Attributes, then, are common properties of bodies that also function as the meanings of concrete general terms. Mill attempted to incorporate this moderate realism into his phenomenalist account of our knowledge of the external world: "[W]e know not, and cannot know, anything of bodies but the sensations which they excite in us or in others." Since we know bodies through their observable attributes, it follows that "those sensations must be all that we can, at bottom, mean by their attributes" (*Collected Works* VII: 65). In his later work, *An Examination of Sir William Hamilton's Philosophy* (1865), Mill defined matter as "a Permanent Possibility of Sensation" (*Collected Works* IX: 183) and in this respect counted himself a follower of Berkeley.

However, unlike Berkeley, Mill attempted to apply phenomenalism to mind as well as to matter. Just as a material object is the possibility of a series of sensations, so the mind of an individual is likewise the possibility of a series of sensations. It seems as if the basic entities in Mill's ontology are sensations ordered in various series. Empiricists usually think of individual sensations as particular, and Mill agrees: "Particulars alone are capable of being subjected to observation" (*Collected Works* VII: 193). It is not clear how this ontology can be made consistent with Mill's moderate realism; there seems to be no room within his phenomenalism for attributes as universals. Mill acknowledged another problem that he felt to be intractable. How can a series of sensations be aware of itself? He does not know how to answer this question and says, "I do not profess to have adequately accounted for belief in mind" (*Collected Works* IX: 196).

Another difficulty with his phenomenalism, one that he fails to recognize, is that he tends to think of material things as the causes of our sensations while simultaneously defining them as possibilities of sensation (*Collected Works* IX: 181). Yet if a cause is an actual entity, possibilities cannot function as causes. In *A System of Logic*, Mill was attracted to Kant's view that phenomena are produced by unknown causes. "For, as our conception of a body is that of an unknown exciting cause of sensations, so our conception of a mind is that of an unknown recipient, or percipient of them"(*Collected Works* VII: 63). His treating possibilities as if they are actualities is likely the product of this residual Kantianism that he never completely shed.

One of the most famous theses of *A System of Logic* is his view of inference and of general propositions: "All inference is from particulars to particulars: General propositions are merely registers of such inferences already made and short formulae for making more" (*Collected Works* VII: 193). This claim is the conclusion of his theory of the role and function of the syllogism. Consider the syllogism "All men are mortal; Socrates is a man; therefore, Socrates is mortal." On one hand, it seems as if the conclusion is already contained within the premises, and thus no new knowledge is produced. In that case the syllogism would be an instance of the fallacy of *petitio principii*. On the other hand, it seems as if reasoning of this sort is capable of convincing us of new truths. Mill attempts to resolve this dilemma by saying that the syllogism is not actually a case of reasoning that yields new knowledge but is an interpretation of what the major premise means in a particular case. The major premise functions as an inference ticket that licenses us to accept the conclusion. General propositions are, in Mill's words, "merely abridged statements, in a kind of short-hand, of the particular facts, which, as occasion arises, we either think we may proceed on as proved, or intend to assume" (*Collected Works* VII: 192). To believe a general proposition is just to be disposed to assert such particular facts as are represented in the conclusion. In order to establish that Socrates is mortal, we do not need to pass through the major and minor premises of the syllogism. Our knowledge of his mortality is in fact based on an induction covering the mortality of countless other men. The major premise merely registers this past induction and reminds us that we can employ its results to new instances.

In Mill's epistemology, "the only things we can observe directly [are] our own sensations, or other feelings" (*Collected Works* VIII: 698). Knowledge of all other facts is attained by inductive inference. As Mill characterizes it, induction is the process of justifying a generalization by sampling, that is, by appealing to observed instances. Every inductive inference assumes that nature is uniform, a principle that Mill explains as equivalent to the law of causation, "the truth that every fact which has a beginning has a cause" (*Collected Works* VII: 325). Consistent with his empiricism is Mill's claim that the uniformity of nature is itself justified by induction. The methods of inductive inference assume that there is a law to be found, and the process of discovering that phenomena are instances of laws provides further confirmation of nature's uniformity.

Mill seems not to have been bothered by Hume's famous SKEPTICISM about induction. Hume would have objected that on Mill's account inductive reasoning is circular because the very law it is alleged to presuppose is itself justified by induction. Mill's way out is to claim that our initial inductions impart some probability to their conclusions independently of the law of causation, which is then inferred from laws previously established. Once the law of causation has been justified, it imparts an additional confirmation to the laws originally inferred without it. This solution does not seem consistent with Mill's claim that all inductions presuppose the uniformity of nature, but perhaps the inconsistency can be removed by interpreting him to mean that the principle of uniformity is necessary to increase the probability of every inductive inference, but not to impart the initial probability. The skeptic would then ask why the fact that Socrates, Plato, Aristotle, and other men have been observed to be mortal imparts any likelihood at all to the generalization that all men are mortal since it includes many facts quite independent of the initial sample. It is not clear what Mill would reply other than to point out that inductive extrapolation from an observed sample is the established practice in rigorous scientific inquiries.

In his discussion of scientific practice, Mill seldom refers to the phenomenalism that constitutes the official foundation of his epistemology. Rather, he frequently sounds like a scientific realist according to whom scientific theories refer to such unobservables as atoms and the ether. He concedes that scientists frequently infer facts beyond what the senses are capable of revealing. But he fails to distinguish the method of inferring such facts (which is today usually called inference to the best explanation) from induction proper, which consists in generalization from an observed sample. When discussing the hypothetical method, he claims that the formation of the hypothesis is a case of induction, not realizing that hypotheses frequently bring into the picture facts about unobservables. Thus, because of the phenomenalism lurking in the background, he does not see the need to clarify the distinction between induction and inference to best explanation.

Mill made some important additions to his empiricist theory of knowledge in the famous second chapter of *On Liberty*, in which he defends the liberty of thought and discussion. He argued there that the political authorities are never justified in preventing people from discussing any question whatever. "To refuse a hearing to an opinion because [the authorities] are sure that it is false is to assume that their certainty is the same thing as absolute certainty. All silencing of discussion is an assumption of infallibility" (*Collected Works* XVIII: 229). This assumption is mistaken. Mill here anticipates the view that C. S. PEIRCE later called fallibilism, according to which no belief is absolutely certain, so that we should be prepared to revise any belief in the light of subsequent experience.

Liberty of discussion is important not merely to fix our beliefs but also to guide our actions in the light of our beliefs. With respect to the relation of belief to practice, Mill puts forward the following principle: "Complete liberty of contradicting and disproving our opinion, is the very condition which justifies us in assuming its truth for purposes of action" (*Collected Works* XVIII: 231). Liberty is a condition of rational belief and action. In his formal epistemological writings, Mill emphasized the role of experience as the basis for justified belief. In his defense of freedom, he claims that experience alone is never sufficient to assure ourselves that we are not mistaken. "There must be discussion to show how experience is to be interpreted" (*Collected Works* XVIII: 231). The only way to be sure that we have interpreted it correctly is to enter the marketplace of ideas and engage strenuously with criticisms. "The beliefs which we have most warrant for have no safeguard to rest on but a standing invitation to the whole world to prove them unfounded" (*Collected Works* XVIII: 232).

Even if it turns out that one's belief is true and is free from all error, it does not follow that our holding it is rational in the absence of discussion. A necessary condition for our belief to be rational is that we know what can be said against it, and we are able to refute criticisms offered by those who hold contrary views. Furthermore, in the absence of critical discussion, beliefs turn into dead formulas, and their meaning fails to be understood.

Moreover, Mill points out, the opinions of people are often one-sided, and the truth frequently resides in some way of synthesizing and reconciling opposing views.

Truth, in the great practical concerns of life, is so much a question of the reconciling and combining of opposites, that very few have minds sufficiently capacious and impartial to make the adjustment with an approach to correctness, and it has to be made by the rough process of a struggle between combatants fighting under hostile banners. (*Collected Works* XVIII: 254)

We see, then, that when we turn to "the great practical concerns of life," an empiricist theory of inferential justification of the sort that Mill worked out in *A System of Logic* must be supplemented by a theory of the interactions that ought to occur within the community of concerned citizens if our beliefs are to count as rational. In *A System of Logic*, Mill recognized that "in almost every act of our perceiving faculties, observation and inference are intimately blended" (*Collected Works* VIII: 641–42). This was really a consequence of the associationist psychology that James Mill advocated and that his son adopted (see ASSOCIATIONISM). We cannot easily separate the data of experience from the interpretations we impose upon it. By the time he came to compose *On Liberty*, he recognized the need for criticism and discussion in order to provide assurance that the interpretations that we are barely conscious of making are not prejudices derived from tradition and authority.

As we can see from his epistemological remarks in *On Liberty*, Mill recognized that reflection on the problem of knowledge had great practical significance and was not merely a topic for abstract speculation. In particular, he believed that a philosophy based on intuitionism and the a priori is an enemy of radical reform:

The practical reformer has continually to demand that changes be made in things which are supported by powerful and widely spread feelings, or to question the apparent necessity and indefeasibleness of established facts; and it is often an indispensable part of his argument to shew, how these powerful feelings had their origin, and how those facts came to seem necessary and indefeasible. There is therefore a natural hostility between him and a philosophy which discourages the explanation of feelings and moral facts by circumstances and association, and prefers to treat them as ultimate elements of human nature; a philosophy which is addicted to holding up favourite doctrines as intuitive truths, and deems intuition to be the voice of Nature and of God, speaking with an authority higher than that of our reason. In particular, I have long felt that the prevailing tendency to regard all the marked distinctions of human character as innate, and in the main indelible, and to ignore the irresistible proofs that by far the greater part of those differences, whether between individuals, races, or sexes, are such as not only might but naturally would be produced by differences in circumstances, is one of the chief hindrances to the rational treatment of great social questions and one of the great stumbling blocks to human improvement. This tendency has its source in the intuitional metaphysics which characterized the reaction of the nineteenth century against the eighteenth. (*Collected Works* I: 269–70)

For Mill, radical empiricism is not merely a correct account of the foundations of human knowledge but is also the precondition for bringing a decent society into existence.

In his ethics, Mill adopted the utilitarianism of Bentham and of James Mill according to which those actions, practices, and institutions are desirable that contribute to the greatest happiness for the greatest number. However, he objected to Bentham's purely quantitative approach to the determination of happiness because it implies that it might be better to be a satisfied fool than a dissatisfied Socrates. In his *Utilitarianism* (1863) (*Collected Works* X), he proposed that quality be taken into account as well as quantity and argued for a preference test among people of wide experience as the way to determine superiority in quality.

For Mill, ethical theory is of interest not merely because it clarifies our existing moral sensibility but because it may lead to improved opinions about moral issues. He opposed the intuitionist epistemology in ethics that appeals to the alleged self-evidence of preferred principles on the grounds that it is just a way of defending prevailing opinions. For Mill, since "the moral feelings . . . are eminently artificial, and the product of culture" ("Dr. Whewell on Moral Philosophy," *Collected Works* X: 179), the appeal to intuition is equivalent to a defense of things as they are. The advantage of utilitarianism is that it appeals to an outward standard rather than to culturally conditioned emotions disguised as self-evident principles. Thus, ethical disagreements are resolvable by an empirical test: just see which course of action produces more happiness in quantity and quality than the alternatives, and that is the one to be chosen. There are, however, well-known difficulties in measuring utility and in determining the fair distribution of benefits, so it is doubtful that the principle of utility is able to provide a direct empirical test as Mill thought.

But even if it did, the question would arise about the status of the principle itself. Is it itself an empirical generalization inductively confirmed? Or is it an a priori truth justified by an appeal to reason and intuition? Mill attempted to answer these questions in the final chapter of *A System of Logic*. There he classified morality as an art that speaks in imperatives and rules rather than a science that refers to matters of fact. The utilitarian morality, then, is a product of art that pronounces the greatest happiness of the greatest number to be the most desirable end of human conduct and the test of the desirability of all other ends. The claim that the greatest happiness of the greatest number is the end of human life is not, according to Mill, an assertion of a matter of fact; it does not assert that anything is the case; it is a recommendation about what ought to be the case. So it is neither an intuitive truth nor an inductively justified empirical claim.

Mill claims, however, that a statement about what ought to be involves a certain type of matter of fact: "The fact affirmed in them is, that the conduct recommended excites in the speaker's mind the feeling of approbation" (*Collected Works* VIII: 949). So it looks as if ethical propositions interpreted as recommendations express feelings of approval and disapproval. This would bring Mill close to Hume's subjectivist moral epistemology. However, he points out that the fact that one person approves of a course of action is no reason anyone else should approve. Approvals themselves need to be justified by an appeal to general premises that specify the proper objects of approbation. Mill thinks that the principle of utility is the "general principle to which all rules of practice ought to conform, and the test by which they should be tried'' (*Collected Works* VIII: 951). But this leaves the principle of utility up in the air. It is either an object of approbation or something else. If it is an object of approbation, it needs to be justified by a more ultimate principle; and if it is something else, what that is has been left undetermined. So it cannot be said that Mill was successful in defending empiricism in ethics against the intuitionists or that he was successful in showing that there is an acceptable, objective, nonarbitrary standard of human conduct.

PRIMARY WORKS

The Collected Works of John Stuart Mill. Gen. ed. J. M. Robson. 33 vols. London and Toronto: Routledge and University of Toronto Press, 1962–1991.

OTHER PRIMARY TEXTS

Frege, Gottlob. ''Sense and Reference.'' In *Translations from the Philosophical Writings of Gottlob Frege*, edited by Peter Geach and Max Black. Oxford: Basil Blackwell, 1952.
Hume, David. *An Enquiry concerning Human Understanding*. In *Enquiries concerning Human Understanding and concerning the Principles of Morals*, edited with an analytical index by L. A. Selby-Bigge; revised with notes by P. H. Nidditch. Oxford: Clarendon Press, 1975.
Locke, John. *An Essay concerning Human Understanding*. Edited with an introduction by P. H. Nidditch. Oxford: Clarendon Press, 1975.

BIBLIOGRAPHY

Anschutz, R. P. *The Philosophy of J. S. Mill*. Oxford: Clarendon Press, 1953.
Berger, Fred R. *Happiness, Justice and Freedom: The Moral and Political Philosophy of John Stuart Mill*. London: University of California Press, 1984.
Britton, Karl. *John Stuart Mill*. London: Penguin, 1953.
Cowling, Maurice. *Mill and Liberalism*. Cambridge: Cambridge University Press, 1963.
Halévy, Elie. *The Growth of Philosophic Radicalism*. Boston: Beacon Press, 1955.
Himmelfarb, Gertrude. *On Liberty and Liberalism: The Case of John Stuart Mill*. New York: Alfred A. Knopf, 1974.
Jackson, Reginald. *An Examination of the Deductive Logic of John Stuart Mill*. London: Oxford University Press, 1941.
Packe, Michael St. John. *The Life of John Stuart Mill*. New York: Macmillan, 1954.
Ryan, Alan. *Mill*. London: Routledge and Kegan Paul, 1974.
Schneewind, J. B., ed. *Mill: A Collection of Critical Essays*. Garden City, NY: Doubleday, 1968.
———. *Sidgwick's Ethics and Victorian Moral Philosophy*. Oxford: Clarendon Press, 1977.
Semmel, Bernard. *John Stuart Mill and the Pursuit of Virtue*. New Haven, CT: Yale University Press, 1984.
Skorupski, John. *John Stuart Mill*. London and New York: Routledge, 1989.
Stephen, James Fitzjames. *Liberty, Equality, Fraternity*. Cambridge: Cambridge University Press, 1967.
Ten, C. L. *Mill on Liberty*. Oxford: Clarendon Press, 1980.

CHARLES LANDESMAN

MIND–BODY PROBLEM. Roughly speaking, "the mind-body problem" has to do with the relation between minds and bodies or between psychological events and physical events. Looked at historically, it has been a shifting cluster of diverse problems. It began with questions like these: Is it, at least in principle, possible for a strictly physical system to have thoughts? If this is not possible, if, for instance, there must be an incorporeal spirit in us that does the thinking, how are these spirits related to our bodies? Does the spirit move the body? How can it do so?

HOBBES was what is now called an "identity theorist." He held that mental events just *are* physical events of various kinds. A human being is a complex physical system. LOCKE was an agnostic in this regard—not a materialist but not a wholehearted dualist. God, he held, may have the power to create strictly material entities that can think and feel. Perhaps we have (or are) physical "spirits." On the other hand, he thought, it seems far more reasonable to suppose that our spirits are immaterial (like God). BERKELEY was bolder. He was certain that we are incorporeal. In fact, as he saw it, there is no such thing as "matter" in the philosophical sense of the term.

In the nineteenth century, John Stuart MILL was in substantial agreement with Berkeley in regard to minds and the physical world. He was a phenomenalist in regard to the physical world (see PHENOMENALISM) and a realist in regard to minds. As he saw it, "matter" is a permanent possibility of sensation, and a "mind" is a series of thoughts linked by memories (and, perhaps, expectations)—a "thread of consciousness." From this perspective, the original mind–body problems seem to vanish, although other problems spring up to take their place.

At the end of the twentieth century, most of the people who worry about "the mind–body problem" are realists in regard to the physical world. Furthermore, there is widespread agreement that it is possible for physical systems (e.g., horses and humans) to have thoughts and feelings. That is no longer a central issue. There are, however, still many problems in this area. Consider the best theory of human psychology presently available. Call it B (for Best). We assume that B employs terms like "pain," "belief," "desire," and so on, terms taken from everyday, common-sense talk about psychological matters. B includes claims like, "Prolonged pain tends to cause depression." Is B reducible to neurophysiology plus various facts about the physical world? Is neurophysiology reducible to chemistry and physics? In short, is our best psychology reducible (via a series of reductions) to physics? Let us call the doctrine that it is thus reducible "reductive physicalism" in regard to psychological facts.

The *identity theorists* (for instance, J.J.C. Smart) held that psychological terms like "pain" designate particular kinds of neurophysiological states, events, propensities, and so on. Pain, they said, just *is* "the firing of c-fibers," or whatever. Clearly, the identity theory was compatible with reductive physicalism in regard to the psychological realm. Unfortunately, the identity theory (in its original "type-type" form, according to which mental properties or "types" are identical with physical properties or "types") seems plainly false. For one thing, aliens from outer space or some actual animals may feel pain but lack c-fibers.

Eliminative materialists (for instance, Paul Churchland) hold that our commonsense psychology is not reducible to neurophysiology. For this and other reasons, they think that it is a bad, false theory, like alchemy or astrology. Presumably, the condemnation would apply to B as well.

Machine functionalism is (or was until recently) a popular replacement for the identity theory. Roughly speaking, machine functionalists (for instance, Hilary Putnam in the 1960s and 1970s) think of mental states as being something like the various states of a Turing machine. That is, a particular mental state is defined by its causal relations to "input," to other mental states, and to behavioral "output."

Functionalism (in a more general sense) is the view that mental terms (e.g., "pain," and "depression") are functional terms, like "valve lifter" and "mousetrap." Mental states are defined by their job, their role, not by the physical setup that happens to embody that state in a particular kind of animal or on a particular occasion. Mental states are "multiply realizable." Functionalism (in the more general sense) is plainly incompatible with the identity theory (in its original "type-type" form).

What about reductive physicalism? Can reductionists accept functionalism? Hartry Field (in "Physicalism") argues for a "weakened" version of reductionism ("quasireductionism") designed, in part, to accommodate functionalism. Both the new version and the old entail that if something (e.g., depression) is correctly explained in B, then it must be possible to transcribe the explanation into the language of physics and to explain in physical terms why the transcribed explanation is correct. "[A]ll good explanations ultimately depend entirely on physical explanations." That is the heart of reductive physicalism. It is a bold claim. But is it true in regard to B? The answer is as yet unclear.

Nothing has been said here about consciousness, intentionality, "qualia" (e.g., the taste of anchovies), and mental representations. These topics (and several others) are at least as interesting and arguably as relevant to "the mind–body problem" as the ones discussed.

BIBLIOGRAPHY

Books

Lycan, William G., ed. *Mind and Cognition, A Reader.* Cambridge, MA, and Oxford: Basil Blackwell, 1990.
Warner, Richard, and Tadeusz Szubka, eds. *The Mind–Body Problem, A Guide to the Current Debate.* Oxford and Cambridge, MA: Basil Blackwell, 1994.

Articles

Field, Hartry. " Physicalism." In *Inference, Explanation, and Other Frustrations, Essays in the Philosophy of Science*, edited by John Earman. Berkeley: University of California Press, 1992.

Putnam, Hilary. "Robots: Machines or Artificially Created Life?" *Journal of Philosophy* 61 (1964): 668–90.

Smart, J J.C. "Sensations and Brain Processes." *Philosophical Review* 68 (1959): 141–56.

HUGH CHANDLER

MODALITY (NECESSITY AND POSSIBILITY). Factual modality pertains to a given world, whereas logical modality encompasses all possible worlds. For instance, in our world it is factually impossible for human beings to survive without oxygen for more than a few minutes, but there are logically possible worlds in which this is common.

Empiricists can find this distinction useful if, like LOCKE and HUME, they ground beliefs about the actual world in experience and maintain that beliefs in MATHEMATICS and LOGIC are a priori beliefs about possible worlds (see A PRIORI/A POSTERIORI DISTINCTION). But some empiricists want to go further than this. They want to establish that even beliefs in logic and mathematics must be empirically grounded. Some argue that they are inductive generalizations (such as MILL, Bolzano). Others treat them as part of a larger explanatory system, the worth of which depends on its ability to accommodate empirical input (see QUINE). This highly aggressive empiricism seems to strip the concept of logical necessity of its application. It argues that theories in logic and mathematics are just as revisable as other theories, and revisable theories do not seem to be necessary truths.

If empiricism wants to keep logical necessity as an object of inquiry, it must do something about revisability. Some (e.g., Alvin Plantinga) think it can solve the problem by invoking the distinction between logical and epistemic modalities and pointing out that uncertain theorems can still be necessarily true. But the argument from revisability is not an argument from uncertainty. It is the argument that confidence in a belief is grounded in an experience of the fate of similar beliefs, an experience that establishes how inquiry probably will develop in the actual world, not how it develops in every possible world. So according to the argument, a revisable belief is not concerned with logical necessity.

The only way to answer the argument is to distinguish confidence in a belief from the belief itself and insist that the ground for confidence is not the same as the reason to hold the belief. For instance, empiricism must be able to say that whereas Euclid's ground for confidence in one of his theorems is the performance of similar theorems, his reason to accept the theorem is his proof. In that case, although his ground for confidence is empirical, his reason to believe the theorem can be a priori, and although his confidence concerns the actual world, his theorem can concern every possible world. So, although the theorem is revisable because his ground for confidence does not guarantee survival in this world, the theorem can be logically necessary. The challenge empiricism faces is to make good on this distinction. Otherwise, it will have to treat logical modality as a matter of purely idle interest.

PRIMARY WORKS

Bolzano, Bernard. *Theory of Science*. 1837. Edited and translated by Rolf George. Berkeley: University of California Press, 1972.
Hume, David. *Enquiries concerning Human Understanding and concerning the Principles of Morals*. Edited with an analytical index by L. A. Selby-Bigge; revised with notes by P. H. Nidditch. Oxford: Clarendon Press, 1975.
Locke, John. *An Essay concerning Human Understanding*. Edited with an introduction by P. H. Nidditch. Oxford: Clarendon Press, 1975.
Mill, John Stuart. *A System of Logic*. London: J. W. Parker, 1843.

BIBLIOGRAPHY

Plantinga, Alvin. *The Nature of Necessity*. Oxford: Clarendon Press, 1974.
Quine, W.V.O. *From a Logical Point of View*. Cambridge: Harvard University Press, 1953.

DOUGLAS ODEGAARD

MOORE, GEORGE EDWARD. G. E. Moore (1873–1958), one of the twentieth century's most distinguished philosophers, was born in Upper Norwood, a suburb of London, and died in Cambridge. Beginning with a famous book, *Principia Ethica*, and an equally celebrated article, "Refutation of Idealism," both published in 1903, Moore continued throughout his long career to make fundamental contributions to topics with which classical and contemporary empiricists had grappled, such as the relationship between PERCEPTION and KNOWLEDGE and the challenges posed by SKEPTICISM. Yet he cannot correctly be described as an "empiricist." Like them, he rejected any form of IDEALISM or pure rationalism or any form of speculative METAPHYSICS, but he also rejected the empiricist doctrines that contingent propositions are never certain and that SCIENCE alone is the key to reality. He is perhaps better described as inheriting and developing the commonsense tradition of Thomas REID, though even this characterization would ultimately have to be qualified. For example, in his last paper, "Visual Sense-Data," published a year before he died, he defended a sophisticated form of the representative realism found in LOCKE.

Moore's personal life was uneventful, being mainly spent in academic circles. In 1911 he became university lecturer in moral science and in 1925 professor of philosophy at Cambridge University, a post he held until his retirement in 1939. He replaced G. F. Stout as editor of *Mind* in 1921 and served in that capacity for more than twenty years. In 1951 he received the Order of Merit. He was forty-three when he married Dorothy Ely. Moore was a man of simple character, completely devoid of affectation, pose, and pretense. He enjoyed the pleasures of eating, drinking, walking, gardening, and talking with his friends. He is described by his contemporaries as an "exceptional and lovable personality.'' Philosophically, he exhibited immense analytical power. C. D. Broad wrote that ''it is doubtful whether any philosopher known to history has excelled or even equaled Moore in sheer power of analyzing problems, detecting and exposing fallacies and ambiguities, and formulating and working out alternative possibilities.''

Moore's approach to problems was piecemeal and critical and almost entirely directed to issues in epistemology and ETHICS. Despite this restricted focus, his writings and his powerful argumentative personality exercised an enormous influence on philosophers and nonphilosophers alike, setting high standards for making sharp distinctions, for talking in straightforward, ordinary discourse, and for advancing lucid arguments. As Tom Regan has pointed out in *Bloomsbury's Prophet* (1986) the Bloomsbury group—Virginia Woolf, Lytton Strachey, J. M. Keynes, et al.—saw in Moore's *Principia* a philosophy that emphasized the liberation of the individual and the rejection of a life led in conformity with the rules of conventional morality. Apart from these literati, Moore influenced such eminent philosophers as RUSSELL, WITTGENSTEIN, Norman Malcolm, J. T. Wisdom, O. K. Bouwsma, and a host of younger persons, many of whom are still writing today. Russell, for example, swayed by Moore's arguments, eventually abandoned a deep commitment to idealism. As he states in *My Mental Development*, ''He [Moore] took the lead in rebellion, and I followed, with a sense of emancipation.''

The best accounts of Moore's life (as distinct from commentaries on his philosophical views) are to be found in his charming autobiography (in *The Philosophy of G. E. Moore*, 3d ed., 1968: 3–36) and in Ray Monk's *Ludwig Wittgenstein: The Duty of Genius* (1990). In the autobiography, Moore describes his schoolboy days, his parental background, and the intellectual ferment he encountered in Cambridge as an undergraduate. His assessments of such persons as Russell (''I have certainly been more influenced by him than by any other single philosopher''), Ramsey, Stout, Sidgwick, Ward, McTaggart, Henry Jackson, and Wittgenstein are fascinating. Of Wittgenstein he says: ''I soon came to feel that he was much cleverer at philosophy than I was and not only cleverer, but also much more profound.'' Nevertheless, he fails to describe certain relationships he had with these individuals, such as the following. Ray Monk relates that Moore was offended by a letter that Wittgenstein, then a twenty-five-year-old graduate student, had written him in 1914. He severed relationships with Wittgenstein until 1929, when the latter returned to Cambridge as a Ph.D. candidate. Moore and Russell served as his dissertation committee, and Wittgenstein submitted the *Tractatus Logico-Philosophicus*, published seven years previously, as his doctoral thesis. In his report Moore wrote: ''It is my personal opinion that Mr. Wittgenstein's thesis is a work of genius; but, be that as it may, it is certainly well up to the standard required for the Cambridge degree of 'Doctor of Philosophy.' '' In his autobiography, Moore does mention that when he retired as professor, he was ''glad to think'' that Wittgenstein was his successor.

Moore's epistemological writings fall into two (sometimes overlapping) categories: those defending certainty against probabilists, mitigated and radical skeptics, relativists, and conventionalists; and those defending the existence of SENSE-DATA. His most important papers in the former category are "A Defense of Common Sense" (1925), "Proof of an External World" (1939), "Four Forms of Skepticism" (1940), and "Certainty" (1941). His major papers concerning sense-data theory are "The Status of Sense-Data" (1913–1914), "Some Judgments of Perception" (1918–1919), "A Defense of Common Sense, Part IV," (1925), and "Visual Sense-Data" (1957).

"A Defense of Common Sense" contains his strongest defense of certitude. In it, Moore describes what he calls "the common sense view of the world." This consists of a set of propositions that virtually every person knows to be true with certainty. Among these are that "the earth exists," "the earth is very old," "my body [said by any speaker] was smaller at one time than it is now," and "I [said by any speaker] am a human being." Moore says of these propositions that they are *wholly* true and that they entail the existence of external objects and the reality of SPACE and TIME. With respect to the potentially skeptical query, "How do you know these propositions?," Moore responds that he does not know how he knows them to be true or at least that he is less sure how he knows than that he does know them to be true.

From this description of the "common sense view" he draws conclusions that rocked the philosophical world. He states, for example, that if no proposition belonging to the "common sense view" is true, then it follows that no philosopher has ever existed, and therefore no philosopher could have held that no proposition belonging to the "common sense view" is true. He states he is more certain that some philosophers have existed and have held some views than any claim to the effect that the "common sense view" is false. Any philosophical theory to the contrary can thus be dismissed without any detailed examination of its arguments.

Moore's attack on radical skepticism (the doctrine that KNOWLEDGE and certainty are unattainable) is equally powerful. He asserts that skepticism is self-contradictory. When a skeptic says, "No human being has ever known of the existence of other human beings," the skeptic is making a statement about human knowledge in general. It entails that he knows that other human beings now exist and have existed in the past. He is thus asserting that he knows the very things that, according to his theory, no human being has ever known. The theory can thus be dismissed as self-refuting.

In "Certainty," Moore attacks both mitigated and radical forms of skepticism. The mitigated skeptic holds that humans can attain probability, but never certainty, about the world. The radical skeptic goes further, denying that any form of certainty is possible. Moore argues that from the fact that a proposition such as "I am now standing up" is contingent, it does not follow that it cannot be known to be true with certainty or that Moore does not know it to be true with certainty. All that follows is that its negation is not self-contradictory. Moore insists that he knows with certainty that he is now (as he speaks) standing up.

He also admits that he cannot *prove* that he is standing up, but from that fact it does not follow that he does not know that he is standing up. He admits that he cannot prove he is standing up because that would require that he prove that he is not now dreaming, and this, he agrees (with the skeptic), nobody can prove. But he concludes by pointing out that his argument, "I know I am standing up and therefore I know I am not dreaming," is at least as good as the skeptic's argument, "If you are dreaming you do not know you are standing up." Though this does not constitute a complete defeat for the skeptic, it is not a defeat for Moore either. The standoff allowed him to continue his philosophical activities unhindered by skeptical challenges.

Because of Moore's defense of sense-data theory, his views about perception have been more controversial. Moore wished to defend a form of direct realism—the notion that we directly perceive at least parts of the surfaces of physical objects. But he never could overcome "the argument from synthetic incompatibility" that seemed to make such direct perception impossible. The argument can be formulated as follows. We know that a penny is circular and that, being metallic, it does not change its shape under normal conditions of temperature and pressure. But one who sees it from an angle will perceive an ellipse in his visual field. Now nothing can be both elliptical and round at the same time. It follows that in seeing an elliptical object, one is not *directly* seeing the surface of the coin. Moore called what is directly perceived in such a situation (i.e., the elliptical entity) a "sense-datum." What, he asked, is the relationship between the elliptical sense-datum and the circular surface of the penny? If the argument from synthetic incompatibility is correct, it cannot be one of identity. If the relationship is not identity, we do not directly perceive the surface of the coin—and therefore direct realism cannot be true. Two other possibilities are suggested: that the datum is a mental representation of the coin or that some form of PHENOMENALISM is true. For many years Moore could not decide among these options, but in his last paper, "Visual Sense-Data," he finally espoused a form of representative realism.

Moore's writings on moral philosophy also had a revolutionary impact. In his time, the ethical systems that seemed most compatible with empiricism were utilitarianism and various forms of preference and evolutionary theories. In *Principia Ethica*, Moore agreed with the proponents of such doctrines that moral judgments can be either true or false. But in support of an intuitionistic form of moral realism, he developed a devastating argument against what he labeled "the naturalistic fallacy." The fallacy, a form of reductionism, consists in trying to give a definition of a moral concept, "good," in nonmoral terms. According to Moore, "[P]ropositions about the good are all of them synthetic and never analytic" (see ANALYTIC/SYNTHETIC DISTINCTION). It follows that such propositions as "Pleasure is the only good" or "The good is the desired" are synthetic and do not capture the meaning of "good." The result applies to any "naturalistic" property, such as preference, desire, or utility. The argument concludes that goodness is a simple property and is therefore not definable. Moreover, since physical science is reductive, no scientific account of goodness, and therefore of morality, is possible. *Principia*'s position is thus clearly incompatible with a strict empiricist outlook. Hume's notion, for instance, that one could introduce the experimental method into moral subjects was thus rejected. *Principia* was important for another reason. In emphasizing the need to clarify the meaning of such key notions as "good," "the good," "ought," and "right," it began a tradition of metaethics that dominated moral philosophy for much of the century.

PRIMARY WORKS

Principia Ethica. Cambridge: University Press, 1903.
Ethics. London: Oxford University Press, 1912.
Philosophical Studies. London: Routledge and Kegan Paul, 1922.
Philosophical Papers. London: Allen and Unwin, 1959.

BIBLIOGRAPHY

Books

Stroll, Avrum. *Moore and Wittgenstein on Certainty*. New York: Oxford University Press, 1994.
White, A. R. *G. E. Moore, A Critical Exposition*. Oxford: Oxford University Press, 1958.

Article

Malcolm, Norman. "George Edward Moore." In *Knowledge and Certainty*. Englewood Cliffs, NJ: Prentice-Hall, 1963.

AVRUM STROLL

MORAL SKEPTICISM. Moral skepticism is usually defined as the denial of an objective basis of MORALITY (see SKEPTICISM). Contemporary defenders of moral skepticism, such as J. L. Mackie in *Ethics: Inventing Right and Wrong* (1977), see the issue as principally a metaethical one: are there independent moral facts? Is there a special ontological realm in which moral universals reside? This is distinct from the normative issue, which concerns whether one holds to a conventional set of moral guidelines (such as prohibitions against lying or stealing). Seventeenth- and eighteenth-century British discussions of moral skepticism similarly focused on the metaethical and ontological question. Even if a philosopher advocated a traditional set of normative guidelines, denying the independence of moral facts implied that the guidelines were only a matter of custom and could change at a future time. Thus, in the seventeenth- and eighteenth-century context, the term "moral skepticism" was an abusive label that signified that a moral theory presented a danger to traditional moral standards.

What counts as a "moral fact" or an "objective basis of morality" depends on historical context. For example, a theory that reduced morality to human instinct would be exceedingly skeptical by eighteenth-century standards but would be considered optimistic by our own. To know what it means to call a philosopher of that period a moral skeptic, then, requires understanding what counted for the eighteenth century as an "objective basis of morality." The phenomenon of moral obligation involved issues at several levels: God's moral mandates, natural laws, universal moral relations, human moral intuition, and human moral motivation. Objectivity was a factor at all of these levels. At the top of the list, perhaps the most objective view was that moral principles are simply commanded by God, and their existence depends directly on God's will. William Law offers such an argument in his *Essay on the Origin of Evil* (1729). Next on the list is the natural law theory, especially as offered by Hugo Grotius in *de Jure Belli et Pacis* (1625). Grotius extends the ancient Roman notion of judicial natural law to the ethical realm, governing all obligatory behavior. Like mathematics, moral natural laws are rational principles, known a priori, and unalterable even by God. A variation on the natural law view was the *eternal fitness* theory of moral obligation, as offered by Samuel Clarke in *A Discourse concerning the Unchangeable Obligations of Natural Religion* (1706). For Clarke, moral conduct is proper when it *fits* or corresponds with universal moral relations. Such fitness is apparent to all rational beings, and, again, the universal moral relations themselves are unalterable by God.

The next level of issues is epistemological and involves how we acquire knowledge of moral truths. Rationalists such as Grotius and Clarke contended that we grasp them purely rationally, just as we intuit mathematical truths. Riding on Locke's account of sense PERCEPTION (see LOCKE), empirically oriented theorists argued that we perceive moral truths through an internal moral sense. This is the view of the earl of Shaftesbury in his *Characteristics* (1711), Joseph Butler in his *Fifteen Sermons* (1726), and Francis HUTCHESON in his *Illustrations on the Moral Sense* (1755).

The final issue of moral obligation involves our motivation to act morally. Rationalists such as Clarke argued that the intellectual grasp of the moral relations themselves is sufficient motivation. In his *Divine Legation* (1738), William Warburton maintains that God's mandate is required as the prescriptive foundation of morality, although moral universals themselves exist independently of God. Others argued that moral motivation is grounded in human psychology—either natural or learned inclinations.

Given these differing issues, moral skepticism involved taking an antirationalist, antiobjectivist, or antitheistic stance on several (although not necessarily all) of these topics. The first philosopher of the modern period branded a moral skeptic in the preceding sense was Thomas HOBBES, whose skeptical views appear in *Leviathan* (1651). Moral values for Hobbes are derived from social agreement and motivated by self-interest alone. Although Hobbes makes verbal concessions concerning divine moral mandates, morality is functionally a societal creation. He describes society's moral principles as natural laws, but they are not grounded in the fabric of the universe as Grotius believes. Knowledge of the moral laws is arrived at through reasoned deductions given our social condition; however, such moral reasoning is not a matter of a priori INTUITION about the fixed nature of the universe. Finally and most important, the motivation for moral conduct is based on self-interest—not on the rational grasping of the moral laws themselves or divine mandates. Hobbes thus runs counter to moral objectivism in virtually every possible way. For almost a hundred years, his name was synonymous with moral skepticism, and his theory was the principal target for succeeding moral philosophers.

Despite Locke's antirationalist orientation, in matters of morality he is anything but skeptical. The moral law is ultimately the law of God, and, like MATHEMATICS, "morality is capable of demonstration" (*Essay* IV.xii.8; see DEMONSTRATION). Further, divine rewards and punishments are important motivators for proper conduct.

Early moral sense theorists such as Shaftesbury came under mild attack from rationalist moral philosophers. In his *Foundation of Moral Goodness* (1728), John Balguy charges that the moral sense theory undermines the objective nature of morality by making it depend on our sensations. However, few could charge moral sense theorists with moral skepticism. Shaftesbury, for example, argues for the objectivist position that morality is grounded "in the nature of things" (*Characteristics* II: 267). Further, our instinctive social inclinations (as opposed to our selfish ones) are the natural foundation of moral motivation. Butler argues similarly that our more altruistic natural inclinations motivate us.

With the publication of *The Fable of the Bees; or Private Vices, Public Benefits* (1714), Bernard Mandeville came to share Hobbes' title as a moral skeptic. Through a poetic allegory, Mandeville argues that individual vices frequently produce public benefit. For example, envy, vanity, and love of luxury make people spend, and this is necessary for profitable trade. So too with even crimes and wars. Mandeville wrote for a degree of shock value and does not offer a systematic account of moral obligation. However, he shared Hobbes' view that we are driven by self-interest, and he attacked Shaftesbury's contention that we have instinctive social inclinations. BERKELEY sharply criticized Mandeville in Dialogue Two of his *Alciphron* (1732). In that work, Berkeley bases morality on an intellectually perceived beauty of proportionality in "a Providence inspecting, punishing, and rewarding the moral actions of men" (*Alciphron* III: 10). Thus, Berkeley is allied with the moral objectivists.

With the publication of Book III of Hume's *Treatise of Human Nature* in 1740, moral skepticism took a more precise form. Hume opens the work insisting that moral judgments do not involve either rationally grasping moral relations or empirical illumination by a moral sense. Further, God plays no role as either author or motivator of morality. Like Hobbes, our motivation to be moral is based on our psychological makeup. However, for Hume, the most important of our moral motivations are artificially instilled, such as our inclinations toward justice, chastity, and political allegiance. Hume was thus quickly accused of "sapping the foundations of morality" (William Wishart, in *A Letter from a Gentleman*, 1745). When Hume popularized his moral theory in *An Enquiry concerning the Principles of Morals* (1751), his discussion of artificially instilled motives was subdued, and his attack on moral relations was placed in an appendix. He in fact opens this work denouncing those who deny the "reality of moral distinctions," and he recommends that we leave such people to themselves. Emphasis was placed instead on the useful and agreeable consequences of an agent's action as they spark a spectator's moral approval (this discussion formerly appeared only at the close of Book III of the *Treatise*). The change of emphasis prompted a reviewer to write that the *Enquiry* was "free from that sceptical turn which appears in his other pieces." The change in emphasis also redirected British moral theory insofar as the notion of *useful consequences* (i.e., utility) became the litmus test of proper moral conduct.

Bentham adapted Hume's theory of *utility* in his *Principles of Morals and Legislation* (1789). Not only does Bentham dismiss ontological discussions of moral relations and the moral sense, but he rejects the relevance of *any* discussion of the psychology of moral motivation or moral perception. For him, pleasing consequences are all that matter, since only these are empirically quantifiable. Bentham's position was no less "skeptical" than Hume's rejection of moral relations. However, the tide had already turned away from the earlier rationalist and objectivist moral ontologies. By the mid-nineteenth century, MILL could freely argue in *Utilitarianism* (1863) that education (convention) was the principal motivating force behind our pursuit of general happiness. Although Mill's position spawned criticism, moral skepticism was not one of the charges.

Moral skepticism in the early twentieth-century empirical tradition involved issues of language as much as ontology. The key representatives are A. J. AYER in *Language, Truth and Logic* (1936) and C. L. Stevenson in *Ethics and Language* (1944). For them, moral utterances do not even rise to the level of factual statements about the world; instead, such utterances are noncognitive uses of language, mere expressions of feelings, or mere prescriptions.

BIBLIOGRAPHY

Books

Darwall, Stephen. *The British Moralists and the Internal "Ought."* Cambridge: Cambridge University Press, 1995.
Raphael, D. D., ed. *British Moralists: 1650–1800*. Oxford: Clarendon Press, 1969.
Schneewind, J. B., ed. *Moral Philosophy from Montaigne to Kant: An Anthology*. Cambridge: Cambridge University Press, 1990.

Articles

Fieser, James. "Is Hume a Moral Skeptic?" *Philosophy and Phenomenological Research* 50 (1989): 89–106.
Schneewind, J. B. "Natural Law, Skepticism, and Method." *Journal of the History of Ideas* 52 (1991): 289–308.

JAMES FIESER

MORALITY (ETHICS). Empiricists in ethics consider observation and experience a basis for moral principles; they typically presuppose a continuity between the methods in SCIENCE and the methods in ethical theory. On this account, an epistemological empiricist need not be a moral empiricist: one may believe that all knowledge of the natural world begins in experience but deny that morality is part of the natural world or that it is known experientially. (John LOCKE is an early modern thinker who exemplifies this view.) More specifically, moral empiricists use observation of human behavior or psychology in two ways. First, some support conclusions about the source and constitution of human value ("the good") and in turn justify norms for conduct and character that dictate how the value in question ought to be realized. Second, those engaged in metaethics explain the origin of our IDEAS of morality (good and bad, virtue and vice) and give psychological and practical explanations for the norms we accept. These explanatory accounts are sometimes seen as justifying our morality as well. What people generally care about, desire, or approve is arguably indicative of what is valuable for human beings or is at least part of the basis of their value concepts. Since pleasure and pain are universal concerns, moral empiricists typically (although not necessarily) identify these as the states salient to value.

Moral rationalism, in contrast, maintains that value and moral principles can be discerned by REASON without an empirical account of human desire, since the basis of the good is not found in contingent human constitution but is built into a necessary structure—of reason itself, of moral concepts, of the universe so conceived, and so on. Rationalists generally see morality in terms of duty and obligation, arguing that what one ought to do in a given case is not wholly dependent on realizing an observable value in particular circumstances. For example, it may be my duty to tell the truth, irrespective of the pain or pleasure produced by the action. Furthermore, while moral empiricists maintain that what we ought to do is constrained by what we are psychologically capable of doing (assuming that what we care about determines what we can be moved to do), moral rationalists assume without empirical investigation that we are capable of doing what reason tells us we ought to do.

The conception of moral empiricism described here is most clearly exemplified in the eighteenth century. However, the ancient philosopher whose views most closely resemble the early modern moral empiricists is EPICURUS. Epicurus taught that the agent's own pleasure was the highest good and defined pleasure as mental tranquillity and absence of pain. ARISTOTLE deserves passing mention as a philosopher with an empirical approach. His views are based on observation of human activity, and although he does not identify the good with pleasure, he considers pleasure to be an essential ingredient in the happy life.

The rise of modern science in the 1600s leads to a theory of the genesis of moral rules based on a scientific view of human nature. The MATERIALISM of Thomas HOBBES has it that desire is an unpleasant agitation causing animals to "endeavor" toward or away from an object (*Leviathan*, Chapter 6). Given the egoistic condition of all animals, "good" can have no normative (moral)

MEANING in ''the State of Nature.'' Rather, morality is constructed by rational animals who, knowing that life under natural conditions will be fraught with conflict, contract to create moral rights (*Leviathan*, Chapters 8, 14). Ideally, the contract produces a Sovereign who embodies the desires of the subjects. Since the rights conferred are derived from human needs, the contrast between nature and constructed morality does not undermine Hobbes' empiricist approach.

The ''moral sense theorists'' in the eighteenth century are known for describing a continuity between our ideas of the natural world and our ideas in morality. Yet Shaftesbury, who introduces the term ''moral sense'' (in his collected essays, *Characteristics of Men, Manners, Opinions, Times*), has a complex view not clearly empiricist. He argues that human beings have a natural sensibility to beauty (a Platonic quality); one's sense also reflects on, and responds with, admiration or disgust to the order or disorder in one's own internal affections. Thus, it discerns moral character. Francis Hutcheson offers an unambiguously empiricist theory of ''moral perception'' that borrows the framework of LOCKE's epistemology to posit a faculty of moral perception analogous to physical sense perception. On this approach, virtue and vice, detected by natural sentiments humans feel when they contemplate actions or characters, are thought akin to Lockean secondary qualities such as redness and bitterness (see PRIMARY AND SECONDARY QUALITIES), which are perceiver-dependent. Hutcheson argues that any explanation we might offer for feeling approval and disapproval (the moral sentiments) must finally appeal to our unanalyzable psychological disposition to take pleasure in benevolence—a motive that promotes the greatest happiness for the greatest number (*An Inquiry into the Original of Our Ideas of Beauty and Virtue*, Treatise II.3).

David HUME, the most significant opponent of moral rationalism in the same century, begins his case with the argument that reason, the ability to discern truth and falsity, cannot motivate to action by itself. Motivation requires a passion, such as anger or kindness, and the PASSIONS, on Hume's epistemology, are not states of mind that represent anything, accurately or inaccurately. So, motivational states are not objects of reason at all (*A Treatise of Human Nature* II.iii.3). Given this, Hume concludes that reason alone cannot be the source of our morality: awareness of moral rules motivates people to action, and reason alone cannot.

Hume's conclusion about the source of morality is consistent with the moral sense school but derives from his own philosophy of mind. Contrary to Hutcheson's positing of a sui generis moral sense, Hume's project of introducing ''the experimental method of reasoning into moral subjects'' (*Treatise*: title page) compels him to produce a unified principle of explanation for the moral (and the aesthetic) sentiments, which are themselves forms of pleasure and pain: they are products of the faculty of sympathy, the ability to convert our ideas of the pleasures and pains of others into our own experiences (impressions). We sympathize with people affected by the qualities of the character in question and judge these qualities as ''natural'' virtues and vices based on our sentiments. At the same time, we assume a shared perspective that "corrects" for the irregularities in the strength of our sympathies created by our particular relationships to the characters we judge. In this "general point of view" we take on the feelings of the acquaintances close to the character in question (*Treatise* III.iii.1), a procedure resembling appeal to standard conditions in physical perception that corrects for variation in observational circumstances. Adam SMITH's *The Theory of Moral Sentiments* is a further attempt to explain moral sentiments scientifically by the psychology of sympathy, but sympathy here is an ability to imagine others' condition and respond with harmonious feelings.

In the nineteenth century Jeremy Bentham dispenses with the moral sense but retains the principle embodied in Hutcheson's theory: produce the greatest happiness (pleasure) for the greatest number. Bentham's hedonic calculus makes morality quantifiable by offering a method that measures along several parameters (including intensity, duration, and purity) the pleasure or pain a given action would produce. While Benthamite utilitarianism has provoked scathing criticisms questioning the legitimacy of a theory in which "the ends justify the means," utilitarianism is made more palatable in J. S. MILL's *Utilitarianism*. Utilitarianism continues in more sophisticated forms in the twentieth century.

Empiricism in epistemology has informed ethics much more significantly than thinking about ethics itself has informed empiricism. In fact, the legacy of empiricism in ethics is multifaceted. Hume is often (controversially) considered a progenitor to the emotivist line popularized by A. J. AYER in the 1930s: moral claims have no factual content in the way scientific claims do and express only emotions. Contemporary expressivists (Blackburn, Gibbard) hold that our moral language expresses attitudes that allow us to perform all the practical tasks moral community requires—to agree, to disagree, to establish social coordination. Yet, one may question whether the noncognitivists remain inside the empiricist tradition, since they hold that moral discourse makes no commitment to moral qualities in the way scientific discourse commits us to natural qualities. The moral sense school is ancestor to the contemporary sensibility theorists (Wiggins and McDowell), who contend that moral judgments are products of certain sensibilities whose objects are not reducible to properties that are part of the causal/explanatory structure of science. These judgments are cognitive since the properties that they concern are, like colors, a feature of experience regulated by rules of proper judgment. The nonreductive naturalists—contemporary moral realists (Sturgeon)—argue that distinctively *moral* facts serve as explanations of our moral judgments, which are true or false by reference to those facts. Reductive naturalists (Railton) argue that moral discourse just *is* about natural properties, properties that are defined by reference to what motivates human beings. These contemporary cognitivist views are united by the theme that moral inquiry is not a wholly different endeavor from scientific inquiry.

PRIMARY WORKS

Ayer, A. J. *Language, Truth and Logic.* New York: Dover, 1952.

Bentham, Jeremy. *An Introduction to the Principles of Morals and Legislation* (1789). Edited by J. H. Burns and H.L.A. Hart. London: Athlone Press, 1970.

Hobbes, Thomas. *Leviathan* (1651). New York: Dutton, 1950.

Hume, David. *A Treatise of Human Nature.* 2d ed., edited with an analytical index by L. A. Selby-Bigge; revised with notes by P. H. Nidditch. Oxford: Clarendon Press, 1978.

Hutcheson, Francis. *Illustrations on the Moral Sense* (1728). Edited by Bernard Peach. Cambridge: Harvard University Press, 1971.

———. *An Inquiry into the Original of Our Ideas of Beauty and Virtue* (1725). New York: Garland, 1971.

Mill, John Stuart. *Utilitarianism* (1863). Edited by George Sher. Indianapolis, IN: Hackett, 1979.

Shaftesbury, Third Earl (Anthony Ashley Cooper). *Characteristics of Men, Manners, Opinions, Times* (1711). New York: Bobbs-Merrill, 1964.

Smith, Adam. *The Theory of Moral Sentiments* (1759). Edited by D. D. Raphael and M. A. Laurence. Oxford: Clarendon Press, 1976.

BIBLIOGRAPHY

Books

Darwall, Stephen. *The British Moralists and the Internal "Ought": 1640–1740.* Cambridge: Cambridge University Press, 1995.

Raphael, D. D. *The Moral Sense.* Oxford: Oxford University Press, 1947.

Articles

Darwall, Stephen, Allan Gibbard, and Peter Railton. "Toward *Fin de siecle* Ethics: Some Trends." *The Philosophical Review* 101 (1992): 115–89.

McDowell, John. "Values and Secondary Properties." In *Morality and Objectivity,* edited by Ted Honderich. London: Routledge and Kegan Paul, 1985: 110–29.

Railton, Peter. "Moral Realism." *The Philosophical Review* 95 (1986): 163–207.

Sturgeon, Nicholas. "Moral Explanations." In *Morality, Reason and Truth,* edited by D. Copp and D. Zimmerman. Totowa, NJ: Rowman and Allanheld, 1985: 49–78.

ELIZABETH RADCLIFFE

N

NATURALISM. Naturalism is the view that all phenomena are natural. Natural religion can be viewed as an extension of naturalism. Naturalist epistemology and genetic epistemology are extensions of naturalism to the study of KNOWL-EDGE.

The concern of the Royal Society of London was natural knowledge, to the exclusion of supernatural knowledge: its founders wanted to preclude discussions about the possibility or impossibility of all sorts of claims for supernatural events, magic or miracles, the appearance of ghosts or angels. (The society did not, however, oppose the witch-hunts that took place in England in its earliest days.) Thus, the dichotomy natural/supernatural was established. Those seeking natural knowledge were not opposed to the marvelous, however. Following GALILEO, they insisted that the natural world is marvelous enough; following him, Descartes and BOYLE specified natural phenomena as those that were both reported repeatedly and deemed repeatable, and they considered the aim of SCIENCE to be the explanation of them. The sentiment that science is marvelous had its clearest expression in the phrase ''natural magick,'' a commonplace in the sixteenth and the seventeenth centuries, traceable to the *Oration on the Dignity of Man* by Giovanni Pico della Mirandola (1463–1494), who is considered one of the heralds of Renaissance philosophy. In line with the preference for natural phenomena over supernatural ones, natural religion was contrasted with revealed religion: it was the religion that comes naturally, the one that needs no aid from revelation or any other miracle; it is the doctrine of natural theology plus its proofs. Its advantage was seen in its universality, in its being supported by nothing more than proofs, which rely on the light of reason that is common to all. The advocates of natural religion viewed its doctrine, but not its proofs, as embodied in revealed religion. All this is a seventeenth-century product.

The term ''naturalism'' was invented by Pierre Bayle (1697) to denote the ancient Epicurean doctrine that the world is devoid of magic, spirits, divinities, and their miracles (see EPICURUS). This doctrine was shared by all of the followers of Epicurus, as well as by Spinoza, HUME, KANT, and most modern nonreligious thinkers. Its major thrust is the opinion that the soul is not immortal, and so it implies the absence of divine providence and debunks traditional religion. Max Weber described it around the turn of the twentieth century as "disenchantment of the world." This can be contested: possibly the world can still be viewed as enchanted, even by such naturalists as Spinoza and by Einstein. The latter spoke of cosmic religious feelings and of the skeptical awe he had toward the universe; he considered himself religious in the same manner in which he viewed Gautama the Buddha and Spinoza as religious.

The picture thus far is very clear, regardless of what opinions one has: the religious and the irreligious, the advocates of myths and their opponents can all understand the description clearly. However obvious this picture is, it has some interesting and not so obvious corollaries. Consider parapsychology, for example. Naturalists claim that there are no repeatable reports of any parapsychological events. Moreover, understood naturalistically, as a mode of communication hitherto unknown, it is not problematic: even though in the view of naturalists there is no channel for parapsychological communication, their naturalism does not depend on this view. In the early twentieth century, Norman Kemp Smith introduced the term "naturalism" in a new sense, to describe Hume's view of belief (see HUME). According to Kemp Smith, naturalism is the view that belief precedes its justification.

In this century, both Jean Piaget and W.V.O. QUINE suggested that knowledge itself should be taken as a natural phenomenon and studied scientifically. (Piaget's term is "genetic"; it comes from the late nineteenth-century writings of Franz Brentano, where it denotes the empirical. Quine's term is "naturalist epistemology.") Piaget, but not Quine, developed the empirical study of the way people (especially children) acquire empirical knowledge.

PRIMARY WORKS

Books

Piaget, Jean. *Judgment and Reasoning in the Child.* Translated by M. Warden. London: K. Paul, Trench, Trubner, 1928.
Pico della Mirandola, Giovanni. *Oration on the Dignity of Man.* Translated A. Robert Caponigri. Chicago: University of Chicago Press, 1956.

Article

Quine, W.V.O. "Epistemology Naturalized." In *Ontological Relativity and Other Essays.* New York: Columbia University Press, 1969: 69–90.

BIBLIOGRAPHY

Gibson, Roger F. *Enlightened Empiricism: An Examination of W. V. Quine's Theory of Knowledge.* Tampa: University of South Florida Press, 1988.

JOSEPH AGASSI

NEURATH, OTTO. Otto Neurath (1882–1945) was a founding member of the Vienna Circle of logical positivists (see LOGICAL POSITIVISM/LOGICAL

EMPIRICISM). He was, throughout his life, interested in various kinds of political action aimed at creating a more equitable social structure to liberate not just the few but all. A lifelong believer in the importance of social planning, he accepted a position with the short-lived Soviet government in Bavaria in 1919. After its overthrow and a brief term in prison, he returned to Vienna, where he was again involved in cooperative and socialist movements. He fled to Holland in 1936 and then from Holland to England in 1940, escaping in a small boat. Like other members of the Vienna Circle, Neurath was interested in developing and improving the language of SCIENCE. But he put his concerns into a broader social context. Thus, he hoped to develop forms of language that would enable scientists and others to communicate more effectively, particularly in the use of pictures and diagrams to present statistical data in a way that would be informative to people who lacked technical knowledge of statistics. Again he was interested in developing the language of science in a way that would promote the unity of science, bringing the various sorts of science together in a single world-picture. Neurath saw this as an important step in social liberation: one could not free people for the pursuit of happiness in the absence of scientific knowledge that would provide the knowledge of the means to human liberation. Neurath envisioned, in particular, the unification of the human sciences, on one hand, for example, sociology and psychology, and the natural sciences such as physics and biology, on the other. These, he argued, were methodologically of a piece. This insistence that the human sciences were sciences exactly like physics was maintained against the views of many philosophers in the Romantic tradition of much philosophy of German-speaking *Mitteleuropa* that there is a sharp methodological distinction between *Geisteswissenschaft* and *Naturwissenschaft*. Neurath was strongly opposed to this sort of irrationalism. He was equally opposed to those who followed G. Lukacs in Hegelianizing Marxism, insisting that if Marxist theory was to be scientific, then it had to be expressed in the unified language of positive science and had to proceed by methods that were not essentially different from those of physics. In both cases, he argued that antiscientific (and antiempirical) views were inimical to social progress. Like Karl POPPER, Neurath argued that transcendental METAPHYSICS, whether of the Platonic sort or the Hegelian sort, was a hindrance to scientific progress and, as ideology, interfered with the development of social democracy.

The unification of science was to be achieved by an "encyclopædia." This encyclopedia of unified science was to make explicit both the data of science and the theoretical connections among these data. This encyclopedia was not only to express the state at which science had arrived but to play a significant methodological role. Some logical positivists in the Vienna Circle, Moritz Schlick in particular, argued, following the early WITTGENSTEIN, not only that the language of science is to be connected to the world as we experience it, a point upon which Neurath agreed, but also that certain basic sense experiences can provide a foundation of incorrigible data upon which the rest of the structure can be constructed, a point where Neurath disagreed. Neurath argued, to the contrary, that there was no such incorrigible basis, that all data were in principle hypothetical, and that each datum could, like any theoretical principle, be revised or even rejected in the light of further experience. Moreover, contrary to Popper, it is not the isolated hypothesis that is compared to experience, perhaps to be rejected, but the whole body of knowledge. Again, contrary to Popper, existential hypotheses are legitimately scientific; though not falsifiable, they are still confirmable when they guide scientists to the discovery of new theories and systems of cross-connections. In any case, the encyclopedia that must be used as the starting point of scientific research is the historically conditioned body of statements that we have inherited. There is no transcendent or ahistorical starting point.

This antifoundationalist empiricism of Neurath was later developed further by W.V.O QUINE, on one hand, and I. Lakatos, on the other.

PRIMARY WORKS

Empiricism and Sociology. Dordrecht, Holland: Reidel, 1973.
Gesammelte Philosophische und Methodologische Schriften. 2 vols. Wein: Hulder-Pichler-Tempsky, 1981.
Philosophical Papers. Dordrecht, Holland: Reidel, 1983.

BIBLIOGRAPHY

Coffa, A. *The Semantic Tradition from Kant to Carnap.* Cambridge: Cambridge University Press, 1991.
Übel, T., ed. *Rediscovering the Forgotten Vienna Circle.* Dordrecht, Holland: Kluwer, 1991.

FRED WILSON

NEWTON, SIR ISAAC. Isaac Newton (1642–1727) was the English scientist and philosopher whose work defined the frame of reference of natural SCIENCE with respect to both its ontology (bodies related by mutual gravitation) and its method of reasoning (INDUCTION). After taking note of Newton's life, career, and relation to his predecessors, this entry traces his articulation of the experimental philosophy in his argument for universal gravitation and responses to criticisms by BERKELEY and Leibniz, among others. It also examines HUME's critique of the fundamental notions of the Newtonian system of the world and contrasts Hume's empiricism with the critical rationalism of KANT.

NEWTON'S LIFE

After his graduation from Trinity College in 1665, Cambridge University closed because of the plague, and Newton retreated to Woolsthorpe, the town of his birth, for eighteen months, during which annus mirabilis, Newton reported many years later:

I found the Method of approximating series and the Rule for reducing any dignity of any Binomial into such a series. The same year in May I found the method of Tangents of Gregory & Slusius, & in November had the direct method of fluxions & the next year in January had the theory of Colours & in May following I hade entrance into ye inverse method of fluxions. And the same year I began to think of gravity extending to ye orb of the Moon. (*Never at Rest*: 143)

In 1667 he returned to Cambridge as Lucasian Professor of Mathematics and resided there until 1696, when he moved to London to become first warden, then master, of the mint. There he increased production of coins tenfold, oversaw their standardization, and urged the death penalty for counterfeiters. He was a member of Parliament for one term, representing Cambridge at the time of the Restoration of the monarchy upon the Glorious Revolution of 1689, during which time he met John LOCKE. Newton was president of the Royal Society of London for Improving Natural Knowledge from 1703 until his death.

Once or twice Newton suffered from disorders of mind or personality that caused him to withdraw from others. These have been variously attributed to an unhappy childhood or alchemical experiments with mercury and other poisons. His father, Isaac Newton, died before he was born; his mother, Hannah Ayscouth, married Barnabas Smith two years later and lived with him and their children in another town, apart from Isaac, during his childhood. Upon the death of his stepfather he was reunited with his mother at age eleven.

Newton recomposed white light from light first separated into colors. He reported this and thirty other experiments with light in two papers presented to the Royal Society, 1672 and 1675, and in *Opticks*, 1704. Robert Hooke and Christian Huygens objected not to his experiments but to his corpuscular theory: Hooke held that light was a pulse in an ethereal medium; Huygens that it was a wave in a dense medium. Newton favored corpuscles because light travels in a straight "line without bending into the shadow." By contrast waves spread after passing a barrier. Newton completed *Mathematical Principles of Natural Philosophy*, 1687, at the urging of Edmund Halley, who prepared its geometrical figures.

Newton engaged in an extended controversy with Leibniz: each disputed the other's claim to original authorship of the calculus. It now appears that each developed it independently. Robert Hooke, Newton's immediate predecessor as president of the Royal Society, accused Newton of plagiarizing Hooke's explanation of the elliptical shape of orbits in terms of a centripetal force that falls off with the square of the distance.

This entry follows the view that Newton's articulation of the experimental philosophy evolved in part out of his effort to avoid controversy. An English law for the burning of heretics was not repealed until 1677. For a thorough contemporary analysis of Newton's caution see Bechler 1990.

RELATIONSHIP TO PREDECESSORS

Newton's work successfully incorporated features of the thought of BACON, GALILEO, Descartes, and BOYLE. Like Bacon, Newton rejected induction by simple enumeration: induction first requires a systematic causal analysis of the phenomena. Like Galileo and Descartes, Newton sought to view phenomena within the context of a systematic mathematical representation. Unlike Descartes, Newton rejected the test of hypothetical doubt. He followed the experimental approach to CAUSALITY of Bacon and Galileo, even though it brought him into conflict with Cartesian views on matter and mechanism. Newton gave priority to experiments.

Interpreters and scholars have differed on what constitutes the distinctive character of Newtonian science. Is it its a priori rationalist system of mathematical representation of what was known piecemeal into a unified system (see A PRIORI/A POSTERIORI DISTINCTION)? Or is it its empiricist restrictions to things known by the senses? On one hand, Einstein appeared to accomplish a great deal from rational reflection on the mathematical representation of physical variables. On the other hand, Benjamin Franklin's formulation of electronic action (e.g., poles repel, opposites attract) followed systematic experimentation without sophisticated mathematical calculation. Like Galileo, Newton excelled in the integration of mathematical argument and experimental analysis.

NEWTON'S ARGUMENT FOR UNIVERSAL GRAVITATION

Newton developed his articulation of the experimental philosophy in justifying the argument for universal gravitation. The argument in *Principles* is complex: first, he *defines* the quantities of matter, motion, and force; second, he provides a unified formulation of the *laws* of motion; third, he states his *rules* of reasoning; fourth, he identifies relevant *phenomena*; and fifth, he derives the universal law of gravitation:

Definitions:

The quantities of matter, motion, and force are products of density, volume, velocity, and acceleration. (*Mathematical Principles of Natural Philosophy*: 1–6)

Laws:

I. Every body continues in its state of rest or of uniform motion in a right line unless it is compelled to change that state by forces impressed upon it.

II. The change of motion is proportional to the motive force impressed and is made in the direction of the right line in which that force is impressed.

III. To every action there is always opposed an equal reaction: or, the mutual actions of two bodies upon each other are always equal, and directed to contrary parts. (Principles: 13)

Rules of Reasoning:

1. We are to admit no more causes of natural things than such as are both true and sufficient to explain their appearances.

2. Therefore to the same natural effects we must, as far as possible, assign the same causes.

3. The qualities of bodies, which admit neither intensification nor remission of degree, and which are found to belong to all bodies within the reach of our experiments are to be esteemed the universal qualities of all bodies whatsoever.

4. In experimental philosophy we are to look upon propositions inferred by general induction from phenomena as accurately or very nearly true, notwithstanding any contrary hypotheses that may be imagined, till such time as other phenomena occur, by which they may either be made more accurate or liable to exceptions. (Principles: 398–400)

Phenomena:

i) Kepler's second and third laws of planetary motion are satisfied by the moons of Jupiter;

ii) the same laws are satisfied by the moons of Saturn;

iii) the orbits of the planets are circumsolar;

iv) the planets describe equal areas in equal times when their orbits are taken to be circumsolar;

v) the orbits of the planets do not satisfy the equal areas law when taken to be geocentric;

vi) the orbit of the moon around the earth satisfies the equal areas law. (*Principles*: 401–5)

Derivation:

Newton derives the law of universal gravitation from the six phenomena by applying the three laws according to the four rules in the following steps:

1. He uses Laws I and II to factor orbital motions into an inertial component tangential to the orbit and a centripetal component accelerated toward the center of the orbit.

2. He cites Rules 1 and 2 to sanction assigning the same cause (gravity) to similar effects (centripetal accelerations):

   a. The force by which the moon is retained in its orbit is the same as the force of gravity responsible for the acceleration of bodies falling freely near the earth;

   b. The forces retaining the moons of Jupiter and Saturn in their orbits are the same as the force that retains the moon of the earth;

   c. The force that retains the circumsolar planets in their orbits is the same as the force retaining the moons.

3. He generalizes on bodies related by gravity to the earth:

Universally, all bodies about the earth gravitate toward the earth; and the weights of all, at equal distances from the earth's centre, are as the quantities of matter which they severally contain. This is the quality of all bodies within the reach of our experiments; and therefore (by Rule 3) to be affirmed of all bodies whatsoever. (*Principles*: 413)

4. Using the third rule again he universalizes to conclude that every planet is attracted to every other, every part to every part, and that every body gravitates toward every other in proportion to the quantity of their matter and inversely with the square of their distance.

5. Finally, by Law III, Newton argues gravity is mutual, "since all the parts of planet A gravitate toward any other planet B; . . . planet B will gravitate toward all the parts of planet A."

Rules 1, 2, and 4 convert analytical, mathematical descriptions of phenomena into causal explanations. Motions of falling bodies near the earth and motions of orbiting bodies are mathematically similar: they satisfy a common formula. Hence, by Rule 2 they must have the same cause. If gravity is the cause of the motion of falling bodies, it must also be the cause of the similar motions of the moons and planets. If gravity is a sufficient cause, no other cause need be hypothesized, given Rule 1. Rule 3 sanctions the universalization of the gravitation relation. Rule 4 protects the explanation from alternative conjectures that lack independent experimental support. Having established the universality of gravity, he uses it to explain the elliptical orbits of the planets and the motions of the seas. For a detailed analysis of Newton's argument for universal gravity in the context of a contemporary theory of inference from experience see Glymour 1980.

Newton was soon famous throughout Europe. After his death he was hailed by Voltaire as one of the finest members of the species and by HUME as "the greatest and rarest genius that ever arose for the ornament and instruction of the species" (Force and Popkin: 186). Nevertheless, he did not escape criticism. Berkeley (1710) criticized *Principles* as MATERIALISTIC and atheistic; Leibniz (1711) faulted Newton's conception of gravity because it involved nonmechanical causality. Rules 3 and 4 cited in Newton's argument for universal gravitation were added in the 1713 and 1726 editions of *Principles*. These rules restrict scientific argument to qualities known by our senses and hypotheses supported by experiments. Newton thereby sought to avoid controversial debate on mere conjectures, whether his own or others'. Newton also introduced arguments for the existence of God in later editions of *Principles* and *Opticks*.

LEIBNIZ: MECHANICAL CAUSALITY AND GRAVITY

According to Newton's theory of gravity, however near or far bodies are from each other, they are related by gravitational attraction, a force that acts, even though the bodies be separated by a vacuum. Newton was aware of this departure from the mechanical conception of causality. He had himself, at an earlier time, found nonmechanical causation problematic and denied it was inherent to matter. In a letter to Bentley dated February 25, 1693, but not published until 1756, Newton wrote:

It is inconceivable that inanimate brute matter should, without the mediation of something else which is not material, operate upon and affect other matter without mutual contact, as it must be if gravitation, in the sense of Epicurus, be essential and inherent in it. And this is the one reason why I desired you would not ascribe innate gravity to me. That gravity should be innate, inherent, and essential to matter, so that one body may act upon another at a distance through a *vacuum*, without the mediation of anything else, by and through which their action and force may be conveyed from one to another, is to me so great an absurdity that I believe no man who has in philosophical matters a competent faculty of thinking can ever fall into it. (*Newton's Philosophy*: 54)

By contrast the Cartesian theory holds that changes in motion are caused by direct encounters of bodies: there is no action at a distance. Descartes held that to endow particles with the power of action at a distance would make them divine powers. Newton leaves the question of whether the cause of gravity is material or spiritual to his readers.

Leibniz held the Cartesian ideal of mechanical explanation for the motion of matter. In a letter to Hartsoeker in 1711 he argued that Newtonian gravity, if not conceived as mechanically explicable, is unintelligible: "[I]f . . . by a simple *primitive property* or by a law of GOD which brings about this effect without using any intelligible means, then it is a senseless occult quality, which is so very occult that it can never be cleared up, even though a Spirit, not to say God himself, were endeavoring to explain it" (cited in *Principles*: 668). In 1712 this letter was published in London.

The second edition of *Principles* appeared in 1713 with additions intended to fend off Leibniz's criticism. Newton added a General Scholium, in which, first, he contended that the hypothesis of vortices is violated since the motions of comets are inconsistent with it: "[F]or comets are carried with very eccentric orbits through all parts of the heavens indifferently, with a freedom that is incompatible with the notion of a vortex" (*Principles*: 543).

For this edition of *Principles*, Newton rewrote the section at the beginning of Book Three originally labeled "Hypotheses" and called it "Rules of Reasoning in Philosophy." The first two rules of reasoning were previously included among the hypotheses. These two rules govern causal explanations of natural appearances in particular instances.

In revising this section Newton added Rule 3 on induction with an explanation that articulates two fundamental features of the experimental philosophy. It restricts what may be universalized to qualities known by the senses, and it rejects hypothetical doubt. He claims that all our knowledge of the qualities of bodies is by experiments; for example, "We no other way know the extension of bodies than by our senses" (*Principles*: 399). He explicitly eschews hypothetical doubt: "We are certainly not to relinquish the evidence of experiments for the sake of dreams and vain fictions of our own devising" (*Principles*: 399). This is a direct rejection of Descartes' method:

never to accept anything as true that I did not know evidently to be so; that is, carefully to avoid precipitous judgment and prejudice; and to include nothing more in my judgments than what presented itself to my mind with such clarity and distinctness that I would have no occasion to put it in doubt. (*Discourse on the Method*: 10)

Descartes used hypothetical doubt in the first of his *Meditations on First Philosophy* to question anything derived from the senses. Newton holds the opposite view. He rejects anything not derived from the senses if it is used to cast doubt on something that is.

Toward the end of the explanation attached to Rule 3, Newton summarizes the argument for universal gravitation:

Lastly, if it universally appears, by experiments and astronomical observations, that all bodies about the earth gravitate toward the earth, and that in proportion to the quantity of matter which they severally contain; that the moon likewise, according to the quantity of its matter, gravitates toward the earth; that, on the other hand, our sea gravitates toward the moon; and all the planets one toward another; and the comets in like manner toward the sun; we must, in consequence of this rule, universally allow that all bodies whatsoever are endowed with a principle of mutual gravitation. For the argument from the appearances concludes with more force for the universal gravitation of all bodies than for their impenetrability; of which among those in the celestial regions we have not experiments, nor any manner of observation.

He adds in the third edition immediately: "Not that I affirm gravity to be essential to bodies: by their vis insita I mean nothing but their inertia. This is immutable. Their gravity is diminished as they recede from the earth." The gravitational relation between two bodies is like the distance between them—it is not something inherent in them.

In the General Scholium to the second edition Newton made his famous statement, *Hypotheses non fingo*:

But hitherto I have not been able to discern the cause of those properties of gravity from phenomena, and I frame no hypotheses; for whatever is not deduced from the phenomena is to be called an hypothesis; and hypotheses, whether metaphysical or physical, whether of occult qualities or mechanical, have no place in experimental philosophy. In this philosophy particular propositions are inferred from the phenomena, and afterwards rendered general by induction. Thus it was that the impenetrability, the mobility, and the impulsive force of bodies, and the laws of motion and of gravitation were discovered. And to us it is enough that gravity really does exist, and act according to the laws which we have explained, and abundantly serves to account for all the motions of the celestial bodies, and of our sea. (*Principles*: 547)

For Newton empiricism is more important than mechanism.

Newton added Rule 4 in the third edition of *Principles* with the explanation: "This rule we must follow, that the argument of induction may not be evaded by hypotheses" (*Principles*: 400). In Newton's view principles of plenitude or sufficient reason that follow from God's nature by Leibniz's conjectures are not reasons to deny the existence of a void or action at a distance, given that these are supported by evidence, and Leibniz's conjectures are not.

In 1718 Newton brought out a second English edition of *Opticks*. In its advertisement he wrote: "And to shew that I do not take Gravity for an Essential Property of Bodies, I have added one Question [Query 31] concerning its Cause, chusing to propose it by way of a Question, because I am not yet satisfied about it for want of Experiments." Again Newton gave priority to the test of experience over preconceptions. He argued that his conception of gravity is not of an occult power but of a manifest principle:

To tell us that every Species of Things is endow'd with an occult specifick Quality by which it acts and reproduces manifest Effects, is to tell us nothing: But to derive two or three general Principles of Motion from Phaenomena, and afterwards to tell us how the Properties and Actions of all corporeal Things follow from those manifest Principles, would be a very great step in philosophy, though the Causes of those Principles were not yet discovered. (*Opticks*: 401)

Gravity, he claimed, is not occult because it is species-neutral; that is, it applies to all species of body.

These additions to the rules of reasoning and scholia of *Principles* and to the Queries of *Opticks* articulated and defended his argument by induction for universal gravitation. Newton repeatedly gives priority of the test of experiments over argument based on mere conjectures and pure hypotheses.

BERKELEY: MATERIALISM AND ATHEISM

Berkeley, commenting on the original edition of Newton's *Principles*, in which Deity is not mentioned, took it to be materialistic and atheistic. Berkeley preferred a relativistic conception of SPACE and motion to avoid "a dangerous dilemma . . . of thinking either Real Space is God, or else that there is something besides God which is eternal, uncreated, infinite, indivisible, unmutable. Both of which may justly be thought pernicious and absurd notions" (*Principles of Human Nature*: Part I, §111, §117, cited by Cajori: 668, 670). Berkeley, like Descartes, identified space (extension) with matter. Newton did not. Space and time are undefined primitives in *Principles*. In the first scholium of *Principles* explicating its initial definitions he wrote: "Absolute, true, and mathematical time, of itself, and from its own nature, flows equably without relation to anything external"; and "Absolute space, in its own nature, without relation to anything external, remains always similar and immovable" (*Principles*: 6). Newton held the existence of space to be independent of matter, and he offered no empirical account of our knowledge of space and TIME.

By contrast Newton confounded charges of atheism by offering an empirical account of our knowledge of God in the added passages to the Queries and scholia of later editions of *Opticks* and *Principles*. In the second edition of *Principles*, Newton suggested that discourse regarding God is appropriate to natural philosophy:

As a blind man has no idea of colors, so have we no idea of the manner by which the all-wise God perceives and understands all things. He is utterly void of all body and bodily figure, and can therefore neither be seen, nor heard, nor touched; nor ought he to be worshiped under the representation of any corporeal thing. We have ideas of his attributes, but what the real SUBSTANCE of anything is we know not. In bodies, we see only their figures and colors, we hear only the sounds, we touch only their outward surfaces, we smell only the smells, and taste the savors; but their inward substances are not to be known either by our senses, or by any reflex act of our minds: much less, then, have we any idea of the substance of God. We know him only by his most wise and excellent contrivances of things, and final causes. And thus much concerning God; to discourse of whom from the appearances of things, does certainly belong to Natural Philosophy. (*Principles*: 546)

Here in the same paragraph in which knowledge of the *substance* of God (or anything else) is denied, knowledge of the *existence* of God is affirmed.

In additions to the third edition of *Principles* (1726) Newton laid an empiricist foundation for knowledge of the unity of God:

Every soul that has perception is, though in different times and in different organs of sense and motion, still the same indivisible person. There are given successive parts in duration, coexistent parts in space, but neither the one nor the other in the person of a man, or his thinking principle; and much less can they be found in the thinking substance of God. Every man, so far as he is a thing that has perception is one and the same man during his whole life, in all and each of his organs of sense. God is the same God, always and everywhere. (*Principles*: 543)

Understanding of the unity of God comes from our knowledge of our own unity by our senses; that the existence of bodies in motion is the cause of our senses and the existence of God is the cause of bodies in motion, we infer from apparent effects.

Newton introduced a more extensive account of self and God in *Opticks*, Query 28, which was one among questions added to the Latin edition of 1706 and revised again for the second English edition of 1718. It meets Berkeley's criticism by accommodation:

Is not the sensory of Animals that place to which the sensitive Substance is present, and into which the sensible Species of Things are carried through the Nerves and Brain, that there they may be perceived by their immediate presence to that Substance? And these things being rightly dispatch'd, does it not appear from Phaenomena that there is a Being incorporeal, living, intelligent, omnipresent, who in infinite Space, as it were in his Sensory, sees the things themselves intimately, and thoroughly perceives them, and comprehends them wholly by their immediate presence to himself: Of which things the Images only carried throughout the Organs of Sense into our little Sensoriums, are there seen and beheld by that which in us perceives and thinks. (*Opticks*: 370)

Can we infer from phenomena that there is such a Being? Newton claimed we can: "By this way of Analysis we may proceed from Compounds to Ingredients, and from Motions to the Forces producing them; and in general, from effects to their Causes, and from particular Causes to more general ones, till the Argument end in the most general" (*Opticks*: 404); and

And if natural Philosophy in all its parts, by pursuing this Method shall at length be perfected, the Bounds of Moral Philosophy will also be enlarged. For so far as we can know by Natural Philosophy what is the first Cause, what Power he has over us, and what Benefits we receive from him, so far our Duty toward him, as well as that toward one another, will appear to us by the Light of Nature. (*Opticks*: 405)

Newton's affirmation of the existence of God as cause of the world appears inferentially similar to gravity as cause of acceleration. It is affirmed a posteriori without dogmatism or doubt. He claimed no certitude, and he feigned no doubt.

He insisted we have knowledge of things only as they appear and not of their substance or how they are innately.

NEWTON AND HUME

Hume's relation to Newton is complex. On one hand, it appears that Hume sought to further the development of the experimental philosophy of Bacon and Newton in applying it to "the science of MAN." On the other hand, he profoundly disagreed with Newton's inference to the existence of God as Cause of the world.

Newton's view of causation sanctioned inference to the existence of a system of bodies, self-identical over time, arrayed across different points of space, whose motions relative to each other are constantly modified by relations of gravitation. Hume denied the validity of this inference. Newton's view sanctioned a second inference, which appears to be of the same form to a numerically identical cause of bodies and the design of their relations to each other, which cause is itself a choice by an intelligent being. This inference to Deity was Hume's primary target. His sweeping critique of the basic concepts of the Newtonian model of the world sought to sever its scientific achievements from theism. (For a thorough examination of Newton and Hume on the design arguments, see Hurlbutt 1965.)

Newton's Rules of Reasoning restricted the *explananda* to natural effects, that is, to sensible effects or appearances. But they did not similarly restrict the *explanans* to natural causes, to sensible or apparent causes. Hume did. Hume cast doubt on explanations of apparent effects in terms of causes that are not also apparent. He argued that the claim that there must be such explanations is unintelligible.

In *A Treatise of Human Nature*, Book I, Hume offered a systematic critique of the primitives and rules of reasoning of Newton's natural philosophy. He claimed that certain ideas of space, time, necessary causal connection, body, and soul that are central to it lack originating impressions and are, therefore, unintelligible (*Treatise*: 26). *Insensible extension*, whether because divided *in infinitum* or because a *vacuum*; *insensible duration*, whether because *without change* or because diminished *in infinitum*; *necessary connection*, whether in the form of the idea that everything that has a beginning must have a cause (*Treatise*: 78) or in the form of the idea that similar causes *must* have similar effects (*Treatise*: 105); *perfect identity*, whether of changing *bodies* external to the senses or of the changing *self* at different times—all are unintelligible.

Each unintelligible idea is a primitive idea in Newton's natural philosophy. According to it, there are empty spaces between bodies that, as such, are neither tangible nor visible; there is motion *in vacuo* that meets no resistance; there are durations and distances diminished *in infinitum*, even though none such are perceived; absolute time is invariant in its flow whether there be change or not and whether events be retarded or accelerated; it is *necessary* that there is no change in motion without an external cause and that the same effects have the same causes; *bodies* are numerically identical from one time and place to another whether or not perceived in the interim; our knowledge of the *identity* of the *self* over time is the basis for our understanding of the identity of God, though God be omnitemporal and omnispatial.

Newton qualified his beliefs regarding these several features of his model. He had revised his presentation of the calculus to minimize ontological commitment to infinitesimals; a vacuum is a relative matter and may be operationally conceived as a relatively nonresisting medium (*Opticks*: 639). But Newton did not appear to qualify his conception of the unity of the self in space and time, our *awareness* of which provides a basis in experience for understanding the omnipresence of Deity (*Principles*: 545).

Just as Newton sought to separate knowledge of the existence of body and God as causes of appearances from knowledge of their substance, Hume sought to separate knowledge of appearances from knowledge of the existence of causes unperceived. Hume disputes as unintelligible the *necessity* of a cause and disputes the validity of the inference from perceived effects to causes apart from perception: he claims we have no idea of body continuing unperceived nor of self continuing without perceptions.

Hume and Newton agree that causal analysis is guided by the rule that similar effects have the same causes, but Hume invariably interprets this rule in a purely qualitative way—similar effects have similar causes. In Section XV, "Rules by Which to Judge of Causes and Effects," Rule 4, Hume writes that "the same effect never arises but from the same cause" (*Treatise*: 173). In Rule 5, he claims that "where several different objects produce the same effect it must be by means of some quality, which we discover to be common amongst them. For as like effects imply like causes, we must always ascribe the causation to the circumstance wherein we discover the resemblance" (*Treatise*: 174]. "[W]hen in any instance we find our expectation disappointed, we must conclude that this irregularity proceeds from some difference in the causes," according to Rule 6. Hume's first three rules require that cause and effect be contiguous in space and time, that the cause be prior to the effect, and that the two be constantly conjoined. Rules 7 and 8 attribute diminution and delay to compounded causes.

Like Newton, Hume urges us to accept universally only what we can find in particular cases. But unlike Newton, Hume holds that we cannot find causation in particular cases:

It appears that, in single instances of the operation of bodies, we never can, by our utmost scrutiny, discover any thing but one event following another; without being able to comprehend any force or power by which the cause operates, or any connexion between it and its supposed effect. (*An Enquiry concerning Human Understanding*: 84–85)

Causality can be concluded only from pluralities of perceptions. Where we appear to infer from a single case of A to an effect B, Hume claims there is a prior repeated association of similar qualities. For example, C and D may have been constantly conjoined, and if C and A are of the same variety (have a common factor), and D and B are of the same variety, then Hume allows one might expect B, given a single instance of A (*Treatise*: 104–5, 131). For Hume we infer a cause for effects previously preceded invariably in our experience by similar causes. But we do not know that there *must* be a cause, that causes are fewer rather than greater, or that similar (independent but correlative) effects *must* have *numerically* the same cause.

KANT agreed with Hume that knowledge of extrasensory causes is not attainable. But Kant held that the idea of such is intelligible and important in giving us the wherewithal to formulate questions and to seek a cause where none is known. For Kant causality was constitutive of representations of sensations because of its indispensable role in sorting genuine from illusory objects. A priori knowledge of objects and causality is limited to the possibilities of experience: what is not part of the causal structure of the world is not a possible object of knowledge.

Like Berkeley, Hume takes spatial relations to be properties of impressions and is thoroughly skeptical about the existence of space separate from perception. Historically, empiricist views of space had difficulty explaining our knowledge, apparently a priori, of geometry. Kant holds that space and time are forms of sensory intuition and that as such they are subjective conditions of objective experience: every actual occurrence is at a time the same as, earlier than, or later than, any other, and every actual body exists at a place near or distant from any other. He holds that we are justified in representing a plurality of objects in different places at the same time, each continuing the same as itself over time.

In the twentieth century Einstein and others brought our conceptions of space, time, and causality under the influence of empirical inquiry. Einstein's revisions of the theory of gravity rejected absolute space and time as unobservable and restored the mechanical conception of causality: in relativity theory there is no instantaneous causal action at a distance. The mechanical model fell again with the development of quantum mechanics, which makes position and velocity not jointly determinable for subatomic particles. It did not fall easily: Einstein, Podolsky, and Rosen (1935) argued for the existence of an unknown (hidden) variable that would restore classical conceptions of causality, position, and motion. Since Bell (1964, 1966) the hidden variable thesis has been shown to be inconsistent with theory and experiment.

CONCLUSION

Newton's work was central to the development of the modern view of empirical science and the natural world. Fundamental questions of the nature of science developed by Newton, his critics, and their successors continue to be debated. Is the structure of causality subjective or objective? What is the relation between theory and evidence? Is it inductive or deductive? Do theories describe or explain? Realists accept inference to the common cause or best explanation;

others tend to view science as aiming at epistemic virtues like empirical adequacy, reliability, testability, reduction of error, or semantic simplicity; some view as problematic the relation of theory to reality because of complex interdependencies among hypotheses and theories in relation to empirical evidence. Advocates of nearly every view claim to have a plausible reading of Newton's accomplishments and methods.

PRIMARY WORKS

Sir Isaac Newton's Mathematical Principles of Natural Philosophy and His System of the World. Translated into English by Andrew Motte in 1729; translations revised, and supplied with an historical and explanatory appendix, by Florian Cajori. Berkeley: University of California Press, 1934.

Opticks or a Treatise of the Reflections, Refractions, Inflections and Colours of Light. Based on the 4th ed.: London: W. Innys, 1730; with a foreword by Albert Einstein; an introduction by Edmund Whittaker; a preface by I. Bernard Cohen; and an analytical table of contents prepared by Duane H. D. Roller. New York: Dover, 1952.

Newton's Philosophy of Nature: Selections from His Writings. Edited and arranged with notes by H. S. Thayer, with an introduction by John Herman Randall, Jr. New York: Hafner Press, 1953.

OTHER PRIMARY TEXTS

Descartes, René. *Discourse on Method and Meditations on First Philosophy.* Translated by Donald A. Cress. Indianapolis, IN: Hackett, 1980.

Hume, David. *An Enquiry concerning Human Understanding.* In *Enquiries concerning Human Understanding and concerning the Principles of Morals*, edited with an analytical index by L. A. Selby-Bigge; revised with notes by P. H. Nidditch. Oxford: Clarendon Press, 1975.

———. *A Treatise of Human Nature.* 2d ed., edited with an analytical index by L. A. Selby-Bigge, revised with notes by P. H. Nidditch. Oxford: Clarendon Press, 1978.

BIBLIOGRAPHY

Bechler, Zev. *Newton's Physics and the Conceptual Structure of the Scientific Revolution.* Boston: Kluwer Academic, 1990.

———. *The Newtonian Revolution.* Cambridge: Cambridge University Press, 1980.

Cohen, I. Bernard. *Franklin and Newton: An Inquiry into Speculative Newtonian Experimental Science and Franklin's Work in Electricity as an Example Thereof.* Cambridge: Harvard University Press, 1980.

Force, James, and Richard H. Popkin. *Essays on the Context, Nature, and Influence of Isaac Newton's Theology.* Boston: Kluwer Academic, 1990.

Glymour, Clark. *Theory and Evidence.* Princeton: Princeton University Press, 1980.

Hurlbutt, Robert H., III. *Hume, Newton and the Design Argument.* Lincoln: University of Nebraska Press, 1965.

Koyre, Alexandre. *Newtonian Studies.* Cambridge: Harvard University Press, 1965.

Wallis, Peter, and Ruth Wallis. *Newton and Newtoniana, 1672–1975.* Folkestone: Dawson, 1977.

Westfall, Richard S. *Never at Rest: A Biography of Isaac Newton.* Cambridge: Cambridge University Press, 1980.

SAMUEL RICHMOND

NOMINALISM. Nominalism is one of the main theories of universals, generally contrasted with realism about universals, the view that there are universals. While, in its strict sense, it must have been held by some philosophers (perhaps by some of the Sophists) as soon as the problem of universals was identified in ancient Greek philosophy, the origin of the term "nominalism" is obscure, though certainly it is not later than the Middle Ages. There were references to the so-called *Nominales* as early as the third quarter of the twelfth century, but the term referred to a theological position regarding the objects of belief or faith. It appears that Albert the Great established the more or less contemporary meaning of the term, though in view of its transparent etymology, surely it must have been used with that meaning before (see Courtenay).

The term has a broad sense, namely, the one stated earlier and employed today most prominently by David Armstrong, as well as a narrow but more useful sense associated with the work of philosophers such as David Pears and Renford Bambrough, who were heavily influenced by the later WITTGENSTEIN. According to this narrow and etymologically more proper sense, the only thing distinctive about the individual things that supposedly exemplify the same universal is the existence of a word conventionally applied to all of them. In this sense, nominalism should be distinguished not only from realism but also from what H. H. Price has called the philosophy of resemblances. There need not be even a unique resemblance among the individuals named by the same word. Wittgenstein's famous example was games. Surely there is no unique resemblance between football, solitaire, and a child's throwing a ball up and down, but all three are correctly called games. Rather, at most the use of the word "game" is governed by what Wittgenstein called "family resemblances."

The implausibility of nominalism so understood has been evident to most recent writers on universals. Perhaps all games have no unique resemblance with each other, but surely games of football do. They would have it even if there were no name for them (i.e., "football").

Sometimes the word "conceptualism" is used as a name for a variety of nominalism. According to this variety, the individuals allegedly exemplifying a universal have in common only the fact that they correspond to one and the same concept, the latter being a mental entity. If the correspondence is understood as resemblance, we have a variety of the philosophy of resemblances. If not, the view is open to objections parallel to those against nominalism in the narrow sense. No concept of a certain rare species of animal need exist in order for there to be members of that species, unless it exists in God's mind, as the medieval conceptualists indeed held.

So let us proceed to the varieties of nominalism covered by the broader sense of the term. The most familiar is the already mentioned philosophy of resemblances, which is explained by Price as holding that an individual object's having a certain property consists in its resembling each of a set of exemplars at least as closely as they resemble each other. The exemplars may be further understood as establishing the sense of a word or the existence of a class or as governing the application of a concept, but then we would really be concerned with other varieties of nominalism, to be mentioned shortly. The crucial notion, of course, is that of the supposed relation of resemblance. Is there such a relation, or does it simply consist in the resembling individuals' exemplifying the same universal? If there is such a relation, it would be expressed presumably in statements of the form "X resembles y." These would have to be genuine statements, with a determinate truth-value. But they are not. It is a familiar remark that everything resembles everything else "in some respect." "Dick resembles that house" is either trivially true, for the reason just given, or has no determinate truth-value. Of course, we could provide it with one by specifying the respect of the resemblance (e.g., color), but this would be in effect to appeal to a universal. We could also say, "X resembles y more than z" or more generally, "X resembles y more than z resembles w," where x could be identical with z. But this would not be a statement asserting a relation of resemblance. It would be a statement asserting a difference in degree between two cases of resemblance. But then we have to conclude that the appeal to this statement casts no light on the alleged relation of resemblance but rather presupposes it. So a resemblance statement of the form "X resembles y" cannot stand on its own, and "resembles" has to be understood as referring to something else, not to a relation. The obvious alternative is that it refers to a universal shared by the resembling individuals, and the statement of difference in degree of resemblance asserts a difference in degree of specificity between two universals. (E.g., Dick may resemble the house in that both are white, but only generically so, not absolutely specifically—i.e., they both are white but not exactly the same shade of white.) This argument is developed by Butchvarov 1967.

Exactly the same problem arises for what recently has come to be known as trope theory, originally proposed by G. F. Stout and later defended by D. C. Williams and Keith Campbell. The theory holds that the qualities of particular things are themselves particulars. But, of course, it has to tell us also what relationship they have—say, what relationship all particular blue qualities have in virtue of which we classify them as blue. Stout gave the unhelpful answer that they just have an ultimate and indefinable unity. Williams and Campbell answer that they resemble each other. If so, then their trope theory is open to the same objection to any appeal to a relation of resemblance that was explained earlier. The introduction of the technical term "trope" has contributed nothing. "Particular quality," which was Stout's term, is at least clear, unambiguous, and unpretentious.

If it is suggested that all blue particular qualities form a distinct class, then we must ask what determines or defines that class, and again the likely nominalist answer would be that they all bear the same name or that they resemble each other.

A somewhat idiosyncratic but philosophically useful sense of "nominalism" has been proposed by Nelson GOODMAN. In this sense, "nominalism" describes any view that is not committed to the existence of classes, even if it is committed to the existence of universals, which he calls "individuals" (see Goodman: 142ff.). Clearly, however, this sense is, at most, of tangential relevance to what has usually been understood by the problem of universals.

Nominalism can be simply the blunt negative thesis that there are no universals, without being supplemented with a positive thesis. But without a positive thesis, the negative thesis would lack a rationale. We can distinguish two versions of the view that there are universals. According to the first, two or more numerically distinct individual things can literally have one and the same quality—for example, all blue things have the quality (presumably generic) blue color, or equivalently, the quality blue color exists in all blue things. In short, universals are qualities that exist (or can exist) at several distinct places at the same time. This is the view of Armstrong and perhaps can be attributed to ARISTOTLE. The argument (e.g., Stout's) against it is simply that nothing can exist at several distinct places at the same time. But, obviously, this merely begs the question against the defender of universals, perhaps by confusing the criteria for the identity of qualities with those for the identity of spatiotemporal individuals. On the other hand, there seems to be some plausibility to the claim. Surely we can distinguish the blue color of one book from the blue color of another book?

But this ignores a lesson philosophers should have learned long ago from Frege. Such distinctness is present in the subject matter of all informative identity-statements, for example, to use Frege's example, in that of "The evening star is identical with the morning star." Frege explained it with his distinction between the different modes of presentation of which one and the same reference is capable. However, the notion of a mode of presentation is unclear and too psychologistic, while that of reference is linguistic. It would be better to replace the former with that of (potentially "intentional") object and the latter with that of entity. Then we can say that an informative identity statement is about two objects but, if true, one entity. The colors of all blue things would be distinct objects but one entity, that is, the universal blue color. In this the plausibility of the view that the qualities of discrete individual things are particulars is combined with that of the view that they are universals (see Butchvarov 1979).

But we could also admit the numerical distinctness of the blue colors of all blue objects and argue that what they have in common is that all are exemplifications of one and the same universal, which, however, cannot be intelligibly assigned spatiotemporal location. This would be the second version of the view that there are universals, arguably held by Plato and perhaps not really different from the view mentioned in the preceding paragraph. Let us call it Platonism. According to it, there are universals (or, in Plato's terminology, forms or ideas), and individual things have their qualities by participating in, exemplifying, imitating the appropriate universals. The latter are not in space and time, while the former are. It follows that there may be, in fact obviously there are, unexemplified universals, for example, perfect justice or any geometrical figure if understood strictly in accordance with its definition. There have been many arguments against Platonism. The least impressive is the baldly empiricist one: we cannot perceive Platonic universals. Plato would have agreed but also concluded that this shows that empiricism is false and that we have cognitive powers that are purely intellectual, as the example of perfect justice makes evident. Another objection to Platonism has been that, being nonspatiotemporal, Platonic universals can have no causal powers. Plato would have replied that this objection rests on a narrow conception of causality. If understood broadly, the cause of x is what explains the nature and existence of x. Think of the Aristotelian doctrine of the four kinds of causes: efficient, material, formal, and final. Platonic universals may not be efficient or material causes, but they certainly can be formal and final causes. The form Blue Color explains what the colors of blue things are and what they aim to imitate. Perfect justice explains what the imperfect justice of individual persons, actions, and institutions is and what it aims to imitate.

PRIMARY WORKS

Aristotle. *Categories* and *Metaphysics*. In *The Collected Works of Aristotle*, edited by Jonathan Barnes. 2 vols. Princeton: Princeton University Press, 1984.

Berkeley, George. *The Works of George Berkeley, Bishop of Cloyne*. Edited by A. A. Luce and T. E. Jessop. 9 vols. London: Thomas Nelson and Sons, 1948–1957.

Hume, David. *A Treatise of Human Nature*. 2d ed., edited with an analytical index by L. A. Selby-Bigge; revised with notes by P. H. Nidditch. Oxford: Clarendon Press, 1978.

Plato. *The Republic* and *Parmenides*. In *The Collected Dialogues of Plato*, edited by E. Hamilton and H. Cairns. Princeton: Princeton University Press, 1961.

Spade, Paul, trans. and ed. *Five Texts on the Medieval Problem of Universals: Porphyry, Boethius, Abelard, Duns Scotus, Ockham*. Indianapolis, IN: Hackett, 1994.

BIBLIOGRAPHY

Books

Aaron, R. I. *The Theory of Universals*. Oxford: Clarendon Press, 1952.

Armstrong, David. *Universals and Scientific Realism*. Cambridge: Cambridge University Press, 1978.

Butchvarov, Panayot. *Being Qua Being: A Theory of Identity, Existence and Predication*. Bloomington and London: Indiana University Press, 1979.

———. *Resemblance and Identity: An Examination of the Problem of Universals*. Bloomington and London: Indiana University Press, 1967.

Campbell, Keith. *Abstract Particulars*. London: Blackwell, 1995.

Courtenay, William J. *Nominales and Nominalism in the Twelfth Century, Lectionum Varirietates. Hommage a Paul Vignaux (1904–1987)*. Edited by J. Jolivet, Z. Kaluza, and A. de Libera. Paris: Vrin, 1991.

Fales, Evan. *Causation and Universals*. London: Routledge, 1990.

Goodman, Nelson. *The Structure of Appearance*. 2d ed. Indianapolis, IN: Bobbs-Merrill, 1966.

Price, H. H. *Thinking and Experience*. London: Hutchinson's University Library, 1953.

Stout, G. F. *The Nature of Universals and Propositions*. London: Oxford University Press, 1921.

Williams, D. C. *The Principles of Empirical Realism*. Indianapolis, IN: Charles Thomas, 1966.

Articles

Bambrough, J. R. "Universals and Family Resemblances." *Proceedings of the Aristotelian Society* 61 (1961): 207–23.

Pears, David. "Universals." *Philosophical Quarterly* 1 (1950–1951): 218–27.

PANAYOT BUTCHVAROV

O

OCKHAM, WILLIAM OF. William of Ockham (1285?–1347) was one of the great theologian/philosophers of late medieval scholasticism. He became a Franciscan as a youth, was educated in the Franciscan school at Oxford, and later taught at the Franciscan house in London. All his nonpolitical philosophy was written between 1317 and 1324 and consists of both theological and purely philosophical works. Among the latter are commentaries on the logical and physical works of ARISTOTLE as well as his *Summa Logicæ*, which transformed the subject of LOGIC. In the second half of his life, Ockham became involved in the dispute over poverty in the Franciscan Order and eventually in polemics against the power of the papacy. He died in Munich under the protection of the emperor, Louis the Bavarian, in 1347.

It would be a mistake to think of Ockham as an empiricist in anything like the modern sense of the term, but his philosophical contributions include ideas that are important for the empiricism of both the early modern period and later logical empiricists. In what follows, both those empiricist features of Ockham's thought that he shared with a great many other scholastics and those which are original to him are briefly sketched.

Most of the later scholastics accepted the Aristotelian approach to science and rejected Platonic doctrines of INNATENESS, and Ockham was no exception. But the way this point was made in the fourteenth century is distinctive. Ockham began from the dichotomy of *intuitive* versus *abstractive* cognition, which he defined in his own way as a distinction between cognitions that naturally cause judgments about contingent matters, such as the actual existence of something, and those that do not but can directly lead to judgments about necessary truths. The paradigm of the former is VISION; that of the latter, IMAGINATION. Ockham believed that there could be nonsensory, that is, intellective, forms of both. The mind has not only cognitions in the form of CONCEPTS by which it can think of things whether or not they are actually present but also cognitions caused by the object itself and leading directly to the judgment that the object exists. Some of the intellectual intuitions are mediated by sensory intuition, but others, like those of one's own thoughts and feelings, are direct. The denial of innateness is the claim that all abstractive cognitions arise out of intuitive ones; that is, the noncomplex elements out of which is constructed the content of any abstractive cognition must first have been intuited. The mind is not equipped with these from birth.

The preceding doctrine is very much mitigated by Ockham's acceptance of the process of ABSTRACTION. Although all intuitive cognitions are of particular things, the mind can construct on the basis of them cognitions that, so far as their intrinsic character goes, could equally well be of any of many different particulars. Ockham thought of any of these cognitions as equally "resembling" the members of some class of objects and thus constituting a mental sign of them. In this way he arrived at concepts of species and genera and UNIVERSALS in general. The relationships between these concepts result in necessary truths; and SCIENCE, even science of the extramental world, is mainly concerned, Ockham thought, with discovering such necessary truths. Although Ockham had a place for contingent generalizations within science, he accepted in a way no modern empiricist would the Aristotelian emphasis on necessity.

Most late scholastics adopted what we would call a "direct realist" position in epistemology, and Ockham was particularly concerned to make sure this was not compromised. Intuitive cognitions are directly of a reality that is not constructed by the process of cognition itself. The intuitive cognition of a horse is directly of the horse, not directly of an idea of the horse. Abstractive cognitions too relate directly to their real objects. The general concept of horse is of horses, not of some abstract idea of a horse. In Ockham's day it was common to think that cognition, at least abstractive cognition, involved a "species"—that is, some sort of likeness, that had a real existence in the senses or mind and served to mediate the extramental object to the cognitive faculty. Ockham thought this proposal led to making the direct object of cognitive acts and states always something mental, and thus raised the possibility of global SKEPTICISM. Instead of "species," Ockham proposed "habits" that are formed by intuitive cognitions and make us ready to form the appropriate abstractive cognitive acts when required. But the "habits" are not at all the objects of the acts they facilitate, although they can become objects of other reflective acts that the mind performs to know its own contents.

What in his own day chiefly set Ockham's thought apart from that of other scholastics was his relentless effort to rid science and METAPHYSICS of types of entities and modes of distinction between entities that he thought were in all cases explanatorily needless and in many cases positively incoherent. (This rejection of needless entities was an ancient principle, but it has come down to us under the name of "Ockham's razor.") In this effort at ontological parsimony, Ockham was greatly assisted by the sophisticated tools of logical analysis, especially terminist logic, which the scholastic tradition had developed and to which Ockham himself was an important contributor. For example, on the topic of universals, which had been a concern since ancient times, Ockham argued that the "moderate realism" of most Aristotelians was mistaken in supposing that there were real, mind-independent natures that were common to many individuals and grounded the classification of those individuals into species and genera. Instead, he claimed, we need only the relational facts that various individuals are the same in species and the same in genus to each other. One of Ockham's most common tactics in defending his ontological parsimony is illustrated here: where others find a need grounded in a priori logical considerations for a set of odd things, Ockham sees the needs of science as satisfied by mere facts about things that are already familiar and widely assumed.

Although Ockham denied that anything extramental was common to many, he was happy to allow that concepts in the mind are common in the sense that they signify each of many things equally well. This was his NOMINALISM as regards universals: commonness results from signification and is not presupposed by it. The result is that many doctrines of Aristotelian science and metaphysics, which the moderate realists had taken as being about extramental things, Ockham argues are really about concepts and their logical relationships.

It will be apparent from the preceding that Ockham was himself no skeptic and was basically conservative when it came to Aristotelian science and methodology. But certain doctrines that he sponsored in theology inadvertently left an opening for the skepticism that did develop soon after Ockham's philosophical period. God's omnipotence, according to Ockham, meant that he could produce anything and make anything be the case, as long as there was no logical contradiction involved in so doing. God could, for example, produce intuitive cognitions even when their objects were not existent. God could make accidents exist without any substrate. Some later thinkers in the fourteenth century, notably Nicholaus of Autrecourt, would use such ideas to argue that most of the principles of Aristotelian science were not genuinely demonstrable or totally certain. But Ockham himself drew no such conclusions.

PRIMARY WORKS

Ockham: Philosophical Writings. Edited and translated by P. Boehner. Edinburgh and London: Nelson and Sons, 1962.

Guillelmi de Ockham Opera Philosophica et Theologica. 17 vols. St. Bonaventure, NY: Franciscan Institute, 1967–1986.

Ockham's Theory of Terms. Part I of the Summa Logicæ. Edited by M. Loux. Notre Dame, IN: University of Notre Dame Press, 1974.

Ockham's Theory of Propositions. Part II of the Summa Logicæ. Edited and translated by A. J. Freddoso and H. Schuurman. Notre Dame, IN: University of Notre Dame Press, 1980.

BIBLIOGRAPHY

Adams, Marilyn M. *William Ockham.* 2 vols. Notre Dame, IN: University of Notre Dame Press, 1987.

Moody, Ernest A. *The Logic of William of Ockham.* New York: Sheed and Ward, 1935.

Panaccio, C. *Les mots, les concepts et les choses. La semantique de Guillaume d'Occam et le nominalisme d'aujourd'hui.* Montreal and Paris: Bellarmin and Vrin, 1991.
Tachau, K. T. *Vision and Certitude in the Age of Ockham.* Leiden: Brill, 1988.

MARTIN TWEEDALE

OPERATIONISM. Operationism (less often, operation*al*ism) is a particular form of CONCEPT empiricism, native to the twentieth century and particularly prominent in the social sciences, which holds that a concept for SCIENCE depends (or ought to depend) in some significant manner on the operations associated with its application. As with most descriptions of philosophical doctrines, making the description of operationism broad enough to be accurate renders it entirely schematic; the views championed by particular "operationists" emerge when specific senses are supplied for key phrases, particularly, "depend in some significant manner" and "operation." As also is often the case, the views of operationists differed dramatically, and arrayed over the decades following the introduction of the "operational attitude" by the Harvard physicist Percy Bridgman in 1927, they do not display the rational development often prized by philosophers. Instead, in the 1930s through the 1950s a variety of "operationisms" was discussed and defended, with no obvious leader emerging at debate's end. The outcome, nevertheless, was salutary for a philosophical doctrine; operationism left its mark on scientific practice, such that introductory and methodology texts from many scientific fields still advocate the "operationalizing" of scientific concepts. In the following I trace operationism historically, addressing Bridgman's "operational attitude," then the development of operationism among psychologists and social scientists, and finally the issues around which the operationism debate revolved and the more general question of its impact.

BRIDGMAN'S "OPERATIONAL ATTITUDE"

Operationism's standing in scientific practice is explained in part by the fact that it was conceived by professional scientists, rather than philosophers. Arguably, operationism originates in Percy Bridgman's 1927 *The Logic of Modern Physics*, although Bridgman did not there use the term "operationism." Indeed, he later disavowed the term and, in the view of some later self-proclaimed operationists, disavowed operationism itself. Somewhat distressed by the conceptual revolutions engendered by special relativity and quantum mechanics, Bridgman drew upon his own attempts to understand these developments (as well as his work in high-pressure phenomena, for which he was awarded the Nobel Prize in physics in 1946) to describe a means of formulating scientific concepts that, he believed, would render science immune to subsequent profound revolutions. Discarded concepts like Newtonian mass and simultaneity had been defined in terms of properties, argued Bridgman, and subsequently these concepts were discovered to be inapplicable to new domains of experience, like the very fast or very small. A *proper* means of formulating scientific concepts would prevent our concepts from being held hostage by future experiences, Bridgman claimed, and thus prevent as well forthcoming conceptual revolutions of the magnitude of special relativity or quantum mechanics. That proper means was to identify a concept's MEANING with the operations that determined when it applied in a given situation. Bridgman's formulation became a reference point for all later operationisms:

In general, we mean by any concept nothing more than a set of operations; *the concept is synonymous with the corresponding set of operations*. If the concept is physical, as of length, the operations are actual physical operations, namely, those by which length is measured; or if the concept is mental, as of mathematical continuity, the operations are mental operations, namely those by which we determine whether a given aggregate of magnitudes is continuous. (*The Logic of Modern Physics*: 5)

If concepts are defined in terms of operations rather than properties—if the having of a given length, for example, simply *means* the outcome of a certain operation—we would never be brought to abandon our concept of length. Empirical discoveries may surprise and excite us, argued Bridgman, but our conceptual repertoire, operationally defined, would remain.

Bridgman regarded his operational attitude as encapsulated in, among other things, Einstein's attitude to simultaneity. Thus, Bridgman made no priority claim to the operational attitude, though neither did he cite those thinkers who influenced its development in his hands (most likely, Stallo, PEIRCE, and MACH).

Among "operationisms," Bridgman's operational attitude occupies a particular niche. Bridgman presented operations as providing the meaning of concepts; this is the manner in which concepts depend on operations. The extension of "operation" for Bridgman included operations in the usual, "concrete" sense—for example, the laying end-to-end of a ruler—as well as what Bridgman called "mental" operations, consisting in such things as the comparison of two objects in thought or the understanding of a mathematical demonstration.

Bridgman's later writings on operationism were typically in response to others' understanding of *The Logic of Modern Physics*, and although Bridgman presented himself as clarifying his 1927 view, in fact he forwarded substantial modifications. In *The Nature of Physical Theory* (1936) and subsequent articles Bridgman claimed that an operational account of a concept was only a necessary, not a sufficient, condition for scientific legitimacy, and he further emphasized the range and importance of "mental," "verbal," and "pen-and-pencil" operations, all of them distinct from concrete operations like the measurement of length by means of a rigid rod. This led to an emphasis in later writings and in correspondence on what Bridgman regarded as science's subjective and private character. Already in 1936, he had written that "in the last analysis science is only my private science" (*The Nature of Physical Theory*: 13); for many, especially those in the social sciences who had regarded Bridgman as the progenitor of operation*ism*, such claims indicated that Bridgman himself had lost the operational attitude.

OPERATIONISM IN THE SOCIAL SCIENCES

Operationism in the social sciences, psychology in particular, is most often associated with one of Bridgman's colleagues, the Harvard psychologist S. S. Stevens. From 1935 to 1939, Stevens published four articles addressing the application of operationism in psychology. Where Bridgman, struck by recent revolutions in physics, had described an attitude designed to prevent future conceptual upheavals, Stevens sought a method that would minimize disagreement among scientists. Stevens' quest stemmed from his conviction that agreement was essential to science; in its absence, science could not be had. Consequently, Stevens sought the general form of the rules that would guide the application of a concept, such that no disagreement could arise over the application of concepts so guided. Taking agreement between individuals to be coextensive with shared discriminatory capacities—by which he had in mind overt, behavioral, and public actions—Stevens proposed that scientific concepts be associated with rules for their application that could be expressed solely in terms of acts of concrete denotation and subsequent discriminations. Indeed, such discriminations were the "*sine qua non* of any and every operation." "In this sense," he continued, "discrimination is the fundamental operation of all science" ("The Operational Basis of Psychology": 324). Stevens' emphasis on agreement and his notion of "operation" as overt discrimination (effectively excluding Bridgman's "mental" operations) distinguished his position sharply from Bridgman's, while at the same time aligning it, at least in the minds of many contemporaries, with behaviorism and the logical positivism of the Vienna Circle (see LOGICAL POSITIVISM/LOGICAL EMPIRICISM), several of whose members, notably Rudolf CARNAP, had recently arrived in the United States and at Harvard. As Stevens recognized, his view also accorded a special role to his own field of psychology—psychophysics—which studied the discriminatory capacities of humans generally. For this reason, Stevens argued, psychology was "propaedeutic" to other sciences, including physics. Finally, it is worth noting that nothing in Stevens' view required taking operationism as a thesis about the meaning of concepts, even in Bridgman's restricted sense of a necessary condition for meaningfulness. Interestingly, in Bridgman and Stevens we have quite different manifestations of a common empiricist program. One, Bridgman's, developed empiricism's traditional emphasis on the private nature of experience, while the other, Stevens', emphasized objectivity and the public character of KNOWLEDGE also traditionally associated with empiricism.

The late 1930s and 1940s saw a proliferation of claims to, and calls for, operational definitions, as well as burgeoning discussion of the appropriate formulation of the doctrine. This is certainly attributable to the different views to which the term lent itself, some of which were arrived at independently and only later associated with Bridgman's attitude (for an argument that this is true of Stevens' operationism, see Hardcastle 1995). B. F. Skinner, for example, had looked to Bridgman's *The Logic of Modern Physics* for theoretical support in his 1930 Harvard Ph.D. dissertation on the behavioral analysis of the reflex. E. C. Tolman, perhaps the most prominent behaviorist after Skinner, offered in 1936 an operational analysis of demand, as did E. G. Boring in the same year for temporal PERCEPTION. The versions of operationism presented in these discussions differed from each other and yet were associated not only with logical positivism but with PRAGMATISM, particularly Charles Peirce's version of that doctrine.

That there was such a "honeymoon" period for operationism in the 1930s and early 1940s gives some credence to Boring's frequent and Whiggish suggestion that operationism was "there all along" (for a competing analysis, in which Boring plays a significant historical role, see Rogers 1989). By the mid-1940s, however, serious worries had been raised over the nature and coherence of operationism.

DEBATE AND LEGACY

At the suggestion of E. G. Boring, a set of questions about operationism was taken up by psychologists and philosophers in a "Symposium on Operationism," published in *The Psychological Review* of September 1945; many of the same questions arose nine years later, in 1954, in a similar exchange in *The Scientific Monthly*. These symposia displayed the diversity and disagreement that operationism had, ironically, engendered.

Chief among the worries was a consequence Bridgman had recognized in associating concepts with operations, namely, that different operations must in turn distinguish the concepts with which they were associated. Bridgman's example was of length; length measured by the laying end-to-end of rigid rods and length measured by triangulation were in fact two different concepts, he argued, and ought not be referred to alike by the term "length." Thus, a thoroughgoing operationism seemed to result, in exchange for clarity and caution in the face of future experience, in a vast array of concepts to be managed. A suggested fix called upon the use of further operations to coordinate the other operationally defined concepts, thus allowing that one sort of length could be identified, albeit tentatively, with another.

Concerns about a multiplicity of concepts arose particularly if one identified the meaning of a concept with the operations associated with it, as had Bridgman in 1927. That identification also raised the related problem of how operations could be good or bad for some purposes, as clearly they seemed to be. As a matter of scientific practice, rigid rods, for example, were recognized as well suited to the measurement of length, while elastic ones were not. But if concepts are *identified* with operations, there could be no such sense in which a proposal for measuring length could be good or bad. The "fix" here most often suggested involved locating the quality of operations not in their ability to capture some property independent of them (e.g., the "actual" length of the object to be measured) but in various pragmatic factors, such as the compatibility of the proposed operations with others antecedently accepted. Even with these problems solved, there remained other worries, many of them put clearly, directly, and nearly devastatingly, in Carl Hempel's 1954 "A Logical Appraisal of Operationism."

Finally, other concerns arose even if one did not take operationism as a theory of the meaning of concepts. There was never an accepted account of what counted as an operation. This was a debate not only over the status of mental and hypothetical operations but over whether all operations must, or can, themselves be defined as well, with some advocating that some operations could be used to define themselves or that some operations were basic and thus needed no definition. In these debates we find analogues to debates in other periods of the history of empiricism over the nature of the fundamental elements of experience.

I have taken a historical approach to operationism not only for expository purposes but to convey something of the current attitude toward operationism. Although it is among the most recent expressions of empiricism, operationism has been relegated to the various strains of empiricism popular in the 1930s and 1940s. Presently, it enjoys less favor than other versions of empiricism. Yet at the same time, the call for operational definitions serves as a rallying cry for scientists when they seek to clarify or legitimate their terms or concepts. In this manner, the operationism of Bridgman and Stevens continues to influence scientific practice.

PRIMARY WORKS

Books

Benjamin, A. C. *Operationism*. Springfield, IL: Thomas, 1955.
Bridgman, P. W. *The Logic of Modern Physics*. New York: Macmillan, 1927.
———. *The Nature of Physical Theory*. Princeton: Princeton University Press, 1936.
Tolman, E. C. *Purposive Behavior in Animals and Men*. New York: Century, 1932.

Articles

Boring, E. G. "Temporal Perception and Operationism." *The American Journal of Psychology* 48 (1936): 519–22.
Bridgman, P. W. "Operational Analysis." *Philosophy of Science* 5 (1938): 114–31.
———. "P. W. Bridgman's 'The Logic of Modern Physics' after Thirty Years." *Dædalus* 88 (1959): 518–26.
Hempel, C. G. "A Logical Appraisal of Operationism." *The Scientific Monthly* 79 (1954): 215–20. Reprinted in C. G. Hempel, *Aspects of Scientific Explanation*. New York: Free Press, 1965, 1970.
Israel, H., and B. Goldstein. "Operationism in Psychology." *Psychological Review* 51 (1944): 177–88.
Stevens, S. S. "The Operational Basis of Psychology" (discussion). *American Journal of Psychology* 47 (1935): 323–30.
———. (1935). "The Operational Definition of Psychological Concepts." *Psychological Review* 42 (1935): 517–27.
———. "Psychology: The Propaedeutic Science." *Philosophy of Science* 3 (1936): 90–103.

———. "Psychology and the Science of Science." *Psychological Bulletin* 36 (1939): 221–63.

"Symposium on Operationism." *Psychological Review* 52 (1945).

"Symposium on Operationism." *The Scientific Monthly* 79 (1954).

Tolman, E. C. "Psychology versus Immediate Experience." *Philosophy of Science* 2 (1935): 356–80.

BIBLIOGRAPHY

Books

Smith, L. *Behaviorism and Logical Positivism: A Reassessment of the Alliance*. Stanford, CA: Stanford University Press, 1986.

Suppe, F. *The Semantic Conception of Theories and Scientific Realism*. Chicago: University of Illinois Press, 1989.

Walter, M. L. *Science and Cultural Crisis: An Intellectual Biography of Percy Williams Bridgman (1882–1961)*. Stanford, CA: Stanford University Press, 1990.

Articles

Hardcastle, Gary L. "S. S. Stevens and the Origins of Operationism." *Philosophy of Science* 62 (1995): 404–24.

Koch, S. "Psychology's Bridgman vs. Bridgman's Bridgman: An Essay in Reconstruction." *Theory and Psychology* 2 (1992): 261–90.

Moyer, A. E. "P. W. Bridgman's Operational Perspective on Physics, Part 1: Origins and Development" and "P. W. Bridgman's Operational Perspective on Physics, Part 2: Refinements, Publication, and Reception." *Studies in the History and Philosophy of Science* 22 (1991): 237–58 and 373–97.

Rogers, T. B. "Antecedents of Operationism: A Case History in Radical Positivism." In *Positivism in Psychology: Historical and Contemporary Problems* ed. C. W. Tolman. New York: Springer-Verlag, 1992.

———. "Operationism in Psychology: A Discussion of Contextual Antecedents and an Historical Interpretation of Its Longevity." *Journal of the History of the Behavioral Sciences* 23 (1989): 139–53.

GARY L. HARDCASTLE

P

PASCAL, BLAISE. Although Blaise Pascal (1623–1662) predates the rise of empiricism as a distinct school of modern philosophy, his innovative work as a scientist and philosopher has considerable bearing on the scope and nature of empirical KNOWLEDGE. Pascal's views were shaped by his involvement in the scientific community of the French elite (including Descartes, with whom he often disagreed) and by his later conversion to Christianity and exposure to Jansenism, a renewal movement within Catholicism that Pascal defended in his *Provincial Letters* but that was finally crushed by the church. Pascal's writings do not offer us a philosophical system; however, his insights into scientific experimentation and general epistemology present challenges to both rationalism and empiricism.

Amid the ferment of seventeenth-century scientific controversies, Pascal questioned the received wisdom that nature abhors a vacuum and devised an ingenious experiment to refute it. Many assumed on traditional or even a priori principles (whether philosophical or theological) that nature's economy eschewed a vacuum and that no experiments were needed to decide this matter. The METAPHYSICS of the great chain of being inherited from the medieval world demanded that nature be a hierarchical plenum or continuum devoid of ontological gaps. In his Preface to *The Treatise on the Vacuum*, Pascal distinguished between authority resting in the tradition found in books—concerning history, geography, language, and theology—and what can be discovered through empirical investigation. We may learn from the ancients in matters of geometry, arithmetic, music, physics, medicine, and architecture, but our knowledge need not be limited to their static opinions. Although nature "is always at work, her effects are not always discovered: time reveals them from generation to generation, and although always the same in herself, she is not always equally known. The experiments which give us our knowledge of nature multiply continually" (Preface to *The Treatise on the Vacuum*; 357). This also questions the deductivism of Descartes' philosophy of nature.

Pascal argued that the ancients erred on the question of the vacuum because of experimental inadequacies. With better experimentation, new discoveries emerge. Pascal broke new ground for a more scientific method by emphasizing PROBABILITY and falsification: "For in all matters whose proof is by experiment and not by demonstration, no universal assertion can be made except by the general enumeration of all the parts and all the different cases." The knowledge of nature is bought at the price of arduous and progressive experimentation. This is captured by the conclusion of Pascal's Preface to *The Treatise on the Vacuum*: "Whatever the weight of antiquity, truth should always have the advantage, even when newly discovered, since it is always older than every opinion men have held about it, and only ignorance of its nature could imagine it began to be at the time it began to be known."

Despite his zeal for inductive methods in scientific knowledge and his prowess as a precocious inventor and mathematician, Pascal grappled with the skeptical ruminations of the influential Montaigne. In a long and vertiginous fragment in *Pensées* (a posthumous collection of his notes on religion and morality), Pascal despaired of knowing the essence or meaning of nature through mere human investigation. Human knowers are strangely situated between "nothingness and infinity," such that certain knowledge of either is impossible. Pascal avers that each person is "a nothing compared with the infinite, a whole compared to the nothing, a middle point between all and nothing" (*Pensées* #199/72). Yet this station is not a comfortable middle because our ignorance of both the infinitesimal and the colossal precludes us from finding our place in the incomprehensible whole. Neither the newly invented telescope nor the microscope could reveal the significance of nature. For every veil they lift, another one appears.

Pascal's reflections on the constraints of empirical knowledge compelled him not to condemn or abandon scientific pursuits but to put scientific knowledge into a more humble philosophical framework. Empirical observation is but one of several paths to knowledge. Some knowledge is a priori, or intuitive (see A PRIORI/A POSTERIORI DISTINCTION), and eludes our empirical efforts: "Knowledge of first principles, like space, time, motion, number, is as solid as any derived through reason, and it is on such knowledge, coming from the heart and instinct, that reason has to depend and base all its arguments" (*Pensées* #110/339). Pascal means that "reason," or computational or discursive capacities (essential for empirical investigations), cannot generate or sustain our most basic epistemic principles. In acknowledging that not all knowledge is empirically derived, Pascal is close to a rationalist like Descartes (despite differing from him in other respects) and far from an empiricist like LOCKE, who thought that what Pascal attributed to "the heart and instinct" could be accounted for through empirical processes.

Yet the knowledge of the heart is not irrational: "Principles are felt, propositions proved, and both with certainty though by different means" (*Pensées* #110/339). Pascal laments that few things can be known through intuition alone: "Would to God . . . that we never needed [reason] and knew everything by instinct and feeling! But nature has refused us this blessing, and has instead given us only very little knowledge of this kind; all other knowledge can be acquired only by reasoning'' (*Pensées* #110/339). Pascal includes in ''reasoning'' the employment of reason in empirical endeavors. In making the distinction between a priori knowledge of the heart and what can be known only by other means, he illustrates that he is neither a rationalist nor an empiricist. His discussion of the heart's epistemic capacities anticipates recent thinking by Alvin Plantinga and others concerning ''properly basic beliefs,'' beliefs that are rationally justified, even though they are neither inferred from empirical data nor logically necessary.

Although not a fideist, Pascal saw the heart as the organ of religious faith, which is able to apprehend realities that are above sense and reason but that are not against them. Part of the philosophical strategy of Pascal's unfinished apology for the Christian faith (the *Pensées*) was to ''humble proud reason,'' precisely through a rational study of its limitations: ''Reason's last step is the recognition that there are an infinite number of things which are beyond it. It is merely feeble if it does not go as far as to realize that. If natural things are beyond it, what are we to say about supernatural things?'' (*Pensées* #188/267). Further: ''Faith certainly tells us what the senses do not, but not the contrary of what they see; it is above, not against them'' (*Pensées* #185/265). This construal of faith as being above reason has parallels to Locke's discussion in *An Essay concerning Human Understanding* (*Essay* IV.xviii), although Pascal differed from Locke in many other respects.

Pascal's discussion of the prudential benefits of religious faith in epistemically impeded situations (the famous ''wager'' argument) raises salient issues regarding the ethics of BELIEF, the relation of will to belief, religious experience, and decision theory. Although often disparaged, the wager argument has recently been gaining philosophical apologists.

Pascal's musings, though typically aphoristic and unsystematic, provide ample resources for further philosophizing on SKEPTICISM, scientific method, and religious belief.

PRIMARY WORKS

''Preface to the Treatise on the Vacuum.'' In *Pascal*, vol. 33 of *Great Books of the Western World*, edited by R. M. Hutchins. Chicago: Encyclopedia Britannica, 1952.
Pensées. Edited by Alban Krailshaimer. New York: Penguin Books, 1965.
The Provincial Letters. Edited by Alban Krailshaimer. New York: Penguin Books, 1967.

BIBLIOGRAPHY

Davidson, Hugh M. *The Origins of Certainty: Means and Meaning in Pascal's Pensées.* Chicago: University of Chicago Press, 1979.
Rescher, Nicholas. *Pascal's Wager: A Study of Practical Reasoning in Philosophical Theology.* Notre Dame, IN: University of Notre Dame Press, 1985.
Wells, A. N. *Pascal's Recovery of Man's Wholeness.* Richmond, VA: John Knox Press, 1965.

DOUGLAS R. GROOTHUIS

PASSIONS. In modern philosophy, passions are motions or disturbances of the mind that direct one toward good objects and away from bad objects. An alternative understanding of the passions in eighteenth-century medicine had them classified as "non-naturals," that is, things that cause diseases when abused (along with air, food, sleep, motion, and retained excretions). The concept of the passions during the modern period is part of a traditional theory developed by the Stoic philosophers, as reported by Cicero (*Tusculan Disputations* IV: 6,11). According to this theory, four passions are the foundation of all others: joy, grief, desire, and fear. Joy results from the *presence* of good objects or situations, and fear from the presence of bad ones. By contrast, desire results from *anticipating* good objects or situations, and fear from anticipating bad ones. A similar catalog of eleven foundational passions was offered by AQUINAS based on a distinction between our *concupiscible* appetites (focusing on easily obtainable objects) and irascible appetites (focusing on not easily obtainable objects; *Summa Theologica*, 1a2ae, Q. 25: 4).

During the next five centuries, treatises on the passions emerged from a variety of disciplines, all firmly grounded in the Stoic and Thomistic tradition (see STOICISM). Rhetoricians, artists, and writers theorized about evoking passions in their audience. Moral philosophers studied the passions to better understand human motivation and the development of virtues to control our base inclinations. Seventeenth-century Continental philosophers such as Descartes (*Passions of the Soul*) and Malebranche (*Search after Truth*) offered physiological explanations of the passions based on turbulences of humors, vapors, or animal spirits in the blood. For Descartes, perceptions and memories trigger a physiological chain of events prompting the pineal gland to cause the "soul to be sensible of this passion" (*Passions of the Soul*: Art. 26). Eighteenth-century British philosophers, who were less involved in the natural sciences, deliberately avoided detailed physiological explanations. Nevertheless, many, if not all, of the passions were thought to depend on bodily mechanisms (Hutcheson, *Nature and Conduct of the Passions* III: 3).

LOCKE briefly describes the passions as modifications of pleasure and pain and follows the standard Stoic and Thomistic account. Joy, for example, "is a delight of the Mind, from the consideration of the present or assured approaching possession of a Good" (*An Essay concerning Human Understanding* II.xx). BERKELEY does not treat the subject in any of his writings. HUME devotes the entirety of *A Treatise of Human Nature*, Book II, to the passions. With little alteration, Hume adopts the Stoic account of the principal passions of joy, sorrow (grief), hope (desire), and fear (collectively classed by Hume as direct impressions of reflection). Hume's unique contribution is the *double relation* involved in the passions of love, hate, pride, and humility (collectively classed as indirect impressions of reflection). Pride, for example, arises when one takes pleasure in a possession, such as one's house. This pleasure triggers an *associated impression* or feeling of pride (relation one). The feeling of pride prompts one to have an idea of oneself, and the idea of oneself triggers an *associated idea* of one's house (relation two).

Traditional discussion of the passions continued into the nineteenth century with only occasional reference to Hume's theory (e.g., T. Cogan, *Treatise on the Passions*, 1813). Interest in the passions tradition among contemporary psychologists has died, as exemplified in James's claim that "its pretences to accuracy are a sham" (*Principles of Psychology* 1890).

BIBLIOGRAPHY

Books

Árdal, Páll S. *Passion and Value in Hume's* Treatise. Edinburgh: Edinburgh University Press, 1966.
Glathe, Alfred. *Hume's Theory of the Passions and of Morals: A Study of Books II and III of the* Treatise. Berkeley: University of California Press, 1950.

Article

Fieser, James. "Hume's Classification of the Passions and Its Precursors." *Hume Studies* 18 (1992): 1–17.

JAMES FIESER

PEIRCE, CHARLES SANDERS. Charles Sanders Peirce (1839–1913) was an American logician and philosopher, best known as the founder of PRAGMATISM and for his development of a systematic theory of signs or semiotic. Although his emphasis on the role of observation and experiment in all spheres of knowledge makes him a major figure in the development of empiricist ideas in the late nineteenth century, he sharply disassociated himself from the NOMINALISM of the classical empiricists and arrived at his ideas through a sympathetic critical engagement with the work of KANT. After describing Peirce's pragmatism and experimentalism, I examine the systematic structure of his thought and the rich conception of experience he employed.

The son of a distinguished Harvard professor, Peirce taught logic and philosophy of science there while developing his pragmatism in regular discussions with William James and others and also working as a scientist for the U.S. Coast Survey. During the 1880s, he lost both the post he had obtained lecturing in logic at Johns Hopkins University and his job with the survey. Although maintaining his contacts with James, Josiah Royce, and others and giving occasional invited lectures, he worked largely in isolation, developing his philosophical system, until his death.

Peirce saw logic as the study of the norms and habits of reasoning that guide us in carrying out inquiries, in trying to replace doubt by settled belief. In "The Fixation of Belief" (1877), the first of a series of "Illustrations of the Logic of Science," he argued that we should employ the "Method of Science," defending rules by reference to the underlying hypothesis that there are real things that affect us through our senses and whose properties can be discovered through responsible inquiry. Later papers in the series developed Peirce's theories of reality and probability in the course of explaining how the method of SCIENCE works. Although Peirce did not use the word "pragmatism" until after 1900, the doctrine appeared in the second of the series, "How to Make our Ideas Clear." Reflective clarity about the contents of our hypotheses is invaluable for carrying out scientific inquiries, and we can gain such clarity by listing the experiential consequences we would expect our actions to have if the hypothesis was true. For example, from the hypothesis that a lump of metal is magnetized, we can predict that if we place iron filings close to it, we shall observe them attracted to it. Pragmatism holds that this process yields a complete clarification of the content of the hypothesis and that any "proposition" that resists such clarification is empty: a consequence was that "ontological metaphysics" is "gibberish."

Applying this principle to the clarification of "Truth" and "Reality," Peirce returned to a theme from his 1870 review of Fraser's edition of BERKELEY. "Nominalists" like LOCKE and Berkeley define reality as the efficient cause of our impressions, as what produces our sensations. Peirce favored the "realist" view of reality as the final cause of inquiry, as the object of the opinion we are destined to accept if we inquire sufficiently well. The method of science ensured the operation of this "destiny" or "fated convergence." The view is realist because, since the destined opinion will involve general concepts, it was favorable to the view that universals were real: the nominalist conception located our encounter with reality in sensations that were supposedly wholly particular. Peirce's later attempts to prove his "pragmaticism"—as he christened his doctrine to distinguish it from the ersatz versions purveyed by James and Dewey—relied heavily on the assertion that it entailed an extreme form of realism.

After 1880, Peirce argued that we directly experience external things: judgments expressing the content of our experience must contain indexical or demonstrative components referring to items experienced as "other than" ourselves. Second, he insisted that his pragmatism depended on a non-Humean theory of laws: reality involves real "mediation." There are objective truths about what would happen if I were to place filings near the magnet or about what would have happened if I had done so. Pragmatism required this doctrine because it explained how knowledge of laws can yield knowledge of particular events that are themselves no longer observable.

Peirce's philosophy was shaped by his revision of Kant's system of categories. He believed that an adequate language would have resources for expressing concepts of three kinds: those like ". . . is blue," which apply to a single object; those like ". . . hits . . . ," which relate two objects; and those like ". . . gives . . . to . . . ," which relate three objects. Calling the phenomena expressed by such concepts "Firstness," "Secondness," and "Thirdness," respectively, he argued that they provide a complete categorization of both experience and reality. He insisted that all three were manifested in experience: direct experience of external things involves Secondness; and experience of real generality, of real mediation, involved Thirdness. Unless he could defend these claims about the richness of the content of experience, pragmatism could not be reconciled with realism. Phenomenological observation of all that we can experience, imagine, dream, and so on was supposed to vindicate this claim. Particularly important for his "empiricist" defense of realism was the claim (which he called "synechism") that experience is continuous—not made up of a succession of discrete elements but welded together, its components all being connected or mediated by general ideas.

Peirce's epistemology combined a fallibilist awareness that the results of inductive reasoning (see INDUCTION) always risked falsification in the light of further experience with the insistence that we always operate against the background of a body of vague, commonsense certainties. Skeptical doubt directed at our everyday view of the world is an illusion encouraged by the discredited nominalist conception of reality. He also developed a sophisticated theory of thought and language. His semiotic theory insisted that meaning was a form of thirdness: a thought or utterance representing an object only through being understood or interpreted as so doing.

PRIMARY WORKS

The Essential Peirce. Edited by N. Houser and C. Kloesel. 2 vols. Bloomington: Indiana University Press, 1992.
The Writings of Charles S. Peirce: A Chronological Edition. Bloomington: Indiana University Press, 1982–present.

BIBLIOGRAPHY

Fisch, Max. *Peirce, Semiotic, and Pragmatism*. Bloomington: Indiana University Press, 1986.
Hookway, Christopher. *Peirce*. London: Routledge and Kegan Paul, 1985.
Ketner, Kenneth, ed. *Peirce and Contemporary Thought*. New York: Fordham University Press, 1995.

CHRISTOPHER HOOKWAY

PERCEPTION. "Perception" was understood by British empiricists to signify either (1) consciousness generally, (2) its most elementary and passive species, or (3) the datum immediately present to consciousness in sensation or reflection.

LOCKE defined perception as "the first faculty of the Mind, exercised about our *Ideas*. . . . [I]n bare naked *Perception*, the Mind is, for the most part, only passive; and what it perceives, it cannot avoid perceiving" (*An Essay concerning Human Understanding* II.ix.1). The objects of perception comprise what we are capable of understanding independently of any reference to past experience, reliance on habit, and exercise of judgment. Because Locke denied innate ideas (see IDEAS and INNATENESS), this means that perception is so extremely primitive a level of awareness that "[w]e may, I think, from the Make of an *Oyster*, or *Cockle*, reasonably conclude, that . . . there is some small dull Perception, whereby they are distinguished from perfect Insensibility'' (*Essay* II.ix.13–14).

Locke's notion of perception diverged significantly from ordinary and scientific conceptions, as is effectively dramatized by his analysis of the famous Molyneux thought experiment, concerning a man blind from birth who, when first made to see, is asked to distinguish a cube from a sphere. According to Locke, he could not perceive the difference, nor, in contrast to what Leibniz would argue in the *New Essays on Human Understanding*, could he reason out the difference on geometrical or other a priori grounds. Instead, such discrimination requires judgment founded on repeated experience of visually perceived objects. So too for all physical properties, irrespective of the sense by which they are apprehended: nothing external or enduring is, strictly speaking, perceived; only momentary ideas are. Deeply ingrained habit, as well as the fact that ''the actions of the Mind are performed'' so ''very quick'' as ''to require no time, but many of them can be crouded into an Instant'' (*Essay* II.ix.10), disguises from us our reliance on higher functions of understanding in what we ordinarily, but falsely, term ''perception.'' From this there follows another important consequence, widely overlooked in discussions of Locke and his successors: since it is presumably only by inference and analysis, not direct inspection, that simultaneous mental actions can be distinguished, it seems that they did not deem it essential to employ introspective means alone in order to determine what is, and is not, given in perception.

Although BERKELEY subscribed to the greater part of Locke's empiricist credo, he dissented on one crucial point, ABSTRACTION, with significant consequences where perception is concerned. According to Berkeley, we can conceive as separate only what is separately perceivable and conceive as conjoined only what is conjointly perceivable (see *Principles of Human Knowledge*, Introduction, §10). Hence, thought is limited to recollecting and rearranging the contents given in perception; we can never, contrary to what Locke believed, discover new ideas by means of higher intellectual operations such as abstraction. For example, Locke held that, through abstraction, we can obtain an idea of shape separable from the qualities specific to tactile and visual perception, which may then be supposed to apply to objects outside and independent of the mind. Berkeley rejected this on the ground that it is impossible for shape and qualities specific to sensation ever to be perceived separately, and what cannot be perceived separately cannot be supposed to exist separately. In the end, he confined the idea of shape, as well as all other ideas of SPACE, exclusively to the sense of touch, with no application to anything outside this sensory field. Similarly, Berkeley limited ideas of TIME to the succession of perceptions in a mind, with no application to anything other than trains of thought; unity and number to the manipulation of perceptible signs; happiness to the perception of pleasure; and so on. Most notoriously, he confined the idea of EXISTENCE to what can perceive or be perceived: ''I think an intuitive knowledge may be obtained . . . by any one that shall attend to what is meant by the term exist when applied to sensible things. . . . Their *esse* is *percipi*, nor is it possible they should have any existence, out of the minds of thinking things which perceived them'' (*Principles*, Part I, §3). Perception thus became criterial for both reality and possibility: only what perceives or is perceived may be ascribed reality, and only what is perceptible can be conceived to exist. To determine whether and to what extent our thought corresponds to reality, we have therefore merely to attend to the unvarnished given of perception as the only genuine standard of objective truth. For whatever else may be said to exist—matter, mathematical objects, and so on—is merely the imposition of language on understanding; "We need only draw the curtain of words, to behold the fairest tree of knowledge, whose fruit is excellent, and within the reach of our hand" (*Principles*, Introduction, §25).

HUME endorsed Berkeley's critique of abstraction, so that both the separability principle and the status of perception as criterial of reality and possibility were basic to his philosophizing. For him, "perception" thus denotes the object immediately and preimaginatively present to consciousness, and the question that divided him from Berkeley was what precisely deserves to be so classified. Hume distinguished perceptions into impressions or ideas, according to their relative vivacity. The exact meaning of "vivacity" is subject to dispute, but it seems most closely to approximate a "reality sense," that is, the degree to which a given perception is regarded as really existing by consciousness. It thus is to be equated not with the fact of its presence to consciousness but with the degree of response—vivacity or "feeling"—its presence evokes within consciousness itself. Sensations and reflections (PASSIONS, volitions) naturally evoke the maximal degree of this feeling; memories and believed ideas approach, but do not equal, impressions in vivacity; while fantasies, hypotheses, and other unbelieved ideas have relatively little vivacity.

Notably absent from Hume's inventory of preimaginative perceptions are relations. To begin with, he denied what Berkeley and everyone else prior to him had taken for granted, namely, that perceptions have intrinsic relations of existential dependence: "[A]ll our particular perceptions . . . are different, and distinguishable, and separable from each other, and may be separately consider'd, and may exist separately, and have no need of any thing to support their existence" (*A Treatise of Human Nature*: 252). Hume traced the idea of necessary connection (existential dependence) to an impression consisting of the *facility* felt in the transition from an impression to an idea customarily associated with it and the *vivacity* felt to pertain an idea thus associated. This means that the only necessary connections we are capable of conceiving or knowing are inextricably bound up with operations and affects immanent to associative IMAGINATION. Consequently, it is impossible to conceive our perceptions as having any intrinsic, preassociative dependence on one another, on anything unperceived, or on the mind (i.e., their *esse* may not be their *percipi*).

Although less certain, it seems likely that Hume also broke radically with tradition by subjectivizing all relations generally. For such claims as that "a relation . . . is not, strictly speaking, a property in the figures themselves, but arises merely from the comparison, which the mind makes betwixt them" (*Treatise*: 46) suggest that relations are bound up with mental activity; and Hume's belief that, if we consider "the nature of relation," we find "that facility of transition . . . is essential to it" (*Treatise*: 99) implies that the affect concomitant with relational activity enters into the very content of ideas of relations. Why would he have held such a view? Hume's prime concern was empirically to determine the nature and causes of what we believe. Even if relations did exist independently of consciousness, they could matter to us and influence our reasoning only if they evoked the appropriate response in associative imagination: facile transitions and vivacity (belief). In the absence of these feelings—or, in the case of philosophical relations, without a foundation in them—the "relation" would be only so much noise in our perceptual input, with no ability whatever to influence our thought or actions. Thus, for Hume, the preimaginative given of perception can be conceived only as a flux of fleeting, relationless, existentially autonomous existents.

What then? For Locke, perception was synonymous with the primitive input of consciousness and had to be kept sharply distinct from its output of objective representation. With Berkeley and then Hume, the data of perception became even more fluxlike and fragmentary, so that, correspondingly, an ever greater representational burden was placed on the imagination and understanding to process and organize these data into consciousness of a world of objects in dynamical interconnection and of self in interaction with other selves. The implications of this progression were decidedly skeptical (see SKEPTICISM), since one had only to peek behind the curtain of imaginary accretions and linguistic obfuscation to ascertain that the true nature of the reality we perceive falls far short of the reality we believe ourselves, in ordinary consciousness, to behold.

Yet, paradoxically, the philosopher who pushed the progression to its utmost limit did so precisely to remove its skeptical sting. According to KANT, there is no such thing as a preimaginative given of perception: "No psychologist ever has even so much as thought that the imagination might be a necessary ingredient of perception itself . . . because it was believed that the senses furnished not impressions alone but their composition as well, and brought images of objects to hand" (*Critique of Pure Reason*: A120n). In Kant's view, simply to have a manifold of perceptions together in one consciousness and represent it as a manifold require a synthesis of imagination, performed in accordance with a priori forms of intuition (pure SPACE and TIME). Since the consequence of this is, in effect, to stitch up the curtain of empirical imagination behind which empiricists like Hume purported to peek, Kant thereby dislodged perception from the special criterial status it had enjoyed with Berkeley and Hume and so denuded it of its skeptical implications vis-à-vis objective representation.

PRIMARY WORKS

Berkeley, George. *The Works of George Berkeley, Bishop of Cloyne*. Edited by A. A. Luce and T. E. Jessop. 9 vols. London: Thomas Nelson and Sons, 1948–1957.

Hume, David. *A Treatise of Human Nature*. 2d ed., edited with an analytical index by L. A. Selby-Bigge; revised with notes by P. H. Nidditch. Oxford: Clarendon Press, 1978.

Kant, Immanuel. *Kritik der reinen Vernunft*. Edited by Raymond Schmidt. Hamburg: Felix Meiner Vorlag, 1990.

Locke, John. *An Essay concerning Human Understanding*. Edited with an introduction by P. H. Nidditch. Oxford: Clarendon Press, 1975.

WAYNE WAXMAN

PERSONAL IDENTITY. The idea (today, we would say, "concept") of IDENTITY presents one of the most difficult challenges for the empiricist project of tracing all our ideas to sense experience. It is one thing to say, as LOCKE does, that "our idea of sameness is not so settled and clean as to deserve to be thought innate"; it is another to show how, with all its instability, it is at least rooted in, if not entirely reducible to, the ideas our senses provide to us. Yet such an account must both undergird and constrain an empiricist explanation of personal identity. Thus, an understanding of the positions and arguments to be described in this entry requires familiarity with those on the more general topic (see the entry on IDENTITY).

"Personal identity" has been used to label a number of different things: the identity of persons, that of minds (or souls), of selves generally, and of one's own self. What makes a person the same over time? A mind the same mind? A self the same self? Wherein does such sameness consist? What are the marks by which it can be recognized? On what basis are we entitled to attribute it? Such questions are, of course, neither new nor only for empiricists. In spite of HUME's gloss on the topic as one that has "become so great a question in philosophy, especially of late years in England," it is worth reminding ourselves that it is a perennial one:

[A]s one develops from childhood to old age, one is said to be the same person, although one never has the same elements in oneself even though one is called the same person. On the contrary, one is always undergoing renewal while losing some element of one's hair, flesh, bones, blood, and all parts of the body generally. This is so not only with regard to one's body, but also with regard to one's soul. One's habits, characteristics, opinions, desires, pleasures, pains, fears, none of these ever stay the same. (Plato, *Symposium*: 207 d–e)

The basic puzzle is much as we find it in Locke and Hume. What is different, of course, is the reluctance to adopt a solution in terms of an underlying SUBSTANCE that is unchanged and thus properly speaking is—as Hume and REID will say, "perfectly"—identical through these alterations. The task then is to provide an answer that is consistent with both empiricism and our everyday judgments of sameness.

Locke is the first to take pains to avoid running together the various questions just listed: "[T]o conceive and judge of [identity] aright, we must consider what idea the word it is applied to stands for ... the difficulty or obscurity that has been about this matter rather rises from the names ill used, than from any obscurity in things themselves" (*An Essay concerning Human Understanding* II.xxvii.7). It is "one thing to be the same *substance*, another the same *man*, and a third the same *person*." He is still able to talk about a mind or soul as "an immaterial substance," in a way that Hume will regard as meaningless. But he is careful to separate the question of personal identity from that of the identity of such a putative spiritual substance, which "concerns not personal identity at all," anymore than does the identity of bodies. On the first score, if, as Locke argues, "consciousness makes personal identity," as long as we cannot rule out the possibility of "the same consciousness [being] transferred from one substance to another, it will be possible that two thinking substances make but one person. For the same consciousness being preserved, whether in the same or different substances, the personal identity is preserved" (*Essay* II.xvii.13). Conversely, even if we suppose, as believers in reincarnation do, the same spiritual substance to inhabit two or more bodies, we are not tempted to regard these as embodying the same person, as long as the second has no memory of the life— the experiences and actions—of the first. On the second score, as far as being the same man goes, this must consist in bodily continuity; otherwise, it would be impossible to secure the identity of a child with the adult it grows into while disallowing the possibility of two or more physically distinct entities—Socrates and Plato, for example—being the same. But being the same man is not the same thing as being the same person, "person" being a forensic term: only conscious, intelligent agents can be the subject of moral judgments and of rewards and punishments:

For should the soul of a prince, carrying with it the consciousness of the prince's past life, enter and inform the body of a cobbler, as soon as deserted by his own soul, every one sees he would be the same person with the prince, accountable only for the prince' actions: but who would say it was the same man? (*Essay* II.xvii.15)

Thus, while "participation [in] the same continued life by constantly fleeting particles of matter" is enough to constitute the sameness of a man, nothing but consciousness can unite remote existences into the same person, a person (or self) being "a thinking intelligent being." (Locke thinks that all thinking is necessarily conscious.) Thus, "consciousness alone makes self."

This has proved to be one of the most disputed aspects of Locke's account. Butler allows that "consciousness does ... ascertain our personal identity to ourselves," but he objects that it "presupposes, and therefore cannot constitute personal identity," an objection echoed by Reid ("[P]ersonal identity is confounded with the evidence we have of our personal identity ... an absurdity too gross to be entertained") and many later writers. (But see Ayer's defense of Locke on the point—Ayer: 196.)

BERKELEY is strangely silent on the topic of personal identity. Hume's treatment is, however, one of the best-known parts of his philosophy and has been often seen as the inevitable skeptical outcome of his basic principles rigorously applied. It has also been regarded as offering, as in the rest of his philosophy, a more positive, constructive account, one that leaves untouched the legitimacy of our ordinary judgments. Like Locke, Hume distinguishes between (what he calls) strict or perfect identity, on one hand, and imperfect identity, on the other. While the former tolerates no change, the latter can accommodate it in the case of both objects and minds or selves. While it is a mistake—though a natural one—to ascribe perfect identity to a mind consisting of perceptions that change with "inconceivable rapidity," it is legitimate to regard it as one thing, capable of being identified at different times as the same in a less demanding sense. That sense requires only a certain kind of relational unity among perceptions connected by memory and causation, the latter itself depending on the former. "[M]emory [is] the source of personal identity. Had we no memory, we never shou'd have any notion of causation, nor consequently of that chain of causes and effects, which constitute our person." Whether Hume is committed to Reid's "gross absurdity" is not clear: he says both that "memory does not so much *produce* as *discover* personal identity" and that "memory not only discovers identity, but also contributes to its production" (*A Treatise of Human Nature* I.iv.6). What is clear, though, is that some of one's perceptions are memories that enable one to think of oneself as the same now as earlier. Thus, at least our *belief* in our own identity is explained—always Hume's immediate and minimum goal. If causal relations among perceptions make those perceptions constitute a person, and if the presence of causal relations itself requires memory, as Hume thinks, then, no less than for Locke, memory, or consciousness, makes for personal identity.

In any case, "the self or person is not any one impression, but that to which our several impressions and ideas are suppos'd to have a reference." It is merely "a bundle or collection of different perceptions," but it is an *organized* bundle. As such, it has perfectly good identity conditions, sufficient for deciding when it is and when it is not one thing, just as does "a ship, of which a considerable part has been chang'd by frequent reparations." We *do* make a mistake if we attribute strict or perfect identity to either, as indeed we are naturally tempted to do. Like so many of our judgments, those of identity are unreflective, arising out of the tendency of the mind to conflate distinct ideas whenever the transition between them is easy and habitual: "That action of the imagination, by which we consider the uninterrupted and invariable object, and that by which we reflect on the succession of related objects, are almost the same to the feeling." But this is a problem only if we invent an unchanging self to be *really* strictly or perfectly identical, something that only philosophers do.

Hume compares the mind to a theater (in the sense of a play, rather than a building) and to a commonwealth; to the former, to illustrate the changing character of its successive contents, and to the latter, to show its essentially relational character. (Rather, as in Ryle's example, in a somewhat different context, it would be a mistake to ask, having been shown all its individual buildings, "But where is the university?" so with commonwealths and minds, it is a mistake to look for something over and above the items they contain and the relations in which these stand.)

Hume is often thought to have rejected, or at least to have expressed grave doubts about, his own account in an appendix to the *Treatise* written later, but the meaning of his remarks there is far from clear. On one interpretation, at least, he is merely elaborating on, in order to make clearer, both his objections to the view of the self as a substance and his own relational account.

While nineteenth-century empiricists, such as MILL, pay little attention to the topic of personal identity, it remains one that engages the attention of many philosophers, particularly of those of an empiricist bent, in our own time.

PRIMARY WORKS

Butler, Joseph. *Dissertation on Personal Identity*. In *The Works of Joseph Butler*, with introduction and note by J. H. Barnard. London: English Theological Library, 1900.

Hume, David. *A Treatise of Human Nature*. 2d ed., edited with an analytical index by L. A. Selby-Bigge; revised with notes by P. H. Nidditch. Oxford: Clarendon Press, 1978.

Locke, John. *An Essay concerning Human Understanding*. Edited with an introduction by P. H. Nidditch. Oxford: Clarendon Press, 1975.

Reid, *Essays on the Intellectual Powers of Man*. In *The Works of Thomas Reid*, 7th ed., edited by William Hamilton. Edinburgh: Maclachlan and Stewart, 1872.

BIBLIOGRAPHY

Ayer, A. J. *The Problem of Knowledge*. London: Macmillan; New York: St. Martin's Press, 1956. Penguin Paperback.

JOHN I. BIRO

PHENOMENALISM. "Phenomenalism" is a term applied, primarily, to the metaphysical (ontological) thesis that the particulars constituting sensible things (bodies) are all *phenomenal*. What is a phenomenal particular? Several approaches to this question are possible, but the approach taken here is historical. The historical recommends itself because it is no exaggeration to say that nearly every version of phenomenalism has roots in the work of George BERKELEY (1685–1753). But the historical approach has the additional advantage that it permits us to explain what phenomenal particulars are supposed to be without begging philosophical questions about their existence.

Seventeenth-century philosophers were largely in agreement on two propositions about our perceptual relation to the world (see EXTERNAL WORLD): (1) perceptual experiences are produced by processes that involve bodies acting on our organs of sense—wherein the proximate cause of a perceptual experience is an event or process taking place in the brain of the perceiver; (2) the perceptual experiences produced in this way are mental representations of bodies. Proposition (1) is at the heart of the causal theory of perception (it has the status of a truism of science), while (2) is central to any ontological account of intentionality, any account of the directedness or aboutness of consciousness.

In the representative realism (or representationalism) of Nicolas Malebranche (1636–1715) and John LOCKE (1632–1704) the production mentioned in (1) and (2) is regarded as a wholly mechanical and linear process—an instance of "billiard-ball causation"—and "representation" is understood iconically (or imagistically). So regarded and understood, representationalists generally hold that (1) and (2) commit us to rejecting the commonsense conviction that we perceive bodies, that bodies are colored, flavored, and so on. Such convictions, "strictly speaking," are false: bodies have, in themselves, at most only a few of the qualities we ordinarily attribute to them; and bodies can be perceived, at best, only *mediately*—where "mediate" means *via the mediation of*—and the mediating item, the *immediate* object of perception, is one that intervenes between the physical object and the mind. The immediate object of perception, then, is a *tertium quid*, a third thing—an item that is neither a body nor a mind. However, although neither a body nor a mind, the *tertium quid* is nevertheless essentially mental, that is, dependent for its existence on a mind.

Now as Berkeley (and many others) read it, Book II of Locke's *An Essay concerning Human Understanding* contains an unambiguous statement of representationalism. (As Berkeley realized, Malebranche's representationalism differs significantly from Locke's, but we restrict ourselves here to the latter.) Locke calls the representational items *ideas of sense*, and, on his account, their character is precisely that ascribed by common sense (by plain men and women) to bodies: most of the simple qualities we normally—but mistakenly, according to Locke—attribute to bodies (thermal qualities, color, flavor, etc.) are held to be attributable, again "strictly speaking," only to ideas or sensations. Locke was fairly confident that ideas resemble bodies in certain respects (specifically, in those respects—solidity, most prominently—required to sustain billiard-ball causation), and he seems to have thought that this resemblance is the ground of the intentionality of perception: ideas of sense are about (they represent) bodies only because, and to the extent that, they resemble bodies.

The principal objection to representationalism is epistemological: if all we ever perceive are the mental effects of external material causes, it is not obvious how we could ever even frame the concept of an external material cause nor, assuming we do frame it, how we could know of the existence and nature of any objects alleged to satisfy that concept. Locke thought he could explain the origin of the concept by means of his theory of abstract ideas (see ABSTRACTION), but he never adequately addressed the objection that his representationalism leads to SKEPTICISM about the existence and nature of the material world. Although representationalists after Locke (particularly in the present century) have advanced several ways of disarming this objection, Berkeley certainly thought it was both serious and fatal. He argued generally that Locke's account of abstraction is incoherent and, more specifically, that the very concept of material substance is either contradictory or empty—and consequently can form no part of the meaning of "body" (or, as he preferred, "sensible thing"). He argued, moreover, that even if we waive these objections, representationalism collapses: since something perceivable cannot be like something unperceivable—as Berkeley put it, "[A]n idea can be like nothing but an idea" (*Principles of Human Knowledge* §8)—the alleged resemblance between an idea and a material substance is unintelligible. Having demolished "materialism" and representationalism, he set himself the task of forging an ontology capable of accommodating (1) and (2) while at the same time avoiding—indeed, refuting—skepticism.

Berkeley argued that his alternative phenomenalistic analysis of bodies makes possible—indeed, ensures—that sense perception is a form of knowing both the existence and nature of bodies. (Indeed, this has long been thought to be one of the principal advantages of phenomenalism.) The ontological account of bodies that he proposes can be stated briefly: bodies are constituted not of material substances but rather of "collections" of sensible qualities inseparably tied and lawfully related to each other. This ontology leads to, and merges neatly with, Berkeley's epistemology, a species of foundationalism: our knowledge of such collections of sensible qualities—our knowledge of phenomenal particulars—provides us with the foundation for our knowledge of bodies. To fully appreciate these two aspects of Berkeley's phenomenalism (and, incidentally, to expose that feature of his phenomenalism for which he is best known) we need to look more closely at his distinction between immediate and mediate perception.

Both Locke and Berkeley take "immediate perception" to stand for a type of infallible awareness, indeed, a bona fide case of perceptual *knowing* that is directed at *mind-dependent* sensible *qualities*. Let us consider these three points in reverse order. Berkeley writes: "Those things alone are [immediately] perceived by any sense, which would have been perceived, in case that same sense had then been first conferred on us" (*Dialogues*: 204). He holds that someone who perceives for the first time experiences nothing but determinate quality-clusters unique to a given mode of perception, what Berkeley sometimes refers to as the "proper objects" of perception. Here are some examples: for vision, there are colored expanses; for touch, thermal qualities, kinesthetic feelings of resistance (or solidity) and texture; for hearing, various auditory qualities such as pitch and volume. (Berkeley's answer to my opening question, then, is that a phenomenal particular is a mode-specific cluster of sensible qualities.) Of special interest in this connection is Berkeley's thesis of the heterogeneity of proper objects, in particular his thesis that visual shape is as different from tactual shape as either is from color, sound, flavor, or odor. Berkeley held that our mistakenly identifying the two types of shape is a result of their lawful connections: they so constantly occur together in our experience that we (and even the philosophers among us) mistakenly suppose that the visual and tactual qualities are identical, that shape is a "common sensible."

Berkeley's second point of agreement with Locke is that the immediately perceived sensible qualities are mind-dependent: they are ideas or sensations; their *esse* is *percipi*. For Locke the mind-dependence of sensible qualities is integral to his realistic analysis of (1) and (2), the ideational (or sensational) character of sensible qualities being premised on the existence and causal efficacy of unperceivable material substances. But having rejected this latter as incoherent, Berkeley's argument for the mind-dependence of sensible qualities must be (and is) grounded in an entirely different way, and, given this IDE-ALISM, he is then required to (and does) advance a different account of (1) and (2), an account in which "production" is explicated as lawfulness, and all of the lawfully related items are perceivable (indeed, *perceived*). In this, Berkeley clearly anticipates the account of causation as regular sequence (or constant conjunction) advanced by David HUME (1711–1776).

Thus, Berkeley's, the first phenomenalistic analysis of bodies, is advanced as idealistic phenomenalism: each sensible quality is an idea, each proper object is a collection of ideas, and the analysis of bodies is exhausted by proper objects, so bodies are themselves ideational. The idealistic side of Berkeley's philosophy is closely linked to the first point of his agreement with Locke about the meaning of "immediate perception." For if we ask why it is held that, in immediate perception, no mistake is possible about the existence and nature of proper objects, Berkeley has a ready, the traditional—indeed, Locke's—answer: it is unthinkable (in their terms, it is an absurdity to suppose) that the mind could be mistaken about its own contents, unthinkable that here, in the mind, "seems" does not entail "is." It is but a short step from this, via Berkeley's phenomenalism, to the conclusion that skepticism is false, that in perceiving we are really knowing both the nature and existence of bodies.

To evaluate this conclusion we need to look a little more closely at the concept of mediate perception. For both Locke and Berkeley the object of a mediate perception is a body. While Berkeley sometimes seems to follow Locke in holding that mediate perception is inferential, he is really committed to rejecting this Lockean position. In the realm of the mind, as just noted, "seems" entails "is," and it seems to me that I see this red globe (a body) with the same "immediacy" that I see a circular colored expanse (a proper object of vision). At the very least it must be admitted that there is typically no conscious process of inferential thought taking place when I see a red globe. (With the possible exception of Gottfried Wilhelm Leibniz [1646–1716], philosophers of the early modern period would generally have regarded as absurd the notion of an unconscious passage of thought.) In any case, Locke's characterization of mediate perception as inferential is inconsistent with both Berkeley's ontology and his epistemology, for he rejects the representationalist view that mediate perception involves a tertium quid and insists instead that mediate perception is "mediated" only in the sense that it is a form of perception that has been conditioned by experience: accumulated experience "converts" immediate perception into mediate perception.

As with Locke's account, mediate perception is about bodies, but since Berkeley holds that bodies are constituted of immediately perceived items, and these latter are infallibly perceived, he appears to be entitled to the conclusion that his account avoids skepticism about both the existence and nature of bodies. The appearance, however, is deceptive. Berkeley writes that "the more a man knows of the connexion of ideas [i.e., proper objects], the more he is said to know of the nature of things" (*Dialogues*: 245); and this suggests that one's knowledge of a proper object does not yield knowledge of a body until one knows how proper objects of this kind are connected to proper objects of other kinds (e.g., how a given proper visual object is lawfully related to a proper tangible object). Indeed, with this statement Berkeley signals the recognition that his account yields not yet knowledge of bodies but at best only the underpinnings of such knowledge: given that knowledge of proper objects can yield knowledge of bodies only by the mediation of inductively based beliefs about the laws of nature, and given that such beliefs can never satisfy the criterion of indubitability—a point that Hume both emphasizes and then exploits to great effect—Berkeley will have to concede that his account yields, at best, only probable belief in the existence of bodies.

We see, then, that from the point of view of epistemology, phenomenalism actually delivers less than it promises. In addition, phenomenalism faces a variety of ontological problems. Three are prominent. The first is the problem of theoretical objects: scientists generally regard the fundamental objects of physical theory (the "corpuscles" of Berkeley's era) to be real (independent) existents. Berkeley's only explicit response to this (*Principles* §§ 62–65) is to permit the existence of theoretical objects if they are perceivable (e.g., by means of powerful microscopes). If it is a theoretical requirement that the fundamental objects be unperceivable, it is open to him (though he does not avail himself of it) to "dissolve" the problem by treating the theories in which references to unperceivable items seem to be made as having instrumental but no ontological import. (This theory, called INSTRUMENTALISM, becomes central to the late nineteenth-century phenomenalism of Ernst MACH.) A second problem is privacy: common sense regards bodies as capable of being perceived by many different perceivers (i.e., they are public). While Berkeley emphasizes that no two people can perceive the same phenomenal particular, he also says that it "is not at all repugnant to the principles I maintain" that "different persons may perceive the same thing" (*Dialogues*: 247). While he does not explain how bodies can be public, it is open to Berkeley to point out that a system of particulars can be perceived without perceiving all of its members, and a thing, or body, just *is* a system of phenomenal particulars, so it follows that (even though no two people perceive the same constituents) more than one person can perceive the same body. The third problem is that of intermittency: common sense regards bodies as items that continue to exist during those intervals in which we are not perceiving them (they are continuants) and, indeed, that bodies might exist, even though *never* perceived.

Intermittency is perhaps, for Berkeley, the most vexing of the ontological problems; and three different solutions, none of them very satisfactory, can be found in his writings. When he emphasizes that phenomenal particulars are "fleeting indeed, and changeable" (*Dialogues*: 258), he seems ready to accept the "gappiness" of bodies and to insist that although we should "speak with the vulgar" (i.e., speak as if bodies were continuants), we should "think with the learned" (recognize that they are not). A second Berkeleian approach (*Principles* §§3, 58) is to treat assertions about unperceived existents as assertions about what would be perceived if certain conditions were satisfied. (Berkeley promptly ignores this suggestion—it plays no role in his system—but many twentieth-century phenomenalists regard it as the cornerstone of their philosophies.) A third approach is to invoke the Deity either to fill in the gaps or to be at the ready to do so. Hume rejected the second and third solutions as, respectively, merely verbal and rationally (as well as empirically) unacceptable. Hume's argument that the commonsense position is based on a "fiction of the imagination" suggests that bodies simply are modally and temporally gappy and private (mind-dependent) entities. But Hume also hints at another solution, one based on his insight that there is no contradiction in supposing the existence of unobserved phenomenal particulars. (If one supposes, as both Locke and Berkeley encourage us to do, that a phenomenal particular is a *sensation*, then, of course, one will insist that Hume's "insight" is just plain wrong: there cannot be unsensed sensations. The implicit argument here, however, is a non sequitur: as Hume remarks in his discussion of "cause" and "effect," from the fact that there cannot be a husband without a wife, it does not follow that every man is a husband.) Hume maintains that there is no demonstrative proof of the non-existence of unperceived phenomenal particulars, and this opens the door to an opposing phenomenalistic analysis of bodies.

If unperceived phenomenal particulars exist, one can advance a thesis of realistic phenomenalism that disposes immediately of Berkeley's second and third problems. The intermittency objection is answered by filling the gaps with unperceived phenomenal particulars; and the publicity problem is solved pretty much along the lines suggested earlier: the phenomenal particulars belonging to a body that I, alone, am currently seeing are constituents of an enormously complex system of phenomenal particulars the vast majority of which exist unperceived; but while no one else can perceive the same phenomenal particulars of which I am now aware, an indefinite number of people can perceive phenomenal particulars belonging to the same system that I am currently perceiving.

After Hume, phenomenalism was to languish until the late nineteenth century. In the meantime, with the rise of transcendental and absolute idealism in the late eighteenth and early nineteenth centuries, it nearly disappeared from the philosophical landscape. It reemerged in ambiguous form in 1866 with the publication of J. S. MILL's *An Examination of Sir William Hamilton's Philosophy.* In this work Mill tried to solve the intermittency and publicity problems by regarding a body as a "Permanent Possibility of Sensation" (198). Unfortunately, however, he did not explain how we are to understand this expression. Were it not for his own description of himself as a "Berkeleian," it would be tempting to suppose that a "permanent possibility" is an unknown material cause with the power to produce ordered sensations in perceivers. But if this antiphenomenalist view is not Mill's, that still leaves us with at least two other possibilities. According to the first, the expression "permanent possibility" refers to lawfully ordered items that have precisely the character of presented sensations except that they are not experienced. (This position would take advantage of both Hume's insight and his analysis of CAUSATION.) According to the second, the permanent possibilities are conceptual constructs; they are the dispositionally expressible contents of our expectations (see DISPOSITIONS). Both of these are phenomenalistic, but while the first (realistic) version gets us a degree of permanence, it seems inconsistent with the modal term (the unobserved phenomenal particulars are actual, not possible), and the second (idealistic) version mislocates the ground of permanence, for Mill unmistakably regards the permanence as independent of the perceiver.

Both of these versions find homes in the twentieth century. In the first several decades, numerous philosophical developments—most notably in logic and philosophy of language—encouraged the reemergence of phenomenalism. Around the turn of the century, acknowledging his debt to Berkeley and Hume, the noted scientist/philosopher Ernst Mach (1838–1916) combined strict empiricism, the quest for certainty, and the ideal of the unity of science (see LOGICAL POSITIVISM) with a "neutral monist" line on phenomenal particulars (the "elements" of science can be treated as mental or material, depending on the context) and an instrumentalist solution to the problem of theoretical objects.

By the end of the third decade, the "linguistic turn" in philosophy brought an increasing emphasis on language either as an object or as a tool of philosophical investigation. Mainstream phenomenalism took the first alternative, construed language as the expression of CONCEPTS, regarded its method as conceptual analysis, and took its principal enterprise to be the translation of ordinary sentences about bodies into conjunctions of sentences about phenomenal particulars. The completion of this task was sometimes said to be a "logical construction" of a body, and while some followed Berkeley in regarding the construction (and/or the constructed elements—now generally referred to as "sense-data") to be mind-dependent, the characteristic preoccupation with epistemology and the adoption of a positivistic (antimetaphysical) stance led many to regard such metaphysical commitments as meaningless (see METAPHYSICS). Mainstream phenomenalism in this century is thus not strictly classifiable as either idealist or realist, and if any label recommends itself, it is conceptual phenomenalism.

Conceptual phenomenalism draws much of the inspiration for its transitional enterprise from Berkeley's suggestion that categorical statements like, "There is a table in the next room" are best understood as conditional: "If a perceiver were in the next room, he or she would perceive such and such phenomenal particulars." The most serious difficulties for the enterprise emerge from reflection on such examples. If it is to be successful, any such translation must eliminate all references to bodies in favor of references to phenomenal particulars (so that, e.g., the word "room" in the antecedent would be impermissible, and the word "perceiver" problematical). But this only magnifies, perhaps beyond tractability, a problem that already exists: even the simplest of ordinary categorical statements about bodies requires an indefinitely (perhaps infinitely) complex translation. From the logical point of view, however, there is an even more devastating objection: while the conditional statement seems clearly to be entailed by its corresponding categorical, it is nevertheless a mistake to regard them as having the same meaning—at the very least it must be admitted that there is an irreducible logical difference between categorical and conditional statements. (These and other objections to conceptual phenomenalism are discussed more fully under the rubric "linguistic phenomenalism" in R. J. Hirst's *Encyclopedia of Philosophy* entry "Phenomenalism.")

The complexity of the analysis should be regarded as a serious problem for mainstream phenomenalists—concerned as they are with the analysis of concepts—but it should not be thought (as it often is) a defect of phenomenalism generally. The versions of realistic phenomenalism advanced by Bertrand RUSSELL, in *Mysticism and Logic* (1918), and H. H. Price, in *Hume's Theory of the External World* (1940), are able to sidestep the difficulty because on these accounts it is not the *concept* of a body, but rather, a body itself, to which the phenomenalistic analysis is applied. Thus, there is nothing to prevent realistic phenomenalists from retorting as follows to the complexity objection: although even the most simple of (macroscopic) bodies is staggeringly complex on the account of modern physicalism—there are billions of atoms, for example, in the dot at the end of this sentence—no one would object to an atomistic-physicalist analysis of a (macroscopic) body on grounds of its complexity.

Although Russell's realistic phenomenalism was advanced in 1914–1915, he soon abandoned it. While Price may have held a similar view, he explicitly advanced it on Hume's behalf. The real champion of the theory appeared at a time when phenomenalism was everywhere in retreat. Midway through the twentieth century Gustav BERGMANN (1906–1987) published *The Metaphysics of Logical Positivism* (1953), a work in which he argued, true to his title, that the logical positivists, though ostensibly eschewing metaphysics, were in fact committed by their empiricism and naturalism to a phenomenalist ontology. For Bergmann, the true spirit of the "linguistic turn" is not to be found in treating language (or concepts) as an *object* of philosophical investigation; rather, its true spirit lies in regarding language (specifically, a logically rigorous language, such as the notation of Russell's *Principia Mathematica*) as a *tool* in such investigations. During the 1950s and 1960s, Bergmann elaborated a sophisticated ver-

PHENOMENALISM 325

sion of realistic phenomenalism, facilitated by the linguistic tool he referred to as the "ideal language method." Within this method, translation is regarded not as something that would capture what ordinary people "mean" by sentences about bodies—indeed, on Bergmann's complementary account of mental acts, the opacity of thought rules out any such enterprise (see "Acts" in *Logic and Reality*). Rather, the purpose of such an enterprise is to represent perspicuously the "ontological structure" of bodies: the properties of, connections within, and relations between, the phenomenal particulars that constitute bodies. For this, all that is required, Bergmann insists, is a "schema."

The contrast between Berkeley's idealism and Bergmann's realism serves nicely to illuminate the defining feature of a phenomenal particular. For both Berkeley and Bergmann, the particulars constituting bodies are "fleeting indeed, and changeable" (*Dialogues*: 253): they are, as Bergmann puts it, "momentary" existents. Concomitantly, both deny that there are any substances, any enduring existents, to be found among the constituents of bodies. Both, in short, are phenomenalists. However, their reasons for adopting phenomenalism are very different. Berkeley thought that the constituents of bodies were momentary because mind-dependent, but he had no convincing argument that substances (continuants) are impossible. Bergmann rejects Berkeley's idealism—insisting that a properly drawn act-object distinction secures the mind-*in*dependence of bodily constituents—and premises the impossibility of substances on the relativity of TIME. The argument exemplifies Bergmann's method: if substances exist, contradictions in the ideal language can be avoided only if time is absolute (see "Some Reflections on Time" in *Meaning and Existence*, esp. 230–31). There is a curious irony here in that Berkeley, too, rejects absolute time (*Principles* §98).

PRIMARY WORKS

Bergmann, Gustav. *Logic and Reality*, Madison: University of Wisconsin Press, 1964.
———. *Meaning and Existence*. Madison: University of Wisconsin Press, 1959
———. *The Metaphysics of Logical Positivism*. Madison: University of Wisconsin Press, 1954. See especially 153–75.
Berkeley, George. *The Works of George Berkeley, Bishop of Cloyne*. Edited by A. A. Luce and T. E. Jessop. 9 vols. London: Thomas Nelson and Sons, 1948–1957. In the present article, page references (to the *Dialogues*) are to Luce and Jessop *Works*, vol. 2.
Hume, David. *A Treatise of Human Nature*. 2d ed., edited with an analytical index by L. A. Selby-Bigge; revised with notes by P. H. Nidditch. Oxford: Clarendon Press, 1978. See especially "Of Scepticism with Regard to the Senses," 187–218.
Locke, John. *An Essay concerning Human Understanding*. Edited with an introduction by P. H. Nidditch. Oxford: Clarendon Press, 1975.
Mach, Ernst. *The Analysis of Sensations*. New York: Dover, 1914. English translation of the greatly enlarged 5th ed. of *Beiträge zur Analyse der Empfindungen*; originally published, Jena: G. Fischer, 1886).
Mill, J. S. *An Examination of Sir William Hamilton's Philosophy*. In *The Collected Works*

of J. S. Mill, vol. 9. Toronto: University of Toronto Press, 1979. See especially Chapter 11.

Price, H. H. *Hume's Theory of the External World*. Oxford: Oxford University Press, 1940. See especially "The Existence of Unsensed Sensibilia," 101–40.

Russell, Bertrand. *Mysticism and Logic*. London: Longmans, Green, 1921. See esp. "The Relation of Sense-Data to Physics" (1914): 145–79; and "The Ultimate Constituents of Matter" (1915): 125–44.

Whitehead, Alfred North, and Bertrand Russell. *Principia Mathematica*. Cambridge: Cambridge University Press, 1962. Originally published 1913.

BIBLIOGRAPHY

Gram, M. S., and E. D. Klemke, eds. *The Ontological Turn: Studies in the Philosophy of Gustav Bergmann*. Iowa City: University of Iowa Press, 1974: esp. 89–113, 148–67, 168–92. Bergmann's philosophy is discussed sympathetically but critically. Also contains a complete bibliography of Bergmann's writings.

Hirst, R. J. "Phenomenalism." In *The Encyclopedia of Philosophy*, edited by Paul Edwards. New York: Macmillan, 1967. There has not been much of a general nature written on phenomenalism since Hirst's article (and its companion on "Sensa") was published. Both articles include good bibliographies of early- and mid-twentieth-century material critical of phenomenalism.

Lewis, Douglas. "Moore's Realism." In *Moore and Ryle: Two Ontologists*, by Laird Addis and Douglas Lewis. Iowa City, 1965: esp. 126–30. A nontechnical exposition of Bergmann's phenomenalism.

ROBERT MUEHLMANN

POPPER, SIR KARL RAIMUND. Karl Raimund Popper (1902–1994) was an Austrian-British philosopher, logician, and epistemologist, the most severe critic of positivism and of neopositivism (see LOGICAL POSITIVISM), a defender of rationalism in the form of critical rationalism (a generalized deductivist empiricism), and the main initiator of a biologically inspired evolutionary epistemology. According to his falsificationist view of scientific method, empirical "evidence" plays a crucial role as the means of testing scientific hypotheses and theories, while playing no role in their formulation or positive validation.

Popper was born in Vienna on July 28, 1902, as the youngest of three children in a moderately prosperous family with close connections to the cultural, scientific, and political life of the prewar Austro-Hungarian Empire. At the age of sixteen Popper left high school, disappointed with the teaching, to study on his own at the University of Vienna, first as a nonmatriculated student and from 1922 as a regular student, attending lectures on history, literature, music, psychology, philosophy, mathematics, physics, and other subjects. Simultaneously an apprentice to a cabinetmaker and a student at a teachers' college in 1922–1924, Popper qualified in 1924 as a teacher in primary schools and for a time worked as a social worker in A. Adler's social guidance clinics for children. In the late 1920s he participated in the launching of O. Glöckel's school reform movement from the Vienna Institute of Education, and in 1928 he defended his doctoral dissertation ("Zur Methodenfrage der Denkpsychologie"), advised by

K. Bühler and examined by M. Schlick. In 1929 Popper qualified as a teacher of mathematics and physics in secondary schools, becoming in 1930 *Hauptschullehrer* in Vienna. In 1930–1933 he worked intensively on a large book manuscript, *Die beiden Grundprobleme der Erkenntnistheorie*, which was discussed and read by some members of the Vienna Circle, with whom he had been in contact since 1922. An abbreviated version of this work was published in 1934 under the title *Logik der Forschung*, and its success led to invitations to London, Oxford, and Cambridge and finally, late in 1936, to Popper's being offered a lectureship in philosophy at Canterbury University College, Christchurch, New Zealand. Here he lived throughout the Second World War, during which period he wrote *The Open Society and Its Enemies*. Returning to Europe in 1946, first as reader in philosophy and then, from 1949 to 1969, as Professor of logic and scientific method at the London School of Economics and Political Science, University of London, Popper's influence in a large number of fields in and outside philosophy made some count him among the greatest philosophers of his century. He was elected fellow of the British Academy in 1958 and of the Royal Society in 1976, knighted in 1965, and appointed Companion of Honour in 1983. He received many prizes and numerous honorary degrees from universities throughout the world. Popper died in Croydon, London, on September 17, 1994.

Being critical from early on of the psychological and philosophical underpinnings of the education he received at all levels, Popper set out to develop a more satisfactory theory of KNOWLEDGE and learning. In so doing not only was he to change the whole conception of how observation and experiment contribute to SCIENCE, but *logical* analyses of scientific discoveries eventually convinced many scientists that his method of conjectures and refutations—and not, as most had believed, that of BACON's *Novum Organum*—was indeed the one that they employed.

The struggle between rationalism and empiricism in the history of Western thought has centered on the validity of statements about reality (synthetic judgments), not on the validity of purely logical statements (analytic judgments), which both traditions agree can only be decided a priori (see ANALYTIC/SYNTHETIC DISTINCTION and A PRIORI/A POSTERIORI DISTINCTION). From the two Kantian distinctions—the distinction between analytic statements and synthetic statements (which is a logical one) and the distinction between a priori and a posteriori (which is an epistemological one)—follow: (1) all analytic statements are valid a priori and (2) all statements whose validity can be decided a posteriori are synthetic. Nothing is said, however, whether or not there are synthetic statements whose validity can be decided a priori.

In *Die beiden Grundprobleme* (published in 1979; English translation in preparation) Popper resumes the historical situation arguing (13ff.) that the real issue between rationalism and empiricism is *whether synthetic judgments can be decided a priori*. Classical rationalism had welcomed this possibility, asserting that a basis of validity for such judgments was to be found in the evident—in the possibility that synthetic judgments may appear to be "rationally or intuitively obvious" ("*Evidenslehre*"). To this, however, empiricism objects that some such "obvious" synthetic judgments have surprisingly turned out to be false. Besides logic as the basis of validity for analytic judgments, empiricism admits no basis of validity for synthetic judgments other than empirical evidence—and thereby rejects the supposition that synthetic judgments can have a priori validity.

Popper argues further that the truly rationalistic thesis "that synthetic judgments may exist a priori" is in no way logically connected with the idea of *deductivism*, with which rationalism is often associated. In a similar way, the basic idea of *empiricism* can be separated from the idea of *inductivism*, which is often associated with it. The four combinations of possible epistemological positions arising from these distinctions are characterized (*Die beiden Grundprobleme*: 15) by the following examples: (1) classical rationalism is deductivist and rationalist (e.g., KANT and Spinoza); (2) classical empiricism is inductivist and empiricist (e.g., MILL); (3) inductive rationalism has been realized in many philosophical systems (e.g., WITTGENSTEIN's *Tractatus*); and (4) deductive empiricism. The latter, Popper's declared position, is a combination only rarely realized in philosophy and epistemology. It combines a strictly *empirical* viewpoint with a strictly *deductivist* approach, assuming, like rationalism, that scientific postulates can initially be put forward without logical or empirical justification. In contrast to rationalism, deductive empiricism regards its postulates not as being *a priori true* (whether or not they appear evident) but as being *problematic*, because "they are only advanced *tentatively*, as unfounded anticipations, working hypotheses, or suppositions. Their corroboration or possible falsification is done, in a strictly empiricistic way, by experience alone, by deducing statements whose content consists of predictions capable of direct testing" (*Die beiden Grundprobleme*: 16). Thus, if we use the expression "a priori" to mean "not *originating* from experience," then DISPOSITIONS, anticipations, hypotheses, and so on do indeed appear as "*a priori synthetic judgments*": the anticipatory types of reaction found in most animal behavior (relating to species-identification, communication, reproduction, etc.) and in much human behavior and action (relating to attachment, nonverbal communication, and the search for regularities) will then correspond to a priori "causal statements," and Popper cautiously ends his account of this deductivist-empiricist "preformation *theory*" with the striking declaration: "*Synthetic judgments may well exist a priori, but they are usually a posteriori false*" (*Die beiden Grundprobleme*: 32).

Popper reached this compromise between rationalism and empiricism, later named *critical rationalism*, as a consequence of his solution in 1927 to the problem of INDUCTION. Following HUME's logical rejection of induction, Kant had developed a theory of knowledge implying that the human intellect does not induce its laws from nature but imposes them upon nature. Accepting this view as fundamentally correct but as claiming too much, Popper modifies Kant's theory, arguing (*Die beiden Grundprobleme*: 30ff.) that such "imposed laws'' are not true a priori, as implied by Kant, but conjectural or problematic, as they may or may not be capable of withstanding empirical tests, that is, a posteriori attempts at refutation. Owing to their strictly universal character, they can never be demonstrated to be true. Theories may, however, be corroborated, and *corroboration* is an account of how a given theory has stood up to empirical tests. Thus, theories with a high degree of corroboration are such highly improbable and powerful theories that they may be good *approximations to the truth* (verisimilitude) within their domains. Progress in science may be assessed by a *criterion of progress*, which implies that a rational choice between competing theories is made preferring the best-tested theory, that is, the theory that has the greater explanatory and predictive power (*Conjectures and Refutations*: 217). Popper also worked on a theory of verisimilitude aimed at describing scientific progress as an approximation to truth through a succession of false theories (*Conjectures and Refutations*: Chapter 10; Miller 1994: 195ff.).

Popper argues further that the basic statements used in testing theories *do not relate to an absolute empirical basis*: basic statements are also open to criticism (testing). In order to test theories, we have, of course, sooner or later to decide by agreement which basic statements are to be accepted as true. Such decisions are governed by rules (conventions). These rules, agreed upon by the scientific community, establish the objectivity of the empirical basis, *objectivity thus being relative*. Popper differs from the conventionalists in holding that the statements decided by agreement are not the universal laws but only the *singular* basic statements; and the conventions govern their acceptance, not their truth. From this follows Popper's *falsificationist* methodology, which states that a theory is scientific if empirical singular statements (potential falsifiers or falsifying hypotheses) can be derived from the theory and its initial conditions. Nonrepeatable single occurrences are not enough to refute a theory, but ''if *accepted* basic statements [basic for the corroboration of hypotheses] contradict a theory, then we take them as providing sufficient ground for its falsification only if they corroborate a falsifying hypothesis at the same time'' (*Logic of Scientific Discovery*: 87). Falsification provides a *criterion of demarcation* between scientific theories (hypotheses) and nonscientific ones: hypotheses must not be considered empirical-scientific unless there are tests that could eliminate them.

Formulation of this criterion hinges on Popper's solution to the problem of induction (*The Philosophy of Karl Popper*: 40ff.). Having accepted Hume's *logical rejection* of induction but not his irrationalist view of induction as a *psychological process*, Popper approached Hume's psychological problem of induction by arguing (*Objective Knowledge*: 23ff.) that there is no induction by repetition, neither in science nor anywhere else. What is mistakenly considered as induction is in reality a Darwinian-like process of bold action and critical selection. Thus, on the scientific level, the ''imposed laws'' may consist of conjectures in the form of more or less elaborated hypotheses—often explanatory theories put forward to solve theoretical or practical problems. In everyday situations, the ''laws imposed'' may be some dogmatic procedure or routines that the agents guess or assume will be functional in the context. On the animal level, the "laws" that animals can be said to impose in the form of behavior may be stirred by preprogrammed knowledge or by modified prior knowledge and thus, in the last analysis, on some inborn knowledge.

This noninductivist theory of knowledge Popper characterizes (*Conjectures and Refutations*: 51ff.) as the mode of discovery by conjectures and refutations, or as learning by trial and error elimination, the same in all living beings "from the amoeba to Einstein." In his evolutionary epistemology, problems and problem solving are considered a distinguishing feature of life (*Alles Leben ist Problemlösen*): life and problems arise simultaneously; only organisms have problems, among them survival problems; and problem solving is their way of adaptation to the world. There is life as long as there are problems.

Popper's realist and almost biologist reading of Kant, from which his critical rationalism and evolutionary epistemology developed, also provided a point of departure for his falsificationist theory of knowledge, of truth, and of scientific objectivity, as well as for his criticism of inductivist ideas in logic, epistemology, and the sciences. Popper's rational and critical approach to all matters made him a follower of the European Enlightenment.

PRIMARY WORKS

Bibliography. Logik der Forschung. Vienna 1934; 10th ed. Tübingen 1994. English translation: *The Logic of Scientific Discovery.* London and New York: Routledge, 1959; 10th impr. London: Routledge, 1980.
The Open Society and Its Enemies. London: Routledge, 1945; 5th ed. 1969.
Conjectures and Refutations. New York: Basic Books, 1962; 5th ed. 1989.
Objective Knowledge: An Evolutionary Approach. Oxford, 1972.
Die beiden Grundprobleme der Erkenntnistheorie. (Ms. from 1930–1933, edited by T. E. Hansen.) Tübingen, 1979.
Postscript to the Logic of Scientific Discovery. Edited by W. W. Bartley. 3 vols. Totowa, NJ, 1982–1993.
(with J. Eccles). *The Self and Its Brain.* Boston: Routledge and Kegan Paul, 1983.
Popper Selections. Edited by D. Miller. Princeton, 1985.
(with K. Lorenz). *Die Zukunft ist offen.* Munich, 1985.
A World of Propensities. Bristol, 1990.
In Search of a Better World. London: Routledge, 1992.
Alles Leben ist Problemlösen. Munich, 1994.
The Myth of the Framework. Edited by M. A. Notturno. London: Routledge, 1994.

BIBLIOGRAPHY

Books

Bunge, Mario, ed. *The Critical Approach to Science and Philosophy. Essays in Honour of Karl R. Popper.* Glencoe, IL, 1983.
Currie, G., et al., eds. *Popper and the Human Sciences.* Dordrecht: Reidel, 1985.
Fischer, H. *Kritik und Zensur; Die transzendentalphilosophie zwischen Empirismus und Kritischen Rationalismus.* Inaugural-Dissertation der Friedrich-Alexander-Universität. Erlangen-Nürnberg: 1981.

Gómez Tutor, J. I. *Das Induktions-und Abgrenzungsproblem in den Frühschriften von Karl R. Popper*. Frankfurt: P. Lang, 1988.

Levinson, P., ed. *In Pursuit of Truth. Essays on the Philosophy of Karl Popper on the Occasion of His 80th Birthday*. Atlantic Highlands, NJ: Humanities Press, 1982.

Miller, D. *Critical Rationalism: A Restatement and Defence*. Chicago: Open Court, 1994.

O'Hear, A., ed. *Karl Popper: Philosophy and Problems*. Cambridge: Cambridge University Press, 1996.

Schilpp, P. A., ed. *The Philosophy of Karl Popper*. 2 vols., La Salle, IL: Open Court, 1974.

Seiler, M., et al., eds. *Heinrich Gomperz, Karl Popper und die Österreichische Philosophie*. Amsterdam: Rodopi, 1994.

   Articles

Albert, H. "Der Kritische Rationalismus Karl R. Poppers." *Archiv für Rechts- und Sozialphilosophie* 46 (1960): 391–415.

———. "Karl Popper (1902–1994)." *Journal for the General Philosophy of Science* 26 (1995): 207–25.

Levinson, P. "In Pursuit of Truth (2)." *Et cetera* 42 (1985): 196–320.

Petersen, A. F. "Review Article on *Die beiden Grundprobleme*." *Philosophy of the Social Sciences* 14 (1984): 239–50.

ARNE FRIEMUTH PETERSEN

PRAGMATISM. Pragmatism was a philosophical tradition that emerged in the United States during the last third of the nineteenth century. The term was first used publicly by William James in 1898, but he credited both name and doctrine to discussions with Charles PEIRCE in a "metaphysical club" in Cambridge, Massachusetts, in the early 1870s. The third of the "classical pragmatists," John Dewey, was active until the 1940s. Subsequently, a growing number of philosophers, including Richard Rorty, Nicholas Rescher, and Hilary Putnam, have emphasized the importance of pragmatism for contemporary philosophy.

It is a mistake to view pragmatism as a homespun American product: Peirce identified BERKELEY and Spinoza as early pragmatists and arrived at his own position through an attempt to purge KANT's philosophy of its transcendental elements; James dedicated his pragmatism to the memory of John Stuart MILL; and Dewey's pragmatism developed out of the impact of Darwinism (see DARWIN) on his early Hegelianism. Moreover, the school had influential followers in Europe: F. C. S. Schiller in Oxford made a substantial impact, and there was a strong pragmatist movement in Italy. Through Dewey and James, especially, pragmatism had a major influence on the development of educational theory and social psychology.

Peirce defended a "pragmatist principle" as a rule for clarifying the meanings of concepts and hypotheses: their whole meanings can be displayed by identifying the experiential consequences we would expect our actions to have if the hypotheses were true or the concepts were applied to some object of experience. Such clarifications provided all the information that was needed to test hypoth-

eses using the scientific method; and any proposition that resisted such clarification could be dismissed as lacking cognitive meaning. This enabled Peirce to
dismiss "ontological metaphysics" and to reject as meaningless the Kantian
idea of a thing in itself. The most important application of this principle was
Peirce's definition of truth in terms of the long-run agreement of inquirers.
Peirce was anxious to show that his principle could be proved within a systematic philosophical system including a theory of categories, a systematic theory
of meaning, and a "scientific metaphysics."

James and Dewey adapted Peirce's rule to provide the foundations for an
overall philosophical system. The former saw pragmatism as a way of dissolving
philosophical conundrums: by clarifying claims through asking what turns practically on their truth or falsehood, he hoped to avoid futile debates. Moreover,
seeing beliefs and theories as instruments that enable us to get into a satisfactory
relation to our experience, he identified true propositions as those that are successful instruments. Although beliefs are often "good" because they yield reliable predictions and enable us to control experienced objects, he was ready to
allow that it was a truth-relevant characteristic of moral or religious beliefs that
they answered to less "cognitive" needs. James' pragmatism was loosely linked
to his "radical empiricism": although serious inquiry must concern items encountered in experience, the atomistic conception of experience favored by earlier empiricists should be rejected. Experience has a rich content, and James
agreed with Peirce that the relations that hold different elements of our experience together are themselves parts of experience.

Drawing on Peirce's account of the nature of inquiry and James' claims about
concepts and theories, Dewey's version of pragmatism was often called "instrumentalism." It emphasizes that inquiries arise out of particular contexts or
situations that become problematic or "indeterminate." He describes how concepts and investigations enable us to remove these indeterminacies and explores
the normative structures that guide us in solving problems intelligently. We are
warranted in asserting propositions that successfully serve this function. Dewey
showed the influence of Darwin's work, emphasizing the continuities between
human processes of inquiry and problem-solving strategies found in nature.

Alongside an emphasis on the richness of experience and on treating inquiry
as an activity that enables agents to reach a satisfactory relation to their experience, this stress upon evolutionary ideas is characteristic of pragmatism. Contemporary pragmatists have been most impressed by two further pragmatist
themes. All of the classical pragmatists reject the traditional correspondence
theory of truth, viewing truth rather as the product of a properly conducted
inquiry. In this spirit Richard Rorty identifies pragmatism with the doctrine that
thought and language do not seek to "represent" an independent reality, and
Hilary Putnam denies that rationality needs a "metaphysical" grounding. Second, they reject the sharp separation of fact and value characteristic of more
traditional versions of empiricism. Dewey uses his account of inquiry to emphasize the parallels between investigations in ethics and in science: in each

case, we are guided by norms and by experience in trying to remove problematic indeterminacies from our understanding of the world. Moreover, the focus on inquiry in epistemology permits an emphasis on the roles of values in reflective reasoning and of interests and values in shaping our theories. Although this is most evident in the work of James and Dewey—both of whom fight against the tendency to distinguish sharply the cognitive and the affective sides of human nature—it is found too in Peirce's writings. In his mature work, he proposes to ground logic in ethics and aesthetics and to emphasize the role of sentimental responses in enabling us to deal rationally with pressing moral, religious, and political matters. Where other empiricists see the influence of emotions or values on our beliefs as a threat to rationality and objectivity, the pragmatists seek an understanding of objectivity that allows for the ineliminable role of evaluations in inquiry.

PRIMARY WORKS

Dewey, John. *Logic: The Theory of Inquiry*. New York: Henry Holt, 1938.
James, William. *Pragmatism: A New Name for Some Old Ways of Thinking*. Edited by F. T. Bowers; vol. 3 of *The Works of William James*. Cambridge: Harvard University Press, 1975; originally published in 1907.
Peirce, Charles S. *The Essential Peirce*. Edited by N. Houser and C. Kloesel. 2 vols. Bloomington: Indiana University Press, 1992.

BIBLIOGRAPHY

Rorty, Richard. *Consequences of Pragmatism*. Minneapolis: University of Minnesota Press, 1982.
Smith, John E. *Purpose and Thought: The Meaning of Pragmatism*. New Haven, CT: Yale University Press, 1978.
Thayer, Henry T. *Meaning and Action: A Critical History of American Pragmatism*. Indianapolis, IN: Bobbs-Merrill, 1968.

CHRISTOPHER HOOKWAY

PRIMARY AND SECONDARY QUALITIES. The distinction between primary and secondary qualities is a metaphysical and epistemological one that corresponds to something like the distinction between the world as it is in itself, and the world as we experience it—or, more generally, to the distinction between appearance and reality. Certain qualities are considered to belong to objects independently of the way in which these objects are perceived by us, while others are considered to belong to them only by virtue of the way in which they affect the different senses. Since the former, primary qualities are intrinsic to objects themselves, they ultimately account for the secondary or "sensible" qualities that are associated with our perceptual experience of those objects.

The distinction between primary and secondary qualities, so understood, may be traced to Greek ATOMISM as the view that the only qualities that belong to atoms are ones such as size, shape, and motion, while these alone are sufficient to explain the causal properties of objects themselves. Perhaps the first empiricist account of the distinction is to be credited to Thomas HOBBES (*Leviathan*, Chapter 1), who ascribes "sensible" qualities to the effects produced on the senses by motions of matter, thereby distinguishing between qualities as they are experienced by us and qualities as they are in the object. The best-known empiricist account of the primary/secondary quality distinction, however, is provided by John LOCKE in *An Essay concerning Human Understanding* (II.viii). Locke's account reflects Robert Boyle's corpuscularian view of the underlying structure of physical objects (see BOYLE), which had provided a new rationale for the distinction between primary (or "first") and secondary (or "second") qualities associated originally with the theory of elements. It should be noted, however, that the primary/secondary quality distinction is not peculiar to empiricism. A version of the distinction occurs in Descartes (e.g., in *Principles of Philosophy*), whose philosophy in this respect displays the influence of GALILEO. But while the distinction is thus associated with quite different philosophical traditions, it reflects in each case a certain kind of scientific world-view—one that sees the physical world atomistically, with material particles possessing only those qualities required for them to interact so as to produce phenomena observable at the macroscopic level. The qualities in question are mathematically measurable, comprising such features as shape, size, and velocity. The outcome, then, appears to be that qualities of this kind alone are real or intrinsic features of objects themselves, or the particles of which they consist, while the qualities we ascribe to objects on the basis of the way they appear to the various senses—color, taste, smell, and so on—are manifestations of our sensory experience of those objects. The epistemological implication is that by applying mathematics to the real or primary qualities we may achieve knowledge of the objects to which they belong, while so long as we are confined to the sensible world, we are capable only of belief or conjecture. Since the universe is mathematical in nature and mechanical in its operation, knowledge of its ultimate constituents and their primary qualities would enable us to account for the appearances of objects associated with secondary qualities like color.

We can see from the preceding how the distinction between the primary and secondary qualities comes to be associated with a more general contrast between appearance and reality. While the primary qualities belong to a scientific conception of the nature of the physical world, the secondary qualities are features only of the way in which observers experience that world. Let us now consider in more detail the empiricist account of this distinction as it is presented by Locke. Locke's crucial claim about the primary qualities concerns their *inseparability* from body and from every particle of matter, perceivable or otherwise. Secondary qualities, he writes, "in truth are nothing in the objects themselves, but powers to produce various sensations in us by experience" (*Essay* II.viii.9). This type of remark has given rise to different accounts of Locke's view of the status of the secondary qualities. Thus, he is sometimes interpreted in accordance with the first part of the quoted remark, as saying that the secondary qualities, since they are "nothing in the objects themselves," are to be identified with

IDEAS. This would align him with the tradition associated with Greek atomism, according to which such qualities cannot, strictly speaking, be considered to belong to objects themselves. On the other hand, the subsequent reference to secondary qualities as "powers to produce various sensations in us" has been taken to represent the view of secondary qualities as features of bodies themselves, albeit *dispositional* features dependent on the primary qualities of the insensible particles in which bodies ultimately consist (see DISPOSITIONS). While the former, subjectivist interpretation appears to gain support from passages in which Locke refers to primary qualities as the only "real" qualities of bodies, the latter is consistent with Locke's own account of the way in which ideas of taste, color, and so on arise in the mind. If we understand Locke in this second way, then he would appear to be saying that a secondary quality like color really does belong to objects themselves (i.e., as a *power*), insofar as their primary qualities enable them to produce certain kinds of sensation in us. Yet, at the same time, it does not belong to objects independently of their relation to us as perceivers. In this context, it is worth noting also Locke's reference to a third kind of quality, consisting in the power of an object, by virtue of its primary qualities, to produce changes in the sensible qualities of other objects—as in the case of fire's effects upon the appearance of wax (*Essay* II.viii.10).

Locke also expresses his claim concerning the difference between the two sorts of quality by suggesting that while our ideas of primary qualities *resemble* the corresponding qualities of objects themselves, no such resemblance obtains between our ideas of secondary qualities and the corresponding qualities of objects. It is hard to know how to assess this claim, unless it is a way of saying that while objects have shapes and sizes, for example, just as we conceive them to do, they fail to possess such qualities as color and smell in the way that these qualities are conceived by us, that is, as qualities that belong to bodies independently of our perception of them (*Essay* II.viii.24). If this is what Locke has in mind, then he appears to be committed to a kind of error theory about the secondary qualities, according to which we mistakenly think of them as "real," or intrinsic, qualities of bodies, rather than as relational qualities (or "powers"). We should note, however, that the primary/secondary distinction does not seem to require the attribution to us of this kind of error, since it might be argued that the distinction itself is implicit in the way that we regard the color of objects, for example, as opposed to, say, their shape. Of course, if we took the latter view, then this might be invoked to provide further support for the Lockean distinction. It is possible that what Locke is saying here also reflects the influence of a certain view of PERCEPTION, according to which the immediate objects of awareness in perception are ideas that represent, more or less faithfully, corresponding qualities in objects themselves. But it is important to recognize that whether or not there is this kind of connection between Locke's own claim about primary and secondary qualities and his commitment to a representational theory of perception, the distinction itself does not seem to depend on any commitment to a theory of this kind.

It is a matter of considerable controversy how we should understand Locke's observations about the differences between the primary and secondary qualities (*Essay* II.viii.16–22). Is this "little excursion into natural philosophy" intended merely to explain the distinction made by Boyle, or is it intended to provide additional philosophical arguments in support of the distinction? Perhaps either of these interpretations would be consistent with Locke's conception of his philosophical role as "Under-Labourer" to scientific "Master-Builders" like Isaac NEWTON and Boyle. But it does appear that, for Locke, the primary/secondary quality distinction can be supported by considerations that do not presuppose the truth of a particular scientific account of the nature of matter. (Hence, the thought-experiment that accompanies Locke's claim about the inseparability of the primary qualities from body, and the appeal to familiar facts about perception in support of his view of the secondary qualities.)

It would certainly be a mistake to suppose that the distinction between primary and secondary qualities is universally accepted by empiricist philosophers. In fact, a fierce critic of this distinction, as formulated by Locke, is George BERKELEY (in *The Principles of Human Knowledge* and the *Three Dialogues between Hylas and Philonous*). Berkeley's principal objection to Locke bears on the supposed ontological distinction between the two sorts of quality (i.e., insofar as the primary qualities are considered to be the only "real" qualities of matter as something that is mind-independent). For, according to Berkeley, the two sorts of quality are inseparable from each other, and they therefore share the same ontological status. Berkeley's argument on the former point appeals to the impossibility of forming by ABSTRACTION an idea of body as possessing qualities like extension and motion independently of any "sensible" qualities (*Principles* §10). The gist of his argument on the latter point is that the considerations that are thought to establish the subjectivity of the secondary qualities apply equally to the primary qualities with which they are contrasted. For instance, if it is true that the color an object appears to have is relative to the circumstances under which the object is perceived, then similar considerations apply also in the case of properties like shape and size (*Principles* §14). Berkeley's view, in fact, is that neither the so-called secondary qualities nor those that are classified as primary may be considered to exist independently of perception. All the qualities involved exist only as ideas that belong to a perceiving mind. There is, of course, an alternative possibility that nevertheless calls Locke's position into question; and this is to reject the distinction between primary and secondary qualities in favor of the view that all qualities of objects are equally "real" or objective. Arguably, this is the outcome of David HUME's critique of Locke as a proponent of what Hume calls the "Modern Philosophy" (*A Treatise of Human Nature* I.iv.4), though it is not easy to be sure what Hume has in mind when he refers to the distinction as one that results in the "annihilation" of objects themselves.

Interest in the distinction is maintained through work in contemporary AN-ALYTIC PHILOSOPHY. A focus of recent discussion has been the distinctive relation between our attribution of qualities like color to objects and the occurrence of distinctive kinds of experience—and the comparison in this respect with our attribution of the types of quality traditionally categorized as primary. To this extent there appears to be some support for the relational view of secondary qualities that, on one interpretation, is to be found in Locke. Yet there is also support for Berkeley's claim that perceptual experience of primary qualities is inseparable from experience of the secondary qualities. It is one of the many fundamental philosophical issues that arise here whether this kind of distinction, between what is true of *per*ception as opposed to *conc*eption, can really be maintained. But it is perhaps fair to say that the view of secondary qualities as relational qualities of objects has become the focus for debate about the secondary/primary quality distinction. For while this kind of view has been quite widely endorsed, it is also the specific target of recent critics of the primary/secondary quality distinction. Thus, the account of color, for example, as a relational quality has been rejected in favor of the view that it possesses the same kind of status as the supposedly more objective primary qualities. This view itself, however, is open to question, if only on the ground that the assumption apparently being made here, that all objects of a certain color share some corresponding physical property or properties, appears to be untenable. So the distinction between primary and secondary qualities retains a considerable resilience, even in the face of recent criticism, which testifies to the value of the arguments of those empiricist philosophers who had earlier attempted to establish the distinction on a secure philosophical and scientific footing.

PRIMARY WORKS

Berkeley, George. *The Works of George Berkeley, Bishop of Cloyne*. Edited by A. A. Luce and T. E. Jessop. 9 vols. London: Thomas Nelson and Sons, 1948–1957.

Boyle, Robert. *Selected Philosophical Papers of Robert Boyle*. Edited by M. A. Stewart. Indianapolis, IN: Hackett, 1991.

Descartes, René. *The Philosophical Writings of Descartes*. Edited and translated by John Cottingham, Robert Stoothoff, and Dugald Murdoch. 3 vols. Cambridge: Cambridge University Press, 1985.

Hobbes, Thomas. *The English Works of Thomas Hobbes*. Edited by William Molesworth. London: J. Bohn, 1839.

Hume, David. *A Treatise of Human Nature*. 2d ed., edited with an analytical index by L. A. Selby-Bigge; revised with notes by P. H. Nidditch. Oxford: Clarendon Press, 1978.

Locke, John. *An Essay concerning Human Understanding*. Edited with an introduction by P. H. Nidditch. Oxford: Clarendon Press, 1975.

BIBLIOGRAPHY

Grayling, A. C. *Berkeley: The Central Arguments*. London: Duckworth, 1986: Chapter 2, section 2.

Hacker, P.M.S. *Appearance and Reality*. Oxford: Blackwell, 1987.

Mackie, J. L. *Problems from Locke*. Oxford: Clarendon Press, 1976: Chapter 1.
McGinn, Colin. *The Subjective View*. Oxford: Clarendon Press, 1983.

ANTONY E. PITSON

PROBABILITY. In the history of empiricism, probability has been a central and distinctive concern, but the understanding of it has proved elusive. It is, of course, difficult to be precise about the nature of empiricism or, as we shall see, the nature of probability, but empiricism is at least concerned to give an account of human knowledge that is strongly grounded in sensory experience and hence has tended to favor caution in claiming certainty and to respect the variable and contingent nature of the realities encountered in experience. One traditional role of probability discourse fits well with these ambitions: we qualify propositions as probable when not in a position to assert them as certain, and the contingencies of experience very naturally give rise to assessments of the probability of outcomes as yet unknown.

HISTORICAL BACKGROUND

The use of expressions like "probable" is presumably as old as conversation itself and was invoked when it was necessary to act or judge in contexts that fell short of yielding certainty or failed to meet some ideal providing for full assurance of outright truth. Nonetheless, the understanding of probability has undergone dramatic changes over the years. A core substrate in the concept is the idea of approvability, but what one takes as the basis for the approvability of views that are less than certain or "fully" guaranteed depends, among other things, on the model of fully guaranteed truth that one adopts. This is one reason concepts of SCIENCE are relevant to probability, and that the rise of the modern sciences has been significantly related to a changed conception of probability. In the ancient and medieval worlds a strong contrast was made between science and opinion: the former solid, systematic, and certain; the latter ephemeral, particular, and unsure. The probable belonged to the world of opinion, where it frequently denoted what was approved by authoritative voices or delivered by expert testimony. Science, by contrast, was a matter of demonstration from first principles, excluding beliefs that seemed true but might be false; it was a realm of universality and necessity, a realm in which the probable had no place. The idea of a systematic and rational determination of the probable, independent of authority, lay latent until the development of the experimental sciences and the discovery of the probability calculus and ideas associated with it. Ian Hacking, who has contributed considerably to our understanding of the development of modern conceptions of probability, has gone so far as to claim (most improbably!) that there was no such thing as probability prior to the middle of the seventeenth century. Hacking's dramatic thesis is influenced by the French theorist Michel Foucault's predilection for the discovery of radical conceptual discontinuities in the history of thought and by holistic theories of concept possession, but even if we resist the idea that medieval and modern farmers could not actually share the thought that their chickens had probably been killed by a fox (rather than a wild dog) and, moreover, do so on a basis independent of authoritative opinion, it remains true that the conceptual landscape of contemporary probability discourse is very different from that of our medieval ancestors.

Much of this is due to the systematic application of MATHEMATICS to calculating chances, an application that can plausibly be said to have begun in 1654, when, as Poisson put it: "A problem about games of chance proposed to an austere Jansenist by a man of the world was the origin of the calculus of probabilities." PASCAL solved the problem and corresponded with Fermat, and before long Huygens had written a textbook. The mathematical theory of probability was on its way. At about the same time, Descartes was attempting to establish science, and knowledge generally, upon new, indubitable foundations. Subsequent empiricists inherited Descartes' project but substituted sensory input rather than rational insight as the foundation. The eventual failure of the project would contribute significantly to an increased epistemological role for probability.

Although seventeenth- and eighteenth-century empiricist philosophers had little to contribute to the theory of chances, both LOCKE and HUME make considerable play with probability as an important reference point in ordinary rational thinking, and Hume's famous explication of CAUSALITY and his critique of the utility of "necessary connection" in reasoning about the natural world helped displace the medieval picture of the science of nature as essentially concerned with deducing truth from first principles and the "essences" or substantial forms that inhabited the natural order. In that picture (as in Descartes') knowledge of causes had been part of demonstrative science, but if Hume's critique of causation as a matter of necessary connection were to be accepted, then we require a different understanding of science. It is symptomatic of the increased philosophical significance of probability that Thomas REID, one of Hume's most astute and persistent critics, concentrates upon Hume's attitude to probability when he tries to defend a commonsense epistemology against Hume's SKEPTICISM about knowledge and REASON. Reid also foreshadows a characteristically modern anti-Cartesianism when he asserts that "many things are certain for which we have only that kind of evidence which philosophers call probable" (*Essays on the Intellectual Powers of Man* VII: Chapter 3).

Yet if it was increasingly clear that knowledge or even reasonable belief about the world of experience involved this new understanding of probability, the nature of probability remained open to dispute. From the beginnings of speculation about probability in its modern sense there has been a marked duality in what the term conveyed. The early pioneers concerned themselves both with its epistemological dimension and with its stochastic or statistical dimension, both with degree of credible belief and with frequency of outcomes. The relation between these dimensions would become particularly important for later empiricists.

CONTEMPORARY DEVELOPMENTS

The concept of probability has had a central, though not unproblematic, role in the recent development of empiricism. On one hand, it has allowed the possibility that empiricism, especially an empiricist account of scientific method, could be articulated without essential appeal to certainty, thereby avoiding the pitfalls of skepticism. On the other hand, however, the concept of probability has itself proved only awkwardly amenable to empiricist analysis.

The empiricist project of uncovering deliverances of the senses that could serve as solid foundations on which scientific method could build a secure body of empirical knowledge failed to deliver. The absolutely certain, incorrigible, infallible "sense-data" statements proved a chimera, and it was seen that the best the senses could provide as a basis for empirical knowledge were fallible, revisable observation statements. Nor were these statements seen as unequivocally foundational, in the light of a growing recognition of interdependence within our system of beliefs. Moreover, no reasoning that leads beyond this evidence was absolutely secure. Neither the senses nor empirical reasoning could completely secure our beliefs about the world from error. But this, the empiricist held (echoing Reid), leads to skepticism only if one requires Cartesian certainty. The proper standard need preclude only normal, serious doubts, not the neurotic doubts based on mere logical possibilities of a Cartesian kind. This reply to the skeptic seems to rest upon a contrast between absolute certainty, which leaves no room whatsoever for error, and practical or empirical certainty, which allows a negligible probability of error. Empiricism thus shifts its focus from Cartesian certainty to very high probability in countering the skeptic. To know something requires that one be entitled to regard it as empirically certain and to have no doubt about its truth. This is a far lesser requirement than to be entitled to regard it as logically certain, that is, holding that there is no logical possibility of it not being so. Thus, while empirical reasoning does not show that a conclusion cannot possibly be false, it can show that it is empirically certain. Insofar as this shift from logical to empirical certainty seems inevitably to introduce some notion of probability, the problems inherent in doing so are poignantly brought out in the "lottery paradox." This paradox shows that empirical certainty, construed as extremely high probability of being true, lacks a crucial characteristic of knowledge, that of conjunctivity. If two propositions are known, their conjunction is known. However, by virtue of the axioms of probability, two propositions may each be empirically certain without their conjunction's being certain. Hence, it is unclear that an appeal to probability can serve the empiricist as a counter to skepticism.

PROBABILITY AND SCIENTIFIC METHOD

For the empiricist, what is learned from the operation of the senses is the central determinant of our system of beliefs. At a sophisticated level, this determination is the operation of scientific method. Hence, it has always been a core concern of empiricism to characterize scientific method. However, the more pervasive intrusion of probability into empiricism has been in the development of theories of scientific method themselves. The proper place, if any, of probability in such an account has been a critical issue in the development of an empiricist account of scientific method. CARNAP's monumental *Logical Foundations of Probability* sought to specify an inductive logic (see INDUCTION) that generated probabilistic conclusions from nonprobabilistic evidential premises. An alternative approach that also gave a central role to the effectiveness of the probability calculus in understanding scientific method is that of the Bayesians. Interpreting the central theorem of Thomas Bayes, Bayesians held that the proper effect evidence should have on our confidence in some hypothesis was a function of the probability of that evidence if our hypothesis were true and the normally quite independent probability of that evidence if our hypothesis were false. However, the very influential work of POPPER is deeply antipathetic to any appeal to probability in characterizing scientific method. Wesley Salmon, in turn, has challenged Popper's claims to give an adequate account of scientific method without essential appeal to the concept of inductive probability. He argues that Popper's own account of scientific method covertly depends on appeal to the legitimacy of inductive probability.

EMPIRICIST ACCOUNTS OF PROBABILITY

The need for an acceptable account of probability has increasingly imposed itself on the attention of empiricists, in part because of its importance in the statement of empiricism itself and in part because of its growing role in scientific inquiry.

The seemingly hybrid character of probability makes it problematic for all philosophers. The empiricist must also contend with its less-than-obvious connection with observational data. Ramsey and others legitimated a notion of probability tied to rational degrees of belief, constrained by the probability calculus, and interpreted these in terms of coherent betting behavior acceptable to the behavioristically inclined empiricist. This, however, appears to fail to do justice to the objective side to probability judgments, for its central constraint of coherence requires only a sort of consistency between probability judgments, yet we habitually suppose individual judgments have some legitimacy in isolation. On the other hand, REICHENBACH and others sought to develop a unified ''objective'' account in terms of frequency. Carnap's landmark ''Two Concepts of Probability'' argued that the puzzlingly ambiguous character of probability dissolves if we distinguish two concepts: degree of reasonable belief, on one hand, and frequency of a certain kind of event in some class, on the other. The frequency account brought problems, since ascriptions of probability outrun actual frequencies, and resort to such notions as mathematical limits is under suspicion for the empiricist.

Some of the problems facing a frequency account may be solved by accepting an account of objective chance as a kind of dispositional property of an object, called a propensity, that yields a range of results in specified circumstances according to a certain probability distribution. As a kind of dispositional property, propensities are problematic for the empiricist because of their counterfactual implications. However, if the interpretation is tenable, the empiricist reduces the problem of objective probability to the problem of DISPOSITIONS. Mellor and others have explored, within roughly empiricist confines, what account one might plausibly give of the relation between degrees of reasonable belief, on one hand, and objective chance, on the other.

BIBLIOGRAPHY

Books

Carnap, R. *The Logical Foundations of Probability*. Chicago: University of Chicago Press, 1962.
Hacking, Ian. *The Emergence of Probability*. Cambridge: Cambridge, University Press, 1975.
———. *Logic of Statistical Inference*. Cambridge: Cambridge University Press, 1965.
Kyburg, H. E., Jr. *Probability and the Logic of Rational Belief*. Middletown, CT: Wesleyan University Press, 1961.
Mellor, D. H. *The Matter of Chance*. Cambridge: Cambridge University Press, 1971.
Popper, K. R. *Logic of Scientific Discovery*. London: Hutchinson, 1959.
Reichenbach, H. *The Theory of Probability*. Los Angeles: University of California Press, 1949.
Reid, Thomas. *Essays on the Intellectual Powers of Man*. Edinburgh: J. Bell, 1785. See especially Essay VII, Chapters 3, 4.
Salmon, W. *The Foundations of Scientific Inference*. Pittsburgh: University of Pittsburgh Press, 1966.

Article

Carnap, R. "Two Concepts of Probability." *Philosophy and Phenomenological Research* 5 (1944–1945).

C.A.J. COADY and L. J. O'NEILL

Q

QUINE, WILLARD VAN ORMAN. Willard Van Orman Quine (1908–) is among this century's most important analytic philosophers (see ANALYTIC PHILOSOPHY), placing him in the ranks of Bertrand Russell, Ludwig WITTGENSTEIN, and Rudolf Carnap. After completing a two-year Ph.D. at Harvard in 1932—where he studied with Clarence I. Lewis and Henry M. Scheffer and wrote a dissertation entitled "The Logic of Sequences: A Generalization of *Principia Mathematica*" under the direction of Alfred N. Whitehead—Quine was awarded Harvard's prestigious Sheldon Traveling Fellowship in 1933. He used the fellowship year to visit Vienna (where he attended meetings of the Vienna Circle), Prague (where he first met Carnap) and Warsaw (where he first met Stanisław Leśniewski, Jan Łukasiewicz, and Alfred Tarski, among other prominent Polish logicians). Quine's Sheldon year had a profound and lasting impact on his philosophical development. Upon his return to the United States, Quine was awarded a three-year fellowship as a junior fellow in Harvard's (then brand-new) Society of Fellows. Subsequently, Quine was appointed to the faculty of Harvard's Philosophy Department. There he remained as Edgar Pierce Professor of Philosophy and senior fellow in the Society of Fellows until his retirement in 1978 at the age of seventy.

During his long career Quine lectured worldwide and published countless articles and some twenty-one books on various philosophical topics, including logic, philosophy of logic, set theory, philosophy of mind, philosophy of language, philosophy of science, epistemology, metaphysics, and ethics. His most famous articles include "New Foundations for Mathematical Logic" (1937), "Two Dogmas of Empiricism" (1951), and "Epistemology Naturalized" (1969); his most famous books include *Mathematical Logic* (1940), *Methods of Logic* (1950), *From a Logical Point of View* (1953), *Word and Object* (1960), *Roots of Reference* (1974), *Theories and Things* (1981), *The Time of My Life* (an autobiography, 1985), *Pursuit of Truth* (1990), and *From Stimulus to Science* (1995). Collectively, Quine's books have been translated into more than a dozen languages. Quine is, incontestably, the century's most influential American philosopher since John Dewey. Though he does not, in any deep sense, share Dewey's pragmatism, Quine throughout his career has been a critic as well as an advocate of empiricism.

QUINE'S CRITICISM OF EMPIRICISM

In many of his writings, but especially in "Two Dogmas of Empiricism," Quine criticizes what he regards as two central dogmas of empiricism: the analytic/synthetic DISTINCTION and epistemological reductionism.

The First Dogma: Analyticity

In the 1930s, logical empiricists (notably Carnap and Alfred J. Ayer) were among the first philosophers to claim that some statements are true solely by virtue of the meanings of their words, while other statements are true, if they are, by virtue of the meanings of their words *together with* how things are in the world. The former statements were said to be *analytic*; the latter, *synthetic*. Presumably, then, statements like, "All bachelors are unmarried men" are analytic, whereas statements like, "All bachelors are lonely" are synthetic. One very important epistemological moral of drawing this venerable distinction in this way is that arithmetical statements like Immanuel KANT's infamous "The sum of seven and five is twelve" (which Kant regarded as synthetic) can henceforth be regarded as analytic: true solely by virtue of the meanings of their words, independently of how the world is. Thus, in the hands of the logical positivists, the analytic/synthetic distinction became a powerful epistemological resource enabling them to confidently rise to the rationalists' challenge to explain the necessity of true mathematical statements without at the same time violating the empiricists' doctrine that all statements based on experience are merely probable. The challenge was to be met by claiming that mathematical truths are necessary because they are analytic—true solely by virtue of the meanings of their words. Furthermore, because they are analytic, mathematical truths are devoid of empirical content. Thus, contrary to Kant, true mathematical statements are not necessary and contentful (i.e., a priori and synthetic); rather, they are necessary and contentless (i.e., a priori and analytic). (See MATHEMATICS and A PRIORI/A POSTERIORI DISTINCTION.)

Quine regards the analytic/synthetic distinction to be a dogma because he believes that no one, including Kant, Carnap, and Ayer, has made adequate theoretical sense of the distinction. The logical empiricists' attempt to explain analyticity in terms of meaning, for example, is an attempt to explain the obscure in terms of the more obscure. This is not to say that Quine requires proponents of the analytic/synthetic distinction to provide necessary and sufficient conditions for analyticity; rather, he requires "no more . . . than a rough characterization [of analyticity] in terms of dispositions to verbal behavior" [*Word and Object*: 207]. However, no such characterization currently exists, and until one is in hand, empiricists' acceptance of the distinction remains a dogma of empiricism.

The Second Dogma: Reductionism

The second dogma of empiricism, according to Quine, is associated with epistemological reductionism, the doctrine that each empirical statement belonging to a scientific theory, considered independently of its fellow empirical statements, has associated with it a unique range of confirming experiences as well as a unique range of infirming experiences. According to Quine, ''The dogma of reductionism survives in the supposition that each statement, taken in isolation from its fellows, can admit of confirmation or infirmation at all'' (''Two Dogmas of Empiricism'': 41). Quine maintains that this dogma betrays a mistaken view of how scientific theory relates to experience. His holistic ''countersuggestion . . . is that our statements about the external world face the tribunal of sense experience not individually but only as a corporate body'' (''Two Dogmas of Empiricism'': 41). But how are we to understand ''corporate body''? In ''Two Dogmas of Empiricism,'' Quine took ''corporate body'' to mean the whole of science: ''The unit of empirical significance is the whole of science'' (''Two Dogmas of Empiricism'': 42).

However, by the time he published *Word and Object* Quine had supplanted this *extreme* holism with a more plausible, *moderate* holism. Quine explains this change as follows: ''It is holism that has rightly been called the Duhem thesis and also, rather generously, the Duhem-Quine thesis. It says that scientific statements are not separately vulnerable to adverse observations, because it is only jointly as a theory that they imply their observable consequences'' (''On Empirically Equivalent Systems of the World'': 313).

Quine moderates this formulation of the holism thesis by articulating a pair of reservations. One reservation, he explains, ''has to do with breadth. If it is only jointly as a theory that the scientific statements imply their observable consequences, how inclusive does that theory have to be? Does it have to be the whole of science, taken as a comprehensive theory of the world'' (''On Empirically Equivalent Systems of the World'': 314) as Quine maintained in ''Two Dogmas of Empiricism''? Quine now believes that it does not:

Science is neither discontinuous nor monolithic. It is variously jointed, and loose in the joints in varying degrees. In the face of a recalcitrant observation we are free to choose what statements to revise and what ones to hold fast, and these alternatives will disrupt various stretches of scientific theory in various ways, varying in severity. Little is gained by saying that the unit is in principle the whole of science, however defensible this claim my be in a legalistic way. (''On Empirically Equivalent Systems of the World'': 314–15)

A second reservation is a function of the fact that in the process of language learning, some sentences become closely linked to observation:

These statements are indeed separately susceptible to tests of observation; and at the same time they do not stand free of theory, for they share much of the vocabulary of the more remotely theoretical statements. They are what link theory to observation, affording theory its empirical content. Now the Duhem thesis still holds, in a somewhat literalistic way, even for these observation statements. For the scientist does occasionally revoke even an observation statement, when it conflicts with a well attested body of theory and when he has tried in vain to reproduce the experiment. But the Duhem thesis would be wrong if understood as imposing an equal status on all the statements in a scientific theory and thus denying the strong presumption in favor of the observation statements. It is this bias that makes science empirical. ("On Empirically Equivalent Systems of the World": 314)

Thus, Quine's moderate holism acknowledges both (1) that it is more accurate of science to think of significant stretches of science, rather than the whole of science, as having observable consequences (or, as having "critical semantic mass") and (2) that, generally, a statement's susceptibility to observational testing is a matter of degree, and that some statements, namely, observation statements, are individually susceptible to such testing. This moderation of the extreme holism of "Two Dogmas of Empiricism" does nothing to mitigate the force of Quine's criticism of the two dogmas, however.

Quine on Mathematical Truth

Where does all this leave Quine when it comes to providing an empiricistic account of mathematical truths' lack of empirical content and necessity? Quine's response to both issues relies on his moderate holism:

Take the first problem: lack of content. Insofar as mathematics gets applied in natural sciences, I see it as sharing empirical content. Sentences of pure arithmetic and differential calculus contribute indispensably to the semantic mass of various clusters of scientific hypotheses, and so partake of the empirical content imbibed from the implied observation [sentences]. As for inapplicable parts of mathematics, say higher set theory, I sympathize with empiricists in questioning their meaningfulness. We do keep their sentences as meaningful, but only because they are built of the same lexicon and grammatical constructions that are needed in applicable mathematics. ("Two Dogmas in Retrospect": 269)

What of the problem of the necessity of mathematical truths?

This again is nicely cleared up by moderate holism, without the help of analyticity. For let us recall that when a cluster of sentences with critical semantic mass is refuted by an experiment, the crisis can be resolved by revoking one *or* another sentence of the cluster. We hope to choose in such a way as to optimize future progress. If one of the sentences is purely mathematical, we will not choose to revoke it; such a move would reverberate excessively through the rest of science. We are restrained by a maxim of minimum mutilation. It is simply in this, I hold, that the necessity of mathematics lies: our determination to make revisions elsewhere instead. ("Two Dogmas in Retrospect": 269–70)

Thus, Quine's moderate holism plays the same important epistemological role that analyticity was supposed to play for the logical empiricists. Whereas individual mathematical truths were necessary and analytic for the logical empiricists, they are neither for Quine. Finally, as Quine's account of mathematical truth evinces, even though he remains firm in repudiating the two dogmas of empiricism, he does not repudiate empiricism altogether.

QUINE'S ADVOCACY OF EMPIRICISM

As a thoroughgoing naturalist, Quine maintains (1) that there is no adequate first philosophy, that is, no a priori or experiential ground outside science upon which science can be based, and (2) that science is the measure of what exists and how we come to know what exists.

Quine argues that attempts at "first philosophy" as disparate as those of René Descartes and Carnap are destined to fail. For example, in his *Meditations on First Philosophy* Descartes sought to deduce all the truths of nature from a foundation of self-evident truths (namely, clear and distinct ideas), but, as Quine points out, not even all the truths of arithmetic can be deduced from a self-evident foundation. Furthermore, Carnap, in his *Der logische Aufbau der Welt*, sought to rationally reconstruct scientific discourse on a foundation of elementary experiences and a similarity relation, but, as Quine points out, Carnap's project failed because a theory's theoretical terms cannot be defined, even contextually, on such a meager basis.

However, despite the failure of the best attempts at first philosophy—the failure to ground science on some nonscientific base—the fact remains that contemporary science (broadly construed) provides the best theory of what exists (ontology) and the best theory of how we know what exists (epistemology). Furthermore, the best scientific theory of what exists supports physicalism, while the best scientific theory of how we know what exists supports empiricism.

Quine's acceptance of *physicalism* indicates different things in different contexts. In the context of philosophy of mind, it indicates the repudiation of Cartesian dualism of mind and body (see MIND–BODY PROBLEM); in the context of philosophy of language, it indicates the repudiation of mentalistic semantics; in the context of general ontology, it indicates the acceptance of the view that nothing happens in the world without some redistribution of microphysical states.

Quine's acceptance of *empiricism* involves his endorsing the following two cardinal tenets of empiricism: "[W]hatever evidence there *is* for science *is* sensory evidence . . . [and] all inculcation of meanings of words must rest ultimately on sensory evidence" ("Epistemology Naturalized": 75).

However, it is noteworthy that since Quine is a fallibilist regarding science, he recognizes that science is changeable. It is at least conceivable (if unlikely) that at some time in the future science might withdraw its support for physicalism and/or empiricism. Thus, Quine's acceptance of physicalism and empiricism is firm but tentative.

The First Cardinal Tenet: Evidence

"Evidence" is not a technical term in Quine's philosophy. So, when he writes that "whatever evidence there *is* for science *is* sensory evidence," we should understand "sensory evidence" as more or less ordinary language and, therefore, as both general and vague. This cardinal tenet of empiricism is offered in the spirit of *nihil in mente quod non prius in sensu* (nothing is in the mind that is not first in the senses). Moreover, it is, according to Quine, a finding of science itself: "Science itself teaches that there is no clairvoyance; that the only information that can reach our sensory surfaces from external objects must be limited to two-dimensional optical projections and various impacts of air waves on the eardrums and some gaseous reactions in the nasal passages and a few kindred odds and ends" (*Roots of Reference*: 2). On the basis of this meager input, humans come to talk of a world of objects, visible and invisible, concrete and abstract. How do we do this, and why do our scientific theories work so well? This, for Quine, is the central question of epistemology, and its answer is to be pursued by philosophers and scientists working together, as naturalized epistemologists, within the best scientific theories available. "A far cry, this, from old epistemology [i.e., first philosophy]. Yet it is no gratuitous change of subject matter, but an enlightened persistence rather in the original epistemo-logical problem [namely, relating evidence to theory]" (*Roots of Reference*: 3).

The Second Cardinal Tenet: Meaning

When Quine writes that "all inculcation of meanings of words must rest ultimately on sensory evidence," the kind of meaning that he is referring to is cognitive meaning, the kind of meaning associated with truth and falsity. However, for Quine, not all cognitive meaning has empirical content:

I think it's a mistake to require that a sentence must have empirical content in order to be [cognitively] meaningful. In fact, I think there is no end to the important . . . beliefs and truths of history and sociology, and perhaps theoretical physics. You can add a whole bunch of them together and they won't be enough to imply any observations, and yet they're important. They seem plausible by virtue of symmetry, simplicity, fitting-in to the things that we have well established by tests. These are indispensable, moreover, in suggesting further hypotheses which one can test. Science would be paralyzed if we excluded the untestables. ("W. V. Quine: Perspectives on Logic, Science and Philoso-phy": 55)

Thus, appearances notwithstanding, the second cardinal tenet of empiricism is not advocating a form of semantic reductionism.

Quine's collective writings on epistemology can be viewed as his attempt to salvage and reorient logical empiricism. From Quine's point of view, the logical empiricists weren't empiricistic enough: they drew the line at the analytic/syn-thetic distinction. By rejecting that distinction and supplanting it with moderate holism, Quine espouses a more thoroughgoing empiricism. His many contri-butions to empiricism make Quine one of the truly great empiricists of the twentieth century.

PRIMARY WORKS

Books

Word and Object. Cambridge, MA: MIT Press, 1960.
Ontological Relativity and Other Essays. New York: Columbia University Press, 1969.

Roots of Reference. La Salle, IL: Open Court, 1974.
From a Logical Point of View. Cambridge: Harvard University Press, 1980.
Theories and Things. Cambridge: Harvard University Press, 1981.
Pursuit of Truth. Cambridge: Harvard University Press, 1990 (rev. edition 1992).
From Stimulus to Science. Cambridge: Harvard University Press, 1995.

   Articles

"Epistemology Naturalized." In *Ontological Relativity and Other Essays*. New York: Columbia University Press, 1969: 69–90.
"On Empirically Equivalent Systems of the World." *Erkenntnis* (1975): 313–28.
"Two Dogmas of Empiricism." In *From a Logical Point of View*. Cambridge: Harvard University Press, 1980: 20–46.
"Two Dogmas in Retrospect." *Canadian Journal of Philosophy* 21 (1991): 265–274.
(Bradley, Edmister, and Michael O'Shea, interviewers). "W. V. Quine: Perspectives on Logic, Science and Philosophy." *The Harvard Review of Philosophy* 4 (Spring 1994): 47–57.

BIBLIOGRAPHY

Barrett, Robert, and Roger Gibson, eds. *Perspectives on Quine*. Oxford: Basil Blackwell, 1990.
Davidson, Donald, and Jaakko Hintikka, eds. *Words and Objections: Essays on the Work of W. V. Quine*. Dordrecht, Holland: D. Reidel, 1969.
Gibson, Roger. *Enlightened Empiricism: An Examination of W. V. Quine's Theory of Knowledge*. Tampa: University of Florida Presses, 1988.
———. *The Philosophy of W. V. Quine: An Expository Essay*. Tampa: University of Florida Presses, 1982.
Hahn, Lewis, and Paul Schilpp, eds. *The Philosophy of W. V. Quine*. La Salle, IL.: Open Court, 1986.
Hookway, Christopher. *Quine: Language, Experience, and Reality*. Stanford, CA: Stanford University Press, 1988.
Leonardi, Paolo, and Marco Santambrogio, eds. *On Quine*. Cambridge: Cambridge University Press, 1995.
Orenstein, Alex. *Willard Van Orman Quine*. Boston: Twayne, 1977.

ROGER F. GIBSON

R

REASON. If the intellect or the understanding is the faculty whereby we come to know truths, reason is perhaps most accurately thought of as the subfaculty whereby we come to know or believe inferentially or via ratiocination. Frequently, however, "reason" is used to describe the broader faculty, and includes our ability to know noninferential truths as well. When used in this larger sense, the expansion is normally limited to INTUITION, which accounts for the immediate awareness of certain truths, truths known "by the light of reason," and does not include sensory truths or noninferential beliefs. Reason is thus usually contrasted not only with IMAGINATION but also with sensation. In the empiricist tradition, this contrast is limited to the activities of the faculties; the items that the faculties manipulate are common to all: IDEAS.

LOCKE defined KNOWLEDGE as "the perception of the connexion and agreement, or disagreement and repugnancy of any of our Ideas" (*An Essay concerning Human Understanding*, IV.i.2). Different ways of perceiving the agreement or disagreement result in different modes or "degrees" of knowledge: "[S]ometimes the Mind perceives the Agreement or Disagreement of two Ideas immediately by themselves, without the intervention of any other: And this, I think we may call intuitive Knowledge" (*Essay* IV.ii.1). Like Descartes, Locke thought that because of its noninferential nature, intuitive knowledge was the most certain of any kind of knowledge "and like the bright Sun-shine, forces it self immediately to be perceived, as soon as ever the Mind turns its view that way" (*Essay* IV.ii.1). Like Descartes, Locke thought that "all the Certainty and Evidence of all our Knowledge" depends on intuition, and like Descartes, he was remarkably economical in providing us with an account of this important component in our faculty of reason (see DEMONSTRATION).

Intuitive knowledge results from the immediate perception of the agreement or disagreement of any two ideas; demonstrative knowledge results from an inferential perception, that is, the perception of the agreement of two ideas via the intervention of one or more intermediate ideas:

[W]hen the Mind cannot so bring its Ideas together, as by their immediate comparison, and as it were Juxta-position, or application one to another, to perceive their Agreement or Disagreement, it is fain, by the Intervention of other Ideas, (one or more, as it happens) to discover the Agreement or Disagreement, which it searches; and this is that which we call Reasoning. (*Essay* IV.ii.2)

A piece of demonstrative reasoning is thus a chain of ideas, the first idea of which is perceived to agree with the last. This perception is not immediate, as in intuition, but indirect or inferential, depending as it does on the intervening ideas or "proofs."

Demonstrative reasoning, although certain, is less certain than intuition because it requires more effort and is indirect. Locke compares it to seeing a face "reflected by several mirrors," in contrast to the direct perception of intuition. Furthermore, demonstration is dependent on intuition. Each idea in a demonstrative chain is intuitively connected to the ideas with which it is adjacent; if two adjacent ideas were not intuitively perceived to agree, then they would in turn need to have an intermediate idea or proof interposed, in order for their disagreement to be perceived (*Essay* IV.ii.7).

As knowledge involves the perception of the certain agreement of two ideas, so judgment is the presumption of their agreement, without the perception (*Essay* IV.xiv). Sometimes we judge two ideas to agree directly, but sometimes intermediate ideas or proofs are required (*Essay* IV.xv), in which case we have PROBABILITY. So reasoning comes in two forms, for Locke: demonstrative reasoning, which extends knowledge beyond that which is intuitively self-evident, and probable reasoning, which extends belief or opinion beyond immediate judgment, including judgment of the senses (*Essay* IV.xiv.2).

By and large, HUME took over Locke's account of reason as the faculty that allows us to engage in demonstrative and probable reasoning. His treatment of intuition and demonstration is not developed in the same detail as Locke's, and it is likely that he simply took over most of that theory. One important difference is this: Hume limited demonstration by subject matter; only relations concerning quantity and number—that is, mathematical relations—are susceptible of demonstration. In contrast to Locke's optimism about the possibility of a demonstrative morality, Hume's limitation is not so much a difference in theories of demonstration as a disagreement about which classes of ideas can be made precise enough to withstand the uncertainties produced by a long chain of ideas. Locke thought that proper definitions of moral concepts were self-evident enough to be known by intuition, thus opening up the possibility of a demonstrative morality based on such intuitive truths. Hume thought that mathematical relations owed their precision to the concept of a "unite" (*A Treatise of Human Nature* I.iii.1). The lack of any such "precise standard" in other relations, he thought, precludes demonstration.

It is likely that Locke's picture of probability was Hume's target in his argument concerning INDUCTION (*Treatise* I.iii.6). Locke's conception of probable reasoning was analogous to his account of demonstrative reasoning: they are each chains of ideas, whereby the first idea is seen to agree with the last idea, via the intermediate ideas or proofs. In demonstration, the links between the adjacent ideas are intuitive; in probability, the links hold only "for the most part" (*Essay*, IV.xv.1). The concept of intuition helps explain what links the ideas in a demonstrative chain. Judgment is supposed to play an analogous role in a probable chain, but it is unclear how this might work. Hume argued that "if we are determin'd by reason," we must make use of the principle of the uniformity of nature. But since that principle is unavailable to us, some other account must be given of probable reasoning. Hume's own explanation of what bound the ideas together in a chain of probable reasoning was the association of ideas.

Reason is the faculty that allows persons to engage in these inferential practices, demonstrative and probable reasoning. But what grounds these practices? It is tempting to think of the empiricist account of demonstrative reasoning as being grounded in a formal conception of inference, but their complete rejection of syllogism rules that out. A better account can be given in terms of the semantic relation between ideas. Locke grounded probability in conformity with our own experience, and the testimony of others (*Essay* IV.xv.3), but Hume argued that such an account could not explain the probable beliefs we have. His own account gives such an explanation but leaves it unclear how such beliefs are rationally grounded in the experience that explains them. One attractive picture is reflexivity: reason is warranted if it survives its own survey. But Hume appears to argue (*Treatise* I.iv.1) that when reason surveys itself, it completely self-destructs. Hume's account, if any, of the warrant of reason, especially probable reasoning, remains a controversial question.

PRIMARY WORKS

Hume, David. *A Treatise of Human Nature*. 2d ed., edited with an analytical index by L. A. Selby-Bigge; revised with notes by P. H. Nidditch. Oxford: Clarendon Press, 1978.
Locke, John. *An Essay concerning Human Understanding*. Edited with an introduction by P. H. Nidditch. Oxford: Clarendon Press, 1975.

BIBLIOGRAPHY

Books

Baier, Annette C. *A Progress of Sentiments*. Cambridge: Harvard University Press, 1991.
Norton, David Fate. *Hume: Commonsense Moralist, Sceptical Metaphysician*. Princeton: Princeton University Press, 1982.

Article

Owen, David. "Hume's Doubts about Probable Reasoning: Was Locke the Target?" In *Hume and Hume's Connexions*. Edited by M. A. Stewart and John P. Wright. Edinburgh: Edinburgh University Press; University Park: Penn State University Press, 1994.

DAVID OWEN

REICHENBACH, HANS. Hans Reichenbach (1891–1953) was one of the central figures of Logical Empiricism, as LOGICAL POSITIVISM later came to be known. Reichenbach's philosophy is distinguished by its engagement with PROBABILITY and physics and by a temperate realism that avows that, conditional upon the adoption of certain conventional or volitional presuppositions, SCIENCE produces knowledge of a mind-independent world.

Hans Reichenbach was born in 1891 in Hamburg, Germany, the son of a prosperous merchant. He pursued studies of mathematics, physics, and philosophy at several universities in Germany, writing a Kantian-inspired doctoral dissertation on the theory of probability at the University of Erlangen in 1916. After brief service in the Signal Corps of the German army, he came in 1917 to Berlin, where in 1918 he was one of the five participants in Einstein's first seminar on the general theory of relativity at the University of Berlin. This encounter with Einstein and the theory of relativity had a profound intellectual influence, convincing Reichenbach that KANT's conception of the a priori (see A PRIORI/A POSTERIORI DISTINCTION) was untenable. Within a few years Reichenbach wrote three books on the philosophical transformation necessitated by the theory of relativity. With the assistance of Einstein, Reichenbach obtained a position at the University of Berlin in 1926 as professor of philosophy of physics in the faculty of natural science. There he also became the central figure in an influential discussion group interested in philosophical aspects of science, a like-minded counterpart to the Vienna Circle. In 1930, together with Rudolf CARNAP, he founded the journal *Erkenntnis*, an official organ of logical positivism. With the advent to power of Hitler in 1933, Reichenbach emigrated first to Turkey and then, in 1938, to the United States, becoming professor of philosophy at the University of California–Los Angeles, where he was to remain until the end of his life. During this period he produced six books, including a philosophical examination of quantum mechanics and a treatise on the theory of probability. He had nearly completed a book on the philosophy of time when he suffered a fatal heart attack on April 9, 1953.

In the theory of probability, Reichenbach was a staunch proponent of the limiting frequency conception of probability, maintaining that the term ''probability'' had a univocal sense as the limit of the relative frequency of positive instances to all cases in a sequence of trials. But while the definition of probability in terms of limits of relative frequencies has the merit of being mathematically precise and thus a suitable basis for the logical development of the calculus of probability, it is not without problems in the application of this calculus to empirical subject matter. In particular, since all empirical tests involve but a finite sequence of trials, some rationale must be provided for applying limit results here—in effect, a justification of the rule of INDUCTION, the inference that goes from an observed number of instances to the prediction of equal results in all future instances.

Probability is given a central role throughout Reichenbach's philosophy. Accommodating the fact that the truth-value of many empirical statements is unknown, Reichenbach based his major work in general epistemology on the concept of probability and not truth, so the schema of logical inference is generalized to include probabilistic implication: a statement A may be said to imply a statement B with *degree of probability p*. At the heart of this program is the substitution of a *probability theory of MEANING* for the exclusive reliance on determinate truth or falsity of a statement presupposed by earlier forms of the verifiability theory of meaning (see VERIFICATION PRINCIPLE). In broad agreement with the outcome of the Protocol Sentence Debate (1932–1935) in the Vienna Circle, Reichenbach held that there is no certain knowledge; even statements about immediate experiences are only probable: ''There is no Archimedean point of absolute certainty left to which to attach our knowledge of the world; all we have is an elastic net of probability connections floating in open space'' (*Experience and Prediction* 1938: 192).

In the absence of absolutely certain statements, the criterion for empirical meaningfulness of a statement cannot consist in showing that the statement is determinately true or false, but only in an assessment of its probability. The rules for a statement's verification become, in principle, inductive rules governed by the calculus of probability, a modification that considerably widens the scope of empirical meaningfulness. Statements about the prehistoric past or about the internal constitution of the sun are accorded empirical meaning on the grounds of their indirect verification through the use of inductive inferences from direct observations. The rightful intent is to salvage the theoretical language of science from the indiscriminate sword wielded by earlier positivist implementations of the verifiability theory, which indeed rendered much of scientific discourse meaningless. At the same time, Reichenbach emphasized that the principle of verifiability is itself a choice that is inherently neither right nor wrong but a volitional decision whose merits can be assessed only by the consequences of its adoption. A similar pragmatic ''justification'' was given for the rule of induction.

In the period after the inception of the general theory of relativity (GTR) in 1915, Reichenbach was among the first to realize that it entailed either a fundamental revision or a complete overthrow of the Kantian doctrine that the structure of SPACE and TIME in physics was synthetic a priori, an immutable condition of the possibility of experience. His first work (1920) on the philosophical significance of the theory attempted a reconciliation. Of the two primary meanings of the Kantian a priori, namely, as valid for all time and as constitutive of the object of knowledge, only the latter is deemed compatible with the new physics of the GTR. The function of a priori principles in knowledge is relocated in ''principles and axioms of coordination'' linking the MATHEMATICS of physical theory with objects in the physical world, in effect, ''constituting'' the latter as objects of knowledge. But it should be noted that not only has the Kantian account been modified but also an empiricism has been rejected that accords concepts no logical independence from the contents of PERCEPTION and sensation, a rejection Reichenbach would always retain. But he quickly came to view the role of coordinative principles in non-Kantian terms, emphasizing instead their character as freely chosen conventions or "coordinative definitions," not derived from experience but essential to the applicability of mathematical theory to physical reality. From this vantage point, "the philosophical significance" of the GTR is that it shows how empiricist analyses of scientific knowledge must be tempered by recognition of the fundamental role of conventional elements among the basic propositions of physical theory. For example, the impossibility of ascertaining whether a physical measuring rod undergoes alterations of length in transport means that measurements of the geometry of physical space rest upon conventions regarding the behavior of rigid bodies. But since there can be no necessity about which convention to choose, the possibility is always open to adopt another, while modifying remaining parts of the total theory to "save the phenomena." The articulation of this compensating interdependence of empirical and conventional elements in a theory was termed the method of "empirically equivalent descriptions," illustrating thereby the underdetermination of theory by empirical evidence. But unlike many others, both then and subsequently, Reichenbach did not view this finding as licensing skeptical or antirealist conclusions about scientific theories.

His analysis of the space-time metric led Reichenbach to hold that the topological properties of the space-time manifold are, upon adoption of a conventional prohibition against causal anomalies (e.g., closed, timelike curves), not only more fundamental than the metrical but "an ultimate fact of nature" (*The Philosophy of Space and Time*: p. 285). But this was only the first stage in a larger reductive program that sought to show that spatial topological properties (such as the relation "between" among points) were reducible to temporal topological properties (in particular, "earlier than") and the (linear) order properties of the latter, in turn, to causal relations. This is the program of a *causal theory of time*. But in addition to order properties, time is also considered to have a determinate direction, manifested in such irreversible phenomena as the melting of snowmen, in the growth and decay of organisms, and in the facility with which we obtain records and knowledge of the past but not of the future. To this problem Reichenbach's posthumously published *The Direction of Time* (1956) is devoted.

The problem of the direction of time had already arisen within physics in the development of the statistical mechanical theory of gases in the last quarter of the nineteenth century. The situation was this: the laws of classical mechanics are time-reversal invariant, yet the Second Law of Thermodynamics affirms that the entropy—or measure of disorder—in the universe never decreases. Beginning in the 1870s, the Austrian physicist Boltzmann argued, not uncontroversially, that the irreversible direction of entropy of a macrosystem is compatible with the statistical behavior of enormous numbers of microprocesses (collisions of gas molecules) governed by the time-reversible laws of classical mechanics.

That is to say, the Second Law is a statistical law: it is only extremely improbable that the entropy of a complex physical system could ever decrease, so that a more ordered (hence, less probable) state would follow a less ordered (more probable) one. Viewing Boltzmann's statistical definition of time direction as his "great contribution to physics and to philosophy" (*The Direction of Time*: 134), Reichenbach sought an empiricist clarification of Boltzmann's definition by considering only the statistics of physical systems at the macrolevel, an analysis that would thus provide an observational basis for the statistical definition of time direction. Temporal anisotropy is to be reduced to entropic increase by considering the statistics of thermodynamic processes in a large number (an "ensemble") of macroscopic subsystems that could be considered as prima facie isolated, having "branched off" from a comprehensive system. Because of their (indefinite) isolation, branch systems may be found to be initially in lower entropy states than their surrounding environment, yet observation shows that their evolution is toward higher and higher relative states of entropy. A simple example, used by Reichenbach, is that of a footprint on a beach (a highly ordered state of grains of sand, presumably traceable to a past interaction before branching), which gradually erodes and disappears through the action of weather or tides. To be sure, any *given* branch system may feature an apparent anti-Second Law fluctuation, such as the creation of a "footprint" by wind without interaction with a wider environment. Still, Reichenbach argued, if one considers an average over an ensemble of branch systems (say, the beach at East Hampton, New York) such anomalous behaviors become statistically insignificant amid the entropy-increasing processes in the vast majority of branch subsystems. Consistent with Boltzmann's statistical explanation of entropic increase, Reichenbach maintained that "we cannot speak of a direction for time as a whole," so the notions of *past* and *future* must be relativized to a "particular section of the entropy curve of the universe" with its attendant branch systems, which alone are observable. Accordingly, the humanly known direction of the temporal order ("positive time") is defined (*The Direction of Time*: 127) in terms of the direction of "most" (indeed, the vast majority of) thermodynamic processes in the branch systems along that section. For it is "only this reflection of the general trend in many individual manifestations" that "is visible to us and appears to us as the direction of time" (*The Direction of Time*: 136).

Reichenbach's entropic approach to the problem of the direction of time can be considered, at best, suggestive, yet this work remains today a centerpiece of discussions in the philosophy of time. For one thing, the very characterization of branch systems—suspended from interaction with a containing environment—apparently relies on the notion of causality, whereas causal relations are supposed reducible to that of entropic increase. But perhaps most unsettling to an empiricist is Reichenbach's reductive *definition* of positive time as entropic increase in the vast majority of branch systems. For how can such a fundamental aspect of experience as the distinction between past and future have merely a probabilistic basis?

PRIMARY WORKS

Experience and Prediction. Chicago: University of Chicago Press, 1938.
The Theory of Probability. Berkeley and Los Angeles: University of California Press, 1949. German original published 1935.
The Direction of Time. Berkeley and Los Angeles: University of California Press, 1956.
The Philosophy of Space and Time. Translated by Maria Reichenbach and John Freund. New York: Dover, 1957. German original published 1928.
The Theory of Relativity and a Priori Knowledge. Translated by Maria Reichenbach. Berkeley and Los Angeles: University of California Press, 1965. German original published in 1920.
Selected Writings, 1909–1953. Edited by Maria Reichenbach and Robert S. Cohen. 2 vols. Dordrecht: D. Reidel, 1978.

BIBLIOGRAPHY

Books

Grünbaum, Adolf. *Philosophical Problems of Space and Time.* 2d enlarged ed. Dordrecht: D. Reidel, 1973.
Salmon, Wesley, ed. *Hans Reichenbach—Logical Empiricist.* Dordrecht: D. Reidel, 1977.
Sklar, Lawrence. *Physics and Chance: Philosophical Issues in the Foundations of Statistical Mechanics.* New York and London: Cambridge University Press, 1993.

Articles

Earman, John. "An Attempt to Add a Little Direction to 'The Problem of the Direction of Time.' " *Philosophy of Science* 41 (1974): 15–47.
Kamlah, Andreas. "Hans Reichenbach—Leben, Werk und Wirkung." In *Wien-Berlin-Prag: Der Aufsteig der wissenschaftlichen Philosophie.* Edited by Rudolf Haller and Friedrich Stadler. Vienna: Verlag Hölder-Pichler-Tempsky, 1993: 238–83.
Nagel, Ernest. "Probability and the Theory of Knowledge." *Philosophy of Science* 6 (1939); as reprinted in *Sovereign Reason.* Glencoe, IL: Free Press, 1954: 225–65.

T. A. RYCKMAN

REID, THOMAS. Thomas Reid (1710–1796) was the central figure in Scottish "common sense realism" and a critic of the "theory of ideas" of BERKELEY and HUME. His most significant works are *An Inquiry into the Human Mind* (1764), *Essays on the Intellectual Powers of Man* (1785), and *Essays on the Active Powers of Man* (1788). The most important themes in each of these will be summarized. The *Inquiry* advances a theory of "direct" PERCEPTION (rather than mediated by ideas) and a geometry of the visibles; the first collection of essays offers an expansive understanding of the powers of the human mind and a novel account of judgment; and the second set of essays defends a libertarian understanding of human freedom (see FREE WILL) and develops an account of the MORAL SENSE.

REID'S LIFE

Born on April 26, 1710, at Strachan near Aberdeen, Scotland, Thomas Reid entered a family connected to both the Scottish clergy and the physical sciences.

(His great-uncle David Gregory had invented the reflecting telescope.) His academic career began at Marischal College, where he studied under the regent George Turnbull, whose pursuit of the scientific investigation of the "furniture of the mind" must have recommended itself. Reid graduated with a degree in theology in 1731 and served the next five years as a Presbyterian clerk and librarian at Marischal; during this time he read Clarke on the freedom of the will. After resigning his office in 1736, he accompanied John Stewart—later a professor of mathematics at Marischal—on a tour of England. While in Cambridge on this tour, Reid met and conversed with the blind mathematician Saunderson—conversations that would bear such remarkable fruit years later with Reid's work on the geometry of the visibles.

On returning to Scotland in 1737, Reid was appointed to pastor the church at New-Machar. The early years of his ministry were difficult but included his marriage to Elizabeth, his uncle's daughter. It is likely that Reid still adhered to Berkeley's interpretation of Locke's empiricism (see LOCKE) when he took the post at New-Machar, but in time he came to see it as leading only to SKEPTICISM. In 1738 he compiled notes on Peter Browne's *Procedure, Extent, and Limits of Human Understanding* (1728), which led to a reexamination of his commitment to Locke's philosophy of mind and Berkeley's extension of it. How quickly Reid abandoned the "Way of Ideas" (see IDEAS) is unclear, but a break is evident in his orations to the graduating class at King's College, Aberdeen, and the rejection is unmistakable by the time he left Aberdeen for Glasgow in 1763.

The seeds of this turning away were probably planted much earlier in the experimental method that he learned from Turnbull, which encouraged Reid to search out the various powers of the human mind. But even if this was not the case, there is adequate reason to believe that prior to the publication of Hume's *Treatise of Human Nature* (1739–1740) Reid was already moving away from the Way of Ideas and its assumptions about the philosophy of mind. His early reading of Hume only confirmed worries Reid already possessed.

Reid served at New-Machar for fifteen years, spending much of his time examining the laws of external perception, and in 1748 published in the *Philosophical Transactions of the Royal Society of London* "An Essay on Quantity, Occasioned by Reading a Treatise in Which Simple and Compound Ratios Are Applied to Virtue and Merit"—a critique of HUTCHESON. Even with his scholarly interests, Reid must have served the congregation well. In 1752, when he was elected professor of philosophy by King's College, Aberdeen, he left behind a congregation sad to see him leave.

While a regent at the University of Aberdeen and in connection with his colleagues in the Aberdeen Philosophical Society, Reid applied himself to his most significant work, *An Inquiry into the Human Mind, on the Principles of Common Sense* (1764). One of his explicit targets in the *Inquiry* was Hume's skepticism, and in order to ensure that he was not misunderstanding Hume's work, he sent a draft to Hume for his inspection. Hume's response praises the perspicuity of Reid's style—and raises no objections to Reid's characterization of Hume's ideas.

In 1763 Reid was invited to succeed Adam SMITH to the professorship of moral philosophy at the University of Glasgow. While at Aberdeen, Reid had become friends with Henry Home (Lord Kames), a justice on Scotland's Court of Sessions and a published critic (and relative) of Hume. Kames was influential not only in securing Reid's appointment at Glasgow but, through years of friendship and correspondence, in the development of Reid's thought as well.

Reid's tenure at the University of Glasgow extended from 1763 until 1781, when he resigned his position in order to pursue writing without distraction while still in good health. Although he left teaching at the age of seventy-one, he was still active enough to compile and organize his lectures into two further volumes: *Essays on the Intellectual Powers of Man*, which was published in 1785; and *Essays on the Active Powers of Man*, which appeared in 1788.

In his final years Reid continued to pursue the researches that had animated his life from his intellectual nonage: mathematics and scientific inquiry. He also wrote essays for a philosophical society, including one on Priestly's treatment of matter and mind and another on More's "Utopia." The report of his friends is that his mind was sound and active until his death on October 7, 1796.

AN INQUIRY INTO THE HUMAN MIND

Reid's first published treatise, *An Inquiry into the Human Mind on the Principles of Common Sense*, gives the first results of his inductive research into the laws governing human thought (see INDUCTION). Although the method and aim Reid identifies for the work are similar to the method and aim proposed by Hume in his *Treatise*, Reid reaches very different conclusions. By careful observation of the progress of the mind, Reid proposed to develop a "mechanics" of thought: to lay bare the "principles of our constitution" (the laws of thought) and to give an inventory of the "furniture of the mind," determining which features of our thoughts are "original" and which are "acquired" through experience. The most noteworthy results of this investigation can be summarized under four headings: the rejection of "the theory of ideas," the development of an account of "direct perception," the introduction of the need for "original" conceptions, and the highly original formulation of the "geometry of the visibles."

Theory of Ideas

Although the target of his attack appears to expand in content as his argument progresses, the core of the "theory of ideas" (which Reid also calls the "ideal hypothesis" and the "Way of Ideas") is that ideas are the only objects of the human mind. This hypothesis Reid thinks has been assumed without argument by thinkers from the "Schoolmen," to Descartes, to Locke, Berkeley, and Hume. Reid argues that it should be rejected, in various passages offering at least three reasons for this conclusion.

The first reason for rejecting the ideal hypothesis is also the one Reid most often gives: it leads to skepticism. Reid concedes that the works of Berkeley and Hume are admirably rigorous explorations of the implications of the theory of ideas, but he insists that both reach conclusions that are unacceptably distant from the dictates of common sense. Hume's *modus ponens* is Reid's *modus tollens*: both grant that *if* ideas are the only objects of human thought, *then* KNOWLEDGE of external bodies is impossible; and while Hume asserts the antecedent and detaches the consequent, Reid denies the consequent and concludes that the ideal antecedent must be false.

Reid's confidence in the trustworthiness of common opinion was not unqualified, but it regularly heads his list of objections: where common sense and speculative philosophy disagree, Reid consistently places the burden of proof on the skeptic. This prominent theme in Reid's thought is not grounded in naive dogmatism but rather is an extension of his clear expectation that the "author of our constitution" has equipped every human—even untutored "vulgar" individuals—with faculties adequate to the demands of ordinary existence. Convinced that the ideal hypothesis requires the abandonment of this expectation, Reid abandons the hypothesis instead.

But Reid's reasons for rejecting the theory of ideas are not limited to worries about its implications. A second objection is that the theory uncritically assumes that ideas (as conceived by the theory) exist at all. On Reid's understanding of the theory, the word "idea" signifies "whatever is the immediate object of thought." Reid admits that he is conscious himself of perceiving, remembering, and imagining; but he will not admit that the object of perceiving, for example, is only an idea. The "idea," according to Reid, is only the act of perceiving, while the object of the perceiving is some external object.

A third objection to the theory of IDEAS can be found in Reid's insistence that there is no reason to think that sensations resemble what they represent. In this objection, Reid appears to add to the ideal hypothesis a commitment to "ideas" as images or pictures of objects, as well as the suggestion that external objects are known—if known at all—by an inference from the images to the external objects. Berkeley's conclusion from these premises is to deny the existence of the non-ideal external things; Reid's is to deny the existence of the ideas that are supposed to be mediating the mind's access to the external world: for Reid, perception of the external world is "direct."

Direct Perception

Some of the most significant "observations" that Reid reports from his close examination of the data of consciousness concern the difference between sensation and perception and in particular the relative inaccessibility of sensations. On Reid's account, "sensations" are the feelings that attend the stimulation of one of the external senses: the "visible object" attending impressions on the retina or the feeling attending the chemical changes on the tongue. "Perceptions," on the other hand, include judgment; and since their objects are the external objects themselves (and not the sensations that occasion them), Reid insists that perception is "direct" and not mediated. (This formulation collapses a development between the formulation of the *Inquiry* and that offered in the *Essays*. In the former, Reid appears to claim that perception is "immediate," while in the latter he settles for "direct." It is likely that in the *Inquiry* he wished to draw the contrast to the theory of ideas as sharply as possible and that by the time of the latter work Reid recognized that calling perception "immediate" would obscure the significant role played by sensation in perception.)

Reid's understanding of the relationship between sensation and perception is crucial to his thought: external perceptions (judgments about external objects) are not derived from sensations; rather, the sensations "signify" the existence of the external object to the mind. Perceptions are sight-translations of the signs given by impressions on the organs of the external senses. These perceptions are "direct" because the sensations themselves are not objects of consciousness. The human mind is constructed in a such a way that it interprets the sensible sign without consciously attending to it. For this conclusion, Reid appeals to the "data" of introspection. While there are sensations, such as pain, that are direct objects of consciousness, we do not find ourselves believing in the existence of some external object in connection with them. On the other hand, sensations that do attend beliefs about external objects are very difficult to make the objects of conscious awareness. Careful attention and patience can bring these sensations before consciousness, but it takes considerable effort to attend, for example, to the "visible object" (which is two-dimensional).

This difference between sensations, Reid contends, is not due to a difference in the sensations themselves—both are only feelings. Instead, the difference lies in the way the human mind is constituted (hardwired?) to interpret the sensible signs. We perceive the presence of a hard surface not because we draw an inference from sensory "givens" but rather because we have been constituted by the Author of Nature to form a BELIEF (perception) about the presence of the surface on the occasion of experiencing the sensible sign. No inferential process is involved in moving from the sign to the thing signified.

On Reid's understanding, the role of sensation in perception is like the role of LANGUAGE in communication: the sensation is not the object of awareness; it is the sign by which the direct object of perception (the external object) is perceived. While it is possible to force ourselves to attend to the sensations as sensations (just as it is possible to attend to words as words), from this it does not follow that we can formulate judgments (perceptions) about external objects (or the thoughts others attempt to communicate) only by reasoning from one to the other. Reid is able to call this "direct" perception because perceptions involve judgment and not just an image; and he can also insist that the direct object of perceptual judgment is the external object and not the sensation or impression that signifies the object: there is no inference from the sensation to the external object because the sensation is not perceived.

An "idea" of an external object, for Reid, is just the act of the mind's attending to the external object. It is not the image or impression that is formed by the object on the external organ(s) of sense and somehow made available to some internal eye.

Original Conceptions

In keeping with the position that perception involves judgment and that sensations do not resemble the things that they signify, Reid maintains that the conceptions involved in ideas of external objects have more content than the bare sensible givens. Unlike Hume and Locke, Reid does not think that every conception can be constructed from simple ideas "of sense" (either of impression or reflection), this because many of our most important conceptions are "original," arising from the "constitution of the mind."

Reid's confidence that the mind must supply content in addition to that contained in the sensations can be traced to two observations. The first is that the concept of an object of external perception involves features that are neither images nor feelings; and the second is that even Hume's attempt to reduce all conceptions to constructs from simple ideas of sensation and reflection failed to preserve commonsense beliefs about external objects. The concepts supplied by the mind in perception are "original" contributions that the mind makes to thought. Each of the external faculties (sight, touch, hearing, smell, tasting) has conceptions original to it (for sight, it is color) and thus is the source of "original perceptions" concerning the possession of those qualities by external objects.

By allowing for conceptions with content not reducible to sensory "givens," Reid moves clearly away from the central empiricists of the eighteenth century. But this departure opens the way for the most significant development in the *Inquiry*: his account of the visual perception of depth.

The Geometry of the Visibles

The most original work in his *Inquiry* is Reid's resolution of a dispute between Berkeley's *New Theory of Vision* (1709) and Martin's *New and Compendious System of Optics* (1740) over the best explanation for the visual perception of depth: our evident ability to make three-dimensional judgments (the distance of an object from the eye or the shape of a solid figure) using only the sense of sight (see SPACE). All parties to the controversy conceded that the sense of sight delivered only a two-dimensional object (the surfaces facing the eye) and that the concept of depth is given only by touch. Martin had contended that judgments of depth from sight alone were possible because REASON (very rapidly) calculated distances from the eye on the basis of a precise awareness of the angle of inclination between the lines of sight of the two eyes. Berkeley insisted that through habitual connection between judgments of sight and touch, the mind comes to be able to "interpret" visible objects as signs for tangible objects. The worlds of sight and touch are disjoint for Berkeley (it is not possible to reason from one to the other), but experience makes it appear that they are related.

Reid finds both of these solutions suggestive but neither satisfactory. Martin's account posits implausibly extensive innate facility with complex geometry, and Berkeley's solution leaves a troubling mystery: if the worlds of sight and touch are disjoint, then why would solid geometry appear to be a simple extension of plane geometry? Reid's solution retains the best of both while avoiding these problems.

With Berkeley, Reid maintains that the signs supplied by the two-dimensional, visible object can become signs for tangible depth (and a three-dimensional, tangible object) by a habitual connection of visual and tangible data. But unlike Berkeley, Reid insists that the object perceived by sight and the object perceived by touch are the very same (external) object; and to show that this is so, he saves Martin's focus on reason by devising a ''geometry of the visibles.''

Assisted by the blind mathematician Saunderson, Reid developed rules by which the appearance of the visible object could be deduced from the data of touch, and vice versa. Because Reid conceived of the visible object as a projection onto the inside of a sphere with the eye at the sphere's center, the result is a crude spherical geometry; and Reid was able to display the success of his system by Saunderson's ability to deduce how objects that he could perceive only by touch would appear to those with sight. The interdeducibility of the visible and tangible objects Reid took as a decisive argument against Berkeley's IDEALISM, since Saunderson's ability showed that even though experience in fact supplies the link between the visible and the tangible for the sighted, experience is not essential for someone in possession of Reid's geometry. At the very least, the rigorous coherence of the visible and tangible object suggests that the best explanation is a unified object external to both senses.

ESSAYS ON THE INTELLECTUAL POWERS OF MAN

In the first of his two collections of essays on the powers of the human mind, Reid extends the investigation of the *Inquiry* beyond the powers of the five senses to the original powers and laws of the human constitution of the other ''senses,'' including memory, consciousness, reasoning, and aesthetic taste. In addition to an expansive account of the various distinct powers, these essays are also noteworthy for their novel treatment of judgment and a seemingly audacious list of ''first principles of contingent truth.''

Faculty Psychology in the *Essays*

In contrast to Hume's effort to reduce all thought to combinations of impressions and ideas of sensation or reflection, Reid is willing to expand his catalog of distinct and primitive faculties of the human mind. Each of the ''faculties'' distinguished as the result of his observations is described as operating on the same input-output model Reid used to characterize the workings of the external senses: given the input appropriate to the faculty, it ''puts out'' a belief employing an original conception proper to the faculty.

For the faculties of external perception, the inputs are all impressions on the organs of sense, but for the "intellectual" powers the inputs are intellectual objects (conceptions). Given conceptions as inputs (whether a complex conception of a person or a conception of an external object), these powers "return" judgments we are disposed to believe. Memory, for example, takes as its input distinct conceptions of (apparently) prior events and delivers a judgment that the events occurred in the past. The faculty of aesthetic taste takes a conception of an external object with particular qualities and returns a judgment about the BEAUTY of the object.

While this may seem simplistic when compared with Hume's ingenious reductions of categories such as beauty and moral virtue, Reid's confidence in his account is grounded in two crucial assumptions. His first assumption is that the creator of the human mind has equipped it in such a way that all well-formed adults not corrupted by prejudice or philosophy are competent to form correct judgments about the world. Philosophical accounts that write off common opinion as fundamentally confused succeed only in revealing the arrogance of philosophers.

Reid's second crucial assumption concerns the accuracy of the content of common conceptions. While he is not anxious to multiply original conceptions and distinct powers where it is unnecessary, neither is he willing to lose or abbreviate conceptions simply to save a simple theory. Concerning the concept of the "beautiful," for example, Reid identifies a distinct faculty that supplies the concept directly. Convinced that beauty cannot be reduced (without loss) to a special combination of feelings, he prefers to identify a distinct faculty to be the source for it, rather than trying to explain the irreducible parts away. Reid's investigations turn up many different faculties because he discovers many conceptions not reducible to combinations of the outputs of other faculties.

Of Judgment, Evidence, and First Principles

The sixth essay among those on the intellectual powers drives to the heart of Reid's epistemology, not only developing his concept of epistemic evidence but also offering lists of "self-evident first principles" of necessary and contingent TRUTH. Reid could have presented his conception of evidence more clearly, and current interpretations typically explain it either in geometrical or naturalistic terms. Pivotal in deciding between these interpretations is the role it is thought the "first principles" are to play in his overall epistemology.

Defenders of the geometrical account of evidence see in the first principles the axioms, certified by "common sense," necessary for providing deductive proofs to justify belief. This interpretation is supported by Reid's insistence that the first principles are "self-evident" and his occasional references to the first principles as "axioms." Advocates for a naturalistic reading of Reid's conception of evidence stress Reid's many references to the inductive-introspective method he claims to be following in his investigations and see in the first principles expressions only of the "laws of the human constitution" displayed in the ordinary belief of honest people with mature intellectual faculties.

Before offering an even more successful account of Reid's conception of evidence, it is worth giving a sample of some of the first principles of contingent truth that Reid identifies. He gives twelve, but the following are typical:

2. That the thoughts of which I am conscious, are the thoughts of a being which I call *myself*, my *mind*, my *person* (*Works*: 443b).

3. That those things did really happen which I distinctly remember (*Works*: 444b).

7. That the natural faculties, by which we distinguish truth from error, are not fallacious (*Works*: 447a).

12. That, in the phænomena of nature, what is to be, will probably be like to what has been in similar circumstances (*Works*: 451a).

This is antiskepticism with its teeth bared, but Reid at least claims not to have crafted his list to plug all the skeptical leaks sprung by Descartes and Hume. In justifying these principles as "first," Reid cites a number of features that they possess besides undermining skepticism: they are learned too early to be the result of prejudice, their contradictories are laughably absurd, and "common sense" approves them.

This last quality—being accepted by all humans who possess that common degree of skill with reason necessary for self-government (Reid's "common sense")—may suggest that the naturalistic interpretation is to be preferred, but it seems that it is best understood only as a certain kind of naturalism. From the outset of his discussion of judgment and running through his various comments on epistemology, Reid makes repeated reference to the practice of the courtroom to illustrate and explain his meaning. In light of Reid's friendship with Henry Home (Lord Kames) and the similarities between Reid's first principles and the first principles of Scottish law found in Viscount Stair's *Institutions of the Law of Scotland* (1693), it seem reasonable to conclude that Reid understands epistemic evidence on the model of evidence in the Scottish courts.

If Reid does have legal evidence in mind when discussing epistemology, then his first principles of contingent truth can be understood as laws of the human constitution discovered by examining the common beliefs of the mature and unbiased. But as laws of thought or common sense, they would figure in his epistemology the way standing laws functioned in the Scottish courts: as legal presumptions. These presumptions were rebuttable but were justified without argument in the absence of sufficient evidence to the contrary.

While more work is needed on Reid's epistemology, a legal interpretation of his intentions seems to get explicit support in his response to Hume's skepticism "with regard to reason." To Hume's contention in the *Treatise* (I.iv.1: 180–83) that all probable evidence must, when appropriately examined by reason, diminish to zero, Reid argues that the force of evidence is never handled that way in court. Competent judges will be sure to carefully examine the trustworthiness of the evidence brought by witnesses; but, contrary to Hume's analysis, even strict scrutiny need not diminish its strength to zero. Reid appears to find two significant faults in Hume's argument: first, Hume neglects the possibility that on examination the judge will find the testimony to be even more valuable than first thought; and second, Hume assumes that the mere fallibility of a witness is sufficient to undermine the significance of her or his testimony. Reid holds Hume to the standards of the court, and since infallibility is not required in court, it ought not be required for KNOWLEDGE.

ESSAYS ON THE ACTIVE POWERS OF MAN

The companion to the essays on the intellectual powers extends the inductive investigation of the powers of the mind to those powers with which humans exercise the will. Here Reid is still concerned with faculties as input-output systems, but with the active powers the "output" is not just a judgment—it is also an action. The active powers are "active" because they lead to action, and while Reid devotes some attention to "mechanical" and "animal" principles, his focus is on the rational principles of action. In connection with the powers relating to the will, Reid also finds it necessary to address the nature of human liberty. These essays are most noteworthy for the defense Reid offers of the liberty of moral agents and for his treatment of the rational principles of action: our regard for the good on the whole and the moral sense.

Of the Liberty of Moral Agents

In striking contrast to Hume's analysis, Reid defends the common belief that humans have free will in the libertarian sense of having the power of alternate choice. Reid bases this conclusion on the fact that humans are accountable for their actions (and so must be free in the libertarian sense) and on the self-evidence of the proposition that we are efficient (originating) causes in our deliberate and voluntary actions. That all humans believe this is evident by their actions, inasmuch as they do not attempt what they do not believe to be within their power. The libertarian conclusion in this essay has far-reaching consequences, since Reid's account of causality, contra Hume, locates the origin of our conception of "cause" in our introspective awareness of what it is like to bring things about through the free exercise of our wills (see CAUSATION).

Rational Principles of Action

While the focus of Reid's account of moral judgment is his discussion of the moral sense or conscience, he also develops a parallel principle of action that embraces elements of what would now be called utilitarianism. "Our regard for the good on the whole" is a rational principle of action, and by it humans judge what action would best meet their ends. What is noteworthy about Reid's analysis of this principle is his concession that even though judgments of the good on the whole are not moral judgments, nonetheless the actions they suggest are extensionally equivalent with the demands of conscience. If given the time necessary to calculate the good on the whole, humans would be equipped to perform what MORALITY requires. Possession of a conscience is necessary only because the Creator of the human constitution thought the matters too significant to be left to such a weak faculty.

The demands of morality require a faculty capable of judging what is required quickly, not through a long calculation of outcomes. Reid discovers through his introspective investigations a "sense" suited precisely to this end: a moral sense that "perceives" duty as the eye perceives color. Some of the details of this doctrine are clear. For example, Reid insists both that the "moral sense" delivers the same judgments to all humans who have reached "years of understanding" and that the moral sense has to be cultivated through education.

Just how this power is supposed to operate is not carefully explained, but it is likely that, as with the intellectual powers, Reid's moral sense is an input-output mechanism that takes intellectual objects as its inputs and returns judgments involving the appropriate original conceptions. Since Reid takes the object of moral judgment to be a relation (between an actor and an action), the input for the moral sense is an ordered pair of conceptions: one for the actor and another for the action. The faculty's output is a judgment about whether or not the action is a duty for the actor—where the concept of obligation or duty is an original conception supplied by the moral faculty or sense.

The moral faculty is a "sense" because its judgments have the same evidential force as the judgments delivered by the external senses. While this faculty operates automatically in all mature adults, moral education is nonetheless useful because there is a voluntary element to how one conceives of particular actors and actions—and feeding the sense inaccurate input conceptions can lead to faulty moral judgments. Reid's treatment of the moral sense exhibits the central features of his philosophical method, combining a search for "mechanical" principles of operation with a deep reluctance to abandon common beliefs for the sake of an artificially simple theory.

PRIMARY WORKS

The Works of Thomas Reid. 7th ed., edited by William Hamilton. Edinburgh: Maclachlan and Stewart, 1872.

The Philosophical Orations of Thomas Reid. Edited by D. D. Todd. Carbondale: Southern Illinois University Press, 1989.

Practical Ethics. Edited by Knud Haakonssen. Princeton: Princeton University Press, 1990.

BIBLIOGRAPHY

Books

Barker, Stephen T., and Tom L. Beauchamp. *Thomas Reid: Critical Interpretations*. Philadelphia: Philosophical Monographs, 1976.

Dalgarno, Melvin, and Eric Matthews. *The Philosophy of Thomas Reid*. Dordrecht: Kluwer Academic, 1989.

Daniels, Norman. *Thomas Reid's Inquiry: The Geometry of the Visibles and the Case for Realism*. New York: Burt Franklin, 1974.

Ellos, William J. *Thomas Reid's Newtonian Realism.* Washington, DC: University Press of America, 1981.
Gallie, Roger. *Thomas Reid and "The Way of Ideas."* Dordrecht: Kluwer Academic, 1989.
Grave, S. A. *The Scottish Philosophy of Common Sense.* Westport, CT: Greenwood Press, 1973.
Lehrer, Keith. *Thomas Reid.* New York: Routledge, 1989.
Marcil-Lacoste, Louise. *Claude Buffier and Thomas Reid.* Kingston: McGill-Queen's University Press, 1982.
McCosh, James. *The Scottish Philosophy.* Hildesheim: Georg Olms Verlagsbuchhandlung, 1966.
Raphael, D. D. *The Moral Sense.* London: Oxford University Press, 1947.
Schultess, Daniel. *Philosophie et Sens Commun chez Thomas Reid.* Berne: Peter Lang, 1983.
Stewart, M. A. *Studies in the Philosophy of the Scottish Enlightenment.* Oxford: Clarendon Press, 1990.

Articles

Alston, William P. "Thomas Reid on Epistemic Principles." *History of Philosophy Quarterly* 2 (1985): 435–52.
Beanblossom, Ronald. "In Defense of Thomas Reid's Use of 'Suggestion.'" *Grazer Philosophische Studien* 1 (1975): 19–24.
Cantor, G. N. "Berkeley, Reid, and the Mathematization of Mid-Eighteenth-Century Optics." *Journal of the History of Ideas* 38 (1977): 429–48.
Faurot, J. H. "The Development of Reid's Theory of Knowledge." *University of Toronto Quarterly* 21 (1952): 224–31.
Immerwahr, John. "The Development of Reid's Realism." *Monist* 61 (1978): 245–58.
Marcil-Lacoste, Louise. "The Seriousness of Reid's Skeptical Admissions." *Monist* 61 (1978): 311–25.
Pritchard, Michael. "Reason and Passion: Reid's Reply to Hume." *Monist* 61 (1978): 282–98.
Ross, Ian. "Unpublished Letters of Thomas Reid to Lord Kames, 1762–1782." *Texas Studies in Literature and Language* 7 (1965): 17–65.
Stewart, Dugald. "An Account of the Life and Writings of Thomas Reid." In *The Works of Thomas Reid*, 7th ed., edited by William Hamilton. Edinburgh: Maclachlan and Stewart, 1872.
Wolterstorff, Nicholas. "Hume and Reid." *Monist* 70 (1987): 398–417.

WILLIAM C. DAVIS

RELATIONS. Despite the importance of relations to both mathematical and everyday KNOWLEDGE, no adequate theory of relations was developed until the twentieth century. ARISTOTLE's formal LOGIC did not account for the validity of arguments using relations, and his METAPHYSICS did not accommodate them. Even with the gradual downfall of Aristotelianism since the seventeenth century, a systematic theory of relations, encompassing both the logical and the metaphysical, did not appear until the twentieth. Although empiricism addresses the issue of relations more than most philosophical movements, its contribution at best paved the way for a complete analysis.

To understand both the metaphysical and logical neglect of relations we must first understand what they are according to modern theory. Bertrand RUSSELL places special emphasis on relations because they are crucial to MATHEMATICS. "If x is less than y, and y is less than z, then x is less than z" is a fundamental law of arithmetic, surely known since the time of the early Greeks. Yet, no logic until that of PEIRCE could handle inferences based on this law, and no metaphysical system could satisfactorily explain how the relation of less-than could hold between *two* entities. We need not turn to arithmetic for examples of relations since they play a fundamental role in our knowledge of the everyday world and its physics, thus making their neglect even more startling. Russell's logical analysis shows that its being at a distance D from b is not a property of an entity a in the same way that its shape is. Rather, that a is D from b is a fact about both a *and* b. The statement that "a is D from b" is as much a reflection of the world as "a is spherical."

Why did Aristotle deny ontological status to relations? He speaks of qualities being "in" substances (see SUBSTANCE) in an almost physical way. But how could a relation (e.g., father-of) be in two substances (the father and the son) and thus be in two places at once? It is also true that in some cases relations that appear to be required are not: if a and b are exactly similar in color, then the fact that both have the same color property is all that there is to their similarity. Also, the implicit or explicit embrace of some form of absolute SPACE and TIME—the view that there are moments and places that are intrinsically ordered—seems to dilute the need for spatial and temporal relations: a is at a place, and that tells us where it is with respect to other things in other places (indeed, one may wonder whether the puzzlement over relations helps generate the doctrines of absolute space and time). Aristotle's subject-predicate logic can even, in a (illusory) sense, accommodate relational truths. That John loves Mary makes John a Mary-lover. However, the logical form of arguments using relations is thereby lost. If a has the nonrelational property being-greater-than-b, and b has the property being-greater-than-c, it does not follow that a is greater-than-c.

Perhaps, had Aristotle's physics been mathematical, the importance of relations would have been inescapable. But the mathematization of physics did not come until the seventeenth century. Not surprisingly, philosophers then began to write more directly about relations. What is surprising is that it was the empiricists, not known for being great mathematicians, rather than the rationalists (who were so known), who motivated the eventual reification of relations. Still, the NOMINALISM (which holds that only individuals exist) of the seventeenth century almost automatically precluded a full theory of relations.

LOCKE, writing in the midst of the scientific revolution, is the first major figure of the seventeenth century to discuss the place of relations in epistemology. Locke claims that relations arise upon a comparison of ideas; since knowledge depends almost exclusively on such comparisons, the status of relations appears crucial (*An Essay concerning Human Understanding* II.xxviii.17–19). Yet, Locke shares the reluctance of his predecessors to grant them objective ontological status: relations are "not contained in the real existence of Things, but [are] something extraneous, and superinduced" (*Essay* II.xxv.8). To say they arise on a comparison is to imply that were there no minds, there would be no relations. BERKELEY follows suit. He claims that relations are notions as opposed to ideas. Ideas arise from sense experience; notions do not. So, whatever relations are, they do not seem to be observable features of what Berkeley calls the physical world (*The Principles of Human Knowledge* I.89, I.142, and editor's note 1).

With HUME we have a major advance in the theory of relations. In his *Treatise of Human Nature* he discusses them extensively. What he calls philosophical relations are divided into relations that "depend entirely on the ideas," for example, resemblance and those that "may be chang'd without any change in the ideas," for example, spatial contiguity and causal connection (*Treatise* I.iii.1). Although he has the tendency to assimilate relations depending entirely on ideas to functions of the qualities of the things related—the resemblance of two red things is a function of the fact that they are both red—spatial and temporal relations are not such functions. What Hume calls *natural* relations are all causal features of mental operations, hence are a species of philosophical relation. These causal features are the laws of the association of ideas (*Treatise* I.i.4, I.iii.7). Nowhere does Hume state that the mind creates any of these relations (although causal relations are a function of others). As he says, the mind *discovers* them: " 'Tis from the idea of a triangle, that we discover the relation of equality." There are many similar passages. Thus, Hume justifies the epistemological importance of relations by claiming they are features of the world. Hume does not work out a logic for relations, but he paves the way for that logic to arise in the late nineteenth and early twentieth centuries.

PRIMARY WORKS

Aristotle. *The Basic Works of Aristotle*. Edited by Richard McKeon. New York: Random House, 1941.

Berkeley, George. *The Works of George Berkeley, Bishop of Cloyne*. Edited by A. A. Luce and T. E. Jessop. 9 vols. London: Thomas Nelson and Sons, 1948–1957.

Hume, David. *A Treatise of Human Nature*. 2d ed., edited with an analytical index by L. A. Selby-Bigge; revised with notes by P. H. Nidditch. Oxford: Clarendon Press, 1978.

Locke, John. *An Essay concerning Human Understanding*. Edited with an introduction by P. H. Nidditch. Oxford: Clarendon Press, 1975.

Russell, Bertrand. *Logic and Knowledge*. Edited by Robert Charles Marsh. London: Macmillan, 1964.

Russell, Bertrand, and Alfred North Whitehead. *Principia Mathematica*. 3 vols., 2d ed. Cambridge: Cambridge University Press, 1925–1927.

BIBLIOGRAPHY

Books

Kneale, William, and Martha Kneale. *The Development of Logic.* Oxford: Clarendon
    Press, 1962.
Weinberg, Julius. *Abstraction, Relation, and Induction.* Madison: University of Wiscon-
    sin Press, 1965.

Article

Hausman, Alan. "Hume's Theory of Relations." *Noûs* 1 (1967): 255–82.
                                    ALAN HAUSMAN and DAVID HAUSMAN

RELIGION. For a belief system to be a religion, some key characteristics are
relevant, such as a belief in a personal Deity of some form or other (GOD); a
moral code, sanctioned by the Deity, that addresses the problems of evil and
free will; a worldview, including a cosmogony and/or creation myth; certain
tenets or dogmas such as beliefs in miracles and/or an afterlife. While it would
be odd, to say the least, to claim that one has a "religion" without having a
central belief in some kind of (supernatural or otherwise) Deity, the other features may or may not be present.

The empiricist commitment to sensory experience as the justification for any
knowledge claims gives rise to questions regarding the propositions of religious
discourse. How can the nature of sensory experience give rise to proofs for the
existence of God, conceived as a supernatural Deity? What system of cosmogony is possible, given that we have sense experience only of the effect and not
the cause? Does sense experience support the belief in miracles and/or an afterlife? How do we know God gives approval to a moral code? How do we
respond to the factual claim that evil exists in the world? The questions here
are concerned not with whether these beliefs can be supported by the evidence
but with determining what would count as evidence and what inference is possible based on that evidence. For example, does the fact that the world presents
itself to us in a certain way constitute evidence for claims about the origin of
the world, in terms of either purposive design or the nature of the originator?
The logical positivists of the 1920s (see LOGICAL POSITIVISM), successors
to David HUME's (1711–1776) empiricism, claimed that any proposition that
was not open to empirical verification or falsification (a Humean "matter of
fact") was meaningless (see VERIFICATION PRINCIPLE) and that the propositions of religion fell into this category. Statements like "God exists" are
neither true nor false, as there are no conditions under which its truth or falsity
can be determined, but are "non-sense" (as without sense). They are, at best,
expressions of emotional attitudes.

The term "natural religion" has been used to designate the belief system that
draws inferences regarding the existence and nature of the Deity from the world
of nature or experience. The propositions of religion are confirmable either by
observation or by inference from observation. The Analogical Argument from

Design, presented and defended by Cleanthes in Hume's *Dialogues concerning Natural Religion* (first published in 1779), is an example. "Look around the world," Cleanthes urges. The world resembles a machine, in that it exhibits certain features that are also exhibited by "manufactured" artifacts in the world. We know that such artifacts, like computers and sewing machines, have intelligent human designers, and so Cleanthes infers that the world has a similarly intelligent divine designer. He claims that the same method of reasoning that is used in the world of experience, inference from observation, is applicable to the world of religion. Through a critique based on the inability of the evidence—the data in the world—to provide any conclusive proof of this claim, Philo shows Cleanthes that his method of investigation, the experimental method, cannot be transferred from this world to the world beyond it. The experimental method is persuasive when there is repeated experience or comparisons of the same species of objects to justify the inferences. However, as we have no repeated experience of worlds being formed and as the universe is a unique item, such inferences are, at best, a guess or conjecture.

Various doctrines of organized religion have come under attack by Hume on similar grounds. In Section XI of *An Enquiry concerning Human Understanding*, "Of a Particular Province and a Future State," Hume claims, "No new fact can ever be inferred from the religious hypothesis; no event foreseen or foretold; no reward or punishment expected or dreaded beyond what is already known by practice and observation."

Hume's critical analysis of miracles is found in Section X of the *Enquiry*, a section he was advised to omit from the earlier published *Treatise of Human Nature*. A miracle is generally regarded to be an occurrence that goes against the laws of nature (or else it would not be considered to be a miracle) and is willed by the Deity; that is, it has religious significance. Hume claims that as such events go against the laws of nature (which laws are derived from constant and regular conjunction), there can be no constant conjunction possible in order for an inference from effect to cause to be justified. Further, Hume states, "there must be uniform experience against every miraculous event, otherwise the event would not merit that appellation" (*Enquiry*: 115). As it is from uniform experience, as constant conjunction, that we draw all our inferences, such experience actually constitutes a proof against miracles.

LOCKE considers miracles to be matters of fact, observed by some and then believed by others based on their testimony. However, according to Hume, this testimony is believed out of proportion to its reliability. In order to be a miracle, an event could not resemble any previous experience, and as such it lacks the force of custom or habit to engender belief. The "passion of *surprise* and *wonder* . . . gives a sensible tendency toward the belief of those events" (*Enquiry*: 117). This further denigrates the credibility of the observer's testimony: "[I]f the spirit of religion join itself to the love of wonder, there is an end of common sense; and human testimony, in these circumstances, loses all pretensions to authority."

George BERKELEY's (1685–1753) doctrine of immaterialism (all that exists are minds and ideas; no idea can exist independently of a perceiver) places God at the core of our perceptual lives. According to Berkeley, LOCKE's theory of the independent existence of objects results in central miracles in the Judeo-Christian tradition—Moses turning his rod into a serpent, Jesus turning water into wine—becoming "so many cheats, or illusions of fancy" (see *Principles of Human Knowledge* §34, §35, and §84). What is real is what is perceived by a mind, and the observers "saw" the serpent and "tasted" the wine. Miracles, however, occur too infrequently to be an effective proof of God's existence (*Principles of Human Knowledge* §63) (see GOD).

PRIMARY WORKS

Berkeley, George. *The Principles of Human Knowledge* in *Berkeley's Philosophical Writings*. Edited by D. M. Armstrong. New York: Collier, 1965.

Hume, David. *Dialogues concerning Natural Religion*. Edited by S. Tweyman. London: Routledge, 1993.

———. "On Miracles" (Section X) and "Of a Particular Providence and of a Future State" (Section XI). In *Enquiries concerning Human Understanding and concerning the Principles of Morals*, edited with an analytical index by L. A. Selby-Bigge; revised with notes by P. H. Nidditch. Oxford: Clarendon Press, 1975.

Locke, John. *An Essay concerning Human Understanding*. Edited with an introduction by P. H. Nidditch. Oxford: Clarendon Press, 1975.

BIBLIOGRAPHY

Davies, B. *An Introduction to the Philosophy of Religion*. Oxford: Oxford University Press, 1993.

Logan, B. *A Religion without Talking: Religious Belief and Natural Belief in Hume's Philosophy of Religion*. New York: Peter Lang, 1993.

Pitcher, G. *Berkeley*. The Arguments of the Philosophers. London: Routledge and Kegan Paul, 1977.

Tweyman, S., ed. *Hume on Miracles*. Bristol: Thoemmes Press, 1996.

———. *Hume on Natural Religion*. Bristol: Thoemmes Press, 1996.

Yolton, John W. *A Locke Dictionary*. Oxford: Blackwell, 1993; see esp. "Miracles," "Revelation," and "Religion."

BERYL LOGAN

RUSSELL, BERTRAND. The British philosopher Bertrand Russell was born in 1872 and died in 1970 at the age of ninety-seven. His parents, Lord and Lady Amberley, died when he was a child. His grandfather, Lord John Russell, was the eminent British prime minister (1846–1852 and 1865) and first Earl Russell, noted for his role in the repeal of the Corn Laws in 1846.

When Russell was four, he and his older brother, Frank, were brought to live with their paternal grandparents. The house in which Russell was raised had been given to his grandparents by Queen Victoria; it was situated on eleven acres from which there was a commanding view of Windsor Castle. The task of Russell's upbringing was assumed by his grandmother, Countess Russell, who, by his own admission, was the most important person to him throughout his childhood. Unlike his brother, Russell was educated by tutors. One gathers from his *Autobiography* that his childhood was a happy one.

Russell entered Trinity College, Cambridge, in 1890, where, for his first three years, he studied mathematics and attended lectures by A. N. Whitehead on mechanics. His fourth year was spent studying philosophy; the British idealist J.M.E. McTaggart appears to have strongly influenced Russell's early philosophical views. G. E. MOORE and Russell overlapped at Cambridge, and it was there that they first became friends. In 1895 Russell was elected a fellow of Trinity College. His dissertation (published in 1897 as *An Essay on the Foundations of Geometry*) was examined by Whitehead and the psychologist James Ward.

Shortly after his fellowship election, Russell married Alys Pearsall Smith, an American Quaker. The marriage was childless and, as it turned out, unhappy. (It was to be followed by three other marriages.) The next fifteen years were largely taken up with philosophical and mathematical work and were intellectually the most productive period of Russell's life. Despite the pressure of intellectual work, Russell found time to stand for Parliament as a Suffragist candidate in a by-election of 1907. He was unsuccessful.

The public person we have come to know as a passionate voice for equality and social justice began to emerge in earnest shortly after his separation from Alys and the completion of this period of his intellectual life. Russell's relationship with Lady Ottoline Morrell was profoundly influential, if not in initiating this transition, then at least in sustaining it.

Russell was outspoken in his opposition to the First World War at a time when public support for the war was almost universal. He paid dearly for his opposition with the loss of many friendships, Whitehead's and McTaggart's among them. In 1918 he was sentenced to six months' imprisonment for an antiwar article he contributed to a pacifist weekly. Russell's championship of unpopular causes, often at considerable personal cost, continued for the rest of his long life. As a democrat and social activist he is best known for his pacifism, his advocacy of nuclear disarmament, and his many acts of solidarity with the underprivileged peoples of the First and Third Worlds.

The uniqueness of Russell's position in philosophy in general and in the empiricist tradition in particular consists in his having combined a broadly empiricist outlook with far-reaching contributions to logic and the philosophy of mathematics. Although empiricist in orientation for most of his philosophical career, his one serious historical work was a study of Leibniz (1900). As we shall see, Russell represented a departure from empiricist tradition not just in his blend of abilities but also by the manner in which he applied his technical contributions to logic and philosophy of mathematics to his other philosophical work.

LOGIC

Russell's contributions to logic, together with their anticipation by Gottlob Frege, constituted a renaissance, far exceeding the logical investigations of any earlier period. It is not possible to survey in any detail the field of mathematical or symbolic logic that Frege and Russell created. Fortunately, it is no longer necessary to do so, since symbolic logic has come to occupy so central a place in the repertoire of analytical tools acquired by every serious student of philosophy.

Russell's logical contributions we shall briefly survey fall into two broad categories: (1) his development of the theory of relations and the modern theory of quantification and (2) his theory of types. In this section we concentrate on the first of these contributions, leaving the theory of types to be discussed in the next section in connection with his philosophy of mathematics. In the third section we again touch upon the theory of quantification.

Russell's theory of relations received its first pedagogical presentation in *The Principles of Mathematics* (1903). But the theory of quantification, as we know it, was not given until the publication of "On Denoting" in 1905. The theory of quantification of *Principles* shows the work to have been incomplete by comparison with Frege's *Begriffsschrift* (1879) and transitional so far as Russell's own development of his logic was concerned. Russell's presentation of his logic was given its final form in *Principia Mathematica* (1910–1913), co-authored with Whitehead and appearing in three volumes. After the revisions occasioned by *Principia*'s second edition (1925), Russell effectively ceased publishing in logic.

What the theory of quantification with relational expressions achieved was quite remarkable both in itself and by comparison with the traditional Aristotelian logic it replaced. Part of this achievement may be illustrated by comparing two subsystems of the so-called first-order fragment of the system of logic of *Principia*. The term "first-order" refers to the character of the quantifiers and variables of quantification: in first-order logic we restrict ourselves to variables that range over individuals. The second-order case contains as well variables for properties of, and relations among, individuals; in second-order logic, property and relation variables may be bound to (second order) quantifiers, and properties and relations are said to be "quantified over." This process may be extended into higher orders as well, but we ignore second- and higher-order extensions and concentrate on two first-order fragments: (1) the *relational (first-order) fragment*, containing just a single binary relation symbol R; and (2) the *monadic (first-order) fragment*, containing the countable collection

$$\{P_n: n \in N\}$$

of one-place predicate letters. We note that the traditional logic can be represented in a part of the monadic fragment.

A striking feature of the relational fragment is its considerably greater expressive power relative to that of the monadic fragment. If, beyond the requirement that R refer to a relation and the P_n to properties, we impose no conditions or restrictions on how the predicate letters of either fragment are to be understood, then we find that the relational fragment allows for the construction of a single sentence that is true only when interpreted over a universe (nonempty set) of infinitely many individuals:

$$\forall x \exists y Rxy \ \& \ \forall x \neg Rxx \ \& \ \forall x \forall y \forall z (Rxy \ \& \ Ryz \rightarrow Rxz) \ \&$$
$$\forall x \forall y (rxy \rightarrow \neg Ryx).$$

However, the same is not true of the monadic fragment: given any sentence of the monadic fragment, we can always find a universe of finitely many individuals in which it holds; indeed, the number of individuals required depends, in a simple way, on the number of unary predicate symbols the sentence contains. The relational fragment thus allows us "to capture the infinite with finite means," in a sense in which this was not possible in the traditional logic of Aristotle.

PHILOSOPHY OF MATHEMATICS

In philosophy of mathematics, Russell is best known for the paradox that bears his name and as the principal exponent, after Frege, of logicism. His chief contributions to the development of logicism were the discovery and analysis of his paradox and his subsequent resolution of it by the simple and ramified theories of types.

Russell's paradox is most directly presented in the context of "naive set theory," rather than in terms of Frege's theory of classes. In the first instance, naive set theory is a theory of set or class existence: a class is thought of as determined by some property that all of its members share. The notion that a class exists if, and only if, there is a property that its members have in common is sometimes referred to as the "logical notion of class." For this notion, the basic axiom of class existence is given by the naive comprehension axiom

$$\forall P \exists x \forall z \ (z \in x \leftrightarrow Pz).$$

On its intended interpretation, the axiom asserts that for every property there is a class that consists of precisely the individuals having the property. It will be observed that the axiom is a sentence of second-order logic and that it implies the first-order instances of the following naive comprehension *scheme*:

$$\exists x \forall z \ (z \in x \leftrightarrow \phi(z)),$$

where $\phi(z)$ is a (first-order) formula in one free variable, not containing the variable x. Russell's paradox follows immediately from the instance

$$\exists x \forall z \ (z \in x \leftrightarrow z \notin z),$$

which asserts the existence of a class consisting of precisely those sets that are not members of themselves. This is easily shown to lead to a contradiction. Since the property expressed by

$$z \in z$$

and, therefore, the property expressed by

$$z \notin z$$

seem to be perfectly legitimate properties, something is seriously amiss with the logical notion of class.

Russell perceived that his paradox arose as well in the context of Frege's theory of classes and that, in consequence, Frege's formulation of logicism was seriously compromised. Since Russell had aligned himself with Frege, the discovery cut very deeply into his own intellectual ambitions. Before proceeding to Russell's solution of his paradox, let us pause to consider the philosophy of mathematics Russell and Frege espoused and the reason the paradox was of philosophical interest to them.

In *Principles* Russell outlined an approach to the philosophy of mathematics that, in his view, would constitute the complete refutation of the Kantian idea that in order to account for our knowledge of certain mathematical truths, such as the infinity of the number sequence or our ability to draw valid inferences from the axioms of Euclidean geometry, a faculty of "intuition," held to fall between sense perception and general logical reasoning, must be countenanced (see KANT). Truths requiring this faculty would constitute a special class of truth that Kant termed "synthetic a priori" (see ANALYTIC/SYNTHETIC, A PRIORI/A POSTERIORI). The substantive point of disagreement between Russell and Kant centered on Kant's contention that logic is forever incapable of accounting for our knowledge of such truths.

In §434 of *Principles*, Russell makes the claim—jarring to a contemporary ear—that Kant was correct to hold that the truths of mathematics are not analytic; his mistake lay in not recognizing that logic is as synthetic as mathematics. This is potentially misleading: Russell is certainly not saying that logical reasoning requires Kant's faculty of intuition. His point is rather that logical reasoning can yield knowledge that we might not have had independently of the reasoning. At this point of his development, Russell rejected the claim that logic is analytic, since the Kantian characterization of an analytic proposition, in terms of the "inclusion" of the predicate in the subject-term of the proposition, seemed to preclude the possibility that knowledge of an analytic proposition could ever lead to *new* knowledge.

It should also be noted that the idea, common among the Vienna Circle of LOGICAL POSITIVISTS, that logic and mathematics consist of tautologies or conventions of language played no role in Russell's thinking on these matters until long after his association with Ludwig Wittgenstein. The notion of *tautology* occurs at the very end of *Introduction to Mathematical Philosophy* (1919), where, after explaining that he does not know how to define the notion, Russell says:

The importance of "tautology" for a definition of mathematics was pointed out to me by my former pupil Ludwig Wittgenstein, who was working on the problem. I do not know whether he has solved it, or even whether he is alive or dead. (*Introduction to Mathematical Philosophy*: 205, n1)

But in *Principia* (I: 12–13, 59) we find Russell and Whitehead confidently arguing hypotheticodeductively in favor of their logical axioms on the ground that from them only the known truths of mathematics follow.

Now in his *Foundations of Arithmetic* (1884), Frege had succeeded in deriving the infinity of the number sequence from the surprisingly simple principle that for any properties P and Q, the number of Ps is identical with the number of Qs if, and only if, $P \approx Q$—that is, the Ps and the Qs are in one–one correspondence or, as we shall sometimes say, P is equinumerous with Q. In *Foundations*, Frege's introduction of this principle is accompanied by a reference to HUME, who, in his *Treatise* (I.iii.1), had written: "When two numbers are so combined as that one has always an unit answering to every unit of the other, we pronounce them equal." In recent literature, this principle has come to be referred to as "Hume's principle," and for brevity of expression, we follow this practice.

In *Foundations*, Frege also presented, for the first time, his explicit definition of the cardinal numbers. The basic idea of Frege's definition is of great importance to the understanding of Russell's philosophy, not only because Russell had independently discovered a very similar definition of number but because variations on the central idea it embodies came to occupy a prominent place in virtually all of Russell's subsequent technical philosophical work. The essential idea is this: given an equivalence relation such as the relation of one–one correspondence, we may form the collection of equivalence classes under the relation. Mathematically, this is called a *partition* of the class on which the equivalence relation is defined. In the present case, the equivalence classes consist of collections of properties. Russell and Frege then proceeded to *identify* the number of the property P with the class of properties equinumerous with P:

$$\{Q: Q \approx P\}.$$

Russell (but not Frege) saw in this procedure a general method by which we might reduce our ontological commitments. For example, we might have supposed that, in addition to properties and classes, there are also numbers. Russell argued that this supposition is not required: while there *may* be numbers, we need neither assert nor deny their existence, since all the purposes served by numbers are also served by classes of equinumerous properties. We therefore achieve a reduction in our ontology without having to engage in a long and potentially unresolvable debate. In particular, many philosophical positions associated with traditional British empiricism received, in Russell's hands, a new formulation and justification by the use of this technique (see following on epistemology and metaphysics.)

To return to the interest of Russell's paradox: as we mentioned earlier, Frege had solved the problem of accounting for the infinity of the number sequence by his derivation from Hume's principle of the axiom: Every natural number has a successor. He then sought to account for the logical—or "nonintuitive"— status of Hume's principle by deriving it from the definition of numbers as classes of equinumerous properties. Russell's paradox showed Frege's account of the notion of class to be defective (inconsistent), and this called into doubt Frege's justification for holding that his notion of number did not depend on Kantian intuition, since this claim was assumed to depend on the reduction of the numbers to classes.

Russell's solution to his paradox, as articulated in his simple theory of types, consisted in maintaining that classes must be regarded as stratified into various levels. The essential idea of the theory was that the naive comprehension scheme

$$\exists x \forall z \ (z \in x \leftrightarrow \phi(z))$$

should be replaced by a family of schemes, one for each "type" of existentially bound variable, where, if the type of z is 0, then that of x is 1; and in general, if the type of z is n, then that of x must be n + 1, for all atomic formulas involving the relation symbol $\in$ of class membership. (In the case of an atomic formula containing the identity symbol, the variables flanking = must be of the same type.) It thus becomes impossible, in the language of the simple theory of types, to formulate the property expression that gave rise to Russell's paradox since, having the form $\neg(z \in z)$, it requires that variables of the *same* type appear on both sides of the relation symbol $\in$ for membership.

While the simple theory of types addressed the problem of inconsistency, Russell was never entirely satisfied with it. He therefore sought to supplement it with the (considerably more involved) ramified theory of types, believing that this theory, in contradistinction to simple type theory, incorporated his analysis of the source of his paradox, as well as that of several other related paradoxes. Space is lacking to expound the ramified theory or even Russell's analysis of the source of his paradox; the interested reader should consult Russell's 1908 paper, "Mathematical Logic as Based on the Theory of Types," as well as the papers of Gödel and Kreisel.

Assuming that the theory of classes based on the theory of types solves the mathematical problem that the various paradoxes presented, how does the philosophical program of logicism fare within type theory? Frege's full solution to the problem of accounting for the infinity of the number sequence—his derivation of the axioms of arithmetic from Hume's principle and his derivation of Hume's principle from the definition of the numbers as classes—demanded that the universe of classes *not* be stratified in the manner required by both the simple and the ramified theories of types. Russell could not, therefore, incorporate Frege's achievement into his own development of logicism but had to articulate a new approach to the problem. Here we note just one of the (more obvious) modifications the theory of types required, namely, the introduction, as a separate axiom, of his and Whitehead's Axiom of Infinity: For every cardinal number n, there is a class of n members.

Intuitively, the axiom requires that the class of individuals—the values of the variables of lowest type—is infinite in the sense that it is enumerable, but not enumerable by any initial segment of the sequence of natural numbers. The necessity of including this axiom is standardly taken to demonstrate the collapse of the logicist program since it introduces an assumption—the infinity of a collection of "nonlogical objects"—whose justification could only be empirical. While there is undoubtedly some merit to this criticism, it fails to recognize Russell's genuine achievement. The natural numbers are not merely infinite; they are *Dedekind* infinite: that is to say, they are mapped one-one by the successor function onto a subset of themselves (namely, $N-\{0\}$). Recall that for Russell, the cardinal numbers are classes of equinumerous classes (or properties—the difference is inessential in this context). In *Principia* (II, *124.57) Russell proves (without the Axiom of Choice) the mathematically significant result that if the class of individuals is infinite, then the class of cardinal numbers is Dedekind infinite. Thus, while it is true that the Axiom of Infinity introduces an empirical element into Russell's system, this axiom does not by itself assert that the numbers, as Russell reconstructs them, are *in the relevant sense* infinite. That fact must be established, rather than merely assumed; and Russell does, indeed, establish it. (For more detail, see the paper by Boolos.)

PHILOSOPHY OF LANGUAGE

It is universally agreed that Russell's main contribution to the philosophy of language is his theory of descriptions, first articulated in "On Denoting." As we shall soon see, this theory forms the technical backbone of many of Russell's theses in metaphysics, theory of knowledge, and philosophy of language.

There are two respects in which, on Russell's view, the traditional logic was inadequate, both of them connected with its commitment to the thesis that all propositions are of subject-predicate form. The first consequence of the adherence to a subject-predicate analysis was the failure to formulate logic with sufficient generality to deal with relations. We have already discussed this issue in the first section. The second consequence is more subtle and has really to do with the understanding of quantification, or what Russell called "denoting phrases"—phrases involving the use of the words "all," "some," "every," "a," and so on and especially "the." In *Principles*, Russell had attempted to deal with the analysis of such phrases by the device of denoting concepts, of which *Principles* contains an elaborate and rather difficult theory. The goal of "On Denoting" was to achieve a theory of how such phrases contribute to the logical form of the sentences in which they occur without the use of the notion of a denoting concept. Fortunately, the central theses of the theory may be explained without going into the details of the theory of *Principles*.

To begin with, Russell placed special emphasis on *definite descriptions*, denoting phrases of the form "the so and so," where "the" is used in its singular sense, as in, The junior author of *Principia* was British. The sentences (*) Russell is mortal and (**) The teacher of Wittgenstein is mortal will be regarded as "in the same form" by anyone who assimilates definite descriptions to proper names. Indeed, on such a view, their form is given by the expression (§) Pa, which, according to the traditional analysis, attributes to the individual a the property P. On Russell's analysis, this is incorrect: (**) is actually a general (i.e., quantified) sentence of the form

$$(\S\S) \; \exists x \forall y \phi \; (x,y).$$

The difference is important, since the logical consequences of (**) will vary according to whether it has the form (§) or (§§), a fact emphasized by Russell in his essay.

The Russellian analysis of (**) sees it as involving the predicate expressions: x taught y and x is mortal; the proper name Wittgenstein; and the logical vocabulary of variables, quantifiers, and sentential connectives of first-order logic with identity. In detail, (**) is given the analysis:

$$\exists x(x \text{ taught Wittgenstein } \& \; \forall y \; (y \text{ taught Wittgenstein } \rightarrow x = y) \; \& \\ x \text{ is mortal}),$$

which, by a well-known procedure—the reduction to prenex normal form—may be reduced to a sentence of the form (§§), as claimed.

Of special interest to us is the manner in which Russell combined his theory of descriptions with a principle he discusses in *The Problems of Philosophy* (1912) and which, aside from changes of detail, he maintained throughout his philosophical career. In *Problems*, Chapter 5, the principle is called "[t]he fundamental principle in the analysis of propositions" and is given the formulation "Every proposition which we can understand must be composed wholly of constituents with which we are acquainted."

Before discussing this principle, it is necessary to recognize that Russell's use of "proposition" is a special, technical one. For Russell, a proposition is a structured object

$$<a_1, \ldots, a_n; P_1, \ldots, P_m >$$

whose "constituents" are generally nonlinguistic entities; thus, the a_i are individuals, and the P_j are properties and relations (what Russell calls "propositional functions," evidently thinking of them in analogy with the *characteristic function* of the corresponding class). As Russell once remarked in response to an incredulous letter from Frege, "I believe that in spite of all its snowfields Mont Blanc itself is part of what is actually asserted in the proposition 'Mont Blanc is more than 4000 metres high' " (Frege, *Philosophical and Mathematical Correspondence*, Letter to Frege of December 12, 1904).

The fundamental principle evidently embodies a very simple theory of linguistic meaning: we grasp the meaning of a sentence if we understand the proposition it expresses. The model of understanding is both compositional and empiricist: our understanding of the whole proposition goes by way of our understanding of its parts (constituents), and the understanding of a part consists in our acquaintance with it. On first hearing, the theory seems wildly implausible and subject to obvious counterexamples. Consider, for example, the sentence

(*) Russell is mortal.

How are we to explain our grasp of the meaning of this sentence if, as would seem to be the case, the proposition $\pi(*)$ it expresses is the structured object

$$\pi(*) \quad <\text{Russell}; \text{x is mortal}>$$

consisting of Russell and the property of mortality? Presumably, none of us have been acquainted with Russell, and therefore, by the fundamental principle, we should all fail to understand $\pi(*)$. But in fact we do understand $\pi(*)$.

Russell's resolution of this difficulty consists in observing that our knowledge of things is only sometimes knowledge by acquaintance. We know many things only by description. For example, I know Russell as the junior author of *Principia*, in which case a sentence that better reflects my grasp of the meaning of (*) is given by its translation into

(T*) The junior author of *Principia* is mortal.

By the theory of descriptions, the nonlogical constituents of the proposition expressed by (T*) are the referents of the predicate expressions:

x authored y,
x is junior to y,
x is mortal;

and the proper name *Principia*.

My grasp of the meaning of (*) thus consists in my grasp of the meaning of its translation into (T*), which, in turn, requires my acquaintance with the reference of the previously mentioned predicate expressions and proper name. Observe that *Russell is not among the constituents of the proposition expressed by* (T*); as Russell would say, he has disappeared under analysis.

Notice that although (*) and (T*) may express different propositions—for someone acquainted with Russell, (*) is a perfectly good reflection of the proposition it expresses—they have the same assertoric content: on the assumption that Russell *was* the junior author of *Principia*, (*) and (T*) are responsible to the obtaining of the same state of affairs, namely, that there should exist a time when Russell dies.

Russell regarded the consequence we have just reviewed as the major epistemological benefit of his theory of descriptions: it gives the key to maintaining a staunchly empiricist theory of meaning while preserving our commonsense belief that our knowledge often extends beyond the limits of our acquaintance.

EPISTEMOLOGY AND METAPHYSICS

Like the great British empiricists who preceded him, Russell placed the theory of PERCEPTION at the center of his theory of knowledge. Russell is differentiated from his empiricist predecessors by the fact that his theory of knowledge is deeply embedded in his logical innovations and philosophy of language. Before Russell, logical doctrines played virtually no role in the articulation of a theory of knowledge of the external world; and the empiricists' contributions to philosophy of language appear very much as an afterthought, rather than a completed theory with a definite subject matter.

Russell's mature theory of perception begins (in *Problems*) as an apparently slight variation on LOCKE's representationalism; it then undergoes a brief cryptophenomenalist transition in *Our Knowledge of the External World* (1914) and finally stabilizes with the articulation, in *The Analysis of Matter* (1927), of a sophisticated, ''structuralist'' variant of his earlier Lockean realism. All three stages are characterized by an adherence to what, for lack of a better term, I call ''Russell's principle of the relativity of perception.'' This principle asserts that no physical object is ever simply given to us in perception: our perceptual knowledge of the physical world is always mediated by our acquaintance with a distinguished and canonical class of propositional functions.

Russell's principle gains in clarity and plausibility if it is seen from the perspective of his philosophy of language. Recall that in our discussion of knowledge by description, any individual whose acquaintance we have not made is presented to us by a definite description. By the theory of descriptions, the propositional constituents of every proposition ''containing'' the description include various propositional functions (and perhaps other individuals) but do not include the individual—Russell, in our example—himself. Here it is important to keep in mind (1) that a Russellian proposition is a nonlinguistic entity and (2) that a description ''occurs'' in a proposition only under its Russellian analysis, according to which it unfolds into propositional functions and individuals with which we are acquainted.

To make the step from the abstract theory of descriptive knowledge to Russell's analysis of perception, it is necessary to specify the distinguished family of propositional functions that are relevant to perception. For Russell, this family comprises sensible qualities and relations—what, in *Problems*, are termed SENSE-DATA. In later work, Russell drops this terminology but maintains the doctrine in the form in which I have explained it. Physical objects do not, of course, occur as constituents in any proposition we can understand; otherwise we would be acquainted with them, and the claim, so central to Russell's view of perception, namely, that our knowledge of the physical world is always mediated, would be false.

There are two respects in which Russell's principle is appropriately called a relativity principle. The first is well known and has to do with his always motivating the principle by traditional arguments that appeal to the relativity of sensible qualities to the conditions of perception and the disposition of our sense organs. The second is more abstract and metaphysical and appears to be based on the intuition that, for us, perception requires that the world is always given in some way or grasped from a particular point of view.

In what I have called his cryptophenomenalist phase, Russell articulated a program of "logical construction" that was directly motivated by his work in philosophy of mathematics. Roughly speaking, we begin with the commonsense assumption that a physical object presents us with a series of experiences of the object, each experience arising from one or another perspective on the object. The program is to show, in general terms, that it is possible to refrain from the postulation of an object "at the center" of the collection of different perspectives and that we can make do with just the series of experiences themselves. Unlike the traditional PHENOMENALISM of BERKELEY, this view is not committed to the denial of the existence of matter; nor does it presume to give a traditional conceptual analysis of *matter*. Its principal interest consists in the technical program of construction—later called "reconstruction"—that it outlines. This program was taken up by CARNAP and GOODMAN.

Returning to Russell's mature, realist theory of our knowledge of the external world: where Locke had distinguished between PRIMARY and SECONDARY QUALITIES of physical objects, Russell distinguished qualitative from structural knowledge. The concept of structure was elucidated in *Principia* under the title "relation arithmetic"—a general and universal-algebraic theory of mathematical structures and the morphisms that relate them. Our perceptual experience has both qualitative and structural dimensions, but only the structural component may be legitimately transferred to the physical causes of our perceptual experience. Of the structure of the world, we may know a great deal; of the qualitative character of the world as it is in itself, we can know nothing.

PRIMARY WORKS

An Essay on the Foundations of Geometry. Cambridge: Cambridge University Press, 1897.

A Critical Exposition of the Philosophy of Leibniz. Cambridge: Cambridge University Press, 1900; 2d ed. 1937.

The Principles of Mathematics. Cambridge: Cambridge University Press, 1903; 2nd ed. 1938.

"On Denoting." *Mind* n.s. 14 (1905): 479–93.

"Mathematical Logic as Based on the Theory of Types." *American Journal of Mathematics* 30 (1908): 222–62.

(with A. N. Whitehead). *Principia Mathematica*, 3 vols. Cambridge: Cambridge University Press, 1910–1913; 2d rev. ed. 1925.

The Problems of Philosophy. Indianapolis, IN: Hackett, 1912; reprint, 1990.

Our Knowledge of the External World. London: George Allen and Unwin, 1914; 2d rev. ed. 1929.

Introduction to Mathematical Philosophy. London: George Allen and Unwin, 1919.

The Analysis of Mind. London: George Allen and Unwin, 1921.

The Analysis of Matter. New York: Harcourt Brace, 1927.
Human Knowledge: Its Scope and Limits. London: George Allen and Unwin, 1948.
My Philosophical Development. London: George Allen and Unwin, 1959.
The Autobiography of Bertrand Russell. 3 vols. London: George Allen and Unwin, 1968.
The Collected Papers of Bertrand Russell. Gen. ed. Kenneth Blackwell et al. London: George Allen and Unwin, 1983. The definitive edition of Russell's papers and manuscripts.

OTHER PRIMARY TEXTS

Books

Frege, Gottlob. *Begriffsschrift: A Formula Language, Modeled upon That of Arithmetic, for Pure Thought.* In *From Frege to Gödel: A Sourcebook in Mathematical Logic, 1879–1931*, edited by Jean van Heijenoort; translated by Stefan Bauer-Mengelberg. Cambridge: Harvard University Press, 1967.
———. *The Foundations of Arithmetic: A Logico-Mathematical Enquiry into the Concept of Number.* Translated by J. L. Austin. Evanston, IL: Northwestern University Press, 1980.
———. *Philosophical and Mathematical Correspondence.* Edited by Brian McGuinness. Chicago: University of Chicago Press, 1980.

Articles

Gödel, Kurt. "Russell's Mathematical Logic." In *The Philosophy of Bertrand Russell.* Edited by Paul Arthur Schilpp. Evanston and Chicago: Northwestern University Press, 1944.
Newman, M.H.A. "Mr Russell's Causal Theory of Perception." *Mind* n.s. 37 (1928): 137–48.

BIBLIOGRAPHY

Books

Griffin, Nicholas, ed. *The Cambridge Companion to Russell.* Cambridge: Cambridge University Press, 1997.
Savage, C. Wade, and C. Anthony Anderson, eds. *Rereading Russell: Essays on Bertrand Russell's Metaphysics and Epistemology.* Minnesota Studies in the Philosophy of Science, vol. 12, Minneapolis: University of Minnesota Press, 1989.

Articles

Boolos, George. "The Advantages of Honest Toil over Theft." In *Mathematics and Mind.* Edited by Alexander George. Oxford: Oxford University Press, 1994.
Kreisel, Georg. "Obituary of Bertrand Russell." *Biographical Memoirs of Fellows of the Royal Society* 19 (1973): 583–620.

WILLIAM DEMOPOULOS

S

SCIENCE. Science is the systematic search for new knowledge about the universe and its inhabitants and the knowledge that results from that search. Scientists are the practitioners of science. We have to fine-tune this definition somewhat, but it tells us something of the nature of science. Some historical background will further our understanding.

The English term "scientist" was suggested by William Whewell, a philosopher of science, in the mid-nineteenth century. The term "scientist" replaced the term "natural philosopher." Most famous scientists were natural philosophers in their day, for example, NEWTON and DARWIN. We retrospectively apply the term "science" to certain kinds of knowledge and activity produced by both contemporary scientists and their natural philosopher predecessors.

Most contemporary science has its roots in ancient philosophy. ARISTOTLE, in particular, pointed toward future sciences in his great works, for example, *The Physics.* Although Aristotle prefigured science, we do not generally classify his systematic search for knowledge as scientific. Aristotle used naked-eye observations and deductive logic to come to conclusions about the nature of the world around him, but the term "science" is reserved for knowledge that derives from experimentally tested general laws. The departure from an Aristotelian approach to understanding nature to what we now call a scientific approach was brought about by many figures in the sixteenth and seventeenth centuries. This transformation is referred to as the "scientific revolution": the period starting with the publication of COPERNICUS' *De Revolutionibus* in 1543 and ending with the publication of Newton's *Principia Mathematica* in 1687.

Several crucial figures contributed to the development of science, not only with their scientific achievements but by their pronouncements on scientific method. We can mention only a few here. GALILEO and Francis BACON were contemporaries who profoundly influenced the development of science. Galileo's contributions to astronomy, mathematics, and mechanics are important to this day, but his contributions to the methods of science (directions for how science should be done) are just as important. First, Galileo believed that there could be scientific laws, for example, laws of motion, that would be applicable to all objects in the universe. These laws would be mathematical in character and would allow for no exceptions. Second, Galileo proposed that experiments on ideal systems could give us information about the natural world. For example, experiments on constrained motion (a ball moving down an inclined plane) could give us information about natural motion (the behavior of natural objects falling to the earth). According to Galileo, MATHEMATICS was the language in which nature was written, and experimental and mathematical investigations would discover truths about nature. Francis Bacon was not a practitioner of science, but his writings on scientific method were very influential. He stressed the importance of systematically collecting observations and inferring hypotheses and generalizations from them.

All arguments about the correct approach to science stem from the work of contributors to the scientific revolution. Galileo and Bacon both shared the view that experimenting on nature could involve experimenting on ideal systems or interfering with nature's processes. This view was also stressed by BOYLE. For example, while Galileo experimented on motion with balls and inclined planes, Boyle experimented on the nature of air with air pumps that created partial vacuums. Debates about the correct method in science during the early scientific revolution pitted various approaches to investigating nature against Aristotelian approaches. As the revolution came to a close, debates about scientific method took on a more familiar tone, pitting empiricist against rationalist approaches. It is often assumed that Newton was the empiricist to Descartes' rationalist in these debates, but Newton blended both strands of thought. Newton's famous fourth Rule of Reasoning in Philosophy is:

In experimental philosophy we are to look upon propositions inferred by general induction from phenomena as accurately or very nearly true, not with standing any contrary hypothesis that may be imagined, till such time as other phenomena occur, by which they may either be made more accurate, or liable to exceptions.

This won him an empiricist following, including HUME, but Newton himself was more concerned about the clear mathematical presentation of results, laws, and hypotheses than he was about their empirical verification. His most frequent criticism of his contemporaries was that they lacked mathematical ability.

Newton also introduced theoretical objects and forces as part of his explanations of phenomena, for example, absolute space and gravity. This approach was resisted by natural philosophers at the time. Leibniz, although he was a rationalist, argued that Newton had introduced occult phenomena or entities. Theoretical objects have posed a long-standing problem for empiricist philosophers of science, as they are, by definition, not available to the senses. Despite objections, the introduction of theoretical entities has become a defining feature of science, for example, elementary particles, electromagnetic waves, and photons.

Debates about whether scientific truths were deduced from first principles or induced for observations have continued into this century. These debates are usually carried out by philosophers of science, but scientists often join in. MILL carried on the empiricist tradition in his debates with Whewell in the nineteenth century. Whewell insisted that pure empiricism was not enough of a methodology for science. Logical empiricist philosophers of science (see LOGICAL POSITIVISM/LOGICAL EMPIRICISM) in the twentieth century have proposed that science rests on a combination of INDUCTION and deduction, scientific laws or hypotheses being confirmed largely inductively, and predictions and explanations being deduced from laws. Philosophers of science often specialize in one scientific discipline, for example, philosophy of biology. This kind of specialization has presented problems for general approaches to defining science. What may be an appropriate methodological characterization of mechanics does not work for parts of biology, and vice versa. Despite these differences, most science is still characterized by the prevalence of experimental testing of results, the collection of results under general laws, and the omnipresence of mathematics as a language of presentation. An alternative approach changes the focus from methods and defines science in terms of the social features of scientific practice. For example, empirical laboratory studies by anthropologists highlight the salient features of scientific practice distinguishing it from other human practices.

BIBLIOGRAPHY

Grinnell, Frederick. *The Scientific Attitude*. 2d ed. New York: Guilford Press, 1992.
Marks, John. *Science and the Making of the Modern World*. London: Heinemann, 1983.
Mason, Stephen. F. *A History of the Sciences*. New York: Macmillan, 1962.
Matthews, Michael R. *The Scientific Background to Modern Philosophy*. Indianapolis, IN, and Cambridge: Hackett, 1989.

STEPHEN M. DOWNES

SENSATIONALISM. Sensationalism is the theory that all knowledge derives from sense experience. Sensations include the qualia or internal content of vision, sound, taste, touch, and smell: pain, pleasure, emotion, proprioception of body unity, position, and motion and related psychological states. Different concepts of sensationalism emphasize different reductions of knowledge to different choices of sensations, thereby providing philosophical foundations for distinct types of empiricist epistemologies.

The modern doctrine of sensationalism begins with Condillac. In his *Traité des sensations* and *Essai sur l'origine des connoissances humaines*, Condillac, following Locke's suggestions in *An Essay concerning Human Understanding*, proposes that all knowledge is nothing but "transformed" sensation. Yet Condillac goes beyond Locke in denying the role of reflection in the production of knowledge from sensation. Condillac investigates the distinguishing characteristics of particular senses by means of an ingenious thought experiment, in which a statue is supposed to be endowed with human psychological abilities but deprived of any sensations. Condillac argues that the statue would be utterly lacking in knowledge despite its full complement of cognitive faculties, until its sense modalities are activated—only then can the statue's epistemic processes be furnished with the raw materials of PERCEPTION to be transformed into knowledge about the world. Condillac's sensationalism finally tries to explain how particular items of knowledge derive from specific kinds of sense experience.

In more recent philosophy, a scientific version of sensationalism has been defended by MACH. Mach's *Die Analyse der Empfindungen* advances sensationalism as a contribution to the logical positivist program to eliminate metaphysics from natural science (see LOGICAL POSITIVISM/LOGICAL EMPIRICISM) and to ground all knowledge on a correct understanding of the scope and limitations of modern physics. Mach, in keeping with the semantic reductivism of Vienna Circle positivism, maintains that the only scientifically meaningful propositions are those that can be verified, confirmed, or disconfirmed by means of empirical evidence based on immediate sense experience. Mach regards the world studied by empirical science as decomposable into "elements" that can be understood alternatively as the most basic possible sensations or as the atomic physical constituents of matter. Phenomenalism and sense-data theory are heir to Mach's pioneering efforts to elaborate a more rigorous formulation of sensationalism as the mind's direct acquaintance with the epistemically infallible psychological contents of sensations.

The philosophical difficulties encountered by sensationalism raise doubts about its acceptability. Sensation as raw experience unpreconditioned by extra-sensational concepts or categories, as KANT argued, is the naive, untenable dogma of radical empiricism. Berkeley, moreover, clearly understood and embraced as an important discovery the conclusion that if all knowledge of the physical world is reducible to sensation, then, since sensations are psychological occurrences, the world itself exists only mentally as a congeries of ideas or immediate sense impressions. That sensationalism implies IDEALISM is avoided in a more robustly realist epistemology and ontology only by admitting that sensations intend or are about something other than themselves, that they represent a mind-independent reality. The contradiction between sensationalism and commonsense realism in its opposition to idealism proves that if there is a world outside sensation, then there is knowledge of an existent reality that does not consist in, and is not fully reducible to, sensation alone.

PRIMARY WORKS

Aristotle. *De Anima.* Translated with commentaries and glossary by Hippocrates G. Apostle. Grinnell: Peripatetic Press, 1981.
Condillac, Étienne Bonnot de. *Essai sur l'origine des connoissances humaine* (1746). Translated by Thomas Nugent as *An Essay on the Origin of Human Knowledge, Being a Supplement to Mr. Locke's Essay on the Human Understanding*, with an

introduction by Robert G. Weyant. Gainesville: Scholars Facsimiles and Reprints, 1971.

———. *Traité de sensations* (1754), translated by Geraldine Carr as *Condillac's Treatise on the Sensations*, with a preface by H. Wildon Carr. London: Favil Press, 1930.

Locke, John. *An Essay concerning Human Understanding* (1690). Edited with an introduction by P. H. Nidditch. Oxford: Clarendon Press, 1975.

Mach, Ernst. *Die Analyse der Empfindungen* (1906). Translated by C. M. Williams as *The Analysis of Sensations*. Chicago: University of Chicago Press, 1914.

DALE JACQUETTE

SEXTUS EMPIRICUS. A late member of the Pyrrhonist school of skepticism, Sextus Empiricus lived during the second century A.D. His surviving writings are *Outlines of Pyrrhonism* and two volumes entitled *Against the Mathematicians*, which provide a compendious survey of the debates that preoccupied the school for five centuries. Translated into Latin in the 1560s, the former shaped the epistemological concerns of modern philosophy and contained many skeptical arguments later discussed by Montaigne and Descartes (see Popkin 1979).

Ancient skepticism had a distinctive character whose contemporary relevance has recently been emphasized (see Fogelin 1994). Most philosophers see in skepticism the threat that none of our beliefs count as knowledge: unless this can be overcome, our epistemological position is unsatisfactory. Pyrrhonism suggests that skeptical challenges should lead us to live without belief, suspending judgment on all things. Abandoning belief turns out to provide the tranquillity (*ataraxia*) that other philosophers sought in dogmatic knowledge.

According to Sextus, skepticism is an ability or mental attitude that opposes appearances to judgments in any way whatsoever, with the result that, owing to the equipollence of the objects and reasons thus opposed, we are brought firstly to a state of mental suspense and next to a state of "unperturbedness" or quietude (*Outlines of Pyrrhonism* [henceforth PH1]: 8). Pyrrhonism invites obvious objections: suspension of judgment is psychologically impossible, and without beliefs, we would have nothing to guide our actions. The "quietude" of total inaction is hardly desirable. However, Sextus rejects this objection by describing the Pyrrhonist's "guide to life." First, skeptics "acquiesce in appearances," allowing their actions to be shaped by sensory appearances, by bodily needs, and by natural desires. Second, they should conform in a detached and uncommitted way to the religious and ethical practices of their community. Third, they are advised to learn a trade: Sextus himself was a physician.

So one can acquiesce in appearances, acting as seems reasonable in the light of experience, while holding no beliefs. This raises a question about what "belief" ("dogma") means. Sextus denied that skeptics "overthrow the affective sense-impressions which induce our assent involuntarily," and he called these impressions "appearances." When we question whether the underlying object is such as it appears, we grant the fact that it appears, and our doubt does not concern the appearance itself but the account given of that appearance (PH1:

19). Since the skeptics talk of ''appearances'' in connection with ethical beliefs and mathematical proofs as well as with sensory information, it is a more general and less theory-laden notion than the more recent concept of an ''IDEA.'' The skeptic uses ''dogma'' in the sense of ''assent to one of the non-evident objects of scientific inquiry'' while the Pyrrhonian philosopher ''assents to nothing that is non-evident'' (PH1: 13–14). Arguably, the only ''beliefs'' to be abandoned are those espoused by dogmatic philosophers and scientists who claim knowledge of the worldly mechanisms and essences underlying our experience.

Pyrrhonists risk another sort of easy refutation: if they believe (dogmatically) that we should suspend judgment on all nonevident things, they contradict themselves and succumb to ''negative dogmatism.'' The description of skepticism as an ''ability'' responds to this, as does the emphasis that a skeptic is ''a lover of his kind'' whose aim is to ''cure by speech, as best he can, the self-conceit and rashness of the dogmatists'' (PH1: 280). The skeptics practiced a kind of philosophical therapy, helping people to obtain tranquillity through seeing how various dogmatic philosophical endeavors tend to self-destruct, judging arguments by their effectiveness in achieving this end.

The core of Pyrrhonist practice is a body of ''modes'' or ''tropes,'' techniques for bringing about the suspension of belief. The most important of these fall into two sets: the ten modes of Aenesidemus and the five modes of Agrippa.

As Sextus' definition of skepticism suggested, the use of these techniques falls into three stages: (1) the opposition of appearances and judgments; (2) the equipollence of reasons and objects; and (3) suspension of belief (*epoché*). Consider a simple example: a tower appears to be round from a distance yet seems to be rectangular when examined closely; the ''appearances,'' when viewed from different distances, are opposed. We can acquiesce in both of these contextually relative appearances, using them to guide our conduct; but the dogmatist will ask which, if either, of these appearances is actually correct. The Pyrrhonist expects to be able to sabotage any attempt to defend one of the appearances over the other, so, while acknowledging that it appears round from a distance and rectangular from close up, he avoids any dogmatic belief about the underlying reality. Any criterion offered for favoring one appearance over another will itself succumb to skeptical criticism.

THE TEN MODES OF AENESIDEMUS (PH1 36–163)

These modes provide a mass of information to be used in ''opposing appearances.'' They are used by skeptics to put their dogmatist rivals on the defensive, forcing them to acknowledge the need for a criterion to justify preferring one of the opposed appearances. To the contemporary reader, these are apt to seem a curious mix of unconvincing ''facts'' and odd speculations—their use depends on their being acknowledged by the dogmatists. The first mode ''shows that the same impressions are not produced by the same objects owing to the differences in animals'' (PH1: 40). Since we admit that our sensory appearances depend on the physical constitution of our perceptual apparatus, any evidence that different animals have very different physical constitutions should raise the question of why our appearances have special authority. We might expect creatures with concave or convex eyes to receive different appearances; those with scales or feathers may have different tactile impressions; those with rough tongues may receive different appearances of taste. Moreover, the best explanation of the fact that animals vary in their tastes and preferences is that the appearances they receive are different. Once we acknowledge that our appearances are determined by accidental features of our constitutions and contexts, we must recognize the need to defend any claim to dogmatic knowledge of the nonevident natures of things.

The next three modes resemble the first in appealing to ways in which appearances reflect possibly accidental features of their subjects. The second exploits variations between people: differences in body shape between "Indians" and "Scythians" reflect varying "predominant humors," which also affect sense impressions. Different people have different tastes—which, again, is best explained by reference to differences in their impressions. We are told of those who shiver in the sun and in hot baths while feeling warm in the shade and of Ethiopians who eat scorpions and snakes with impunity. Since people vary in intelligence and judgment, we cannot take everyone's views as of equal standing: we need a rule for deciding whose judgment should be trusted, who possesses expertise in different areas—it would be question-begging for dogmatists uncritically to claim authority for their own appearances.

The third and fourth modes show that we can oppose appearances solely by appeal to the impressions of a particular person. First, I receive different appearances from different senses: honey "seems to some pleasant to the tongue but unpleasant to the eye; so that it is impossible to say whether it is absolutely pleasant or unpleasant" (PH1 92). Mode four: our appearances are affected by our "circumstances," whether we are awake or asleep, old or young, drunk or sober, afraid or bold, full of grief or joy. If something seems dangerous when we feel timid or are sober but not when we are in a confident frame of mind or drunk, then is it really dangerous?

The fifth mode appeals to ways in which appearances depend on locations and distances: a tower appears round from a distance but square to close inspection (PH1: 118); an oar will appear bent when in the water but straight when out of the water (PH1: 119). Further aspects of the object and its context are invoked by the sixth and seventh modes. My impression of your complexion will vary according to whether you are hot or cold, so I must be able to discount for such "environmental" variations before deciding what your complexion "really" is; silver filings appear black when they are by themselves, white when combined into a mass; and so on.

The remaining modes are rather a mixed bag. The tenth, applicable primarily in ethics, points to the variety in laws, habits, and ethical standards found in different societies at different times, and the ninth notes that we are differently impressed according to whether an object is rare or common: gold, unlike water, is precious; comets, unlike the sun, are portentous. The eighth, based on "relativity," seems to describe the pattern common to all the others: appearances are relative to subjects and contexts. Once we have concluded that "all things are relative," we are "plainly left with the conclusions that we shall not be able to state what is the nature of each of the objects in its own real purity" (PH1: 140).

THE FIVE MODES OF AGRIPPA (PH1 164–177)

Developed, according to Sextus, by "the later skeptics," these modes clarify the strategy behind skeptical challenges and introduce themes familiar to contemporary epistemology. Two of these are already familiar. The first (based on "discrepancy") challenges a belief by showing that it has been a matter of endless dispute, and the third ("relativity") observes that appearances are relative to judgers and their contexts. The other Agrippan modes reflect the familiar regress of justification. When we try to prove some proposition—or to justify preferring one appearance over another—the skeptic can point out that "the thing adduced as a proof . . . needs a further proof, and this again another, and so on *ad infinitum*" (PH1: 166). The mode based on hypothesis comes into play when dogmatists try to block this regress through adopting hypotheses that are assumed to be true without demonstration; and the final mode ("from circular reasoning") is used when the proof makes use of claims themselves depending on what the proof is supposed to establish. Although not listed among the original ten modes, these styles of argument are employed there when skeptics try to block dogmatist attempts to justify preferring one appearance over another.

Sextus illustrates the strength of these modes by arguing that "every matter of inquiry admits of being brought under these modes" (PH1: 169ff.). The mode of discrepancy enables us to see that any matter of dogmatic belief is an object of controversy. Anything used to settle the debate can itself be challenged: an infinite regress emerges that can be avoided only by circular reasoning or by hypothesizing something as granted without demonstration.

During the Hellenic period, many epistemological debates concerned proper methods of medical diagnosis. "Rationalists" relied on scientific theories invoking unobservable pores, atoms, and functions, while empiricists held that medical practice could be grounded only in experience. Although he suggested that Pyrrhonists should favour a third ("Methodist") school, Sextus' name supports the common assumptions that the school was associated with a moderate and detached medical empiricism (Frede 1987: Chapters 12–15).

Pyrrhonist ideas were used for a variety of purposes after their rediscovery in the sixteenth century but were most commonly associated with a moderate kind of empiricism. Noting that Sextus did not question knowledge of appearances, Mersenne proposed that science should describe the systematic relations between appearances, and GASSENDI suggested that the atomic theory be adopted as a fruitful and effective way of making sense of experience while agnostic about whether it gave a correct account of the underlying nature of matter. Several scholars have emphasized the parallels between HUME's philosophy and characteristics of Pyrrhonism (see Hookway 1990: Chapter 5).

PRIMARY WORK

Sextus Empiricus. *Works.* 4 vols. Translated by R. G. Bury. Loeb Classical Library. London: Heinemann, 1933–1949. Vol. 1 is *Outlines of Pyrrhonism* (referred to as PH); the other three volumes contain *Against the Mathematicians.*

BIBLIOGRAPHY

Books

Annas, Julia, and Jonathan Barnes. *The Modes of Skepticism.* Cambridge: Cambridge University Press, 1985.
Barnes, Jonathan. *The Toils of Skepticism.* Cambridge: Cambridge University Press, 1990.
Burnyeat, Myles, ed. *The Skeptical Tradition.* Berkeley and Los Angeles: University of California Press, 1983.
Fogelin, Robert. *Pyrrhonian Reflections on Knowledge and Justification.* Oxford: Oxford University Press, 1994.
Frede, Michael. *Essays in Ancient Philosophy.* Oxford: Oxford University Press, 1987.
Hookway, Christopher. *Scepticism.* London: Routledge, 1990.
Popkin, Richard. *The History of Skepticism from Erasmus to Spinoza.* Berkeley and Los Angeles: University of California Press, 1979.

Article

Barnes, Jonathan. "The Beliefs of a Pyrrhonist." *Proceedings of the Cambridge Philological Society* 19 (1982): 1–29.

CHRISTOPHER HOOKWAY

SIMPLE/COMPLEX DISTINCTION. An idea is either simple or complex. A complex idea can be separated into other ideas of which it is composed. Simple ideas are those ideas that cannot be so decomposed. Ideas received through experience are already bundled into complex ideas. For example, the idea of a white horse is a complex idea. Through ABSTRACTION, one can separate it into the ideas of white and horse. The idea of a horse, in turn, is composed of further ideas. The idea of white, however, is simple; it cannot be broken down into component simpler ideas. Since all complex ideas are composed of simple ones, what is received from experience are simple ideas, typically packaged with others to form complex ideas. Thus, LOCKE calls simple ideas "the Materials of all our Knowledge" (*An Essay concerning Human Understanding* II.ii.2).

Locke's simple ideas present "one uniform Appearance" either through sensation or reflection. Each simple idea is completely distinct from all others, including those simple ideas with which it may be conjoined in experience. Ideas of color, sound, tastes, and odors are simple ideas of sensation received from one sense. Space, figure, rest, and motion are simple ideas received from more than one sense. Pleasure, pain, power, existence, and unity are simple ideas of sensation and reflection, in Locke's view.

HUME employs the simple/complex distinction in his codification of perceptions. Simple ideas are derived from simple impressions, which they resemble. Complex ideas are composed of simple ones; a complex idea need not have an antecedent resembling complex impression, though each of its component simple ideas must have an antecedent resembling simple impressions. Hume shares Locke's view that ideas, such as the ideas of colors, tastes, and sounds, are simple, but he parts company with Locke on others, such as the idea of existence. Reflection on any idea, Hume argues, is reflection on it as existent. There is no separate simple idea of existence. BERKELEY, contra Locke, holds that the idea of unity is a complex idea abstracted from all others (*The Principles of Human Knowledge*: Part I §13).

While Berkeley holds that ideas can be collected and ''marked by one name'' or separated from such collections by abstraction, he does not claim that there are simple ideas (*Principles*: Part I §1). Winkler chronicles several arguments from Berkeley's notebooks, arguments not prominent in his published works, against the simplicity of color ideas. Our ability to compare two ideas of shades of the same color, Berkeley argued, shows that they must have constituent ideas that make the comparison possible. Thus, the ideas of the shades are not simple. Berkeley also held that the complexity of the cause of an idea of color shows that the idea itself must be complex. This second argument is open to the objection that Berkeley failed to distinguish the phenomenological character of ideas from the character of their causes.

Both Locke and Hume offer descriptions of the mental operations that give rise to complex ideas. Locke describes three kinds of complex ideas—modes, SUBSTANCEs, and RELATIONS, representing three different types of complexity in ideas. With his view that our ideas of substances are complex ideas, Locke sets himself against a tradition begun by ARISTOTLE and followed by the modern rationalists, which took substances to be simple. Descartes held that the mind, for example, was a simple substance. For Locke, the notion of an immaterial substance is as much a complex idea as is any idea of material substance. Hume finds that there is no simple impression of substance; so there can be no simple idea. The idea of substance, then, is nothing but a collection of simple ideas. Hume sees a philosophical liability in the use of the notion of substance. Philosophers are likely to forget that it is just a complex idea and to mistakenly infer that it represents a basic metaphysical category.

PRIMARY WORKS

Aristotle. *Categories*. In *The Complete Works of Aristotle*, vol. 1, edited by Jonathan Barnes. Princeton: Princeton University Press, 1984.

Berkeley, George. *The Works of George Berkeley, Bishop of Cloyne*. Edited by A. A. Luce and T. E. Jessop. 9 vols. London: Thomas Nelson and Sons, 1948–1957.

Descartes, René. *The Philosophical Writings of Descartes*. Edited and translated by John

Cottingham, Robert Stoothoff, and Dugald Murdoch. Cambridge: Cambridge University Press, 1984–1985.

Hume, David. *A Treatise of Human Nature.* 2d ed., edited with an analytical index by L. A. Selby-Bigge; revised with notes by P. H. Nidditch. Oxford: Clarendon Press, 1978.

Locke, John. *An Essay concerning Human Understanding.* Edited with an introduction by P. H. Nidditch. Oxford: Clarendon Press, 1975.

BIBLIOGRAPHY

Ayers, Michael. *Locke: Epistemology and Ontology.* London: Routledge, 1991.
Winkler, Kenneth P. *Berkeley: An Interpretation.* Oxford: Oxford University Press, 1989.

SAUL TRAIGER

SKEPTICISM. The term "skepticism" may refer loosely to a doubting disposition of mind or more precisely to any one of a number of related philosophical stances or doctrines. Anciently, it comprised as well a certain style of life, which had peace of mind (*ataraxia*) as its principal objective and within which suspension of judgment (*epoché*) was cultivated as the means to that end.

So as to be able to deal with the subject in brief compass, we restrict our discussion to *epistemological skepticism*, defined here as the reasoned nonacceptance of knowledge claims falling under some specified general description. Epistemological skepticism may be *limited* (partial, restricted, circumscribed), applying only to claims pertaining to particular subject matters, such as moral or aesthetic value, or to claims deriving from the employment of particular faculties, principles, or methods, such as the senses, introspection, or inductive inference; or it may be *universal* (total, unrestricted, global), taking in all knowledge claims.

Epistemological skepticism may also be *mitigated* or *unmitigated*. Mitigated skepticism holds that while *strong* or *strict* knowledge claims are not to be accepted, certain *weaker* epistemological claims, for instance, claims to justified or "probable" belief, may in principle be accepted as claims to what may be called *virtual knowledge*; that is, they may under certain conditions be accepted as robust stand-ins for knowledge claims in the strict sense. Unmitigated skepticism resists even these weaker claims. The distinction between mitigated and unmitigated skepticism is one of *depth*, while the distinction between limited and unlimited skepticism is one of *scope*.

The term "skepticism" is also commonly applied to the reasoned refusal to countenance certain kinds of entities, such as mental states, values, or nonobservable physical entities like subatomic particles. Such *ontological skepticism*, as it may be called, will not be specifically treated here, although it generally goes hand in hand with an associated variety of epistemological skepticism.

Any brand of epistemological skepticism takes for granted a particular characterization of knowledge on the basis of which the skepticism is raised. The distinction between mitigated and unmitigated skepticism presupposes, in addition, a distinction between stronger and weaker varieties of knowledge or between genuine and virtual knowledge. If two parties characterize knowledge differently, one of them may be considered a skeptic from the standpoint of the other without being in any way skeptical according to his or her own lights. So, for instance, if Theaetetus declares that it is impossible to be certain of anything, he will presumably be considered a universal skeptic by anyone who thinks that to know a thing requires being certain of it. Theaetetus, on the other hand, may think that knowledge does not require certainty and so may deny that his position is a skeptical one. Since any form of skepticism rests, at least covertly, upon a correlative characterization of knowledge, discussions or attributions of skepticism in which the operative notion of ''knowledge'' is never resolved are bound to be unenlightening.

DOGMATISTS, ACADEMICS, AND PYRRHONISTS

Within the Western tradition, philosophical skepticism is very old. Its beginnings are traceable to philosophers such as Xenophanes (sixth century B.C.); Heraclitus (sixth–fifth century B.C.); Parmenides and Zeno of Elea (early to mid-fifth century B.C.); Protagoras, Gorgias, and Socrates (fifth century B.C.); Democritus (fifth–fourth century B.C.), and, finally, Pyrrho of Elis (c. 365–270 B.C.), who is traditionally (but somewhat misleadingly) recognized as the founder of Greek skepticism. While skeptical thinking thus extends back to the very beginnings of Western philosophy, Skepticism as a distinct type of philosophical movement, with a theoretical and methodological apparatus of its own, seems to have arisen at the beginning of the third century B.C. in reaction to Stoicism and Epicureanism.

Even the most recent discussions of skepticism retain important elements of the ancient debates, for which our main sources are Cicero (106–43 B.C.), Diogenes Laërtius (probably early third century A.D.), and, especially, SEXTUS EMPIRICUS (c. 160–210 A.D.).

Reviewing the positions of his predecessors, Sextus distinguishes between (1) *Dogmatism*, including the philosophies of Aristotle and the Peripatetics, of Plato and the Old Academy, and of the Stoics and Epicureans; (2) *Academic Skepticism*, the philosophy of Arcesilaus (c. 315–240 B.C.) and the New Academy; and (3) *Pyrrhonism*, which is the skepticism expounded by the breakaway school of Aenesidemus (c. 100–40 B.C.). The difference between these three styles of philosophy lies in the positions taken toward judgment-making or *assent* (*synkatathesis*) and toward the *objective knowledge claims*, as we may call them, that ostensibly express such assent: an objective knowledge claim is one that reaches beyond subjective presentations or appearances (*phantasia*) to the objective facts, conditions, or situations that these presentations seemingly discover to us. To *assent* (in the technical language of the Stoics) is to accept a subjective presentation as true.

Dogmatic philosophers assent to at least some presentations, generally to quite a few. Accordingly, they advance claims to objective knowledge; they argue—or are at least prepared to argue—that their assent is warranted, which amounts to arguing for the truth of their claims. We may note here that for all of the parties to the ancient discussions, from the Stoics onward, a knowledge claim is understood to be a claim to certainty. In any event, assent and the knowledge claims that reflect it are precisely what the skeptical philosopher is concerned to avoid.

Academic Skeptics maintain that assent is never warranted and that no objective knowledge claims are sustainable; they assert, and essay to demonstrate, that we can have no knowledge of anything lying beyond our subjective presentations. Arcesilaus, the founder of Academic Skepticism, seems to have been the first to exploit *isostheneia*, or the equipollence of opposed arguments, as a kind of demonstration that assent and the claims that express it are never warranted; and it is this kind of demonstration upon which Academic Skeptics all rely. The rhetorical technique of balancing every argument with a counterargument already had a long history within Greek philosophy; Arcesilaus' contribution was to make use of it to justify a far-reaching *epoché*, or suspension of judgment. Aside from Arcesilaus, the most important of the Academic Skeptics was Carneades (c. 213–128 B.C.). He seems to have argued that while we are never justified in assenting to any subjective presentation (which would imply certainty), we are entitled to accept some of them as "probable" (which does not imply certainty). In other words, while objective knowledge claims are never warranted, objective "probability" claims may be. No more than "probability" is really needed, Carneades maintained, as a guide to life. Carneades' position therefore represents a kind of mitigated skepticism.

The Pyrrhonist declines on principle to assent to any presentation and declines as well to advance any thesis about the possibility of objective knowledge. Aenesidemus, the founder of the Pyrrhonist school, sought to make skepticism consistent and self-covering. This was the reason for his break with the New Academy: he thought that in asserting and seeking to demonstrate that we can have no knowledge of anything beyond our own subjective presentations, Academic Skepticism dogmatized and thereby betrayed its own principles. Maintaining a consistent, self-covering position is always a problem for a universal skeptic; limited skepticism is not as vulnerable to this difficulty, for obvious reasons. Ancient skepticism was not, it is true, quite universal, since it never questioned our knowledge of our own subjective appearances or presentations, but only of the objective realities lying beyond them. This is, however, quite enough to generate the consistency problem. The Pyrrhonist view is that consistent skeptics can assert no doctrine about the impossibility of objective knowledge; indeed, they can assert no doctrine whatever. Still, Pyrrhonists can, and do, indulge in argument, and their basic style of argumentation is that of the Academic Skeptic: they generate an equipollence of opposing considerations, and thereby an *asynkatathesis*, or avoidance of assent. Aenesidemus, indeed, made a detailed compendium of these equipollences, classified into ten "tropes" or "modes"; and this compendium has served as a storehouse of examples for all later skeptical discussions. Aenesidemus' tropes comprise arguments from illusion, from the relativity of perception, and so on. Unlike the Academic Skeptic, however, the Pyrrhonists use such arguments only to *show* (in the sense of exhibiting), not to *demonstrate*, that assent is unwarranted and that the reasonable man must therefore suspend judgment; they take up a *stance* but advance no *doctrine*, a posture that is reflected in the Pyrrhonist slogan, "I determine nothing."

THE HERITAGE OF ANCIENT SKEPTICISM

As may be gathered from the preceding discussion, Dogmatism, Academic Skepticism, and Pyrrhonism—at least as described by Sextus—all began from a certain set of common premises. These premises were implicit (at least) in a great deal of earlier philosophy, but they were first regimented into a system by the Stoics (see STOICISM). Let us take stock of them: the first premise is that our subjective experience consists of a variety of appearances or presentations (*phantasia*), the phenomenal character and qualities of which are evident per se. A person's subjective presentations thus constitute, in themselves, a kind of knowledge, a knowledge of the way in which things appear to him or her. Since knowledge is understood to require certainty, the idea is that a person cannot go wrong concerning his or her own subjective presentations.

Furthermore, these presentations seem to represent, or to make manifest to us, various objective facts or states of affairs; they are in that sense not only presentations but (ostensibly) representations. Objective reality can be known only, if at all, through our subjective presentations. We may accept a presentation as true, which is the same as judging that such-and-such is the case: a correspondence conception of truth is operative here. This act of accepting or judging is assent (*synkatathesis*), which finds its expression in language in the form of objective knowledge claims. However, nothing forces us to assent to our presentations; we may suspend judgment, and indeed, as experience seems to show, not every appearance is true or trustworthy. The question is, then: To which presentations are we entitled to assent? Which of them are indubitable representations of objective reality and identifiable as such? This problem of distinguishing indubitable, or veridical, from dubitable, or nonveridical, presentations was known anciently as the *problem of the criterion*.

It was over this question, finally, that the schools diverged. Dogmatic philosophers pretended to a criterion that enabled them to identify indubitable presentations and to distinguish them, with certainty, from those that are doubtful or false. In particular, the Stoics alleged that there existed a species of infallible presentations, "cognitive" or "apprehensive" presentations (*phantasia kataléptiké*), surely recognizable by their intrinsic qualities. The Academic Skeptics tried to demonstrate that no such criterion was to be found. Responding to the Stoics, Arcesilaus and Carneades argued against both the existence and the infallible recognizability of apprehensive presentations. The Pyrrhonists neither pretended to such a criterion nor denied that one does or could exist; they suspended judgment on this question. To take a position on the problem of the criterion would, they thought, be to dogmatize or worse: According to Aenesidemus, Carneades not only dogmatized in maintaining that the probable can be distinguished from the improbable, but inconsistently argued against the existence of any criterion adequate to distinguish the indubitable from the dubitable while failing to apply similar arguments against the criterion by which he sought to distinguish the probable from the improbable.

Notwithstanding their divergent responses to the problem of the criterion, the common base of all of these schools is the *representational epistemology* described earlier, along with a commitment to the idea that knowledge requires certainty and to the correspondence conception of truth. If we assume that we can know objective reality only *through* subjective appearances or presentations that are not, or not all, necessarily reliable, skeptical questions are bound to arise. It is surely no accident that Academic Skepticism (the first Skeptical school) was launched in reaction to Stoicism, which articulated and regimented this representational epistemology. There may well be other vehicles through which insistent skeptical questions can arise; but it is through this vehicle that they have in fact arisen in almost every case. The skepticism to which representational epistemology conduces is, as we have seen, not strictly universal but is nearly such: it attaches to all objective knowledge or "matters of fact."

In the later tradition of Western philosophy, practically every response to threatened skepticism has consisted in either (1) an acceptance of skepticism (whether in the Academic or the Pyrrhonist style) in the wake of having adopted representational epistemology in something like its classical form; or (2) an attempt to overcome (in the Stoic manner) the skepticism invited by this representational epistemology, through finding a positive solution to the problem of the criterion; or (3) an attempt to disconnect the skeptical engine by reforming (but usually not by abandoning completely) representational epistemology; this third approach is the rarest.

SOME INSTRUCTIVE EXAMPLES

By looking very briefly at a few examples from modern philosophy (and pushing aside all complexities and disputed questions of interpretation), we can illustrate the three kinds of responses mentioned at the end of the last section.

It is not difficult to discern René Descartes' (1596–1650) commitment to a representational epistemology, with all of the relevant trappings described earlier. With this as a starting point, Descartes deepened and radicalized the skeptical challenge, generating "hyperbolic doubt" out of the "dream argument" (already raised, and responded to, by Plato) and the specter of the *malin génie* (often translated as "evil demon"). Radical as these devices are, they are still highly reminiscent of a number of Aenesidemus' tropes. Descartes' purpose was, of course, to make the strongest skeptical case that he could, precisely in order to answer it and thereby to quash the skeptical challenge—the *crise pyrrhonienne*—once and for all. His proposed solution is very much in the spirit of the Stoics: he produces and defends a criterion, that of clarity and distinctness. These are meant to be intrinsic and patently recognizable properties of certain presentations that together guarantee the veracity of those presentations. Descartes' clear and distinct ideas are obviously at no great remove from the *phantasia kataléptiké* of the Stoics.

George BERKELEY (1685–1753) was mindful of the radical skeptical challenge mounted by Descartes but was unconvinced by Descartes' solution. Well aware of the way in which the skeptical arguments were grounded in representational epistemology and greatly exercised about the vulnerability to skepticism that he perceived in the ''materialistic'' realism of John LOCKE (1632–1704), Berkeley proposed a drastic reform, namely, collapsing the received distinction between subjective presentations and real, or objective, things. A world lying entirely beyond our ''IDEAS,'' like the ''material'' world imagined by Locke and others, would be unknowable, Berkeley argued; and all talk of such a world is otiose. But this is no obstacle to objective knowledge, that is, to knowledge of and about ''real things''; for real things (including tables, chairs, trees, animals, and so on) do not lie beyond our ideas but *are* ideas or collections of such, and it is therefore the things *themselves* that are presented to us, Berkeley maintained. Presentations do not, as in the classical theory, stand *between* us and objective reality. Berkeley's theory seems, indeed, to yield knowledge far too easily, for he has difficulty accounting for the difference between ''real things'' and ''chimeras'' (as he calls them), which are equally ''ideas.'' The correspondence between ideas and an underlying reality can no longer be appealed to for help in explaining this difference, and, indeed, Berkeley's reform implies a retreat from the correspondence conception of truth. His ultimate solution to this conundrum is not fully clear, but Berkeley appeals to both intrinsic features (vivacity) and extrinsic features (coherence, dependency on the will) of presentations in trying to make out the difference between real things and mere fancies. In an odd way, he is thus drawn back into trying to solve the problem of the criterion. Since he still thinks of subjective presentations as the vehicles of objective knowledge, Berkeley can perhaps not be said to have entirely abandoned representative epistemology; but even if this term can still be applied in some sense to the reformed theory (despite the notion of ''representation'' having lost most of its purchase), it is an epistemology drastically different from that of the Stoics. Very few have taken it up.

David HUME (1711–1776), in particular, may be seen as declining Berkeley's proposed reform and cleaving to the classical position, including the correspondence conception of truth. Hume is, however, prepared to swallow the skeptical consequences, admitting and, indeed, arguing that there is no way in which we can be sure that our subjective presentations correctly represent ''matters of fact'': this ''philosophical'' skepticism comes directly out of his representative epistemology, as Hume points out himself with admirable clarity. Like the Academic Skeptics, Hume sees no positive solution to the problem of the criterion. His philosophical skepticism is softened, however, by his view that our nature constrains us (and perhaps even entitles us, in a certain sense) to believe the sorts of things that we need to believe for the sake of the successful conduct of life; and these beliefs—or at least those to which moral or practical certainty attach—comprise a kind of "virtual knowledge" (to revert to a term used earlier), even if they fail to pass strictly philosophical muster. On these counts, Hume emerges as a mitigated skeptic, perhaps more Carneadean than Pyrrhonian.

SKEPTICISM AND EMPIRICISM

There is evidently no very tight connection between skepticism and empiricism. One can be an empiricist without being a skeptic, and one can likewise be a skeptic without being an empiricist. Nevertheless, a nontrivial association between skepticism and empiricism derives from the fact that empiricist epistemology has been characteristically representational (although the reverse is not the case, and important modern rationalists, like Descartes and KANT [1724–1804], have been representationalists). For this reason, empiricist theories, both ancient and modern, have in almost every instance generated skeptical questions that have had, sooner or later, to be addressed; and we have spoken earlier about the types of response they have evoked. In later modern philosophy, most especially during the twentieth century, epistemological theories have become ever more subtle and sophisticated, and novel solutions to traditional problems have begun to appear. Some contemporary empiricists have, wittingly or unwittingly, moved perceptibly away from representational epistemology in its classic form. Nelson GOODMAN (b. 1906), a latter-day Berkeleian, is one example; Willard van Orman QUINE (b. 1908) is another. Should empiricism take a definitively nonrepresentationalist turn, its traditional flirtation with skepticism would surely lose much of its ardor.

PRIMARY WORKS

Berkeley, George. *The Works of George Berkeley, Bishop of Cloyne.* Edited by A. A. Luce and T. E. Jessop. 9 vols. London: Thomas Nelson and Sons, 1948–1957.

Cicero. *Academica.* With an English translation by H. Rackham. The Loeb Classical Library. London: William Heinemann, 1951.

———. *De Finibus Bonorum et Malorem.* With an English translation by H. Rackham. The Loeb Classical Library. London: William Heinemann, 1983.

———. *De Natura Deorum Academica.* With an English translation by H. Rackham. The Loeb Classical Library. London: William Heinemann, 1951.

Descartes, René. *The Philosophical Writings of Descartes.* Edited and translated by John Cottingham, Robert Stoothoff, and Dugald Murdoch, vols. 1 and 2. Cambridge: Cambridge University Press, 1984–1985.

Diogenes Laërtius, *Lives of Eminent Philosophers.* Vols. 1 and 2, with an English translation by R. D. Hicks. The Loeb Classical Library. London: William Heinemann, 1979–1980.

Hume, David. *An Enquiry concerning Human Understanding.* In *Enquiries concerning Human Understanding and concerning the Principles of Morals,* edited with an analytical index by L. A. Selby-Bigge; revised with notes by P. H. Nidditch. Oxford: Clarendon Press, 1975.

———. *A Treatise of Human Nature*. 2d ed., edited with an analytical index by L. A. Selby-Bigge; revised with notes by P. H. Nidditch. Oxford: Clarendon Press, 1978.

Locke, John. *An Essay concerning Human Understanding*. Edited with an introduction by P. H. Nidditch. Oxford: Clarendon Press, 1975.

Sextus Empiricus. *Against the Ethicists*. With an English translation by R. G. Bury. Loeb Classical Library. London: William Heinemann, 1968.

———. *Against the Logicians*. With an English translation by R. G. Bury. Loeb Classical Library. London: William Heinemann, 1967.

———. *Outlines of Pyrrhonism*. With an English translation by R. G. Bury. Loeb Classical Library. London: William Heinemann, 1967.

Wittgenstein, Ludwig. *On Certainty*. Oxford: Blackwell, 1977.

BIBLIOGRAPHY

Annas, Julia, and Jonathan Barnes, eds. *The Modes of Scepticism: Ancient Texts and Modern Interpretations*. Cambridge: Cambridge University Press, 1985.

Brochard, Victor. *Les Sceptiques grecs*. Paris: F. Alcan, 1887.

Burnyeat, Myles, ed. *The Skeptical Tradition*. Los Angeles and London: University of California Press, 1983.

Fogelin, Robert J. *Hume's Skepticism in the Treatise of Human Nature*. London: Routledge and Kegan Paul, 1985.

Hankinson, R. J. *The Skeptics*. London and New York: Routledge, 1995.

Hookway, Christopher. *Scepticism*. London and New York: Routledge, 1990.

McGinn, Marie. *Sense and Certainty*. Oxford: Blackwell, 1989.

Naess, Arne. *Scepticism*. London: Routledge and Kegan Paul, 1968.

Popkin, Richard H. *The History of Scepticism from Erasmus to Descartes*. Rev. ed. New York; Evanston, IL; London: Harper, 1964.

Putnam, Hilary. *Reason, Truth and History*. Cambridge: Cambridge University Press, 1981.

Richter, Raoul. *Der Skeptizismus in der Philosophie und seine Überwindung*. Vols. 1 and 2. Leipzig: Verlag der Dürr'schen Buchhandlung, 1904–1908.

Robin, Léon. *Pyrrhon et le scepticisme Grec*. Paris: Presses Universitaires, 1944.

Schofield, Malcolm, Myles Burnyeat, and Jonathan Barnes, eds. *Doubt and Dogmatism: Studies in Hellenistic Epistemology*. Oxford: Clarendon Press, 1980.

Stough, Charlotte. *Greek Skepticism: A Study in Epistemology*. Berkeley: University of California Press, 1969.

Strawson, P. F. *Skepticism and Naturalism: Some Varieties*. London: Methuen, 1985.

Stroud, Barry. *The Significance of Philosophical Scepticism*. Oxford: Oxford University Press, 1984.

MIKAEL M. KARLSSON

SMITH, ADAM. Adam Smith (1723–1790) was born in Kirkcaldy, Scotland. He studied at Glasgow University (1737–1740) with Francis Hutcheson and later at Oxford (1740–1746). Between 1748 and 1751 Smith, under the patronage of Henry Home (Lord Kames), lectured at Edinburgh and in 1751 became a professor at Glasgow University until he resigned in 1764. He held no other university position, but in 1778 Smith was named commissioner of customs for Scotland and commissioner of salt duties for Scotland and relocated to Edinburgh, where he died. During the Glasgow period Smith published the first of his two published works, the *Theory of Moral Sentiments* (TMS) in 1759. Although remembered today mostly for the second work—*An Inquiry into the Nature and Causes of the Wealth of Nations* (WN) (1776)—the TMS was an immediate international success, and it is truer to Smith to understand the WN in light of the TMS than to do the reverse.

Throughout his life Smith was close friends with David HUME, and Hume's influence is clearly evident in Smith's work. But unlike Hume, Smith was not primarily an epistemologist, so his empiricism manifests itself through his published works on ethics and economics and in his unpublished writings on a variety of subjects (many of which are now available). In general, his works show a marked interest in the development and evolution of systems, be they linguistic, moral, or social, as demonstrated by experience. His works are, consequently, replete with examples, cases, and historical references, and he prefers this approach to abstract and speculative theorizing. There is, in addition, a consistent skepticism about metaphysical and theological matters. There is no a priori knowledge or innate ideas (see INNATENESS) for Smith, and he repeatedly attacks philosophy for its excesses of ABSTRACTION.

In ethics, empiricism is reflected in an emphasis on the PASSIONS and IMAGINATION. The basic theoretical framework of TMS, then, is within the empiricist tradition. It is also clearly inspired by Hume. But Smith is much more liberal with his use of examples, particular cases, and historical references than is Hume, and discussion of theory is left alone until the very end of the work. There is, as a result, a strong empirical and sociological quality to TMS that is not shared by many other works in ethics prior to Smith. The reader more directly experiences the moral sentiments and seems less removed from human conduct than would be the case with theoretical reflection alone. Moreover, since the line between describing conduct or moral experience, on one hand, and recommending courses of action, on the other, is deliberately obscured, the transition to social science comes easily.

Human beings are portrayed in TMS as creatures whose moral imaginations allow them to identify with the sentiments of others (sympathy) and thus to be bound to them by norms evolving from social interaction and monitored by an "impartial spectator"—itself a creation of our moral imagination. Self-interested motivation, though powerful and important, is by no means the whole of our nature. Consequently, Smith saw economics as circumscribed by both law and morals, but the exact relationship between economic and ethical conduct has been the source of scholarly controversy for some time. It is perhaps a sign of Smith's empiricism that he seems less concerned to identify explicitly the exact connection between his works than he is with accurate portrayals of human nature and conduct.

After leaving Glasgow, Smith spent a few years traveling in France, where he met many of the leading *philosophes* and economists of the day. He then returned to his native Kirkcaldy. Drawing upon his conversations, research, and the collection of a large amount of data, Smith wrote the WN, which finally appeared in 1776 (the year of Hume's death). The same attention to example, circumstance, and evidence found in TMS is exhibited by the WN. While it would be misleading to say that the WN is more empirical than TMS, WN does pay more attention to the actual effects of public policy as demonstrated by the evidence of historical experience and causal reasoning. In this respect its empiricism is perhaps more obvious and more influential.

PRIMARY WORKS

The Glasgow Edition of the Works and Correspondence of Adam Smith. Oxford: Clarendon Press, 1976–1987. Includes *The Theory of Moral Sentiments*; *An Inquiry into the Nature and Causes of the Wealth of Nations*; *Essays on Philosophical Subjects*; *Lectures on Rhetoric and Belles Lettres*; *Lectures on Jurisprudence*; *Correspondence of Adam Smith.* The Glasgow editions are available in paperback from Liberty Classics, Indianapolis, IN.

BIBLIOGRAPHY

Brown, Maurice. *Adam Smith's Economics: Its Place in the Development of Economic Thought.* London: Croom Helm, 1988.
Campbell, T. D. *Adam Smith's Science of Morals.* London: Allen and Unwin, 1971.
Cropsey, Joseph. *Polity and Economy: An Interpretation of the Principles of Adam Smith.* The Hague: Martinus Nijhoff, 1957.
Haakonssen, Knud. *The Science of the Legislator: The Natural Jurisprudence of David Hume and Adam Smith.* Cambridge: Cambridge University Press, 1981.
Ross, I. S. *The Life of Adam Smith.* Oxford: Clarendon Press, 1995.

DOUGLAS J. DEN UYL

SOLIPSISM. Solipsism is the following theory: I and only I exist. Everything else, the theory is understood to claim, including other people and other things, is a figment of my experience—perceived by me in the way they are perceived in motion pictures. This is the whole theory; it is associated with, and often confused with, IDEALISM, the denial that material things exist, the claim that only people exist. The reason for this fusion lies in the fact that solipsism is the most extreme version of idealism, which suggests that the arguments that lead to idealism (Ockham's razor) lead also to the conclusion that no proper things exist except for one's own self. Solipsism is the most frivolous version of idealism, yet it was taken seriously by quite a few thinkers. For a conspicuous example, Dennis Diderot, one of the editors of the famous *Encyclopedie*, said that refuting it is one of the most important and challenging intellectual tasks. Immanuel KANT declared that the inability to refute idealism is a scandal in philosophy. Why? Why do we have to refute frivolous theories? After all, we normally take it for granted that other people exist and that many things other than people exist; why assert that only I exist? Or that only we exist?

There is a historical explanation of why solipsism was taken seriously. Consider ''I and only I exist'' a bit more carefully. Who is that fortunate or unfortunate individual designated by the word "I" here? By the first-person singular is meant not the individual who wrote these words, nor even the one who reads them; it designates the same person who is designated in the famous tag of Descartes: "I think, therefore I am." The first-person singular here is not Descartes. Perhaps it is the reader: it is hard to decide, as the definite article in the expression "the reader" is somewhat misleading. Still, clearly, any reader may identify with the first-person singular of the statement, "I think, therefore I, the reader, am," even though it is meant in the abstract, as the *res cogitans*.

What transpires from the context is this. The premise "I think," which (presumably) leads to the conclusion "I exist," is very specific: the situation it emerges from is known as Descartes' thought-experiment: "I recognize that to be rational I must reject all that I was taught, doubt everything, start afresh, and endorse from now on no statement except ones that I can prove. From now on I act in the light of this recognition. I now doubt everything. Therefore, I now think; I think, therefore, I exist." In order to grant the view that you also exist, that my body also exists, and the armchair on which I am sitting exists, and so on, I have to prove their existence. Suppose that I (i.e., the individual who is performing Descartes' thought-experiment) can prove that I exist, and then I become stuck. I then become stuck in solipsism. If so, then Descartes' thought-experiment becomes an unfortunate failure, a dangerous journey from which one never returns, the irretrievable loss of one's mind. Descartes was afraid of this. As he reports, he postponed performing his thought-experiment until suitable conditions were found. He first vowed to go on a pilgrimage upon a successful result.

The crucial point is the view that in order to be rational one must undertake the performance of Descartes' thought-experiment. If it is not successful, then rationally one must end up doubting that anything exists; if, however, it is successful, then one ends up allowing that other things exist. Hence, what imposes solipsism on one is the view that rationality requires the performance of Descartes' thought-experiment and that it succeeds only in part: it establishes the existence of the individual who performs it and no more. The ways out of solipsism are clear, then: the simplest but hardest is to deny that the performer of Descartes' thought-experiment becomes stuck in solipsism; the most unpleasant but easiest is to eschew rationality; the most revolutionary way out is to deny that rationality requires that Descartes' thought-experiment should be performed. This, however, invites a totally new idea of what constitutes rationality.

The denial that Descartes' thought-experiment gets one stuck in solipsism is the assertion that either it imposes the denial of the existence of any thing whatsoever or that it imposes the claim that other things exist as well. The first disjunct was probably invented by David HUME; it was revived by Ernst MACH and perhaps endorsed by Ludwig WITTGENSTEIN. (Solipsism is endorsed explicitly in his *Tractatus Logico-Philosophicus* 5.6ff., though in a qualified manner: it is true but not given to proper assertion, he says there.) The second disjunct is the assertion that other things exist. This was claimed repeatedly but never successfully. In particular, Rudolf CARNAP called his view "methodological solipsism" to stress that beginning from admission of my own sense experiences alone I can build up the world-picture of common sense. He relinquished the label because, he said, he was misunderstood. More likely he was not misunderstood but disbelieved. One may also reject rationality and with it the need to undergo Descartes' thought-experiment. Giving up reason, however, is a great sacrifice, of course, and even to no avail: one who went on the dangerous mission with Descartes cannot wipe out the memories. The only remaining way out of solipsism is to deny that rationality demands following Descartes' thought-experiment. This is why an increasing number of philosophers are emulating Karl POPPER and his followers in the study of non-Cartesian rationality.

PRIMARY WORKS

Carnap, Rudolf. *The Logical Structure of the World*. Translated by R. A. George. Berkeley: University of California Press, 1967. Original German published in 1928.
Descartes, René. *Meditations on First Philosophy,*. In *The Philosophical Writings of Descartes*, 3 vols., edited and translated by John Cottingham, Robert Stoothoff, and Dugald Murdoch. Cambridge: Cambridge University Press, 1984–1985.
Wittgenstein, Ludwig. *Tractatus Logico-Philosopicus*. Translated by D. F. Pears and B. F. McGuinness. London: Routledge; New York: Humanities Press, 1961.

BIBLIOGRAPHY

Oliver, W. Donald. "A Sober Look at Solipsism." *American Philosophical Quarterly* 4 (1970): 30–39.

JOSEPH AGASSI

SPACE. The concept of space was arguably forged only in recent times. Plato conceived of space (*chora*) as "an invisible and formless being" that is "hardly real" but that serves as the "receptacle" of sensible things—both in the sense of being occupied by sensible things but also in the sense that it comes to constitute sensible things by having geometrical shapes impressed upon it (*Timaeus* 48e–53e). This view led ARISTOTLE to remark that Plato identified space with matter (*Physics* 209b11–16).

For his part, Aristotle had absolutely no use for a concept of space distinct from body. He preferred instead to talk about place (*topos*), which he took to be a property of body—or, more precisely, of those bodies surrounding the body that is said to be in a place (*Physics* 212a6–7).

Prior to Plato and Aristotle, Parmenides and Melissus had gone so far as to deny the intelligibility of space distinct from body. A space with no body in it would be a place where nothing exists. But Parmenides argued that it is absurd to maintain that what is not, is, and hence that nothingness or not-being might exist anywhere (Kirk, Raven, and Schofield, eds., *The Presocratic Philosophers* DK28B7; "DK" refers to the standard fragment numbers for pre-Socratic philosophers originally established by Hermann Diels and Walther Kranz and now used in all standard editions of pre-Socratic fragments). Melissus had taken this one step further and argued that there can be no motion, since, if there can be no empty space, there can be no room for anything to move (DK30B7).

The ancient Greek atomists Leucippus and Democritus and, later, EPICURUS and Lucretius turned this argument on its head and observed that, since motion obviously does occur, void space and hence nothingness must exist for bodies to move in, however absurd this might seem (DK67A19; Lucretius, DRN i 334–39). This argument, grounded as it is in an appeal to sensory evidence, represents one of the earliest instances of the triumph of empiricist principles over the dictates of pure reason. However, the atomists drew the distinction between void (*kenon*) and body in such strong terms that it is a serious question whether they did not conceive of void as quite literally nothing or "what is not" and to be such as to exist only in the intervals between bodies (or "what is") (DK67A7, DK68A37). If so then they, too, would be a long way from more recent notions of space as a kind of thing that contains bodies and exists coincidentally with them.

Modern thought about space and place arguably began in 1277, when Etienne Tempier, bishop of Paris, attempted to rein in the subversive views of the Paris Arts Masters by condemning as heretical a number of Aristotelian doctrines that tended, among other things, to limit the omnipotence of God. Included in the condemned propositions was the thesis "that God cannot move the heavens in a straight line, the reason being that he would then leave a void." The condemnation led late scholastic thinkers to consider how Aristotelian physics and cosmology might be reconciled with the possible existence of vacua within the world or actual existence of void beyond its limits. The speculations of the late scholastics about how a body would move were it placed in a void foreshadowed the counterfactual speculations GALILEO and NEWTON engaged in when formulating the concept of inertial motion.

However, the difficulties the ancient Greek philosophers had with the notions of void and with space conceived as something distinct from body continued to be felt, particularly in rationalist quarters. Appealing to reasoning in the spirit of Parmenides and Melissus (that empty space is nothing, and nothing cannot exist), Descartes identified space with body, holding, on one hand, that bodies just are shaped and movable pieces of space (*Principles of Philosophy* II.4) and, on the other, that space is body, so that there can be no such thing as empty space (*Principles* II.18).

Descartes' equation of body with space was later rejected by Leibniz, Newton, and LOCKE, all of whom claimed that body has to possess impenetrability, repulsive force, or solidity. This view entailed that space must be at least conceptually distinct from body (since space would be a penetrable extension, and body an impenetrable one). At this point the notion of space as a container, distinct from bodies and permeating them, was arguably first forged, though the question of whether space could exist apart from body continued to be hotly debated.

Leibniz maintained that our concept of space is abstracted from the RELA-TIONS of place observed among coexisting bodies. On this view, were there no relatively placed coexisting bodies, there would be no space, so that pure space is merely an idea formed by abstracting the relations of placement from the bodies that exhibit those relations (Fifth Letter to Clarke, PP47).

Earlier, Descartes' contemporary GASSENDI had maintained that space is neither SUBSTANCE nor accident nor idea but a special kind of incorporeal nature that, like a substance, exists independently of being conceived and independently of other substances and their properties or relations.

The opposed views of Gassendi and Leibniz can be referred to as substantivalist and relationist, respectively. Initially, both sides of the debate between substantivalists and relationists were carried out largely by appeal to a priori considerations (see A PRIORI/A POSTERIORI DISTINCTION). While some attempted to defend Gassendi's position on the independent existence of space empirically, by appeal to experiments with suction pumps and barometers, the results were open to rival interpretation and so not convincing. Moreover, even if an empty space exists at the top of a barometric tube, it is still perceived and located relatively to surrounding bodies, so it remains open to the relationist to maintain that were there no bodies, there would be no space, empty or full. Alternatively, even if a vacuum cannot be created, it remains open to the substantivalist to claim that this is merely because the forces of nature will not allow the evacuation of a space, not because space cannot in principle exist apart from body.

But while the question of the actual existence of empty space might have little bearing on the dispute between substantivalists and relationists, another question, concerning the existence of absolute space, does have significant bearing on this dispute. Absolute space is space conceived as the ultimate reference frame for motion. The view that there is an absolute space is opposed to relativism, the view that all motion is relative to other bodies. Relativism is obviously consonant with relationism, the former holding that were there no other bodies, there would be no motion, and the latter that were there no bodies whatsoever, there would be no space. But absolutism is inimical to relationism, for if a body can be supposed to be in motion relative to space itself, independently of reference to other bodies, then space is being treated not as a relation but as something that *stands in* relation to other things, hence, as something substantival.

Thought about the relational or substantival nature of space was revolutionized when, in the Scholium to Definition 8 of his *Principia*, Newton offered an apparently empirical argument for the existence of absolute, and so of substantival, space. Newton observed that if all motion were relative, it would make no difference whether one took a given body to be in motion with respect to certain others or rather took those others to be in motion at the same speed in the opposite direction and the given body to be at rest. But, he claimed, this is not in fact the case. There is a fact of the matter about whether, say, the earth rotates or the heavens do or whether a bucket of water is rotating relative to certain landmarks or whether, rather, these landmarks are rotating relative to it. For if the water is really rotating, the water will rise up the sides of the bucket as its parts endeavor to recede from the axis of motion due to centrifugal force, whereas if the bucket is at rest, and the landmarks are rotating in the opposite direction, the water will stay flat. Thus, there are "force effects" present in bodies when they change speed or direction, and the presence of these effects is proof that those bodies are really (or, as Newton put it, "absolutely") in motion.

But, Newton proceeded to observe, motion is change of place. If there are real or absolute motions that can be said to occur independently of any reference to a relation to landmark bodies, then there must be real or absolute places that are where they are independently of any reference to landmark bodies and with reference to which accelerating bodies must be said to be changing speed or direction. These absolute places constitute absolute space. Moreover, since this absolute space can be supposed to exist independently of reference to the extension of bodies or the relations of landmarks, it is not dependent on body but can exist on its own, and it could be, at least in principle, empty.

Despite this argument, the Newtonian conception of space did not gain universal acceptance. Initially, the strongest opposition came from what might be called the "rationalist" camp and from Leibniz in particular. Leibniz's main objections to Newton's position on space and time were that it violates the principles of sufficient reason and the identity of indiscernibles. In a limitless, substantival space God would have had no sufficient reason to create the universe where it is rather than three feet to the left or earlier rather than later. Were space absolute, it would be possible for the entire universe to be in uniform, rectilinear motion through absolute space. But a universe in such motion does not differ from one at rest, so by the principle of the identity of indiscernibles, the two must be identical, contrary to the hypothesis.

Leibniz is less clear in response to Newton's "bucket experiment"—as was almost every other critic of Newton of the period other than KANT. Kant claimed that the bucket experiment demonstrates only that we must accept a distinction between true and apparent motion, not one between absolute and relative motion (*Kant's gesammelte Schriften* IV 560–63). A body is said to be in true motion insofar as it is acted upon by a moving force, and, according to Kant, we can think that certain bodies are in "true" motion without having to invoke absolute space. In the case where the water moves up the sides of the bucket, we say there is true motion, but we do not say this because we suppose that the parts of the water are changing place in absolute space but because there is a *relative* motion of the parts of the water away from a common axis. This particular kind of relative motion indicates that there is a moving force acting on the water, rather than on its surroundings, and this is all that is required to establish the distinction that the bucket experiment calls for.

The most influential challenge to the Newtonian concept of space in the early modern period came neither from Leibniz nor Kant but from Pierre Bayle. In the article on Zeno of Elea in his *Dictionnaire Historique et Critique*, Bayle revived the paradoxes of motion and extension propounded by Parmenides' disciple Zeno and used them to attack the intelligibility of space. Bayle's conclusion, that the concept of space is so deeply incoherent that no such thing could exist, except, perhaps, as an idea in the mind, influenced BERKELEY and HUME and gave comfort to Leibniz in his fight with the Newtonians. His arguments were repeated in the second of the four "antinomies" discussed in Kant's *Critique of Pure Reason* and arguably led Kant to develop his view of space and time as forms of sensory intuition.

One of the most surprising facets of the reception of the Newtonian conception of space is that the attacks did not come merely from rationalist quarters. In the early eighteenth century the traditional allegiance between empiricists and those advocating void, absolute, or substantival space broke down. Newtonian substantival space came to be perceived as a piece of vestigial, metaphysical baggage that had to be tossed out of a purely empiricistic account of the world and replaced with (ironically) a relationist account of just the sort advocated by Leibniz. The instigator of this revolution was George Berkeley.

Berkeley's opposition to Newtonian space was based on the empiricist principle that all meaningful terms must ultimately name some sensory experience (see VERIFICATION PRINCIPLE, MEANING). Berkeley insisted that an independently subsisting space is not an object of sensory experience. No space could ever be experienced apart from visual or kinesthetic qualities such as color or the free motion of the limbs (*Principles of Human Knowledge* §§9–15 and *Dialogues between Hylas and Philonous* I). In a striking passage, he rejected the ideas of absolute and substantival space as so refined and ABSTRACT as to be virtually meaningless.

And so let us suppose that all bodies were destroyed and brought to nothing. What is left they call absolute space. . . . That space is infinite, immovable, indivisible, insensible, without relation and without distinction. That is, all its attributes are privative or negative. It seems therefore to be mere nothing. The only slight difficulty arising is that it is extended and extension is a positive quality. But what sort of extension, I ask, is that which cannot be divided nor measured, no part of which can be perceived by sense or pictured by the imagination? . . . From absolute space then let us take away now the words of the name, and nothing will remain. . . . Such an idea . . . I find to be the purest idea of nothing, if indeed it can be called an idea. (*De Motu* §§54–55)

Berkeley's challenge to specify what space is, given that all the terms used to describe it are negative or privative, is one that Newton could answer by maintaining that space is the reference frame with respect to which inertial forces operate. This is not a reply that Berkeley handles very well (*Principles* §114; *De Motu* §§63–64).

However, later empiricists made up for the deficiency. Ernst MACH famously observed that the bucket experiment is not an empirical experiment at all but a thought experiment. When we observe the water rise against the sides of the bucket, we do so in this world, against the backdrop provided by the fixed stars and with huge masses of matter surrounding us. We have no way of knowing for sure what we would observe were we enabled to adopt a vantage point outside this galaxy and observe the entire galaxy being rotated while the bucket is held stationary. Perhaps then the water would rise as well. Or perhaps, if we stayed on the earth and watched the bucket rotate relative to the fixed stars, but its walls were ten miles thick, the water would fail to rise. Perhaps it would also fail to rise if the universe were completely empty of everything but the bucket and the water. Mach accordingly drew the positivist conclusion (see LOGICAL POSITIVISM) that the most we can know is that inertial forces operate relative to the fixed stars, not relative to absolute space.

While the substantivalist/relationist and absolutist/relativist issues have continued to figure in more recent thought about space and space-time (despite its name, the theory of relativity does not necessarily enjoin a relationist view of space-time), the question of which side in these disputes is implied by empiricist commitments has grown increasingly muddied. A different issue has come to have more immediate relevance to empiricists: the status of geometrical principles (see MATHEMATICS). This issue first became acute when Kant famously argued that the principles of geometry are neither trivial, analytic truths nor propositions established by experience but are both nontrivial and a priori, thus attacking the empiricist ANALYTIC/SYNTHETIC DISTINCTION.

The nineteenth-century discovery of non-Euclidean geometries allowed empiricists such as Mach and Hermann von HELMHOLTZ to argue that Kant had been wrong about the a priori status of geometry. If there is not just one geometry, but many, it becomes a question which correctly describes space, and this is a question that is to be resolved by experience, not a priori.

However, this position was challenged at the turn of the century by Poincaré, who argued for a thesis that has since come to be called geometrical conventionalism. By means of an ingenious example, Poincaré showed that, even if physical measurements were to uncover apparent violations of Euclidean principles, it would be open to us to maintain that there are certain universal forces operating to distort our measuring instruments. Thus, there may be no fact of the matter about which geometry (in combination with a theory of the operation of universal forces) correctly describes space, and, if that is so, then it is open to us to simply pick one—perhaps on the basis of such neo-Kantian considerations as what we find most simple or elegant, given the constitution of our knowing powers.

A standard empiricist response to conventionalism, classically offered by Hans REICHENBACH, has been to raise the verificationist claim that there is no meaningful difference between a theory that postulates the existence of a "flat" (Euclidean) space together with forces that distort the length of measuring rods over large distances and a theory that postulates a curved space together with nondistorting forces. Both theories are merely alternative ways of describing the same observed facts and make no meaningful or significant claims beyond predicting and describing these facts.

The issues that arise in this connection—of whether observation can be neatly distinguished from theory, of the underdetermination of theory by observation, of the verification principle of meaning, and of INSTRUMENTALISM, OPERATIONISM, and positivism—have made discussions of the nature of space and space-time one of the prime test cases for current thought about empiricism in the philosophy of science.

PRIMARY WORKS

Aristotle. *Physics* IV 1–9. In *The Complete Works of Aristotle*, vol. 1, edited by Jonathan Barnes. Princeton: Princeton University Press, 1984.

Berkeley, George. *De Motu, Principles of Human Knowledge*, and *Three Dialogues between Hylas and Philonous*. In *The Works of George Berkeley, Bishop of Cloyne*. Edited by A. A. Luce and T. E. Jessop. 9 vols. London: Thomas Nelson and Sons, 1948–1957.

Descartes, René. *Principles of Philosophy*. In *The Philosophical Writings of Descartes*, vol. 1, edited by John Cottingham, Robert Stoothoff, and Dugald Murdoch. Cambridge: Cambridge University Press, 1985.

Gassendi, Pierre. *Syntagma Philosophicum*. In *The Selected Works of Pierre Gassendi*. Translated by Craig B. Brush. New York: Johnson Reprint Corporation, 1972: Physics, Section I, Book II.

Helmholtz, Hermann von. ''The Origin and Meaning of Geometric Axioms.'' In *Selected Writings of Hermann von Helmholtz*. Edited by Russell Kahl. Middletown, CT: Wesleyan University Press, 1971.

Kant, Immanuel. *Kant's gesammelte Schriften*. Edited by the Königlichen (later Deutschen) Akademie der Wissenschaften. Berlin: Georg Reimer (later Walter de Gruyer). 1990–.

Kirk, G. S., J. E. Raven, and M. Schofield. *The Presocratic Philosophers*, 2d. ed. Cambridge: Cambridge University Press, 1983. These authors use the fragment numbers established by Hermann Diels and Walther Kranz in *Die Fragmente der Vorsokratiker* (Berlin: Weidmann, 1960).

Leibniz, Gottfried Wilhelm, and Samuel Clarke. *The Leibniz–Clarke Correspondence*. Edited by H. G. Alexander. Manchester: Manchester University Press, 1956.

Mach, Ernst. *The Science of Mechanics*. 6th ed. Translated by Thomas J. McCormack. LaSalle, IL: Open Court, 1960: Chapter 2, Section VI.

Newton, Isaac. *Principia Mathematica* Scholium to Definition VIII and General Scholium to Book III. In *Sir Isaac Newton's Mathematical Principles of Natural Philosophy*, 2 vols., translated by Florian Cajori. Berkeley: University of California Press, 1934.

Plato. *Timaeus*, in *The Collected Dialogues of Plato*, edited by Edith Hamilton and Huntington Cairns. Princeton: Princeton University Press, 1961.

Reichenbach, Hans. *The Philosophy of Space and Time*. Translated by Maria Reichenbach and John Freund. New York: Dover, 1958.

BIBLIOGRAPHY

Grant, Edward. *Much Ado about Nothing: Theories of Space and Vacuum from the*

Middle Ages to the Scientific Revolution. Cambridge: Cambridge University Press, 1981.

Sklar, Lawrence. *Space, Time, and Spacetime.* Berkeley: University of California Press, 1974.

LORNE FALKENSTEIN

SPACE COGNITION. Theories of space cognition have traditionally been divided into just two camps: the empirist, which seeks to show that our knowledge of space is obtained from experience, and the nativist (see INNATENESS), which argues that experience is inadequate to yield this knowledge and that innate ideas or innate abilities must be invoked to explain how it arises. (The term "empirist" is used in preference to "empiricist" because we are not here dealing with an account of the *justification* for our claims about space [for that, see SPACE] but one of the *origin* of our ability to perceive the world in spatial terms.)

However, a second dispute cuts across the empirist and nativist camps. This is the dispute between intuitionists, who believe that our knowledge of space is direct or immediate, and constructivists, who believe that it arises only through cognitive processing of more primitive data. The issue is further complicated by the fact that space cognition is a complex activity that can be broken down into a number of simpler performances: localization, pattern recognition, distance perception, perception of size constancy, eye–hand coordination, and more. One can be an empirist or nativist, intuitionist or constructivist about some of these processes but not others.

The only significant account of space cognition to be developed in the ancient Greek world was that of ARISTOTLE, but it defined the terms in which research has been conducted ever since. Aristotle was perhaps the first to distinguish between two levels of perceptual activity, later referred to as sensation (see SENSATIONALISM) and PERCEPTION.

The former treats of the physiological processes leading to production of the most primitive elements of our conscious experience, often called sensations or the sensory core. The latter deals with the subsequent processing of sensations— with their retention in memory, their modification by IMAGINATION, their integration by a "common sense" (which is not really a "sense" but a perceptual function), their ASSOCIATION by an "estimative power," and their ABSTRACTION by intellect. These latter processes are often referred to as cognitive processes and are taken to involve acts of judgment. Sensation, in contrast, does not involve judgment (though it may involve attention and oversight).

Aristotle further distinguished the data that are specifically delivered through physiological stimulation of each of the sense organs, which he referred to as "proper sensibles," from the "common sensibles." Spatial features, like figure and magnitude, are included among the common sensibles.

It was a feature of Aristotle's theory that sensation and perception occur when the matter of the sense organ (and, in turn, of common sense, memory, and imagination) takes on the form of the object and so ''becomes'' the object. With the demise of Aristotelian hylemorphic metaphysics and its replacement by corpuscularian and mechanistic accounts of nature in the early modern period, this account lost its metaphysical underpinnings. Early modern theories of perception retained Aristotle's distinction between proper and common sensibles but reinterpreted it as a distinction between those IDEAS that do not, and those that do, represent the real world of shaped particles in motion (see PRIMARY AND SECONDARY QUALITIES).

According to Descartes, our ideas of extension in general are innate ideas, not obtained from sensation (as the argument from the wax in *Meditations* II notoriously claims) but knowable by a ''clear and distinct perception'' on the part of the intellect alone. However, even for Descartes, our knowledge of exactly how extension in general is divided into the particular, figured, and moving bodies that exist in the world requires sense experience. This experience is not always reliable (e.g., it represents the sun as being only a few feet in diameter), but without it we would be at a loss to know particulars.

Sense experience occurs when objects in the external world hit the sense organs, causing motions in the attached nerves. These motions are communicated to the brain, where they are combined in the common sense, stored in the memory, and/or imprinted on the pineal gland. Motions on the pineal gland are the occasion of the formation of ''ideas of sense'' by the mind. These ideas include both those of extension and its modes and those of qualities like color. Descartes supposed that neither set of ideas resembles its physical cause (the motions on the pineal gland) in any way, though those of extension and its modes may resemble the external objects that originally affected the sense organ.

Where vision is concerned, Descartes followed a theory originally propounded by Euclid, according to which our ideas of magnitude vary with the size of the angle subtended by light rays coming from the ends of the object and intersecting at the eye, and those of shape correspond to the pattern imprinted by light on the retina. This theory has no ready account to provide for the perception of depth or size constancy, since the lines of vision may be of any length, and the same object can subtend the different angles at different distances. Descartes accordingly accepted that our spatial sensations are only two-dimensional. In his *Dioptrics* he identified various processes that the mind subsequently performs to construct ideas of relations in the third dimension. Some of these processes are explicitly described as involving innate mechanisms (AT VI 137–40). Thus, in addition to invoking innate ideas of extension in general, Descartes postulated innate perceptual mechanisms to add depth to our immediate sensations of the spatial features of particulars.

LOCKE accepted the general Cartesian picture of ideas as effects on the mind of corpuscular motions induced in the body, as well as Descartes' distinction between those ideas that can, and those that cannot, be taken to represent the features of bodies. But he rejected the nativist elements of Descartes' program.

For Locke, our ideas of space and extension are obtained only through the senses. He did not delve into the details of how space cognition occurs, but he did attack the notion that our ideas of space and its modes are common sensibles. The point was suggested to him by William Molyneux, who asked him to consider whether a person blind since birth and suddenly made to see would be able to tell a cube apart from a sphere without first touching them. Both Locke and Molyneux thought that the way a space feels to the touch is so different from the way it looks to the eye that the answer would have to be no (*An Essay concerning Human Understanding* II.ix.8).

The implications of a negative answer to this "Molyneux question" were far-reaching—perhaps farther-reaching than Locke himself realized. If there are distinct visual and tangible spaces, and we are not born knowing which visual shapes go with which tangible shapes, then Cartesian nativism about extension must be wrong—there cannot be an "intelligible extension" to which we have innate access via clear and distinct perception. But even more seriously, if there is no such thing as space distinct from either visual sensible qualities, on one hand, or tangible ones, on the other, then how can there be a real world of corpuscles that are in space and possess "primary qualities" but do not have color or tactile qualities? If there were such a space, would it not have to be a third and as yet unconceived (and inconceivable?) entity, as different from the visual and tangible spaces of our experience as they are from one another?

It is but a small step from this last realization (a step mediated by an attack on the ability to form abstract ideas of pure space) to BERKELEY's idealism, which has as one of its central premises the claim that sensible qualities exist only when perceived and that space (and therefore objects in space) cannot be conceived apart from sensible qualities.

Berkeley also attacked Descartes' acceptance of innate mechanisms in the theory of vision. Whereas Descartes had claimed that we get ideas of depth "as if by an innate geometry" from the angles at which the eyes must be turned to bring the lines of sight to converge on the object, Berkeley argued that it is neither by an innately determined response nor by calculation from the angles of convergence of the lines of vision (which are in any case themselves invisible) that we come to perceive depth. Rather we learn by experience to associate certain degrees of strain in the ocular muscles with certain tangible measures, like how far we must reach or how long we must walk in order to touch an object, and afterward we associate this degree of strain with a particular tangible distance. Berkeley went on to identify a number of other such associative mechanisms responsible for our perception of depth, size constancy, orientation, and the coordination of visual with tangible space.

Whereas Berkeley's idealism never gained any adherents, this empirist and constructivist theory of vision was immediately and enthusiastically accepted. It is important to note, however, that there are limits to what Berkeley achieved. He did not consider how we come to localize objects and their parts on the two-dimensional field of view, and it remains a question whether he was not forced to consider two-dimensional visual spatial relations to be immediately sensed, rather than inferred.

Berkeley's empirist successors aimed to rectify this omission. Among other devices, one proved to be particularly fruitful, both of research projects and of controversies: Rudolf Hermann Lotze postulated that localization might be effected through reference to what were called "local signs" or "nerve signatures." According to this theory, our visual sensations exhibit peculiar, purely qualitative characteristics that are specific to the nerve that is being affected. (Compare how in the case of touch we are aware whether it is the nerves in the hand or the foot that are being affected, even though the sensation coming from each may be identical.)

One of the major subjects of controversy for visual theorists of the nineteenth century was whether we learn by experience to associate particular nerve signatures with particular locations in space or whether we are innately so constituted that particular nerve signatures are automatically interpreted as signifying locations. The empirists, among them HELMHOLTZ, MACH, Wundt, James and John Stuart MILL, and Bain, opted for the former alternative; those who opted for the latter, most notably Hering, were called "nativists." Empirical evidence, such as the speed with which previously blind patients were able to acquire the ability to localize objects, played a large role on both sides of the debate. But, as is so often the case, sufficiently ingenious theorists were able to preserve their positions in the face of recalcitrant experimental results. Wundt and Helmholtz postulated that the speed with which the previously blind are able to localize objects might be due to the fact that the local signs exhibit degrees of similarity and difference, like colors. If the local signs from the most closely adjacent nerves are also the most similar in quality, the process of learning their order could be greatly abbreviated.

However, not all critiques of the Berkeleian paradigm were "nativist" in Hering's sense. William James was far more critical of the constructivist aspect of Berkeley's paradigm than the empirist aspect. James (like Locke at *Essay* II.xiii.2–3) took a primitive kind of spatiality or "voluminousness" to be immediately evident in our sensations, prior to association or any other cognitive activity. Though the rhetoric of his day was so overpowering that he himself believed this position to have affinities with Hering's nativism (as if all the opponents of Berkeleianism had to be collected together in a single "nativist" camp), there is nothing nativist in supposing that space is given as a quality of sensations. This position is more aptly described as intuitionistic empirism or sensationalism.

Another example of a response to Berkeley that does not fit the traditional categories can be found earlier, in the mid-eighteenth century, in Thomas REID's account of vision. Reid accepted Berkeley's constructivist accounts of depth, size constancy, and orientation. But he completely undercut the latter's empirism with a nativist account of the origin of the immediate objects of vision. According to Reid, the immediate objects of vision are concave, two-dimensional figures that are not given in sensation but rather are the intentional objects of beliefs that have been "suggested" to us by physiological effects on the retina. We are innately so constituted that the occurrence of these effects leads us to form beliefs in the sorts of objects that generally tend to cause them—or, more exactly, in the sorts of images those objects project on the back of the retina. This is an intuitionist nativism, quite different in character from Hering's constructivist nativism. For Hering the immediate objects of vision are not already spatial in character, though they do exhibit qualitative "nerve signatures" that we are innately disposed to interpret as signifying locations in space. But for Reid the datum that first arises in consciousness already carries information about space. Reid was explicit, however, that this datum is not a sensation, as it was for James, but an innate perception.

The cases of James and Reid are examples of two kinds of *intuitionist* response to Berkeley. Both take space, or at least certain very primitive spatial features such as two-dimensional layout, to be present in the immediate objects of vision. James' intuitionism is sensationist (and hence empirist) in character, whereas Reid's is nativist.

There are two other intuitionist positions on space cognition in the eighteenth-century literature, and these are even more unorthodox than those of Reid and James. They were formulated by HUME and KANT. To appreciate them it is necessary to first note that all of the theories of space cognition so far considered, from Aristotle right down to James, have tacitly accepted that cognition is of SUBSTANCES or their properties. Those who accept this view have a special problem dealing with RELATIONS, especially with spatiotemporal relations, which must be somehow reduced to properties or substances. Berkeley's theory of vision and the later developments of the theory of local signs attempt to account for spatial relations as products of association of individual mental representations. James' sensationism and Reid's "innate ideas nativism" attempt to identify space with the properties of individual mental representations (or of their intentional objects). All of these approaches attempt to do away with spatial relations by reducing them to something else.

Elsewhere, I have argued that HUME and KANT reject this entire paradigm and instead maintain that spatial relations are directly and immediately sensed. According to them, the immediate objects of sensory experience do not just consist of a collection of sensations. They consist of a collection of sensations *presented in a certain order*. This order of presentation, which Hume called the "manner of disposition" of impressions (*A Treatise of Human Nature* I.ii.3), and Kant called their "form of intuition" (*Critique of Pure Reason* A20/B34) is the original datum from which our ideas or concepts of space are drawn.

For Hume, the manner of disposition is simply a brute fact of the way impressions are given, so his "formal intuitionism" is empirist in character. For Kant, the form of intuition is supposed to be grounded on the constitution of our receptor system. Thus, Kant's "formal intuitionism" is nativist in character, though this nativism (where what is innate is the capacity for receiving data in a certain order) has as little in common with Reid's nativism (where what is innate is a perception) or Hering's (where what is innate is a mechanism for processing previously received data) as it does with most forms of empirism.

One of the features that characterize such minority recent accounts of perception as Gestalt theory and Gibson's "ecological approach" is an increased sensitivity to the possibility that the "sensory core" may also consist of more than just sensations but may also consist of relations—that, in effect (and as Gibson has insisted), the traditional distinction between sensation and perception may be illegitimate. However the current debate between Gibsonian intuitionism and more traditional constructivism plays itself out, the cases of Hume and Kant, James and Reid, and Helmholtz and Hering indicate that one can envision either nativist or empirist variants. Where space cognition is concerned, the fault lines between the core disputes and between empirism and its opponents run orthogonal to one another, so that it is impossible to characterize a standard empirist approach to these matters.

PRIMARY WORKS

Aristotle. *On the Soul* (De Anima) II and III. In *The Complete Works of Aristotle*, vol. 1, edited by Jonathan Barnes. Princeton: Princeton University Press, 1984.

Berkeley, George. *New Theory of Vision* and *Theory of Vision Vindicated and Explained.* In *The Works of George Berkeley, Bishop of Cloyne.* Edited by A. A. Luce and T. E. Jessop. 9 vols. London: Thomas Nelson and Sons, 1948–1957.

Descartes, René. *Optics* (Dioptrics) VI and *Meditations* VI. In *The Philosophical Writings of Descartes*, vols. 1 and 2, translated by John Cottingham, Robert Stoothoff, and Dugald Murdoch. Cambridge: Cambridge University Press, 1984–1985.

Helmholtz, Hermann von. "Recent Progress in the Theory of Vision." In *Selected Writings of Hermann von Helmholtz.* Edited by Russell Kahl. Middletown, CT: Wesleyan University Press, 1971.

Hume, David. *A Treatise of Human Nature*, 2d ed., edited with an an analytical index by L. A. Selby-Bigge; revised with notes by P. H. Nidditch. Oxford: Clarendon Press, 1978.

James, William. *The Principles of Psychology.* Vol. 2, Chapter 20. New York: Henry Holt, 1890.

Kant, Immanuel. *Critique of Pure Reason.* Edited and translated by Norman Kemp Smith. New York: St. Martin's Press, 1965.

Locke, John. *An Essay concerning Human Understanding.* Edited with an introduction by P. H. Nidditch. Oxford: Clarendon Press, 1975.

Reid, Thomas. *Inquiry into the Human Mind.* Chapter 6. In *Philosophical Works*, vol. 1, edited by William Hamilton. Reprint edition. Hildesheim: Olms, 1967.

BIBLIOGRAPHY

Boring, Edwin. *A History of Experimental Psychology.* 2d ed. New York: Appleton-Century-Crofts, 1950.

Hatfield, Gary. *The Natural and the Normative: Theories of Spatial Perception from Kant to Helmholtz.* Cambridge: MIT Press, 1990.

Pastore, Nicholas. *Selective History of Theories of Visual Perception 1650–1950.* New York: Oxford University Press, 1971.

Schwartz, Robert. *Vision. Variations on Some Berkeleian Themes.* Cambridge: Blackball, 1994.

LORNE FALKENSTEIN

STEWART, DUGALD. Dugald Stewart (1753–1828), according to S. A. Grave, gave the commonsense philosophy of Thomas REID the "dignity of an institution." Stewart certainly deserves much credit for the widespread popularity of Reid's philosophy. However, it is not often appreciated that he made significant contributions of his own to the tradition, especially in the areas of metaphilosophy, philosophy of science, aesthetics, and agency theory.

BIOGRAPHY

Stewart was born in Edinburgh, where his father was professor of mathematics at the university, and he spent his early years there and at the family home in Ayrshire. He attended Edinburgh University starting in 1765 and studied under John Stevenson, professor of logic and metaphysics, and Adam FERGUSON, who held the chair of moral philosophy from 1764 to 1785. At the urging of Ferguson, Stewart went to the University of Glasgow in 1771 to study under Reid. He wholeheartedly endorsed Reid's philosophy, even though his time there was brief; he returned to Edinburgh in 1772 to take over classes in mathematics for his ailing father. Stewart continued as professor of mathematics at Edinburgh until 1785, when he was appointed to the chair of moral philosophy. When his son George died in 1809, Stewart retired from his teaching duties, although he retained his chair jointly with Thomas Brown until 1820.

Stewart retired to Kinneil House, Linlithgowshire, where he devoted his time to writing. During this period most of his work was completed. Prior to his retirement he had published the first volume of the *Elements of the Philosophy of the Human Mind* (1792) and *Outlines of Moral Philosophy* (1793) and presented an "Account of the Life and Writings" of Adam SMITH (1795), William Robertson (1801), and Reid (1803) to the Royal Society of Edinburgh. After retiring, he published volumes 2 and 3 of the *Elements* in 1814 and 1827, respectively; *Philosophical Essays* in 1810; part one of the *Dissertation* in 1815; and part two in 1821. *Philosophy of the Active and Moral Powers of Man* was published just weeks before his death in 1828.

METAPHYSICS AND METAPHILOSOPHY

Following the lead of Reid, the commonsense philosophers believed that certain concepts such as SPACE and TIME cannot be generated from experience. LOCKE understood the importance of the concepts but mistakenly believed they could be obtained through experience. The Scottish realists held that these concepts come from the input of the intellect itself. Space, for instance, is not directly experienced through the senses but is a presupposition of our having experience of any object. If objects exist, then there must be space in which they exist. Thus, concepts such as space come not from experience but from our constitution.

The preceding serves as the foundation for Reid's principles of common sense. These principles are either evident or self-evident and require no justification. Any proposition that denies one of these principles is rejected out of hand, since it is always more likely that the premises of an argument that attempts to undercut them are false rather than that the evident or self-evident ones are mistaken. Denying these principles of common sense leads to absurd consequences, and the job of the philosopher is to show the premise that yields the absurd conclusion. The idealism of BERKELEY and the SKEPTICISM of Hume are good examples of the absurd conclusions some philosophers accept. According to Reid, their reasoning is good, yet we have conclusions that are unacceptable to the principles of common sense. They erred in accepting the premise of Descartes and Locke that we are directly aware of sensations or ideas instead of the objects themselves.

Not all commonsense beliefs count as principles of common sense. In order to be a genuine principle certain criteria must be met. Following from the evident or self-evident nature of these principles is the fact that they will be universally held, since we all have the same nativistic epistemic input. They will also be unavoidable—it is pointless to deny one of these principles since one cannot help but act as if it were true. Hume may call in question our ability to know necessary connections, but in practice he cannot help but act like everyone else who believes that one event necessarily produces another.

Stewart and the other commonsense philosophers were empiricists, but in a different way than were the British Empiricists. The commonsense philosophers were influenced by BACON and believed that in SCIENCE we reach laws by generalization rather than hypotheses. Thus, the method of INDUCTION came to be important not only in science but also for their philosophy of mind. However, experience was not the only component necessary for knowledge—a nativistic epistemic component is also essential. Thus, Stewart's form of empiricism is opposed to both rationalism and British empiricism. It is contrary to rationalism because knowledge had to be activated by empirical events. The nativistic concept of space is not activated until we perceive an actual object that has to be seen in space. There is no knowledge without the empirical dimension. However, that is not to say that all we know comes from sensation and PERCEPTION. Along with the experience is the nativistic element provided by the understanding.

Any number of examples might be given to illustrate the nativistic input of the intellect, but the following should suffice to provide the framework. Hume's argument against any knowledge of the self is centered upon our inability to experience it. Without that direct experience we can, Hume concluded, make no knowledge claim regarding its existence. Put simply, we have no empirical grounds for asserting the existence of self. Stewart concurred with Hume that we have no direct experience of self but came to a different conclusion. Stewart argued that we are conscious of sensation, volition, thought, and so on but are not directly conscious of mind or self. However, the experience of these activities is the occasion for the intellect to provide knowledge of the self who experiences the sensations. Stewart wrote:

The moment that, in consequence of such an impression, a sensation is excited, we learn two facts at once;—the existence of the sensation, and our own existence as sentient beings;—in other words, the very first exercise of consciousness necessarily implies a belief, not only of the present existence of what is felt, but of the present existence of *that* which feels and thinks; or (to employ plainer language) the present existence of that being which I denote by the words *I* and *myself*. (*Collected Works* II: 42)

Stewart endorsed Reid's framework and the principles of common sense but criticized Reid's use of the term "common sense." "Common sense" for Reid had a technical meaning—his principles were essentially synthetic a priori, since they arise from the nativistic epistemic input of the understanding. Stewart believed that "common sense" as it is ordinarily used indicated a kind of practical judgment well suited to the affairs of daily living. The unhappy consequence of Reid's use of "common sense" was that many believed the commonsense philosophy allowed the opinion of the multitude to dictate to the philosopher. Stewart preferred to call these principles "fundamental laws of human belief." Others in the tradition followed Stewart's lead and used descriptions such as "common consciousness" or "basic intuitions."

Reid and his followers, then, believed that any proposition that contravened common sense could be dismissed, since it is always more likely that the discursive philosophical argument that undercuts it is mistaken than it is that an evident or self-evident belief is false. However, Stewart argued that this aspect of Reid's metaphilosophy was not sufficient. Berkeley, after all, claimed that his views were compatible in every way with common sense. Any ordinary proposition about objects has the same truth-value whether the object is understood as a physical object that exists apart from a perceiver or as a group of sensations. Thus, Stewart argued that Berkeley must have violated common sense by using a meaning contrary to the ordinary one. If we carefully analyze the word "existence," we find "not only that we are irresistibly led to ascribe to the material world all the independent reality which this word expresses, but that it is from the material world that our first and most satisfactory notions of *existence* are drawn" (*Works* III: 54). So Stewart claimed that any philosophical analysis must not violate either the truth-value of ordinary propositions or the meanings of terms.

PHILOSOPHY OF SCIENCE

Stewart studied mathematics and physics while a student at Edinburgh and held the chair of mathematics there for ten years. This provided him with the necessary tools for work in the philosophy of science. Of all the Scottish realists, only James McCosh surpassed Stewart's acumen in this area. (Stewart's philosophy of science can be found in the *Works* III: 230–357.) One particularly interesting aspect of Stewart's work is the tension that resulted from being drawn in opposing directions. The tradition stressed the inductive method and believed science was extrapolation from empirical fact. It took literally NEWTON's "hypotheses non fingo." Reid held that hypotheses are virtually useless and maintained a rigid inductivism. Stewart knew physics well, and he was drawn to the mechanics of Boscovich, which were based on a hypothetico-deductive system. Thus, Stewart, as part of the commonsense tradition, claimed that hypotheses should be used only as heuristic devices, but in reality he had accepted Boscovich's doctrines, which violated this view.

AESTHETICS

Many of the Scottish realists—and Stewart was no exception—wrote on aesthetics (see volume 5 of the *Works*). The most interesting part of Stewart's work occurs in his discussion of BEAUTY. He argued that beauty has no unifying essence, and we cannot, therefore, provide a definition to say what beauty is. Suppose that we have five objects—A, B, C, D, and E. A may be like B, and both can be beautiful; B like C, and again both beautiful; C like D, and both beautiful, and so on. However, it is not necessary that they be deemed beautiful for the same reason or even alike for the same reason. This analysis of beauty is interesting for two reasons. The first is that Stewart's treatment of this concept is different from his analysis of other concepts in epistemology or the philosophy of science. The second is that Stewart's argument is suggestive of the contemporary concept of family resemblances we find in Wittgenstein (*Philosophical Investigations*: 65–77). This notion was adapted to aesthetics by Maurice Mandelbaum in "Family Resemblances and Generalization concerning the Arts" (*American Philosophical Quarterly*, 1965). Instead of focusing on a definition of beauty, then, Stewart attempted to show how the concept of beauty has evolved over the centuries and how human perceptual and mental mechanisms have evolved, the first enterprise being naturalistic, and the other linguistic.

AGENCY THEORY

The Scottish realists were opposed to any form of determinism, and most adopted Reid's agency theory, agent causality. On this view, freedom is maintained by showing that the concept of cause is not applicable to human action. Motives do not necessitate actions but should be viewed as giving advice that the agent either accepts or rejects. Stewart supported Reid's view but suggested that there was a metaphysical component necessary in order to maintain freedom (see FREE WILL). Some argued that GOD's foreknowledge and freedom are incompatible. The commonsense philosophers generally claimed that there was no inconsistency. Stewart, however, suggested that they may be inconsistent, but he saw no reason to abandon freedom and embrace determinism. He wrote, "[I]f it could be demonstrated . . . that the prescience of the volitions of moral agents is incompatible with the Free-agency of man, the logical inference would be, *not* in favour of the scheme of Necessity, but that there are some events, the *foreknowledge of which implies an impossibility''* (*Works* VI: 398). If genuine possibilities remain until a decision is made, then there is nothing to be known by God until the agent chooses. Therefore God's omniscience is not in jeopardy.

Stewart played a crucial role in spreading the influence of the commonsense philosophy, especially in America, where this philosophy dominated for over sixty years. Besides being a superb lecturer, he was a clear writer whose books were enormously popular and used as texts more often than Reid's in American colleges. *Active and Moral Powers* was reprinted ten times between 1849 and 1868. In addition, Stewart added significantly to the tradition with points as relevant today as they were in the nineteenth century.

PRIMARY WORK

Stewart, Dugald. *The Collected Works of Dugald Stewart*. Edited by William Hamilton. 11 vols. Edinburgh: Thomas Constable, 1854–1860.

BIBLIOGRAPHY

Books

Grave, S. A. *Scottish Philosophy of Common Sense*. Oxford: Oxford University Press, 1960.
McCosh, James. *The Scottish Philosophy, Biographical, Expository, Critical, from Hutcheson to Hamilton*. London: Macmillan, 1874.
Olson, Richard. *Scottish Philosophy and British Physics, 1750–1880*. Princeton: Princeton University Press, 1975.
Wittgenstein, Ludwig. *Philosophical Investigations*. New York: Macmillan, 1953.

Article

Madden, Edward H. "Stewart's Enrichment of the Commonsense Tradition." *History of Philosophy Quarterly* 3 (1986): 45–63.

TODD L. ADAMS

STOICISM. The Stoic school was founded around 300 B.C. in Athens by Zeno of Citium (334–262). The school was named after the Stoa Poikile, a public hall in which Zeno and his disciples taught. At that time the Greek philosophical tradition was less than three centuries old. Socrates had been put to death one century before. Plato had been dead for five decades, ARISTOTLE for two. The city-states, the political foundation of Greek civilization in the classical period, had recently been reduced to the status of mere cities within the Hellenistic Empire, whose vast territory extended all the way to India. From this beginning, the Stoic school as both institution and movement developed and evolved until it began to fade away in the third century A.D. The long history of the school has been divided into three periods of early, middle, and late. Zeno, Cleanthes (331–232), and Chrysippus (c. 280–c. 206) represent the early period, during which basic Stoic theories were systematically set forth. Panaetius (c. 185–c.

110) and Posidonius (c. 135–c. 50 B.C.) represent the middle period, during which the earlier system was modified. Seneca (c. 2 B.C.–c. 65), Epictetus (c. A.D. 55–c. 135), and Marcus Aurelius (121–180) represent the final, Roman imperial period during, which the earlier interest in theorizing tended to yield to insistent moral exhortation.

Most of the original Stoic literature has been lost, and what little that remains is mostly in fragments. The fragments have been collected and arranged by von Arnim and, in a more accessible form, by Long and Sedley.

The following account of Stoicism deals first with philosophical influences upon Stoicism and then with the Stoic divisions of philosophy. Stoic epistemology, LOGIC, physics, and ETHICS are dealt with in that order. The entry concludes with a look at the influence of Stoicism upon the subsequent philosophical culture of Europe in general and British Empiricism in particular.

There are two sources of philosophical influence upon the formation of Stoicism, namely, the Stoics' predecessors and their contemporaries. The earlier Stoics were eclectic in developing their distinct system of thought. For philosophical inspiration, perspectives, doctrines, and conceptual apparatus they drew freely, though selectively, upon Heraclitus, Socrates, Plato, ARISTOTLE, the Megarians, and the Cynics. At the same time, they engaged in vigorous dialectic exchanges with the contemporary school of SKEPTICISM (see also SEXTUS EMPIRICUS) and Epicureanism (see EPICURUS). The Skeptics denied the knowability of the real nature of things and dismissed the Stoics for being dogmatic. The Epicureans held the constitution of the universe to consist exclusively of matter and the void (see MATERIALISM). Observation by means of the senses was the Epicurean foundation of KNOWLEDGE, and the hedonistic principle was the basis of Epicurean ethics. The challenges of these rival schools afforded the Stoics much philosophical stimulation and occasions for discipline and sophistication in their theory construction.

The Stoics divided philosophy and the philosophical curriculum into logic, physics, and ethics. Their division of logic included philosophy of language and epistemology as well as logic proper; that of physics included ontology, cosmology, and theology; and that of ethics included value theory, moral psychology, and political philosophy. For the Stoics these three divisions came together because the ethical end of living a reasoned life requires a reasoning mind fully in tune with the rational constitution of the universe, on one hand, and principles of rational discourse, on the other.

The Stoic epistemology is empiricist. There are no innate ideas or knowledge (see INNATENESS). The mind in its initial state is like an impressionable slab without impressions on it. External objects as they are sensed impress themselves upon the mind. CONCEPT formation results from the accumulation of particular types of impressions. This way of picturing the origin of knowledge, coupled with an analysis of definition, yields for the Stoics a conceptualist position on the issue of universals. Definition calls for no supramundane individual as definiendum. For a definition is just a handy way of summarizing conditional statements about the individuals subsumed under a concept: "[W]hoever says 'Man is a rational mortal animal' says the same thing in meaning as whoever says 'If something is a man, that being is a rational mortal animal' " (Long and Sedley I.30I). For the Stoics, the foundation of our knowledge of the universe, whose denizens are corporeal individuals, lies in a certain type of impression they call *kataleptikē*. Translated as "cognitive" by Long and Sedley, this term in this context literally means *enabling the mind to grasp the object*. The cognitive impression, which "arises from what is and is stamped and impressed exactly in accordance with what is [40C], reveals its object just as it is to the mind [40B]" (see PERCEPTION). Assent to the cognitive impression is cognition, while cognition secured is scientific knowledge.

Upon this self-authenticated epistemic foundation the scientist builds by reasonable conjecture as well as by valid inference. In this connection the Stoics faced a problem of INDUCTION, formulated it, and proposed a solution to it. Calling it a problem of "sign-inference," they formulated the problem as follows: when we infer from known cases to unknown ones, we are using the implicit hypothesis that the unknown is relevantly similar to the known. Let us therefore make this hypothesis explicit and build it into the inference, for example, "Since the men familiar to us are mortal, so too if there are elsewhere men resembling the men familiar to us . . . in respect of being mortal, they would be mortal" (42G3). This, however, strikes us as vacuously true. Eliminate the hypothesis then. But this alternative won't do either, for then the inference becomes invalid. To this problem the Stoics proposed the following solution: the sign-inference is valid if, and only if, the respect in which similarity is supposed is essential to the subject (see ESSENCE). For example, "Since the men familiar to us are mortal in that and insofar as they are men, men everywhere are mortal" (42G4). It remains to be established by empirical studies that human beings are indeed mortal *in that and insofar as* they are human beings. (This could not be done, objected the Epicureans, without smuggling in the sign-inference.) If, on the other hand, the respect in which similarity is supposed to hold is accidental to the subject, then the inference would have to be judged invalid. "After all, just because the men familiar to us are short-lived, we won't say that the Acrothoites are short-lived too!" (42G4). Some Stoics added that the conclusions of some such invalid inferences could still be probable. For, as the Stoics generally held, whatever is reasonably conjectured to be the case, albeit not known, is worthy of acceptance, or else "all life would surely be abolished" (42I).

Logic proper, for the Stoics, is part of the essence of rational discourse whether human or divine and part of the virtue of reliably discriminating the true from the false. The Stoics believed that the human capacity for rational discourse and epistemological discrimination, when fully developed, is a manifestation of cosmic and divine reason. Thus, logic for them is at once of scientific, ethical, cosmological, and theological significance.

Logic for the Stoics takes the form of propositional calculus with its elements of propositions, propositional connectives, and validity. A proposition is conceived of as the bearer of truth-values, the meaning of a declarative sentence, and the intentional object of a judgment. Propositions are either simple or compound. Simple ones have the form "S is P," while compounds consist of simple propositions connected by logical connectives. The Stoics introduced a set of propositional connectives, defining some truth-functionally, some non-truth-functionally, and established such equivalences as that between "If p, then q" and "Not both: p and not−q." They had at their disposal both what we call "material implication" and "strict implication." They defined the validity of an argument as the truth of the conditional proposition whose antecedent is the conjunct of the argument's premises and whose consequent is the argument's conclusion.

The Stoic division of "physics" is the study of the universe and the place of humanity in the universe. Since the end of Stoic ethics, "living in accordance with nature," requires the knowledge of what accords with nature, and the human activity of living includes physics as one of its constituents, physics turns out to be both a methodological necessity for, and an essential part of, ethics. Without physics human perfection is impossible.

Stoic physics teaches the following: the universe is a finite, all-inclusive corporeal entity situated within an infinite void and coextensive with an infinite duration of time. Both void and time are incorporeal. The universe is constituted by matter, an inert, amorphous, and passive principle, and GOD, an active, formative principle. The universe, God-in-matter or matter permeated with God, is internally differentiated, cohesive, organized, rationally articulated, and strictly regulated by god or cosmic reason. God is also called "fate," as the course of nature is completely causally determined. Between the polar metaphysical principles of matter and God, both of which are corporeal, there lie in ascending order elements, material objects, plants, and animals, nonrational ones first and then rational ones. A nonrational animal is receptive of impressions, and the nexus of sensory stimulus, impulse, and behavior is automatic. "A rational animal, however, in addition to its impressionistic nature, has reason which passes judgment on impressions, rejecting some of these and accepting others, in order that the animal may be guided accordingly" (53A5). We human beings are vegetative as embryos, animal-like as infants, and as we grow, the seed of REASON in us germinates. Human ontogenesis is a preparation for ascent toward divinity.

Stoic physics concerning humanity's place in the universe lays for Stoic ethics a functionalist foundation epitomized by the formula "life in accordance with nature." Let us see how this formula applies to the universe, the animal, and the human being. The universe as a whole, vitalized by God-in-matter, necessarily lives in accordance with nature (see MODALITY). It is the best possible universe by virtue of its own rational constitution. An animal *qua* animal naturally strives to live according to its constitution. Its impulse to preserve itself is the primary form of this striving. The essential rationality of humankind introduces a special variation on the functionalist theme: "What is best in men? Reason: with this he precedes the animals and follows the gods" (63D1). Thus, for humankind the formula comes to mean living in accordance with right reason, which is common to human nature and the nature of the universe. A life that satisfies the formula constitutes human perfection or happiness, whereas failure to lead such a life may well be called fatal dysfunction.

To this functionalism Stoicism gives a strict moral interpretation, wherein lies the most distinct feature of Stoic ethics:

> The virtues—prudence, justice, courage, moderation and the rest—are good. . . . The opposites of these—foolishness, injustice and the rest—are bad. . . . Everything which neither does benefit nor hurts is neither of these: for instance, life, health, pleasure, beauty, strength, wealth, . . . and their opposites, . . . For these things are not good but indifferents of the species "preferred." (58A2–4)

The consequence of this interpretation is that moral virtues constitute happiness, and that happiness is untouched by the vicissitude of fortune. What human beings naturally desire, that is, what they would desire if they were fully rational, coincides with the dictate of morality.

An injunction against PASSIONS marks Stoic moral psychology. A passion is defined as an excessive or irrational impulse. An impulse itself, however, need not be excessive or irrational. On the contrary, the Stoic wise man would have rational impulses, and a wise man devoid of impulses would be inconceivable, if not dead. The Stoics' use of expressions like "disobedience to the dictates of reason," which would suggest political subjugation and subordination or the lack thereof within the individual soul, is not meant to indicate a hierarchical psychological partition. A person's "commanding faculty" is unitary, the Stoics insist, and it includes all judgments and impulses. One insight involved in this psychological monism is the crucial role evaluative judgment plays in the etiology of emotion: "[A]ppetite and anger and fear . . . are corrupt opinions and judgments" (65G3).

The Stoics liked to represent humanity in the world order as citizenship in a political order, and they drew political implications from this representation: "[Y]ou are a citizen of the world and a part of it, not one of the underlings but one of the foremost constituents. For you are capable of attending to the divine government" (59Q3) and "There will not be a different law at Rome and at Athens, or a different law now and in the future, but one law, everlasting and immutable, will hold good for all peoples and at all times" (67S4). This cosmopolitanism reflects the union of the following Stoic conceptions: God as the rational regulator of the universe, the universality of rationality and of reason-based ethics, eudaemonistic ethics, the prescriptive character of morality, and the human race as a moral community.

Stoicism's influence has been vast. Already in late antiquity Stoicism enjoyed a commanding presence in the European intellectual scene. Many scientists like Geminus (first century B.C.), Strabo (b. c. 63 B.C.), and Cleomedes (second century A.D.), religious thinkers like Philo Judaeus (c. 20 B.C.–c. A.D. 40), St. Paul (d. c. A.D. 67), Clement (d. c. A.D. 215), and Origen (185–254), and writers like Cicero (106–43 B.C.) came under Stoicism's influence. Cicero bequeathed to posterity the Stoic conceptions of divinely ordained universal law, the brotherhood of man, and human rights. When St. Paul said, "[F]or in him we live and move, in him we exist; as some of your own poets have said, 'We are indeed his offspring' " (Acts XVII.28), he may have been quoting from Cleanthes' "Hymn to Zeus" (54I1). Clement, who called the Stoics "the most refined of the natural philosophers" (49G), and Origen took much interest in Stoicism, particularly Stoic theology.

Early modern philosophers of Europe like HOBBES, Descartes (1596–1650), and LOCKE found the Hellenistic schools of Epicureanism, Skepticism, and Stoicism particularly interesting. This was because these philosophers were seeking to liberate themselves from Christian theology and medieval scholasticism, in both of which Platonism and Aristotelianism had been deeply implicated, while the Hellenistic schools, free from a notion of transcendent divinity, seemed to offer fresh perspectives as well as rich conceptual resources.

Marks of Stoicism's influence are distinct in much of modern European philosophy, particularly in the philosophy of Locke, Spinoza (1632–1677), Leibniz (1646–1716), and KANT (1724–1804). To take Spinoza as an example, most of his main conceptions—"god or nature," *natura naturans* and *natura naturata*, universal causal determinacy and freedom as self-causation (see FREE WILL), the necessary dependence of freedom on knowledge, the fundamental unity of the bodily and the mental (see MIND–BODY PROBLEM), the connection between cognition and emotion, ethics based on impulse for self-preservation, and intellectual love of God—are in some of their aspects directly traceable to Stoic roots.

On the issue of knowledge acquisition, where we begin and how we proceed, Stoicism and British Empiricism are in basic agreement. Being inclined toward materialism on the metaphysical constitution of the universe and also toward particularism on the issue of universals, the Stoics mistrust any notion of abstract entity, a mistrust they share with the Empiricists. The Stoic picture of the mind born blank, a tabula rasa upon which sense impressions are stamped by external objects, is accepted by Locke and remains operative as a root metaphor even after BERKELEY's rejection of the external world and HUME's dissolution of the mind. Accordingly, for both Stoicism and Empiricism, sense perception is logically and temporally prior to human understanding, and human knowledge is a construct on the foundation of sense impressions. As neither Stoicism nor Empiricism clearly distinguishes logical and temporal priority, for a given mental construct logical analysis either retraces the process of constructing it or, in the absence of such a process, declares the construct to be a figment, a candidate for metaphysical elimination. In the course of construction and analysis both the Stoics and Hume face the problem of induction. There is one critical difference between the schools. While for Empiricism the root picture of the mind is that it is the mere receptacle of impressions, for Stoicism, as one matures, one comes to exercise reason in assenting to, or rejecting, impressions.

Stoic influences on Locke's ethics and political philosophy are noteworthy. His belief in the innate goodness of humankind, his conceptions of the original state of nature characterized by reason, tolerance, and equality, natural law as the foundation for positive law, and human rights, particularly property rights, all have some of their roots in Stoicism. The sociopolitical environment of Locke and that of Zeno and Chrysippus are far apart indeed. Yet in the intellectual heritage of Locke, the political theory of the Stoics must have been prominent.

Important as Stoicism's influence is upon the subsequent philosophical tradition of the West, its sphere extends far beyond a narrow circle of philosophers. As a consciousness-molding cultural force, Stoicism has done much to perpetuate the outlook on human existence according to which reason is supreme, and moral judgment reflects the structure of human knowledge and cosmic reality, not the structure of the social culture in which we live. The public visibility of the Stoic wise man, immune to passion and impregnable to misfortune, is well attested to by the common usage of "stoical" and "philosophical." The Stoic teaching concerning "the brotherhood of mankind" presumably applied to women as well as to men. But if it did, the Stoic philosophers failed to make this implication clear. Even in these late days one seldom hears of "the Stoic wise woman" or "the sisterhood of humankind."

PRIMARY WORK

Long, A. A., and D. N. Sedley. *The Hellenistic Philosophy*. Vol. 1, *Translations of the Principal Sources with Philosophical Commentary*. Cambridge and New York: Cambridge University Press, 1987: 158–437.

BIBLIOGRAPHY

Books

Inwood, Brad. *Ethics and Human Action in Early Stoicism*. Oxford: Clarendon Press; New York: Oxford University Press, 1985.

Rist, John M. *Stoic Philosophy*. Cambridge and New York: Cambridge University Press, 1969.

———. *The Stoics*. Berkeley: University of California Press, 1978.

Article

Annas, Julia. "Stoic Epistemology." In *Epistemology*. Edited by Stephen Everson. Cambridge and New York: Cambridge University Press, 1990: 116–42.

YUKIO KACHI

SUBSTANCE. The ontological category of substance was invoked from the time of ARISTOTLE through the seventeenth century to answer the question, What is a thing (a horse, a star)? An entity like an individual horse maintains an IDENTITY over time, is different at any given moment from every other thing in the universe, yet changes in ways characteristic of horses. Classically, metaphysicians wished to account for these facts by specifying the entities that justify our claims about the horse (see METAPHYSICS).

Aristotle believed the facts can be explained by the category of substance (*Metaphysics* Z). A substance is a combination of *form* and *matter*. Its form is a set of essential properties (see ESSENCE), characteristic of what all things of a *kind* do *naturally*. Essential properties include both immediately observable characteristics, for example, the horse has four hooves, and POWERS (dispositions), for example, the horse, if thirsty, will drink when led to water. Being a horse, it has these properties *necessarily* (see MODALITY). *Accidental* properties, those a thing has that do not flow from its essence, are merely *contingently* connected to the substance. Aristotle thus analyzes the idea of *predication*, what it means for a thing to have a property, by giving it an ontological ground, an advance of incalculable importance in logic and metaphysics. The matter of the horse is the *stuff* that the form molds. This matter accounts for the fact that this horse is at this moment different from all other things in the universe. Two chunks of *prime* matter, the ultimate stuff of the universe, differ merely numerically; they are simply *two* chunks. The substance persists through TIME, the horse's fundamental identity through change.

Though there is a close relationship between matter and form, they are of ontologically different kinds, just as the category of substance, though closely related to both, is a *third* kind. The notion of matter is an extremely difficult one for Aristotelians. Matter is not itself a property but a *substrate* for properties. Sometimes it was said that a substance *supports* its properties, that properties must *inhere* in substances. These metaphors are especially puzzling to the empiricists, but they add to a temptation to identify substance with matter *alone*: the phrases "supporting or standing under the properties," and "properties inhering in substance" can both be understood if we think of the marble of the bust of Socrates as a model. Aristotle thought the marble provided the matter for the sculptor, who then imposed a form, properties, on it. The marble is "under" the essential shape: if we could strip away the shape of Socrates, all we have is the chunk of marble that enables the shape to exist in this place. If substance is identified with matter, we have reduced the Aristotelian categories to two: a substance is no longer form plus matter but stuff to which form is superadded.

Is it then the matter as substrate that *has* the essential properties, a kind of pincushion in which they stick? Certainly, this is a discernible strand of the substance tradition, one which is discussed by LOCKE (*An Essay concerning Human Understanding* II.xxiii). On this view, the matter is what unifies its properties into one thing. Problems loom when we now try to recover the place in this scheme of our original horse. It is tempting, if we think of the substrate as having the properties of the horse, to identify the horse with the substrate. However, commonsensically, if we ask what has the properties of the horse, there is a clear answer—"Dobbin" names both the stuff of the horse *and* its properties. If what possesses the properties is the *combination* of form and matter, the problem is to specify the relation of form to matter, given that it is no longer true to say the *matter has* the properties. Problems about predication loom large as seventeenth-century metaphysicians struggle with the doctrine of substance. Examples include the traditional problems of PERCEPTION. A round object appears oval from a certain perspective. It cannot be both round and oval; yet if the property of being oval is present, it must be *supported*. It cannot be in the object; hence, it must be in the mind. Yet, if it attached to the substantial mind, the mind would be oval. Of the British empiricists, BERKELEY resolves the issue by rejecting material substance and its (to him) mysterious role in predication, then redefining support in terms of perception; HUME rejects the whole notion of substance.

Aristotle held that a substance is a source of activity and thus of change. Citing the nature of the horse alone to explain why it gallops is unsatisfactory. The horse is not always galloping; something is needed to activate the disposition to gallop. Perceiving the whip, the horse *wants* to gallop. Aristotle invokes *desire*, explicitly or implicitly, to explain all natural change, even in inanimate objects. It is as if the acorn perceives the climatic conditions and then wills itself to grow in response to them; to Aristotelians, the external conditions are not the deepest-level explanation for the change. Rather, it is the activation of the disposition by desire because it involves *action*.

The rise of science brought about the downfall of the doctrine of substance. Descartes begins the modern attack on Aristotle by showing that, given the law of inertia, bodies cannot change themselves. Since bodies are all totally subject to the mathematical laws of physics (see MATHEMATICS), Descartes was able to reduce the number of kinds of substance to two—minds, whose essence is thought, and extended bodies (*Meditations on First Philosophy*, Third Meditation). Locke (*Essay* II.xxiii) analyszs the notion of substance as substrate, stressing the unknowability, that is, unperceivability, of a mysterious something that is not a property. He confuses that notion with substance as form and matter combined, with the physical notion of microstructure, and even with substance as external object compared to the ideas by means of which we know it (see Bennett 1971). He attacks the Aristotelian notion of essence (*Essay* III.vi), thus the distinction between accidental and essential properties, and paves the way for Hume's analysis of causation in terms of constant conjunction. Without essences, one must look to external conditions as causes as well as for a new analysis of predication. Locke's final stance on the question of the existence of substance is unclear. He *is* clear that our ideas of bodies are merely collections of ideas of qualities we have perceived the bodies to have. Berkeley retains mental substance but attacks the notion of physical substance as a crucial step in his march toward idealism, the view that everything that exists is either a mind or a quality of a mind (*The Principles of Human Knowledge* I §§1–89). Berkeley adopts and adapts to idealism Locke's view that physical objects are collections of quality *ideas* (*Principles* I.1, I.3, I.49). Since his arguments against material substance seem to be against the essential *logic* of the category, for example, that properties are supported by substances or inhere in them, as well as their unperceivability, one wonders whether he is entitled to mental substance. Thus, HUME (*A Treatise of Human Nature* I.i.6; I.iv.5–6) questions its existence and analyzes both bodies and minds as collections of (in some sense) mind-dependent qualities.

The attack on a substance analysis of bodies thus seems to end in idealism. In the twentieth century, Bertrand RUSSELL ("Logical Atomism" II–III in Russell 1964) has championed the view of momentary substrata all of whose properties are only contingently related to it, while Nelson Goodman (*The Structure of Appearance* VI–VII) has advocated a collections analysis akin to Berkeley's and Hume's. Neither, however, is an idealist.

PRIMARY WORKS

Aristotle. *The Basic Works of Aristotle*. Edited by Richard McKeon. New York: Random House, 1941.

Berkeley, George. *The Works of George Berkeley, Bishop of Cloyne*. Edited by A. A. Luce and T. E. Jessop. 9 vols. London: Thomas Nelson and Sons, 1948–1957.

Descartes, René. *The Philosophical Writings of Descartes*. Edited and translated by John Cottingham, Robert Stoothoff, and Dugald Murdoch. 3 vols. Cambridge: Cambridge University Press, 1985.

Goodman, Nelson. *The Structure of Appearance*. Boston: D. Reidel, 1977.

Hume, David. *A Treatise of Human Nature*. 2d ed., edited with an analytical index by L. A. Selby-Bigge; revised with notes by P. H. Nidditch. Oxford: Clarendon Press, 1978.

Locke, John. *An Essay concerning Human Understanding*. Edited with an introduction by P. H. Nidditch. Oxford: Clarendon Press, 1975.

Russell, Bertrand. *Logic and Knowledge*. Edited by Robert Charles Marsh. London: Macmillan, 1964.

BIBLIOGRAPHY

Books

Bennett, Jonathan. *Locke, Berkeley, Hume: Central Themes*. Oxford: Clarendon Press, 1971.

Loux, Michael J. *Substance and Attribute*. Boston: D. Reidel, 1978.

Article

Haring, Ellen Stone. "Substantial Form in Aristotle's Metaphysics Z." *Review of Metaphysics* 10 (1956–1957): 308–32, 482–513, 698–713.

ALAN HAUSMAN and DAVID HAUSMAN

T

TIME. In his *Essay concerning Human Understanding,* LOCKE tells us that "by reflecting on the appearing of various ideas one after another in our understandings, we get the idea of succession" (*Essay* II.xiv.6). He claims that "the distance between any parts of that succession, or between the appearance of any two ideas in our mind, is that we call duration" (*Essay* II.xiv.3). A further claim is that "the constant and regular succession of ideas in a waking man is, as it were, the measure and standard of all other successions" (*Essay* II.xiv.12). BERKELEY would appear to endorse this account of duration and its measurement when he says, "Time therefore being nothing, abstracted from the succession of ideas in our minds, it follows that the duration of any finite spirit must be estimated by the number of ideas or actions succeeding each other in that spirit or mind" (*Principles of Human Knowlege* §98).

Locke argues that "any constant periodical appearance or alteration of ideas, in seemingly equidistant spaces of duration, if constant and universally observable, would have as well distinguished the intervals of time as those that have been made use of," such as the diurnal and annual revolutions of the sun. While this argument may dispose of the need to use the regular motion of a continually existent body as a measure of duration—and of the thesis that time is such motion—it clearly does not give any support to Locke's proposed standard. For the allegedly constant and regular succession of ideas in a waking man is surely not publicly accessible in the way that a sunrise is.

In his *Treatise,* HUME addresses the crucial question of how the idea of time is derived from the succession of perceptions. As usual Hume insists that "every idea, with which the imagination is furnished, first makes its appearance in a correspondent impression."

What impression is then available to supply the idea of time? Hume declares:

The idea of time is not deriv'd from a particular impression mix'd up with others, and plainly distinguishable from them; but arises altogether from the manner, in which impressions appear to the mind, without making one of the number . . . since [time] appears not as any primary distinct impression, [it] can plainly be nothing but different ideas, or impressions, or objects dispos'd in a certain manner, that is, succeeding each other.

Hume may not have successfully distinguished a temporal from a spatial disposition here. Nevertheless, for anything like a tune to be perceived, the mind must take notice of the manner in which its different sounds make their appearance. Malherbe emphasizes that the manner is not intuited a priori as in KANT (see A PRIORI/A POSTERIORI DISTINCTION).

In the *Intellectual Powers*, REID claims that "it is impossible to show how we could acquire a notion of duration if we had no memory." For "if we speak strictly and philosophically, no kind of succession can be the object of the senses or of consciousness." An operation of the memory is "a calling to mind of what is past." Without a notion of the past, there is no awareness of succession.

PRIMARY WORKS

Berkeley, George. *The Principles of Human Knowledge*, Part I [Dublin 1710]. In *The Works of George Berkeley, Bishop of Cloyne*. Edited by A. A. Luce and T. E. Jessop. 9 vols. London: Thomas Nelson and Sons, 1948–1957. See esp. §98.

Hume, David. *A Treatise of Human Nature*. 2d ed., edited with an analytical index by L. A. Selby-Bigge; revised with notes by P. H. Nidditch. Oxford: Clarendon Press, 1978. See esp. II.i.3.

Locke, John. *An Essay concerning Human Understanding*, edited with an introduction by P. H. Nidditch. Oxford: Clarendon Press, 1975.

Reid, Thomas. *Essays on the Intellectual Powers of Man*. Essay III, Part V. Edinburgh: J. Bell, 1785.

BIBLIOGRAPHY

Malherbe, Michel. *La Philosophie Empiriste de David Hume*. 3d ed., Chapter 3. Paris: J. Urin, 1992.

ROGER GALLIE

V

VERIFICATION PRINCIPLE. The principle of verification was used by members of the Vienna Circle (see LOGICAL POSITIVISM/LOGICAL EMPIRICISM) to distinguish meaningful from meaningless expressions. Roughly, the principle of verification states: if there are empirical circumstances under which it is deemed legitimate to utter an expression, then this expression is meaningful and worthy of analysis (i.e., philosophic investigation). Otherwise, the expression should be branded as nonsense and, for the purpose of analysis, is to be ignored. According to the members of the Vienna Circle (e.g., CARNAP, Schlick, Hahn, NEURATH, Hempel), all of whom adhered to one form or another of the principle of verification, the claims one finds in METAPHYSICS fall into the latter category. As such, philosophic investigation into these claims was considered by them to be a futile pursuit.

The exact formulation of the principle of verification varied from one positivist to the next. Indeed, some never formulated it explicitly, though it was clear that they were tacitly using this principle in their work (Carnap in the *Aufbau* is a case in point). One of the earliest formulations of the principle, from Friedrich Waismann's "Logische Analyse des Wahrscheinlichkeitsbegriffs," is, "[T]he meaning of a statement is the method of its verification," a version subsequently adopted by Schlick (see "Meaning and Verification": 148). Without a doubt (as Max Black pointed out in his 1934 *Analysis* article "Principle of Verifiability"), it is not entirely clear what it means to identify the meaning of a statement with the method of its verification. Schlick made steps toward clarifying this issue in his "Meaning and Verification," where he expressed his agreement with (what today we know as) a Wittgensteinian use-theory of meaning. Schlick comments: "[S]tating the meaning of a sentence amounts to stating the rules according to which the sentence is to be used, and this is the same as stating the way in which it can be verified (or falsified)" ("Meaning and Verification": 148). It should be emphasized that Schlick's views in this paper crucially diverge from the later Wittgenstein's in that Schlick avows the usefulness of ostensive definition in setting the meaning of an expression (see WITTGENSTEIN).

Underlying the principle of verification as a theory of MEANING is an entirely appropriate and relatively uncontroversial account of what constitutes the meaning of an expression. Carnap expresses this core idea in his "Testability and Meaning" as follows: "[I]f one knew what it would be for a given sentence to be found true then we would know what its meaning is" (47). In other words, the meaning of a sentence is its truth conditions; as such, one would say that two expressions possess the same meaning if they are true under the same circumstances. But, of course, the principle of verification as it was interpreted by the members of the Vienna Circle (including Carnap) requires more than this core idea: it requires that one also be able to *tell* whether the expressions are true under the same circumstances. As Carnap continues, "[I]f for two sentences the conditions under which *we would have to take them as true* are the same, then they have the same meaning" (emphasis added).

Interpreting the principle of verification in this way—as identifying the meaning of an expression with how we go about verifying this expression—leads to innumerable difficulties, simply in light of the fact that we are led to greatly abuse traditional conceptions about meaning. For instance, we have no idea what procedure one might use to verify that the center of the sun is extremely hot; nonetheless, we clearly know what it means to say that the center of the sun is hot. Or, to borrow an example from Isaiah Berlin (1939: 239), the claim "If I were now at the North Pole, I should feel colder than I do" has an obvious meaning. But how does one verify it, if I am not *now* at the North Pole? Carnap was candidly dismissive of these sorts of problems concerning the divergence between what we normally understand to be the meaning of an expression and what the principle of verification tells us is the meaning of an expression. For instance, Carnap comments:

[W]e are concerned only with the problem of meaning as it occurs in methodology, epistemology or applied logic, and not with the psychological question of meaning. We shall not consider here the questions whether any images and, if so, what images are connected with a given sentence. (1953: 75)

In other words, if the criterion of verifiability does not succeed in capturing what we take to be the meaning of an expression, so much the worse for what we take to be the meaning of an expression. We would be exhibiting a psychological tendency that has no epistemological/logical/methodological bearing.

Without a doubt, the principle of verification, as a criterion of meaning, is highly contentious. Yet for many positivists, the principle of verification was *not* interpreted as a theory of meaning, but as a theory of meaning*fulness*. For example, A. J. AYER in his second edition of *Language, Truth and Logic* (1946) offers as his version of the principle: "[A] statement is held to be literally meaningful if and only if it is either analytic or empirically verifiable" (9).

Similarly, Hempel in his 1950 survey article, "The Empiricist Criterion of Meaning," understands the principle of verification as describing those conditions under which a sentence has empirical meaning—it does not aspire to tell us what that meaning is. Even under this weaker interpretation, the principle of verification is burdened with some serious defects. Consider Ayer's formulation: here, one could interpret "verifiable" as (1) "conclusively established in experience" (Ayer 1946: 9)—this is "strong verifiability"—or as (2) having the determination of its truth-value depend on the occurrence of some possible sense experience—this is "weak verifiability." The criterion interpreted along the lines of (1), as was often pointed out, is too strong, ruling out all universal propositions, including perfectly meaningful ones (e.g., "All cats spend time sleeping"). But how does one interpret the criterion using (2)? Ayer suggests interpreting (2), to begin with, in the following way: a statement is (weakly) verifiable if "some observation-statement can be deduced from it in conjunction with certain premises, without being deducible from those other premises alone" (1946: 11). Unfortunately, under this interpretation, any statement S, no matter how ridiculous, will count as meaningful (let a "certain other premise" be "If S, then O," for some observation report O). Ayer subsequently revised (2), restricting the "certain other premises" to observation and analytic statements (see Ayer 1946: 13). Yet the flaws in this revision were clearly pointed out in Alonzo Church's 1949 review of the second edition of Ayer's *Language, Truth and Logic*; Church demonstrated that the criterion is still too weak, allowing any statement to count as verifiable and, hence, literally meaningful.

The principle of verification suffers further difficulties. An interesting problem described by Morris Lazerowitz (1937) asks: How can we decide that an expression is verified and so meaningful on the verification criterion, unless we have some prior idea about what this expression is *saying*? For in saying that an expression is verified we are saying that the world has the features the expression says it has. Yet, if we have such a prior idea, it must follow that the expression says *something* (i.e., that it is meaningful). Accordingly, what need do we have for the principle of verification as a tool that decides for us whether an expression can be meaningful? In his second edition of *Language, Truth and Logic*, Ayer attempts to sidestep this problem by using what he thought to be the neutral expression "statement." A "statement" for Ayer is neutral between "proposition" or "putative proposition," each of which assumes the presence of meaning, and "sentence," which assumes an inherent *lack* of meaning. Ayer's account, more exactly, is this: "[E]very indicative sentence, whether literally meaningful or not, shall be regarded as expressing a statement" (1946: 8). With this account, he hopes to circumvent Lazerowitz's objection.

Apart from such semantic difficulties, there is the question of the epistemological status of the principle of verification. Is it an empirical hypothesis (see Ewing 1937; Stace 1944)? A definition (Ayer 1946: 16)? An explication of what it means for an assertion to be meaningful (Hempel 1959: 124)? Is the principle, indeed, self-referentially consistent—does it satisfy its own requirement for meaningfulness?

Such problems have traditionally been thought to subvert whatever value the principle of verifiability was initially thought to have. Nevertheless, leaving these problems aside, it is worthwhile to remember what motivated discussion about the principle of verification in the first place. The dedication expressed by logical positivists to such a principle stemmed from their frustration with what seemed to them to be a complete lack of progress in philosophy, as compared to the sciences. Their "spiritual leader" in this respect was Bertrand RUSSELL. The difficulties of actually getting the principle of verification to work notwithstanding, its motivation is soundly scientific: to use logical analysis in rendering philosophic claims empirically significant. For the positivists, adopting this approach amounts to a "turning-point in philosophy" (to borrow from the title of the first paper—written by Schlick—to appear in the positivist journal *Erkenntnis*). As Schlick remarks, "I am persuaded that we are at present in the midst of an altogether final change in philosophy, and are justly entitled to consider the fruitless conflict of systems at an end" (Schlick 1979: 155).

Why have the previous conflicts between philosophic systems been unproductive? Russell explains: "Philosophy, unlike science, has hitherto been unprogressive, because each original philosopher has had to begin work again from the beginning, without being able to accept anything definite from the work of his predecessors" (1918: 113).

Conversely: "A scientific philosophy such as I wish to recommend will be piecemeal and tentative like other sciences; above all, it will be able to invent hypotheses which, even if they are not wholly true, will yet remain fruitful after the necessary corrections have been made" (1918: 113).

This new image of philosophy, expressed by Russell in his 1914 lecture "On Scientific Method in Philosophy," appears practically verbatim in *Wissenschaftliche Weltauffassung: Der Wiener Kreis*, the 1929 manifesto of the Vienna Circle, written by Neurath, Hahn, and Carnap. With this image in mind, we can understand in a proper light the value and significance of the principle of verification. For it is true that the principle of verification was difficult to formulate adequately, that it underwent a series of questionably successful revisions, and that it was eventually discarded. But that is what is supposed to happen. It is with the spirit of an empirical scientist that philosophers should formulate hypotheses—in this case, regarding the meaningfulness of expressions—respond to criticisms by revising hypotheses, and then under the weight of criticism, discard hypotheses. In other words, some version of verificationism was, in fact, in play during the disputes that led to the discarding of the principle of verification.

PRIMARY WORKS

Books

Ayer, Alfred J. *Language, Truth and Logic*. 2d ed. New York: Dover, 1946.
————, ed. *Logical Positivism*. New York: Free Press, 1959.
Carnap, Rudolf. *Der Logische Aufbau der Welt*. Translated by Rolf George. Berkeley: University of California Press, 1967.

Articles

Berlin, Isaiah. "Verification." *Proceedings of the Aristotelian Society* 39 (1938–1939): 225–48.
Black, Max. "The Principle of Verifiability." *Analysis* 2 (1934): 1–6.
Carnap, Rudolf. "Testability and Meaning." Reprinted, in abridged form, in *Readings in the Philosophy of Science*. Edited by Herbert Feigl and May Brodbeck. New York: Appleton-Century-Crofts, 1953: 47–92.
Church, Alonzo. "Review of *Language, Truth and Logic* (2nd edition)." *Journal of Symbolic Logic* 14 (1949): 52ff.
Ewing, Alfred Cyril. "Meaninglessness." *Mind* 46 (1937): 347–64.
Hempel, Carl. "The Empiricist Criterion of Meaning." Reprinted in *Logical Positivism*. Edited by A. J. Ayer. New York: Free Press, 1959: 108–29.
Lazerowitz, Morris. "The Principle of Verifiability." *Mind* 46 (1937): 372–78.
Neurath, Otto, Hans Hahn, and Rudolf Carnap. "Wissenschaftliche Weltauffassung: Der Wiener Kreis." Reprinted in *Otto Neurath: Empiricism and Sociology*. Edited by Marie Neurath and R. S. Cohen. Dordrecht: Reidel, 1973: 299–318.
Russell, Bertrand. "The Scientific Method in Philosophy." In *Mysticism and Logic*. London: Allen and Unwin, 1918: 95–119.
Schlick, Moritz. "Meaning and Verification." Reprinted in *Readings in Philosophical Analysis*. Edited by Herbert Feigl and Wilfred Sellars. New York: Appleton-Century-Crofts, 1949: 146–70.
————. "The Turning-Point in Philosophy." Translated by Peter Heath. In *Moritz Schlick: Philosophical Papers*, vol. 2, edited by Henk L. Mulder and Barbara F. B. van de Velde-Schlick. Dordrecht: Reidel, 1979: 154–60.
Stace, Walter. "Positivism." *Mind* 53 (1944): 215–37.
Waismann, Friedrich. "Logische Analyse des Wahrscheinlichkeitsbegriffs." *Erkenntnis* 1 (1930–1931): 228–48.

BIBLIOGRAPHY

Hanfling, Oswald. *Logical Positivism*. Oxford: Basil Blackwell, 1981.

ROBERT G. HUDSON

W

WILL. LOCKE described the will as "a power we find in ourselves to begin or forbear, continue or end, several actions of our minds and motions of our bodies, barely by a thought or preference of the mind ordering, or as it were commanding, the doing or not doing such or such a particular action." "The actual exercise of that power," he added, "is that which we call *volition* or *willing*" (*An Essay concerning Human Understanding* II.xxi.5). That we have the power of will is indisputable, in Locke's opinion; but this power is not free: what is free is the person, not the will (see FREE WILL). "So far as any one can, by the direction of choice of his mind preferring the existence of any action to the nonexistence of that action, and vice versa, make it to exist or not exist, so far he is free" (*Essay* II.xxi.21); this freedom is not a power to choose the direction of one's choice.

Although he uses such terms as "choosing" and "preferring" to describe the act of volition, Locke confessed to their inadequacy: they signify desire equally well, he thought; yet desire is very different from volition, frequently running counter to it. The confusion that may arise from the use of these words is easily avoided, he thought; for to obtain a distinct understanding of volition, one need only "reflect" on one's own mind and "observe what it does when it wills." If one does this, one will see that volition is "nothing but that particular determination of the mind, whereby barely by a thought the mind endeavors to give rise, continuation, or stop, to any action which it takes to be in its power" (*Essay* II.xxi.35). Empiricist views on volition and the will amount to a series of footnotes on these claims by Locke.

Following Locke's advice to attend carefully to what goes on in our minds when we exercise our power of volition, HUME declared that by "the will" he means nothing but "the internal impression we feel and are conscious of when we knowingly give rise to any new motion of our body or new perception of our mind." This impression, he said, is "impossible to define" (*A Treatise of Human Nature* II.iii.1). Gilbert Ryle, claiming that no distinguishable impression is actually discernible whenever we knowingly give rise to changes in our body or mind, made fun of what he called "the myth of volitions" in *The Concept of Mind*. Later empiricists, rejecting Ryle's BEHAVIORISM, have defended conceptions of the will that have much in common with Locke's incidental remarks about it. According to Bruce Aune, for example, the will can be understood as the power Locke said it is, and an act of the will (volition) can be understood as the sort of thought by which a person (rather than a mind) "endeavors," in Locke's terms, "to give rise, continuation, or stop to any action" that she or he takes to be in her or his power. A thought of this kind is not a self-directed command, as Locke suggested; it is expressed in words not by an imperative but by a declarative sentence indicating resolve or determination—for example, "I *will* raise my arm."

PRIMARY WORKS

Hume, David. *A Treatise of Human Nature*. 2d ed., edited with an analytical index by L. A. Selby-Bigge; revised with notes by P. H. Nidditch. Oxford: Clarendon Press, 1978.
Locke, John. *An Essay concerning Human Understanding*. Edited with an introduction by P. H. Nidditch. Oxford: Clarendon Press, 1975.

BIBLIOGRAPHY

Aune, Bruce. *Reason and Action*. Dordrecht: Reidel, 1977: Chapter 2.
Ryle, Gilbert. *The Concept of Mind*. London: Hutchinson, 1949.
Sellars, Wilfrid. *Science and Metaphysics*. Atascadero, CA: Ridgeview, 1991: Chapter 7.

BRUCE AUNE

WITTGENSTEIN, LUDWIG. Ludwig Wittgenstein (1889–1951) is one of the major philosophers of the twentieth century. The best English biography is Monk (1990). Born into an extremely wealthy and cultivated Viennese family, he initially studied engineering but turned to philosophy as a result of conversations with Bertrand Russell during a visit to England in 1911. He studied at Cambridge until the outbreak of the First World War, during which he served with conspicuous gallantry in the Austrian army. In 1929 he returned to Cambridge and became first a fellow of Trinity College and, from 1939 until 1947, G. E. Moore's successor in the chair of philosophy. During his lifetime he published only one book, the *Tractatus Logico-Philosophicus* (1921), and a few papers. The enormous fame and influence he enjoyed during his lifetime resulted in great part from his teaching and from the circulation of a small number of manuscripts. He left, however, an immense body of unpublished work, the editing and publication of which began with the *Philosophical Investigations* (1953) and is still continuing.

Wittgenstein stands in an ambiguous relation to twentieth-century empiricism. The *Tractatus* deeply impressed Moritz Schlick and other leading members of the Vienna Circle, of which for a time, beginning in 1927, Wittgenstein was a somewhat peripheral member. Then, and for some time to come, the *Tractatus* was read as a central work of logical positivism (see LOGICAL POSITIVISM/ LOGICAL EMPIRICISM). In retrospect, some sharp differences appear. Notoriously, the *Tractatus* makes room for doctrines—the ones commonly cited involve the remarks concerning "the mystical" and the distinction between "saying" and "showing"—not obviously compatible with the logical positivists' belief in the power of natural science to offer a complete explanation of reality. It is doubtful, though some of his remarks of the period have led some to think otherwise, that the Wittgenstein of 1927–1930 accepted the Verification Theory of Meaning (see VERIFICATION PRINCIPLE). As the notion of verification was ordinarily understood by members of the Vienna Circle (e.g., by AYER 1936), there can be no question of conclusively verifying an empirical claim, "x is an F," since it can never logically be ruled out that further investigation will reveal x not to be an F after all. Wittgenstein, on the other hand, held that if a proposition cannot be conclusively verified it "signifies nothing whatsoever" (Waismann 1979: 47); a move which in effect, by placing considerations of sense beyond the scope of epistemic doubt, breaks with the general tendency of empiricism to conflate the categories of the empirical and the semantic.

The tendency to resist such an assimilation becomes more evident in Wittgenstein's later work. Two central doctrines of empiricism are (1) that all assertions about the world are, if true, contingently true, and hence (2) that there are no necessary truths beyond those whose necessity derives from linguistic or formal stipulation. Traditional metaphysics assumed other kinds of modality, and such claims have been reanimated over the past quarter century even in analytic philosophy, as witness Kripke's (1980) and Putnam's (1974) arguments for the existence of metaphysically necessary statements concerning the identity of individuals and kinds and Putnam's (1992) weaker claim that both ordinary and scientific talk of causality offers support for some notion of physical necessity, however defined.

The empiricist's best line of attack against such attempts to reanimate metaphysics can still seem to lie (Putnam 1992; Ayer 1992) with the traditional empiricist claim that there is a level of discourse below which notions of causality and ontic commitment sufficiently rich to sustain such proposals arise; a level at which meaning is established simply by correlating linguistic expressions with recognizably recurrent sense-qualities. In making such a move, empiricists need not commit themselves to any claim about the ontology of sense-qualities. They need not, that is, opt for traditional talk of "sense-data," with its implied assimilation of the observational to the mental, since it is open to them to lean at this point, for instance, on the notion of a "stimulus" current in behavioral psychology. Nor need they commit themselves to any large-scale program of reductive analysis of nonobservational statements in favor of observational ones. Empiricists can simply put the onus on the would-be metaphysician to say what, for instance, the kind of causality-talk capable of sustaining physical modality adds to talk of observable regularities in experience

(Putnam 1992: 448), or why the ontic distinctions that fuel talk of necessary truths concerning individual or kind identity are not simply empirically underdetermined by the totality of true evidential claims articulable in the empiricist's "basic," altogether nontheoretically-loaded language whose terms simply pick out recurrent features of sensory experience (Quine 1960).

The later work of Wittgenstein, however, puts into question the possibility, even in principle, of the empiricist's "basic" language of bare sensory description. For such a language to get off the ground, it must be possible, *ex hypothesi*, to identify without recourse to language the sensory feature that each general name of the language is to pick out. Ostensive definition has been the technique generally favored by philosophers for accomplishing this end, just because pointing, as a way of associating a basic term with a corresponding sensory feature, has been assumed to be (1) unambiguous and (2) in need of no linguistic supplementation. Both these assumptions are attacked by Wittgenstein (*Philosophical Investigations* I.25–35). Suppose one attempts to establish the reference of "red" by pointing at a red book. Is the pointing gesture to be understood as indicating the color of the book, its functional character, its shape, or one of the other indefinitely numerous features of such an object that such a gesture might serve to indicate? The meaning to be ascribed to the term which the gesture is supposed to define ("red," "rectangular," "book," "paper," etc.) depends, clearly, on the choice between competing interpretations of the intention of the pointing gesture. But, equally clearly, nothing determines that choice; or rather, and fatally from the empiricist's point of view, nothing *extralinguistic* determines it. If we are allowed to use language to specify the intent of the pointing gesture (if we are allowed to say things like, "That *color* is called N," "That *shape* is called N," and so on), then the problem vanishes. But, of course, to allow moves like that is to allow the empiricist's would-be "pure" language of reference to sense-qualities to be contaminated by the conceptual structure of "ordinary" language, with all its potential for metaphysical excess.

A related issue arises in connection with Wittgenstein's celebrated "Private Language Argument" (*Philosophical Investigations* I.256f.). The question here is whether it is possible to give a name to an inner state irrespective of whether that state stands in any intrinsic relationship to the body and to the physical world; or, in other words, whether the disembodied or, what comes to the same thing, only contingently embodied consciousness envisaged by Descartes as constituting what is essential to a human being would, even in principle, be able to invent for itself a language in which to name and describe its own conscious states. Wittgenstein answers that it would not. His argument, in effect (Harrison 1991), is that one can be said to have given a meaning to a sign S by means of a procedure P, only if P results in the setting up of some criterion by appeal to which it can be determined, in the future, whether S is being used wrongly. In the case under discussion, in which a Cartesian consciousness LW attempts to establish S as a name of one of its states, no such P is available. All that LW can do in the circumstances is to concentrate its attention on the state in question while also bringing before it the sign S. But, manifestly, no criterion of wrongful future use is thereby established since the bare subjective conviction of LW, in the absence, *ex hypothesi*, of any intrinsic connection between LW's inner states and LW's body, or the physical world, must remain the only court of appeal on the question of whether a given inner state is relevantly similar to the one by appeal to which the reference of S was established and thus on whether S is being correctly used to refer to the new state.

If, on the other hand, there is some connection between the inner state and the body or the physical world, then the situation changes, since that connection can provide the required criterion for wrongful use of S, in which case the sign S no longer belongs to a "private language." Thus, "pain" both picks out an inner state and is a term in a public language, because pain has what Wittgenstein calls a "natural expression" (*natürlich Empfindungsausserung*). By its intrinsic character, that is, pain, when its intensity rises above a certain level, forces its possessor to exhibit bodily symptoms of distress. It follows both (1) that to call an inner state that lacked such a connection with the body "pain" would be to misuse the word "pain" and (2) that such a use of the term would be objectively assessable as wrong. As Wittgenstein says (*Philosophical Investigations* I.580), "[A]n inner process stands in need of outward criteria."

"Pain," of all words, might have been expected to conform to the empiricist model according to which the reference of a basic term of sensory description is established simply by associating it with the appropriate sensory state. But if Wittgenstein is correct, that model fails here also. The issues of what different speakers are referring to when they speak of pain, of whether they are referring to the same thing, and of whether or not the term, on a given occasion, is or is not being misapplied (issues that must be settled if "pain" is to function as a term in a public language) can be settled only because of the presence in our lives of a relationship (between pain and its overt bodily expression) that, because it is an "intrinsic" relationship, resists assimilation to the empiricist partitioning of all truths between the categories of the contingent and the formal or stipulative.

Ayer (1963) interprets Wittgenstein as suggesting that memory cannot be trusted in the absence of "outward criteria." He answers that to question the validity of memory as an ultimate source of epistemic warrant amounts, absurdly, to denying the possibility of kinds of recognitional capacity that must simply be postulated as fundamental unless we wish to deny the possibility of learning, including animal learning, per se. If, however, we admit the existence of basic recognitional capacities, there seems no reason that we should not determine the reference of a term by associating it with such a capacity.

But this begs Wittgenstein's question in two ways. First, the focus of Wittgenstein's argument is logical, not epistemic or psychological. What interests him is not what must be the case if one is to recognize an inner state but what must be the case if the reference of a name for such a state is to be rendered determinate. His suggestion is that determinacy of reference requires the possibility of distinguishing between correct and incorrect applications of a term and that only the existence of intrinsic connections between ''inner'' and bodily states can found that possibility. The in-principle feasibility of determining the reference of a term by associating it with a bare recognitional capacity, therefore, is just what the argument places in question. Second, of course, and more generally, the argument raises a question concerning the transferability of such notions as ''reference'' from the everyday physical world, presumed both by everyday discourse about pain and by animal learning experiments, to the phenomenal realm frequently supposed by empiricists and certainly by the Ayer of 1963 to be that in which observational content is to be sought, and it is unclear, to say the least, that such doubts do not also infect the notion of memory.

Despite these well-known differences over whether a satisfactory account of reference is possible for a language of pretheoretic sensory description, it has often been claimed that many of Wittgenstein's own arguments in the later work, particularly those that found his opposition to METAPHYSICS and SKEPTICISM, rest on covert appeals to some form of verificationism in the theory of meaning. Thus, Chihara and Fodor (1965) take the Private Language Argument to assert a ''logical connection'' between behavior and pain and suggest, reasonably on this assumption, that there could be such a connection only if the meaning, in the sense of the observational or operational content, of ''x is in pain'' is capturable by some set of statements about x's behavior. But this is once again to assume that the main focus of Wittgenstein's argument must be epistemic, ignoring the sharp separation between the epistemic and the logical that informs Wittgenstein's work at all periods. The connection between pain and behavior of which Wittgenstein's actual text (1953; I.256–57) speaks is not the ''logical'' one credited to him by Chihara and Fodor but a natural one, namely, the connection that consists in the fact that pain by virtue of its phenomenal character forces one to exhibit overt signs of distress when its intensity rises above a certain level. What this ''connection'' opens up is not the possibility of asserting, counterintuitively, a ''logical''— or, to speak plainly, analytic—equivalence between ''x is in pain'' and ''x is exhibiting pain behavior,'' but simply the possibility of an incorrect use of ''x is in pain'' (Marconi 1995: 108), and thus the possibility of agreement between different speakers on what is being asserted by a statement of that form (or, in other words, the possibility of satisfying Frege's [1952: 59] demand that the sense of a sentence be ''objective'' [i.e., publicly accessible to all speakers in common]), irrespective of whether any actual assertion made by means of it turns out to be true or not.

There is, in any case, no need to look for covert verificationism or OPERATIONISM in Wittgenstein's thought in order to make sense of his opposition to metaphysics and skepticism. It can plausibly be seen as springing, rather, from the thought that, since reference can be rendered determinate only by criteria rooted in practices whose applicability depends on the presence in our lives of specific, concrete sets of circumstances, such as the intrinsic connection between pain and the exhibition of bodily distress, the power of any such criterion to render reference determinate will always be, in principle, limited in scope. While the natural connection between pain and its bodily expression may allow us to make clear to one another to what state of Henry's we intend to refer when we say that Henry is in pain, it will not allow us to make clear to one another, to use an example of Wittgenstein's, to what state of the pot we intend to refer when we say, "The pot is in pain." If the error of skepticism and metaphysics lies, as many philosophers since KANT have supposed, in exceeding some "limit" or other (of "experience," of "sense," of "language"), these are the sort of limits that, for Wittgenstein, they exceed, rather than the sort envisaged by verificationism as a theory of meaning. Here, as elsewhere, Wittgenstein's thought, while it shares a number of features with empiricism, is not, in the end, consonant with it.

PRIMARY WORKS

Philosophical Investigations. Oxford: Blackwell, 1953.
Blue and Brown Books. Oxford: Blackwell, 1960.
Tractatus Logico-Philosophicus. Translated by D. F. Pears and B. F. McGuinness. London: Routledge; New York: Humanities Press, 1961.

BIBLIOGRAPHY

Books

Ayer, A. J. *Language, Truth and Logic.* London: Gollancz, 1936.
Kripke, S. *Naming and Necessity.* Oxford: Blackwell, 1980.
Monk, R. *Ludwig Wittgenstein: The Duty of Genius.* New York: Free Press, Maxwell Macmillan International, 1990.
Quine, W.V.O. *Word and Object.* Cambridge: MIT Press, 1960.
Waismann, F. *Wittgenstein and the Vienna Circle.* Oxford: Blackwell, 1979.

Articles

Ayer, A. J. "Can There Be a Private Language?" In *The Concept of a Person and Other Essays.* New York: St. Martin's Press, 1963.
———. "Reply to Hilary Putnam." In *The Philosophy of A. J. Ayer.* Edited by Lewis Edwin Hahn. La Salle, IL: Open Court, 1992.
Chihara, C. S., and J. A. Fodor. "Operationalism and Ordinary Language: A Critique of Wittgenstein." *American Philosophical Quarterly* 2 (1965): 281–95.
Frege, G. "On Sense and Reference." In *Translations from the Philosophical Writings of Gottlob Frege.* Edited by P. Geach and M. Black. Oxford: Blackwell, 1952.
Harrison, B. "Wittgenstein and Skepticism." In *Meaning-Skepticism.* Edited by Klaus Puhl. Berlin and New York: de Gruyter, 1991.
Marconi, D. "Fodor and Wittgenstein on Private Language." In *Wittgenstein: Mind and Language.* Edited by R. Egidi (Synthese Library no. 245). Dordrecht: Kluwer, 1995.

Putnam, H. "Is It Necessary That Water Is H$_2$O?" In *The Philosophy of A. J. Ayer*. Edited by Lewis Edwin Hahn. La Salle, IL: Open Court, 1992.

———. "The Meaning of 'Meaning.' " In *Mind, Language and Reality, Philosophical Papers, Volume 2*. Cambridge: Cambridge University Press, 1974.

BERNARD HARRISON

INDEX

Page numbers referring to main entries on a topic are indicated in **boldfaced** type.

Willis, Thomas, 119–20
Winkler, Kenneth, 50
Wittgenstein, Ludwig, **442–48**; analytic philosophy, 6; external world, 101–2; logical positivism/logical empiricism, 218–22; Moore and, 263; nominalism, 290; solipsism, 406; tautologies, 377–78; verification principle, 437; Vienna Circle and, 60–61
Wolff, Christian, 120
Wollaston, William, 83–84
Woolston, Thomas, 83–84

About the Editors

DON GARRETT is Professor of Philosophy at the University of Utah. He is the author of *Cognition and Commitment in Hume's Philosophy* and an editor of *Hume* studies.

EDWARD BARBANELL is a Ph.D. candidate in Philosophy at the University of Utah.

ISBN 0-313-28932-8

HARDCOVER BAR CODE